THE JOURNAL

OF

PHARMACOLOGY

AND

EXPERIMENTAL THERAPEUTICS

FOUNDED BY JOHN J. ABEL

OFFICIAL PUBLICATION
OF THE AMERICAN SOCIETY FOR PHARMACOLOGY AND
EXPERIMENTAL THERAPEUTICS INCORPORATED

VOLUME 72
1941

BALTIMORE, MARYLAND

CONTENTS

NUMBER 1, MAY, 1941

I. The Scientific Proceedings of the American Society for Pharmacology and Experimental Therapeutics, Incorporated........................ 1

II. A Comparison of Ephedrine and Eserine. J. D. P. Graham and M. R. Gurd.. 48

III. Action of Adrenaline and Potential Changes in the Cat Uterus. G. Balassa and M. R. Gurd... 63

IV. A Method for Determining Loss of Pain Sensation. Fred E. D'Amour and Donn L. Smith.. 74

V. On the Action of Prostigmine on the Circulatory System. Rafael Mendez and Abe Ravin.. 80

VI. The Action of Pitocin and Adrenalin on Different Segments of the Rabbit Uterus. D. D. Bonnycastle and J. K. W. Ferguson......... 90

VII. Comparative Effects of Sulfonamide Compounds as to Anemia and Cyanosis. Arthur P. Richardson.................................... 99

VIII. The Relationship Between the In Vitro and the In Vivo Activity of Sulfonamide Compounds. H. J. White, A. Calvin Bratton, J. T. Litchfield, Jr. and E. K. Marshall, Jr............................ 112

NUMBER 2, JUNE, 1941

IX. A Study of the Effects of Morphine and of Carbon Tetrachloride on the Rate of Disappearance of Ethyl Isoamyl Barbituric Acid. H. J. Tatum, D. E. Nelson and F. L. Kozelka.............................. 123

X. Effects of Certain Drugs on Temperature Regulation, and Changes in their Toxicity, in Rats Exposed to Cold. Julian B. Herrmann...... 130

XI. Excretion of Combined Morphine in the Tolerant and Non-Tolerant Dog. Vincent Thompson and E. G. Gross......................... 138

XII. The Toxicity and Local Anesthetic Activity of Three New Biphenyl Derivatives. Edwin J. Fellows.................................. 146

XIII. The Effect of Atropine, Pilocarpine, Prostigmine, Eserine, Mecholyl and Ephedrine on the Tonus and Contraction Mechanisms of the Urinary Bladder, with Observations on the Clinical Application of these Drugs. Harry A. Teitelbaum and Orthello R. Langworthy.... 152

XIV. The Influence of Gold Sodium Thiomalate (Myocrysin) on the Prevention of Hemolytic Streptococcus Arthritis in Rats. Sidney Rothbard, D. Murray Angevine and Russell L. Cecil............... 164

XV. The Effect of Barbituric and Thiobarbituric Acid Derivatives on the Pyloric Sphincter and Stomach in Unanesthetized Dogs. Charles M. Gruber and Charles M. Gruber, Jr............................ 176

XVI. The Toxicity of Optically Inactive, *d*- and *l*-Selenium-Cystine. A. L. Moxon, K. P. Du Bois and R. L. Potter........................... 184

XVII. The Toxicity of Orally-Ingested Tungsten Compounds in the Rat. F. W. Kinard and John Van De Erve.................................. 196

XVIII. Studies on Fat Metabolism and Susceptibility to Carbon Tetrachloride. J. C. Forbes, B. E. Leach and E. L. Outhouse..................... 202

XIX. The Quantitative Effect of Fifteen Chemically Related Glycosides and Genins on the Embryonic Chick Heart. Arthur C. DeGraff, George H. Paff and Robert A. Lehman 211

NUMBER 3, JULY, 1941

XX. Toxicity and Actions of Trimethylene Glycol. W. Van Winkle, Jr.... 227
XXI. Anesthesia. IV. The Anesthetic Action of Cyclopropyl Ethyl Ether. John C. Krantz, Jr., C. Jelleff Carr, Sylvan E. Forman, William E. Evans, Jr., and Henry Wollenweber 233
XXII. Further Studies on the Fate of Selenium in the Organism. Benton B. Westfall and M. I. Smith 245
XXIII. The Absorption and Elimination of Phenolphthalein in Normal and Pathologic States: With Particular Reference to Liver and Kidney Diseases. Bernard Fantus, Frederick Steigmann and J. M. Dyniewicz 252
XXIV. Comparative Physiological Actions of Phenyl-, Thienyl- and Furylisopropylamines. Gordon A. Alles and George A. Feigen 265
XXV. A Method for the Determination of *5,5* Diphenylhydantoin in Biological Material. F. L. Kozelka and C. H. Hine 276
XXVI. Distribution and Rate of Metabolism of *5,5* Diphenylhydantoin. C. H. Hine and F. L. Kozelka 280
XXVII. Distribution, Excretion, and Rate and Site of Detoxification of Metrazol. H. J. Tatum and F. L. Kozelka 284
XXVIII. The Mode of Action of Neoprontosil in Streptococcus Infections in Mice. J. T. Litchfield, Jr., H. J. White and E. K. Marshall, Jr.... 291
XXIX. The Effect of Sulfanilamide and Some of its Derivatives on the Reaction of Mice to Anesthetics. Thomas C. Butler, H. L. Dickison, Wm. M. Govier, C. M. Greer and Paul D. Lamson 298
XXX. Further Observations on the Action of Drugs on the Caliber of Coronary Vessels. Papaverine Hydrochloride, Digitalis Derivatives, Aminophyllin, Caffein, Glucose, Calcium Gluconate and Metrazol. E. Lindner and L. N. Katz 306
XXXI. The Response of Sulfapyridine-Resistant Pneumococci to Hydroxyethylapocupreine. L. H. Schmidt and Clara L. Sesler 311
XXXII. Studies on Shock Induced by Hemorrhage. I. Effect of Thiamin on Survival Time. Wm. M. Govier and C. M. Greer 317
XXXIII. Studies on Shock Induced by Hemorrhage. II. Effect of Thiamin on Disturbances of Carbohydrate Metabolism. Wm. M. Govier and C. M. Greer 321
XXXIV. Histone Zinc Insulin—Its Pharmacologic Characteristics and Its Application in the Treatment of Diabetes Mellitus. Charles A. Barnes, Tracy D. Cuttle, and Garfield G. Duncan 331
XXXV. Quantitative Gastrointestinal Absorption and Renal Excretion of Propylene Glycol. W. Van Winkle, Jr. 344
XXXVI. The Production in Cultures Containing Sodium Paranitrobenzoate of a Substance That Affects the Action of Sulfathiazole. John K. Miller 354
XXXVII. The Effect of Posterior Pituitary Preparations on the Large Intestine of the Unanesthetized Dog. Edward Larson 363
XXXVIII. Influence of Cocaine on the Uterine Reactions Induced by Adrenalin and Hypogastric Nerve Stimulation. John S. Labate 370

XXXIX. The Effects of Sodium Diphenyl Hydantoinate (Dilantin) on the Blood Ascorbic Acid Level in Guinea Pigs. Miles E. Drake, Charles M. Gruber, Victor G. Haury and E. Ross Hart 383

XL. Antagonistic Effect of Asphyxia to Curare Paralysis of the Vagus Nerve. Hans Mautner and Aldo Luisada 386

XLI. The Effect of Digoxin on the Cold Blooded Heart and Its Bearing on the Mechanism of Digitalis Action. A. M. Wedd, H. A. Blair and G. K. Dwyer 394

XLII. The Effects of Sedative Drugs on the Pial Vessels. Theodore P. Sohler, Gladys N. Lothrop and Joan Wilkinson 409

XLIII. Index 417

THE SCIENTIFIC PROCEEDINGS OF THE AMERICAN SOCIETY FOR PHARMACOLOGY AND EXPERIMENTAL THERAPEUTICS, INCORPORATED

THIRTY-SECOND ANNUAL MEETING, CHICAGO, ILLINOIS, APRIL 15–19, 1941

Anesthetic Potency and Biochemical Effects of 1 and 2 Chlor-Propene-1 and 1 and 2 Brom-Propene-1. B. E. ABREU, S. A. PEOPLES, C. A. HANDLEY AND D. F. MARSH (introduced by C. D. Leake), University of Oklahoma, University of Alabama, University of South Dakota and University of California.

Previously published experiments (*Anesthesia and Analgesia*, 18:156, 1939) indicate that certain mono-halogenated olefins might have possibilities as general anesthetic agents. Atropinized dogs were maintained in the second plane of the third stage of anesthesia (Guedel) for 60 minutes, with appropriate concentrations of 1 and 2 Chlor-Propene-1 and 1 and 2 Brom-Propene-1. A modification of the Waters' absorption technique was employed for anesthetizing the animals. At 20 minute intervals after the start of anesthesia, blood and bag concentrations of the anesthetic agents were determined by a method devised by one of us (S. A. P.) to be described elsewhere. Plasma carbon dioxide combining power, blood glucose and blood lactate were determined at the same time intervals as the anesthetics, and at 30, 60 and 120 minute intervals after the cessation of anesthesia. There is no significant difference between the brominated and chlorinated compounds with respect to anesthetic potency or ease of production of biochemical changes. In the case of all of the compounds no marked changes in blood constituents were observed.

The Determination of Chloral Hydrate in Blood and the Absorption Curve of Chloral Hydrate. W. LLOYD ADAMS (Introduced by Byron B. Clark), Albany Medical College

The Fugiwara color reaction (R—C—halogen$_3$ + pyridine → red or pink color) is extremely sensitive (1:1,000,000) but the color fades rapidly. Consequently, previous adaptations of this reaction to quantitative methods have necessitated simultaneous control determinations. An extended study of the conditions under which chloral hydrate may be determined quantitatively by this color reaction has been made. A method which eliminates the necessity of controls, increases accuracy, and shortens the time of determination has been developed using an appropriate filter and a photoelectric colorimeter. This was possible only after finding the means of producing an optically clear solution without filtration, and after finding a means of significantly retarding color-fading. Duplicate determinations can be made on blood containing only 0.025 mgm. of chloral hydrate per cc. with an error of less than 5%.

Chloral hydrate has been administered by stomach tube to dogs, and samples of blood taken at 10 minute intervals for several hours, and once daily thereafter. The absorption curves, which will be shown, reveal the presence of a small amount of the drug for several days before the blood is free of chloral.

Effects of Chlorination of Alkyl Cresols on Their Local and Systemic Activity. HAMILTON H. ANDERSON AND M. H. HU (by invitation), Peiping Union Medical College.

Brown and Lamson (J. Pharmacol. and Exp. Therap., **53**: 264, 1935) determined the oral toxicity of a complete series of alkyl phenols and found 6-hexyl-m-cresol to be no more toxic for man than hexylresorcinol. Unlike hexylresorcinol, it does not cause any whitening of mucous membranes (J. Pharmacol. and Exp. Therap., **53**: 227, 1935). Hartman and Schelling (Amer. J. Surg., **46**: 460, 1939) reported 4-chloro-6-hexyl-m-cresol to be an efficient and non-irritant antiseptic having low local and systemic toxicity.

For the present study 6-hexyl-m-cresol, its isomers and their chlorinated derivatives were prepared in this laboratory by Prof. Peter P. T. Sah. Systemic toxicity in inbred white rats was determined by Brown and Lamson's method. Local application on mucous membranes showed no untoward effects on the tongues of dogs and men, but there was slight redness of the conjunctivae of dogs which persisted for from 5 to 7 hours.

On gastric administration, the lethal range for all agents was found to be from more than 10 cc. to 1.5 cc. per kgm. in 110 rats treated. Of the 6 compounds tested, 6-chloro-2-hexyl-p-cresol was least toxic. Other compounds, in order of increasing toxicity, were 4-chloro-6-hexyl-o-cresol, 4-chloro-6-hexyl-m-cresol, 6-hexyl-m-cresol, 6-hexyl-o-cresol and 2-hexyl-p-cresol.

Severe convulsions developed immediately after lethal amounts of 2-hexyl-p-cresol were administered. Less severe convulsions developed in rats given smaller doses and appeared in one animal given 4-chloro-6-hexyl-m-cresol. At necropsy congested lungs and kidneys were observed in most animals and with 2-hexyl-p-cresol gastric and renal hemorrhages were noted.

Chlorination reduced systemic toxicity of all compounds; reduction in toxicity was most pronounced in 6-chloro-2-hexyl-p-cresol.

Side Chain Oxidations and Their Possible Pharmacological Significance. GEORG BARKAN, Evans Memorial, Massachusetts Memorial Hospitals, and Boston University School of Medicine.

In previous investigations it was observed that under certain experimental conditions, sulfanilamide solutions when treated with oxygen form H_2O_2 and a blue-violet compound which is reversibly reducible and oxidizable. The hypothesis that the formation of the blue-colored product might be due to the influence of nascent H_2O_2 found support in further experiments.

Nascent hydrogen peroxide as formed on autoxidation of hydrazine solutions, in presence of cupric ions, oxidizes sulfanilamide to blue-violet derivatives, which are also reversibly reducible and oxidizable. It was found that arsanilate under the same conditions, with hydrazine, copper and oxygen, gave a blue product spectroscopically identical with that from sulfanilamide. On oxidation both sulfanilamide and arsanilate, obviously lose their characteristic side chains. There result identical, or at least similar, and chemically very reactive products, derived from rather different original substances. The significance of this type or reaction is discussed from the pharmacological and toxicological point of view.

Pharmacological Studies on levo-N-Ethyl-Ephedrine Hydrochloride (Nethamine Hydrochloride). I. Toxicity and Effect on the Respiratory and Circulatory Systems. T. J. BECKER, M. R. WARREN, D. G. MARSH, AND R. S. SHELTON (introduced by E. M. K. Geiling), Research Laboratories, The Wm. S. Merrell Company.

Curtis, in 1929, reported preliminary results obtained with some tertiary amines closely related to ephedrine and suggested that a number of these might be more suitable for therapeutic purposes than levo-ephedrine. One of these compounds, levo-N-ethyl ephedrine hydrochloride, has been prepared in pure form and its pharmacological action studied.

The toxic effects of this compound have been observed in rabbits following both oral and intravenous administration. Results indicate that prolonged daily administration of levo-N-ethyl ephedrine in doses of 25 mgm./kg. intravenously or 50 mgm./kg. orally produces no apparent pathological changes. The M.L.D. following intravenous administration is 50 mgm./kg. or approximately the same as that of levo-ephedrine.

The effect of levo-N-ethyl ephedrine on respiration has been determined in both normal and anesthetized dogs. In normal dogs doses of 1 to 5 mgm./kg. administered intravenously produce no significant change in the rate but increase the depth of respiration.

The pressor effect of this compound has been determined in anesthetized and decerebrate dogs. Results indicate that levo-N-ethyl ephedrine hydrochloride in doses of 1 mgm./kg. administered intravenously exerts about one tenth the pressor action of similar amounts of levo-ephedrine. The site of action of levo-N-ethyl ephedrine hydrochloride on the heart has been determined.

Results of experiments on rats indicate that levo-N-ethyl ephedrine hydrochloride produces very little central stimulation. The results have been compared to those obtained with similar doses of levo-ephedrine.

Attempted Immunization of Canaries against Plasmodium Cathemerium by Injection with Filtered whole Mosquito Substance. HARRY BECKMAN, Marquette University School of Medicine.

Uninfected canaries were divided into two lots of 8 each. One lot was injected intramuscularly with 0.05 cc. of the Berkfeld filtrate from a large number of uninfected mosquitoes ground up in physiological saline solution, the injected amount representing the substance from one mosquito; injections at intervals of three days for a series of eight. The other lot of birds was similarly injected with saline alone. Two days after the last injections, mosquitoes carrying the sporozoites of *Plasmodium cathemerium* were allowed to bite all the birds and six days thereafter blood smears began to be made and were continued daily to death or recovery (latency) of the individual bird. The injected material failed to show any immunizing properties as all save 1 of the treated birds developed a typical infection and all save 2 of the controls. The 3 resistant birds became infected upon being bitten again sixteen days after the original bites.

Action Potentials in Isolated Nerve as a Measure of Local Anesthetic Potency. A. L. BENNETT AND J. C. WAGNER (by invitation) AND A. R. MCINTYRE, University of Nebraska College of Medicine.

Frog sciatic nerve maintained under constant temperature and humidity in a special chamber was driven by single spike shocks of controllable intensity and frequency. The action potentials were amplified and made to drive a cathode ray oscilloscope where the action current could be photographically recorded. Solution containing local anesthetics could be applied to the nerve without causing movement of the nerve on the electrodes and without opening the chamber surrounding the nerve. Observations of the extent and rate of change of the action potentials were used as a measurement of anesthetic potency.

It was found that when the concentration of procain was kept constant

$$\frac{T}{2 \log D} = k_1 \qquad (1)$$

It was also found that for a given diameter of nerve

$$T \times \log R = k_2 \qquad (2)$$

Thus

$$k_1 k_2 = \frac{\log T}{\log D} \times \log R = K \qquad (3)$$

Where T = time to 80 percent block
D = diameter of nerve in micra
$R = \frac{(\text{molarity} - \text{minimum effective molarity})}{\text{minimum effective molarity}}$

Nitrophenol as an Antiseptic. R. Beutner and (by invitation) A. Cohen, and K. R. Beutner, Hahnemann Medical College and Hospital of Philadelphia.

Due to chemical change when in contact with body tissue and a subsequent inactivation, phenol and its derivatives have been at a disadvantage as wound antiseptics. Searching for a more stable, non-poisonous, non-irritant phenol derivative, o-nitrophenol seemed to satisfy these requirements.

When injected (500 mgm. in oil) intramuscularly into rabbits, it was recovered, unchanged, 85 to 95 per cent, from urine collected for 2 days after injection. Using p-chlorophenol similarly, about 60 per cent was recovered; from phenol itself only 11 per cent (or 30 per cent in another case).

Repeated application to a rabbit's cornea showed o-nitrophenol was non-irritant. Intramuscular injection of 600 mg./kg. was necessary to kill mice.

The effects of the drug on temperature and metabolism were also tested: 50 mgm. in a 2 kg. rabbit caused no significant temperature change during 6 hours (in agreement with older findings by Tainter, et al.), while in another rabbit injected as a control with only 20 mgm. of dinitrophenol, the temperature rose 2° after 2 hours. Since metabolic stimulation is absent, o-nitrophenol is not likely to cause late poisoning as does dinitrophenol. Orthonitrophenol was found highly penetrant since traces can be found in human urine even after inunction. Its phenol coefficient is about 20.

Accordingly, in clinical tests it proved of value in burns and many skin diseases.

The Effect of Narcotics on Diuresis.[1] R. C. de Bodo and (by invitation) H. I. Bloch, New York University College of Medicine.

[1] Aided by a grant from the American Philosophical Society.

When normal dogs on constant diet are brought into water equilibrium and then given water either by stomach tube (40 cc./kg.) or intravenously (25 cc./kg.), or given saline intravenously, they excrete the fluid quantitatively within three hours. Dogs with permanent diabetes insipidus induced by destruction of the entire neurohypophysis give the same results.

Morphine, as shown previously,[2] decreases markedly the excretion of the water in normal dogs (excreted amount 2–15 per cent), whereas in those with permanent diabetes insipidus it does not have this effect.

To determine whether other narcotics act in the same way, further experiments were carried out with sodium phenobarbital, sodium amytal, nembutal, chloralosane, chloral hydrate, and avertin. The drugs were given intravenously in varying doses. If the water was administered by stomach the drugs were injected intravenously forty minutes later to allow time for complete absorption of the water. The amount of water excreted prior to the drug administration was measured.

Phenobarbital in small, nonanesthetic doses (0.035–0.040 grams/kg.) decreased the excretion of the water approximately 50 per cent in normal dogs; in diabetes insipidus dogs it had no effect on water excretion.

Sodium amytal and nembutal in anesthetic doses decreased the excretion of water approximately 50 per cent in the majority of normal dogs.

Avertin, chloralosane and chloral hydrate were given in full anesthetic doses. While avertin had a marked antidiuretic action in normal dogs, the other two had no such action.

The study of the effect of sodium amytal, nembutal and avertin on diuresis in the diabetes insipidus dogs is in progress.

Metabolic Fate of Evipal. Milton T. Bush and Thomas C. Butler, Vanderbilt University School of Medicine.

It was previously reported (J. Pharmacol., **69:** 277, 1940) that after administration of *nor*-evipal to dogs about 10 per cent was recovered unchanged from the urine; that after administration of evipal such small amounts of narcotic material were recovered as to show that relatively little of the evipal is converted to *nor*-evipal (by demethylation). From the *nor*-evipal urine there has been obtained a new substance, in amount equivalent to more than 10 per cent of the *nor*-evipal administered. It is relatively inactive as a narcotic, has m.p. 213–217° corr. (decomp.); its physical properties and elementary analyses correspond to a C-cyclohexenonyl-C-methyl-barbituric acid. This substance has also been isolated from the urine after evipal administration, in an amount equivalent to about 5 per cent of the evipal. In addition two other substances, having respectively m.p. 141–142° corr. and m.p. 161–162.5° corr., have so far been obtained from this urine. Physical properties and elementary analyses indicate that these are isomeric C-methyl-C-cyclohexenonyl-N-methyl-barbituric acids.

Further studies are necessary and are being made to establish these relationships.

The Action of Ergot Alkaloids on the Virgin Rat Uterus. R. A. Bussabarger (by invitation), L. D. Seager and O. S. Gibbs, University of Tennessee.

Isolated uterine segments from virgin Wistar rats were placed in Tyrode solution in a Gibbs constant temperature bath and contractions mechanically recorded. 38 segments from 17 rats were studied.

[2] Journal of Pharmacology & Experimental Therapeutics, **69,** 276, 1940.

In 176 administrations of ergotoxine ethanesulfonate, 1:1,000,000, to 1:50,000, 7 gave slight increase in amplitude, 2 gave increase in rate only, 28 a decrease in both rate and amplitude, 71 a decrease in amplitude, and 55 gave no change.

In 21 administrations of ergotamine tartrate, 1:1,000,000 to 1:100,000 one gave increased tone, 6 a decrease in amplitude, and 14 no change.

In 22 administrations of ergonovine, 1:1,600,000 to 1:400,000, 2 gave increase in amplitude, 9 a decrease in amplitude, and 11 no change.

The depressant effect of epinephrine and histamine was confirmed. These also depress after ergotoxine causing an additive effect. No reversal to epinephrine was noted.

Acetyl choline constantly stimulates the uterus and this may be reduced or antagonized by ergotoxine as well as epinephrine.

The Delay in Onset of Action of Intravenously Injected Anesthetics. THOMAS C. BUTLER, Vanderbilt University School of Medicine.

Some anesthetics do not produce their full effect immediately after intravenous injection. The delay in onset of anesthesia has been measured in mice for a number of drugs at a dose 1.25 times the median anesthetic dose. Lags were found only for the chloraloses and the 5,5-disubstituted derivatives of barbituric acid and hydantoin. Among the seventeen 5,5-disubstituted barbituric acids studied, the mean lags varied from zero to 23 minutes. In this group there is a rough correlation between anesthetic dose and lag, the more active drugs having the more rapid onset. If the comparison is limited to the subgroup having an ethyl group as one of the 5-substituents or that having an allyl group as one of the 5-substituents, the correlation is much more striking. No delay in onset was found for any N-alkyl barbituric acid or for any thiobarbituric acid.

The Effect of Ethyl Yohimbine in Experimental Hypertension. H. F. CHASE (by invitation), F. F. YONKMAN AND A. J. LEHMAN, Wayne University School of Medicine.

Direct blood pressure tracings were taken from the femoral artery in five healthy dogs of both sexes under pentobarbital anesthesia as control records; following which, four dogs were laparotomized and, after one adrenal gland was extirpated, the kidneys were encased in cellophane following the method of Page. The fifth, or control dog, was treated similarly except that the kidneys were merely stripped of their capsules and not wrapped in cellophane. Increase in tension developed in all dogs except in the control as shown by subsequent readings under pentobarbital anesthesia. In acute experiments on these hypertensive dogs, Ethyl Yohimbine, 3 mgm. per kg. when injected intravenously produced its well-known hypotensive effect in all animals. The percentage drops of systolic blood pressure from hypertensive levels were 19, 29, 51, and 52 per cent, and in the control was 32 per cent. These effects were temporary as are those in normal animals. Epinephrine's effect was remarkably reversed (dose 0.005 mgm. per kg.) after Ethyl Yohimbine, and this normally pressor amine accentuated the hypotensive effect of Yohimbine in all animals including the control. In dogs made hypertensive by this method the hypertension produced does not interfere with the hypotensive effects of Ethyl Yohimbine, or with the well-known "epinephrine reversal" effect as induced by the Yohimbine radical.

The prolonged effect of daily administration of Yohimbine and Yohimbine salts and other hypotensive agents in experimental perirenal hypertension is now being investigated. Further studies are now in progress in which blood pressure determinations are obtained directly from unanesthetized, hypertensive animals.

The Effect of Posterior Pituitary Extract on the Water Uptake in Frogs after Complete or Partial Hypophysectomy, Infundibular Lesions and Thyroidectomy. GRAHAM CHEN (introduced by E. M. K. Geiling), University of Chicago.

The effect of posterior pituitary extract on the water uptake of frogs subjected to various operative procedures has been studied. While normal frogs showed a maximal weight increase averaging 20 per cent following injection of 1 unit of posterior pituitary extract per ten grams of frog, completely hypophysectomized animals or those in which either the anterior or neuro-intermediate lobes were removed showed a maximal weight increase of only about 5 per cent. Similar results were obtained in frogs in which wide lesions were made in the infundibular region. If, however, the infundibulum were merely punctured in the mid-line, the reduction in response to posterior pituitary was not so marked (maximal increase averaging 12.5 per cent). Thyroidectomy resulted in some reduction in water uptake (maximal value averaging 15 per cent).

The LD_{50s} of Neoarsphenamine and Thio-Bismol for Mice and Chinese Hamsters. Y. P. CHEN AND H. Y. SOONG (Introduced by Hamilton H. Anderson), Peiping Union Medical College.

While extensive biological studies have been made on neoarsphenamine and thio-bismol (sodium bismuth thioglycolate), the subcutaneous LD_{50s} of these agents on inbred mice and Chinese hamsters are not available. Since both animals are useful in the study of experimental spirochaetal infections, the present study was undertaken as a preliminary step in the evaluation of drugs used as spirochaetocides.

Using normal inbred, white mice, and healthy stock hamsters, ten animals at each dose, the LD_{50s} were determined by the method of Gaddum et al. (Med. Res. Counc., Spec. Rep. Ser., no. 128 and 183).

The LD_{50s} of neoarsphenamine for mice and for hamsters were 235 mgm. per kgm. and 190 mgm. per kgm. respectively, and of thiobismol for mice and hamsters, 32 mgm. per kgm. and 16 mgm. per kgm. respectively. Eighty-five mice and 55 hamsters were used. These results indicate that commercially available neoarsphenamine and thiobismol are more toxic for Chinese hamsters than for inbred mice.

The Comparative Narcotic Potency of 1-diethylacetyl-5,5-cyclopentamethylene biuret, Paraldehyde and Sodium Barbital. CHARLES H. CHENG (by invitation), HAMILTON H. ANDERSON and S. Y. P'AN (by invitation), Yenching University and Peiping Union Medical College.

Hill and Degnan (J. Amer. Chem. Soc., **62:** 1940) reported 1-diethylacetyl-5,5-cyclopentamethylene biuret to have hypnotic properties and low toxicity. In an effort to compare this agent with commonly used hypnotics, it was prepared according to their method and its narcotic potency was tested in inbred white mice, together with paraldehyde and sodium barbital following the technique of Emerson and Abreu (Univ. Calif. Publ. Pharmacol., **1:** 93, 1938). The results are summarized in table 1.

TABLE 1

HYPNOTIC	DOSE	MORTALITY RATIO*	NARCOSIS	
			Onset	Duration
	mgm./kgm.		*minutes*	*minutes*†
Paraldehyde	800	0/20	3.6 ± 0.6	44 ± 5
	1600	8/20	1 ± 0	195 ± 13
1-diethylacetyl-5,5-cyclopentamethylene biuret	450	1/20	8 ± 0.4	159 ± 17
	600 (single)	4/10	7 ± 0.4	169 ± 15
	600 (divided)	0/10		
Sodium barbital	300	0/20	40 ± 3	202 ± 18
	400 (single)	0/10	16 ± 2	526 ± 38
	400 (divided)	1/10		

* During 24 hours.
† During 12 hours.

Under the conditions of this experiment the biuret produced narcosis more rapidly than barbital and less promptly than paraldehyde. The duration of narcosis was between that of paraldehyde and sodium barbital at lower dose levels. At higher dosage, in single or divided amounts, given in 2 hours, the period of narcosis was significantly shorter than that of sodium barbital.

The Effect of Hydro-alcoholic Solutions of Pyrethrum on Drosophila Flies. YIN-CH'ANG CHIN (Introduced by Hamilton H. Anderson), Peiping Union Medical College.

Patterson (Ann. Rept. Entomol. Soc. Ontario, **65:** 78, 1934) has used *Drosophila ampelophila* Loew to test the toxicity of poisonous baits, and Maxwell and Lord (Ann. Rept. Entomol. Soc. Ontario, **68:** 33, 1937) employed Drosophila flies to test the efficacy of nicotine. In the present study *Drosophila melanogaster* has been used for testing the insecticidal potency of hydro-alcoholic solutions of pyrethrum as a standard for comparison with other contact insecticides now being prepared.

Ten grams of powdered pyrethrum flowers was macerated with 95 per cent ethyl alcohol for 3 days and percolated until the solvent was colorless. The extract was diluted to a volume of 50 cc. and for spraying further dilutions were made with distilled water.

Wild-type fruit flies were bred according to the method of Li (Peking Nat. Hist. Bull., **5:** 29, Pt. 4, 1931) in an incubator at 26°C., and were used during the first five days after hatching.

The method of Peet (Ind. Eng. Chem., **20:** 1164, 1928) for evaluating contact insecticides was adopted, using a smaller cage, a temperature of 27°C., a spray pressure of 120 mm. Hg and an exposure time of 10 minutes. Under such conditions a dilution of 2.5 per cent of pyrethrum powder was found to be the smallest concentration sufficient to kill 95 per cent of the flies. A similar concentration of alcohol was not effective.

The Acute Effects of Aniline on Circulation and Blood of Dogs. Byron B. Clark and (by invitation) E. J. Van Loon and R. W. Morrissey, Albany Medical College.

The acute effects of aniline on respiration, blood pressure, heart rate, and electrocardiogram were determined and correlated with the changes in hemoglobin pigments (Evelyn method).

With continuous intravenous injection of 2 per cent aniline in saline to dogs anesthetized with pentobarbital, the lethal dose was between 500 and 600 mgm. per kgm. (range 400 to 1052). Initially the heart rate, blood pressure, and respiration increased. The hyperpnea continued until sudden respiratory failure. After 300 mgm. per kgm. of aniline, the heart rate slowly decreased and blood pressure fell progressively. The methemoglobin increased to a maximum of 60 to 70 per cent of total hemoglobin. Prior to death the most consistent electrocardiographic change was a progressive decrease in the height of R which became marked after the maximal rise in methemoglobin; T wave and ST segment changes appeared irregularly; no PR or QRS prolongation occurred; the rhythm was of sinus origin except in one experiment where a transitory bigeminy developed. At death, respiration usually stopped first with a blood pressure of 25 to 80 mm., and the heart showed gross arrhythmias.

The effects of single doses, and the relation of dosage and time to methemoglobin formation will be discussed.

These experiments suggest that the severe hemic hypoxia is a major factor in the production of the respiratory, and cardio-circulatory changes.

The Similarity in Basic Functions of Various Bismuth Compounds Used in the Therapy of Syphilis. N. M. Clausen and B. J. Longley (by invitation) and A. L. Tatum, University of Wisconsin.

When the maximal tolerated dose (M.T.D.) determined by the intravenous route was found to be almost the same for bismuth sodium tartrate, bismuth citrate, bismuth ethyl camphorate, iodobismitol and thiobismol, it, was decided to try to determine the minimal curative dose (M.C.D.) for each compound by the same route in rabbit syphilis. Our purpose in using this route of administration is to abolish the obvious factors of absorption, thus putting the compounds on a more common basis for comparison. Using the usual method of popliteal lymph node transfer as the criterion of cure, four out of four compounds tried were curative when fractions of the M.T.D. were given in three weekly intravenous administrations, each giving a M.C.D. in the neighborhood of one or two milligrams per kilogram. When the therapeutic indices are calculated from these data, each of the compounds appears to have an index between one and three. Hence, methods have been presented which have better enabled us to compare the toxicity and therapeutic efficiency of various bismuth compounds on a more common basis than has been accomplished heretofore. From the data presented further evidence has been developed to support the contention that the various bismuth compounds ultimately act in a common manner.

Sweat Responses to Drugs with a Nicotine-like Action. Julius M. Coon and Stephen Rothman (introduced by E. M. K. Geiling), University of Chicago.

Intradermal injection of high dilutions of drugs with a nicotine-like action caused an outbreak of sweat on the human skin in an area about 3 cm. in diameter around the wheal. A similar response was seen on the foot pad of the cat's paw when these drugs were injected into the pad. The optimum concentration of acetylcholine hydrobromide was 1:40,000; of nicotine sulphate, 1:200,000; and of alpha-lobeline hydrochloride, 1:2,000,000. The reaction was demonstrated to be an axon reflex by the criteria ordinarily accepted as proof for this phenomenon.

Intradermal acetylcholine was seen to produce sweating in two ways: (1) by its nicotine-like action and (2) by its direct muscarine-like action. These two reactions could easily be distinguished by the difference in onset, extent, and the concentrations of acetylcholine which produced the optimum response.

The axon reflex response to these drugs was totally abolished by mixing the nicotine sulphate solution, before injection, with a procaine solution as dilute as 1:100,000. This indicates that the nerve fibers responsible for the axon reflex are far more sensitive to procaine than are the sensory nerves.

Nicotine alkaloid, applied topically to the skin of man, causes a sweat response to appear in about ten minutes in the area penetrated by the drug.

A Comparison of Blood Pressure Effects and Toxicity of Ephedrine and Racephedrine. Elizabeth M. Cranston (Introduced by Raymond N. Bieter), University of Minnesota Medical School.

Due to disagreement in the literature concerning the relative toxicity and action of ephedrine and racephedrine, a study was conducted to compare the action of the two drugs, 1) on blood pressure in rabbits anesthetized with sodium phenobarbital, 2) on maintenance of blood pressure following procaine spinal anesthesia in rabbits and 3) on toxicity in normal rabbits.

In barbitalized rabbits, ephedrine intravenously in doses of 2–10 mgm./kgm. produced a greater rise in blood pressure than racephedrine in equal doses, but the toxicity was the same, early toxic symptoms appearing with 20 mgm./kgm., and 60 mgm./kgm. killing 4 out of 5 animals with either drug. Only one dose was injected per animal.

In the spinal anesthesia experiments, 40 mgm./kgm. racephedrine intravenously was required to maintain the blood pressure above 100 mm. of Hg as compared to only 10 mgm./kgm. ephedrine. However, 40 mgm./kgm. racephedrine completely prevented any initial fall in blood pressure following spinal anesthesia, whereas in the case of ephedrine 30 mgm./kgm. was needed to prevent a fall.

The $L.D._{50}$ as determined intravenously in 83 normal rabbits was 60–70 mgm./kgm. for ephedrine and 90 mgm./kgm. for racephedrine.

The Pharmacology of Certain Derivatives of Phenyl Triazole Carboxylic Acid. Raymond W. Cunningham (by invitation), Edwin J. Fellows and A. E. Livingston, Temple University, School of Medicine.

A series of 1-phenyl, 1,2,3-triazole 4-carboxylic acid derivatives has been made available to us for pharmacological study. A stimulant or convulsant action has been reported for certain other compounds containing the triazo group, but subcutaneous injection of large doses of the more soluble members of the present series failed to produce convulsions in rats. Oral administration of the triazole compounds to rats lowered normal temperature as much as 7°F. In view of this fact comparisons with aminopyrine were made with these compounds in normal and febrile rats. Utilizing a technique similar to that employed by Eddy it was found that as much as a four fold increase in pain stimulus was necessary to elicit a response in cats after the triazole compounds. Comparisons of the analgesic action of the triazole compounds and aminopyrine also were made in these animals.

Vioform-N.N.R. and "Diodoquin": Animal Toxicity and Iodine Absorption in Man. NORMAN A. DAVID AND (by invitation) NILKANTH PHATAK AND F. B. ZENER, University of Oregon Medical School.

Previous studies (University of California 1930–32) and recent work show that iodochlorhydroxyquinoline (Vioform-N.N.R.) has a definite toxicity regularly killing 7 out of 10 guinea pigs given single oral doses of 200 mg./kg. and a majority of the animals when given in doses over 300 mg./kg. Diiodohydroxyquinoline, however, appears to have no definite L.D. 50 since small doses (50–100 mg./kg.) kill as many guinea pigs as large doses (2000 mg./kg.). Similar results were noted when the two drugs were given to 4–5 months old kittens. This irregularity in toxicity with "diodoquin" is possibly due to its relative insolubility and to inconstant absorption by the animal.

Nine male medical students given 0.25 gram capsules of vioform t.i.d. for 10 days (total amount—7.5 grams) showed increases in blood iodine varying from 145 to 327 y per cent with an average increase of 223 y per cent. "Diodoquin" given in a dosage of 0.21 grams (1 tablet) t.i.d. for 10 days to 10 individuals (total amount—6.3 grams) showed blood iodine increases ranging from 45.6 to 437 y per cent with an average increase of 172 y per cent. Our toxicity results and studies on blood iodine contradict the manufacturer's claim for "diodoquin" that, ". . . even with enormous dosage, no absorption takes place."

Correlation of the Structure of the Cardiac Glycosides with Their Action on the Embryo Chick Heart. ARTHUR C. DEGRAFF, AND (by invitation) GEORGE H. PAFF AND ROBERT A. LEHMAN, New York University College of Medicine and Long Island College of Medicine.

The influence of the chemical structure of cardiac glycosides and genins on their pharmacological action has been studied and tentative conclusions have been drawn as to the importance of various configurations. The embryo chick heart has been found suitable for this study since fewer variables are operative than in other methods of bio-assay. The procedure and the qualitative effects have been previously described. In this investigation dosage response curves were obtained for K-strophanthoside, lanatosides A, B, and C, convallatoxin and oleandrin and their hydrolysis products, making a total of 15 pure crystalline drugs. Except at the upper limits of concentration, log dose was found to be a linear function of log reciprocal time and the methods of Bliss and co-workers were used for determining the most probable value for the relative potency of each of the drugs with respect to digitoxin. In general, the progenins, which are genins conjugated with desoxy sugars, were found to be many times as potent as the genins and slightly more potent than the corresponding "genuine" glycosides which contain glucose in addition to the desoxy sugars. Furthermore, it was found that the nature and position of the substituent groups on the steroid nucleus is of considerable importance in determining activity, whereas the nature of the desoxy sugar conjugated with the progenins seems not to be of significance.

Sodium Citrate as a Protective Agent Against Injury by a Heavy Metal. G. L. Donnelly and R. L. Holman, (introduced by W. deB. MacNider), University of North Carolina.

Twelve dogs were given subcutaneous injections of 5.0 mg. of uranium nitrate per kilo. Between the sixth and tenth days all animals became acutely ill, and eleven of these died in the acute stage, while one survived.

Another group of ten dogs was given daily intravenous injections of trisodium citrate, 0.33 cc. per kilo of a saturated solution, for five consecutive days. On the fifth day each animal received subcutaneously 5 mg. of uranium nitrate per kilo. The trisodium citrate was continued for five additional days. In this group the clinical evidence of acute illness was either mild or absent. Nine of the ten animals lived, making a survival rate of 90 per cent as compared to the survival rate of 8 per cent in the control group.

The mode of action of trisodium citrate is not known. Whether it is due to the influence of the substance in the maintenance of the alkaline reserve of the body, or whether it is due to one or both ions, or to a combination of both factors remains to be determined by studies now in progress.

Effects of Irritation of the Upper Airway on Spleen Volume. M. S. Dooley, Syracuse University.

It will be shown that, in most instances, constriction of the spleen occurs on irritation of the upper airway, whereas, as was shown by Dooley and Wells in 1929, the kidney invariably constricts. Variations from this usual response seem to depend upon the intricate innervation of the spleen. Other modifications of this response arise from drugs acting on the spleen (lantern slides).

The Determination of the pH of the Skin of Man and Common Laboratory Animal. John H. Draize, Food and Drug Administration, Federal Security Agency, Washington, D. C.

Variations of the pH of human skin in health and disease, and their possible significance on the skin absorption of remedial or other agents warrant study. By use of a glass electrode and a vacuum tube potentiometer, determinations of the pH of skin were made on man (white and colored) and the monkey, dog, cat, rabbit, guinea pig and rat. Whenever possible, the animal subjects were divided equally as to sex and age groups. In man, determinations were made on the skin surfaces of the back of the hand, inner aspect of the forearm, antecubital fossa, inner aspect of the upper arm, axilla, cheek, and forehead. Exclusive of the pH values for the axilla, the following results were obtained:

NUMBER OF SUBJECTS	RACE	SEX	AGE RANGE	VARIATIONS IN pH VALUES	AVERAGE pH VALUE
52	White	Male	21–58	4.0–6.2	4.5
50	White	Female	27–60	4.7–6.7	5.4
25	Negro	Male	26–59	4.3–6.7	5.0

The axilla readings varied from 5.1 to 7.6. In the female subjects there seemed to be no correlation between pH values of the skin and the stage of the menstrual cycle; however, in post menopause (7 subjects) the values were lower than for the general female average.

All laboratory animals with the exception of certain age groups of guinea pigs were higher in value than that of the human range, e.g.,

ANIMAL	NUMBER OF SUBJECTS	NUMBER OF AGE GROUPS	AVERAGE pH OF SKIN
Monkey	3	—	6.3–6.8
Dog	34	6	7.1–7.9
Dog (in estrus)	6	—	7.2–8.2
Cat	27	3	6.0–7.4
Rabbit	20	—	6.1–7.5
Rabbit	5	(6 mo. of age)	6.4–6.8
Guinea pig	67	9	5.0–6.0
Rat	60	13	6.0–7.0

The effect on the pH of the skin of inunctions with the following ointments were studied: 3–25 per cent ammoniated mercury, 2–20 per cent salicylic acid, 5 per cent sodium hydroxide and 15 per cent lactic acid. All ointments, excepting the lactic acid, caused a rise in the pH values of the skin; however, the salicylic acid caused a momentary drop before it rose above the normal level.

A Pharmacologic and Toxicologic Study of Mannitol and Sorbitol. FRED W. ELLIS AND C. JELLEFF CARR, University of Maryland, School of Medicine.

In experiments on the Rhesus monkey the feeding of 3 grams per day of the sugar alcohols mannitol and sorbitol over a period of three months produced no histopathological findings or toxicological indications. The blood sugar level did not change significantly and the blood urea nitrogen was not influenced. In mice and rats the laxative action of these sugar alcohols limits nutritional studies when the compounds comprise a portion of the diet. It has been shown previously that when mannitol or sorbitol is administered by stomach tube to the rat only a small portion of the compound is utilized to form liver glycogen. In the Rhesus monkey mannitol and sorbitol are capable of storage as glycogen in the liver of the fasting animal. In man the administration of 10 grams per day for thirty days produced no significant change in the non-protein nitrogen or CO_2 combining power of the blood, or red blood cell count. The phenolsulphonphthalein test indicated no kidney damage. Mannitol or sorbitol were not excreted in the urine when fed in this quantity. In normal humans sorbitol causes a rise in the R.Q. comparable to that observed after the administration of an equal quantity of glucose while the blood sugar level remains practically normal.

The Anesthetic Action of Methyl Allyl Ether and n-Propyl Ethyl Ether. WILLIAM E. EVANS, JR., University of Maryland.

Anesthesia was produced in dogs by both methyl allyl ether and n-propyl ethyl ether but was accompanied by undesirable side actions in each case.

Methyl allyl ether was extremely irritating to the mucous membranes. It failed to cause complete relaxation of the musculature of the abdomen and the extremities during surgical anesthesia. There occurred a progressive fall of blood pressure with the depth of anesthesia.

n-propyl ethyl ether was a more powerful anesthetic than diethyl ether. Although the blood pressure was only slightly lowered during surgical anesthesia, the respiration was severely depressed both in rate and volume.

A Roentgenkymographic Study of the Effect of Intravenous Lanatoside C Upon the Diastolic Volume and Stroke Output on the Failing Heart. GEORGE FAHR AND JOHN S. LA DUE (by invitation), University of Minnesota.

The intravenous administration of lanatoside C to ten patients with severe heart failure associated with normal sinus rhythm resulted in a prompt increase in the stroke volume of the heart. Control teleoroentgenkymograms,[1] blood pressure and circulation time measurements were made at the start of the experiment. Then 1.6 mg. of lanatoside C (a crystalline cardiac glycoside of Digitalis lanata) were given intravenously and all measurements repeated thirty, sixty and one hundred and twenty minutes after administration of the drug.

All patients showed optimal improvement after thirty to sixty minutes; the transverse diameters of the hearts were 0.5 to 2 cm. smaller than at the beginning of the experiment; the stroke output, as measured by systolic and diasolic volume differences, increased 10 to 40 per cent within the same period of time. With but one exception, the elevated stroke output was accompanied by a parallel increase in pulse pressure and a decrease in circulation time.

The Local Anesthetic Activity of Three New Biphenyl Derivatives. EDWIN J. FELLOWS, Temple University, School of Medicine.

In the present experiments the hydrochlorides of β-diethylaminoethyl-4-amino-4′-biphenylcarboxylate (compound V), di(β-diethylaminoethyl)-2-2′-diamino-5-5′-biphenylcarboxylate (compound VI) and di-(β-diethylaminoethyl)-5-5′-diamino-diphenate (compound VII) were found to exhibit marked local anesthetic properties. Intradermally in guinea-pigs all of the biphenyl compounds without epinephrine were found to produce anesthesia of longer duration than the hydrochloride of p-aminobenzoyl diethylamino-ethanol (procaine) under the same conditions. Compound VII is non-irritating and produces anesthesia *without* epinephrine after intradermal injection for longer periods of time than procaine *with* epinephrine and is more toxic than procaine. All of the biphenyl compounds produce anesthesia of rabbit cornea. In addition to comparing the activity of the biphenyl compounds with procaine and cocaine hydrochlorides the effect of position substitution on local anesthetic activity has been noted and compared with related derivatives.

The Pharmacology of Piperidine and Morpholine Derivatives of α and β-Naphthol. EDWIN J. FELLOWS, RAYMOND W. CUNNINGHAM (by invitation) AND A. E. LIVINGSTON, Temple University, School of Medicine.

In the present studies the hydrochlorides of α-morpholino methyl-β-naphthol (I), α-piperidino methyl-β-naphthol (II), β-piperidino methyl α-naphthyl p-aminobenzoate (III), β-morpholino methyl α-naphthyl p-aminobenzoate (IV), α-morpholino methyl β-naphthyl p-aminobenzoate (V), α-piperidino-methyl β-naphthyl benzoate (VI) and α-piperidino methyl-β-naphthyl p-amino-benzoate (VII) were found to produce local anesthesia. Compounds I and II produce marked anesthesia but cause irritation and are more toxic than procaine subcutaneously in guinea pigs. Compounds III, IV and V are very unstable in solution and produce anesthesia of poor depth and variable duration. Compound VI is stable in solution and pro-

[1] We are indebted to Dr. Ancel Keys for the use of a roentgenkymograph in the Laboratory of Physical Hygiene and for the determination of the systolic and diastolic outline of the hearts and the stroke outputs as calculated by his formula.

duces definite anesthesia which is potentiated by epinephrine intradermally in guinea pigs. It is a more active anesthetic than the hydrochloride of p-aminobenzoyl-diethyl-amino-ethanol (procaine), is also less toxic than the latter after subcutaneous injection in the guinea pig and it produces irritation. Compound VII is the most active of all the compounds. Its intradermal anesthetic activity is ten times greater than that of procaine, it is approximately one-third as toxic subcutaneously in guinea pigs and produces irritation. In one-per cent solution VII produces anesthesia of rabbit cornea of approximately the same duration as one per cent cocaine hydrochloride.

The Chronic Toxicity of Cadmium. O. GARTH FITZHUGH AND FRED H. MEILLER (by invitation), Food and Drug Administration, Federal Security Agency.

Recently DeEds and associates (Science **90,** 498, 1939; J. Pharmacol. and Exper. Therap., in press) have reported experiments on the toxicity of cadmium. We have conducted similar experiments for a longer period of time and have studied the effects of different diets on the toxicity of cadmium. Albino rats at the age of three weeks were placed on diets containing cadmium (cadmium chloride) in concentrations of 15, 45, 75, and 135 p.p.m. All of the animals that now survive have been on their diets for at least six months. Four hundred animals were used in the experimental and control groups.

There was evidence of the toxicity of cadmium at concentrations of 45, 75, and 135 p.p.m. In animals on 135 p.p.m. marked anemia, and in many instances, early death occurred. These animals were stunted in growth, hemoglobin levels were as low as 4 grams, and the erythrocyte counts were as low as two million. From 40 to 50 per cent of the red cells were reticulocytes. Anemia developed later in the rats on the lower concentrations of cadmium. Some animals on 45 p.p.m. of cadmium showed no blood changes after one year, while only one animal on 15 p.p.m. of cadmium has had marked anemia. Bleaching of the incisor teeth was observed in all animals, with the possible exception of some animals on 15 p.p.m.

The toxicity of cadmium was increased by low protein diets.

The Elimination of Prostigmine. DALE G. FRIEND (by invitation) AND OTTO KRAYER, Harvard Medical School.

The inhibition of the cholinesterase activity of the serum was used as an indicator for the presence of prostigmine. Determinations were made by a manometric method[1] using the procedure of Van Slyke and Neill.

After a single intravenous dose of 0.25 mgm. of prostigmine methylsulfate to dogs of 10–15 kgm., the maximum inhibition of cholinesterase in the serum was reached within a few minutes. In 7 animals it took between $4\frac{1}{2}$–9 hours, or an average of 7 hours, for the activity of cholinesterase to return to the normal level.

The following factors have been shown to influence the cholinesterase activity of the serum:

1. *The distribution of prostigmine.* Immediately after the injection, prostigmine begins to exert its inhibitory effect upon the cholinesterase beyond the confines of the circulatory system. For example, it has been shown that samples of thoracic lymph collected within 20 minutes after the intra-

[1] Friend, D. G. and Krayer, O.: J. Pharmacol. and Exper. Therap. (in press).

venous injection of prostigmine to dogs already showed the maximum inhibition of lymph cholinesterase. During the period of distribution, the curve of the cholinesterase activity in the serum shows an initial steep return toward the normal level.

2. *The destruction of prostigmine.* About one-half hour after the injection, the increase in cholinesterase activity in serum begins to proceed much more slowly. Some of the destruction of prostigmine takes place in the serum. This can be demonstrated in vitro. 30 cc. of blood were removed under sterile precautions from 4 dogs 30 minutes after 0.25 mgm. of prostigmine methylsulfate was administered intravenously. The serum was collected and incubated under sterile conditions at 38°C. The enzyme activity returned to a normal value in the serum in vitro during a period of 12–16 hours, while the average time for the recovery of the cholinesterase activity of the same serum in vivo was 7 hours. The increase in cholinesterase activity in the serum in vitro was a linear function of time.

3. *The removal of prostigmine by the kidney.* The kidneys were ligated in 4 dogs under ether anesthesia and the animals allowed to recover. After the intravenous injection of 0.25 mgm. of prostigmine methylsulfate into such animals the recovery of the cholinesterase activity of the serum does not show a distinct difference from the recovery of the cholinesterase activity of the serum in vitro removed from the animals 30 minutes after the injection. This indicates that a large part of the recovery of cholinesterase activity in vivo is probably due to the removal of prostigmine by the activity of the kidney.

Yohimbine and the estrous cycle in rats. N. W. Fugo (by invitation) and E. G. Gross, State University of Iowa.

A series of experiments have been undertaken in this laboratory in view of studying drug effects upon the various endocrine systems. The scope of this report is concerned with the action of Yohimbine HCl on the estrous cycle of rats. The sex cycle of young rats (25–30 days of age) was followed by means of the vaginal smear technique. Experimental animals receiving suitable daily doses for several months showed periods of constant estrous of from three to nine days duration. There were also marked changes in sexual behavior, females acting as males. However, reproduction at the lower dosage is apparently unaffected, since litters of normal size and sex ratio are obtained from treated animals. Castrates treated with Yohimbine show neither estrous cycle or sexual behavior. There were no toxic symptoms developed even after the prolonged administration of the drug with the range of dosage used. The experimental animals showed normal body size, weight and appetite.

It is believed that the action of Yohimbine is related to the sex endocrines.

Toxicological Studies on Ammoniated Mercury. O. S. Gibbs and (by invitation) H. Pond and G. A. Hansmann, University of Tennessee and Columbia Hospital.

Studies have been conducted on animals and man to determine whether the ordinary use of ammoniated mercury is practically dangerous. We made over 20,000 applications to cats, dogs, rabbits, rats and humans: the latter for one month only; the animals for periods up to one year. Our analytical plant with a capacity of 100 analyses per week carried out over 2000 estimations for this study. Pathological studies were made by Hansmann to whom, in order to avoid post-mortem changes, animals were shipped alive, the tissues necessary for analysis being returned.

Results.

1. Nearly all common foods contain mercury. This varies from 0.1–6.0 gamma per 100 grams (or cc.).

2. From estimations of food and total excreta content, in the order of 20 gamma mercury per day is ingested by man.

3. Much larger amounts can be accidentally ingested.

4. The ingestion of traces of mercury and their presence in the excreta, have no toxicological significance.

5. One gram of 10 per cent ammoniated mercury ointment applied daily to man for one month, causes a total increase of 0.5 mg. mercury in the excreta for that period.

6. Erythrematous doses of quartz-light do not increase the absorption.

7. Transient skin rashes (average duration 2.2 days) often appear in the human only, especially in hot, sweaty weather. They may be reproduced by the base alone.

8. All animal tissues including cat, dog, rabbit, rat, cow, pork, fish, frog, foetus (rat and cat), new born (cat and human) contain mercury.

9. The distribution is irregular. Kidney, liver and gut usually highest; spleen, skin, lungs next; brain and bone lowest.

10. The equivalent of 5 mgs. per day per man given to animals caused no pathological lesions. The figure necessary to cause these was not established.

11. Mercury does not form dangerous storage pools in the tissues.

12. It is excreted by urine, gut and skin. This latter is a new finding.

13. The danger of chronic poisoning from insoluble mercury compounds has been overestimated. It depends not only on the amount of ingestion, but also importantly on the state of the animal.

Are the Results of the U.S.P. Frog Method for the Assay of Digitalis Applicable to Man? HARRY GOLD, MCKEEN CATTELL AND (by invitation) NATHANIEL T. KWIT AND MILTON KRAMER, Cornell University Medical College.

The answer is: No. Prior to any official method of assay, specimens of digitalis on the American market were reported to vary in potency by as much as about 300 per cent. Evidence has been adduced indicating that the intensive work on the assay of digitalis during the past 35 years has not improved that situation sufficiently, and preparations of outstanding tinctures of digitalis at the present time vary by nearly 300 per cent when assayed by the cat method, although they are all labeled U.S.P. XI. The cat and the frog methods do not necessarily yield comparable values. Which values are applicable to humans has never been satisfactorily determined. In the present study, results by the two methods have been applied to tests on humans with auricular fibrillation and regular sinus rhythm by a technique in which comparisons are carried out on one and the same subject. These experiments show that animal assay values are misleading, that assays with the U.S.P. frog method are not applicable to humans, that assays with the cat method give results that are more nearly applicable to man in the case of digitalis leaf. The results also indicate that neither overcomes all the obstacles to uniformity among digitalis preparations and that a final evaluation of the potency of a preparation of digitalis must be based on determinations on man directly.

Effect of Dilantin on Metrazol Convulsions. LOUIS GOODMAN AND BJÖRN LIH (by invitation), Yale University School of Medicine.

The effect of sodium diphenyl hydantoinate on metrazol-induced convulsions in mice and rats has been studied. Metrazol, 85 mgm./kg., injected subcutaneously produced characteristic convulsions in 124 of 129 mice (CD_{96}), caused severe seizures in 64 per cent and death in 44 per cent. Dilantin, 20 to 30 mgm./kg., was administered in aqueous solution *per os* to 91 mice twice daily for 4 to 7 days. When the CD_{96} of metrazol was injected within 24 hours after the last dose of dilantin, only 24 per cent showed typical convulsions, 13 per cent had severe convulsions, and 9 per cent died. Best protection was obtained when 30 mgm./kg. of dilantin were given twice daily and metrazol injected within 8 hours after the last dose,—typical convulsions appearing in only 5 per cent and no deaths occurring. Single large doses of dilantin administered parenterally were not protective and appeared to act synergistically with metrazol to produce severe convulsions lasting many hours. In all, 350 mice were employed. Preliminary results in 100 rats indicate that metrazol-induced convulsions in this species may also be favorably modified by chronic dilantin medication. Electroencephalographic studies are contemplated further to elucidate the inhibitory action of dilantin on drug-induced convulsions.

Further Studies on the Mechanism of the Vasomotor Reversal. MELVIN W. GREEN (introduced by Theodore Koppanyi), Georgetown University, School of Medicine.

The following facts have been ascertained concerning the vasomotor reversal of epinephrine following ergotamine: (1) The observations of Herwick, Koppanyi and Linegar concerning the role of anesthesia in vasomotor reversal have been confirmed. Under nembutal anesthesia there is no vasomotor reversal; on the contrary, ergotamine here acts as cocaine or ephedrine, potentiating the epinephrine pressor effect often in height, and always in duration. (2) In animals under urethane anesthesia, the vasomotor reversal obtained following ergotamine administration can be diminished, abolished or converted into a pressor effect by gradually increasing doses of atropine. The larger the dose of epinephrine, the more atropine is required to abolish the reversal. (3) In analyzing the vasomotor reversal the height of blood pressure must be taken into account. The same dose of epinephrine in border-line cases produces a reversal from high levels, but a diminished reversal or a pure rise from lower levels. (4) Ephedrine in appropriate doses may potentiate the reversal-producing effect of ergotamine. The conclusion of Koppanyi and associates that the vasomotor reversal is not entirely or even chiefly due to a sympatholytic action of ergot alkaloids is upheld by these experiments.

The Effect of Barbituric and Thiobarbituric Acid Derivatives on the Pyloric Sphincter and Stomach in Unanesthetized Dogs. CHARLES M. GRUBER AND CHARLES M. GRUBER, JR. (by invitation), Jefferson Medical College.

The actions of many of the barbiturates and thiobarbiturates on excised segments of small intestine, intact stomach, small intestine and colon have been thoroughly investigated. As far as we have been able to determine, no one has studied the effects of these drugs upon the pyloric sphincter. Ohmsted and Girogossintz in 1929 studied the effect of amytal anesthesia on glucose tolerance in dogs. Amytal, they believed, caused a prolonged contraction of the pyloric sphincter and in this manner prevented the passage of glucose from the stomach into the intestine, thus delaying absorption of the sugar.

This investigation was undertaken to determine if these drugs have no action on the pyloric sphincter different from their effects on other portions of the alimentary canal. The effects of the thiobarbiturates and some of the less studied barbiturates on the stomach were also investigated.

Six trained dogs with permanent fistulae of the stomach and duodenum were used. A balloon was placed in the stomach and another in the pyloric sphincter for recording their contractions and general tonus. Sodium amytal was injected 17 times, sodium pentobarbital 11 times, and sodium evipal and ortal sodium 8 times each. Sodium thiopentobarbital and sodium thioethamyl were injected 15 and 8 times respectively.

With the use of the barbiturates, the activity of the pyloric sphincter was either completely inhibited or the contractions were decreased in force in every experiment. The duration of decreased activity, 27 to 165 minutes, depended upon which drug was used, the amount injected and on the animal employed. Often as the animal recovered from the anesthetic effect of the drug it became very excited and abdominal contractions resulting from this excitement made it impossible to determine the absolute recovery time in many of these experiments. Decreased general tonus and muscular activity of the stomach was noted in all of the experiments with the use of barbiturates. The time necessary for recovery varied from 38 to 198 minutes.

The results with the use of the thiobarbiturates were variable. In some experiments the general tonus of the stomach and pyloric sphincter increased, in others they were decreased. The height of the contractions of both was always temporarily decreased and in some experiments they were completely inhibited. The time required for the recovery of the organs varied from 10 to 293 minutes.

N-Allyl-Norcodeine and N-Allyl-Normorphine, Two Antagonists to Morphine. E. Ross Hart (introduced by C. M. Gruber), Jefferson Medical College and University of California.

In 1915, Pohl reported a study on N-allyl-norcodeine. He found that this compound, while almost inactive when given alone, would antagonize the respiratory depression of morphine whether given before or after the morphine. These observations appear to have been neglected by subsequent workers. Our experiments on rabbits show that this antagonism is valid. However, contrary to Pohl, the allyl compound stimulates respiration when given alone. Intravenous administration of N-allyl-norcodeine will antagonize the respiratory effects of about twice the quantity of morphine similarly administered. Our experiments seem to indicate that the allyl compound will modify some other effects of morphine.

N-allyl-normorphine was synthesized by Hart, McCawley and Marsh. It was hoped that this drug might retain some of the analgesic and narcotic potency of morphine and still possess some of the characteristics of N-allyl-norcodeine. Our preliminary experiments thus far have shown that the N-allyl-normorphine has an action similar to that of the codeine derivative in antagonizing the effects of morphine on the respiratory mechanism.

The Influence of Aloe and Podophyllum on the Flow of Bile. Lloyd W. Hazleton, The George Washington University.

Adult dogs were anesthetized with sodium pentobarbital and arranged for continuous recording of respiration and carotid blood pressure. The neck of the gall bladder was clamped to eliminate smooth muscle action and the common bile duct was cannulated so that only hepatic bile was collected. Under these conditions acute biliary fistulas give results which are constant within a narrow range for each animal, but the rate of flow varies somewhat with individual dogs.

The volume of bile was measured at half hour intervals, four or five such periods serving as the control for each animal previous to medication, with an equal number of periods being measured after the drug was administered. Three dogs, serving as controls for the entire period, receiving no drug, the mean biliary flow being 1.5 cc. per period.

Four dogs were given 5 mgm. per kgm. of Extract of Aloe intravenously. The rate of biliary flow was increased uniformly, from a mean of 1.1 cc. to 1.84 cc. per period.

Two dogs were given 5 mgm. and three received 2 mgm. per kgm. of Resin of Podophyllum intravenously. The drug was dissolved in 95 per cent alcohol which was then diluted to 40 per cent with sodium phosphate solution. The mean biliary flow increased from 1.7 cc. to 3.1 cc. per period after the drug.

It is concluded that intravenous injection of Extract of Aloe or of Resin of Podophyllum causes an increased production of hepatic bile in the dog.

The Atropine-Like Action of Pilocarpine. Robert P. Herwick and Theodore Koppanyi, Georgetown University, School of Medicine.

Pilocarpine in doses from 0.5 to 2.0 mgm./kgm. has two atropine-like actions: a) it gradually abolishes the electrical excitability of the vagus; b) it antagonizes the vasodepressor effects of small doses of acetylcholine and pilocarpine. A dose of 2.0 mgm. of pilocarpine produces complete vagal paralysis and reduces markedly the vasodilator effects of relatively large doses of cholinotropic drugs. Prostigmine or eserine antagonizes these actions by a) releasing vagal paralysis and, b) by restoring the vasodepressor effects of acetylcholine. Barium chloride was found to have a similar action being capable of diminishing or abolishing the vasodilator effects of cholinotropic drugs.

Studies on the Metabolism of Diphenylhydantoin. C. H. Hine (by invitation) and F. L. Kozelka, University of Wisconsin.

Employing the method previously reported for the determination of diphenylhydantoin, the investigation of the metabolic fate of the drug in dogs and man has demonstrated that 2 to 10 milligrams are excreted in the urine unchanged. Approximately 9 to 10 per cent of the drug is excreted as diphenylhydantoic acid. This was demonstrated by reconjugation of the hydantoic acid derivative to the hydantoin form by refluxing the urine with sulfuric acid. The diphenylhydantoin was subsequently extracted with ether and identified by melting point and mixed melting point determinations.

The presence of diphenylacetic and benzilic acids could not be demonstrated. Organic sulfates and phenolic compounds remain within normal limits.

The possibility of the further degradation of diphenylhydantoic acid to alpha-diphenylaminoacetic acid or any intermediate products is being investigated.

Anthelmintic Properties of Alkyl Cresols and Their Chlorinated Derivatives. M. H. Hu (by invitation), Peter P. T. Sah (by invitation) and Hamilton H. Anderson, Peiping Union Medical College.

Lamson and Brown (J. Pharmacol. and Exp. Therap., **53**: 227, 1935) found 6-hexyl-m-cresol an effective anthelmintic without local or systemic toxicity in therapeutic amounts. Using their techniques we have studied the isomers and chlorinated derivatives of this compound, which were prepared in this laboratory.

In vitro 6-hexyl-m-cresol killed 10/10 pig ascarides in one hour; 6-hexyl-o-cresol and 2-hexyl-p-cresol were less effective; the para isomer required 2 hours to kill all worms. Chlorinated derivatives also were less effective, 4-chloro-6-hexyl-m-cresol and 2-hexyl-6-chloro-p-cresol at 2 hours were not lethal, while 4-chloro-6-hexyl-o-cresol in this time was effective.

Of the 6 compounds tested *in vivo* in 25 dogs, 2-hexyl-p-cresol was the most active; 66 per cent of ascarides were killed at a dose range of 0.2 to 0.4 cc. per kgm. Other agents, in similar amounts, in decreasing order of effectiveness were 6-hexyl-o-cresol, 2-hexyl-6-chloro-p-cresol, 6-hexyl-m-cresol, 4-chloro-6-hexyl-m-cresol and 4-chloro-6-hexyl-o-cresol.

It would appear that chlorination depresses anthelmintic activity of alkyl cresols.

Acute Fatal Insulin Poisoning. Eugene L. Jackson (Introduced by Torald Stollmann), Emory University and Western Reserve University.[1]

In acute fatal insulin poisoning in unanesthetized rabbits the following observations were made: 1) respiratory failure, even when artificial respiration was instituted, was followed promptly by circulatory failure; 2) respiratory failure was not due to anoxemia; 3) aeration of the blood in the lungs proceeded normally.

Local anesthesia for operative procedures avoided the possible complicating factor of general anesthesia.

To demonstrate, if possible, the cause of respiratory failure a series of experiments was carried out in which respiratory and circulatory activity, etc. were recorded. Departures from the normal were observed but they were not sufficient to explain the death. The significant fact emerged, however, that cessation of respiration, even if artificial respiration was started at once, was followed almost immediately by circulatory failure.

In a second series of experiments analyses of the O_2 content of arterial blood samples, drawn before and after insulin administration, gave average values of 14.6 and 13.7 volumes per cent, respectively. Statistically this difference was not significant. Therefore, the conclusion was drawn that anoxemia did not develop in insulin poisoning.

In a third series of experiments arterial and venous (right ventricle or external jugular) blood samples were drawn simultaneously before and after insulin injection. Analysis of the samples for their O_2 and CO_2 content gave the following average results: arterial-venous O_2 differences before

[1] Aided by a grant from the Committee on Therapeutic Research, Council on Pharmacy and Chemistry, American Medical Association.

and after insulin were 5.7 and 7.2 volumes per cent, respectively, while arterial-venous CO_2 differences before and after insulin were 4.0 and 7.4 volumes per cent, respectively. It was concluded from these data that during insulin poisoning there was no interference with the gaseous exchange either in the tissues or in the lungs. Therefore, respiratory failure could not be attributed to events occurring in the periphery, hence must be ascribed to those taking place in the central nervous system. A study of these events is now in progress.

The Rôle of Blood Cells in the Anaphylactic Histamine Release. GERHARD KATZ, Tulane University.

In a preliminary communication, it was reported that blood cells from sensitized dogs, guinea pigs and rabbits release histamine *in vitro* when they are incubated with antigen. These findings were confirmed on rabbits' blood (C. F. Dragstedt). Further investigations have shown that the greater part of this histamine is released from the white cells, but that red cells, too, release some histamine in *in vitro* shock. The presence of plasma is not essential for this phenomenon: sensitized white, red and whole blood cells release histamine when they are washed and suspended in Locke's solution containing antigen. At 37°C., the greater part of the histamine release takes place within 2 minutes; the release is completed within 7 minutes. The minimal antigen (crystalline egg albumin) concentration giving a maximal release is around 1:1,000, the minimal concentration occasionally giving a detectable release is around 1:250,000. Blood cells from animals sensitized up to 100 days previous to the experiment released histamine in *in vitro* shock. If it be true that the life span of blood cells is below this period, this would mean that cells can become sensitized without necessarily having been in contact with the antigen. In experiments on rabbits' blood, the appearance of an active principle beside histamine was occasionally observed: this substance does not stimulate the isolated, atropinized guinea pig's ileum; it lowers the atropinized cat's blood pressure and causes an epinephrine secretion in cats. It was not seen after the plasma was subjected to the chemical extraction of histamine (method of Barsoum-Gaddum, Code).

Some Effects of Potassium Salts in Man. N. M. KEITH AND (by invitation) A. E. OSTERBERG AND H. B. BURCHELL, Mayo Clinic.

The rapid intravenous injection into a dog of a potassium salt, for example potassium chloride containing 20 to 30 mg. potassium per kg., is quickly fatal. If the same dose is injected slowly in ten minutes, no untoward symptoms develop. In man the rapid injection into a vein of a 1 per cent solution of potassium chloride may cause intense pain along the course of the injected vessel. This pain will not occur if the solution is injected very slowly. On the other hand, a man can ingest quickly by mouth relatively large doses of potassium salts, up to 100 mg. potassium per kg., without demonstrable harmful effects. However, in some individuals large doses of 80 to 100 mg. of potassium per kg. will have a toxic effect on the kidney as revealed by distinctly reduced urinary clearances of inulin and urea. In two normal individuals, each ingesting 80 to 85 mg. potassium per kg., paresthesia subsequently developed in the hands and feet and at that time the serum concentration of potassium was found to be increased to approximately 30 mg. in 100 cc. In a third individual ingesting 104 mg. of potassium per kg., the serum potassium rose to 26 mg. per cent but no paresthesia developed. These latter findings and the production of local pain with intervenous injections, suggest that a sudden increase in the concentration of potassium ion to 30 mg. per cent in the circulating blood plasma acts as a pain stimulus to certain peripheral nerve endings. There is evidence that a less rapid elevation of serum potassium to this level, which may sometimes accompany renal insufficiency, does not cause such paresthesia. We are also at present investigating the relation of rapid increases in serum potassium after the ingestion of potassium salts to changes in the electrocardiogram. An increase in the height of the T wave seems to be a frequent finding as Thompson pointed out in 1939.

Effect of Drugs on Blood Lipids. F. E. KELSEY (introduced by E. M. K. Geiling), University of Chicago.

The mechanism for the control of blood lipids has been reported to be disturbed in certain types of neuroses, as evidenced by a greater spontaneous variation of the blood lipids of such patients, and by their abnormal fat tolerance curves. Studies were undertaken to determine (1) which drugs cause a marked, rapid and consistent effect on the blood lipid level in the normal animal, and (2) the response of the normal and psychotic patients to injections of these drugs.

Bloor's methods were used for the determination of the total lipid, phospholipid, total and ester cholesterol and neutral fat of the heparinized plasma of normal fasting dogs after the injection of mecholyl and both anterior and posterior extracts. With mecholyl a rise of 35 per cent of the phospholipids was uniformly observed after 30 minutes, with a return to the original level usually by the end of the first hour. No consistent changes were found in the other lipid fractions. Pituitary extracts were without effect on the normal dog.

The Effect of Sparteine on the Autonomic Nervous System. THEODORE KOPPANYI AND CHARLES R. LINEGAR, Georgetown University, School of Medicine.

Owing to the conflicting data in recent literature, the effects of sparteine on autonomic neuro-effectors were reinvestigated. It appeared that sparteine possesses two principal actions: a) a nicotine-like, and b) an ephedrine-like action. In doses from 10 to 40 mgm./kgm. it paralyzes the parasympathetic and sympathetic ganglia as evidenced by abolishing of the electrical excitability of the vagus and the pressor effects of the nicotine. The parasympathetic and sympathetic effectors peripheral to the ganglia are not affected; acetylcholine, pilocarpine, and epinephrine effects are not diminished. On the contrary, the epinephrine pressor effects are markedly potentiated both in height and duration following the administration of sparteine (ephedrine-like action).

Prostigmine or eserine which were shown to antagonize the ganglionic depressant actions of nicotine and amytal also antagonized the nicotine-like action of sparteine. Prostigmine in doses from 0.05 to 0.1 mgm./kgm. restored the electrical excitability of the vagus and the pressor effects from stimulant doses of nicotine after they had been abolished by previous administration of sparteine. It also interfered with the potentiation of epinephrine pressor effects by sparteine.

Anesthetic Action of Cyclopropyl Aliphatic Ethers. JOHN C. KRANTZ, JR. AND SYLVAN E. FORMAN (by invitation), University of Maryland.

Through a new chemical reaction the authors have found it possible to synthesize a series of cyclopropyl aliphatic ethers. Two of these compounds namely, cyprome ether and cypreth ether have been studied pharmacologically and the former has been employed in man. The structures of the two ethers are shown by the following formulas:

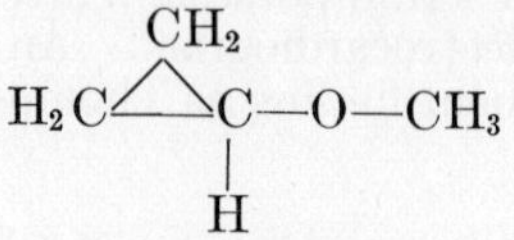

Cyprome Ether

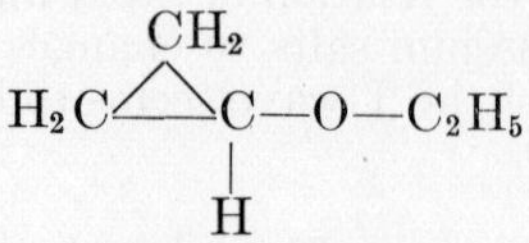

Cypreth Ether

It will be observed that cypreth ether is a true hybrid molecule between ethyl ether and cyclopropane. Its potency in laboratory animals vies with that of chloroform and its anesthetic index is more than twice as great as that of ethyl ether. In man cyprome ether produces an anesthetic syndrome with characteristics of ethyl ether and cyclopropane anesthesias.

Interrelations of Pharmacodynamic Properties of Morphine and its derivatives. HUGO KRUEGER, St. Louis University School of Medicine and University of Michigan.

In attempting to derive relationships between pharmacodynamic actions and chemical structure, the question arises, to what extent the measurable pharmacodynamic properties may be interrelated. A partial answer to this question can be obtained by plotting the minimal effective doses of one property against the minimal effective doses of another property. Such a treatment of the data presented by Small, Eddy, Mosettig and Himmelsbach (Studies on Drug Addiction, 1938) indicates that toxicity and convulsant action in mice were closely related properties, but convulsant action decreased with increase in the magnitude of the fatal dose of *morphine derivatives.* Respiratory depressant doses in rabbits ran parallel to general depressant doses for rats. Analgesia (cats) and general depressant action in rats were also closely associated properties. Also closely associated were convulsant doses for mice and respiratory depressant doses for rabbits. Toxicity in mice and general depression in rats were less closely associated than toxicity and convulsant action in mice. There was no clear cut direct or inverse relation between convulsant doses and general depressant doses or between convulsant and analgesic doses. In only two out of 95 derivatives was emetic action increased relative to toxicity, when compared to morphine. Emetic action was depressed in most derivatives. Convulsant action was enhanced in more derivatives, and more extensively, than respiratory depression, general depression, or analgesia.

Methylation induced slightly more consistent changes in the ratio between fatal and depressant doses than in the ratio between fatal and convulsant doses. If the effective toxic dose was low, methylation decreased the toxicity and respiratory action, but if the effective dose was high, toxicity was altered but little while the respiratory dose was decreased. Methylation decreased respiratory, depressant and analgesic action, but the decrease in depressant action became negligible if the dose of the non-methylated compound was high, while the decrease in respiratory action became very prominent.

Effect of Sulfanilamide and Some of its Derivatives on the Sensitivity of Mice to Anesthetics. PAUL D. LAMSON, THOMAS C. BUTLER, H. L. DICKISON (*by invitation*), WM. M. GOVIER (by invitation), AND C. M. GREER, Vanderbilt University School of Medicine.

Mice fed sulfanilamide for two and one-half days in such amounts as to give a final mean blood concentration of 5 mgm. per cent are anesthetized with smaller doses of pentobarbital, diethyl ether, divinyl ether, and chloroform than are control mice. Sulfanilamide reduced the median anesthetic dose of pentobarbital from the control value of 42.3 ± 0.7 to 30.4 ± 0.8 mgm. per kgm.; the median lethal dose from 120.5 ± 2.2 to 110.5 ± 3.5 mgm. per kgm.

Since the lethal dose of pentobarbital is reduced by about the same absolute amount as is the anesthetic dose, these experiments furnish no basis for the belief that anesthesia by pentobarbital should be either more or less dangerous in the sulfanilamide treated animals than in the normal.

The anesthetic effect is not found one-half hour after the intravenous injection of 100 mgm. per kgm. of sulfanilamide.

The effects of several derivatives of sulfanilamide are being studied.

The Effect on the Blood Picture of the 11 Day Embryo of Liver Extract Injected into the Pregnant Rat. JULES H. LAST AND EDWIN E. HAYS (introduced by E. M. K. Geiling), University of Chicago.

A study was made to determine whether the administration of anti-anemia factors in the form of liver extracts to pregnant rats would alter the blood picture of the developing embryos. Pregnant rats were fed diets containing 2.5 per cent Ventriculin or injected with 12 to 75 units of a potent liver preparation. The pregnant rats were treated before, during and after the anlage of the mesoderm which gives rise to the blood forming tissues in the fetus. Nuclear diameters of the immature cells in the pre-hepatic or "megaloblastic" generation of red cells were measured by means of a camera lucida. A decrease in nuclear diameters would be indicative of accelerated maturation of primitive erythropoiesis. In a series of 132 fetuses from 33 pregnant rats (litter mates), no evidence of a response could be detected in the treated animals over the controls. Embryogenesis of blood in the rat fetus cannot be altered by administration of the anti-pernicious anemia factors to the pregnant rat.

The Influence of Autonomic Drugs and of Nerve Stimulation on the Spasm of the Cardiac Sphincter Following Bilateral Vagotomy. G. LEHMANN, University of Louisville.

In barbitalized, vagotomized dogs stimulation of the peripheral right vagus has a diphasic effect. Strong stimuli cause a fall in tone followed by a rise. Weak stimuli cause only a fall in tone. The secondary rise is abolished by atropine and augmented by eserine. Stimulation of the left splanchnic nerve causes only a rise in tone.

Epinephrine injected intravenously and in the left gastric artery produces a rise in tone which is greatly augmented after cocaine and reduced or reversed after ergotamine. The response to epinephrine is not dependent on the original tone of the sphincter. Small doses of ergotamine alone cause a fall in tone. The sensitivity of the cardiac sphincter to epinephrine is greatly increased by vagotomy. These findings suggest that an adrenergic mechanism may take part in the production of the cardiospasm.

Intraarterial injections of acetyl-choline cause a rise in tone. Atropine produces relaxation. These data suggest that a cholinergic mechanism contributes to the cardiospasm.

The Effect of "Vitamin P" on the Circulatory System. A. J. Leser (by invitation), C. F. Lombard (by invitation), C. H. Thienes, Cecil Wawra (by invitation) and J. L. Webb (by invitation), University of Southern California and California Institute of Technology.

A crude water soluble extract from lemon peel (supplied by Mr. A. J. Lorenz, California Fruit Growers Exchange) has been studied as to its effects on the arterial pressure of the cat and rabbit and on frog and turtle hearts. A definite drop in blood pressure was obtained after intravenous injection of an aqueous solution of the substance. This blood pressure lowering principle could be concentrated by fractional precipitation from a solution of the crude material in ethyl-alcohol. Cutting of both vagi did not change the blood pressure response; however complete atropinisation of the cat abolished it. The isolated frog heart was slowed, its systolic contractions were decreased, spontaneous heart block of the hypodynamic heart could be overcome. The isolated intestine was slightly depressed; toxicity to mice was low. Animal tests on capillary fragility are in progress.

Intravenous Toxicity of the Acetins in Dogs and Rabbits. R. C. Li (by invitation) and Hamilton H. Anderson, Peiping Union Medical College.

It has been shown that with increase in acetylation increase in toxicity of the acetins occurs on subcutaneous administration to rats and mice (Proc. Soc. Exper. Biol. and Med., in press). As an extension of this study, the lethal range for monacetin, diacetin and triacetin, on intravenous injection in dogs and rabbits, was determined. Again, monacetin was least toxic, killing at 5 cc., diacetin, at 3 cc., and triacetin from 1.5 to 2 cc. per kgm. in a group of 12 dogs treated. In rabbits, the same relationship held, monacetin was lethal at 4 cc., diacetin at 1.5 cc., and triacetin at 0.75 cc. per kgm. Twenty-three rabbits were used. Tolerated doses in rabbits were, 2 cc. per kgm. for monacetin, 1 cc. for diacetin and less than 0.5 cc. for triacetin.

Animals exhibited severe dyspnea, muscular tremors, retraction of the neck and occasionally convulsions immediately before death which occurred usually from 2 to 22 minutes after injection. Animals dying from diacetin and triacetin showed varying degrees of hemorrhage in lung tissue, while those dying after monacetin showed less frequent and less severe changes. Sections of the heart, liver, spleen and kidneys were essentially negative on microscopic study.

The Mode of Action of Neoprontosil in Streptococcus Infections in Mice. J. T. Litchfield, Jr., H. J. White (by invitation) and E. K. Marshall, Jr., The Johns Hopkins University.

It is well known that neoprontosil (sodium 4-sulfonamido-phenyl-2-azo-7-acetylamino-1-hydroxynaphthalene 3,6-disulfonate) is reduced in the animal organism to sulfanilamide, but satisfactory data have not been obtained to decide if neoprontosil owes its chemotherapeutic activity entirely to the sulfanilamide formed. In a β-hemolytic streptococcus infection in mice, the Median Survival Blood Concentration of sulfanilamide was determined for neoprontosil and for sulfanilamide. The drug in each case was administered in the diet. The data obtained indicate that in a streptococcus infection of the mouse, the entire chemotherapeutic activity of neoprontosil is due to the sulfanilamide formed from it.

Cathartic Effectiveness of Parenterally Administered Phthalein Laxatives in the Monkey. S. LOEWE, The Montefiore Hospital.

A clue to the unknown mechanism of action of the phthalein laxatives may be expected from information on their parenteral effectiveness. It can be obtained only through experiments in rhesus monkeys. This report deals with determinations of the minimum, intramuscular, laxative doses of representatives from the three sub-groups of phthalides, indolinones and anthraquinones, namely phenolphthalein, isacen and peristaltine. The former were injected in freshly diluted alcoholic or acetone solution, the latter in aqueous solution. In all the monkeys, the orally laxative dose (D_{50}) was previously determined. Results were expressed in per cent of the oral D_{50}. No laxative action was obtained intramuscularly with isacen doses up to 120 per cent of the oral D_{50}, nor with peristaltine doses 100 times the oral D_{50} of phenolphthalein. The minimum intramuscularly effective dose of U.S.P. phenolphthalein was 65 per cent of the oral D_{50}. The intramuscular action of phenolphthalein was persistent, but nevertheless mild. The differences in water-solubility may be important for these differences. The value (200 per cent, i.e., 3×65 per cent) found for commercial ("yellow") phenolphthalein, which, by mouth, is 3 times as potent as U.S.P. phenolphthalein, indicates that the factor responsible for its superior oral activity is not effective intramuscularly.

The Action of Chemical Components of Cannabis Extracts. S. LOEWE AND W. MODELL (by invitation), Cornell University Medical College (in collaboration with Roger Adams, University of Illinois).

Recent advances in the chemistry of American hemp (Cannabis Americana) have made it possible to study the actions of several purified fractions and to determine whether the various biological actions used or recommended for bio-assay purposes are due to one or to more than one active principle.

The biological activity of compounds isolated from American hemp by Dr. Adams and identified by him, were compared with respect to three prominent marihuana actions, namely: 1) The ataxia action, as measured by the "approximation method" in dogs. This action is produced by the isomeric tetrahydrocannabinols. Two isomers, D $-164°$ and D $-240°$, were of high and almost equal potency (about twice that of our standard, a highly purified oil fraction). A synthetic tetrahydrocannabinol was also effective (about 0.20 as potent as the standard). Other compounds which produced ataxia were two hexahydrocannabinols (0.70 and 0.15 that of the standard). 2) The synergistic hypnotic action in the mouse. Cannabidiol is responsible for this action, which parallels the Beam color test, a test which has been shown by Dr. Adams to be specific for cannabidiol. 3) Corneal areflexia, which is produced by Cannabis extracts, and must be due to an as yet unidentified principle. This is indicated by the observation that the natural tetrahydrocannabinols are less than 0.2, and the synthetic tetrahydrocannabinol is less than 0.1 as potent as the less purified standard preparation in producing corneal areflexia, while cannabidiol is virtually ineffective.

Damage to the Optic Tract Produced in Monkeys by Tryparsamide. B. J. LONGLEY, N. M. CLAUSEN, F. A. DAVIS, M. E. NESBIT (by invitation) AND A. L. TATUM, University of Wisconsin.

Since disturbances in vision result occasionally from the clinical use of certain arsenical drugs, it seemed highly desirable to attempt to reproduce such an action in laboratory animals. It is naturally to be hoped that by means of some adequate tests the propensity of drugs to produce optic nerve damage can be determined experimentally. Such a means should open up the possibility of determination of the nature of, and conditions favorable to, the production of this unfortunate side-action.

Five rhesus monkeys were treated with increasing doses of tryparsamide. Four of the five monkeys which received higher doses became blind. The blindness was, for all practical purposes, complete except for the light reflex which was maintained. There was a paling of the optic nerve head and a searching nystagmus. Histological studies are in progress. Other compounds studied include acetarsone and atoxyl. These compounds produced more muscular weakness and incoordination than did tryparsamide but, in the relatively short period of observation, have not produced blindness.

Correlation Between Structure and The Ratio of Inhibitory to Pressor Activity of Sympathomimetic Amines.[1] AMEDEO S. MARRAZZI, New York University College of Medicine.

Having demonstrated adrenergic inhibition in the superior cervical ganglion by recording the reduction in size of postganglionic action potentials, this preparation was used as a readily quantitative and advantageous method of estimating the inhibitory potency of sympathomimetic amines.

The series β phenylethylamine to epinephrine and amphetamine to dioxynorephedrine (cobefrine) have been further examined. Any change in structure modifies pressor as well as ganglionic inhibitory activity to independent degrees. With a view to selecting compounds with predominantly inhibitory properties, the extent of inhibitory potency was expressed by the ratio of the amount necessary to produce the same degree of ganglionic inhibition as epinephrine to the amount necessary to produce the same pressor effect as epinephrine in the same experiment.

These ratios indicate that with respect to predominance of inhibitory effect the sympathomimetic nucleus, as exemplified by β phenylethylamine and amphetamine, is as good as or better than epinephrine. With the addition of the phenolic parahydroxyl group the ratio is maintained or bettered. The further addition of other groups although enhancing activity in general produces a poorer ratio until the full epinephrine structure is reached (ratio = 1). It seems that if one group is to be singled out for addition to the sympathomimetic nucleus in order to improve inhibitory potency, it would be the phenolic parahydroxyl; but the relation of the side groups to each other is equally important and may outweigh the influence of a single group.

Effect of Quinine on Urinary Metabolites of Fasting Dogs. A. T. MILHORAT AND W. E. BARTELS (by invitation), Cornell University Medical College.

Quinine administered to fasting female dogs reduced the urinary output of total nitrogen, urea, phosphorus, and inorganic sulfur, but did not affect the amounts of ammonia, amino acid nitrogen, preformed creatinine, creatine, organic sulfur or vitamin C. This effect usually was slight or absent on the

[1] Aided by a grant from the Committee on Therapeutic Research, Council on Pharmacy and Chemistry, American Medical Association.

day when quinine was given; in fact, the urinary output of total nitrogen and urea often was increased during this period. However, on the subsequent two days, when the urinary elimination of the drug practically was completed, significant effects were observed. The reduction in the urinary output of these substances was greater after a single dose of quinine had been given than when the drug was given daily for periods of several days. Moreover, the effect of quinine diminished after the drug had been given for prolonged periods.

Effect of Quinine on Metabolism in Patients with Muscular Wasting and Creatinuria. A. T. MILHORAT AND V. TOSCANI (by invitation), Cornell University Medical College.

Quinine was administered daily for periods of 5 days to 2 patients with extensive muscular wasting and considerable creatinuria. The diet was kept constant from day to day and the urine and feces were quantitatively collected. The results were as follows: during the period of quinine administration the urinary output of total nitrogen was increased, the fecal nitrogen was unchanged, and the nitrogen retention was decreased, whereas in the control period following the drug administration the urinary output of nitrogen was reduced, and the nitrogen retention was increased. No effect on the urinary creatinine, creatine and vitamin C was observed. The retention of calcium and phosphorus was decreased slightly during the period when quinine was given, but the reduction in calcium retention was more definite during the post-quinine control period. Since the fecal elimination of these substances was practically unaffected, the changes in urinary output cannot be related to changes in intestinal absorption. The findings suggest further that quinine has an effect on protein metabolism, but is without significant effect on the metabolism of creatine in the muscles.

The Use of Digitalis to Prevent the Exaggerated Acceleration of the Heart During Physical Exercise in Patients with Auricular Fibrillation. By WALTER MODELL (by invitation) AND HARRY GOLD, Cornell University Medical College.

Sir Thomas Lewis stated that "Although it is usually possible to control the rate in cases of auricular fibrillation, when the patients are at rest or quietly exercising, it is rarely possible to control the rates adequately in conditions of freer exercise." This view is generally held. Our previous experiences with "vagal" and "extravagal" digitalization suggested that this view might be incorrect. We examined this question in 27 experiments on 11 patients with auricular fibrillation. We found that physical exercise to the limits of endurance produced the same acceleration as complete blocking of the vagi by atropine. However, after "extravagal" digitalization complete blocking of the vagi rarely allows the ventricles to beat faster than 100 a minute. The present results show that exercise to the limits of endurance similarly fails to accelerate the ventricle appreciably above 100 a minute when a similar grade of digitalis action is obtained, namely, "extravagal" digitalization.

This study therefore shows that, contrary to the customary belief, the exaggerated acceleration of the heart during free physical exercise may be satisfactorily controlled by "extravagal" digitalization in patients with auricular fibrillation.

Organotropy of Tribromoethanol, Tribromoacetaldehyde and Tribromoacetic Acid. James L. Morrison (by invitation) and G. A. Emerson, West Virginia University.

Br content of various parts of the brain and of several glands, muscles and secretions was estimated by the method of Brodie and Friedman (J. Biol. Chem., **124**: 511, 1938) in normal and treated cats. The agents were given intramuscularly, in neutral dilute solutions, in amounts equivalent in Br content to 0.2 gm./kg. One-hour absorption periods were allowed. As judged from relative Br contents of blood and tissues, tissue affinities are high for avertin, particularly with brain, glands, bile, heart, lungs and red bone marrow. Tissue affinities for the other 2 agents are low; Br distribution following their administration roughly resembles that of NaBr, or the Br distribution in untreated cats, although there are notable exceptions for certain tissues. Although avertin and bromal are potent narcotics, several tissues other than brain show higher affinities; i.e., there is no specific attraction of brain tissue for these agents. Pathologic side-effects are correlated with distribution.

A Simple and Rapid Qualitative Test for Barbiturates. Hurley L. Motley (introduced by D. E. Jackson), University of Missouri Medical School.

The addition of 5 to 25 mgm. of a soluble barbiturate to ten cubic centimeters of water in a clean test tube containing 0.04 cubic centimeters or one drop of mercurous nitrate test solution (U.S.P. XI.) produces a white to gray colored gelatinous or flocculent precipitate, except for sodium barbital and pentothal sodium where the precipitate was of a finer type with less tendency for flocculation. The addition to the above of 0.08 cubic centimeters or two drops of potassium iodide test solution (U.S.P. XI.) produced a greenish colored colloidal solution, with a change in the character of the precipitate to one with no visible particles. The addition of potassium iodide to a blank produced a canary yellow colored colloidal solution. Determinations on light transmission from 400 to 700 angstroms with a spectrophotelometer revealed specific differences in the control from those with a barbiturate present.

The test is useful for quick differentiation of the barbiturates from other sedatives, particularly the opiates. Many of the drugs tested formed a precipitate with mercurous nitrate, but on adding the potassium iodide either a visible precipitation occurred or the solution was yellow or some other color than green if colloidal. A number of the drugs gave no precipitate with mercurous nitrate. Theobromine and theophyllin, were the only two drugs tested which gave similar results to the barbiturates and on a basis of chemical structure this was not surprising. These two drugs may be differentiated by modifications of the test.

The Liver Histamine in Canine Anaphylaxis. Gaylord Ojers and Carl A. Holmes (by invitation) and Carl A. Dragstedt, Northwestern University Medical School.

Biopsy specimens of liver were obtained before and after the shocking injection of serum in horse-serum sensitized dogs and analyzed for their histamine-equivalent content. The results in 16 animals indicate that the histamine lost by the liver is substantially adequate to account for the degree of shock experienced in each case, and that, therefore, the liver plays the major role in the anaphylactic reaction in the dog.

Distribution of Sulfapyridine and its Sodium Salt in Ocular Fluids and Tissues after Local Application. S. Y. P'AN (introduced by Hamilton H. Anderson), Peiping Union Medical College.

Following a technique previously described (Proc. Soc. Exp. Biol. and Med., in press), 100 mgm. of finely divided sulfapyridine was applied topically to one eye (using the other as a control) of each of 8 albino rabbits. One hour after application, the concentrations of the drug in the various ocular fluids and tissues were: conjunctiva 47.1 ± 11.2, cornea 30.3 ± 6.0, sclera 10.9 ± 3.6, aqueous humour 4.7 ± 1.2 and lens 2.4 ± 0.8 mgm. per cent. The chorioretinal layers and vitreous humour, all tissues and fluids of untreated eyes, and the blood contained no sulfapyridine.

Similar determinations were made after local application of 100 mgm. of sodium sulfapyridine to 8 rabbits. Concentrations of this drug one hour later were: cornea 156.7 ± 22.0, aqueous humour 88.3 ± 9.7, conjunctiva 75.8 ± 13.2, sclera 21.9 ± 5.7, lens 17.7 ± 2.4 and chorioretinal layers 11.7 ± 4.4. No drug was found in the aqueous humour, blood or in untreated eyes.

No tissue reactions were observed following application of sulfapyridine. In eyes to which sodium sulfapyridine was applied marked congestion and chemosis of the conjunctiva appeared almost immediately. These reactions did not subside until from 2 to 5 days after treatment.

A Method for Determining the Solubility of Gases and Vapors in Liquids by Means of the Van Slyke-Neill Apparatus. S. ANDERSON PEOPLES, University of Alabama.

The usual apparatus is modified by the introduction of a heating coil in the water jacket by means of which the chamber temperature can be controlled.

A suitable volume of gas is admitted to the chamber and the mercury level dropped to the 50 cc. mark and reading R_1 is made. If the vapor of a volatile liquid is to be studied a quantity of the liquid is admitted which will be entirely vaporized when the mercury level is at the 50 cc. mark. A quantity S of the absorbing liquid is then admitted into the chamber and while keeping the mercury level at the 50 cc. mark, the chamber is shaken until equilibrium is reached as shown by the constancy of the manometer reading R_2. A correction, C_1 is the manometer reading with the chamber empty and the mercury level at the 50 cc. mark. Correction C_2 is the manometer reading obtained by admitting volume S of the absorbing liquid into the chamber and lowering the mercury level to the 50 cc. mark.

The calculations are as follows:

$$\alpha' = \frac{50(R_1 - C_1) - (50 - S)(R_2 - C_2)}{(R_2 - C_2)S} = \text{Van Slyke–Neill expression}$$

$$\alpha = \alpha' \times \frac{273}{273 + T} = \text{Bunsen Coefficient}$$

The Effect of Varying the Intake of Dietary Salts on the Formation of Galactose Cataracts. CARL PFEIFFER AND (by invitation) HOWARD G. GLASS, AND ROBERT H. DREISBACH, Wayne University and the University of Chicago.

The marked polyuria which occurs with galactose diets in rats prompted this study of water and salt balance in galactose cataract formation. In a series of 30 control rats fed for 3 weeks on Day's galactose diet the incidence of severe cataracts was 45 per cent. In 20 galactose fed rats given 0.2 to 0.3 per cent KCl solution as drinking water the incidence was 20 per cent. In 22 rats given 0.3 per cent of other salt (NaCl, $MgCl_2$, and $CaCl_2$) solutions as drinking water the incidence of severe cataracts was 52 per cent. When 3 per cent K_2HPO_4 was incorporated in the diet, the incidence of severe cataracts fell to 22 per cent compared to 55 per cent for an equal number of control rats fed on the identical diet without the K_2HPO_4. The incidence with 6 per cent K_2HPO_4 was 25 per cent. The acid salt KH_2PO_4 (4 per cent) did not prevent severe cataract formation, for in a series of 10 rats the incidence was 50 per cent. Examination of the eyes at weekly intervals indicated that the primary lens damage is not prevented, but the severity of secondary calcification is decreased by adequate potassium administration.

Addiction Potentialities of "Seconal" and Sodium Amytal in Rats. NILKANTH M. PHATAK AND JOHN R. HILL (by invitation) AND NORMAN A. DAVID, University of Oregon Medical School.

Barlow's (1932) method, used at Dr. Sollmann's suggestion by Stanton (1936) for studying the addiction tendencies of the barbiturates by a "tranquilization" technique is simple and reliable for objective purposes, provided certain modifications in the technique and the recording procedures are observed. We wish to report here on the addiction potentialities of "Seconal" and Sodium Amytal as determined by this technique.

The drugs used and the daily dosages administered subcutaneously to 5 groups of 5 rats each during a period of 8 weeks is given in the table:

GROUP	DRUG	DAILY DOSE	MINIMAL I.P. ANESTHETIC DOSE	MINIMAL I.P. FATAL DOSE
		mg./kg.	*mg./kg.*	*mg./kg.*
1	Controls 0.5 cc. 0.9 per cent NaCl			
2	Sodium phenobarbital	40	150	250
3	"Seconal"	25	40	110
4	Sodium amytal	35	80	180
5	Sodium pentobarbital	30	50	110

The results of weekly 24 hour abstinence irritability of rats as recorded by this technique show no increase to either drug. Some differences in action were noted, however. With Sodium Amytal (35 mg./kg.) the rat irritability decreases steadily and continues even into the withdrawal period indicating a cumulative effect. With "Seconal" (25 mg./kg.) the weekly preinjection struggle response is always the same and the tranquilization at this dose is almost complete. Recovery is prompt and throughout the withdrawal period the abstinence response is the same as the original control level. Results with phenobarbital and pentobarbital-sodium are qualitatively similar to those for Sodium Amytal.

The Effect of High Fat-Low Protein Diets on the Nitrogen and Fat Metabolism of Hypophysectomized and Normal Rats[1]. ROGER M. REINECKE (by invitation), LEO T. SAMUELS, AND HOWARD A. BALL (by invitation),

[1] This investigation was supported by grant from the Committee on Research in Endocrinology, National Research Council.

University of Minnesota Medical School, and the San Diego General Hospital.

A study has been made of the nitrogen excretion, and liver fat of hypophysectomized and normal male rats fed equicaloric quantities of diets by stomach tube in which 15, 10, 5, and 0 per cent of the calories were furnished by protein, the balance being supplied by butterfat. The amounts fed were sufficient to maintain the normal weight when the 15 per cent protein was fed. The results indicate that the hypophysectomized rat can maintain life without any large supply of either exogenous or endogenous carbohydrate if sufficient amounts of fat are available. There seems to be a limited labile supply of protein upon which such animals can draw, however. The implications of this in the problem of pituitary influence on metabolism will be discussed.

Toxicity of Theophylline-Ephedrine-Barbiturate Mixtures. R. K. RICHARDS (introduced by E. M. K. Geiling), Abbott Laboratories.

Combinations of Theophylline, Ephedrine and barbiturates are used clinically. The LD50 of Glucophylline (methylglucamine + Theophylline) orally in mice was 625 mg./kg. and for Ephedrine HCl 900 mg./kg. Both produced marked excitement. The drugs were mixed in the proportion of 16 to 3. The calculated LD50 would be 674 mg./kg. However, actually it was 435 mg./kg., proving a potentiation of the effects. This was corroborated by intraperitoneal injection. The LD50 for Glucophylline was 400 mg./kg. and for Ephedrine HCl 360 mg./kg. Mixed in a proportion of 20 to 3 parts, the LD50 was 250 mg./kg. against 393 mg./kg. which would correspond to the simple summation of effects. 3 parts of pentobarbital or neonal were added to the above mixture. 393 mg./kg. of this mixture with a barbiturate were tolerated by about one-half of the animals. None died on 250 mg./kg. Only slight twitching, but no or very short sleep, followed. These findings show that, pharmacologically, such mixtures are rational.

Comparative Effects of Sulfonamide Compounds in Producing Cyanosis and Anemia. ARTHUR P. RICHARDSON, Stanford University School of Medicine.

Details of methods are described by which bacterial chemotherapeutic and other agents may be compared for their ability to produce anemia and cyanosis in mice. On the basis of drug intake per kilo per day sulfanilamide was found to be 2.1 times as injurious as sulfapyridine, 4.3 times as injurious as sulfathiazole, and 10.9 times as injurious as sulfanilylguanidine. When corrections were made for differences in absorption, excretion, molecular weight, and partition between red cells and plasma, the above compounds were of approximately the same toxicity. Cyanosis characterized by the formation of sulfhemoglobin was produced in direct proportion to the degree of anemia.

The Influence of Metrazol on the "Neurotic Pattern" in Rats. JACOB SACKS AND (by invitation) NORMAN R. F. MAIER AND NATHAN M. GLASER, University of Michigan.

Several investigators have produced a type of abnormal behavior in rats by auditory stimuli. The reaction, called the "neurotic pattern," consists of a period of violent, undirected running, which may be followed by a convulsion.

This abnormal reaction is not shown by all rats. The incidence of reactors varies from 20 to 60 per cent in different strains. Some animals which do not ordinarily show the abnormal reaction can be made to do so by the introduction of other conditions of a psychological nature.

The present experiments were undertaken to determine whether this abnormal reaction is an hereditary character present only in certain rats, or is latent in all. This was done by exposing non-reacting rats to the auditory stimuli after the injection of a sub-convulsive dose of metrazol.

It was found that the abnormal reaction can be produced by this means in the majority of such non-reacting rats tested. The reactions so produced resemble those occurring in reactive animals by exposure to the auditory stimuli or other psychological situation, and differ from the convulsions produced in these rats by larger doses of metrazol.

The percentage of individuals that can be made to show the abnormal reaction is increased much more by metrazol than by any of the purely psychological measures that have been used.

It is therefore concluded that the drug gives rise to effects beyond those which can be produced by purely psychological processes.

It is also concluded that the abnormal response cannot be completely accounted for on the basis of an hereditary trait.

Balance Studies in Hypophysectomized Rats Fed High Carbohydrate and High Fat Diet.[1,2] LEO T. SAMUELS AND (by invitation) ROGER M. REINECKE, AND HOWARD A. BALL, University of Minnesota Medical School, and the San Diego General Hospital.

Hypophysectomized male rats and similar rats with sham operations were fed equicaloric amounts of diets containing 15 per cent of calories as protein and the balance supplied either entirely by fat or entirely by carbohydrate. The diets were fed by stomach tube in quantity sufficient to maintain body weight providing no shift in water occurred and the nutrients were used as fed. Littermates were killed and analyzed at the beginning of the feeding. At the end of 17 days feeding the remaining animals were killed and analyzed for fat, carbohydrate, and protein. Liver, gastrocnemius muscle, and perirenal and gonadal fat depots were analyzed separately.

The hypophysectomized rats were able to maintain themselves on either the fat or carbohydrate diet, but lost small amounts of protein and considerable amounts of water. The fat-fed and carbohydrate-fed hypophysectomized rats all resembled each other in composition, except that the last group had stored more fat and lost more water. The additional fat in the hypophysectomized rats was in the body fat since the liver fat was lower than the corresponding controls. The carbohydrate-fed controls differed from all three of the above groups since they stored less fat and retained more water.

Calculation of the energy equivalents used showed that the hypophysectomized rat can utilize either carbohydrate, fat or protein when supplied in the food, but the carbohydrate-fed hypophysectomized rat stores fat because of a lowered metabolic rate. This was not found in the fat-fed hypophysectomized rats however.

[1] This investigation was supported by grant from the Committee on Research in Endocrinology, National Research Council.

[2] Assistance in the preparation of these materials was furnished by the personnel of the Works Projects Administration, Official Project No. 8750, Sub-project No. 355.

The Action of Various Agents on the Gall Bladder of the Frog. LLOYD D. SEAGER, University of Tennessee.

Intracardial injections of various agents were made into pithed frogs and response of the gall bladder directly observed. Of the ten agents used, as shown in the following table, Posterior Pituitary and Barium Chloride were the only ones that had any appreciable effect. Lack of effective parasympathetic control of the gall bladder in this animal is substantiated by the finding in 32 experiments that vagus stimulation sufficient to stop the heart produced no observable effect.

PREPARATION	DOSE PR. 30 GM.	NUMBER OF EXPERIMENTS	CONTRACTION	NO CONTRACTION
Atropine sulf.	0.02–1 mg.	56	6	50
Acetyl choline	0.02–0.2 mg.	20	4	16
A. C. after:				
Physostigmine	0.02–0.2 mg.	12	3	9
Physostigmine	0.02–0.1 mg.	36	2	34
Pilocarpine	0.2 –0.5 mg.	24	3	21
Epinephrine	0.01–0.2 mg.	45	0	45
Histamine	0.01–0.2 mg.	42	0	42
Post. Pituitary	0.3 –1 unit	48	16	32
Barium Chloride	0.2 –0.1 mg.	36	26	10
Normal Saline	0.2 cc.	40	0	40

On the Oxidative Metabolism of Skeletal Muscle from Chronically Morphinized Rats. M. H. SEEVERS AND F. E. SHIDEMAN (by invitation), University of Wisconsin.

The data presented in the table represents the oxygen uptake (Warburg technic) of minced skeletal muscle from normal rats and indicates the marked increase in oxygen consumption of muscle from rats to which ascending doses of morphine sulfate (20 to 240 mgm. per kgm.) were administered for 13 to 15 weeks. The animals were killed at varying intervals after the last injection.

	NUMBER OF ANIMALS	TIME AFTER LAST INJECTION	MEAN Q_{O_2}	RANGE Q_{O_2}	MEAN PER CENT CHANGE FROM .12 PER CENT MORPHINE
Normal	32		1.55	.97–2.33	+34
Chronic morphine	2	1 hour	2.26	1.67–2.84	+13
	15	24 hours	2.27	1.19–3.83	+16
	2	48 hours	3.37	3.37–3.38	+11
	2	72 hours	3.41	2.52–4.30	+29
	2	96 hours	2.14	1.56–2.71	0
	1	12 days	1.98		−3

The effect of morphine added "in vitro" (last column) is greater in normal than in chronically morphinized muscle.

The extra oxygen uptake due to added pyruvate is significantly less in chronically morphinized than in normal rat muscle and the synergistic effect of morphine on pyruvate oxidation observed in normal muscle is absent in chronically morphinized muscle.

Malonate (.02 M) produces a somewhat greater percentage inhibition of oxidation in chronically morphinized than in normal muscle.

Morphine on the "In Vitro" Respiration of Certain Tissues of the Rat, Rabbit and Cat. F. E. SHIDEMAN (by invitation) AND M. H. SEEVERS, University of Wisconsin.

These observations represent preliminary data obtained in the initial phases of a comprehensive survey of the actions of morphine on the oxidative metabolism of various tissues of several animal species. They are presented for comparison with the action of morphine on the respiration of skeletal muscle detailed elsewhere in these abstracts.

The effects of .12 per cent morphine on the no-substrate Q_{O_2} of various tissues are as follows:

Rat. The respiration of cerebral mince and kidney mince is not affected significantly.

Rabbit. The respiration of spleen, pancreas and adrenal, and to a lesser extent liver and submaxillary gland, is inhibited; heart muscle is unaffected. The respiration of skeletal muscle, uterus and spinal cord is significantly increased.

Cat. The oxygen uptake of cerebral cortex, cerebellar cortex, supramedullary ganglia, and medulla are all inhibited, the latter to the greatest extent. No uniform effect on spinal cord has been obtained.

Skeletal muscle is the only tissue examined thus far in which oxidations are uniformly increased by the addition of morphine "in vitro," although further studies on smooth muscle and spinal cord may yield results of a similar qualitative nature.

Some "In Vitro" Effects of Morphine on the Respiratory Metabolism of Skeletal Muscle. F. E. SHIDEMAN (by invitation) AND M. H. SEEVERS, University of Wisconsin.

The Warburg technic was used to determine the effects of morphine on the Q_{O_2} of rat skeletal muscle mince (Latapie). Morphine (.12 per cent) added "in vitro" produced a mean increase of 34 per cent above the no-substrate Q_{O_2}. An even greater effect was obtained with four year old, brown, morphine stock solutions. This extra oxygen uptake produced by morphine is due not to the increased oxidation of glucose, lactate, citrate, fumarate or acetate since the mean morphine increase remains the same and is superimposed upon the substrate Q_{O_2} when these substances are added. Morphine appears however to affect synergistically the oxidation of pyruvate, and to a lesser extent succinate; e.g., the mean increase above the no-substrate Q_{O_2} in four pyruvate experiments was: morphine, +31 per cent; pyruvate, +63 per cent; morphine and pyruvate, +135 per cent.

The morphine increase persists in the presence of added coenzymes I and II, hence is not due to an inhibition of dephosphorylation of these substances.

Malonate (.02 M) abolishes completely the increase above the no-substrate Q_{O_2} produced by morphine.

Iodoacetate (1:10,000), which does not reduce the no-substrate Q_{O_2}, partially prevents the morphine increase, presumably by diminishing the available substrate, since the full morphine effect is obtained when sufficient lactate is added.

A similar augmentary effect of morphine on the no-substrate Q_{O_2} was observed in a few experiments on rabbit and human skeletal muscle.

Further Observations on the Pharmacological Effects of Trypsin. M. ROCHA E SILVA (by invitation) AND CARL A. DRAGSTEDT, Northwestern University Medical School.

We have previously reported that trypsin has the capacity of liberating histamine when perfused through the lungs of guinea pigs and that it leads to the appearance of histamine in the blood when injected intravenously into intact dogs. That the capacity to liberate histamine from various tissues is a fundamental characteristic of trypsin is supported by experiments on the isolated smooth muscle of guinea pigs, the blood of rabbits, and rabbit's skin.

Effect of Pentothal-Sodium on Urine Output Under Various Experimental Conditions.[1] HERBERT SILVETTE, University of Virginia.

Using a standardized procedure and groups of 12 white rats, the influence of anesthetic doses of Pentothal-Sodium (Abbott) has been determined on the antidiuresis due to the injection of post-pituitary extract and on the diuresis brought about by the administration of hypotonic sodium chloride solution and mercurial and xanthine diuretics.

White rats, given intraperitoneal injections of 0.2 per cent sodium chloride solution, were placed in individual metabolism cages, where the urine output was recorded at half-hourly intervals over a period of 12 hours. After an initial latent period, a marked diuresis was shown which lasted for 6–8 hours. The administration of Pentothal-sodium (6 mgm. per 100 grams) 2 hours after the initial injection of sodium chloride solution brought about an inhibition of urine flow which lasted as long as the animals were kept in the anesthetic state. Soon after the animals' awakening, however, the urine output attained the normal rate of excretion, although the volume of excreted urine had not reached the control level by the end of the 12-hour period.

If, simultaneously or following the administration of Pentothal-sodium, 1.5 units of Post-Pituitary Solution (Squibb) were injected, no antidiuresis occurred. In contrast, if the animals were first rendered antidiuretic by a preliminary injection of post-pituitary extract, and then injected with Pentothal-sodium, the antidiuresis was not overcome, but followed the normal expected course.

Another group of animals was given two priming doses of 0.75 mgm. Mercupurin (N.N.R.) per 100 grams body weight. Then 0.2 per cent sodium chloride solution was administered as usual, and 2 hours afterwards Pentothal-sodium was injected into half the animals. No decrease in the effect of the mercury diuretic was brought about by Pentothal-sodium. On the other hand, similar experiments performed using theophylline diuretics (Phyllicin and Theocin) in place of the mercurial diuretic indicated that Pentothal-sodium exerted an inhibiting influence on xanthine diuresis.

These experiments are being continued and amplified in the expectation that the mechanism by which the barbiturates inhibit the secretion of urine will be thereby resolved.

Some New Aspects of Morphine Action: Influence on Excretion and Blood Level by Prostigmin. DONALD SLAUGHTER AND (by invitation) C. R. TREADWELL AND J. W. GALES, Baylor University College of Medicine.

The excretion of morphine in addicted and non-addicted dogs, receiving three daily subcutaneous doses of 20 mg./kg. of morphine sulfate followed by a three day withdrawal period, has been determined. After a suitable time interval the same dogs were given this standard dose of morphine plus 0.1 mg./kg. of prostigmin methylsulfate and the excretion compared with the

[1] This investigation has been made with the assistance of a grant from the Committee on Therapeutic Research, Council on Pharmacy and Chemistry, American Medical Association.

control period. In non-addicted dogs, prostigmin exhibited no influence on morphine excretion, while in addicted dogs there was a 9 per cent decrease. The addicted dogs also showed less severe withdrawal symptoms when they received prostigmin in addition to their morphine. The total percentage and proportions of morphine excreted as "free" and "combined" were approximately the same in addicted and non-addicted dogs.

Preliminary experiments suggest that morphine disappears from the blood stream more rapidly when prostigmin and morphine are given simultaneously than when morphine is given alone.

Experiments are in progress to ascertain what substance is the "binding agent" for the "combined" morphine in the urine and also to account for these blood differences in morphine content when a cholinergic drug is given.

This is a preliminary report.

The Oxytocic Assay of Posterior Pituitary Fractions. Blackwell Smith, Jr. (introduced by E. M. K. Geiling), University of Chicago.

A comparison of the chicken method of Coon and the official (U. S. P. XI) method for the oxytocic assay of posterior pituitary fractions was carried out. Preparations having pressor:oxytocic (P:O) ratios ranging from 1:15 to 29:1 were assayed by these methods and by the guinea pig uterine method using Locke-Ringer solution with a Mg concentration adjusted to 2.5 mg. per cent, the approximate Mg titre of human and chicken blood sera. Preparations having P:O ratios ranging from 1:15 to 3.5:1 exhibited equal potencies by all three methods. When the P:O ratio exceeded 3.5:1, the chicken method and the uterine method using Locke-Ringer containing 2.5 mg. per cent Mg gave equal results, and the official method gave lower values. This discrepancy, increasing with the P:O ratio, reached 300 per cent. Results indicate that the lower values obtained by the official methods are due to the low, unphysiological Mg titre of the official Locke-Ringer solution. The chicken method, with its simplicity and economy of time and funds, may therefore have the additional advantage of predicting more accurately the oxytocic activity of pressor preparations.

The Ratio of Bromide to Chloride in Body Fluids. Paul K. Smith and (by invitation) Alexander W. Winkler and Anna J. Eisenman, Yale University School of Medicine.

Bromide and chloride are not completely interchangeable in the body fluids. The extent to which they exchange across cell membranes has been studied in experiments of several types. In one group monkeys receiving a constant intake of chloride in the diet were given daily oral doses of potassium or sodium bromide. The ratio of bromide to chloride in serum was regularly greater than the corresponding ratio in urine. At higher levels of serum bromide (up to 60 mEq per liter) the difference between the ratios were somewhat less. In another group of experiments bromides were administered intravenously to dogs. The ratio of bromide to chloride in serum was likewise greater than that in urine. The inequality of the ratios was little affected by diuresis induced in various ways and was independent of the cation associated with the bromide. In still another type of experiment sodium bromide was added to defibrinated human blood *in vitro*. Equilibrium was completely established in a few minutes. The ratio of bromide to chloride in erythrocytes was always greater than that in serum.

The Effect of Morphine and Certain New Derivatives Upon the Fetus. FRANKLIN F. SNYDER AND KHA TI LIM (introduced by E. M. K. Geiling), University of Chicago and Peking Union Medical College.

The effect of morphine upon the fetus, following intravenous injection of the mother, was determined by changes in rate of fetal respiratory movements observed directly through the wall of the unopened uteri of rabbits at full term, the animals having been prepared by a method previously described.

Results showed that rhythmical respiratory movements of the fetuses were not abolished by dosage which produced definite analgesia and respiratory depression in the maternal animal. In a typical experiment a dose of 1 mg. per kg. of morphine sulphate was repeated three times at intervals of about 20 minutes, and finally a dose of ten times the initial one was given. Depression of intrauterine respiratory movements may occur as the dose is increased, and occasionally a transient interruption of rhythmical respiration. The outstanding result during observation of two hours or longer is the rhythmical breathing of the fetuses despite administration to the mother of more than 15 times the analgesic dose of morphine.

Through the courtesy of the Committee on Drug Addiction, National Research Council, we have assayed certain morphine derivatives having exceptional analgesic potency, namely, dihydromorphine, dihydro-a-isomorphine alcoholic ethyl ether, dihydro-a-isomorphine alcoholic methyl ether, dihydrodesoxymorphine D, and methyldihydromorphinone. The results suggest obstetrical usefulness.

The Toxicity of Bismuth Salts by Intravenous Injection. TORALD SOLLMAN AND JOSEPH SEIFTER, Western Reserve University.

Fast, slow, and repeated slow injections of water soluble ionic bismuth compounds (sobisminol, Na Bi citrate and thiobismol) were made intravenously in rabbits and dogs in order to compare the influence of rate on toxicity, symptomatology, sojourn of Bi in the blood and distribution of Bi in the organs.

Slow injections decreased the renal toxicity of sobisminol and Na Bi citrate, so that the LD_{66} obtained for fast injections was more than doubled; but the toxicity of thiobismol appeared unaltered. Dividing the dose in equal portions and injecting slowly for five successive days did not further decrease toxicity in rabbits. Liability to flocculation death decreased by slow injections, especially in dogs, except that slow injection of thiobismol appeared to be more toxic to rabbits than were the fast injections.

Deaths occurring during or shortly after injections were typical of flocculation. Animals which died later showed only the lethargy of uremia. Neither these animals nor those which were sacrificed thirty to sixty days after injection developed any of the striking features observed with administration of more freely diffusible Bi compounds (trimethyl bismuth).

The sojourn of Bi in dogs' blood followed the characteristic rapidly descending parabolic curve of crystalloid substances, except that thiobismol when injected slowly behaved more like a colloid.

The per cent of Bi in the organs paralleled the amount administered and decreased with the time elapsed after administration. Kidney and lung store Bi more rapidly than liver and spleen. The concentrations were fifteen times those obtained by intramuscular injection of similar doses of water soluble bismuth compounds and approximately the same as with like doses of intramuscular injections of the oil suspensions.

Effect of Convulsants at Low Body Temperatures. R. T. STORMONT AND W. E. HOOK (introduced by E. M. K. Geiling), University of Chicago.

Cats were anesthetized with sodium barbital (250 mg./kg. I.V.) and placed in a room at 4°C. The body temperature of the animals was reduced to between 20° and 23°C. and then maintained at this level for the duration of the experiment. The body temperature of control animals, likewise anesthetized with sodium barbital, was maintained between 37° and 39°C. Picrotoxin, metrazol, and strychnine were administered intravenously to both cooled and control animals.

The lethal dose of picrotoxin in the cooled animals was approximately twice as great as in the controls. The lethal dose of metrazol was approximately the same in both groups, whereas strychnine was slightly more toxic in the cooled animals.

Convulsions in the cooled animals were much less severe but greatly prolonged. The survival time of the cooled animals averaged 18 times that of the controls.

Further Studies on Substituted Oxazolediones. ROGER W. STOUGHTON AND J. H. BAXTER, JR. (by invitation), Vanderbilt University School of Medicine.

More examples of 5,5-dialkyl-2,4-oxazolediones, R, R′—C—CO—NH—CO,
└———O———┘

showing hypnotic action have been synthesized. Several short-acting hypnotics, with substituents in the 5-position totaling eight to ten carbon atoms, and showing a greater margin of safety between the effective and lethal doses than those previously reported, have been investigated. One series of phenyl alkyl compounds has also been studied.

The pharmacological examination of one long-acting compound, 5,5-di-n-propyl-2,4-oxazoledione, has been completed. No contraindications against giving it a clinical trial were found. Doses up to 100 mgm. per kilogram have been given to patients without unfavorable consequences and with good sedation and relaxation.

Effects of Chronic Nicotine Poisoning of Rats on Viability of the Young and on the Adrenal Gland. C. H. THIENES AND (by invitation) C. F. LOMBARD AND A. J. LESER, University of Southern California.

Litters of in-bred rats were divided into two groups of 25 pairs each. Both males and females of one group received 2 mg./kilo. of nicotine (in N.S.) twice daily by subcutaneous injection for 8 months; the second group served as controls and received normal saline in corresponding volume. As young were born the litters were divided equally, both males and females. Half of the young received nicotine injections, half saline, so there were four groups of second generation rats, which were injected for a period of 8 to 12 months. Records of 3rd generation young were kept. The nursing period mortality among the young of the nicotine series was 73 per cent of the first generation, 47 per cent of the second generation, while in the control series, mortality was 31 and 34 per cent respectively. These differences were statistically significant.

To determine whether the effect of nicotine was on males, females or both, three groups of 40 pairs each were tested for 6 months. In one group, only females were injected with nicotine, in another group, only males were injected and the third group were controls. Mortalities during the nursing period were 62, 41 and 42 per cent respectively.

Adrenal glands of both injected males and females were enlarged and contained nearly twice as high a concentration of epinephrine as adrenals from controls.

The Transfer of Bismuth into the Fetal Circulation after the Maternal Administration of Sobisminol. H. E. THOMPSON, JR., PH.D., L. T. STEADMAN, PH. D. AND W. T. POMMERENKE, M. D. (introduced by G. P. Grabfield), University of Rochester School of Medicine and Dentistry and Strong Memorial Hospital.

Using a recently developed spectro-chemical procedure capable of measuring less than 0.1 micro-gram of bismuth, the authors were enabled to determine quantitatively the prompt appearance of bismuth in the maternal and fetal blood streams, and in the placenta and exsanguinated umbilical cord, after the oral administration of Sobisminol to parturient women. The sensitivity of the method commends it for the analysis of biological material in which the bismuth concentration is low.

Studies on the Absorption of Some Digitalis Preparations from the Gastro-Intestinal Tract in the Cat and Man. JANET TRAVELL AND HARRY GOLD, Cornell University Medical College.

Absorption after oral administration was determined in the cat by the method of intravenous titration with ouabain, and in patients by a comparison of the effects of oral and intravenous doses of the preparation under controlled conditions at different times, usually in the same individual.

In cats only a small proportion, usually about 25 per cent, of the potent principles in the dose of tincture of digitalis is absorbed from the gastrointestinal tract, and the per cent varies for different specimens of leaf. The tincture of digitalis is as well absorbed from the gastrointestinal tract when it is freshly prepared as when it is several years old. Digitoxin-like preparations are practically completely absorbed after oral administration. Their absorption occurs not only from the small intestine but also from the ligated stomach under suitable conditions. We have indications that the pH and the concentration of alcohol influence absorption from the stomach. Lanatoside C is absorbed much less rapidly and completely than is digitoxin.

Experiments in man support the statement of Hatcher and Eggleston that the gastrointestinal absorption of digitalis and its purified preparations parallels that in the cat. Lanatoside C which is poorly absorbed in the cat is also poorly absorbed in humans, as indicated by the fact that equivalent therapeutic doses of this glucoside are about 4 cat units by intravenous injection and about 40 cat units by oral administration. The digitoxin-like materials which are almost completely absorbed in the cat, are also well absorbed in man since the intravenous and oral digitalizing doses are the same, about 3 cat units. This dose has the same effect as about 20 cat units of digitalis given orally.

Solubility Experiments with Posterior Lobe Pituitary Powder in 0.25 Per Cent Acetic Acid. JOHN A. VAICHULIS (introduced by Harold N. Ets), Loyola University School of Medicine.

Posterior lobe pituitary powder was prepared according to the official U. S. P. XI method, and solutions containing varying amounts of powder per cc. were made up according to the official method. The minimum total volume had to be 10 cc. for an accurate transfer of the macerated powder from the mortar. From the original solutions, dilutions were made with 0.25 per cent acetic acid so that each solution would contain 1 mgm. of powder per cc. The assays on cats and chickens are summarized in the following table:

NUMBER OF EXPERIMENTS	POWDER PER CC.	PRESSOR HORMONE RECOVERED	OXYTOCIC HORMONE RECOVERED
	mgm.	*per cent*	*per cent*
4	20	100	100
4	30	95–100	90–95
4	40	90–100	85–90
2	50	80	80
2	100	50	50

Effects of Anterior Pituitary Like Substance on Carbohydrate Metabolism. BEN VIDGOFF AND ROSA KUBIN (introduced by N. A. David), University of Oregon Medical School.

Since recent work has indicated the diabetogenic effects of certain pituitary extracts, we thought it pertinent to undertake a study of the effects of continued administration of the much used anterior pituitary-like substance on carbohydrate metabolism.

Twelve white male rabbits were divided into 3 equal groups, one animal in each group serving as a control. One of the treated animals received 100 I.U. of A.P.L. daily, another received 500 I.U. of A.P.L. daily and the third was given 1000 I.U. of this substance daily. Prior to treatment the rabbits were kept on a stock diet (rabbit pellets and greens) for 2 weeks after which a sugar curve (normal control) was obtained by injecting 1 unit Insulin per Kilogram body weight. After treatment, additional sugar curves were obtained on both normal and treated animals at intervals of 2 weeks to 1 month. Several of the animals were sacrificed after 9 weeks of treatment in order to investigate short interval and high dosage effects. The remainder of the animals were treated for 7 months to investigate the effects of lower dosage over a long period of time. No significant change in the sugar curve was noted for any animal. Histological study of the tissues is now being made.

On the Mechanism of Carbon Monoxide Poisoning. W. F. VON OETTINGEN AND (by invitation) D. D. DONAHUE AND P. J. VALAER, the National Institute of Health, Bethesda, Maryland.

One of the most oustanding features of CO poisoning is a rise of the spinal and intracranial pressure which presumably is responsible for the immediate or late effects of CO on the central nervous system. In order to establish the best therapeutic procedure for the prevention and reduction of these pressure changes, experiments were carried on in dogs anesthetized by the intraperitoneal injection of sodium amytal. Changes of spinal and intracranial pressure, of arterial and venous blood pressure, of heart and respiratory rate, of minute and respiratory volume, and of the carbon dioxide, carbon monoxide and oxygen content of the blood were studied during exposure to different concentrations of CO.

Exposure to concentrations of 1 per cent CO in air resulted within a few minutes in a progressive increase of the spinal and intracranial pressure which in the beginning was affiliated with stimulation of the respiratory rate and a primary increase of the blood pressure, but which continued to rise after both respiratory and circulatory functions were on the decline. The increase of the respiratory rate was not paralleled by a proportionate increase of the minute volume, so that the respiratory volume was reduced. The carbon dioxide content of the blood was moderately increased and the oxygen content was decreased as the concentration of CO in the blood increased. The concentration of CO hemoglobin at death was 81.5 per cent (median of 8 experiments) and death occurred within a median of 35 minutes.

With exposure to concentrations of 0.25 per cent CO in air the action was delayed and animals survived for 112 minutes, the final concentration of CO hemoglobin in the blood being 73 per cent (median of 10 experiments). Changes of the physiological functions were of similar nature as observed in the first series, although more protracted, and several phases could be distinguished which may overlap each other: (1) a primary stimulation of the medullary centers resulting in increased respiration, rise of blood pressure and slowing of the heart rate; (2) a depression of the peripheral vascular tone, characterized by a fall of the arterial and venous blood pressure; (3) a depression of the cardiac action indicated by a fall of the arterial and rise of the venous pressure; and (4) a final rise of the venous pressure shortly before death which we are inclined to believe associated with a reduction of the intrathoracic space caused by stasis and possibly by edema of the lungs. During the first stages the spinal and intracranial pressure tended to rise, during the final stages they were generally on the decline, presumably on account of a shift of the blood from the periphery to the splanchnic organs. In the second stage of the poisoning the increase of the respiratory rate is presumably due to a stimulation of the carotid sinus.

When the exposure to CO was discontinued after approximately 60% of the hemoglobin was converted to CO hemoglobin and the animals were allowed to inhale air, the spinal pressure first continued to rise, which increase was paralleled by disfunctioning of the peripheral and central circulatory apparatus. As the animals recovered from the acute exposure the spinal pressure decreased but persisted on an elevated level for from 3 to 4 hours, during which time the circulation had apparently partly recovered from the acute exposure to CO. After this period the heart and circulation gave again evidence of beginning failure and this was paralleled by a second rise of the spinal pressure. This delayed failure of the circulation occurred at a time when the CO hemoglobin concentration in the blood was reduced to about 15 per cent so that it cannot be explained on the basis of an existing anoxemia but that it is evidently due to some slowly developing injury of the circulatory apparatus.

Effect of Acetylcholine, Derivatives, and Certain other Drugs upon Artificially Induced Auricular Fibrillation in the Intact Dog. EDWARD W. WALLACE, University of Cincinnati.

Dogs were anesthetized with Nembutal and auricular fibrillation induced with a Jackson esophageal electrode and a variable electronic inductorium. After throwing the auricles into fibrillation a time or two the effect became more permanent and would last several hours without further stimulation.

A series of drugs acting on the conduction and refractory period of the heart were then injected intravenously to observe effects on cardiac arhythmio.

Quinidine and other cinchona alkoloids reestablished normal rhythm.

Epinephrine and derivatives had no effect on the auricular fibrillation. Parasympathetic paralysants such as atropine did not disrupt the arhythmia, nor did nicotine. Acetylcholine, however, in doses which caused a sharp fall in the blood pressure, and momentary arrest of the heart, repeatedly and almost invariably restored normal rhythm. Derivatives of Acetylcholine such as Acetyl-beta-methylcholine, and Carbaminoylcholine, also restored normal rhythm if given in doses large enough to cause an appreciable, sudden drop in blood pressure, and cardiac arrest. However, it was necessary to administer atropine, along with cardiac massage in order to prevent secondary collapse from an overdose of these drugs. In this respect Acetylcholine is superior in that the body has its own automatic antidote for the large dose necessary to momentarily arrest the heart and permit reestablishment of the normal rhythm. Clinical experiments are now under way.

Observations on Kation Shifts following Magnesium and Calcium Injections.[1] George B. Wallace and Bernard B. Brodie (by invitation), New York University College of Medicine.

When magnesium is injected, a part varying up to 30 per cent is bound by the tissues and the remainder is extracellular. This extracellular magnesium is diffusible since it passes readily into peritoneal cavity fluid. Whereas the extracellular magnesium is all excreted within 24 hours, the intracellular portion is still retained after 48 hours, at a time when the magnesium serum level and excretion have returned to normal.

The injected magnesium has difficulty in passing into the cerebrospinal fluid. With a serum level of 18 mg. per cent, the C.S.F. magnesium rises from a level of 2 to a maximum of 3.5 mg. per cent. Coincident with the rise in C.S.F. magnesium, there is a small but consistent rise of C.S.F. calcium. Apparently there exists a corresponding barrier for injected calcium, for with a serum calcium of 26.0 mg. per cent, the C.S.F. calcium rises from a level of 5 to only 6.3 mg. per cent. With the rise in C.S.F. calcium after calcium injection, there was found a small rise in C.S.F. magnesium, as well as in serum magnesium. During magnesium narcosis there is a pronounced drop in serum potassium, but little change in the C.S.F. potassium.

Pharmacological Studies on levo-N-Ethyl Ephedrine Hydrochloride (Nethamine Hydrochloride). II. Effect on Bronchioles, Uterus, Small Intestine, Stomach, and Pupil. M. R. Warren, T. J. Becker, D. G. Marsh, and R. S. Shelton (introduced by E. M. K. Geiling), Research Laboratories, The Wm. S. Merrell Company.

The perfusion method was used in preliminary experiments to determine the effect of levo-N-ethyl ephedrine hydrochloride on isolated lungs of rabbits and cats. Results indicate that levo-N-ethyl ephedrine hydrochloride and levo-ephedrine hydrochloride relax normal bronchioles to approximately the same degree.

Results of experiments on decerebrate dogs indicate that levo-N-ethyl ephedrine possesses both musculotropic and neurotropic action. This response was compared to that of the hydrochloride salts of levo-ephedrine and dl-phenyl-1-amino-2-propanol-1.

The effect of levo-N-ethyl ephedrine hydrochloride on isolated uteri of

[1] Aided by a grant from the Dazian Foundation.

virgin guinea pigs and rabbits was compared to that of the hydrochloride salts of levo-ephedrine, dl-β-phenylisopropylamine and dl-phenyl-1-amino-2-propanol-1. All of these compounds produce the same qualitative effect but differ quantitatively.

Levo-N-ethyl ephedrine usually relaxes strips of the isolated small intestine of rabbits. At times a stimulation is produced. Similar reactions were obtained with the hydrochloride salts of levo-ephedrine, dl-phenyl-1-amino-2-propanol-1 and dl-β-phenylisopropylamine. Preliminary experiments on the stomach in situ indicate that levo-N-ethyl ephedrine produces a definite inhibition of gastric peristalsis.

The mydriatic action of levo-N-ethyl ephedrine is negligible following irrigation of the eye with a 1 per cent solution. Intravenous administration of 25–50 mgm./kg. increases mydriasis but to a lesser degree than similar amounts of levo-ephedrine hydrochloride.

Oxygen Therapy in the Relief of Fatigue in Relation to Flying. R. A. WAUD AND WARD SMITH (by invitation), University of Western Ontario and London Association for War Research.

The effects of administration of various drugs including oxygen on fatigue was studied in guinea pigs. The animals were exercised on a tread-mill while being subjected to a rarefied atmosphere in a decompression chamber. It was found that if oxygen was supplied when the working ceiling of the particular animal was reached, fatigue did not set in and that the ceiling of the animal could be raised by at least 8,000 to 10,000 feet.

The Effects of Benzedrine, Coramine, Metrazol and Picrotoxin on Body Temperature and Gaseous Metabolism in Rabbits Depressed by Alcohol. H. W. WERNER (introduced by A. L. Tatum), University of North Dakota.

Previously reported experiments indicated that, with doses used, benzedrine and coramine were more effective than metrazol and picrotoxin in antagonizing the depression of body temperature which followed the oral administration of 7 cc. per kgm. of alcohol. An attempt to explain these results led to work herein partially summarized.

In control experiments the administration of alcohol was usually followed in $2\frac{1}{2}$ hours by a maximal lowering of body temperature which remained nearly constant until at least $9\frac{1}{4}$ hours after giving alcohol. Although in some experiments metabolic rate increased $2\frac{1}{2}$ to 4 hours after alcohol administration, at later periods the rate was near or, in one of six experiments, considerably below the pre-alcohol level.

Determinations $1\frac{1}{4}$ to $2\frac{3}{4}$ hours after giving analeptics ($5\frac{1}{2}$ to 7 hours after alcohol) showed that benzedrine and coramine were most effective in increasing body temperature while benzedrine and metrazol most consistently increased metabolic rate at this period.

At the period $5\frac{1}{4}$ to $6\frac{3}{4}$ hours after giving analeptics ($9\frac{1}{2}$ to 11 hours after alcohol) rectal temperatures and metabolic rates were usually near the pre-analeptic level, but increased metabolic rates were observed in some experiments with each of the analeptics.

The Inactivation of Choline Esterase by Morphine and Derivatives. CHARLES I. WRIGHT, National Institute of Health.

Bernheim (J. Pharm. & Exper. Therap. **57,** 427, 1936), using a pharmacological method, found that choline esterase was inactivated by morphine. Slaughter and Lackey (Proc. Soc. Biol. & Med. **45,** 8, 1940) were unable to confirm the *in vitro* inhibition of choline esterase by morphine. That serum and brain choline esterase are inactivated by morphine, dilaudid and dihydrodesoxymorphine-D can be shown by the manometric method. The measurements were made at 37.5°C. under an atmosphere of 95 per cent N_2 and 5 per cent CO_2. All materials were dissolved in bicarbonate Ringer's solution. Acetylcholine (2.5 mg.) was placed in the side arm and the choline esterase and morphine in the main vessel. Total solution volume was 3.0 cc.

The table shows the percentage inactivation of serum and rabbit brain choline esterase by the three drugs at concentrations (mg. in 3.0 cc.) shown in the first column. The inactivation was calculated on the basis of the CO_2 produced at 45 minutes.

DRUG CONCENTRATION	DOG SERUM (0.04 CC.)			BRAIN (8.0 MG.)		
	Morphine	Dilaudid	Desoxy-D	Morphine	Dilaudid	Desoxy-D
	Per cent inactivation					
mg.	*per cent*	*per cent*	*per cent*	*per cent*	*per cent*	*per cent*
0.25	18	20	37	15	18	46
0.50	27	33	52	25	26	64
1.0	45	44	69	40	38	80
2.0	60	58	81	53	41	94
4.0	77	63	85	73	67	100

The inactivation by dihydrodesoxymorphine-D was much greater than by morphine or dilaudid. The degree of inactivation of choline esterase by codeine varies widely, depending on the source of the enzyme.

A Study of the Possible Toxic Effects of Prolonged Formaldehyde Ingestion. F. F. YONKMAN, A. J. LEHMAN, C. C. PFEIFFER, AND H. F. CHASE (by invitation), Wayne University.

Two male subjects were placed on daily consumption of pure formaldehyde in water. Beginning with 22 mgm. per day for the first fourteen days, every seven or fourteen days the daily dosage was increased until 200 mgm. were consumed daily during the thirteenth week. Contrary to Wiley's findings in 1908, periodic blood samples revealed no significant changes in hemoglobin, red or white cell number or morphology and all urines were persistently negative when tested for free formaldehyde and albumin. One subject complained of mild pharnygeal and gastric discomfort when the formaldehyde reached a concentration of about 1:3500. This was obviated when the same daily dose of formaldehyde was taken in two glasses of water or a concentration of approximately 1:7000. The second patient did not experience this mild discomfort until a concentration of about 1:2500 was attained. This likewise was rectified by increasing the dilution. How long this consumption of pure formaldehyde could have been endured is problematic, but one concludes that when taken in large amounts but sufficiently diluted so as to cause no or only slight pharyngeal or gastric discomfort, formaldehyde ingestion might be long continued without significantly altering the blood or urinary picture. Feeding of formaldehyde-containing foods to rats confirmed the low toxicity of this aldehyde.

Effect of Lipoiodine-N.N.R. Therapy on Maternal and Fetal Blood Iodine. F. B. ZENER AND NILKANTH PHATAK (by invitation) AND NORMAN A. DAVID, University of Oregon Medical School.

We have already reported that blood iodine values of both iodine treated (Lipoiodine-Ciba, N.N.R., 1 tablet daily during six months before delivery) and iodine untreated pregnant individuals attain a high normal level (24.2 y per cent) at term. This value falls to between 15 and 18 y per cent by 6 weeks post partum. During this time, much of the mother's blood iodine is lost through colostrum and milk (Leipert 1934).

In 47 treated and untreated cases simultaneous determination of maternal and fetal (cord) blood iodine content at parturition showed no correlation between these two blood iodine values. When the mothers were given Lipoiodine during pregnancy, the maternal blood iodine at term was relatively high (27.2 y per cent) but the fetal blood iodine values were still within normal (adult) range of 8.0 to 14.0 y per cent. The actual average blood iodine values for the 47 cases were: maternal blood iodine 24.1 y per cent and cord blood iodine 11.6 y per cent. Apparently an increase in maternal blood iodine does not raise the fetal blood iodine level. It is believed that the increased maternal blood iodine is in some organic combination with the maternal blood proteins or lipids in an "inactive" form. Our results indicate that iodine therapy meets the metabolic needs of the gravid individual without affecting the fetal metabolism.

DEMONSTRATIONS

1. *An All-Glass Ludwig Stromuhr.* JACK NICHOLS (by invitation) AND C. H. THIENES, University of Southern California.
2. *Artificial Respiration Pump Using Compressed Air and Vacuum.* C. H. THIENES AND H. F. WILKINS (by invitation), University of Southern California.
3. *Composite Graphs, Made by Students, as a Means of Presenting and Controlling All Experimental Results Obtained in Class-Work.* J. AUER, A. O. SHAKLEE (by invitation) AND H. KRUEGER, St. Louis University School of Medicine.
4. *A Mouse Holder.* PAUL D. LAMSON. Vanderbilt University School of Medicine.
5. *An Electrical Stimulator for Class Use in Physiology Entirely Operated by 110 Volts A.C.* S. A. PEOPLES, University of Alabama School of Medicine.

MOTION PICTURES

1. Metrazol convulsions in normal and neurotic rats. N. R. F. MAIER (by invitation) AND JACOB SACKS, University of Michigan.

A COMPARISON OF EPHEDRINE AND ESERINE

J. D. P. GRAHAM AND M. R. GURD

From the Nuffield Institute for Medical Research, Oxford

Received for publication January 20, 1941

A new conception of the action of ephedrine was advanced by Gaddum and Kwiatkowski in 1938. They showed that ephedrine in low concentrations increases the action of adrenaline on a variety of preparations. They showed later that a substance indistinguishable from adrenaline is liberated by sympathetic stimulation in the perfused rabbit ear, and that this also is increased in action by ephedrine (Gaddum and Kwiatkowski, 1939). They suggested that ephedrine acted in this way by inhibiting the amine oxidase described by Blaschko, Richter and Schlossmann (1937), which Gaddum and Kwiatkowski held to be responsible for the physiological inactivation of adrenaline; the suggestion was, in fact, that ephedrine acted upon the adrenaline-amine oxidase system in a manner analogous to the action of eserine on the acetylcholine-cholinesterase system. Further evidence (Richter, 1940) has indicated that amine oxidase is probably not concerned in the physiological inactivation of adrenaline, but the basic theory of Gaddum and Kwiatkowski need not necessarily be abandoned, it can be shown that the physiological destruction of adrenaline is enzymic and that the enzyme is inhibited by ephedrine.

There is already considerable evidence of an analogy between the actions of eserine and other anticholinesterases on the one hand, and ephedrine and some other phenylisopropylamine derivatives on the other. Both groups have been shown to increase some of the actions of the corresponding autonomimetic substances under particular conditions, while under other conditions these actions are depressed. Direct comparisons between members of the two groups do not however appear to have been made, and it seemed to us desirable to compare the effects of various concentrations of ephedrine and eserine on the actions of adrenaline and acetylcholine respectively, in a variety of preparations under similar conditions, and to examine the relations between concentration and effect with the object of finding how far the two effects are analogous. The following preparations were used: perfused frog heart, cat blood pressure, cat limb volume, perfused rabbit ear, isolated rabbit gut and cat nictitating membrane.

Perfused frog heart. Frog hearts were perfused *in situ* with frog-Ringer solution (Howell) using a Greene's cannula. The perfusing fluid was led from a Marriotte bottle to the cannula, which was tied into the venous end of the heart; the fluid escaped from cuts in the aortae. In this way a continuous flow of Ringer was maintained at any required pressure. Another Marriotte bottle and a two-way tap permitted of perfusion at the same pressure with Ringer solution containing drugs. The effect of 0.5 μg adrenaline in 0.2 cc. saline, injected directly into the cannula, was recorded first. After acting for one minute the Ringer was washed out three times *via* the side tube and the heart allowed to rest for five minutes. When repeated administrations of adrenaline gave similar effects the perfusing fluid was altered to Ringer solution containing ephedrine. After fifteen minutes perfusion of the heart, and again after thirty minutes, the same dose of adrenaline was repeated. The perfusing fluid was then changed back to plain Ringer and further doses of adrenaline given in fifteen and thirty minutes. In this way the effect of constant perfusion of ephedrine solution upon the action of a fixed

TABLE 1

Summary of experiments on isolated organs

CONCENTRATION OF EPHEDRINE OR ESERINE	FROG HEART		RABBIT EAR	
	Effect of ephedrine on action of adrenaline	Effect of eserine on action of acetyl choline	Effect of ephedrine on action of adrenaline	Effect of eserine on action of acetyl choline
10^{-9}	0	0	+	0
10^{-8}	+	+	+	+
10^{-7}	+	+	+ or −	+
10^{-6}	+	+ or −	−	+
10^{-5}	−	−	−	−
10^{-4}	−	−	Abol.	−
10^{-3}	Abol.	Abol.	Abol.	Abol.

0, no effect; +, potentiation; abol., abolished; −, depression.

dose of adrenaline could be recorded. The same technique was used in determining the effect of perfusion with various concentrations of eserine on the action of 0.1 μg acetylcholine.

A summary of the results of these experiments is given in the second and third columns of table 1, and it will be seen that low concentrations of both drugs increase, while high concentrations diminish the action of adrenaline or acetylcholine.

Figure 1 illustrates some of the results. Ephedrine 10^{-6} increases (a), while ephedrine 10^{-5} diminishes (b), the action of adrenaline. Figure 1 (c) shows the potentiation of acetylcholine action by eserine 10^{-7}. Eserine in a concentration of 10^{-5} usually diminished the action of acetylcholine, but in one experiment a curious reversal of the customary effect was seen at this concentration (fig. 1 d). At this and stronger concentrations eserine was markedly toxic to the frog heart; ephedrine also was toxic at concentrations of 10^{-4} or more.

It is evident that the effects of ephedrine and eserine are similar and that the relations between concentration and effect are also similar in the two cases.

Blood pressure of cat. Some twenty spinal and nembutalized cats were used for these experiments. The majority of the ephedrine experiments were done on spinal cats, while most of the eserine experiments were carried out on nembutalized cats, as it was difficult to obtain a spinal preparation with a sufficiently high initial blood pressure for the latter experiments, in which the

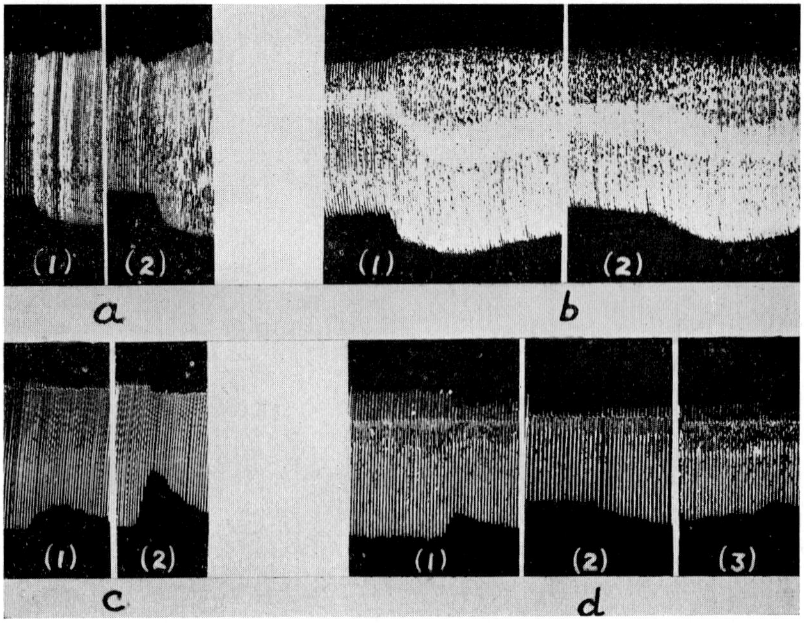

FIG. 1. ISOLATED FROG HEART

(a) Action of 1 μg of adrenaline, before (1) and during (2) perfusion with ephedrine 10^{-6}.
(b) Action of 1 μg of adrenaline, before (1) and during (2) perfusion with ephedrine 10^{-5}.
(c) Action of 0.05 μg of acetylcholine, before (1) and during (2) perfusion with eserine 10^{-7}.
(d) Action of 0.05 μg of acetylcholine, before (1), during (2) and after (3) perfusion with eserine 10^{-5}.

blood pressure level was liable to get progressively lower owing to the large amounts of eserine and acetylcholine given. Some experiments with eserine were made however on spinal cats, and some with ephedrine on nembutalized cats; the results were substantially the same on either preparation. Blood pressure was recorded from the carotid artery and all injections were made into the external jugular vein; in nembutalized animals the vagi were cut and artificial respiration was given if and when necessary.

The doses of adrenaline which were used varied, from 1.66 to 12.5 μg per kilogram and those of acetylcholine from 0.12 to 0.66 μg per kilogram. In any one experiment the dose of one of these drugs was constant throughout the experiment and doses were given at regular intervals until a series of constant responses had been obtained, after which an intravenous injection of ephedrine or eserine, as the case might be, was given, and the series of doses of adrenaline or acetylcholine continued. Further larger doses of ephedrine or eserine were then given and further increase or diminution of the action of adrenaline or acetylcholine observed. The range of doses of ephedrine used was from 0.005 to 28.0 mgm. per kilogram and of eserine from 0.0012 to 1.7 mgm. per kilogram.

The results of the blood pressure experiments are summarized in the second and third columns of table 2.

As in other preparations both ephedrine and eserine in small concentrations increased the action of the corresponding autonomimetic substance,

TABLE 2

Summary of experiments on entire animals

DOSAGE OF EPHEDRINE OR ESERINE	CAT BLOOD PRESSURE		CAT LIMB VOLUME	
	Effect of ephedrine* on action of adrenaline	Effect of eserine on action of acetyl choline	Effect of ephedrine on action of adrenaline	Effect of eserine on action of acetyl choline
mgm. per kgm.				
0.003	+	+	+	+
0.03	+	+	+	+
0.01	+	+	+	+
0.1	+ or −	+ or −	+ or −	+ or −
0.3	+ or −	+ or −	+ or −	+ or −
1.0	−	−	−	−
3.0	−	−	−	Abol.

* In one experiment on the effect of ephedrine on cat blood pressure the dosage levels differed from those given above. This experiment is described in the text.

and in higher concentrations diminished these actions. These effects were never very great, and did not occur at all in some animals.

Figure 2 shows the effect of ephedrine on the action of a constant dose of adrenaline in spinal cats. The upper tracing shows the increase in the adrenaline action produced by a dose of 0.003 mgm. per kilogram of ephedrine (a) and the further small increase produced by a further dose of 0.03 mgm. per kilogram (b). The lower tracing (from another animal) shows the diminution in adrenaline action produced by a dose of 0.05 mgm. per kilogram of ephedrine (c) and the further diminution produced by a dose of 0.5 mgm. per kilogram (d). To facilitate comparison the actual heights of the rises in mm. of Hg have been marked on the tracings.

The dosage level at which the effect of ephedrine changed from an increase in adrenaline action to a diminution was usually within the limits 0.05 to 0.5 mgm. per kilogram as shown in table 2. In one exceptional case however a dose of 5.0 mgm. per kilogram of ephedrine still increased the action of adrenaline, and the adrenaline response did not begin to diminish until nearly twice this dose of ephedrine had been injected.

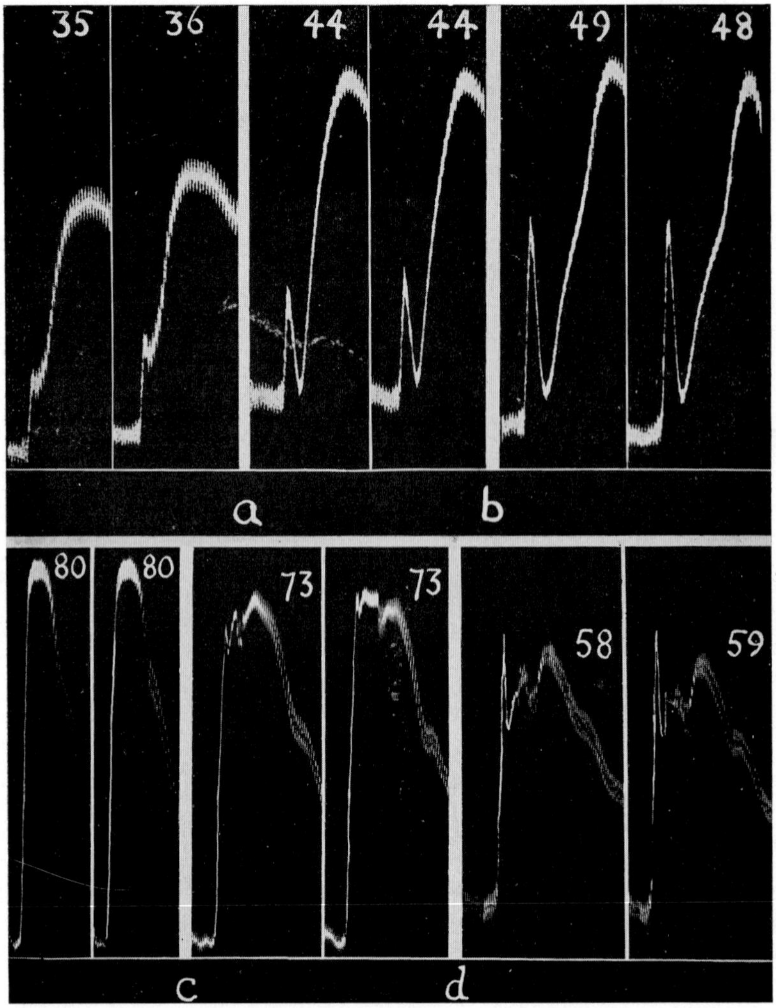

FIG. 2. BLOOD PRESSURE OF SPINAL CAT

Effect of ephedrine on pressor action of a constant dose of adrenaline. Numbers indicate height of rise in mm. of mercury.

Upper tracings: Pressor responses to equal doses of 5 μg/kgm. of adrenaline. A dose of 0.003 mgm./kgm. of ephedrine injected at (a), and 0.03 mgm./kgm. of ephedrine injected at (b).

Lower tracings: From another animal. Pressor responses to equal doses of 5 μg/kgm. of adrenaline. A dose of 0.05 mgm./kgm. of ephedrine injected at (c), and 0.5 mgm./kgm. of ephedrine injected at (d). (The two tracings are not reproduced to the same scale.)

Figure 3 shows the effect of eserine on the action of acetylcholine in a nembutalized cat. Successive doses of 0.0012 (a), 0.012 (b), and 0.12 (c) mgm. per kilogram of eserine caused successive increases in the depressor action of 0.12 μg per kilogram of acetylcholine. A dose of 0.70 mgm. per kilogram (d) reduced the response approximately to its original size, although its duration was greater, and a further dose of 1.70 mgm. per kilogram (e) lowered the blood pressure level considerably, and the action of acetylcholine was still further diminished, part of this diminution doubtless being due to the lower initial level.

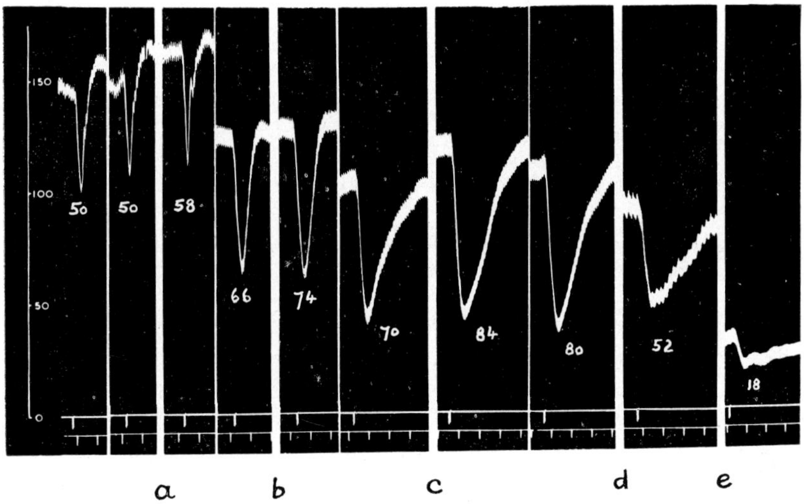

FIG. 3. BLOOD PRESSURE OF NEMBUTALISED CAT

Effect of eserine on depressor action of a constant dose of 0.12 μg/kgm. of acetylcholine. Numbers indicate depth of fall in mm. of mercury. Doses of eserine injected as follows: 0.0012 mgm./kgm. (a); 0.012 mgm./kgm. (b); 0.12 mgm./kgm. (c); 0.7 mgm./kgm. (d) and 1.7 mgm./kgm. (e).

Blood vessels of cat's limb. The vascular effects in the skeletal vessels of the cat were investigated by enclosing the forelimb in a plethysmograph and recording the volume changes in the limb; injections were made intravenously.

The upper tracing in figure 4 shows the effect of ephedrine on the vasoconstriction produced in a spinal cat by a dose of 3.0 μg per kilogram of adrenaline. A fall in the tracing represents constriction and the figures give the depth of the fall in mm. on the original tracing. A dose of 0.0003 mgm. per kilogram of ephedrine (a) increased the action of adrenaline; doses of 0.003 (b) and 0.03 (c) mgm. per kilogram increased it further, while 0.30 mgm. per kilogram (d) reduced it to about its original size and 1.40 mgm. per kilogram (e) diminished it still further.

The lower tracing in figure 4 shows the effect of eserine on the vasodilatation produced in a nembutalized cat by a dose of 0.3 μg per kilogram of acetylcholine. A dose of 0.0003 mgm. per kilogram of eserine (a) had no effect, while 0.003 mgm. per kilogram (b) caused a small increase in the action of acetylcholine. A dose of 0.03 mgm. per kilogram (c) increased the action further, but 0.30 mgm. per kilogram (d) reduced the response to about its original size, and a further dose of 1.30 mgm. per kilogram (e) abolished the action of acetylcholine.

The results of the plethysmograph experiments are summarized in the fourth and fifth columns of table 2. The number of experiments was not sufficient to establish the dosage levels with certainty, but here again the effects of ephedrine and eserine were closely parallel and the relations between concentration and effect were similar.

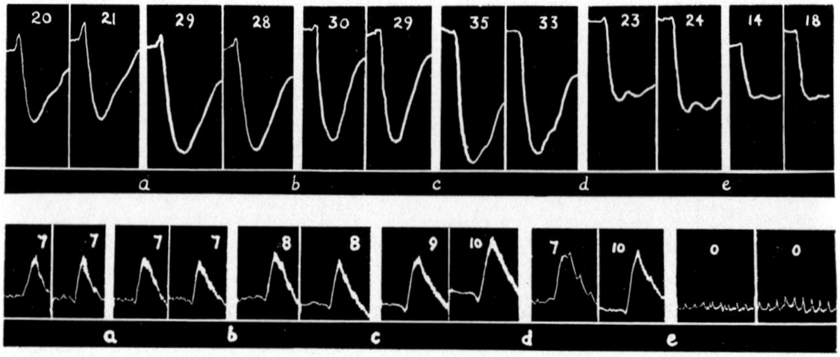

FIG. 4. VOLUME OF FORELIMB OF CAT

Fall in tracing indicates vasoconstriction, rise indicates vasodilatation. Numbers indicate height in mm. of rise or fall on original tracing.

Upper tracings: Vasconstrictor responses to equal doses of 3μg/kgm. of adrenaline in a spinal cat. Doses of ephedrine injected as follows: 0.0003 mgm./kgm. (a); 0.003 mgm./kgm. (b); 0.03 mgm./kgm. (c); 0.3 mgm./kgm. (d) and 1.4 mgm./kgm. (e).

Lower tracing: Vasodilator responses to equal doses of 0.3 μg/kgm. of acetylcholine in a nembutalised cat. Doses of eserine injected as follows: 0.0003 mgm./kgm. (a); 0.003 mgm./kgm. (b); 0.03 mgm./kgm. (c); 0.3 mgm./kgm. (d) and 1.3 mgm./kgm. (e).

Perfused rabbit ear. Both ephedrine and eserine were investigated on the perfused rabbit ear preparation of Gaddum and Kwiatkowski (1938). The ear was perfused with cold oxygenated Locke solution, and by means of a two-way tap the perfusion fluid could be changed quickly to Locke solution containing ephedrine or eserine. The perfusion pressure was varied by using an adjustable stand. Injections of adrenaline or acetylcholine were made directly into the arterial cannula.

Adrenalin in doses of 0.01 to 0.1 μg produced vasoconstriction, indicated in the tracings by an increase in height. After a number of doses of adrenaline had been given, the perfusion fluid was changed to Locke containing a known concentration of ephedrine and a further series of adrenaline doses was given. Figure 5 (a) shows the increase in the constrictor action of 0.01 μg of adrenaline produced by perfusion with ephedrine in a concentration of 10^{-7}, and (b) shows the big diminution in adrenaline action produced by ephedrine 10^{-6}.

The action of acetylcholine in the perfused rabbit ear is variable. Dale (1914) observed a brisk vasodilatation after the injection of 5.0 μg of acetylcholine, but Hunt (1914) was at first unable to obtain a vasodilatation. He observed no effect with small doses, but obtained vasoconstriction with doses over 200 μg. Later Hunt (1918) was able to obtain the vasodilatation observed by Dale with small doses; he found that if the drug was injected into

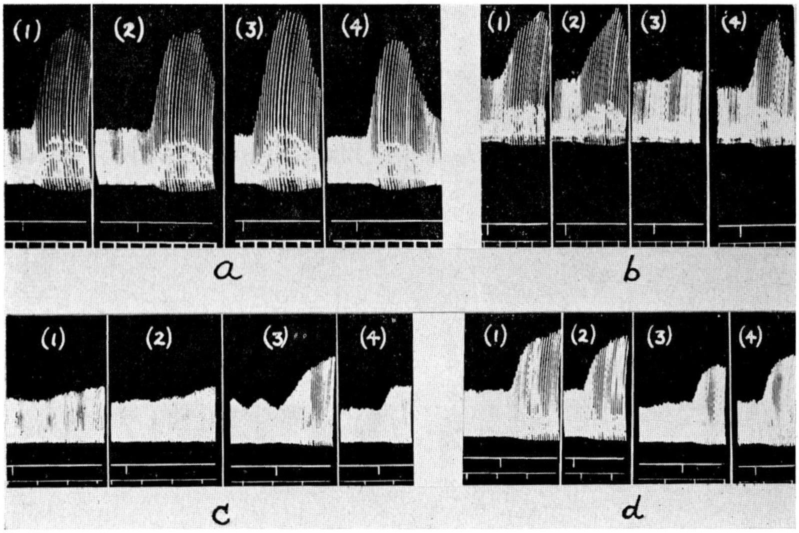

FIG. 5. PERFUSED RABBIT EAR

Rise in tracing indicates vasoconstriction.

(a) Constrictor action of 0.01 μg of adrenaline, before (1, 2), during (3), and 30 minutes after (4), perfusion with ephedrine 10^{-7}.

(b) Constrictor action of 0.01 μg of adrenaline, before (1, 2), during (3), and 30 minutes after (4) perfusion with ephedrine 10^{-6}.

(c) Constrictor action of 0.05 mgm. of acetylcholine, before (1, 2), during (3), and 30 minutes after (4) perfusion with eserine 10^{-7}.

(d) Constrictor action of 0.05 mgm. of acetylcholine, before (1, 2), during (3), and 30 minutes after (4) perfusion with eserine 10^{-5}.

a fresh rabbit ear preparation small doses were without effect while large doses (over 0.1 mgm.) caused constriction, but if the preparation had been perfused for some time, or treated with a small dose of atropine, then small doses of acetylcholine produced vasodilatation.

In our experiments we found that acetylcholine in doses from 0.001 to 1.0 μg had no action at all, while larger doses (5.0 μg to 1.0 mgm.) caused constriction. These results were obtained constantly on a large number of preparations, both fresh and otherwise. On the other hand we found that intravenous doses of 0.1 to 1.0 μg of acetylcholine in the intact rabbit produced vasodilatation in the ear, as recorded by a plethysmograph. For the purpose of the present investigation the type of response to acetylcholine was unimportant provided it was modified by eserine. Figure 5 (c) shows the increase in the constrictor action of 0.05 mgm. of acetylcholine produced by perfusion with eserine in a concentration of 10^{-7}, and (d) shows the diminution in acetylcholine action produced by eserine 10^{-5}.

The results of the rabbit ear experiments are summarized in the fourth and fifth columns of table 1. The effects of the two drugs were again similar and parallel; the concentration levels at which changes of effect occurred were throughout about ten times greater for eserine than for ephedrine.

Isolated intestine of rabbit. Isolated strips of rabbit jejunum were suspended in oxygenated Tyrode solution at 38.5°C. and a series of equal doses of either adrenaline or acetylcholine given until a constant response was obtained. A dose of ephedrine or eserine was then added to the bath and allowed to act for a definite time, after which a further dose of adrenaline or acetylcholine was given. Any alteration in response was confirmed by washing out the ephedrine or eserine and repeating the initial doses of adrenaline or acetylcholine.

Unfortunately it was not possible to demonstrate with certainty all the effects of ephedrine and eserine which were observed in other preparations. The only effect which was established without doubt was the diminution of the action of adrenaline by high concentrations of ephedrine (10^{-4}), which has already been shown by Finkleman (1930). Careful consideration of the results of a large number of experiments leads us to believe that potentiation did occur with low concentrations of ephedrine (10^{-8} to 10^{-7}) and eserine (10^{-8}), and also that depression occurred with high concentration of eserine (10^{-5} to 10^{-4}), but the differences were very small and we do not consider the results conclusive.

Nictitating membrane of the cat. The contractions of the nictitating membrane were recorded in nembutalized cats in which the superior cervical ganglion on the side recorded was excised immediately before the experiment. All injections were made intravenously.

The upper row of tracings in figure 6 shows the effect of ephedrine on the contraction produced by 10 μg per kilogram of adrenaline. The figures show the heights in mm. of the contractions on the original tracings. Successive doses of 0.001 (a), 0.01 (b), and 0.1 (c) mgm. per kilogram of ephedrine produced successive increases in the height of the adrenaline contraction. The last dose of 0.1 mgm. per kilogram ephedrine started the slow contracture of the membrane which was observed by Gaddum and Kwiatkowski (1938). A further dose of 0.5 mgm. per kilogram (d) of ephedrine caused an increase in the contracture, and the adrenaline contraction was now no greater than its original size; a further dose of 1.0 mgm. per kilogram (e) of ephedrine caused a further increase in the contracture and a further diminution of the adrenaline contraction. These diminutions in the adrenaline contraction are however of little significance, since when the later doses of adrenaline were given the membrane was almost completely contracted owing to the action of ephedrine.

The normal nicititating membrane is unaffected by acetylcholine and Rosenblueth and Bard (1932) have shown that there is no parasympathetic nerve supply to the membrane. Nevertheless Rosenblueth (1932) has shown that acetylcholine will cause a contraction of the acutely denervated nictitating membrane. The lower row of tracings in figure 6 shows the effect

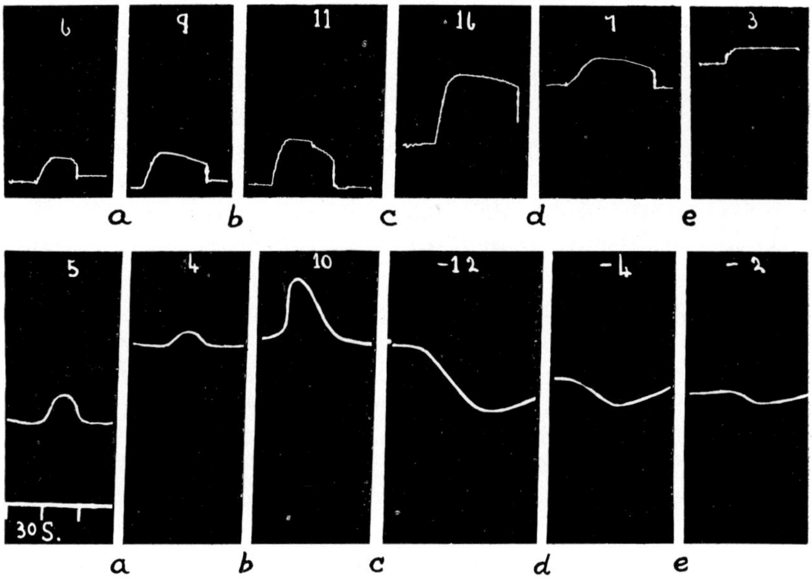

FIG. 6. NICTITATING MEMBRANE OF CAT

Rise in tracing indicates contraction. Numbers indicate height in mm. of rise or fall on original tracing.

Upper tracings: Responses to equal doses of 10 μg/kgm. of adrenaline. Doses of ephedrine injected as follows: 0.001 mgm./kgm. (a); 0.01 mgm./kgm. (b); 0.1 mgm./kgm. (c); 0.5 mgm./kgm. (d) and 1.0 mgm./kgm. (e).

Lower tracings: Responses to equal doses of 10 μg/kgm. of acetylcholine. Doses of eserine injected as follows: 0.001 mgm./kgm. (a); 0.01 mgm./kgm. (b); 0.1 mgm./kgm. (c); 0.5 mgm./kgm. (d); 1.0 mgm./kgm. (e).

of eserine on this action of acetylcholine (10 μg per kilogram). A dose of 0.001 mgm. per kilogram of eserine (a) produced a slow contracture of the membrane somewhat similar to that produced by ephedrine, and slightly diminished the acetylcholine contraction, while a dose of 0.01 mgm. per kilogram (b) considerably increased the latter. A further dose of 0.1 mgm. per kilogram of eserine (c) reversed the response of the membrane to acetylcholine, which now caused a slow and lasting relaxation. Further doses of 0.5 mgm. per kilogram (d) and 1.0 mgm. per kilogram (e) diminished the relaxing action of acetylcholine.

The experiments on the nictitating membrane are difficult to interpret. Low concentrations of ephedrine and eserine cause potentiation, but the effects of high concentrations are not clear. The ephedrine results are complicated by the prolonged contracture which makes it impossible to determine whether or not the adrenaline effect is diminished by high concentrations of ephedrine, while the reversal by eserine of the acetylcholine action cannot be regarded as a diminution of the initial contractile action.

DISCUSSION

In the preparations which we have examined the effects of ephedrine and eserine on the actions of adrenaline and acetylcholine respectively have shown a close similarity. Considering first the experiments on isolated organs, i.e., frog heart and perfused rabbit ear, in which the concentration of ephedrine or eserine in the fluid bathing the tissues was accurately known, concentrations of either drug up to 10^{-9} had no effect, while concentrations of 10^{-8} (and usually 10^{-7} also) produced potentiation i.e. an increase in the action of adrenaline or acetylcholine. Transition from potentiation to depression occurred in the region from 10^{-7} to 10^{-6}, and at concentrations of 10^{-5} and 10^{-4} the action of adrenaline or acetylcholine was diminished, the degree of diminution becoming greater until at 10^{-3} the action was generally abolished. Considering next the blood pressure and plethysmograph experiments, in which the drugs were given intravenously to the entire animal, the transition from potentiation to depression occurred within the dosage range 0.05 to 0.5 mgm. per kilogram (with one exception mentioned below). Assuming the blood volume to be 5 to 7 per cent of the body weight, this range of dosage corresponds with a range of concentration in the blood of from rather less than 10^{-6} to rather less than 10^{-5}, which is in reasonably good agreement with the transitional concentration of 10^{-7} to 10^{-6} found in experiments on isolated organs. The results of experiments on rabbit intestine and on the nictitating membrane of the cat were inconclusive and cannot be included in this scheme, although they do not contradict it.

The precise concentration or dosage levels at which these changes in effect occurred showed some variation both between different types of preparation and between different experiments on the same type of preparation, but when the limitations of the experimental methods are taken into account the variation was not great. In one experiment only was the transitional dosage level outside the limits just mentioned. This was in an experiment on the modification by ephedrine of the pressor action of adrenaline in the cat, in which potentiation still occurred after a dose of 3 mgm. per kilogram of ephedrine, the total amount of ephedrine given being then over 5 mgm. per kilogram. A further 3 mgm. per kilogram was necessary before a diminution of adrenaline action occurred. The transitional level in this case was therefore well over 5 mgm. per kilogram whereas in no other instance was it more than 0.5 mgm.

per kilogram. This transition from potentiation to depression was the most characteristic and definite of the changes produced. The dosage level at the lower end of the scale at which sensitization began to be apparent, and the higher level at which depression passed into abolition, were not so well defined.

It is significant that the tables showing the effects produced by different concentrations of either ephedrine or eserine are practically identical in widely different preparations. The close similarity in type between the concentration-effect tables for ephedrine and those for eserine clearly favors the assumption that the two drugs act in an analogous manner. The fact that the actual concentrations which produce particular effects are almost the same for ephedrine as for eserine has no significance at present, but will be important if it becomes possible in the future to discuss the quantitative aspect of the actions of these substances.

The potentiating effect of eserine on the action of acetylcholine is accepted as being due to the inhibition by the former substance of the enzyme cholinesterase which is responsible for the physiological inactivation of acetylcholine. The opposite effect of higher concentrations of eserine does not appear to have received much attention. Feldberg and Vartiainen (1934) found that perfusion of a sympathetic ganglion in the cat with eserine 1 in 10^{-4} diminished or abolished the action of acetylcholine or of preganglionic stimulation. Manning, Lang and Hall (1937) have shown that the action of eserine is of a double nature, the primary action evident in low concentrations being the inhibition of cholinesterase and consequent increase of parasympathetic effects, while with higher concentrations it has a direct parasympathetic stimulant action, after the enzyme system has been maximally inhibited, which they state occurs at about the level of 0.05 mgm. per kilogram. In our experiments this was the level at which potentiation began to give way to depression of the action of acetylcholine, but we did not observe any direct parasympathetic stimulant action of eserine itself until much larger doses were given.

The inactivation of adrenaline has been discussed by a number of authors, including Blaschko and Schlossmann (1940), Philpot (1940) and Richter (1940). They have pointed out that the majority of the work on the destruction of adrenaline by enzymes has been done *in vitro*, and that these experiments provide little evidence as to the normal mechanism *in vivo*. In addition to the possibility of non-enzymic destruction, adrenaline might be inactivated by one of several oxidase systems, among which are amine oxidase (Blaschko, Richter and Schlossmann, 1937), the cytochrome system, and various other polyphenol oxidases (Blaschko and Schlossmann, 1940). All these enzymes have been shown to oxidize adrenaline readily *in vitro*.

Gaddum and Kwiatkowski (1938) suggested that oxidation by amine oxidase was the normal method of inactivation, but Richter and Tingey

(1939) have shown that the rate of destruction is probably too slow to account for the observed rapidity of inactivation *in vivo*, and also that amine oxidase is not present in appreciable quantity in the rabbit ear, in which Gaddum and Kwiatkowski observed the ephedrine sensitization. These objections are however based on experiments *in vitro*, and as Philpot (1940) points out, owing to the great difference in conditions obtaining between experiments *in vivo* and *in vitro*, great caution must be observed in arguing from one to the other. The same caution is necessary in considering the cytochrome system, especially in view of its wide distribution in mammalian tissue.

The problem has been approached in a different way by Richter (1940) who has attempted to identify reaction products in the urine after oral administration of adrenaline in man. He found that about 70 per cent of the adrenaline administered was excreted in the form of a conjugated derivative in which esterification had taken place at one of the phenolic hydroxyl groups. Preliminary experiments suggested that this substance was the sulphate ester, and that the sulphosynthase system was the enzyme responsible.

The property of modifying the action of adrenaline is by no means exclusive to ephedrine. Kwiatkowski (1940) has shown that veritol acts in the same way, and is in fact more potent than ephedrine. We have found that some other phenylisopropylamine derivatives have the same effect (unpublished work). Macgregor (1939) has shown that cocaine and procaine modify the action of adrenaline in the same way as ephedrine, and Tripod (1940) has extended this work to other local anesthetics, butyn, percaine and stovaine.

Ephedrine can both increase and diminish the action of adrenaline under different conditions. It has long been known to abolish the action of adrenaline on isolated smooth muscle organs (Curtis, 1928 and Finkleman, 1930), and our experiments have demonstrated that while small doses of ephedrine potentiate adrenaline, large doses diminish or abolish its action. A possible explanation of this apparent anomaly lies along the lines of that advanced by Macgregor (1939) for the very similar action of cocaine. Augmentation of the adrenaline effect would be due to competition for the available enzyme, which would result in a diminished rate of destruction of adrenaline, while the depressant effect of higher concentrations of ephedrine would be due to the ephedrine, having saturated all the available enzyme, occupying the sympathetic receptors and preventing the access of adrenaline to them. Bussell (1940) has shown that in general substances which are synergists of adrenaline in low concentrations are usually antagonists at higher concentrations.

The depression of the action of acetylcholine by high concentrations of eserine observed by Feldberg and Vartiainen (1934) and in our experiments could be explained similarly; after the cholinesterase has become fully inhibited by eserine, further amounts of eserine will block the receptors and prevent the approach of acetylcholine.

The position is further complicated by the fact that the enzyme antagonists of cholinergic systems are apparently not specific, and act to some extent on adrenergic systems as well. Thus Secker (1937) has shown that the response of the nictitating membrane of the cat to adrenaline or sympathetic stimulation is increased by eserine and inhibited by atropine. Agar (1940) has shown that the inhibition of young guinea pig uterus by adrenaline is altered by eserine to a diphasic response in which the relaxation is followed by a secondary contraction a few minutes later. Whether substances of the ephedrine and cocaine types have any effect on the action of acetylcholine has apparently not yet been investigated, except for an observation by Macgregor (1939) that cocaine and procaine reduce the nicotine-like action of acetylcholine on sympathetic ganglia. An even more curious observation is that of Thornton (1940), who found that ephedrine potentiated the action of prostigmine in a case of myasthenia gravis.

As long as it was possible to regard amine oxidase as the most probable means of inactivation of adrenaline *in vivo*, the general theory of correspondence between ephedrine and eserine, as outlined above, received considerable support from the fact that the amines behaved towards the oxidase *in vitro* in the way the theory demanded, i.e., ephedrine inhibited the oxidase and slowed down the destruction of adrenaline, and veritol inhibited the enzyme even more powerfully than ephedrine (Blaschko, 1938). Now that the balance of evidence seems to be against amine oxidase in the rôle of physiological inactivator of adrenaline, this support vanishes, and the theory clearly awaits further work on the conjugating system described by Richter (1940). Until more positive evidence is forthcoming, however, the close parallelism which our experiments have demonstrated between the actions of ephedrine and eserine affords some support for the theory.

SUMMARY

1. The effects of various concentrations of ephedrine and eserine on the actions of adrenaline and acetylcholine respectively were examined in the following preparations under similar conditions: perfused frog heart, cat blood pressure, cat limb volume, perfused rabbit ear, isolated rabbit gut, and cat nictitating membrane.

2. In the first four of these preparations the effects of the two drugs showed a close similarity. Low concentrations of either drug up to about 10^{-9} were without effect, while concentrations from about 10^{-9} to 10^{-7} produced potentiation, i.e. an increase in the action of the corresponding hormone. At a concentration in the range from 10^{-7} to 10^{-6}, a transition occurred, the effect being reversed from potentiation to depression, and at higher concentrations the degree of depression became greater, until at about 10^{-3} the action was completely abolished. These concentration levels were practically identical for the two drugs. The experimental results on isolated rabbit gut and cat

nictitating membrane were inconclusive, but as far as they went were in general agreement with the statement above.

3. The action of ephedrine is discussed, and it is concluded that while the close parallelism which exists between the effects of ephedrine and eserine affords some support for the theory that ephedrine acts, in part at least, by inhibiting the enzyme which is responsible for the inactivation of adrenaline, the development of this theory must await further evidence as to the nature and properties of the enzyme.

REFERENCES

AGAR: J. Physiol., **98,** 492, 1940.
BLASCHKO: Ibid., **93,** 7P, 1938.
BLASCHKO, RICHTER AND SCHLOSSMANN: Ibid., **90,** 1, 1937.
BLASCHKO AND SCHLOSSMANN: Ibid., **98,** 130, 1940.
BUSSELL: THIS JOURNAL, **69,** 128, 1940.
CURTIS: Ibid., **35,** 333, 1928.
DALE: Ibid., **6,** 147, 1914.
FINKLEMAN: J. Physiol., **70,** 145, 1930.
FELDBERG AND VARTIAINEN: Ibid., **83,** 103, 1934.
GADDUM AND KWIATKOWSKI: Ibid., **94,** 87, 1938.
GADDUM AND KWIATKOWSKI: Ibid., **96,** 385, 1939.
HUNT: THIS JOURNAL, **6,** 477, 1914.
HUNT: Amer. J. Physiol., **45,** 197, 1918.
KWIATKOWSKI: THIS JOURNAL, **69,** 198, 1940.
MACGREGOR: Ibid., **66,** 393, 1939.
MANNING, LANG AND HALL: Ibid., **61,** 350, 1937.
PHILPOT: J. Physiol., **97,** 301, 1940.
RICHTER: Ibid., **98,** 361, 1940.
RICHTER AND TINGEY: Ibid., **97,** 265, 1939.
ROSENBLUETH AND BARD: Amer. J. Physiol., **100,** 537, 1932.
ROSENBLUETH: Ibid., **100,** 443, 1932.
SECKER: J. Physiol., **89,** 296, 1937.
THORNTON: Ibid., **98,** 4P, 1940.
TRIPOD: Ibid., **97,** 289, 1940.

ACTION OF ADRENALINE AND POTENTIAL CHANGES IN THE CAT UTERUS

G. BALASSA AND M. R. GURD

From the Nuffield Institute for Medical Research, Oxford, England

Received for publication January 20, 1941

The electrical potentials occurring in the uterus of the cat have not received so much attention as the corresponding phenomena in the rabbit (see (1) for literature). Bozler (2) showed that isolated uteri of cats in estrus give rise to bursts of spike potentials, both spontaneously and after electrical stimulation. Bacq and Monnier (3) investigated the potential changes in anestrous and pregnant cat uteri; they observed no spike potentials, but found a slow potential change of long duration, occurring simultaneously with the mechanical contraction or relaxation.

In the rabbit uterus, Balassa (1) found that both spike potentials and slow potential waves could accompany contraction, and that their occurrence depended on the sexual condition; in anestrous uteri and those showing progestational proliferation the slow waves predominated, while in estrous uteri and those in late pregnancy the spikes predominated.

The mechanical response of the cat uterus to adrenaline is reversed during pregnancy (4) and during progestational proliferation (5, 6, 7, 8). Since the potential changes in the rabbit uterus are also influenced by pregnancy and the administration of sex hormones, it was considered of interest to investigate the potential changes in the cat uterus in different sexual states and the connection between these potentials and the reversal of the adrenaline response.

METHODS

Cats were anesthetised with nembutal (0.75 cc. of a 5 per cent solution per kilogram, intraperitoneally) and placed in an insulated metal box. The abdomen was opened in the midline and the uterus arranged for electrical and mechanical recording, as described in a previous paper (1). The mechanical movements were either recorded optically together with the electrical record, or recorded separately on a kymograph and synchronised with the electrical record. The electrical records were made with a string galvanometer and a two-stage direct-coupled amplifier. The galvanometer, amplifier and leads were all shielded so that the 50 cycle A.C. used for the motors did not interfere with the record. The input resistance of the amplifier was 3 megohms and the resistance of the string about 7000 ohms. The full output of the amplifier was not used, since a sensitivity of about 1 to 4 cm. per mV. was found to be sufficient. No qualitative difference could be detected between records made with and without the amplifier.

A few experiments were made on isolated uteri, which were kept in a shielded moist chamber at 40°C, both ends being fixed, with the electrodes between. Where mechanical records only were required the uterus was suspended in Locke solution in the ordinary way.

The electrodes in all the experiments were silver-silver chloride half-cells connected to the uterus through Ringer-agar wicks.

Estrous was produced by daily subcutaneous injections of 100 i.u. of estroform (B.D.H.) for 8 days. Progestational proliferation was produced by daily injections of 25 r.u. of gonadotrophic substance (Prolan, Pregnyl) for 10 days, the injections being subcutaneous on the first three days, intraperitoneal on the fourth and fifth days, and subcutaneous on the last five days.

RESULTS

Anestrous uteri

Attempts were made to use the uteri from immature cats, but in such uteri there were hardly any spontaneous potentials and electrical responses to drugs were very slight. Later experiments were therefore carried out on adult cats during the period from September to February, since Foster and Hisaw (6) have shown that cats are in permanent anestrus during this period.

These uteri showed spontaneous slow potential waves in a more or less regular rhythm. The magnitude was usually about 1 mV. and the average frequency was about 15 to 20 per minute. The regularity of the waves was variable: some uteri showed a quite regular rhythm, in others small secondary changes of a similar nature were superimposed on the main waves, and sometimes two or three waves were missing from an otherwise regular series. In every case some rhythmic potential variations occurred.

An intravenous injection of 5 to 25 μg per kilogram of adrenaline relaxed the uterus, but the slow potential waves continued uninterrupted during the relaxation (fig. 1, a), and generally became larger and more regular. After one to one and a half minutes these effects disappeared, and the original rhythm was restored. The effects of pitocin and histamine on the slow waves were similar to those of adrenaline (fig. 1, c), in spite of the fact that these substances produced contraction of the uterus.

Ephedrine (1 to 2 mgm. per kilogram) relaxed the uterus in the same way as adrenaline, but the potential waves were diminished or abolished (fig. 1, b). The full inhibition lasted about half a minute, and the waves returned to their original size and rhythm in one to one and a half minutes, while the uterus was still relaxed.

Agar (9) has stated that the reaction of the isolated guinea-pig uterus to adrenaline can be changed by eserinization from a simple relaxation to a diphasic response, in which initial relaxation is followed by a delayed contraction. We have examined the anestrous cat uterus to see whether a similar phenomenon occurs in this species. The reaction to adrenaline of the uterus *in vivo* was unchanged by eserinization of the animal with 1 mgm. per kilogram of eserine given gradually, although the reaction to acetylcholine was increased. Similarly in experiments *in vitro* with the uterus suspended in Locke solution (Agar's modification) the reaction to adrenaline was unchanged by two to four hours treatment with eserine in a concentration of 5×10^{-7} to 2×10^{-6}. The phenomenon described by Agar therefore does not occur in the anestrous cat uterus, although a latent adrenaline contractile mechanism could be more readily expected in the cat uterus than in the guinea-pig uterus, in view of the contraction which occurs in the former during pregnancy. The reactions to adrenaline of the uteri of the two animals follow the scheme of table 1.

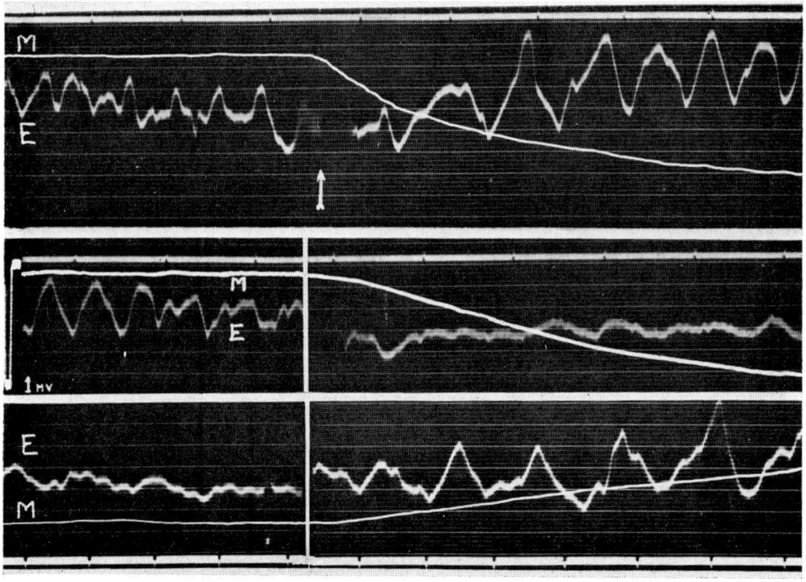

FIG. 1. ANESTROUS CAT UTERI IN VIVO

Electrical record (E) and mechanical record (M). Downward movement of mechanical record indicates relaxation. Time markings; *a* and *b*, 10 secs.; *c*, 5 secs.

a. Injection of adrenaline 5 µg/kgm. (at arrow). Showing increase of slow potential waves, and mechanical relaxation.

b. Injection of ephedrine 2 mgm./kgm. (at white line). Showing diminution of slow waves, and mechanical relaxation.

c. Injection of pitocin 0.2 i.u./kgm. (at white line). Showing increase of slow waves, and mechanical contraction.

Intestine

Berkson (10) has shown that rabbit intestine gives rise to slow rhythmic potential waves similar to those described in anestrous cat uteri, and that these potential waves do not correspond with the peristaltic movements.

We have investigated the potential changes in cat intestine by the same methods used for the uterus, and observed spontaneous slow potential waves as in the anestrous uterus. It was found that adrenaline relaxed the intestine and slightly increased the size of the potential waves (fig. 2, a), while ephedrine also relaxed the intestine, but almost abolished the potential waves (fig. 2, b). This corresponds both with our findings in the anestrous cat uterus, and with those of Berkson in the rabbit intestine. The latter has also shown that nicotine in suitable doses abolishes the potential changes without affecting the contractions of the intestine.

TABLE 1

Reactions of cat and guinea-pig uteri to adrenaline

SEXUAL STATE	CAT	GUINEA-PIG
Anestrous	Relaxes	Relaxes (Gunn & Gunn (11))
Anestrous eserinized	Relaxes	Relaxation and secondary contraction (Agar, (9))
Estrous	Relaxes	Contracts (Holtz & Wollpert (12); Balassa & Gurd (13))
Progestational proliferation	Contracts	Relaxes
Pregnant	Contracts	Relaxes (Gunn & Gunn (11))

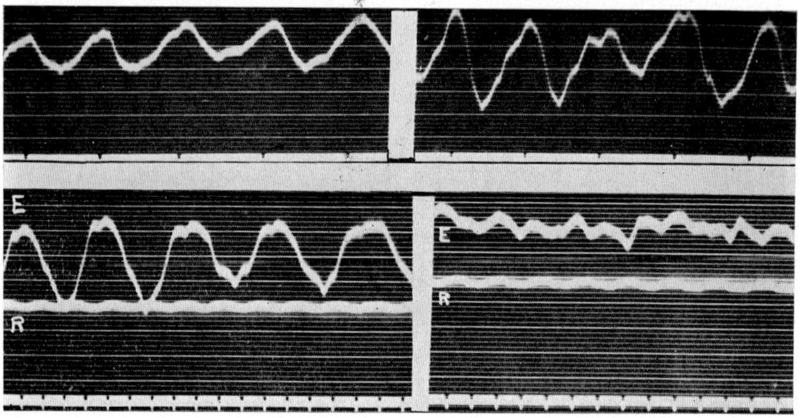

FIG. 2. CAT INTESTINE IN VIVO

Electrical record (E) and respiration (R).

a. Injection of adrenaline 5 μg/kgm. (at white line). Showing increase of slow waves. Time markings; 5 secs.

b. Injection of ephedrine 2 mgm./kgm. (at white line). Showing abolition of regular potential waves. Time markings; 1 sec.

Note independence of slow waves and respiration.

It therefore appears that the anestrous uterus behaves in a similar way to the intestine in regard to the spontaneous potential waves and their modification by adrenaline and ephedrine.

Estrous uteri

The uteri of estrous cats were larger than those in anestrus and showed strong spontaneous contractions both *in vivo* and *in vitro*. Each contraction of the uterus was accompanied by a burst of spike potentials (fig. 3, a), but these uteri did not show spontaneous slow potential waves. The duration of each spike was about 0.2 to 0.4 second; their frequency was usually one or two per second; the total number varied with the strength of the contraction, and the burst of spikes ended before the muscle relaxed. Contractions pro-

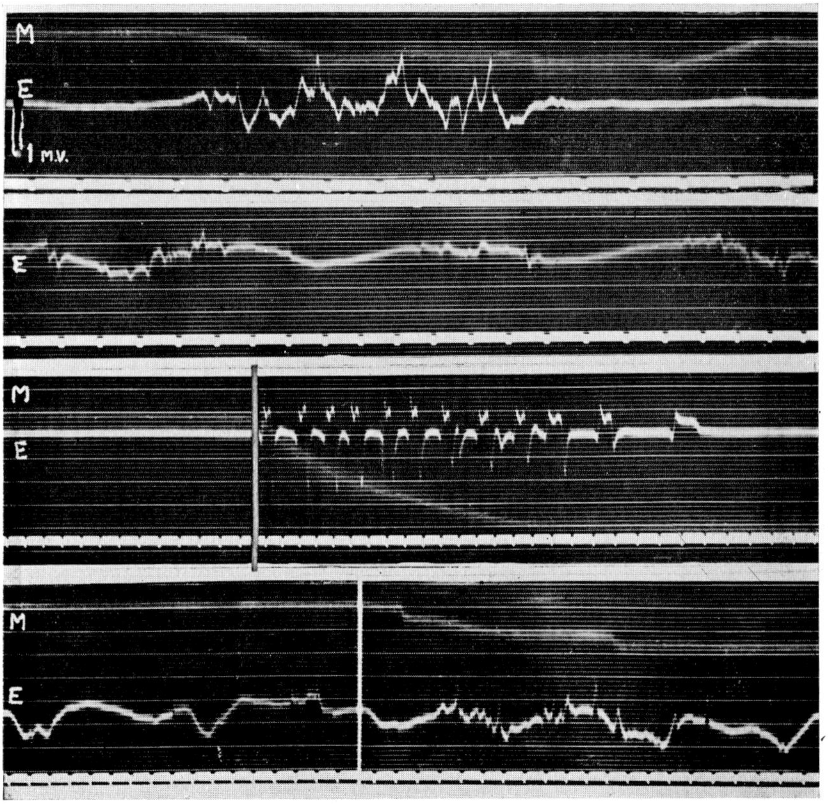

FIG. 3. ESTROUS, PROLIFERATED AND PREGNANT CAT UTERI IN VIVO

Electrical record (E) and mechanical record (M). Downward movement of mechanical record indicates contraction. Time markings; 1 sec.

a. Estrous uterus. Spontaneous contraction.

b. Progestational proliferated uterus. Spontaneous contraction.

c. Late-pregnant uterus. Injection of adrenaline 5 μg/kgm. (at white line). Contraction accompanied by large regular spikes.

d. Progestational proliferated uterus. Injection of adrenaline 5 μg/kgm. (at white line).

duced by the injection of pitocin or histamine were accompanied by similar potentials, the frequency and total number of the spikes being greater than with spontaneous contractions and dependent on the amount of drug injected. These spikes were similar to those observed in estrous rabbit uteri (1), and to those observed by Bozler (2) on isolated estrous cat uteri.

Adrenaline relaxed the estrous uterus, and no electrical changes occurred during the relaxation. Spontaneous contractions ceased during the adrenaline relaxation and spike potentials did not occur until the contractions recommenced.

In two experiments spontaneous slow potential waves were observed in addition to the spikes which occurred during contraction. In view of the resistance of cats to sex hormones and their individual variation, there seems little doubt that these two animals had not yet reached a fully developed estrus, and therefore showed a mixed response.

Uteri showing progestational proliferation

There was considerable variation in the response of the cats treated with gonadotropic hormone. In five of the eight cats treated, the uteri showed progestational proliferation and contracted with adrenaline (fig. 4, a, b); two showed no proliferation and relaxed with adrenaline (fig. 4, c, d), and in one uterus a mixed response to adrenaline occurred.

Those uteri which showed proliferation and contracted with adrenaline showed great variation in their sensitivity to this substance. They showed little spontaneous movement and gave rise to spontaneous slow potential waves similar to those observed in anestrous uteri; the waves were however smaller and less regular. On these slow waves there were superimposed occasional bursts of small spike potentials (fig. 3, b). This was the type of electrical record usually obtained; in some uteri however the spikes were larger and more numerous, and in these uteri spontaneous contractions occurred. In the former case the small size and number of the spikes, and their irregularity, appear to be connected with the absence of mechanical contraction. Probably a small number of fibers only were excited; the coarse mechanical recording system used would only indicate gross contractions.

Contractions produced by adrenaline were accompanied by bursts of spike potentials, the size and number of which depended on the amount of the drug given (fig. 3, d). The slow potential waves continued, either unaltered or slightly increased. Pitocin and histamine produced similar reactions.

Pregnant uteri

Uteri in late pregnancy did not show slow potential waves; while contractions, whether spontaneous or produced by adrenaline or any other drug, were accompanied by large and regular spike potentials (fig. 3, c). These spikes differed from those observed in estrous uteri by their greater magnitude and regularity, but they were qualitatively similar.

In early pregnancy both slow potential waves and spikes could be observed together, as was previously found with rabbits (1).

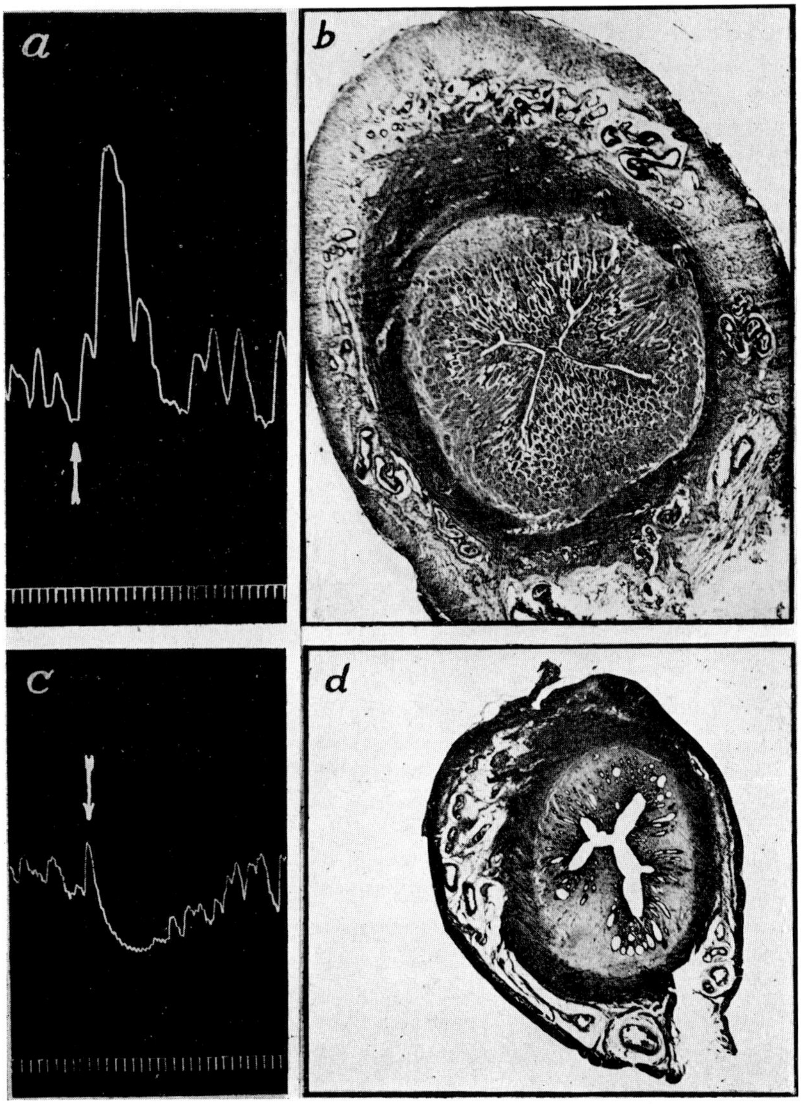

FIG. 4. VARIATION IN RESPONSE OF CAT UTERUS TO GONADOTROPHIC HORMONE

Two animals treated simultaneously with same doses. Downward movement of mechanical record indicates relaxation.

Upper figures: First cat uterus.

a. Injection of adrenaline 5 μg/kgm. (at arrow). Showing contraction of uterus in vivo.

b. Section showing progestational proliferation of endometrium.

Lower figures: Second cat uterus.

c. Same dose of adrenaline as at *a*. Showing relaxation of uterus. *d.* Section showing non-proliferated endometrium.

DISCUSSION

Recent literature includes considerable discussion as to how far artefacts are responsible for certain electrical phenomena observed in smooth muscle, particularly slow potential changes such as those described in this paper. Bozler (2) came to the conclusion that every slow potential change recorded in smooth muscle is an artefact. He used a condenser-coupled amplifier which may possibly have distorted the slow potential changes. Even so he found some structures, e.g., the ureter of the rat, which showed only slow potentials. Bourdillon *et al.* (14), in adequately controlled experiments, demonstrated the existence of slow potential changes in the rabbit vagina.

Various possible origins of such artefacts have been excluded by our experimental procedures. Some experiments were carried out on isolated anestrous uteri suspended in a moist chamber, both wick electrodes and chlorided silver needles being used. This method was not used in the majority of our experiments owing to the difficulty of administering drugs under these conditions, but the fact that the spontaneous electrical records obtained were similar to those in the living animal, i.e., rhythmic slow potential waves, excluded the possibility that these changes were due to drying of the muscle or electrodes or to respiratory movements. The latter possibility was also excluded in the living animal, by recording respiration synchronously with the potential changes: their independence was obvious (see fig. 2, b).

It seems improbable that any artefacts arising from drying of muscle or electrodes, or from muscular movement, or originating in the electrical recording apparatus, should cause regularly occurring rhythmic potential changes. The possibility that such potential changes were due to alterations in the inter-electrode resistance is also remote, since the input resistance of the apparatus was 3 megohms, in comparison with which the tissue resistance was negligible. Moreover, as has previously been pointed out (1), it is highly improbable that any electrical artefact would be influenced in a regular manner by the administration of sex hormones or drugs. Slow potential changes have been demonstrated in a number of laboratories under very varied experimental conditions (1, 2, 10, 14, 15) and their existence is now established beyond doubt. It should be remembered that this characteristic of smooth muscle is not unique, for a number of other structures show relatively slow potential changes in addition to spike potentials; thus nerve fibers show slow after-potentials in addition to spikes, and various relatively slow changes are seen in the electroencephalogram.

The electrical phenomena in the cat uterus differ considerably from those in the rabbit uterus. In the rabbit uterus and vagina there is a close connection between the mechanical contractions and the potential changes (1), while in the anestrous cat uterus and in the intestine of both cat and rabbit, there is no connection between the mechanical movements and the spontaneous slow potential waves. There is a corresponding difference in the mechanical reaction to adrenaline: rabbit uterus contracts, while intestine and anestrous cat uterus relax. Berkson (10) suggested that the slow potential waves which he observed in intestine might be nervous in origin, and it has been shown (16) that there is a difference in the amount of nervous tissue present in cat and rabbit uteri, but there is not sufficient evidence at present to connect this difference with the difference in the electrical phenomena.

There is a striking difference between the effects of adrenaline and ephedrine on the slow potential waves in cat intestine and anestrous uterus. Although both substances cause relaxation of the muscle, the potential waves are increased by adrenaline, diminished or abolished by ephedrine. No explanation of this phenomenon can at present be offered.

Estrous appears to be always accompanied, in every species so far investigated, by powerful and coordinated contractions of the uterus (for references see Reynolds (17)). It seems also, in the three species investigated (cat, rabbit and guinea-pig), that estrus results in the appearance of spike potentials which coincide with the beginning of the contractions (Morisson (18) has observed such spikes during the whole of the contraction in rabbit uterus). The appearance of spikes, and the development of electrical excitability during estrus, led Bozler (2) to believe that, in this condition, excitation is conducted from one muscle cell to another, and that in this state the uterus behaves as a syncytium.

Progestational proliferation of an estrous cat uterus leads to a decrease in spontaneous contractions and a smaller mechanical response to drugs; at the same time spontaneous spike potentials disappear, and those which occur when contraction is produced by a drug are smaller and fewer than in estrus. The luteal hormone therefore appears to inhibit partially the mechanism responsible for the conducted impulses which may be supposed to occur in estrous uteri; this mechanism still functions to some extent, since spike potentials are produced by the injection of drugs and occasionally occur spontaneously, although they are much smaller and fewer than in estrus.

During early pregnancy the mechanical and electrical responses of the cat uterus are similar to those occurring during progestational proliferation, but in late pregnancy the uterus reverts to the estrus type of response; powerful spontaneous contractions occur, and these contractions, as well as those produced by drugs, are accompanied by spike potentials which are even more powerful and regular than during estrus.

In the cat uterus during estrus and late pregnancy a burst of spike potentials always occurs at the beginning of a contraction, whether the contraction is spontaneous or is produced by adrenaline or by pitocin or by any other drug. In the estrous uterus adrenaline causes relaxation, which is not accompanied by any potential changes, while contractions occurring spontaneously or produced by pitocin show a burst of spike potentials. The spikes therefore do not appear to arise from the combination of a substance such as adrenaline with a receptor, but apparently arise from a later stage in the chain of events leading to contraction. According to Bozler's view, the spikes indicate the conduction of impulses from cell to cell.

Contractions of the anestrous cat uterus, e.g., those produced by pitocin, are feeble and are not accompanied by spike potentials. Conduction from cell to cell therefore does not appear to occur in anestrous uteri, and the occurrence of such conduction may be related to the presence of estrogenic hormone. This conduction also seems to be partially suppressed during early pregnancy, possibly owing to the action of the luteal hormone.

In estrous cat uteri spontaneous contractions and spike potentials occur readily, but adrenaline relaxes the muscle just as it does the anestrous uterus. It is clear therefore that the occurrence of spike potentials is not in itself sufficient to reverse the inhibitory action of adrenaline on the uterus, although it appears to be a necessary condition for adrenaline contraction. A further factor is also necessary, and this is probably the development in some of the muscle cells of a receptor capable of combining with adrenaline and setting the contractile mechanism in motion. Since adrenaline reversal only occurs when the uterus is in a state of progestational proliferation, this adrenaline receptor may be related to the presence of luteal hormone. The chain of events when adrenaline causes contraction of a pregnant cat uterus may be as follows: The adrenaline combines with receptors present in or on some of the cells, which are thereby excited and contract; the contractile impulse is conducted to neighboring cells, giving rise to the burst of spike potentials; and lastly contraction occurs in all the cells to which the impulse has spread. The observed time relations between the mechanical contraction and the spike potentials are in agreement with this scheme.

Pitocin produces contraction of the cat uterus whatever the sexual state, and it must be supposed that the receptors for this substance exist independently of the sexual conditions. The contractions produced in anestrous uteri are however much less powerful than in estrous and pregnant uteri; this fact suggests that receptors are present only in some of the muscle cells, and that in anestrus only these cells contract, while in estrus the impulses are conducted to neighboring cells which also contract.

The adrenaline relaxation which occurs in anestrous and estrous uteri is presumably due to another mechanism of unknown character, which is inhibited during pregnancy or progestational proliferation. The significance of the slow potential waves observed in anestrous uteri is also unknown.

SUMMARY

1. In the anestrous cat uterus spontaneous slow rhythmic potential changes occur. They continue, and are slightly increased, during a relaxation produced by adrenaline, but they are abolished or greatly diminished during a relaxation produced by ephedrine. Very similar phenomena occur in the intestine.

2. Eserine has no effect on the action of adrenaline in the anestrous cat uterus.

3. In estrus and in late pregnancy uterine contractions, whether occurring spontaneously or by the action of a drug, are accompanied at the beginning of the contraction by short bursts of spike potentials, with a frequency of 1 to 3 per second and an individual duration of 0.2 to 0.4 second.

4. In early pregnancy and during progestational proliferation, spike potentials accompanying spontaneous contractions are greatly diminished in number and magnitude and are often abolished. In this state the mechanical reaction to adrenaline is reversed. Uterine contractions produced by drugs are accompanied by more spike potentials than are spontaneous contractions, but much fewer than arise from contractions of the estrous uterus.

5. It is suggested that the conduction of impulses from cell to cell is a characteristic of estrous uteri (in all species so far examined), and is responsible for the strong and coordinated contractions which occur during this period. In anestrous uteri such conduction does not occur, and during progestational proliferation it is partially suppressed; the uterine contractions are correspondingly feeble during these phases. Conduction may or may not occur during pregnancy, depending on whether the estrogenic or luteal hormone predominates.

6. The reversal of the mechanical response of the cat uterus to adrenaline during pregnancy and progestational proliferation is discussed, and a possible mechanism outlined.

We wish to record our thanks to Mr. Reginald Duffett for preparing the histological slides used in figure 4.

REFERENCES

(1) Balassa: This Journal, **70**, 189, 1940.
(2) Bozler: Amer. J. Physiol., **124**, 502, 1938; **127**, 301, 1939.
(3) Bacq and Monnier: Arch. Int. Physiol., **40**, 467, 1935; **41**, 334, 1935.
(4) Dale: J. Physiol., **34**, 163, 1906.
(5) van Dyke and Gustavson: This Journal, **37**, 379, 1929; **41**, 139, 1931.
(6) Foster and Hisaw: Anat. Rec., **62**, 75, 1935.
(7) Kennard: Amer. J. Physiol., **118**, 190, 1937.
(8) Robson and Schild: J. Physiol., **92**, 1, 1938.
(9) Agar: J. Physiol., **98**, 492, 1940.
(10) Berkson: Amer. J. Physiol., **105**, 405, 1933.
(11) Gunn and Gunn: This Journal, **5**, 527, 1914.
(12) Holtz and Wollpert: Arch. exp. Path. Pharm., **185**, 20, 1937.
(13) Balassa and Gurd: Unpublished experiments.
(14) Bourdillon: J. Physiol., **97**, 138, 1939; Bourdillon and Lidwell: J. Physiol., **98**, 480, 1940.
(15) Hasama: Arch. exp. Path. Pharm., **153**, 140, 1930.
(16) Reynolds and Kaminester: Amer. J. Physiol., **112**, 640, 1935.
(17) Reynolds: Physiol. Rev., **17**, 304, 1937.
(18) Morisson: Amer. J. Physiol., **128**, 372, 1940.

A METHOD FOR DETERMINING LOSS OF PAIN SENSATION

FRED E. D'AMOUR AND DONN L. SMITH

From The Biologic Research Laboratory, University of Denver

Received for publication January 27, 1941

In a recent study by Schumacher, Goodell, Hardy and Wolff (1) the variation of the pain threshold in humans was determined under a variety of conditions. This paper aroused our curiosity as whether the great uniformity observed in humans also held for animals and also suggested the possibility of adapting the method to the assay of analgesic drugs. The method used by the above workers was a simple one, namely the focusing of a beam of light upon a blackened spot on the forehead for exactly three seconds, with the intensity controlled by a rheostat; determinations were repeated every 30 seconds until an intensity was reached at which the subject just perceived pain. An extremely great stability in the pain threshold was found to exist under a variety of conditions.

In adapting the method to rats the rays from a Mazda 1184, 6 to 8 volt bulb, with reflector, were focused on the tip of the rat's tail, which was placed in a grooved board some six inches below. The set-up includes a voltage regulator, transformer and rheostat; a stop-watch is operated by the same switch which makes and breaks the current. In using this device the operator places the rat's tail in the groove, switches on the light and stop-watch and waits for the response, which is a sudden, typical twitch of the tail, when the animal feels the pain. The switch is then reversed and the time noted. After a few trials we found that a light intensity which produced a reaction in about 5 seconds was most convenient.

RESULTS

Normal variation. We were greatly surprised at last to find a biologic reaction subject apparently to very little individual variation. Up to the present some 10,000 individual tests have been made on several hundred rats. It happened that rats were available from another study in which many states of endocrine dysfunction had been produced. The following is a list of conditions under which tests were made: Adrenalectomized versus hyper-cortin, thyroidectomized versus hyper-thyroid, castrate (male and female) versus hyper-estrin, hyper-progestin, hyper-testosterone, day versus night, cold room versus hot room, and starvation. Tests were also run twice per week for two months on the same rats and no conditioning effect was

TABLE 1

REACTION TIME	PER CENT RESPONDING
seconds	
3–4	0.1
4–5	82.0
5–6	17.6
6–6.5	0.3

TABLE 2

Assay of cobra venom

NUMBER OF RATS	DOSE	AVERAGE REACTION TIME	
		After 30 min.	After 2 hours
	m.u. per kgm.	*sec.*	*sec.*
12	0	4.8	4.6
12	4	4.7	4.5
12	8	4.8	4.9
12	16	5.0	4.9

TABLE 3

Assay of opiates

MATERIAL	DOSE	PER CENT COMPLETELY ANALGESIC
	mgm. per kgm.	
Dilaudid	1	8
Dilaudid	2	75
Dilaudid	4	100
Heroin	1	0
Heroin	2	33
Heroin	4	83
Morphine sulfate	6	0
Morphine sulfate	8	50
Morphine sulfate	10	66
Morphine sulfate	12	92
Codeine sulfate	12	0
Codeine sulfate	18	17
Codeine sulfate	24	75
Codeine sulfate	30	100
Pantopon	12	8
Pantopon	18	66
Pantopon	24	92

All injections were made intraperitoneally, the material being dissolved in approximately 0.5 cc. of saline.

noted. None of the conditions mentioned affected the reaction time significantly, as is shown in table 1, which includes all conditions.

TABLE 4

Details of morphine assay

RAT NUMBER	WEIGHT	REACTION TIME: Control	After 30 minutes	After 1 hour	After 2.5 hours
Dose: 6 mgm. per kgm. intraperitoneally					
	gm.				
1	240	5.0	5.0	4.9	5.0
2	220	4.5	4.8	4.3	4.8
3	240	4.0	9.0	7.5	4.5
4	230	4.4	4.7	4.3	4.2
5	270	4.1	4.2	4.2	4.7
6	240	5.0	5.0	5.3	4.6
7	235	4.6	4.2	4.7	4.2
8	265	4.7	5.0	5.5	5.0
9	250	5.0	4.2	4.9	4.8
10	225	4.4	5.8	4.7	4.7
11	240	4.2	4.6	4.6	4.6
12	220	4.7	4.9	4.2	4.5
Dose: 8 mgm. per kgm.					
13	240	5.5	6.0	6.0	4.0
14	220	4.5	7.0	7.0	4.5
15	250	4.0	Comp.	9.0	5.5
16	260	5.0	7.0	Comp.	4.0
17	180	4.5	8.0	8.0	5.0
18	200	4.0	Comp.	8.0	5.0
19	200	6.0	Comp.	6.0	4.0
20	230	5.0	7.0	6.0	4.5
21	190	4.5	9.0	8.0	4.0
22	200	4.5	8.0	6.0	5.0
23	230	4.5	Comp.	8.0	5.0
24	250	5.5	Comp.	Comp.	5.5
Dose: 10 mgm. per kgm.					
25	250	6.0	Comp.	8.0	4.5
26	240	4.0	8.0	8.0	4.0
27	230	5.0	Comp.	Comp.	5.5
28	200	5.0	8.0	7.0	4.0
29	180	5.0	7.0	Comp.	4.0
30	200	4.0	Comp.	Comp.	6.0
31	220	5.5	8.0	Comp.	4.0
32	250	4.5	Comp.	7.0	7.0
33	200	4.0	Comp.	Comp.	5.0
34	240	4.0	7.0	7.0	4.5
35	230	5.0	7.0	4.5	5.0
36	210	4.0	Comp.	7.0	5.0

"Comp." means complete analgesia.

TABLE 4—*Concluded*

RAT NUMBER	WEIGHT	REACTION TIME:			
		Control	After 30 minutes	After 1 hour	After 2.5 hours
Dose: 12 mgm. per kgm.					
	gm.				
37	220	5.0	Comp.	Comp.	5.0
38	210	4.5	Comp.	Comp.	4.0
39	220	4.0	Comp.	Comp.	4.0
40	250	5.0	Comp.	Comp.	4.5
41	190	4.5	Comp.	Comp.	4.5
42	210	4.5	Comp.	Comp.	5.0
43	210	5.0	Comp.	Comp.	4.5
44	260	6.0	Comp.	Comp.	4.0
45	250	4.0	Comp.	Comp.	6.0
46	200	5.0	8.0	8.0	6.0
47	240	4.0	Comp.	Comp.	5.5
48	200	5.0	Comp.	Comp.	7.0

The assay of drugs. The method was next applied to the assay of the "analgesic" properties of several drugs. (It is of course realized that the subject of analgesia is a complex one and we are here using the term analgesia as synonomous with loss of reaction to pain merely for convenience sake.) The following materials showed no analgesic properties: Cobra venom,[1] in doses of 4, 8 and 16 m.u. per kilogram; Sodium amytal, in doses of 25 and 50 mgm. per kilogram; Tarantula venom, in doses of 10 milkings per rat; Black widow spider venom, in doses of $\frac{1}{8}$, $\frac{1}{4}$ and $\frac{1}{2}$ lethal doses. Results of the tests on cobra venom are given in table 2.

Five of the opiates, dilaudid, morphine sulfate, codeine sulfate, heroin and pantopon, were assayed at either 3 or 4 dosage levels, using 12 animals per dose. The results are given in table 3, the assay of morphine being reproduced in table 4 as an example. By complete analgesia is meant the complete loss of reaction to pain: the animal makes no movement of the tail whatever even though it is being burned to a crisp. It is, of course, not necessary to burn it to that extent, a white blistering appearance being sufficient. Incidentally this does the animal no permanent harm, for if the tail tip is badly burned it merely sloughs off.

DISCUSSION

Since the function of analgesic drugs is to alleviate human pain the human is the best subject for their study. But when the study concerns new and untried drugs or an extensive assay of old ones the human subject is obviously unavailable. As far as animal methods are concerned, the literature is by

[1] The cobra venom used in this study was supplied through the kind cooperation of Dr. Macht, of Hynson, Westcott and Dunning, Inc.

no means replete with descriptions of means for measuring analgesia experimentally, and no method seems to have gained widespread acceptance. Such methods as the piling of weights on a cat's tail, or heating the skin by means of hot water passing through tubes, have been described, but these suffer from two main defects: doubt exists as to the stimulus, i.e., whether it is pain or merely touch, and there are great individual variations in test animals. The method most recently reported is that of Macht (2) who used an electric shock applied to the scrotum. Here again the effective stimulus in control animals varied from 100 to 800 volts.

Of greatest value, of course, would be the development of methods for measuring true analgesia, i.e., the loss of conscious sensation of deep seated, continuous pain, such as that occurring in carcinoma. This is a much more difficult problem and the method described in this paper makes no pretense of measuring analgesia of this sort. It is, however, interesting to note that our rather thorough assay of the opiates gave results in good agreement with their accepted clinical value. A survey of doses recommended in a number of treatises on pharmacology indicates that dilaudid and heroin are considered to be approximately four times as active as morphine, and codein and pantopon about half as active as morphine. This is approximately the ratio of effectiveness found in this study.

We are unable to explain the discrepancy between our findings and those of Macht (2) concerning cobra venom. On a dosage of 0.5 m.u. (using 7 rats) he found an increase in the pain threshold, but in no case did the increase exceed the maximum stimulus (809 volts) found necessary at times in control rats. Only two rats were used on each of the higher doses and the two on 2.0 mμ gave inconsistent results in that the pain threshold in one was increased significantly (from 185 to 1080 volts) but in the other only from 185 to 445 volts. The weight of the rats was not mentioned. In our study, using 12 rats per dose and dosages of 4.0, 8.0 and 16.0 m.u. per kilogram (the rats weighed approximately 250 grams, therefore the dose was about 1.0, 2.0 and 4.0 m.u. per rat) we found no effect whatever on the reaction time. A dose of 16.0 m.u. per kilogram is approximately one-half the lethal dose.

Although, as stated, no claim is made that this method is capable of determining the analgesic power of drugs when deep-seated, continuous pain is involved, nevertheless a method as simple and rapid as this should have value in making it possible to submit to experimental verification many statements found in books on pharmacology, the evidence for which rests usually on uncontrolled clinical impressions. Such questions are: the influence of route of administration upon dosage and duration of analgesia, the possession of analgesic properties by anti-pyretics, barbiturates and other drugs, the potentiating effects of one drug upon another, and the testing for analgesic properties of new drugs. We are at present engaged on certain of these studies.

SUMMARY

1. A simple, rapid method for determining the pain threshold in the rat is described.

2. The individual variation, under a variety of conditions, was found to be surprisingly small.

3. The method was applied to the determination of analgesic properties of several substances, including cobra venom. No analgesic property in the latter could be demonstrated.

4. A comparative assay of five opiates gave results in good agreement with clinical experience.

REFERENCES

(1) Schumacher, Goodell, Hardy and Wolff: Science, **92**, 110, 1940.

(2) Macht and Macht: J. Amer. Pharm'l Ass'n., **29**, 193, 1940.

ON THE ACTION OF PROSTIGMINE ON THE CIRCULATORY SYSTEM

RAFAEL MENDEZ AND ABE RAVIN[1]

From the Department of Pharmacology, Harvard Medical School

Received for publication January 29, 1941

Since Aeschlimann and Reinert (1) described the pharmacological actions of prostigmine in 1931, this drug has found an increasing usefulness in therapeutics. Articles have appeared on the use of prostigmine in myasthenia gravis, in post-operative distention, in urinary disorders, in deafness, as a test for pregnancy, and recently in treatment of certain peripheral vascular diseases. The meagerness of experimental investigations on the action of prostigmine on the circulatory system and the increasing clinical use of the drug seemed to warrant a detailed study of its action on the heart and blood vessels.

METHODS

Isolated frog heart. The experiments were carried out in May on Rana pipiens. The Fühner technique and Clark's solution were used.

Heart-lung preparation. Dogs of from 7 to 11 kgm. were anesthetized with chloralose (0.09 gram per kgm.) and the preparation made in the usual way (2). The bled dog was usually anesthetized with ether after a preliminary dose of morphine (5 mgm. per kilogram), and the blood was defibrinated. Arterial resistance was maintained at 80 to 90 mm. of mercury. The total amount of blood in the system was approximately 1,000 cc. and injections were made into the tube leading to the reservoir (600 cc. capacity). Arterial pressure was recorded with a mercury manometer and venous pressure from the right auricle by a water manometer. During the course of most experiments the inflow level was raised 5 and 10 cm. in order to determine the ability of the heart to respond to increased blood supply (3). In the experiments on coronary flow a Morawitz cannula was introduced into the coronary sinus and the flow measured with a Condon recorder. To record pulmonary pressure a cannula was introduced into a branch of the pulmonary artery and a bromoform manometer used.

Auricular fibrillation was produced by direct stimulation of the right auricle with an induced current from a Harvard inductorium. The movements of the auricle were recorded by means of a spring lever. A Harvard inductorium and a metronome were used for vagal stimulation; shocks were maximal and the intensity of stimulation was varied by changing the frequency.

Nembutal (50 mgm. per kilogram) was used most commonly for anesthesia in cats. Spinal cats were prepared by the Elliot method as described by Burn (4). Blood pressure was recorded by a mercury or membrane manometer, using a very slow continuous infusion of M/6 sodium carbonate in order to prevent clotting (5). Leg volume was recorded by means of an air plethysmograph and a Marey tambour.

---

[1] Medical Fellow of the National Research Council.

Rabbit's ear. The artery and vein were both cannulated as described by Rischbieter (6) and perfusion carried out with Locke's solution at a height of 30 to 40 cm.

The drugs used were prostigmine methylsulfate (Hoffmann-LaRoche), acetylcholine bromide (Eastman), adrenaline (Parke-Davis), atropine sulfate, and nicotine.

RESULTS

Isolated frog heart. Concentration of 1:10,000 of prostigmine produced either no effect or a slight increase in rate and amplitude of contractions. Concentrations of 1:1,000 or 1:500 increased the rate and amplitude more markedly. With a concentration of 1:100 or 1:50 the rate and amplitude showed an initial increase followed by a decrease with development of irregularities. The effect of weaker solutions was completely reversible by washing; that of the stronger solutions was only partially reversible. Atropine in concentrations up to 1:50,000 did not prevent these actions of prostigmine.

Heart-lung preparation. An injection of 0.05 to 0.1 mgm. of prostigmine produced a slow decrease in heart rate associated with an increasing stroke volume (table 1). The total output remained little affected at the onset, but tended to decrease gradually as the rate became more markedly slowed. Arterial pressure showed no appreciable change and venous pressure increased as the output began to decrease.

The decrease in heart rate was evident in 3 to 5 minutes and most marked in 25 to 35 minutes. The decrease ranged from 16 to 40 beats per minute. The higher the initial rate the greater the fall. A second dose of prostigmine produced a further, although smaller, decrease in rate.

Since the increase in stroke volume at the onset of the experiment compensated for the slower rate, the total output per minute remained unchanged (table 1). With the pericardium intact the ability of the heart to dilate was limited and the total output began to decrease early. The venous pressure rose as the output decreased (figure 1). Removal of the pericardium permitted a greater degree of dilation and the total output was maintained at the original level for a longer period (table 1). Even under these circumstances, however, a tendency to a decrease in output and a rise in venous pressure usually became evident within thirty minutes.

The increase in heart volume following an injection of prostigmine was somewhat more than could be accounted for by the increase in stroke volume. This suggests a negative inotropic action on the heart.

Atropine (0.1 to 0.2 mgm.) quickly reversed the changes produced by prostigmine; the rate, stroke volume, and total output returned to original, or slightly below original values (fig. 1). Doses of 5 to 10 mgm. of prostigmine were given after atropine to see if the heart rate could again be slowed, but no clear effect was obtained although the rate sometimes decreased by 4 to 6 beats per minute. These large doses of prostigmine were markedly depressant to the heart in one instance.

Occasionally with doses of 0.05 mgm. prostigmine and more often with larger doses irregularities occurred. These were usually of ventricular origin, but in a few instances marked irregularities occurred which seemed to be of auricular origin. Atropine usually stopped the irregularities, but doses of atropine of over 0.2 mgm. tended of themselves to produce irregularities.

TABLE 1

Action of prostigmine on the heart-lung preparation

Weight of heart-lung dog, 7.6 kgm. Weight of heart, 70 grams. Arterial resistance, 75 mm. of mercury. Pericardium opened. Total blood added to system, 950 cc.

TIME	TEMPERATURE	HEART RATE PER MINUTE	INCREASE OF INFLOW LEVEL	OUTPUT	STROKE VOLUME	ARTERIAL B. P.	VENOUS B. P.
			mm.	*cc. per minute*	*cc.*	*mm. Hg*	*mm.* H_2O
12:50	39.0	156	0	392	2.51	96	24
12:53	38.9	156	50	642	4.12	101	28
12:55	38.9	158	100	857	5.43	104	30
12:57	39.1	158	0	395	2.50	96	24
12:59	Prostigmine 0.1 mgm.						
1:02	39.0	156	0	395	2.53	96	24
1:04	39.0	152	0	392	2.58	96	24
1:06	39.0	144	0	389	2.71	96	24
1:08	39.0	138	0	389	2.82	96	24
1:10	38.9	132	50	642	4.86	101	29
1:13	38.8	130	100	869	6.69	104	30
1:19	39.0	124	0	389	3.14	96	26
1:22	39.0	120	0	382	3.19	96	26
1:25	38.9	118	50	631	5.35	101	31
1:27	38.8	118	100	857	7.26	103	33
1:40	38.9	118	0	380	3.22	95	27
2:10	38.9	120	0	368	3.07	95	28
2:12	38.8	120	50	619	5.16	105	32
2:15	38.8	128	100	844	6.60	105	36
2:38	38.8	124	0	353	2.84	96	30
2:40	38.8	126	50	600	4.76	104	35
2:42	38.8	132	100	832	6.31	105	40
2:44	39.0	130	0	349	2.68	96	30

In the heart-lung preparation pulmonary pressure did not appear to be significantly influenced by fairly large doses of prostigmine (fig. 1).

Action on coronary blood flow. As is evident from figure 2, prostigmine produced a small decrease (or retarded the steady increase) in coronary flow in the heart-lung preparation in the absence of any significant change in the blood pressure. The decrease in coronary blood flow was associated with a decrease in heart rate, but the coronary blood flow in such denervated preparations has been shown to be almost independent of changes in heart rate of a range similar to that encountered in our experiments (7). Atropine produced a prompt increase in the coronary blood flow and after atropine large doses of prostigmine did not produce any appreciable effect.

Action on auricular fibrillation produced by electrical stimulation. The auricles of the cat's heart may be made to fibrillate by stimulation with a faradic current. The persistence of the fibrillation following the cessation of stimulation depends upon the strength and duration of the stimulating current. With weak currents the cessation of the fibrillation is almost synchronous with the cessation of stimulation. With stronger currents the fibrillation persists for a short period after stimulation. Prostigmine in

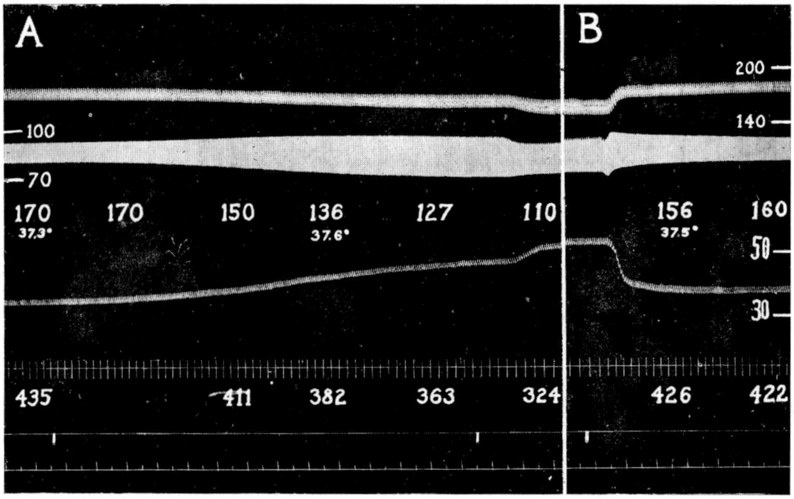

FIG. 1. ACTION OF PROSTIGMINE ON HEART-LUNG PREPARATION

Weight of heart-lung dog, 9 kgm. Weight of heart, 65 grams. Total blood added, 1,000 cc. Arterial resistance, 80 mm. of mercury. Pericardium not opened. Tracings from top to bottom: Pulmonary arterial pressure (scale on right in mm. of water); arterial blood pressure (scale on left in mm. of mercury); venous blood pressure in right auricle (scale on right in mm. of water); cardiac output, each signal indicating 100 cc.; signal indicating injection of drug; time in 30-second intervals. The numbers under the arterial blood pressure indicate the heart rate and the temperature of the blood. The numbers under the output tracing indicate output in cc. per minute. *A*, 0.1 mgm. of prostigmine methylsulfate was injected at the first signal and repeated at the second signal. *B*, 2 minutes after *A*; at signal, 0.1 mgm. of atropine sulfate was injected.

dosage of 0.05 mgm./kgm. markedly prolonged the duration of after-fibrillation (fig. 3). The prolongation of the fibrillation was most evident shortly (3 to 5 minutes) after an intravenous injection and then gradually diminished. Repeated injections greatly increased the after-fibrillation. Atropine antagonized this action of prostigmine. Winterberg (8, 9) has shown that after-fibrillation may be prolonged by stimulation of the vagus and by physostigmine.

Action on the heart rate in the cat. In the cat an injection of prostigmine of less than 0.05 mgm. per kilogram usually had no evident effect upon heart rate. Larger doses produced a gradual decrease in heart rate. The decrease was not evident for about 40 seconds and was most marked in 3 to 5 minutes. The heart rate returned to normal in 30 to 60 minutes. The effect of a second injection while the heart was still slowed was less than that of the first injection. Atropine prevented the decrease in rate and restored the rate to normal after it had been slowed. Decrease in heart rate occurred in animals with

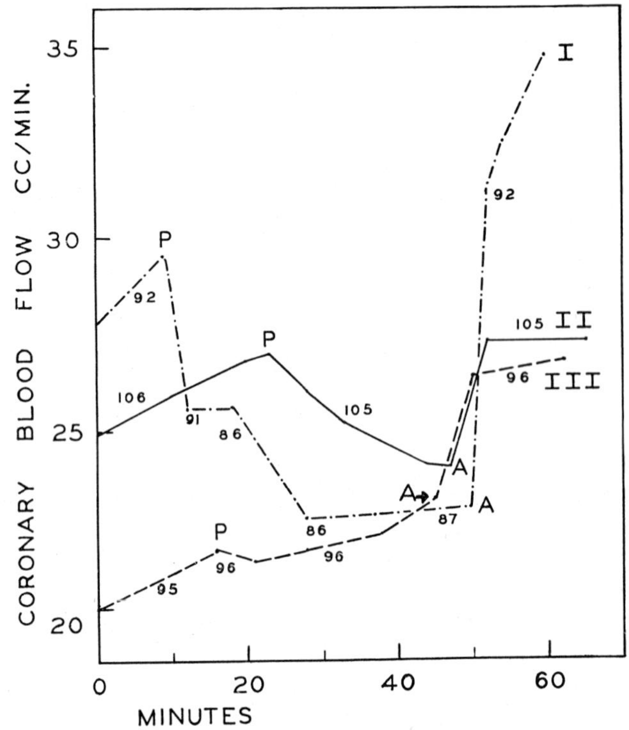

FIG. 2. THE ACTION OF PROSTIGMINE ON CORONARY FLOW IN THE HEART-LUNG PREPARATION

The arrows indicate when prostigmine and atropine were given: I, 0.1 mgm. prostigmine and 0.2 mgm. atropine; II, 0.05 mgm. prostigmine and 0.2 mgm. atropine; III, 0.05 mgm. prostigmine, and 0.2 mgm. atropine. The numbers under the graphs indicate the blood pressure in mm. of mercury.

the vagi cut and the stellate ganglia and upper thoracic sympathetic ganglia acutely removed.

Effect on blood pressure in the cat. Doses of prostigmine of less than 0.05 mgm. per kilogram often produced no change in blood pressure. In cats under nembutal the most common response to doses of 0.05 to 0.1 mgm. per kilogram was an initial fall in blood pressure followed by a rise above the normal level (fig. 4a). The drop in blood pressure was rather sharp but of short duration; the rise in blood pressure was more gradual and more persistent. In a number of animals, including all four spinal cats, only the rise in blood pressure occurred. Fall in blood pressure occurred before any great change in heart rate and was not dependent on the change in heart rate. Rise in blood pressure was seen in one eviscerated animal.

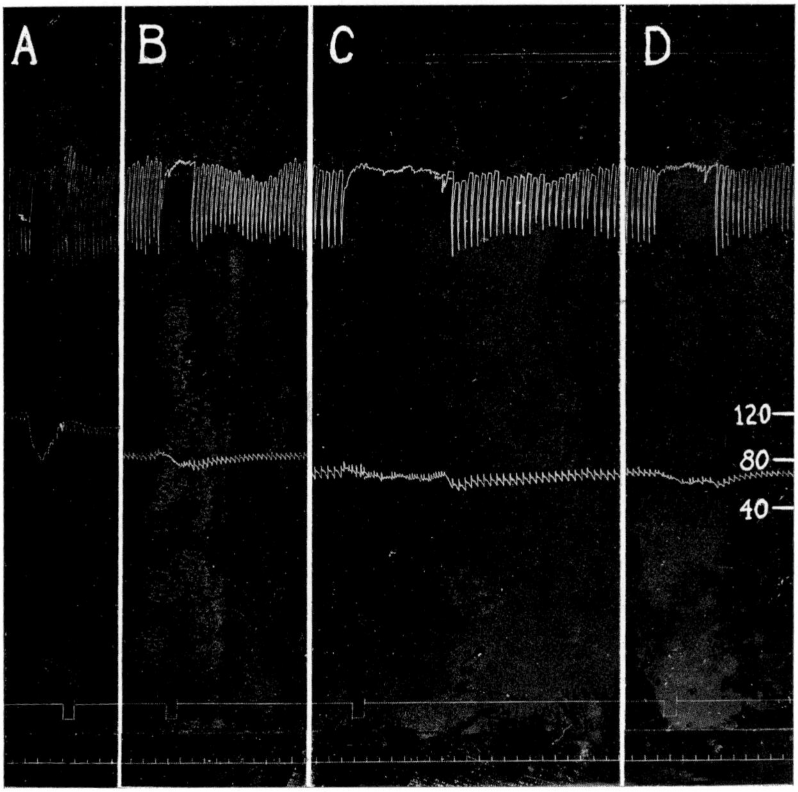

FIG. 3. EFFECT OF PROSTIGMINE ON AURICULAR FIBRILLATION PRODUCED BY ELECTRICAL STIMULATION OF THE RIGHT AURICLE

Cat, weight 3.5 kgm.; nembutal (50 mgm. per kgm.) anesthesia. Right auricle stimulated by means of Harvard inductorium. Tracings from top to bottom: movements of right auricle; arterial blood pressure (scale on right in mm. of mercury); signal indicating duration of stimulation; and time in seconds. *A*, before giving prostigmine. *B*, four minutes after the intravenous injection of prostigmine (0.05 mgm. per kgm.). *C*, ten minutes after B and four minutes of a second injection of prostigmine (0.1 mgm. per kgm.). *D*, nine minutes after C.

A second dose of prostigmine, or a large initial dose, produced in most cases only a fall in blood pressure with a tendency to gradual recovery (fig. 4b). By repeated doses the blood pressure could usually be brought to very low levels. The greater part of the fall in blood pressure occurred before the decrease in heart rate.

Following atropine, prostigmine produced only a rise in blood pressure which lasted 4 to 6 minutes and could be obtained repeatedly in the same animal (fig. 4c). The rise in blood pressure occurred in animals under nembutal anesthesia and in spinal animals. Ligating the adrenals did not seem to affect greatly the rise in blood pressure; in one animal the same increase (45 mm. of mercury) was obtained before and after this operation. In other animals the rise after ligation was not as great as before.

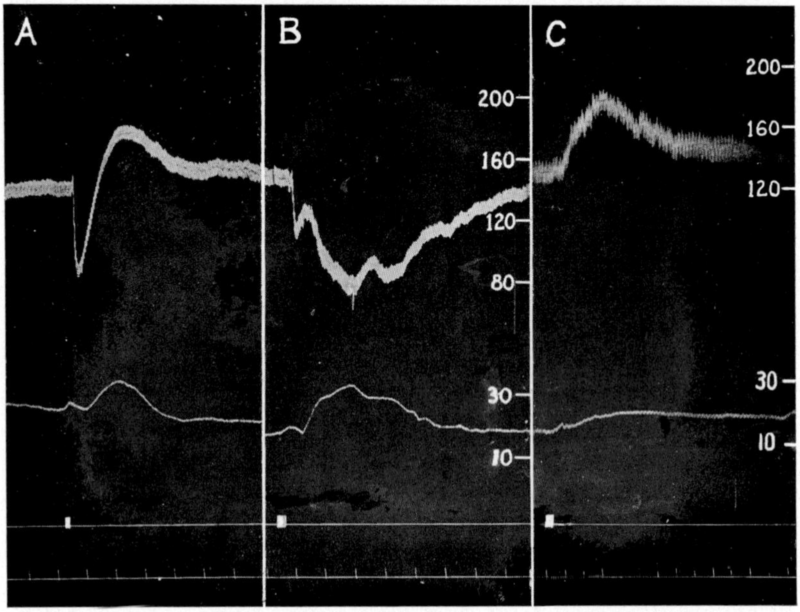

FIG. 4. EFFECT OF PROSTIGMINE ON BLOOD PRESSURE

A shows the effect of the first injection of prostigmine and *B* of a second injection in the same cat. Cat's weight, 3.66 kgm; anesthesia, nembutal (50 mgm. per kgm. intraperitoneally). Upper tracing, arterial blood pressure (scale in B); lower tracing, venous blood pressure (scale in B in mm. of water). Time in 1-minute intervals. *A*, at signal, prostigmine (0.082 mgm. per kgm.) was injected into femoral vein. *B*, 26 minutes after *A;* at the signal a second injection of prostigmine (0.082 mgm. per kgm.) was given. *C* shows rise in blood pressure obtained 14 minutes after 1 mgm. atropine sulfate had been given to a cat of 3.54 kgm. under nembutal (60 mgm. per kgm. intraperitoneally) anesthesia. At signal, prostigmine (0.4 mgm. per kgm.) was injected.

The rise also occurred in spinal eviscerated animals and in eviscerated animals under nembutal. Although it is difficult to compare the results obtained in different animals, the rises produced in eviscerated animals seemed somewhat less than in the uneviscerated animals. The rise also occurred in eviscerated animals with the adrenals ligated; here again it was less than in the intact animals.

The rise in blood pressure is apparently not due to stimulation of sympathetic ganglia as in the case of acetylcholine. In two animals the abdominal sympathetic chain was removed on one side and the volume of both legs recorded. No difference in behavior of the two legs was evident following prostigmine; acetylcholine produced vaso-constriction only in the innervated leg. Full nicotinization did not prevent the fall in blood pressure produced by repeated doses of prostigmine or the rise in blood pressure produced by prostigmine following atropine.

The increase in blood pressure was usually associated with a decrease in leg volume, but in one experiment out of four the leg volume increased slightly.

The rise in blood pressure occurred in many instances before any visible evidences of fibrillary twitching and it also occurred when the twitchings were abolished by curare.

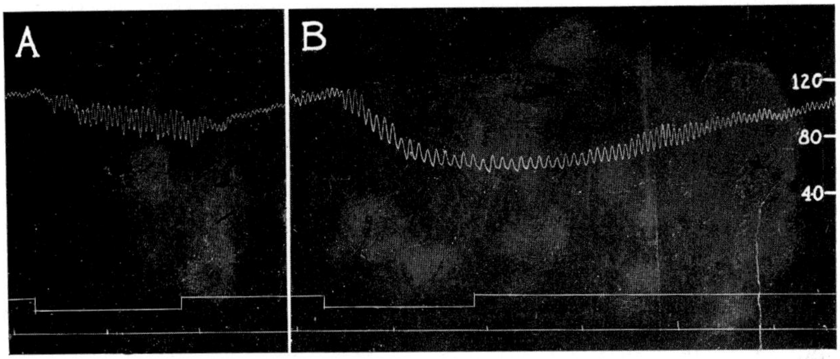

FIG. 5. EFFECT OF PROSTIGMINE ON VAGAL STIMULATION

Cat, weight 2.9 kgm.; nembutal (50 mgm. per kgm. intraperitoneally) anesthesia. Both vagi cut and peripheral end of right vagus stimulated with maximal induction shocks from a Harvard inductorium timed by a metronome; thoracic sympathetic chains removed, and adrenals ligated. Time (lower tracing) in 10-second intervals. Signal (middle tracing) indicates period of vagal stimulation. *A*, before prostigmine; *B*, 10 minutes after *A* and three minutes after injecting prostigmine (0.05 mgm. per kgm.).

Effect on vagal stimulation. Following prostigmine the response of the heart to vagal stimulation was greatly increased (fig. 5). Not only was the degree of slowing of the heart much greater but the slowing persisted for some time following the cessation of the stimulus. The maximal slowing obtained by a given strength of stimulus was practically attained with the first or second injection of prostigmine; therefore, when the heart had been markedly slowed by repeated injections of prostigmine, vagal stimulation produced relatively less slowing than when the heart rate was more rapid. Physostigmine also increases the response to vagal stimulation (*Winterberg* (*9*)). In our experiments, even large doses of prostigmine did not make the heart refractory to vagal stimulation.

Action on the effect of acetylcholine. Prostigmine accentuated the drop in blood pressure produced by acetylcholine. This was usually clearly seen following the intravenous injection of very small (0.05 to 0.10 microgram) quantities of acetylcholine but was more evident with larger doses of acetylcholine (0.5 to 1 microgram). The response to very small doses of acetylcholine often decreased after repeated injections of prostigmine, and at times became less than it was originally. Simultaneous vagal stimulation showed no decrease in effectiveness. The drop in blood pressure produced by prostigmine appeared to be one factor in decreased response to small doses of acetylcholine, but the phenomenon was also seen in an animal in whom no significant drop in blood pressure occurred.

Influence of prostigmine on the pressor response to adrenaline. The pressor effect of adrenaline, under certain conditions, was decreased by prostigmine in dosage of 0.10 to 0.15 mgm. per kilogram. This was observed clearly in three of five spinal cats. Of the other two, one showed only a questionable decrease in response; the other, which was eviscerated, showed no change. Five cats under nembutal anesthesia showed no distinct change in response.

Action of prostigmine on the perfused rabbit's ear. Injections of 0.5 cc. of prostigmine in concentrations of from 1:10,000 to 1:100 produced no obvious effect on the caliber of the vessels of the perfused rabbit's ear.

DISCUSSION

The pronounced ability of prostigmine to inhibit cholinesterase appears to explain many of the actions of this drug on the cardiovascular system. The increased response to vagal stimulation, the slowing of the heart rate, the fall of blood pressure and the increased response to injected acetylcholine which follow the administration of prostigmine can all be attributed to the slower destruction of acetylcholine. Since the electrically produced auricular fibrillation is prolonged by vagal stimulation and vagal stimulation may be simulated by prostigmine, this phenomenon probably falls in the group of actions explained by the ability of prostigmine to inhibit cholinesterase. The decrease in coronary flow observed following prostigmine probably has its origin in the ability of prostigmine to simulate vagal stimulation. Anrep and Segall (7) have shown that the coronary flow in an innervated heart-lung preparation can be decreased by vagal stimulation.

No clear evidence was obtained as to why prostigmine decreases the pressor response to adrenaline in spinal cats.

The increase in the rate and amplitude of the contractions of the frog heart are not the result of an increased acetylcholine action and must be due to a direct effect of prostigmine on the heart muscle. This is in accord with the inability of atropine to prevent this action of prostigmine.

The increase in the blood pressure of the cat after atropine presents a complex problem in which the various factors may be evaluated as follows: *1)* Stimulation of the adrenal glands plays only a small part in the observed effect. With the nictitating membrane as an indicator of adrenal secretion, an injection of prostigmine can be shown to cause liberation of adrenaline by the adrenal glands. Increase in blood pressure, however, was easily obtained after ligation of both adrenals. *2*) An effect on the intestinal tract, especially in the unatropinized animal, may play some part in the response. Although in some animals quite marked pressor responses were obtained after evisceration, the pressor effect in eviscerated animals was smaller than in those which were not eviscerated. *3*) Stimulation of ganglia probably plays no part. This conclusion follows from the experiments in which one lumbar sympathetic chain was removed and from the experiments with nicotine. *4*) Constriction of some portions of the peripheral vascular system by direct stimulation must play an important rôle in the rise in blood pressure, but this conclusion receives only partial confirmation in the results of leg volume experiments and no support from the experiments on the rabbit's ear.

SUMMARY

The actions of prostigmine on the circulatory system have been studied on the heart-lung preparation of the dog, on the isolated frog heart, and on the cat.

Of these actions, the following are referable to the inhibition of cholinesterase: the actions on the heart rate, stroke volume, total output, and coronary flow of the heart-lung preparation of the dog; the increased response to vagal stimulation, the slowing of the heart rate, the drop in blood pressure, and the more pronounced effect upon the blood pressure following injection of acetylcholine in the cat.

The action of prostigmine on the isolated frog heart and the increase in blood pressure in the cat usually produced by the first injection of prostigmine and always produced after atropine are not explained by the inhibition of cholinesterase.

We wish to express our thanks to Professor Otto Krayer for his guidance and criticism during this work.

REFERENCES

(1) Aeschlimann and Reinert: This Journal, **43,** 413, 1931.
(2) Patterson and Starling: J. Physiol., **48,** 357, 1913.
(3) Krayer: Arch. f. exper. Path. u. Pharmakol., **162,** 1, 1931.
(4) Burn: Biological Standardization. Oxford Medical Publication, 1937.
(5) Trendelenburg: Arch. f. d. ges. Physiol., **203,** 413, 1924.
(6) Rischbieter: Ztschr. f. d. ges. exper. Med., **1,** 355, 1913.
(7) Anrep and Segall: Heart, **13,** 239, 1926.
(8) Winterberg: Arch. f. d. ges. Physiol., **117,** 223, 1907.
(9) Winterberg: Ztschr. f. exper. Path. u. Therap., **4,** 636, 1907.

THE ACTION OF PITOCIN AND ADRENALIN ON DIFFERENT SEGMENTS OF THE RABBIT UTERUS

D. D. BONNYCASTLE AND J. K. W. FERGUSON

From the Department of Pharmacology, University of Toronto

Received for publication February 10, 1941

It has been shown by Newton (1) that strips of circular muscle from the *cervix uteri* in several species (goat, rat and guinea pig) can rarely be stimulated to contraction by even high concentrations of oxytocic principle of the posterior pituitary (Pitocin), while relatively low concentrations cause contraction of other parts of the uterus. This characteristic of the oxytocic principle is obviously favorable for the promotion of parturition. It seemed of interest to determine whether different parts of the rabbit uterus showed a similar differential sensitivity to the oxytocic principle, particularly because of the evidence presented by Haterius and Ferguson (2) for the release of an oxytocic hormone by electrical stimulation of the pituitary stalk in rabbits shortly after parturition. Further observations by Ferguson (3) indicate that the motility of the uterus may be influenced by the release of oxytocic hormone as a result of dilatation of the cervix and uterine horn, while dilatation of the vagina appears to modify the uterine activity in a manner similar to that of adrenalin. Consequently a study of the effects of adrenalin on different segments of the uterus also seemed desirable.

The most widely quoted classification of the actions of adrenalin on the uterus in different species is that of Gunn and Gunn (4), which has been extended recently (with due reservations) by Reynolds (5). This describes the reactions merely as motor or inhibitor in the gravid and non-gravid states. The inadequacy of such classification may be illustrated by one example. The effect of adrenalin on the rabbit uterus is alleged to be motor in both the gravid and non-gravid states, while on the cat uterus it is alleged to be motor in the gravid and inhibitor in the non-gravid state. Actually at parturition (the most important motor function of the uterus) the typical reaction of both cat and rabbit uteri to adrenalin is biphasic (Ferguson (3)). Bozler (6) concludes that a mixture of excitation and inhibition is by far the most typical reaction of most uteri most of the time.

The classification of Gunn and Gunn not only fails to describe important facts, but it also fails to suggest the functional rôle of adrenergic nerves or of adrenalin in uterine motility. We believe that the present study has given some insight into their functions.

METHODS

Rabbits three days prepartum to two days postpartum were used in these experiments. Both a circular and longitudinal strip, 1–1.5 cm. long and 2–4 mm. wide, were cut from three sites, the tubal end, a placental site and the cervical end of the uterus. The six strips were placed in Dale's solution (7) in a water bath of 250 cc. capacity and were connected to levers which wrote on a smoked drum. The water bath and its reservoir were contained in a larger electrically heated water bath. The temperature of the inner bath was held at 37.5° ± 0.1°C. The inner bath was aerated with compressed air which was bubbled through at a rate sufficient to produce complete mixing of added drug in about six seconds. The segments were allowed to work in the bath for two hours before drugs were added.

Low concentrations of drugs were used first and followed by higher ones till maximal effects were produced. The solution in the inner bath was changed after a series of drugs or dilutions of the same drug had been applied. The segments were allowed 20–30 minutes to recover from the washing and the series was then repeated. The sequence of drugs was varied so that reactions to one drug with and without the previous administration of another were recorded. For comparison of the sensitivity of different segments every application of a drug which produced a definite effect on one or more segments was considered. Only one experiment was discarded and this because one segment failed to respond to any stimulus.

The concentration of adrenalin chloride used ranged from 1:1000 million to 1:10 million and of pitocin from 8×10^{-6} unit/cc. to 4×10^{-3} unit/cc. Concentrations of chloretone in excess of those in the solutions of drugs used were tested and found to be without effect on the uterine contractions.

RESULTS

Examples of the various effects obtained from adrenalin and pitocin are shown in the illustrations. A statistical analysis of the results as a whole is presented later.

In figure 1, a record from a uterus 24 hours postpartum, 1×10^{-2} unit pitocin in 250 cc. produced no observable effect on the cervical segments, but initiated vigorous contractions in all other segments. Adrenalin in concentration of 1×10^{-8} produced contractions in both cervical segments. It also increased the frequency of contraction in the placental circular segment, had little effect on the placental longitudinal segment, and if anything decreased the activity of the tubal segments.

Figure 2, recorded from a uterus 36 hours postpartum, also illustrates the failure of the cervical circular segment to respond to the addition of 1×10^{-2} unit of pitocin to the bath, while increased activity is produced in all the other segments. On the other hand, adrenalin in concentration of 1×10^{-8} and 4×10^{-8}, elicited increased contractions from the cervical circular segment, mixed and varied effects from the others.

Figure 3 is from the same experiment as figure 2 and illustrates that different doses of adrenalin may have effects which are apparently qualitatively different on segments other than the cervical circular. By comparing the responses with those in figure 2 it can be seen that even the same dose at different times may produce qualitatively different effects on the same segment. In figure 2 adrenalin in concentrations 1×10^{-8} and 4×10^{-8} are

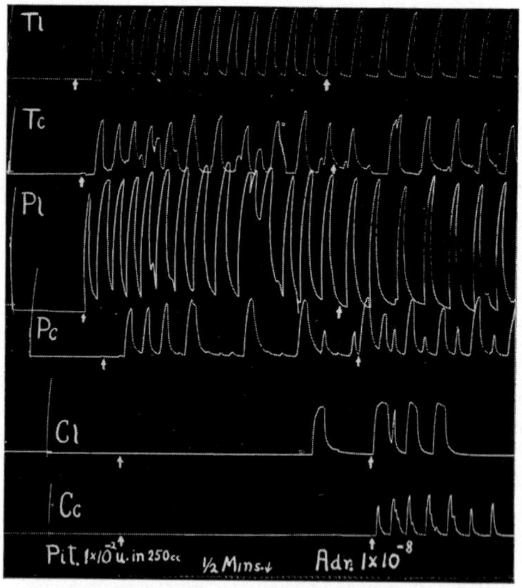

FIG. 1. Rabbit 24 hours postpartum. Uterine segments in water bath in the order marked on illustration as T.L. and T.C., indicating tubal longitudinal and circular segments respectively. Similarly P.L. and P.C. and C.L. and C.C. indicate the placental and cervical segments. The arrows mark the introduction of pitocin 1×10^{-2} unit and adrenalin 1×10^{-8}. Time in half minute intervals.

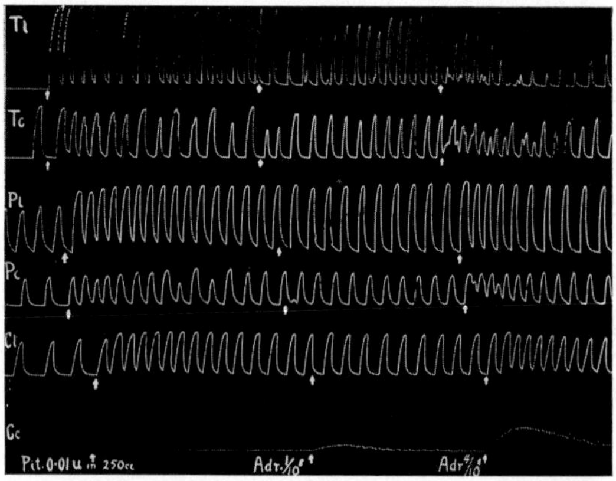

FIG. 2. Rabbit 36 hours postpartum. Uterine segments in water bath in order and marked as in figure 1. Arrows mark the point of application of pitocin 0.01 unit, adrenalin 1×10^{-8} and 4×10^{-8}.

added to a uterus in high activity as a result of pitocin and produce inhibition of the tubal longitudinal segment. In figure 3 the addition of adrenalin 4 ×

10^{-8} to an inactive uterus (pitocin had been washed out), produced marked stimulation.

The figures illustrate clearly that pitocin, when it produces any appreciable effect, is purely augmentor to frequency and contraction. Adrenalin, on the other hand, may have simple augmentory or inhibitory effects, or mixed or biphasic effects on the same segment depending on the dose and previous treatment of the segment. For purposes of quantitative description of the results as a whole, a comparison was made of the proportion of applications of each drug producing augmentation in each segment. Since each segment was exposed to identical concentrations of each drug (and the concentrations used were close to the threshold for definite action), such a comparison should give a measure of differences in the sensitivity of different segments to each

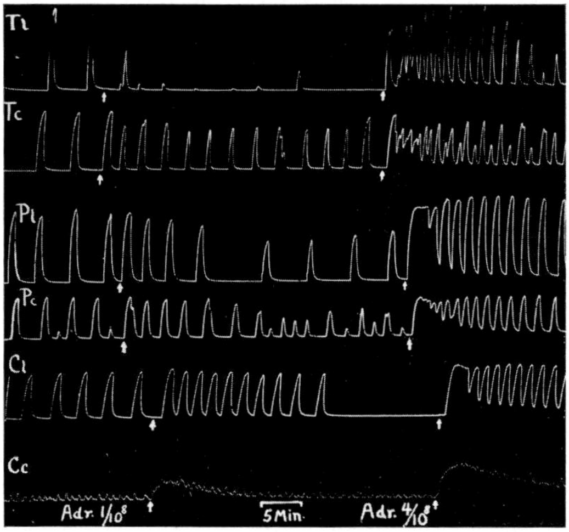

FIG. 3. From same experiment as figure 2. Arrow marks the point of application of adrenalin 1×10^{-8} and 4×10^{-8}.

drug. The effect of adrenalin was arbitrarily described as augmentation when the area under the graphic record was increased above that for an equal period of time preceding the application of the drug. The periods used for comparison were between five and fifteen minutes. In most cases an increase in area under the curve could be easily detected by the eye, but when some doubt existed the graphic record was transferred by carbon paper to letter paper and the area under the curve cut out and weighed. An increase in weight of 10 per cent or more was considered augmentation. Clear-cut differences in the sensitivity of different segments to the augmentor actions (as defined above) of the two drugs are shown in tables 1 and 2.

Table 1 shows that the cervical circular segments responded much less frequently than any other segment to the applications of pitocin, but responded much more frequently than the other segments to adrenalin. In each zone of the uterus the longitudinal segments are more sensitive to pitocin than the circular segments, while the circular segments respond with augmentation more frequently to adrenalin. The standard error of each percentage (S) was calculated by the formula $S = \sqrt{\frac{P \times (100-P)}{N}}$ where P is the per cent of augmentory responses and N the number of applications of the drug (Bradford Hill 1939) and the standard error of the difference between percentages (Sd) by the formula $Sd = \sqrt{S_1^2 + S_2^2}$. When the difference is more than twice the standard error of the difference it is considered significant.

TABLE 1

Per cent of applications of pitocin and adrenalin which produced augmentation of activity in different segments of postpartum uteri

	NUMBER OF UTERI	NUMBER OF APPLICATIONS	TUBAL		PLACENTAL		CERVICAL	
			Long.	Circ.	Long.	Circ.	Long.	Circ.
Pitocin	12	58	86	62	88	65	47	12
Adrenalin	12	78	40	46	37	56	88	91

TABLE 2

Per cent of applications of pitocin and adrenalin which produced augmentation of activity in different segments of prepartum uteri

	NUMBER OF UTERI	NUMBER OF APPLICATIONS	TUBAL		PLACENTAL		CERVICAL	
			Long.	Circ.	Long.	Circ.	Long.	Circ.
Pitocin	5	21	29	29	100	49	10	0
Adrenalin	5	43	58	35	35	58	95	84

By this criterion the only percentages that are not significantly different are the difference between 40 and 46 for the per cent responses of tubal longitudinal and circular segments to adrenalin, and the difference between 88 and 91 for the per cent responses of cervical longitudinal and circular segments to adrenalin.

The sensitivity to the augmentor effect of adrenalin is significantly greater at the cervical end in both circular and longitudinal segments, while the sensitivity of both cervical segments to pitocin is significantly less than that of all other segments. The sensitivity of all longitudinal segments to pitocin is significantly greater than that of all circular segments.

The proportion of augmentor responses to adrenalin was not significantly different whether the administration of adrenalin preceded or followed the administration of pitocin. The larger doses of adrenalin (concentrations of

4×10^{-8} and higher), however, gave a definitely higher proportion of augmentor responses.

Prepartum uterus

The number of experiments is less than on the postpartum uteri but table 2 shows that as in the postpartum uterus the cervical segments are less sensitive than the others to pitocin, but more sensitive to adrenalin. These differences are statistically significant.

In spite of the use of higher concentrations of pitocin on the prepartum uteri, the per cent of positive responses obtained from all segments was only 37, as compared with 60 for the postpartum uteri. The responses of the prepartum uteri were also noticeably less in magnitude and duration. A point of probable importance is the relative insensitivity of the segments from the tubal end of the prepartum uteri to pitocin. It is curious that the per cent responses to a concentration of pitocin as low as 4×10^{-4} unit/cc. is as great or greater in one segment of the prepartum uteri, namely the placental longitudinal segment as in the same segment of the postpartum uteri, although the magnitude and duration of the responses of the prepartum segments were less.

No significant difference was observed in the per cent of response to the same concentrations of adrenalin by prepartum and postpartum segments.

Inhibitory effects of adrenalin

Biphasic effects of adrenalin are not so consistently obtained from the isolated segments as they are from the intact uterus *in situ*. Inhibitory effects, however, were observed much more frequently in placental longitudinal segments than in any other. Two circumstances make the appearance of biphasic responses more frequent *in situ*. In the first place the vasoconstrictor effect of the adrenalin might be expected to inhibit the activity of the uterine muscle by anoxia. Secondly, recording from a whole uterine horn often gives a record of apparent inhibition when inspection reveals irregular and asynchronous activity of different parts of the horn. Inhibition thus recorded is the inhibition of co-ordinated synchronous contraction, or the conversion of what might be called uterine systole to something like uterine fibrillation.

Observations in situ

The foregoing observations indicate that although adrenalin frequently augments the activity of uterine strips, its net effect on the expulsive activity of the uterus must be entirely different from that of pitocin. To test this implication adrenalin and pitocin were administered to rabbits within 24 hours of the expected time of parturition. The abdomen was opened under chloralose and urethane anaesthesia and the uterus observed through a sheet of cellophane arranged to protect the organs from drying. Under these conditions a considerable degree of activity of the uterine musculature was usually observed. The movements are best described as pendular, by which is meant an alternation of contractions beginning at the ends of each ampulla, with contractions beginning at the middle of each ampulla. These contractions draw the uterine wall over the fetus, first towards the ends of the ampulla and then towards the middle.

In three experiments adrenalin, 1 to 1.8 cc. of 1:50,000 was given intravenously and produced intense contractions of the whole uterus, with blanching which lasted three or four minutes. It was particularly noticeable that the cervical region and interampullary nodes were tightly contracted. The tetanic contraction gradually broke up into frequent and intense activity of the pendular type previously described. No fetuses were ever expelled by the stimulation of muscular activity produced by adrenalin. In all these experiments a single intravenous injection of pitocin (0.05 unit in one case and 1 unit in the others) produced immediate expulsion of one or more fetuses. The dose of 0.05 unit caused the expulsion of a fetus within 30 seconds. These experiments clearly demonstrate the nonexpulsive nature of the intense uterine contractions produced by adrenalin as contrasted to the expulsive activity induced by pitocin. Although actual antagonism of the effects of pitocin and adrenalin has not been demonstrated directly in the intact animal, it may be deduced from the experiments on the excised uterus and from considerations to be discussed, that the effects of adrenalin are not only nonexpulsive but definitely anti-expulsive.

Pitressin

In a few experiments pitressin was used as well as pitocin. Roughly about ten or more pressor units of pitressin gave effects equivalent to one oxytocic unit of pitocin. The oxytocic activity of the pitressin on these postpartum uteri seemed to be not much greater than would be expected from the figures for oxytocic activity, very kindly supplied with the solutions of pitressin by Dr. Oliver Kamm of Parke, Davis and Co. The cervical segments showed the same relative insensitivity to pitressin that they showed to pitocin.

DISCUSSION

The results presented in tables 1 and 2 show clearly that augmentor effects (as defined above) are produced by adrenalin most frequently on the cervical end of the uterus and more frequently as a whole on circular strips than on longitudinal. The net effect of circulating adrenalin or of sympathin liberated at nerve endings in the uterus would probably be anti-expulsive by two mechanisms: (a) by keeping the cervical end of the uterus tightly contracted, (b) by promoting contraction of circular muscle in the inter-ampullary regions which would oppose expulsive movements.

It might be postulated that the augmentor component of the reaction of longitudinal muscle to adrenalin, although inconstant, indicates the presence of certain adrenergic nerve fibers which favor expulsive activity. It seems more likely, however, that even the augmentor effect of adrenalin on longitudinal muscles is of a type to interfere with propagated expulsive contractions rather than to reinforce them. It has been shown by Morison (9) that contractions produced by adrenalin in cat and rabbit uteri are not propagated as are spontaneous contractions or those produced by electrical or mechanical stimulation. Thus adrenalin must in some way block the very contractions it produces and hence would likely block propagated expulsive movements. Bozler (6), in fact, suggests that the effect of adrenalin is a dual one on the muscle itself, causing excitation with diminished excitability. The immediate net effect depends on a variety of factors, including the effective concentration of the drug. This view is attractive, since it obviates the necessity of postulating two sets of adrenergic nerve fibers with antagonistic functions in the same organ.

The view that the function of the sympathetic innervation of the myometrium is anti-expulsive in the guinea pig, rat and related species, receives ample support from the literature (Reynolds, Chapter XIII). It has been repeatedly demonstrated that adrenalin almost invariably inhibits the contractions of longitudinal muscle induced by pituitrin in these species. The hypothesis that the function of the sympathetic innervation of the uterine musculature in all species is anti-expulsive is rendered at least very plausible by the present demonstration that in a species in which contraction is a prominent feature of the action of adrenalin, the net effect of adrenalin is almost certainly anti-expulsive.

It has been suggested elsewhere (3) that the anti-expulsive functions of the sympathetic nervous system may be useful in promoting the orderly expulsion of a series of fetuses. For example, when a fetus is expelled into the vagina the dilatation of the vagina has been observed to cause a powerful contraction of the cervix. If this is a part of a generalized discharge of the sympathetic innervation to the uterus (as it appears to be), the net effect would be to delay the expulsion of other fetuses till the vagina was emptied.

SUMMARY

Strips of longitudinal and circular muscle were taken from three zones of rabbit uteri shortly before and shortly after parturition. The zones used were the cervical end, the tubal end and a placental site. All six strips were suspended in a common water bath and exposed to the action of the same concentrations of adrenalin chloride, pitocin and pitressin.

Striking differences were observed in the sensitivity of different parts of the uterus to adrenalin and posterior pituitary extract. Most striking was the relative insensitivity of the cervical end to pituitary extract, and relatively great sensitivity to adrenalin.

It is deduced that the complex action of adrenalin is in effect anti-expulsive and thus antagonistic to the action of oxytocin.

REFERENCES

(1) Newton: J. Physiol., **79**, 301, 1933.
(2) Haterius and Ferguson: Am. J. Physiol., **124**, 314, 1938.
(3) Ferguson: Surg., Gynec. and Obst., 1941 (in press).
(4) Gunn and Gunn: This Journal, **5**, 527, 1914.
(5) Reynolds: Physiology of the Uterus. Hoeber, New York, 1939.
(6) Bozler: Am. J. Physiol., **130**, 627, 1940.
(7) Dale and Laidlaw: This Journal, **4**, 75, 1912.
(8) Hill: Principles of Medical Statistics. The Lancet Ltd., London, 1939.
(9) Morison: Am. J. Physiol., **128**, 372, 1940.

COMPARATIVE EFFECTS OF SULFONAMIDE COMPOUNDS AS TO ANEMIA AND CYANOSIS

ARTHUR P. RICHARDSON

From the Department of Pharmacology, Stanford University School of Medicine, San Francisco

Received for publication February 17, 1941

Marshall, Litchfield and White (1, 2) have described quantitative methods by which the therapeutic value of chemotherapeutic drugs may be determined in mice, but at present there are no accurate methods for determining the comparative toxicity of sulfonamide compounds for the host. The most common and often the most serious complications in the therapeutic use of sulfonamide compounds are those concerned with blood. Until recently it has been impossible to investigate these side actions experimentally due to the difficulty in producing cyanosis and anemia in suitable animals. This difficulty has now been circumvented (3, 4, 5) thus permitting the development of methods by which an accurate comparison of the injuriousness of these compounds, and probably other agents, may be made. This report presents the details of such methods and the results obtained with four of the more widely used sulfanilamide compounds, i.e., sulfanilamide, sulfapyridine, sulfathiazole, and sulfanilylguanidine.[1]

METHODS

The experimental basis for the method employed has already been described (3, 6). White mice were used because they have proved to be the most sensitive animals for the production of blood changes with sulfanilamide. All drugs in appropriate concentration were administered by being incorporated in a diet consisting of powdered Purina Dog Chow. The advantages of this method of medicating mice have been fully described by Marshall *et al.* (1, 2); chief among them is the maintenance of a constant blood level of the drug.

After control examinations of the blood each mouse was placed in an individual cage and allowed to eat the medicated diet freely. Drug-diet intake per mouse was measured periodically, and from this the daily drug intake per kilogram body weight was calculated. All mice used were young adults of 18 to 25 grams obtained from the same strain of Swiss white mice. After 2 weeks on the drug-diet the blood examinations were repeated.

---

[1] Sulfanilamide and sulfapyridine used were furnished by the Abbott Laboratories, North Chicago, Illinois; sulfathiazole was furnished by Winthrop Chemical Co., New York; and sulfanilylguanidine was furnished by Dr. E. K. Marshall, Jr., Johns Hopkins Medical School, Baltimore, Md., and by E. R. Squibb & Sons, New Brunswick, N. J.

Hemoglobin was determined as acid hematin, using a photoelectric colorimeter. Reticulocytes and Heinz bodies were estimated by the wet cover slip method, using brilliant cresyl blue. Previous studies of sulfanilamide anemia in mice showed that changes in hemoglobin and reticulocytes were the most sensitive indication of the action of this drug on blood (6). In the present study both determinations were made. A decrease in hemoglobin indicated hemolysis in the peripheral blood stream, and an increase in reticulocytes pointed to compensation of the bone marrow to the blood destruction. The blood concentration of each drug was determined by the method of Marshall and Bratton (7) for each mouse. Blood for this analysis was obtained by cardiac puncture between 9:00 and 12:00 a.m. of the day of the last blood count. The blood levels reported in this paper therefore represent the minimum concentration of drug maintained in the blood during the medication period (2). A quantity of 0.1 cc. of blood, diluted 1:150, was used for each determination and a final reading was made with a photoelectric colorimeter. Changes in hemoglobin were determined in pooled blood by methods described previously (5). Oxygen capacity was determined by the method of van Slyke (8), blood iron by the method of Coombs (9). Spectroscopic examination was made on a concentrated sample of blood with a replica grating spectroscope.

The general plan was to correlate the intake of each drug with the blood changes produced; thus it was possible to determine for each compound the minimum effective dose which caused a change in hemoglobin or in reticulocytes. The drugs were administered for 2 weeks because it has been shown previously that any particular blood concentration produces its maximum effect within this period (6).

RESULTS

Hemoglobin changes. Comparative results with the four sulfonamides as to blood destruction are presented in figure 1, each point representing the change in hemoglobin in a single mouse in 2 weeks of medication. A total of 62 mice were used for sulfanilamide, 52 for sulfapyridine, 54 for sulfathiazole, and 49 for sulfanilylguanidine. In order to handle the data more conveniently the animals on each drug were divided into four groups according to increasing dosage and the mean loss of hemoglobin was calculated for each group. In figure 1 these mean values are represented by the double circles.

It is seen that when the data are summarized in this manner the points relating the logarithm of the dose to gram per cent changes in hemoglobin lie along a straight line. For each compound the equation to this regression line was calculated according to the method of Fisher (10). In this way it was possible to determine accurately the minimum dose necessary to produce blood changes. From the drug concentration in the blood of each mouse it was possible to convert the minimum effective dosage to minimum effective blood concentration.

An interesting feature of the relation of dosage to destruction of blood was that an increase in intake of drug did not necessarily result in a corresponding increase in anemia for all the compounds. This is indicated in figure 1 by the differences in the slope of the regression lines. At first this result was confusing, but when blood levels were correlated with dosage it became apparent that much of the difference could be accounted for by differences

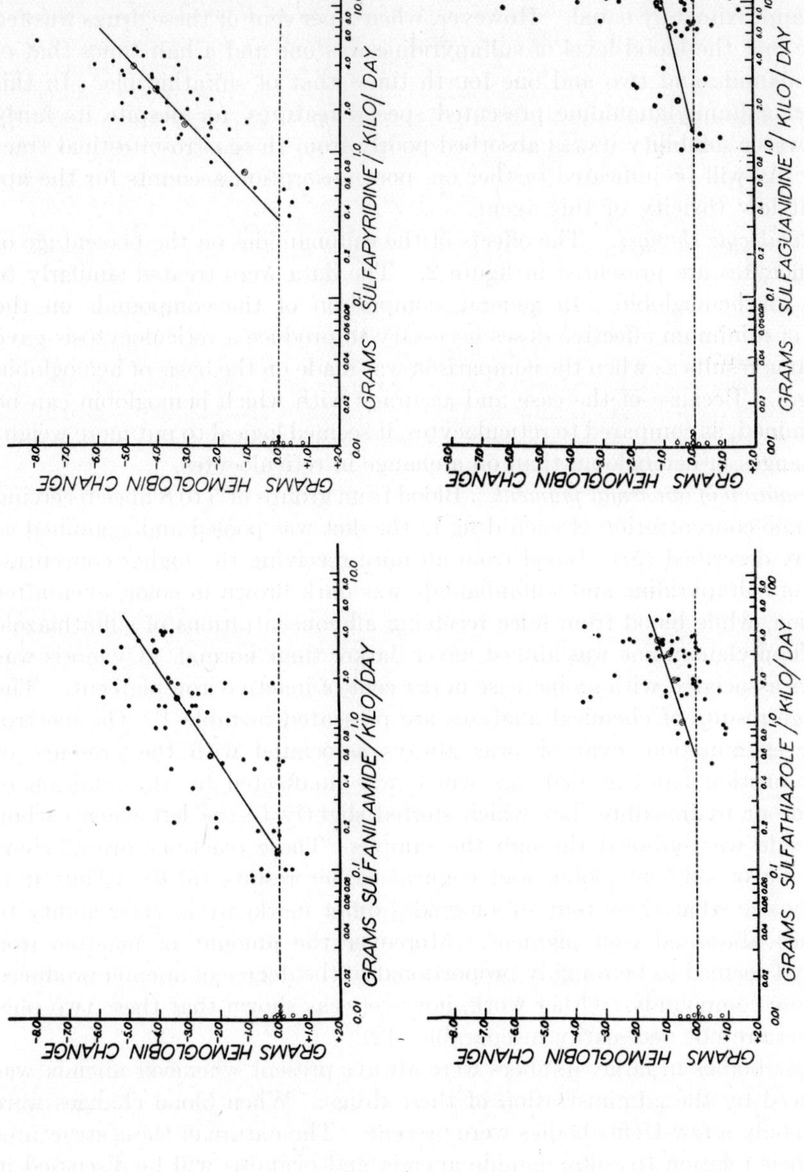

FIG. 1. EFFECT OF SULFONAMIDE COMPOUNDS ON HEMOGLOBIN
Open circles represent changes in hemoglobin of mice receiving no drug

in absorption or excretion, particularly with the higher concentrations in the diet. Details of the results concerning this point are presented in table 1. From this it is seen that, when 0.5 per cent of each drug was administered, the blood levels obtained with sulfanilamide, sulfapyridine, and sulfathiazole were approximately equal. However, when 2 per cent of these drugs was fed in the diet the blood level of sulfapyridine was one and a half times that of sulfanilamide and two and one fourth times that of sulfathiazole. In this respect sulfanilylguanidine presented special features, for despite its fairly high water solubility it was absorbed poorly from the gastro-intestinal tract (11). As will be indicated farther on, poor absorption accounts for the apparent low toxicity of this agent.

Reticulocyte changes. The effects of the sulfonamides on the percentage of reticulocytes are presented in figure 2. The data were treated similarly to those for hemoglobin. In general, comparison of the compounds on the basis of minimum effective doses necessary to produce a reticulocytosis gave the same results as when the comparison was made on the basis of hemoglobin changes. Because of the ease and accuracy with which hemoglobin can be determined, as compared to reticulocytes, it seemed logical to put more weight on changes in hemoglobin than on a change in reticulocytes.

Formation of abnormal pigment. Blood from groups of 5 to 8 mice receiving the same concentration of each drug in the diet was pooled and examined as already described (5). Blood from all mice receiving the higher concentrations of sulfapyridine and sulfanilamide was dark brown in color, even after aeration, while blood from mice receiving all concentrations of sulfathiazole or sulfanilylguanidine was almost never darker than normal. Cyanosis was always associated with an increase in per cent of inactive iron pigment. The average results of chemical analyses are presented in table 1. On spectroscopic examination, cyanosis was always associated with the presence of an absorption band at 620 mμ, which was unaffected by the addition of cyanide or hydrosulfite, but which shifted slightly to the left when carbon monoxide was bubbled through the sample. These reactions are all characteristic of sulfhemoglobin and confirm earlier results (5, 6). Thus it is readily seen that these four sulfonamides differ markedly in their ability to produce abnormal iron pigment. Moreover the amount of inactive iron pigment seemed to be roughly proportional to the degree of anemia produced by these compounds. Other work, however, has shown that these two phenomena are not necessarily inseparable (12).

Heinz bodies in large numbers were always present whenever anemia was produced by the administration of these drugs. When blood changes were slight, only a few Heinz bodies were present. The nature of these structures and their relation to sulfanilamide anemia and cyanosis will be discussed in another report (13).

Distribution of sulfonamide compounds between plasma and erythrocytes.

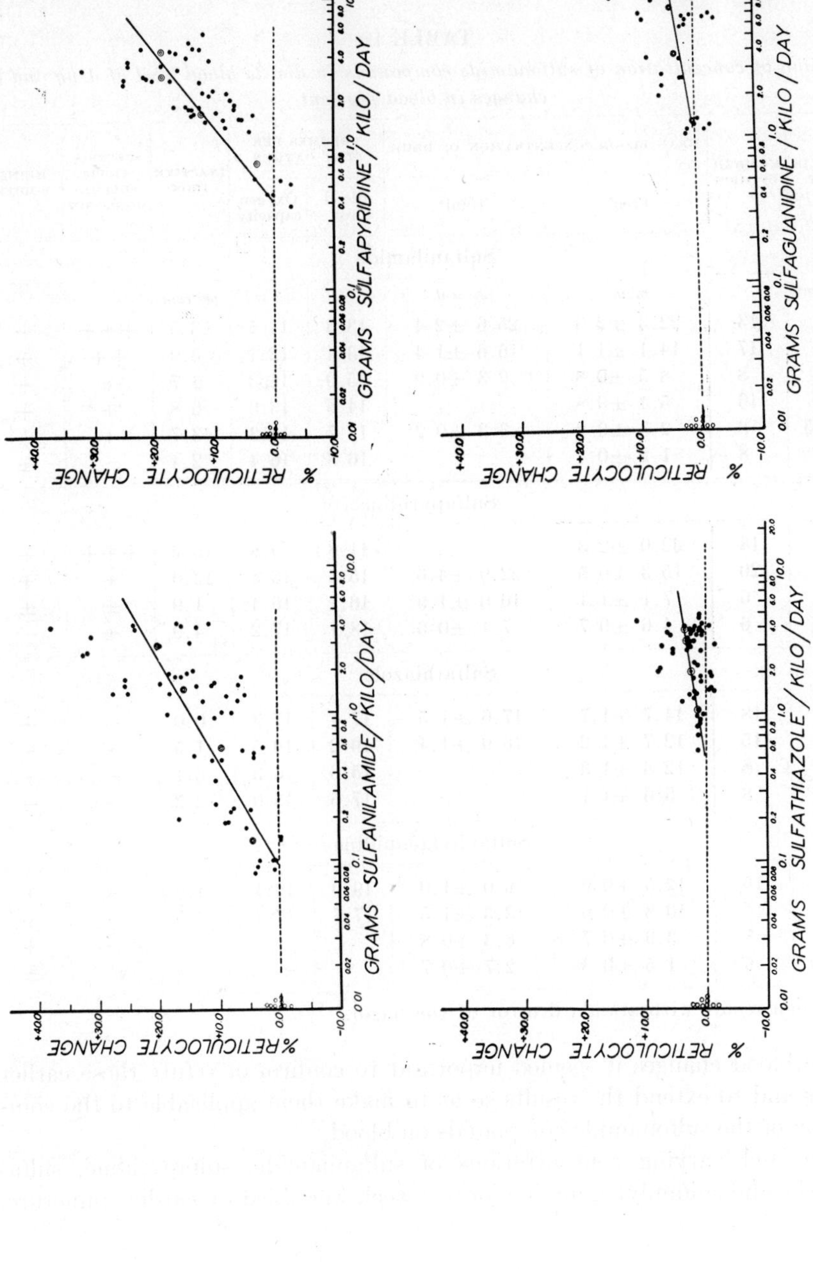

FIG. 2. EFFECT OF SULFONAMIDE COMPOUNDS ON RETICULOCYTES
Open circles represent changes in reticulocytes of mice receiving no drug

It has been claimed that sulfanilamide is not distributed evenly between plasma and red cells in the proportion that would be expected from the known water content of the two media (14, 15). In addition there are claims that the various derivatives now in use differ from sulfanilamide in this respect (16). Because of the possible importance of these characteristics in relation

TABLE 1

Relation of concentration of sulfonamide compounds in diet to blood level of drug and to changes in blood pigment

DRUG IN DIET	NUMBER OF MICE	MEAN BLOOD CONCENTRATION OF DRUG		VOLUMES PER CENT OXYGEN		INACTIVE IRON	SPECTROSCOPIC SULFHEMOGLOBIN	HEINZ BODIES
		Free*	Total*	Blood iron	Oxygen capacity			
				Sulfanilamide				
per cent		*mgm.*	*per cent*			*per cent*		
2.0	13	22.3 ±2.3	25.6 ±2.4	13.3	11.5	13.5	+++	+
1.0	17	14.1 ±1.1	16.6 ±1.4	13.4	12.1	9.9	++	+
0.5	8	8.5 ±0.8	9.3 ±0.9	15.0	14.3	4.7	+	+
0.25	16	5.4 ±0.8		14.6	13.6	6.8	+	+
0.125	8	2.3 ±0.2	3.3 ±0.2	14.7	14.3	3.7	+	+
0.06	8	1.2 ±0.1		16.8	16.4	2.4	−	±
				Sulfapyridine				
2.0	18	32.0 ±2.3		11.8	9.8	16.9	+++	+
1.0	20	15.3 ±0.5	22.9 ±4.6	15.3	13.3	13.0	+	+
0.5	6	7.1 ±1.1	10.0 ±1.9	16.7	16.4	1.9	±	±
0.25	6	4.6 ±0.7	7.1 ±0.6	18.1	17.2	4.9	±	−
				Sulfathiazole				
2.0	18	14.7 ±1.7	17.6 ±1.5	17.4	17.3	0.0	−	+
1.5	15	12.7 ±1.2	16.9 ±1.4	19.2	19.5	1.5	−	±
1.0	8	12.8 ±1.3		15.8	16.3	3.1	−	−
0.5	8	6.6 ±1.1		17.6	18.0	2.2	−	−
				Sulfanilylguanidine				
5.0	15	12.5 ±0.9	16.0 ±1.0	19.9	19.1	4.0	−	+
3.0	15	10.8 ±0.6	13.3 ±1.5	17.7	17.1	3.5	−	+
1.5	8	3.9 ±0.7	6.3 ±0.8				−	+
0.75	6	1.5 ±0.3	2.7 ±0.7					±

* Mean result with standard error of the mean.

to the blood changes it seemed important to confirm or refute these earlier claims and to extend the results so as to make them applicable to the comparison of the sulfonamide compounds on blood.

Mice fed varying concentrations of sulfanilamide, sulfapyridine, sulfathiazole, and sulfanilylguanidine for one week were bled by cardiac puncture.

Blood from each mouse was kept from coagulating by the addition of potassium oxalate and immediately centrifuged. Plasma and erythrocytes, thus obtained, were used for analysis of drug content by the methods described above. The results obtained are summarized in table 2, in which each value is the mean result for each group of mice, plus or minus the standard error of the mean of the observations.

TABLE 2

Distribution of sulfonamide compounds between erythrocytes and plasma

NUMBER OF MICE	DRUG IN DIET	FREE COMPOUND			CONJUGATED COMPOUND		
		Plasma	Erythrocytes	Mean P/E ratio*	Plasma	Erythrocytes	Mean P/E ratio*
				Sulfanilamide			
	per cent						
6	2	13.7 ±1.5	19.7 ±1.9	0.69 ±0.03	2.5 ±0.4	3.6 ±0.5	0.75 ±0.14
6	1	6.9 ±0.5	9.6 ±1.0	0.72 ±0.02	1.6 ±0.1	2.6 ±0.1	0.59 ±0.03
6	0.5	5.5 ±0.7	6.6 ±0.7	0.83 ±0.04	2.0 ±0.3	2.9 ±0.2	0.67 ±0.10
6	0.25	2.4 ±0.3	3.1 ±0.4	0.77 ±0.07	0.8 ±0.2	1.4 ±0.2	0.62 ±0.16
6	0.125	0.4 ±0.4	1.2 ±0.2	0.28 ±0.05	0.5 ±0.1	1.0 ±0.1	0.49 ±0.07
				Sulfapyridine			
6	2	21.4 ±1.8	32.4 ±3.2	0.68 ±0.07	3.3 ±0.7	2.5 ±0.3	1.40 ±0.35
7	1	7.1 ±0.9	11.6 ±2.5	0.71 ±0.01	1.1 ±0.2	1.2 ±0.6	3.06 ±0.10
6	0.5	5.2 ±0.7	6.6 ±0.6	0.88 ±0.09	2.5 ±0.3	2.0 ±0.5	1.19 ±0.22
6	0.25	2.3 ±0.7	1.9 ±0.01	1.10 ±0.08	1.2 ±0.02	1.2 ±0.03	1.30 ±0.3
				Sulfathiazole			
11	2	8.1 ±1.2	4.7 ±0.7	1.75 ±0.09	3.7 ±1.0	1.7 ±0.01	1.9 ±0.48
8	1	6.2 ±0.9	3.3 ±0.8	2.0 ±0.25	2.6 ±0.3	2.3 ±0.4	1.3 ±0.28
5	0.5	3.7 ±0.6	1.9 ±0.4	2.48 ±1.7	1.8 ±0.3	1.8 ±0.2	1.04 ±0.14
6	0.25	2.4 ±0.3	0.9 ±0.3	3.04 ±0.12	1.0 ±0.03	0.9 ±0.3	2.8 ±1.45
				Sulfanilylguanidine			
7	5.0	7.1 ±1.0	8.3 ±1.5	0.84 ±0.06	1.7 ±0.1	2.0 ±0.1	1.2 ±0.6
6	1.5	3.4 ±0.4	4.5 ±0.4	0.76 ±0.05	1.8 ±0.4	2.2 ±0.1	0.84 ±0.04
6	0.75	1.6 ±0.1	2.5 ±0.4	0.70 ±0.01	0.7 ±0.2	1.4 ±0.1	0.5 ±0.00

* P/E ratio means plasma-erythrocyte ratio.

It is seen that, after all doses of sulfanilamide, the concentration of drug in the erythrocytes was considerably greater than in the plasma. On the lower doses of sulfanilamide this difference was greater than on the higher doses. With sulfapyridine, however, the difference in concentration between the two blood components was not so marked. As the concentration of drug in the diet decreased the concentration of this drug in plasma and erythrocytes was about equal. The distribution of sulfathiazole was strikingly different from the other compounds studied. In all mice, and on all concentrations of the drug in the diet, the greater part of the sulfathiazole was found in the plasma. As the total concentration of the drug was decreased the plasma:cell ratio tended to increase. Sulfanilylguanidine resembled sulfanilamide in its distribution between red cells and plasma.

The differences in distribution of sulfanilamide and sulfathiazole were further investigated in rabbits which received gastrically 0.25 gram per kilogram of each drug. The concentration of the drugs was determined in plasma and erythrocytes at suitable intervals. The results are summarized in figure

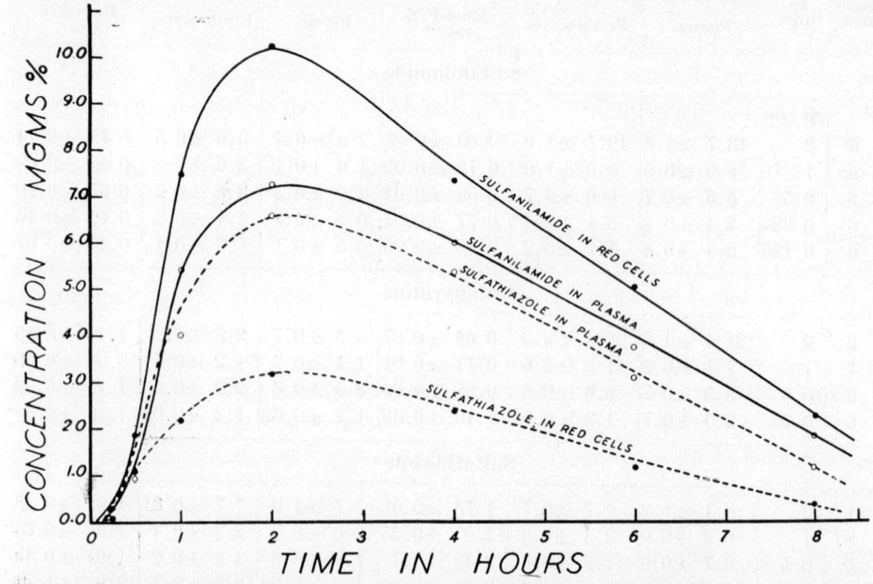

FIG. 3. DISTRIBUTION OF SULFANILAMIDE AND SULFATHIAZOLE IN THE BLOOD OF RABBITS FOLLOWING GASTRIC ADMINISTRATION OF 0.25 GRAM PER KILOGRAM BODY WEIGHT

3, which indicates the averages of determinations on three animals for each compound.

It is seen that, 15 minutes after administration, the characteristic distribution of each drug was established and maintained as long as any drug remained in the blood. It is therefore obvious that, whatever the mechanism responsible for the differences in distribution, an equilibrium was established almost immediately in spite of a constantly shifting concentration. Other results, to be reported elsewhere, have shown that this difference between sulfanilamide and sulfathiazole can be demonstrated for several other species of animals, and is not confined to mouse and rabbit blood. The reason for the increase in erythrocytic concentration of sulfanilamide is not clear at present. Unpublished results by Marshall (17), obtained by adding varying concentrations of drug directly to blood, indicated that as the concentration decreased the erythrocytes took up increasing amounts of the sulfanilamide, thus suggesting that adsorption might be an important factor in this phenomenon. Why sulfathiazole should differ so much from sulfanilamide is not clear, but the difference re-emphasizes the difficulties in making predictions of pharmacological activity from purely physical and chemical data.

DISCUSSION

In evaluating most pharmacological data relating dose to response it is generally considered that figures midway between the maximum and minimum possible effect are most reliable; thus in determining fatal doses the accepted procedure is to determine the amount of the drug killing fifty per cent of the animals. In the present study it was obviously impractical to employ such a method, as only a few mice, even on lethal doses, showed a 50 per cent decrease in hemoglobin. Nor was it practical to select any change less than this which could be used for a comparison. Because of the straight line relationship between the *log* of the dose and the effect on reticulocytes or hemoglobin, the determination of the minimum effective concentration necessary to produce blood changes was determined by calculation of the equation to the regression line. By this procedure data obtained from all the animals were used in making the comparison. Comparing compounds on the basis of the dose just necessary to produce injurious reactions has another advantage. Such information is of the greatest usefulness in therapeutics, since it is desirable to know the maximum amount of drug which can be tolerated without producing side effects.

The administration of these four closely related sulfonamides resulted in what at first appeared to be striking differences in injury to blood. A partial explanation for such results might be obtained by a correlation of all data thus far obtained. On the basis of drug intake, sulfanilamide was the most injurious, being 4.3 times as injurious as sulfathiazole and 10.9 times as injurious as sulfanilylguanidine. Some of this difference can be accounted for by lack of absorption, especially with sulfanilylguanidine. However, even when the minimum blood concentrations necessary to produce anemia were determined for these drugs, sulfanilamide still ranked as the most injurious agent, being 3.5 times more injurious than sulfathiazole.

In any comparison of closely related compounds it is a matter of opinion whether they should be compared according to straight weight or molecular weight. Since one of the ultimate goals of the current studies of blood in this laboratory is to correlate, if possible, chemical structure and destructive action on blood, it is possible that molecular concentration might give interesting relationships for the sulfonamide compounds. This has been done in the third column of table 3, in which the minimum effective blood concentration has been expressed as micromolar concentration in 100 cc. of whole blood. Such a correction brings the injurious doses of each drug closer together, thus suggesting that the chemical grouping responsible for toxic effect on erythrocytes and hemoglobin is inherent in the sulfanilamide nucleus.

Since it has been clearly shown that the injurious action of the sulfonamides is directly on blood in the peripheral circulation (6), the actual concentration attained in the erythrocytes must be an important factor in determining whether or not hemolysis will occur. From the data on the distribution of these agents between plasma and erythrocyte it is obvious that determination of concentration of this drug in whole blood is misleading as an indication of concentration in the erythrocytes. It is important, therefore, to make corrections for any abnormalities of distribution. This may be done by simple calculation. Since the minimum effective blood concentration is that which just barely produces a change in blood, it is safe to assume that the packed

TABLE 3

Minimum effective amounts of sulfonamide compounds necessary to produce anemia in mice

DRUG	DRUG INTAKE	CONCENTRATION IN WHOLE BLOOD		CONCENTRATION IN RED CELLS MICROMOLS* PER 100 CC.
		Mgm. per cent	Micromols* per 100 cc.	
	gm./kgm./day			
Sulfanilamide	0.12	1.41	8.2	11.3
Sulfapyridine	0.31	2.96	11.9	11.9
Sulfathiazole	0.52	4.23	16.6	10.6
Sulfanilylguanidine	1.30	1.72	8.1	10.0

* Micromols equal 10^{-6} mols.

cell volume in these mice was essentially the same as in normal mice kept under the same conditions. In a previous report (6) it has been shown that erythrocytes of normal mice made up 43.0 ± 1.0 per cent of whole blood. Therefore it may be assumed that 0.43 × concentration in erythrocytes + 0.57 × concentration in plasma = concentration in whole blood. From the ratio of concentration in plasma/concentration erythrocytes it is possible to state that, for any particular concentration in whole blood, the concentration in plasma is equal to the appropriate P/E ratio, as determined from table 2, multiplied by the concentration in the erythrocytes. Substitution of this value in the above equation leaves only one unknown concentration in erythrocytes to be solved for.

There is a striking uniformity in the micromolar concentration of each of these drugs which is necessary for minimum effects on blood, as can be seen from the last column of table 3. The fundamental implications of such a result seem fairly obvious, namely, that the chemical grouping in this series of compounds responsible for hemolysis is in sulfanilamide itself. Furthermore, the action of this group is unaffected by substitutions made in the N_1

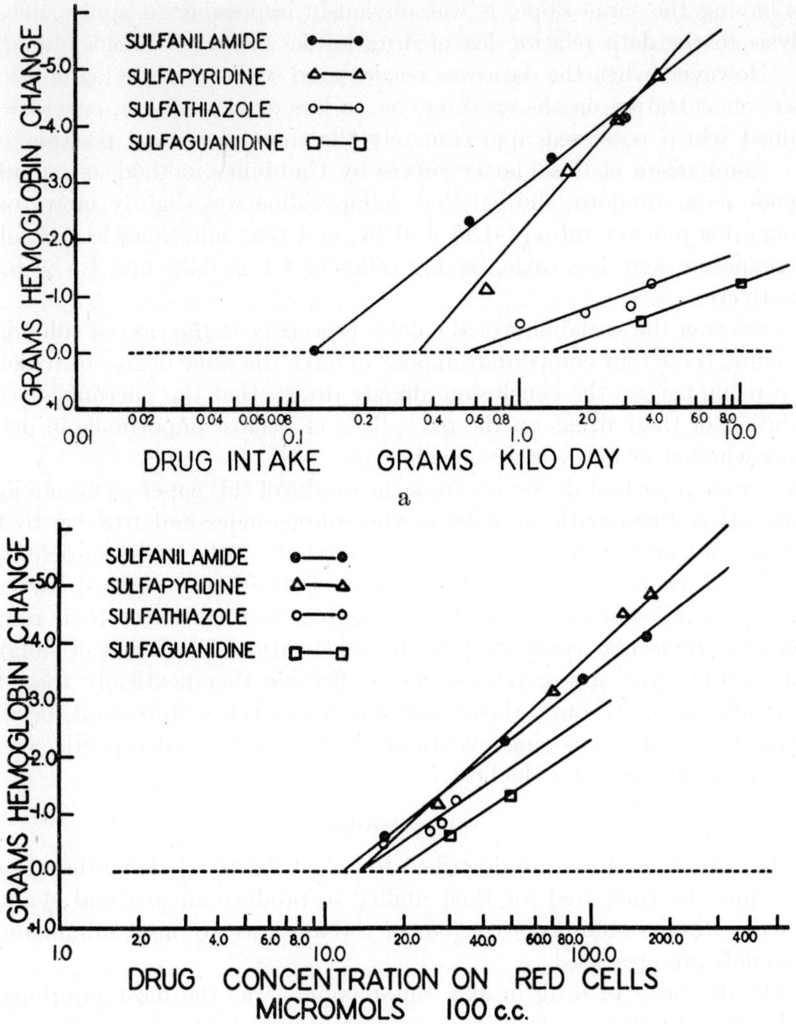

FIG. 4. EFFECT OF SULFONAMIDE COMPOUNDS ON HEMOGLOBIN

position, except as such modification of the molecule changes the absorption or distribution of the compound.

Since objection might be raised to the comparison of these drugs at only one point of the curves, it seemed desirable to make the comparison by some additional method of statistical analysis. For this purpose the relative activity of sulfapyridine, sulfathiazole and sulfanilylguanidine were each compared to sulfanilamide by the log potency method of Gaddum (18, 19). Since Gaddum's method is dependent on the comparison of two regression lines having the same slope, it was obviously impossible to apply such an analysis to the data relating log of drug intake to loss of hemoglobin (fig. 4a). However, when the data was recalculated so as to relate log of micromolar concentration on the erythrocytes to loss of hemoglobin, curves were obtained which possessed approximately the same slope and position (fig. 4b). Comparison of these latter curves by Gaddum's method, using sulfanilamide as a standard, showed that sulfapyridine was slightly more toxic, having a log potency ratio of 0.85 ± 0.26[2], and that sulfathiazole and sulfanilylguanidine were less toxic, having ratios of 1.1 ± 0.28[2] and 1.5 ± 0.64[2] respectively.

Considering the variability of the data, especially in the case of sulfanilylguanidine, these four compounds appear to have the same degree of toxicity, which reëmphasizes the conclusion already drawn that the micromolar concentration of these drugs on the red cells is of utmost importance in determining whether or not hemolysis will occur.

One more important deduction from the results of this paper seems obvious, namely, that therapeutic activity of the sulfonamides and toxicity to the blood are not necessarily related. Marshall *et al.* (2) have shown definitely that these drugs have quite different degrees of effectiveness against bacteria. It may be suggested that if these investigators had calculated their results in terms of molecular concentration the substitution derivatives of sulfanilamide would have appeared even more effective therapeutically than the parent substance. From a theoretical standpoint this is important, because it gives hopes of developing eventually more effective therapeutic agents with even less toxicity for the host.

CONCLUSIONS

1. Details of methods are described by which bacterial chemotherapeutic agents may be compared for their ability to produce anemia and cyanosis in mice. Results obtained with four of the more widely used sulfanilamide compounds are presented.

2. On the basis of drug intake, sulfanilamide was the most injurious to blood, being 2.1 times as injurious as sulfapyridine, 4.3 times as injurious as sulfathiazole, and 10.9 times as injurious as sulfanilylguanidine.

3. When corrections were made for differences in absorption, excretion, molecular weight, and partition between erythrocytes and plasma, all four compounds were of the same order of injuriousness.

4. Cyanosis, characterized by sulfhemoglobinemia, was observed only with higher doses of sulfanilamide and sulfapyridine.

[2] Sampling error was determined by Gaddum's method (19) of calculating 2 times λ, and therefore represents the range of error which would include 21 out of 22 results.

REFERENCES

(1) Litchfield, White and Marshall: This Journal, **67**, 437, 1939.
(2) Marshall, Litchfield and White: Ibid., **69**, 89, 1940.
(3) Richardson: Ibid., **67**, 429, 1939.
(4) Machella and Higgins: Am. J. Med. Sci., **198**, 804, 1939.
(5) Richardson: Bull. Johns Hopkins Hosp., **60**, 445, 1939.
(6) Richardson: This Journal, **70**, 370, 1940.
(7) Bratton and Marshall: J. Biol. Chem., **128**, 537, 1939.
(8) Peters and Van Slyke: Quantitative Clinical Chemistry. Methods. Vol. 2. Williams & Wilkins Co., Baltimore, 1931.
(9) Coombs: Biochem. J., **30**, 1588, 1936.
(10) Fisher: Statistical Methods for Research Workers, p. 117. Oliver and Boyd, Edinburgh.
(11) Marshall, Bratton, White and Litchfield: Bull. Johns Hopkins Hosp., **67**, 163, 1940.
(12) Richardson: This Journal, **71**, 203, 1941.
(13) Richardson and Morton: (to be published).
(14) Size: Proc. Soc. Exp. Biol. and Med., **40**, 451, 1939.
(15) Hansen: J. Lab. Clin. Med., **25**, 669, 1940.
(16) Reinhold, Schwartz, Flippin and Bethlahmy: Proc. Soc. Exp. Biol. and Med., **45**, 317, 1940.
(17) Marshall: Personal communication.
(18) Gaddum: Medical Research Council, Special Report, Series **183**, 23, 1933.
(19) Burn: Biological Standardization, p. 33. Oxford University Press, London, 1937.

THE RELATIONSHIP BETWEEN THE IN VITRO AND THE IN VIVO ACTIVITY OF SULFONAMIDE COMPOUNDS[1]

H. J. WHITE, A. CALVIN BRATTON[2], J. T. LITCHFIELD, JR. AND E. K. MARSHALL, JR.

Department of Pharmacology and Experimental Therapeutics, The Johns Hopkins University, Baltimore

Received for publication March 21, 1941

Numerous *in vitro* studies of the effect of sulfonamide drugs against different species of bacteria have been reported. These have had two purposes: an elucidation of the mode of action of these drugs, and their appraisal for clinical use. However, little information is available concerning the relationship between the *in vitro* and the *in vivo* activity of sulfonamide derivatives. The present communication presents the results of a qualitative study of the antibacterial activity, both *in vitro* and *in vivo*, of 126 compounds against the β-hemolytic streptococcus. The *in vitro* activity of the compounds against a strain of pneumococcus (type I) and a strain of Streptococcus viridans has also been investigated. Derivatives of sulfanilamide, a number of other sulfonamides, and certain sulfones, sulfoxides, sulfides, and miscellaneous compounds have been included in this study.

Our object was to correlate the *in vitro* activity of these compounds, as determined by our standard procedure described below, with their activity against streptococcus infections in mice as reported by other investigators. This procedure required only a very small sample of any particular drug. Since in the case of certain compounds, reports in the literature were inconsistent, we have obtained our own data on *in vivo* activity of such of these and other compounds in the present series as were readily available in sufficient quantity. The activities of some of these compounds have not been previously reported.

METHODS

Mouse-virulent stock blood-broth cultures of β-hemolytic streptococcus strain C 203 (Lancefield group A) and the Neufeld strain of type I pneumococcus were stored at 5°C. Virulence was maintained by weekly mouse passage. Test cultures were obtained, as required, by transferring 1.0 cc. of these stock cultures to 9.0 cc. of buffered peptone-

[1] This investigation has been aided by a grant from The John and Mary R. Markle Foundation.

[2] Lalor Foundation Fellow.

dextrose (PD) broth (1). After incubation at 37°C. for 5 to 6 hours, suitable dilutions of the test cultures were made to provide inoculums for the test mixtures. Our test strain of Streptococcus viridans was one recently isolated from a case of subacute bacterial endocarditis. This strain was subcultured daily in PD broth and cultured and diluted for test mixtures as described above.

Compounds were weighed into broth (5.2 mgm. into 50 cc.), dissolved by heating to 100°C., and dispensed in 5.0 cc. amounts in test tubes. After autoclaving at 110°C. for 10 minutes the drug solutions were held overnight before inoculation with test cultures.

The inoculum consisted of 0.2 cc. of a 10^{-5} broth dilution of test culture which brought the total volume of each test mixture up to 5.2 cc. The final concentration of drug in each case was 10 ± 1 mgm. per cent. Plain broth tubes were seeded with each inoculum

TABLE 1

N^1-acyclicsulfanilamides

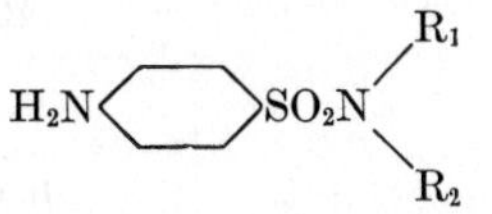

NUMBER	R_1	R_2	ACTIVITY				
			In vitro			In vivo	
						Streptococcus	
			Streptococcus	Pneumococcus	Viridans	Literature	Our data
76	$—OH$	H	++	++	0		+
107	$—NH_2$	H	++	++	0		0
60	$—COCH_3$	H	++	++	+	+ (5)	+
97	$—CH_2COOH$	H	+	++	+	+ (6), 0 (7), + (8)	+
46	$—CH_2CH_2OH$	H	+	++	+	+ (6), + (9)	+
74	$—CH_2CH_2OH$	$—CH_2CH_2OH$	+	++	++	+ (9)	+
173	$—CH_2CH(OH)CH_3$	H	0	++	++	+ (9)	+
174	$—CH_2CH_2CH_2OH$	H	0	++	++	± (9)	
175	$—CH_2C(OH)CH_3{\cdot}CH_3$	H	0	+	+	0 (9)	
176	$—CH_2CHOH{\cdot}CH_2OH$	H	0	++	++	0 (9)	
106	$—CO(CH_2)_{10}CH_3$	H	++	++	++	+ (10)	+
172	$—C{=}NH{\cdot}NH_2$	H	++	++	++	+ (11)	+

for observation of control growth. The initial concentration of bacteria was determined by averaging blood-agar pour-plate counts. The average initial bacterial concentrations per cubic centimeter in test mixtures were as follows: for β-hemolytic streptococcus, 400; for the pneumococcus, 900; for Streptococcus viridans, 700.

Drug-bacteria mixtures were incubated for 48 hours in water baths (2). Activity against the hemolytic streptococcus and pneumococcus strains was determined at 39°C.; against the viridans strain at 41°C. Turbid growth in the control tubes of broth without drug occurred in less than 24 hours.

Classification of compounds, according to their antibacterial activity under our test conditions, was based on the following criteria:

(0), *Inactive,* visible growth in less than 24 hours.

(+), *Inhibitory,* absence of visible growth for at least 24 hours followed by growth in blood broth subculture.

(++), *Bactericidal,* absence of visible growth for 48 hours followed by no growth in blood broth subculture (2).

It should be emphasized that the compounds have been classified as active or inactive on the basis of results with only a single concentration (10 mgm. per cent), and under test conditions which were selected in such a manner as to insure bactericidal activity with sulfanilamide in a concentration of less than 10 mgm. per cent. Repeated titrations

TABLE 2

N^1-isocyclicsulfanilamides

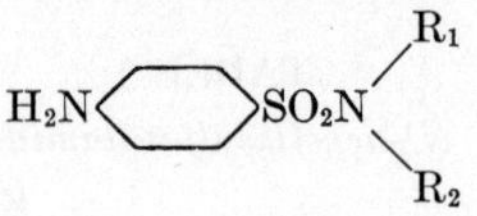

NUMBER	R_1	R_2	ACTIVITY: In vitro: Strepto-coccus	In vitro: Pneumo-coccus	In vitro: Viridans	In vivo: Streptococcus: Literature	In vivo: Streptococcus: Our data
87	$—C_6H_5$	H	++	++	++	+ (12), ± (13), + (14)	+
167	$—C_6H_4OH$-*2*	H	++	++	++	0 (4)	+
33	$—C_6H_4OH$-*3*	H	++	++	++	± (4)	+
169	$—C_6H_4OH$-*4*	H	++	++	++	+ (4), ± (4)	+
105	$—C_6H_4 \cdot NH_2$-*2*	H	++	++	++	± (4)	+
80	$—C_6H_4NH_2$-*3*	H	++	++	++	+ (4), + (15)	
79	$—C_6H_4NH_2$-*4*	H	++	++	++	+ (15), + (6)	+
6	$—C_6H_4COOH$-*2*	H	++	++	++	+ (16)	+
8	$—C_6H_4COOH$-*3*	H	++	++	++	+ (16)	±
4	$—C_6H_4COOH$-*4*	H	+	++	0	+ (16), + (6)	+
5	$—C_6H_4SO_2OH$-*2*	H	+	++	+	+ (16)	±
7	$—C_6H_4SO_2OH$-*3*	H	++	++	+	+ (16)	±
9	$—C_6H_4SO_2OH$-*4*	H	+	+	0	+ (16)	±
12	$—C_6H_4SO_2NH_2$-*3*	H	++	++	++	+ (16)	
36	$—C_6H_4SO_2NH_2$-*4*	H	++	++	+	+ (6), + (17)	+
16	$—SO_2 \cdot C_6H_4NH_2$-*4*	H	++	+	0	+ (16)	
111	$—C_6H_3OCH_3$-(3)OH-*4*	H	++	++	+	0 (4)	0
98	$—C_6H_3OH$(4)COOH(3)	H	0	0	0	0 (4)	0
22	$—CH_2CH_2OH$	$—C_6H_5$	0	+	0	+ (4)	±

for the minimal bactericidal concentration of sulfanilamide under these conditions gave a mean value of 2.5 ± 0.5 mgm. per cent against each of the three bacterial strains. Thus, any compound listed as "+" was less than one-quarter and any compound listed as "++" was at least one-quarter as active as sulfanilamide.

Twenty-seven of the compounds (Nos. 20, 21, 26, 34, 35, 37, 51, 55, 57, 59, 83, 91, 94, 100, 103, 106, 113, 114, 126, 127, 138, 141, 144, 152, 161, 163, 164) were not soluble to 10 mgm. per cent in broth. These compounds have been classified on the basis of their activity in saturated solution.

TABLE 3

N^1-heterocyclicsulfanilamides

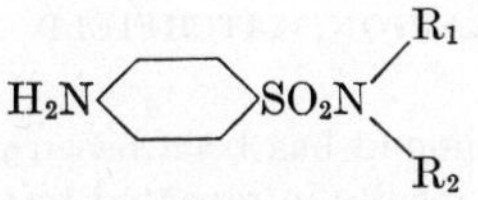

NUMBER	R_1	R_2	ACTIVITY: In vitro: Strepto-coccus	Pneumo-coccus	Viridans	In vivo: Streptococcus: Literature	Our data
2	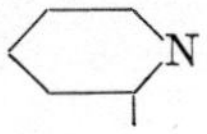	H	++	++	++	+ (18)	+
165	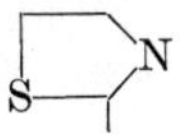	H	++	++	++	+ (19)	+
39	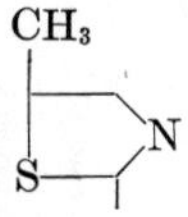	H	++	++	++	+ (19)	+
100	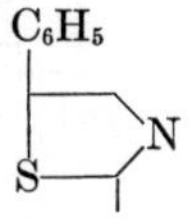	H	++	++	++	+ (20)	+

TABLE 4

N^4-substituted sulfanilamides

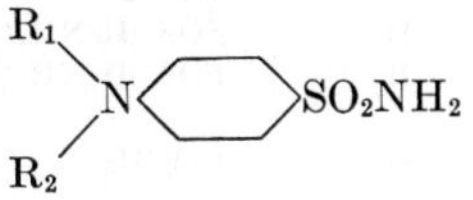

NUMBER	R_1	R_2	ACTIVITY: In vitro: Strepto-coccus	Pneumo-coccus	Viridans	In vivo: Streptococcus: Literature	Our data
162	$—CH_3$	H	++	0	0	+ (21)	
50	$—COCH_3$	H	0	0	0	± (12), + (13)	0
95	$—CH_2SO_2Na$	H	++	++	+	+ (14), + (22)	
51	$—CH_2C_6H_5$	H	++	++	0	+ (23)	+
25	$—SO_2C_6H_4NH_2$-*3*	H	+	+	0	+ (16)	
86	$—COCHCH_2CH_2CONH$	H	0	+	0	+ (17)	
171	$—COCH_3$	—OH	++	++	++		+
84	$—C(=NH)NH_2$[1]	H	++	++	++	+ (7)	
20	(*4*)-$SO_2C_6H_4NHSO_2C_6H_4NH_2$(*4'*)	H	++	++	0	+ (16), + (6)	

[1] The structure of this compound is incorrectly given (7). The sample obtained from the Wellcome Foundation diazotizes and couples, is insoluble in alkali, has the identical melting point of the N^1-derivative (sulfanilylguanidine) and its melting point is not depressed by admixture with sulfanilylguanidine.

Classification of each compound has been based on at least four tests against each bacterial strain. Consistent results in repeated tests were obtained with all but 26 of the compounds (Nos. 15, 22, 25, 26, 38, 43, 57, 59, 64, 71, 113, 114, 130, 132, 137, 146, 149, 153, 154, 158, 159, 161, 163, 164, 173, 174). These discrepancies were to be expected since

TABLE 5

N^1, N^4-substituted sulfanilamides

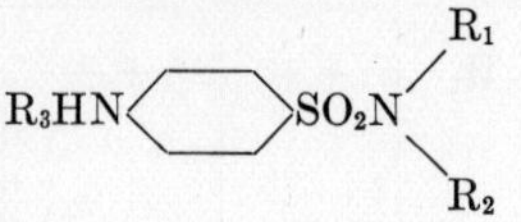

NUMBER	R_1	R_2	R_3	ACTIVITY: In vitro: Streptococcus	In vitro: Pneumococcus	In vitro: Viridans	In vivo: Streptococcus: Literature	In vivo: Streptococcus: Our data
35	$-CH_3$	$-CH_3$	$-SO_2C_6H_4NH_2(4)$	++	++	++	+ (24), + (7)	+
30	$-CH_2CH_2OH$	H	$-SO_2C_6H_4NH_2(4)$	++	++	0	+ (16)	
13	$-CH_2CH_2OH$	$-CH_2CH_2OH$	$-SO_2C_6H_4NH_2(4)$	++	++	0	+ (16)	
27	$-CH_2CH_2OH$	H	(4)-$SO_2C_6H_4NHSO_2C_6H_4$-$NH_2(4')$	++	++	0	± (16)	
28	$-CH_2CH_2OH$	$-CH_2CH_2OH$	(4)-$SO_2C_6H_4NHSO_2C_6H_4$-$NH_2(4')$	+	++	0	+ (16)	
31	$-SO_2C_6H_4NH_2(4)$	H	$-SO_2C_6H_4NH_2(4)$	++	++	0	+ (16)	
15	(4)-$SO_2C_6H_4NHSO_2C_6H_4$-$NH_2(4')$	H	$-SO_2C_6H_4NH_2(4)$	+	+	0	0 (16)	
40	$-CH_2CH_2OH$	H	$-COCH_3$	0	0	0	0 (9)	

TABLE 6

Nuclear-substituted sulfanilamides

NUMBER	FORMULA	ACTIVITY: In vitro: Streptococcus	In vitro: Pneumococcus	In vitro: Viridans	In vivo: Streptococcus: Literature
92	4-(NH_2)-3-$(NH_2)C_6H_3SO_2NH_2$	0	0	0	0 (12)
96	4-(NH_2)-5-$(COOH)C_6H_3SO_2NH_2$	0	0	0	0 (22)
18	4-(NH_2)-3-$(CH_3)C_6H_3SO_2NHC_6H_4SO_2OH$-$4$	+	+	0	+ (16)

activity was based on the use of a single concentration (10 mgm. per cent) under test conditions which were subject to unavoidable variations in such factors as size of inoculum and amount of anti-drug factor present in the medium.

In vivo tests were carried out by the drug-diet procedure (3). Groups of 10 mice were

TABLE 7

Sulfonamides

NUMBER	FORMULA	ACTIVITY: In vitro: Strepto-coccus	In vitro: Pneumo-coccus	In vitro: Viridans	In vivo: Streptococcus: Literature	In vivo: Streptococcus: Our data
61	$C_6H_5SO_2NH_2$	0	0	0	0 (12)	
69	*4*-$OHC_6H_4SO_2NH_2$	0	0	0	0 (12), ± (13), ± (25)	
70	*4*-$O_2NC_6H_4SO_2NH_2$	++	++	0	+ (23)	+
48	*4*-$ClC_6H_4SO_2NH_2$	0	0	0	0 (12)	
47	*4*-$CH_3C_6H_4SO_2NH_2$	0	0	0	+ (12), 0 (13)	±
89	*2*-$NH_2C_6H_4SO_2NH_2$	0	0	0	0 (13)	
93	*3*-$NH_2C_6H_4SO_2NH_2$	0	0	0	0 (13)	
72	*4*-$COOHC_6H_4SO_2NH_2$	0	0	0	0 (22)	
34	*4*-$CH_3C_6H_4SO_2NHC_6H_5$	++	++	0		±
23	*2*-$NH_2C_6H_4SO_2NHC_6H_4COOH$-*2*	+	0	0	+ (16)	
11	*3*-$NH_2C_6H_4SO_2NHC_6H_4COOH$-*2*	0	0	0	+ (16)	±
10	*3*-$NH_2C_6H_4SO_2NHC_6H_4SO_2NHCH_2CH_2OH$-*3*	0	0	0	± (16)	
14	*3*-$NH_2C_6H_4SO_2NHSO_2C_6H_4NH_2$-*3*	0	0	0	+ (16)	0

TABLE 8

Sulfones, sulfoxides, sulfides

NUMBER	FORMULA	ACTIVITY: In vitro: Streptococcus	In vitro: Pneumococcus	In vitro: Viridans	In vivo: Streptococcus: Literature	In vivo: Streptococcus: Our data
71	$C_6H_5SO_2CH_3$	0	0	0		0
56	*4*-$O_2NC_6H_4SO_2CH_3$	+	+	+	0 (7)	
55	$C_6H_5SO_2C_6H_5$	+	0	0		0
41	*4*-$HOC_6H_4SO_2C_6H_4OH$-*4*	++	++	0	0 (7)	±
37	*4*-$O_2NC_6H_4SO_2C_6H_4NO_2$-*4*	++	++	+	+ (26), + (27)	
3	*4*-$H_2NC_6H_4SO_2C_6H_4NH_2$-*4*	++	++	++	+ (26)	+
59	*4*-$CH_3COHNC_6H_4SO_2C_6H_4NHCOCH_3$-*4*	0	+	0	+ (27)	
83	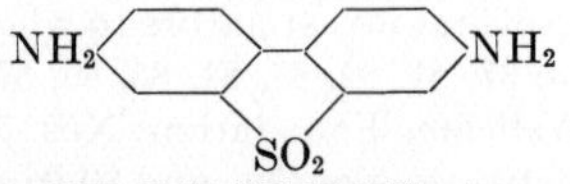	+	0	0	0 (7)	
94	*4*-$NH_2C_6H_4SC_6H_4NH_2$-*4*	++	++	+	+ (27)	+
91	*4*-$NH_2C_6H_4S—SC_6H_4NH_2$-*4*	++	++	++	0 (27), + (7)	
153	$HOCH_2CH_2SCH_2CH_2OH$	++	0	0		0
82	[CO—NC_6H_5—N(CH_3)—C(CH_3)=C—S—]$_2$	++	+	0	+ (7)	
90	*4*-$NH_2C_6H_4SOC_6H_4NH_2$-*4*	++	++	+	+ (7), + (27)	

placed on powdered diets containing 0.5 per cent of the compounds in question. After three days preliminary feeding, the mice were infected intraperitoneally with 100 to 500 lethal doses of a four hour culture of β-hemolytic streptococcus (strain C 203), and maintained on the drug-diet for an additional three days. Both the average survival time and the percent survival (30 days) were taken as criteria of therapeutic activity. If a single experiment failed to classify a compound, the test was repeated with additional mice on diets containing higher or lower drug concentrations.

TABLE 9

Amino-compounds

NUMBER	FORMULA	ACTIVITY				
		In vitro			In vivo	
					Streptococcus	
		Streptococcus	Pneumococcus	Viridans	Literature	Our data
49	4-$NH_2C_6H_4OH$	++		+		±
75	4-$NH_2C_6H_4COOH$	0	0	0	0 (28), 0 (29)	0
53	4-$NH_2C_6H_4CONH_2$	0	0	0	0 (13)	
155	4-$NH_2C_6H_4CH_2COOH$	+	0	0		±
129	4-$NH_2C_6H_4N(CH_3)_2$	++	++	0		0
135	4-$NH_2C_6H_4NH_2$	+	+	0	0 (13)	
145	4-$NH_2C_6H_4NHCOCH_3$	0	0	0	0 (12)	
158	5-NH_2-2(OH)C_6H_3COOH	0	0	0		0
152	2,4,6-$(NH_2)_3C_6H_2COOH$	++	0	0		0
43	4-NH_2-3(OH)$C_6H_3COOCH_3$	0	0	0		0
77	4-$NH_2C_6H_4SO_2OH$	0	0	0	+ (12), 0 (13)	+
154	2,5-$(NH_2)_2C_6H_3SO_2OH$	+	0	0		0
136	4-$NH_2C_6H_4NHC_6H_5$	++	++	+		0
140	Benzidinedisulfonic acid	+	0	0		+
81	2-NH_2—naphthalene—SO_2OH-1	0	0	0	0 (12)	
88	4-NH_2—naphthalene—SO_2OH-1	0	0	0	+ (12)	
52	$NH_2CSNHC_6H_5$	++	++	0		0
45	$NH_2C(=NH)C_6H_5$	0	0	0		0
125	$NH_2CH_2CH_2NH$—naphthalene	++	++	++		0
133	1-NH_2-8-OH—naphthalene—$(SO_2OH)_2$-3,6	0	0	0		0

The data available on most of the compounds either in the literature or as a result of own experiments allow only a qualitative expression of *in vivo* activity. For this reason we have classified compounds as active (+), inactive (0) or of questionable activity (±).

Samples of various compounds were obtained from several investigators to whom we wish to express our thanks for their courtesy. Nos. 3, 37, 81, 82, 83, 84, 85, 86, 87, and 88 were obtained from Drs. Henry and Smith of the Wellcome Foundation; Nos. 59, 89, 90, 91, 92, 93, and 94, from Dr. Nitti of the Pasteur Institute; Nos. 79, and 80 from Dr. Whitby of Middlesex Hospital; Nos. 95, and 97, from Dr. Bauer of the National Institute of Health; No. 96 from Dr. Fischer of the Chinoin Chemical and Pharmaceutical Works; Nos. 40, 173, 174, 175 and 176 from Dr. Long of the Johns Hopkins Medical School; Nos. 46 and 76 from Dr. Chen of Eli Lilly and Company; Nos. 35, 36, 39, 50, and 100 from Dr. Barlow of the Winthrop Chemical Company; No. 51 from Dr. Molitor of Merck and

Company; Nos. 60 and 164 from Dr. Gilbert of the Schering Corporation; No. 165 from Dr. Harrop of E. R. Squibb and Son; Nos. 41, 55, 56, 71, 127 and 133 from Dr. Lubs of the DuPont Company; No. 101 from Dr. Johnston, Mellon Institute; No. 162 from Dr. R. A. Lewis; and Nos. 4, 5, 6, 7, 8, 9, 10, 11, 12, 13, 14, 15, 16, 18, 20, 22, 23, 25, 27, 28, 30, 31, 98, 106, and 111 from Drs. Crossley and Feinstone of the American Cyanamid Company.

TABLE 10

Miscellaneous

NUMBER	FORMULA	ACTIVITY				
		In vitro			In vivo	
					Streptococcus	
		Streptococcus	Pneumococcus	Viridans	Literature	Our data
164	$4\text{-}NH_2C_6H_4SO_2NCH_2CH_2OCH_2CH_2$	+	++	0	± (9)	±
68	$4\text{-}NO_2C_6H_4COOH$	0	0	0	+ (28), + (29)	+
64	$4\text{-}NO_2C_6H_4CONH_2$	+	0	0	+ (28), + (29)	
65	C_6H_5COOH	0	0	0		0
117	$C_6H_5SO_2OH$	0		0	0 (12)	
120	$4\text{-}OHC_6H_4SO_2OH$	0	0	0		0
42	$2\text{-}COOHC_6H_4SO_2OH$	0	0	0		0
123	Anthraquinone-β-SO_2OH	0	0	0		0
131	Nicotinic acid	0	0	0		0
85	*2*-Pyrrolidine-*5*-carboxy-*4′*-amino-benzene sulfinic acid	++	+	0	+ (7)	
73	$C_6H_5NHCOCH_3$	0	0	0	0 (12)	
149	$C_6H_5NHCSCH_3$	++	++	0		0
124	$4\text{-}NOC_6H_4OH$	+	+	0	0 (29)	
143	$4\text{-}OHC_6H_4OH$	++	++	+		0
62	$C_6H_5CONH_2$	0	0	0		±
141	$4\text{-}OHC_6H_4C_6H_4OH\text{-}4$	++	++	+		±
146	$H_2NOCCH_2CONH_2$	+	0	0		0
150	$H_2NOCCH_2CH_2CH_2CH_2CONH_2$	0	0	0		±
156	$C_2H_5NHCSNHC_2H_5$	++	++	0		0
161	$C_6H_5NH\cdot C(=NH)NHC_6H_5$	++	0	0		0
160	$C_6H_5NHC(=NC_6H_5)NHC_6H_5$	++	++	+		0
127	*1*-(HOC_2H_4NH-)naphthol-*5*	++	+	0		0
159	*1*-Benzoyl-*2*-thiohydantoin	++	++	0		0
122	Allantoin	0	0	0		0
144	Benzoin	++	++	0		0
101	Hydroxyethylapocupreine	++	++	++		±

Nos. 74, 172, 167, 33, 169, 105, 171, 22, 61, 69, 70, 47, 48, 34, 53, 125, 64, and 62 as well as additional quantities of Nos. 79, 80 and 87 were prepared by us.

Nos. 153, 49, 75, 155, 129, 135, 136, 145, 152, 154, 140, 68, 117, 149, 146, 150, 156, 161, 160, 159, 122, and 144 were purchased from Eastman Kodak Company. Nos. 158, 43, 72, 77, 52, 45, 65, 42, 123, 131, 73, 124, 120, 141 and 143 were available among our laboratory chemicals.

RESULTS

The results of the present investigation are summarized in tables 1 to 10. In the columns under *Activity in Vitro* are given the classes (++, +, 0) in which the compounds are placed for β-hemolytic streptococcus (*Streptococcus*), pneumococcus (*Pneumococcus*) and Streptococcus viridans (*Viridans*). Under *Activity in Vivo* (infection with β-hemolytic streptococcus) are given the results reported in the literature for β-hemolytic streptococcus infection (first column) and the results of the present investigation (second column). Reference is given to the article reporting the activity of the compound except where the report is contained in the patent literature or in a personal communication to Northey, in which case the reference is to Northey's review article (4). In the arrangement of the tables of sulfanilamide derivatives, Northey's classification (4) has been followed.

DISCUSSION

Due to the errors inherent in any *in vitro* method for testing antibacterial activity, the qualitative nature of our classification cannot be too strongly emphasized. Likewise, the estimation of *in vivo* activity of the compounds against β-hemolytic streptococcus infections in the mouse whether as reported in the literature or from our data is qualitative. Furthermore, the results in the literature are often inconsistent and many of them have been obtained with the use of strains of group A streptococci other than C 203. Due to these facts, it was to be expected that discrepancies which were more apparent than real would occur in our comparison.

Taking our own determinations of *in vivo* activity as correct when a discrepancy occurs, the data in the tables appear to justify the following conclusions.

1. No compound is active *in vivo* (+) if it is inactive *in vitro* (0) on streptococcus unless it is decomposed in the animal organism to a compound which would be active *in vitro*. Thus, the only compounds of the group of sulfonamides, sulfones, sulfoxides and sulfides which are active *in vivo* and inactive *in vitro* are Nos. 59 (table 8), 86 (table 4), and 173 (table 1). The first two of these are N^4-acyl derivatives of sulfanilamide. No. 59 is known to be decomposed in the body to a compound (diaminodiphenylsulfone) very active *in vitro* while No. 86 presumably is decomposed to sulfanilamide. No. 173, although inactive on streptococcus, is active against the other two organisms. The other exceptions are No. 68 (table 10), No. 88 (table 9), and No. 77 (table 9). The first of these, (*p*-nitrobenzoic acid, No. 68), is reduced in the body and probably gives rise to a compound active *in vitro*; the second (*4*-aminonaphthalene-*1*-sulfonic acid, No. 88) is not known to be changed to a compound active *in vitro*. Sulfanilic acid (No. 77) is only very slightly active *in vivo*.

2. Several compounds are very active *in vitro* (++) but inactive *in vivo.* Among the sulfanilamide derivatives, Nos. 29, 111, 102, and 164, and, among other compounds, Nos. 129, 152, 136, 52, 125, 149, 143, 156, 161, 160, 127, 159, 144 and 101 fall into this category.

3. A certain amount of specificity for the three species of bacteria appears to exist *in vitro* under our test conditions. Thus, compounds Nos. 76, 16, 121, 19, 162, 51, 69, 20, 30, 13, 27, 31, 41, 70, 34, 82, 152, 52, 85, 149, 156, 161, 127, 159 and 144 are all "++" for β-hemolytic streptococcus and "0" for Streptococcus viridans. Compounds Nos. 162, 153, 152 and 161 are "++" on β-hemolytic streptococcus and "0" on pneumococcus. Compounds Nos. 173, 174 and 176 are "0" on β-hemolytic streptococcus and "++" on both pneumococcus and Streptococcus viridans.

Certain compounds may owe their *in vitro* activity to partial decomposition to a compound containing an aryl amino group under the conditions of our test. Thus, Nos. 37, 51, 56, 59 and 108 have been found to be partially changed to a compound giving a red color on diazotization and coupling with *N*-(*1*-naphthyl)ethylenediamine (30). No. 162 (N^4-methylsulfanilamide) is apparently not demethylated under the conditions of the *in vitro* test (21).

The above conclusions support the generally accepted idea that bacterial chemotherapeutic drugs act directly upon the bacteria. They also would appear to indicate that a preliminary selection of compounds for more detailed study *in vivo* can be made by an *in vitro* test.

SUMMARY

A qualitative comparison of the *in vitro* and *in vivo* activity on β-hemolytic streptococcus of 126 compounds consisting of sulfanilamide derivatives, sulfonamides, sulfones, sulfoxides, sulfides and certain miscellaneous compounds has been made. It has been shown that no compound is active *in vivo* unless it is active *in vitro* or can be decomposed in the animal body to a compound which would be active *in vitro,* and that compounds can be active *in vitro* but inactive *in vivo.*

REFERENCES

(1) WHITE: Proc. Soc. Exper. Biol. & Med., **43:** 214, 1940.
(2) WHITE: J. Bact., **38:** 549, 1939.
(3) LITCHFIELD, WHITE AND MARSHALL: THIS JOURNAL, **67:** 437, 1939.
(4) NORTHEY: Chem. Rev., **27:** 85, 1940.
(5) DOHRN AND DIEDRICH: München. med. Wchnschr., **85:** 2017, 1938.
(6) BAUER AND ROSENTHAL: Public Health Reports, **53:** 40, 1938.
(7) BUTTLE, DEWING, FOSTER, GRAY, SMITH AND STEPHENSON: Biochem. J., **32:** 1101, 1938.
(8) COOPER, GROSS AND LEWIS: J. Chemotherapy, **15:** 31, 1938.
(9) ADAMS, LONG AND JOHANSON: J. Am. Chem. Soc., **61:** 2342, 1939.
(10) CLIMENKO AND SCHMIDT: Proc. Soc. Exper. Biol. & Med., **43:** 622, 1940.
(11) ROBLIN, WILLIAMS, WINNEK AND ENGLISH: J. Am. Chem. Soc., **62:** 2002, 1940.

(12) BUTTLE, GRAY AND STEPHENSON: Lancet, **1**: 1286, 1936.
(13) TRÉFOUEL, TRÉFOUEL, NITTI AND BOVET: Ann. Inst. Pasteur, **58**: 30, 1937.
(14) ROSENTHAL, BAUER AND BRANHAM: Public Health Reports, **52**: 662, 1937.
(15) WHITBY: Lancet, **1**: 1517, 1937.
(16) CROSSLEY, NORTHEY AND HULTQUIST: J. Am. Chem. Soc., **60**: 2217, 1938; **60**: 2222, 1938; **60**: 2225, 1938.
(17) GRAY, BUTTLE AND STEPHENSON: Biochem. J., **31**: 724, 1937.
(18) WHITBY: Lancet, **1**: 1210, 1938.
(19) FOSBINDER AND WALTER: J. Am. Chem. Soc., **61**: 2032, 1939.
(20) BARLOW AND HOMBURGER: Proc. Soc. Exper. Biol. & Med., **42**: 792, 1939.
(21) LEWIS AND TAGER: Yale J. Biol. & Med., **13**: 111, 1940.
(22) FISCHER: Arch. Internat. Pharm. et Therap., **56**: 131, 1937.
(23) MAYER: Biologie Médicale, *27* (Supplement) 45, 1937.
(24) DOMAGK: Klin. Wchnschr., **15**: 1586, 1936.
(25) MCLEOD: Biochem. J., **32**: 1770, 1938.
(26) BUTTLE, STEPHENSON, SMITH, DEWING AND FOSTER: Lancet, **1**: 1331, 1937.
(27) FOURNEAU, TRÉFOUEL, TRÉFOUEL, NITTI AND BOVET: Bull. de l'Acad. Med., **118**: 210, 1937.
(28) MAYER AND OECHSLIN: Arch. Internat. Pharm. et Therap., **62**: 211, 1939.
(29) ROSENTHAL, BAUER AND ELVOVE: Public Health Reports, **54**: 1317, 1939.
(30) BRATTON AND MARSHALL: J. Biol. Chem., **128**: 537, 1939.

A STUDY OF THE EFFECTS OF MORPHINE AND OF CARBON TETRACHLORIDE ON THE RATE OF DISAPPEARANCE OF ETHYL ISOAMYL BARBITURIC ACID[1]

H. J. TATUM, D. E. NELSON AND F. L. KOZELKA

From the Department of Pharmacology and Toxicology, University of Wisconsin, Madison

Received for publication November 29, 1940

This investigation was undertaken for the purpose of studying the mechanism of the increased duration of anesthesia produced by the less stable barbituric acid derivatives when administered to animals premedicated with morphine or to animals with liver injury produced by carbon tetrachloride. Straub (1), Loewe (2), and Baker (3) observed the synergistic action of morphine with the barbiturates. Zerfas (4) and Isenberger (5) noted that premedication with morphine greatly reduced the amount of amytal necessary for narcosis. Vogeler and Kotzoglu (6) observed that 100 mgm. of morphine per kilogram administered to rabbits produced a tenfold increase in the duration of action of evipal. They also found that 20 mgm. of evipal per kilogram produced a depression lasting for six minutes, whereas the same amount administered to animals premedicated with morphine produced a depression lasting for sixty minutes. Pavel, Milco and Radvan (7), investigating the effect of morphine on liver function, observed that 10 mgm. of morphine caused a twice normal retention of bengal rose in dogs, and 20 mgm. caused a retention of the dye four times that normally found. These authors (8) also reported that morphine significantly inhibits biliary secretion. They concluded, therefore, that morphine depresses secretory activity as well as detoxification processes.

Experimental liver injury in animals has been observed to produce an increased duration of action of the less stable barbiturates. Pratt (9) reported that injury of the liver by the administration of carbon tetrachloride or chloroform increased the duration of action of these barbiturates. These conclusions were essentially confirmed by Cameron and de Saram (10) and by Koppanyi *et al.* (11). The latter, however, postulated a non-hepatic factor in addition to liver injury for the explanation of these findings. They suggested that the non-hepatic factor responsible for the prolonged hypnosis is the increased susceptibility of the central nervous system to the barbiturates.

[1] Aided by grants from the Wisconsin Alumni Research Foundation.

Preliminary report published in the Proceedings of the American Pharmacological Society for 1938.

Their analytical data failed to show consistently a decreased rate of disappearance of the drug from animals having been premedicated with chloroform. Because of the clinical importance of this problem it seemed pertinent to reinvestigate the question in order to determine whether or not the relationship existing between the less stable barbiturates and morphine or liver injury may be explained at least in part by a decreased rate of detoxification of the barbiturate.

METHODS

Ethyl isoamyl barbituric acid was used in these experiments as a representative member of this group of hypnotics. The method employed for the quantitative determination of amytal has been described previously (12). The rate of disappearance of bromsulphalein from the blood was used as a criterion of the effect of morphine, morphine and amytal, and CCl_4 on liver function. It was necessary to modify the technic as commonly employed because even a slight amount of hemolysis tends to mask the bromsulphalein color and renders the proper matching of the colors practically impossible.

Twenty-five milligrams of bromsulphalein per kilogram of body weight were injected intravenously and exactly 2 cc. of blood withdrawn at 1-, 5-, 10-, and 15-minute intervals following the injection. Eight cubic centimeters of absolute alcohol were added to each specimen to precipitate the proteins and simultaneously to extract the dye. The specimens were then centrifuged and the supernatant fluid decanted off into test tubes of uniform size. Two drops of concentrated NaOH were added to each specimen and the solution stirred. The percentage retention of the dye was determined by comparing the specimens obtained at the various time intervals with a series of standards. Blood withdrawn one minute after the injection of 25 mgm. of bromsulphalein per kilogram of body weight was assumed to represent 100 per cent dye retention. The standard solution of this strength was prepared by pooling specimens from five rabbits in order to minimize individual variation. Standards containing from 5 to 100 per cent of this original standard solution were prepared by appropriate dilution with an extract of normal blood precipitated and extracted in the same manner. With this procedure the errors due to hemolysis are eliminated, and the quality of the color in the standards is the same as in the unknown specimens, permitting a satisfactory degree of accuracy.

Preliminary studies were made on rabbits in order to determine the effects of morphine, amytal, CCl_4, and the combination of morphine and amytal on the rate of disappearance of the dye from the blood stream. In these experiments 10 mgm. of morphine per rabbit were given subcutaneously. Amytal was given intravenously in a dose of 35 mgm. per kilogram and the CCl_4 was given orally in doses of 0.5 cc. per kilogram per day for three consecutive days prior to the use of the animals for the experiment. When morphine and amytal were used in combination, the morphine was given fifteen minutes prior to the administration of the amytal.

To determine the rate of disappearance of amytal normally and following premedication with morphine or CCl_4, pooled materials from animals in groups of three were obtained at one hour intervals ranging from fifteen minutes to six hours and fifteen minutes after the injection of the barbiturate. The amytal content of blood, liver, muscle and brain was determined. The purity of the recovered amytal was checked by melting point and mixed melting point determinations and was found to agree with the accepted value for the drug.

RESULTS

The results of the liver function tests are given in table 1. It will be noted that fifteen minutes is approximately the time required for the complete disappearance of bromsulphalein from the blood of normal animals under the conditions of this experiment. The rate of disappearance of the dye is slightly retarded by morphine but quite significantly retarded by the combination of morphine with amytal and greatly retarded in the animals previously treated with carbon tetrachloride. Preliminary tests demonstrated that the dye had no effect on the duration of amytal anesthesia normally or after morphine or carbon tetrachloride premedication.

The concentrations of amytal found in the tissues at the various time intervals are shown graphically in figures 1, 2 and 3. Every point on these curves represents an average of three separate determinations each of which was based on pooled specimens from a series of three animals. The deviation of these values from the mean was less than 1 mgm. per cent. Concentrations of amytal found in the blood in the three series at the various time intervals parallel the duration of anesthesia observed on control animals under the same conditions. The control animals regained all of their righting reflexes in approximately 150 minutes, those which were premedicated with morphine in 250 minutes, and the animals treated with CCl_4 in 430 minutes. At the time the animals regained their righting reflexes the concentration of amytal in the blood is approximately 2.9 mgm. per cent in each of the series.

TABLE 1

*Average percentage of bromsulphalein retention fifteen minutes after the injection of the dye**

Normal	trace†
Amytal (35 mgm. per kilogram)	1.7 per cent
Morphine (10 mgm. per animal)	4.0 per cent
Morphine plus amytal	8.8 per cent
Carbon tetrachloride	30.0 per cent

* All of these tests were performed on the same group of ten rabbits.

† Six of the ten rabbits showed no trace of the dye while three in the amytal group were negative.

It is of interest to note that the concentration of amytal in the liver tissue of animals premedicated with morphine decreases very rapidly during the first two hour period, at the end of which time it reaches approximately the same concentration as that found in the blood and muscle, while in the controls the concentration in the liver remains considerably higher than in the blood and muscle. This difference in distribution suggests that morphine decreases the rate of blood flow through the liver, and consequently less barbiturate is brought to this organ. We are unable to account for the initial high concentration of amytal in this tissue. The rapid fall in the concentration of amytal in the liver during the first two hours would indicate that morphine has no depressant effect on the functional capacity of this organ to destroy the drug. The concentration of amytal in the liver tissue of the animals having received CCl_4 remains at approximately the initial level

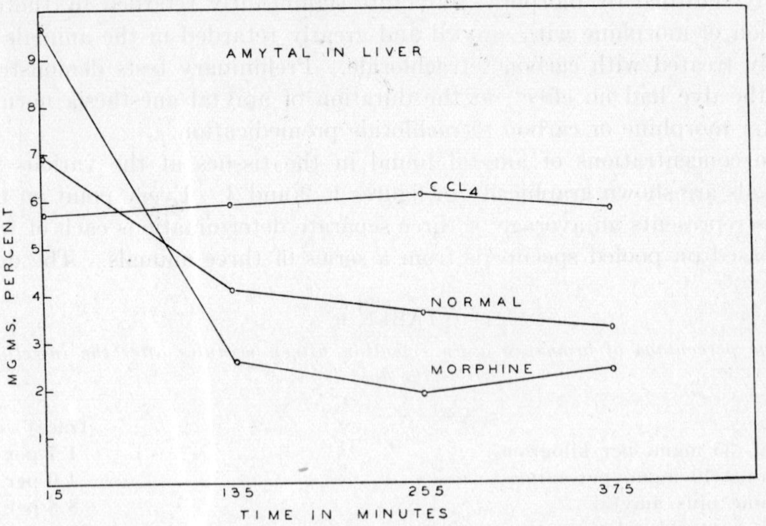

FIG. 1

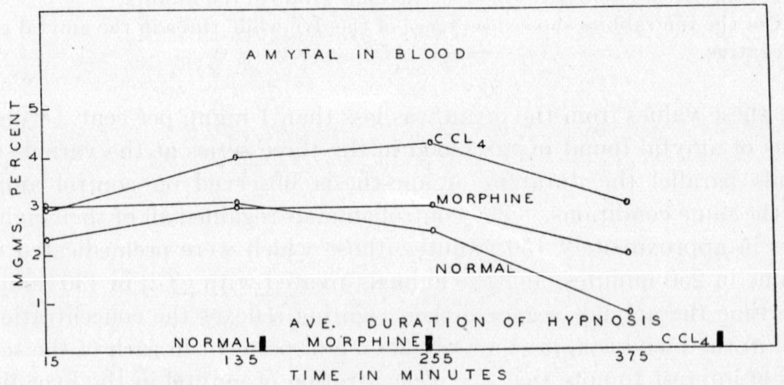

FIG. 2

throughout the period of observation, indicating an inability of this organ to detoxify the drug. No significant difference in the concentration of amytal was found in the muscle from the three series of animals. Although this was also true of the brain tissue, the lack of difference in the concentration of the drug in this tissue could not be considered significant because of the small amount of material available. The presence of the barbiturate could be demonstrated in any of the tissues studied in each of the three series eight hours and fifteen minutes after the administration of the drug, indicating that appreciable quantities are present in the body for a considerable period after the rabbits regained their righting reflexes.

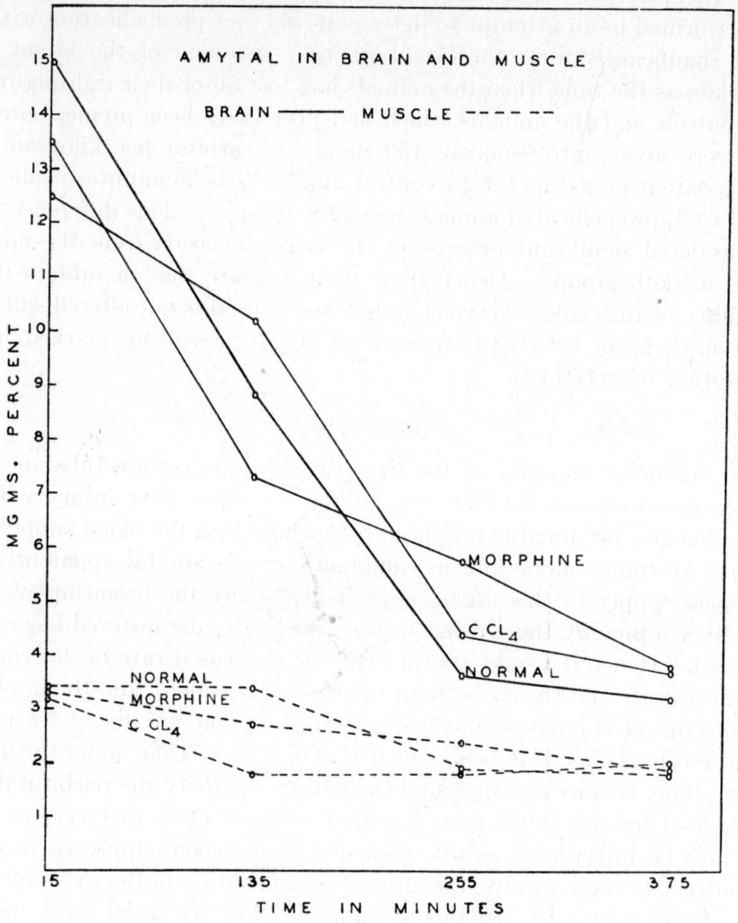

FIG. 3

To determine whether the treatment with CCl_4 increased the susceptibility of the central nervous system to the barbiturates, the maximal tolerated dose of amytal for normal rabbits was administered to rabbits having received CCl_4. A dose of 65 mgm. per kilogram of body weight administered intravenously proved lethal to seven of a group of twelve rabbits previously premedicated with CCl_4, whereas twelve of a group of fourteen normal animals survived a similar dose. These results would tend to indicate an increased susceptibility of the central nervous system to the barbiturate; however, other factors such as abnormal metabolism and a prolonged high concentration of amytal in the system must also be considered. Since the length of the latent period preceding barbital anesthesia has been presumed to be a measure of the susceptibility of the central nervous system to the drug, an experiment was performed in an attempt to determine whether premedication with CCl_4 would significantly alter the latent period. The end of the latent period was taken as the time when the animals had lost all of their righting reflexes. The controls and the animals which had previously been premedicated with CCl_4 were given intravenously 150 mgm. of barbital per kilogram. The average latent period in the 15 control animals was 26 minutes while that of the 17 CCl_4-premedicated animals was 22.8 minutes. This difference cannot be considered significant because of the large deviation from the mean observed in both groups. Hence these data indicate that in rabbits the susceptibility of the central nervous system to barbital is not altered sufficiently by premedication with CCl_4 to account for the resulting marked increase in duration of anesthesia.

DISCUSSION

The functional capacity of the liver to withdraw certain substances from the blood stream was found to be altered by either liver injury with CCl_4 or by changes, presumably produced by morphine, in the blood supply to this organ. Morphine alone and in combination with amytal apparently alters the blood supply to this organ, as is indicated by the bromsulphalein test, since liver injury by these drugs in the quantities administered has not been observed. Hence it would appear that the decreased rate of destruction of the barbiturate and the consequent increased duration of anesthesia observed in the series of animals premedicated with morphine are due at least in part to this mechanism. If it be assumed that the liver, while under the influence of morphine, retains its functional capacity to detoxify the barbiturate, then the marked decrease in the amytal content of the livers in this series of animals may also be interpreted as due to a decreased blood supply to this organ. In contrast to these results, the amytal concentration in the livers of the animals treated with CCl_4 remains at approximately its initial level, indicating the inability of this organ to detoxify the drug. Liver dysfunction is indicated also by the marked decrease in the rate of disappearance of bromsulphalein from the blood stream. It would appear that the increased duration of anesthesia observed in animals treated with CCl_4 is due primarily to the decreased rate of disappearance of the barbiturate from the tissues. Since the concentration of amytal in the blood reaches approximately the same level in the three series at the time when the animals regain their righting reflexes, it seems reasonable that this concentration represents a critical level of the drug for this particular reflex mechanism.

SUMMARY

The rate of disappearance of amytal from the tissues was studied in (*a*) normal rabbits, (*b*) rabbits premedicated with morphine, and (*c*) rabbits premedicated with CCl_4. Observations were made on the rate of disappearance of bromsulphalein from the blood stream on a similar series of rabbits.

The increase in duration of anesthesia produced by the combination of morphine or CCl_4 with amytal is closely correlated with the effects which these drugs have on the retention of bromsulphalein in the blood stream. The duration of anesthesia in the three series of animals parallels the rate of disappearance of the amytal from the blood stream. The animals of each series regain their righting reflexes when the concentration of the amytal in the blood reaches approximately the same level, viz, 2.9 mgm. per cent. Morphine decreases the rate of disappearance of the barbiturate at least in part by altering the blood supply to the liver, while the primary effect of CCl_4 appears to be the production of liver injury.

REFERENCES

(1) STRAUB: Münch. med. Wchnschr., **60**, 1823, 1913.
(2) LOEWE: Deutsche med. Wchnschr., **38**, 947, 1912.
(3) BAKER: Northwest Med., **31**, 126, 1932.
(4) ZERFAS: Brit. Med. J., **2**, 897, 1930.
(5) ISENBERGER: Am. J. Surg., **9**, 35, 1930.
(6) VOGELER AND KOTZOGLU: Chirurg (Berlin) **7**, 242, 1935; Abstract in Internat. Surg. Digest., **20**, 18, 1935.
(7) PAVEL, MILCO AND RADVAN: Compt. rend., Soc. de biol., **102**, 131, 1929.
(8) PAVEL, MILCO, AND RADVAN: Compt. rend., Soc. de biol., **100**, 913, 1929.
(9) PRATT: THIS JOURNAL, **48**, 285, 1933.
(10) CAMERON AND DE SARAM: J. Path. & Bact., **48**, 49, 1939.
(11) KOPPANYI, DILLE AND LINEGAR: THIS JOURNAL, **58**, 119, 1936.
(12) KOZELKA, NELSON AND TATUM: Ibid, **67**, 71, 1939.

EFFECTS OF CERTAIN DRUGS ON TEMPERATURE REGULATION, AND CHANGES IN THEIR TOXICITY, IN RATS EXPOSED TO COLD

JULIAN B. HERRMANN

From the Laboratory of Pharmacology, Yale University School of Medicine

Received for publication December 3, 1940

Current interest in general cooling for the treatment of cancer (1, 2) led to the investigation herein detailed. Hypothermia is produced by administering paraldehyde or a barbiturate in sufficient amount to produce unconsciousness after which the individual is placed nude in an environmental temperature of 10°C. and surrounded by cracked ice. Body temperature falls promptly. Normal mammals, being homeothermous, resist any attempt to lower the body temperature by various phenomena such as shivering, vasoconstriction and body water shift. Deeply narcotized mammals become poikilothermous because their heat-regulatory mechanism is paralyzed. What effect do non-narcotizing doses of CNS depressants have on temperature regulation when test animals are subjected to severe cold and what effect does a reduction of the environmental temperature have on the toxicity of these substances? The experiments to be described below were undertaken in the hope of securing answers to these questions.

PROCEDURE

A number of depressant drugs were administered to young, male albino rats averaging 250 grams in weight. A representative of each of three important groups of depressants was chosen, viz. pentobarbital, paraldehyde, and morphine. The doses were so small that the animals never appeared depressed. Besides the above drugs aspirin (acetyl salicylic acid) and magnesium chloride were also tried.

The rats were deprived of food and water only during the experiment. Body temperatures were first taken by a rectal mercury thermometer and the animals were then divided into three groups. The first group, receiving the drug, was left at room temperature (25.5°C.). The second group, immediately after receiving the drug, was placed in a cold room (3°C.) as was the third group which received no drug and served as a control. In some instances the animals in the cold room were placed over ice cubes. Nembutal (pentobarbital sodium), 25 mgm. per kilogram in 2 cc. of distilled water, or paraldehyde, 0.2 cc. or 0.3 cc. per kilogram in 2 cc. distilled water, were administered intraperitoneally. Morphine sulfate was given in 10, 20, 30, 50 and 70 mgm. per kilogram doses hypodermically. Aspirin in doses of 25, 50 and 75 mgm. per kilogram with acacia was given in 2 or 3 cc. of distilled water by stomach tube. Magnesium chloride in 15 per cent solution was administered intraperitoneally, 300 mgm. per kilogram, or subcutaneously in doses of 700 and 800 mgm. per kilogram. The above doses were chosen because they lie just below the normal threshold for neuromuscular depression. In every case the undrugged control received the same amount of distilled water by the same route.

The animals were placed in cages divided into individual compartments large enough to allow them to move about. Rectal temperatures were taken at intervals throughout the experiment.

RESULTS

Rats exposed to cold after the administration of nembutal, paraldehyde or morphine, in the above-mentioned doses, exhibited a marked drop in tem-

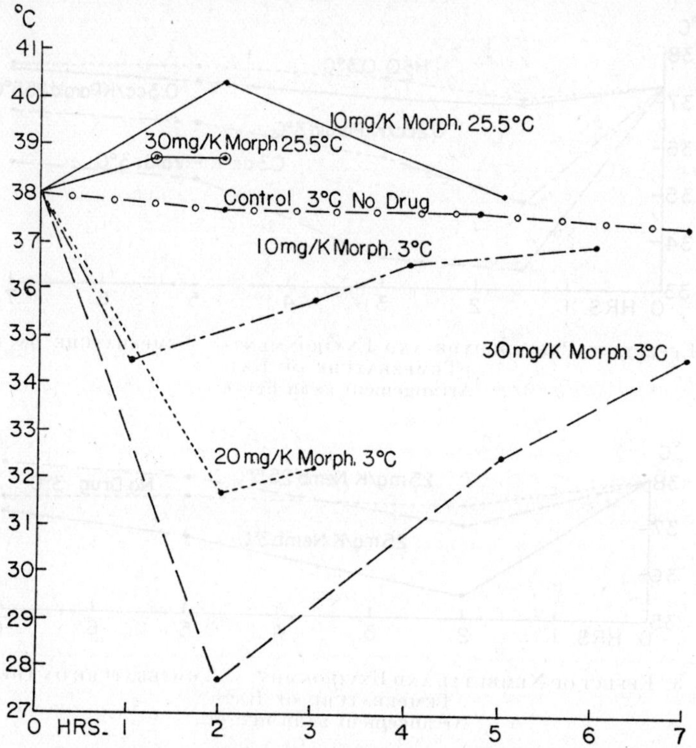

FIG. 1. EFFECT OF MORPHINE AND ENVIRONMENTAL TEMPERATURE ON THE BODY TEMPERATURE OF RATS

Abscissae, time in hours after the administration of the drug. Ordinates, body temperature changes of rats in degrees centigrade. Each curve represents the average body temperature of four or more animals. Room temperature is given with each curve.

perature. This reached its lowest point in about two hours, after which it gradually rose. After seven hours those animals receiving the smallest doses of morphine (10 mgm. per kilogram) and of nembutal (25 mgm. per kilogram) developed a temperature but slightly less than that of the undrugged control. The greatest drop in temperature, with the non-narcotizing doses employed, was produced by morphine; the effects of paraldehyde were intermediate, and those of nembutal were least. A similar relationship between nembutal and morphine is seen in the "tranquilizing doses" of Stanton (3) and of Barlow (4). These results are represented graphically in figures 1, 2 and 3.

In the experiment on morphine (fig. 1) a rise in temperature occurred in all animals receiving doses up to 30 mgm. per kilogram when the animals were kept at room temperature. This phenomenon will be described elsewhere in more detail. All rats receiving morphine developed a well marked catalepsy both at room temperature and in the cold room. Doses of 50 and 70 mgm.

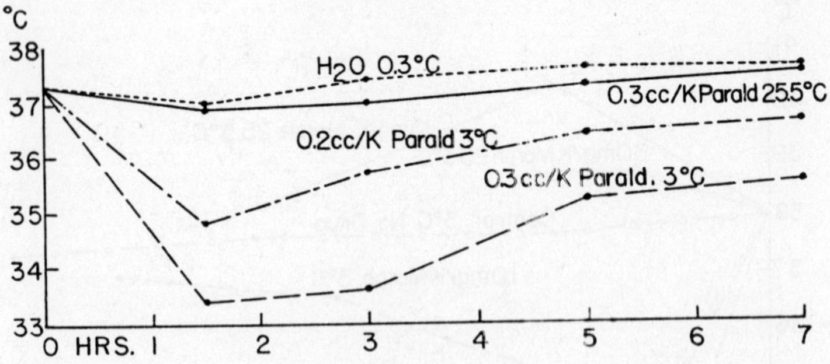

Fig. 2. Effect of Paraldehyde and Environmental Temperature on the Body Temperature of Rats
Arrangement as in figure 1

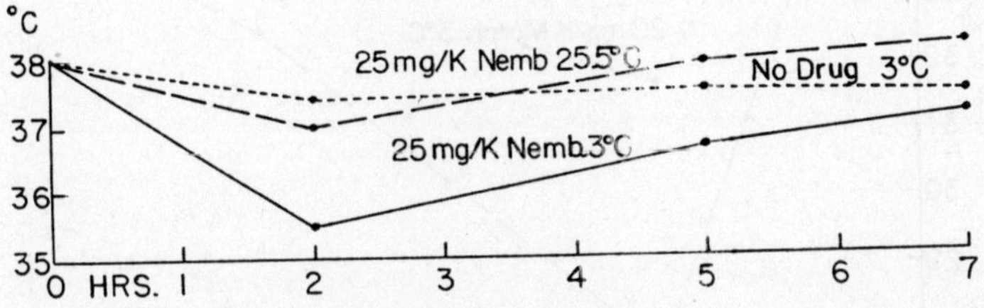

Fig. 3. Effect of Nembutal and Environmental Temperature on the Body Temperature of Rats
Arrangement as in figure 1

per kilogram were fatal to animals exposed to a temperature of 3°C. overnight. Even in dosage of 30 mgm. per kilogram morphine sulphate proved to be more toxic at this temperature than at room temperature. Three out of 4 rats which received this dose and were left in the cold room over night were found dead the next morning while undrugged controls under the same conditions survived.

When the environmental temperature in the cold room (3°C.) was further reduced by ice cubes placed 0.5 to 1 cm. beneath the wire mesh on which the animals rested, 10 and 20 mgm. per kilogram doses of morphine sulphate produced a marked drop in body temperature and death ensued in some instances. Under the same conditions, which are not fatal for undrugged rats, nembutal (25 mgm. per kilogram) and paraldehyde (0.3 cc. per kilogram) become lethal. Table 1 is typical of these experiments.

These results indicate that paraldehyde, morphine and nembutal become more toxic for rats as the environmental temperature is decreased. Rat 1 is interesting in that it established temperature equilibrium at about 32°C. which was maintained for several hours and was still in force when the experiment was terminated. Also, rat 2 was unique in that its temperature fell to

TABLE 1

Effects of cold on body temperature and toxicity after morphine, nembutal and paraldehyde

HOURS	DRUGS AND COLD					DRUGS WITHOUT COLD			COLD
	1	2	3	4	5	6	7	8	9
	38°C.	38°C.	37.5°C.	37.5°C.	38°C.	38°C.	37.4°C.	37.2°C.	37.7°C.
−¼	Morphine, 10 mgm. /kgm.	Morphine, 20 mgm. /kgm.	Nembutal, 25 mgm. /kgm.	Nembutal, 25 mgm. /kgm.	Paraldehyde, 0.3 cc./ kgm.	Morphine, 10 mgm. /kgm.	Nembutal, 25 mgm. /kgm.	Paraldehyde, 0.3 cc./ kgm.	No drugs, 2 cc. H_2O
0	Placed over ice cubes in 3°C. room					Left in 25.5°C. room			Placed over ice in 3°C. room
½	35.5	36.0	36.5	33.0					
1½	34.5	33.5	36.0	31.5	33.5	39.0	36.6	36.9	38.0
2½	32.0	33.0	32.5	29.5	33.0	40.0		37.0	38.3
4	32.0	34.5	28.0	25.0	31.5	38.9	37.8	37.3	38.0
5	32.5	27.5	25.0	20.5	30.5				
6	32.5 (Lively)	23.0 (Slight depression)	19.0 (In extremis)	Dead		38.0	38.0	37.5	38.0
6½	Returned to 25.5°C. room		Dead						
20	37.5	38.5			Dead		36.7	37.4	37.5 (Lively)

23°C. at which level the animal was active and appeared normal except for some sluggishness of movement.

Another series of experiments was conducted to determine the effect of restriction of activity on the ability of the rat to maintain temperature homeostasis in a cold environment after the administration of a sub-hypnotic dose of paraldehyde. To this end rats, after receiving 0.3 cc. of paraldehyde per kilogram hypodermically, were placed in the cold room (3°C.) and spread-eagled on wire mesh frames over ice cubes reaching to within 0.5 to 1 cm. of the ventral surface of the animal. The body temperature dropped quickly to very low levels and those animals which were not returned to a warm room at this juncture succumbed. The undrugged controls under similar conditions also showed a drop in temperature, dying if left exposed to the cold for many hours.[1] However, they survived longer than the drugged animals.

Magnesium chloride, injected hypodermically in the non-depressant doses of 700 and 800 mgm. per kilogram, was also found to cause a temperature drop after exposure to cold (fig. 4). Under the same conditions magnesium chloride (300 mgm. per kilogram administered intraperitoneally) produced no change in body temperature in one animal while in another there was a transient drop of 1.5°C. lasting one hour.

Aspirin, although an excellent drug for reducing fever, had no effect on the temperature of normal rats exposed to cold. Even 75 mgm. per kilogram produced no change in body temperature of animals exposed to an environmental temperature of 3°C. This dose is three times that found by Dickerson and Barbour (6) to reduce temperature by about 0.5°C. constantly in a large, controlled series of fevered rats.

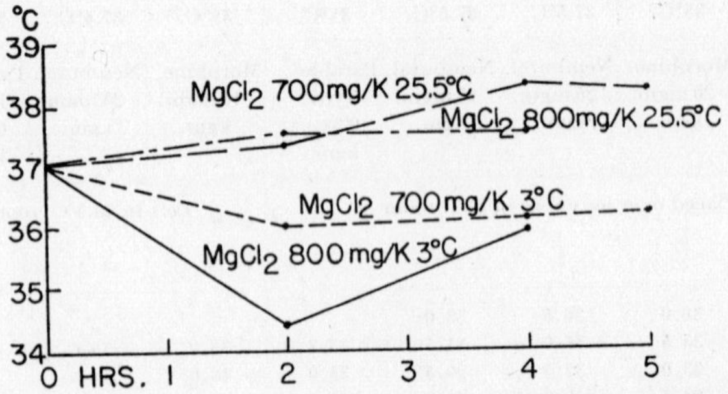

Fig. 4. Effect of Magnesium Chloride and Environmental Temperature on the Body Temperature of Rats

Arrangement as in figure 1. Curves for doses of 700 mgm. of $MgCl_2$ represent the average of two experiments and the curve for the dose of 800 mgm. at room temperature (25.5°C.) represents one experiment. The curve for dosages of 800 mgm. at 3°C. represents the average body temperature obtained in three experiments.

DISCUSSION

Hypnosis produces a poikilothermic condition in which exposure to cold causes a drop in body temperature (Rumf (7)) whereas exposure to heat produces a rise (Dontas (8)). However, it is not necessary to depress deeply in order to produce a fall in body temperature by exposure to cold. Subhypnotic amounts of hypnotic drugs (as exemplified above by nembutal, morphine and paraldehyde) do not paralyze the central mechanism, yet they cause temporary loss of some control over temperature regulation.

Morphine caused a greater drop in body temperature than either paraldehyde or nembutal. The condition of catalepsy may have contributed to this

[1] DiMacco (5), using guinea pigs, found that they succumbed within two hours if tied down and surrounded with ice. We had the same experience with rats.

result, although a consistent rise in body temperature developed after small doses of morphine in ordinary environments. Nembutal was the least effective of the drugs employed, producing the smallest temperature drop and the shortest duration of hypothermia with the dosages used.

The toxicity of paraldehyde, nembutal and morphine appears to be greatly increased by low environmental temperatures. The ordinarily harmless dose of 0.3 cc. per kilogram of paraldehyde was fatal after a number of hours at 3°C., a temperature successfully resisted by normal rats. Similarly, nembutal, in a dose of 25 mgm. per kilogram, was fatal in six hours in the cold. These results agree with those reported by Raventos (9), who found that the median lethal dose of phenobarbital at 20°C. is about two-thirds that at 30°C. Morphine sulphate in the relatively small dose of 30 mgm. per kilogram is lethal to rats at 3°C. after a number of hours. Of interest was a pre-mortal trend back to normal temperature in many instances with this dose of morphine. The thermotaxic centers recover to some extent from their initial depression but insufficiently to enable the animal to survive.

On the other hand, Lambruchini (10) found that frogs kept at an environmental temperature of 3°C. tolerated large doses of morphine but if brought to a warm room, even several days after receiving the drug, the animals died within a few hours. In these conditions the decrease in toxicity at low temperatures is probably due to such factors as a slower absorption. Similarly, drugs such as thyroid and thyrotoxin are considerably less toxic at relatively low temperatures, according to Stoland and Kinney (11), Draize and Tatum (12), and Bodansky (13).

A lowering of the resistance of the thermotaxic centers to the effects of cold may be the cause of increased toxicity of paraldehyde, morphine and barbiturates rather than any direct effects on respiration or circulation.

Since paraldehyde and the barbiturates are the drugs most commonly used as depressants preliminary to and during the general cooling treatment of cancer, the above findings have some practical importance. Although no fatalities have been ascribed to these uses of the drugs, Lawrence Smith (14) has considered edema of the brain, as found at autopsy on patients who died shortly after treatment, as due to barbiturates. The edema may, however, have been merely the result of damage to the brain by the cold.

The temperature drop after the use of magnesium chloride accords with the findings of Rossi (15) and of Caltabiano (16) in rabbits and with those of Burton (17) in cats. The first, working with magnesium chloride, and the second, with calcium chloride, found that the intraperitoneal injection of these substances, followed by the subjection of the animals to low temperatures (surrounding them with salt and ice), caused a more rapid drop in temperature and earlier death than in undrugged controls exposed to the same low temperature. When magnesium was employed there developed a decrease in the water content of the liver, spleen and blood. Rossi interpreted the decreased resistance to cold after administration of magnesium chloride as a depressive phenomenon involving the vegetative nervous system.

A decrease in temperature at the base of the brain causes a movement of water into the cells of viscera, e.g., the liver, leading to an increase in total osmotic pressure of serum (Barbour (18, 19)). By this means, together with vasoconstriction, heat loss by conduction and radiation is diminished, enabling the body to maintain its temperature despite adverse environmental conditions. Therefore it would seem more logical in explaining the temperature fall produced by calcium and magnesium to include disturbances of water balance.

Aspirin was studied as a member of the antipyretic group of drugs. This group is known to reduce temperature in the smaller dosage range only when the organism has been sensitized by fever. Inasmuch as the onset of fevers, which sensitize to aspirin, mimics the complex reaction of the body to cold, it was thought that a cold environment might also sensitize to the antipyretic action of aspirin. Contrariwise, our results show that aspirin does not at all influence the temperature of rats in cold environments.

CONCLUSIONS

1. Morphine, paraldehyde and nembutal produce a temporary fall in the body temperature of rats exposed to a cold environment (3°C.) which does not occur in the undrugged rat. This hypothermia results from doses which are obviously non-depressant to the neuromuscular system either at this low temperature or in ordinary environments.

2. The toxicity of paraldehyde, morphine and pentobarbital sodium for rats is increased at low environmental temperatures.

3. Magnesium chloride in non-depressant doses produces moderate hypothermia in rats exposed to cold.

4. Aspirin, in doses markedly antipyretic for fevered rats, causes no lowering of body temperature on exposure to cold environments. Therefore, the reaction to cold is not the factor in the onset of fever which sensitizes to aspirin.

REFERENCES

(1) Fay and Henny: Surg., Gyn. and Obs., **66**: 512, 1938.
(2) Gerster: Bull. N. Y. Acad. Med., **16**: 312, May 1940.
(3) Stanton: This Journal, **57**: 245, 1936.
(4) Barlow: J. Am. Med. Assoc., **99**: 986, 1932.
(5) DiMacco: Rassegna di terapia e patolog. clin., **4**: 454, August, 1932.
(6) Dickerson and Barbour: Personal communication.
(7) Rumf: Pflüger's Arch. f. d. ges. Physiol., **33**: 538, 1884.
(8) Dontas: Ibid., **241**: 612, 1939.
(9) Raventos: This Journal, **64**: 355, 1938.

(10) LAMBRUCHINI: Compt. rend. Soc. de biol., **129:** 1213, 1938.
(11) STOLAND AND KINNEY: Am. J. Physiol., **49:** 135, 1919.
(12) DRAIZE AND TATUM: Arch. int. Pharm. et Thér., **43:** 237, 1932.
(13) BODANSKY, PILCHER AND DUFF: Journ. Exper. Med., **63:** 523, 1936.
(14) SMITH: Arch. Path., **30:** 424, 1940.
(15) ROSSI: Riv. di Patol. Sper., **20:** 185, 1938.
(16) CALTABIANO: Folia Medica, **23:** 141, 1937.
(17) BURTON: Personal communication.
(18) BARBOUR AND AYDELOTTE: Am. J. Physiol., **104:** 127, 1933.
(19) BARBOUR AND GILMAN: Ibid., **107:** 70, 1934.

EXCRETION OF COMBINED MORPHINE IN THE TOLERANT AND NON-TOLERANT DOG

VINCENT THOMPSON AND E. G. GROSS

From the Department of Pharmacology, State University of Iowa, Iowa City

Received for publication February 12, 1941

That there may be some differences in the handling of morphine by the tolerant and non-tolerant animals which might explain tolerance has long been intimated. Recently Gross and Thompson (1) have demonstrated the presence of a combined form of morphine in the urine of dogs after morphine administration and found further that there are distinct differences in amounts of this "combined" morphine in the tolerant and non-tolerant animals, the non-tolerant dog excreting approximately twice as much of the combined form as the tolerant dog. It has been previously established by Pierce and Plant (2) that there is no marked difference in the excretion of free morphine, since both the tolerant and non-tolerant dog excrete approximately 10 to 20 per cent of a given dose as free morphine. Oberst (3) has established the presence of "bound" morphine in the urine of human addicts. By his method the amount of "bound" morphine was three to thirty-six times the quantity of free morphine.

The fact that the non-tolerant dog excretes a much larger proportion of a given dose of morphine in a combined form as compared to the amount excreted by the tolerant dog indicates at least a partial difference in the handling of morphine as tolerance is established, but this difference is insufficient to explain the question of tolerance. It was therefore thought important to study further the properties of this combined fraction. While these studies do not shed any more light on the question of tolerance, we have established a further difference in the metabolism of morphine in the tolerant and non-tolerant dog.

METHODS

Both tolerant and non-tolerant dogs were employed. The tolerant animals were on a constant 20 mgm./kgm./day morphine sulfate dosage for two to three years, while the non-tolerant dogs were given the same dosage for not over two days. Diet and water intake were controlled before and during the experimental periods. For greater detail concerning care and handling of the animals see Plant and Pierce (4).

The method of analysis has been described by Gross and Thompson (1).

RESULTS

1. Demonstration of two types of combined morphine

At the beginning of a study on the properties of the combined morphine excreted in urine,[1] we thought that some data of interest would be secured from following the rate of hydrolysis of this combined morphine. Accordingly, the urine was made acid with hydrochloric acid, maintained at 100°C., and aliquots were removed at various intervals for analysis. We soon discovered that only a small fraction of the morphine was set free by this method, the rest being hydrolyzed only by thirty minute treatment with 5 per cent concentrated hydrochloric acid in the autoclave under 15 pounds pressure. Figure 1 summarizes the results. A fairly uniform rate of hydrolysis was found for the first sixty minutes, with subsequent very slow rate. This rate of break-down was fairly constant from pH 1 to 3; below this hydrogen ion concentration the hydrolysis proceeded very slowly or did not occur in appreciable amounts. The pH was attained by addition of suitable amounts of hydrochloric acid, and was determined by a Beckman pH meter. These hydrogen ion concentrations were checked after the hydrolysis period and found to be practically unchanged.

This morphine fraction which is set free by two hour hydrolysis at pH 1 to 2 at 100°C. we have designated as the "easily hydrolyzable" fraction. The remainder of the paired morphine, set free by thirty minute hydrolysis with 5 per cent of concentrated hydrochloric acid (by volume) in the autoclave under 15 pounds pressure, has been called the "difficultly hydrolyzable" fraction.

Thus we have four morphine fractions to consider in morphinized dogs:

[1] The compound which gives the morphine color reaction after hydrolysis of the urine has been identified as morphine by Dr. L. F. Small at the National Institute of Health, Washington, D. C.

Morphine hydrate isolated from dogs' urine after hydrolysis showed the following analysis:

52.5 mgm. in 10.0 ml. of N 0.0998 sulfuric acid showed $\alpha = -0.61°$ at 30°.

$$[\alpha]_D^{30} = -116.2° \quad (c = 0.0525)$$

Pure morphine in the same solvent: $[\alpha]_D^{20} = -117.6°$

62.8 mgm. of the base was dissolved in 12 drops of pyridine with 7 drops of acetic anhydride, and allowed to stand at room temperature for 16 hours. The solvent was removed in a vacuum at 50°, the residue dissolved in 2 ml. of water, and the product was precipitated as fine white crystals by slow addition of solid sodium bicarbonate; yield 69 mgm. It was recrystallized twice from ethyl acetate and compared with diacetylmorphine:

Melting point of the acetylation product	172 –173°
Melting point of pure diacetylmorphine	172.6–173.4°
Mixed melting point	172.5–173.2°

All melting points with total stem immersion.

(*1*) Free morphine, extracted from untreated urine; (*2*) "Easily hydrolyzable" morphine; (*3*) "Difficultly hydrolyzable" morphine; and (*4*) a fraction of the injected morphine which is lost, being either destroyed in the animal or excreted in a form so markedly changed that it is not possible to detect it as morphine by our method.

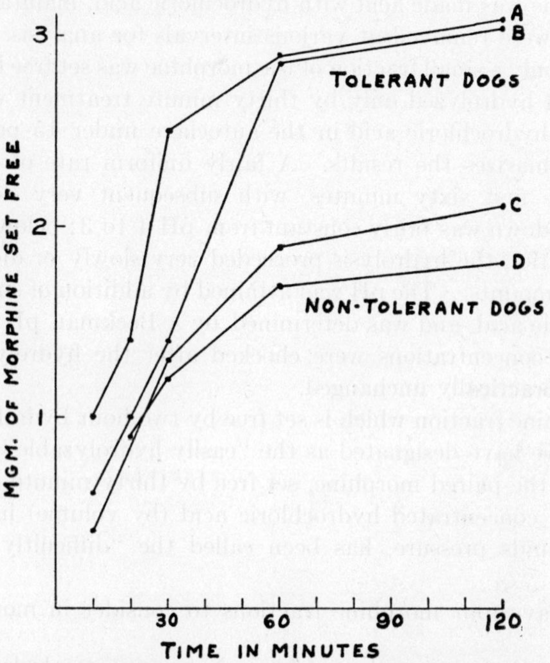

FIG. 1. HYDROLYSIS OF COMBINED MORPHINE IN URINES OF MORPHINIZED DOGS
Morphine set free in aliquots of urine made acid to pH 2 and maintained at 100°C. for the indicated times. *A* and *B*, urine of tolerant dogs. *C* and *D*, urine of non-tolerant dogs.

2. Excretion of the two types of combined morphine in tolerant and nontolerant dogs

Urine was collected for a period of twenty-four hours following injection of morphine and analyzed as described. Ten animals of each group were used; the results are shown in table 1. The percentages are given in the percent of the total dose of morphine that was excreted during a period of 24 hours for tolerant dogs, 72 hours for non-tolerant dogs. It will be observed that the tolerant dog excretes a greater amount of "easily hydrolyzable" morphine than does the non-tolerant, while the reverse situation obtains with the "difficultly hydrolyzable" morphine.

If the calculations are based on the amount of morphine injected, the results are equally striking. In figure 2 is demonstrated graphically the fate of injected doses of morphine in a tolerant (24 hour urine specimen) and a non-tolerant dog (urine collected for 72 hours after single dose). The free morphine is the same in both cases. The "easily hydrolyzable" morphine accounts for 8 per cent of the injected dose in the non-tolerant, 16 per cent in

TABLE 1

Morphine partition in urine after a single injection of the drug

	FREE MORPHINE	EASILY HYDROLYZABLE	DIFFICULTLY HYDROLYZABLE
	per cent	*per cent*	*per cent*
Tolerant dogs	19–26	16–34	42–59
Non-tolerant dogs	13–25	1–12	65–85

The figures are given in terms of total morphine recovered from urine. The urine excreted over 24 hours (i.e., between daily doses) from tolerant dogs was analyzed, while the urine from non-tolerant animals was pooled for 72 hours after a single dose and the morphine fraction determined. For further explanation see text.

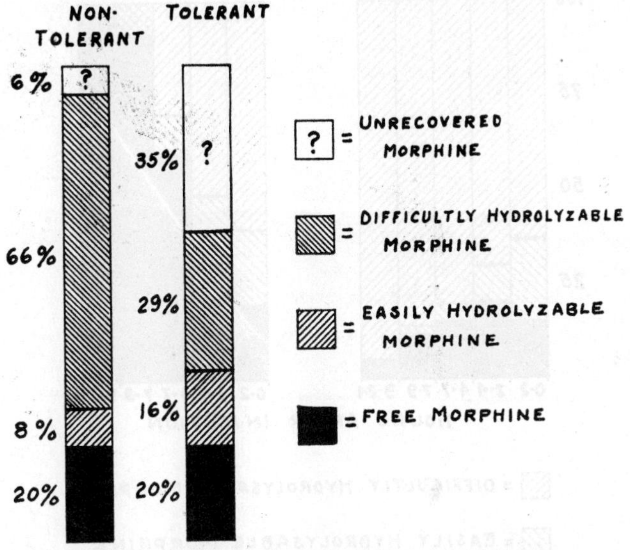

FIG. 2. FATE OF AN INJECTED DOSE OF MORPHINE

Recovery of morphine from urines of morphinized dogs. Results are in percentage recovery of the injected dose (20 mgm./kgm.). The urine of the tolerant dog was collected for 24 hours, that of non-tolerant dogs for 72 hours.

the tolerant dog. "Difficultly hydrolyzable" morphine is represented by an excretion of 66 per cent of the injected morphine from the non-tolerant dog, 35 per cent from the tolerant dog. About 6 per cent of the morphine is unaccounted for in non-tolerant dogs, while 35 per cent is destroyed or altered in tolerant dogs.

TABLE 2

Total morphine excretion

	TOLERANT	RATE PER HOUR	NON-TOLERANT	RATE PER HOUR
	per cent	*per cent*	*per cent*	*per cent*
At end of 2 hours	28	14.0	20	10.0
At end of 4 hours	45	8.5	44	12.0
At end of 7 hours	51	2.0	67	9.0
At end of 9 hours	52	0.5	72	2.5
At end of 24 hours	65	0.6	88	1.+

Excretion of morphine in urines of tolerant and non-tolerant dogs at various intervals after an injected dose (20 mgm./kgm.). The columns headed *Tolerant* and *Non-tolerant* indicate the total morphine excreted at the end of the indicated hours. The *Rate per hour* columns show the percentage of the injected dose excreted during the interval the urine sample was collected.

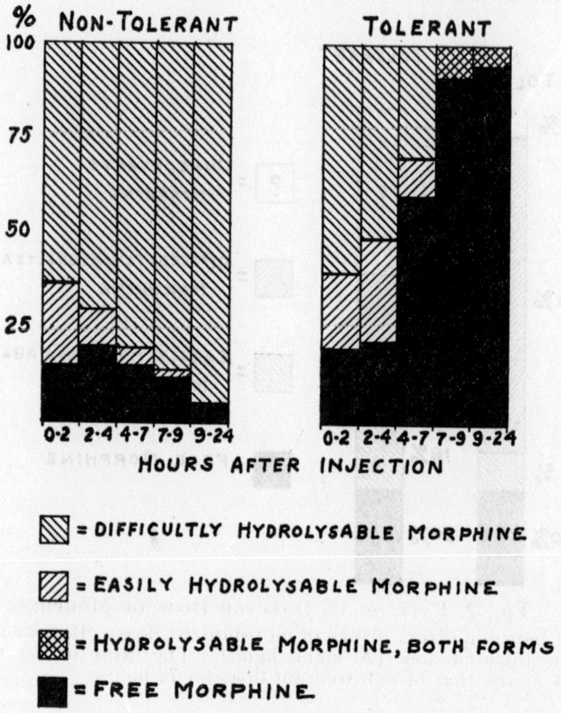

Fig. 3. Morphine Fractions in Urine

Urine was collected from morphinized dogs at the indicated intervals after injection, and the samples analyzed for the various fractions of morphine. The results are given in the per cent of total morphine found in the sample of urine for each period.

3. *Rate of excretion, and relative amounts of fractions of morphine excreted after injection*

The animals were catheterized at definite intervals after morphine injection. The urine was analyzed for total morphine and for free and combined fractions. It was not possible to obtain a sample for the first hour after injection; samples were drawn 2, 4, 7, 9, and 24 hours following the administration of the morphine. The peak in rate of excretion is reached in tolerant dogs during the first 2 hours, later in non-tolerant dogs. At the end of 4 hours, the excretion of injected morphine is about the same in both groups of dogs, i.e. 45 per cent of the injected dose. At that time the tolerant dog has excreted about 70 per cent of the total amount he is going to lose, and morphine appears in small amounts from that time on. Non-tolerant dogs at 4 hours have excreted less than 50 per cent of the total to be excreted, and these animals have therefore much larger amounts of morphine in the urine.

The rate of excretion of the morphine fractions is not constant (see fig. 3). During the first 4 hours there are relatively large amounts of all three fractions of morphine present in the urine of both types of animals. After this a definite trend appears; in tolerant animals the relative amounts of combined fractions decrease until the excretion consists almost entirely of free morphine. In the non-tolerant dogs, on the other hand, free morphine decreases in relative amounts, "easily hydrolyzable" entirely disappears after the first 9 hours, and the morphine is excreted largely as the "difficultly hydrolyzable" fraction.

DISCUSSION

It has been demonstrated that approximately 100 per cent of injected morphine can be recovered from urine of non-tolerant dogs, while but 50 to 65 per cent is reclaimed from tolerant dogs (1). In this paper further differences in the mode of handling morphine have been shown. The combined morphine has been separated into two fractions, (*1*) an "easily hydrolyzable" fraction, excreted in larger amounts in the non-tolerant dog, and (*2*) a "difficultly hydrolyzable" fraction which is excreted in greater quantities in the tolerant dog. Furthermore, the free morphine fraction predominates in the urine of tolerant dogs after the other fractions have nearly disappeared. This is in marked contrast to the excretion in non-tolerant dogs. Here the "difficultly hydrolyzable" fraction of the combined morphine is relatively higher toward the end of excretion, free morphine is low, and "easily hydrolyzable" fraction completely disappears.

The presence of several fractions of morphine in urine of morphinized animals was suggested by Stolnikow (5) and by Marquis (6); the latter named his fractions, "free," "paired," and "altered" form of morphine. Endo (7) found an increase in morphine yield after urine was treated with acid; this increase probably corresponds to the fraction we have called "easily hydrolyzable" morphine. None of these workers showed any difference in excretion of these fractions in tolerant and non-tolerant individuals. Oberst (2), using urine from human addicts, found an increase in morphine yield after three hour hydrolysis at 100°C. with one-fifth volume of concentrated hydrochloric acid.

The results reported in this paper clarify to some extent the findings of Pierce and Plant (8). It should be realized that these workers were determining only the free morphine in tissues and excretions of tolerant and non-tolerant dogs. The excretion at the end of four hours was approximately identical for both groups of animals. This also holds for excretion of free plus combined morphine (table 1). However, Pierce and Plant (8) reported the morphine yield in the excretion of tolerant dogs during the next twenty hours was greater than from non-tolerant dogs. From our data the excretion of the tolerant dogs 4 to 24 hours post-injection consists largely of free morphine, that of the non-tolerant dogs of combined morphine. Taking into consideration this combined morphine, the non-tolerant dog excretes about 44 per cent of an injected dose during this 4 to 24 hour period after injection, the tolerant dog only 20 per cent. From the tissues examined, Pierce and Plant (8) recovered more "free" morphine (42.8 per cent) in the non-tolerant dog four hours after injection, while at the end of twenty-four hours the tissues of the tolerant dog contained more morphine (46 per cent) than the non-tolerant animal. It was rather difficult to explain what happened to the morphine in the body of the non-tolerant dog. From the data presented in this paper it is evident that the non-tolerant dog excretes this excess morphine, largely as combined morphine.

The rôle which these fractions of morphine play in the metabolism of morphinized animals will be discussed in a subsequent publication.

SUMMARY

1. The "combined morphine" in urine of morphinized dogs may be separated into "easily" and "difficultly hydrolyzable" fractions.

2. Tolerant dogs excrete relatively greater amounts of the "easily hydrolyzable" fraction of the combined morphine than do non-tolerant dogs.

3. Seven to twenty-four hours after injection of morphine, urine of tolerant dogs contains mostly free morphine. During this same period, non-tolerant dogs excrete relatively large amounts of the "difficultly hydrolyzable" morphine fraction.

4. Tolerant dogs reach a peak in rate of morphine excretion more quickly than do the non-tolerant animals. The latter, however, continue to excrete relatively large quantities of morphine after the drug has practically disappeared from the urine of tolerant dogs.

REFERENCES

(1) Gross and Thompson: This Journal, **68:** 413, 1940.
(2) Pierce and Plant: Ibid., **46:** 201, 1932.
(3) Oberst: Ibid., **69:** 240, 1940.
(4) Plant and Pierce: Ibid., **33:** 329, 1928.
(5) Stolnikow: Z. Physiol. Chem., **8:** 235, 1884.
(6) Marquis: Inaug. Dissert, Dorpat, 1896.
(7) Endo: Jap. J. Med. Sc. IV Pharmacol., **11:** 140, 1938.
(8) Pierce and Plant: Ibid., **59:** 432, 1933.

THE TOXICITY AND LOCAL ANESTHETIC ACTIVITY OF THREE NEW BIPHENYL DERIVATIVES[1]

EDWIN J. FELLOWS

From the Department of Pharmacology, Temple University School of Medicine, Philadelphia

Received for publication February 18, 1941

Numerous modifications of para-aminobenzoic acid have been made since Einhorn (1) demonstrated in 1899 that esters of this compound produced local anesthesia but Einhorn's (2) diethyl-aminoethyl ester of para-aminobenzoic acid (procaine) still is the most extensively used of all the local anesthetic agents.

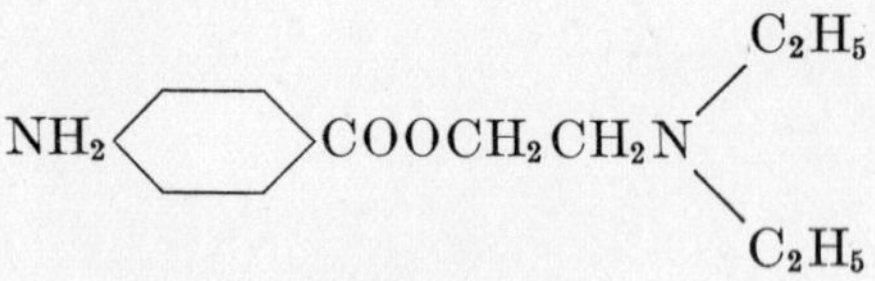

I (Procaine)

Braker and Christiansen (3) deviated slightly from the basic benzoic acid nucleus and synthesized the following biphenyl compounds:

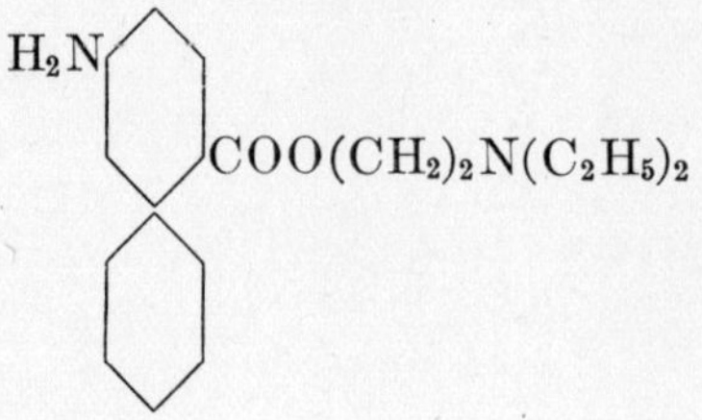

II

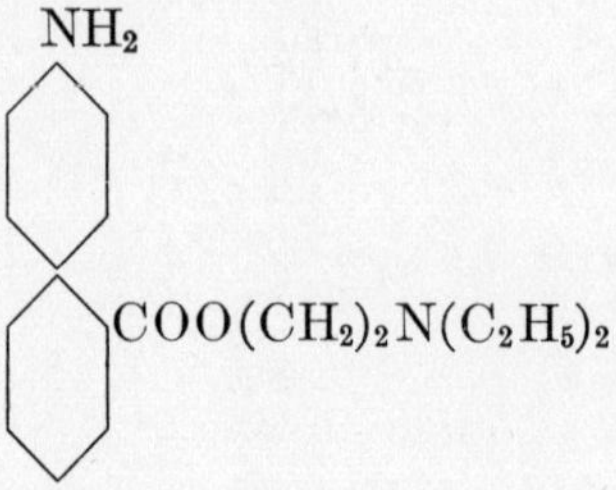

III

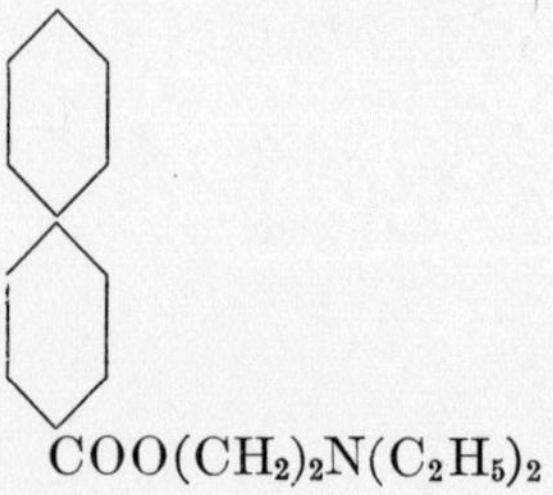

IV

[1] This investigation was supported in part by the D. J. McCarthy Foundation.

These authors found that II was a more active local anesthetic than procaine or cocaine but of no apparent therapeutic value because of its irritant properties; III was comparatively inactive and IV too acid for testing.

The following biphenyl compounds were prepared by Case and Koft (4) and have been made available[2] for the present studies:

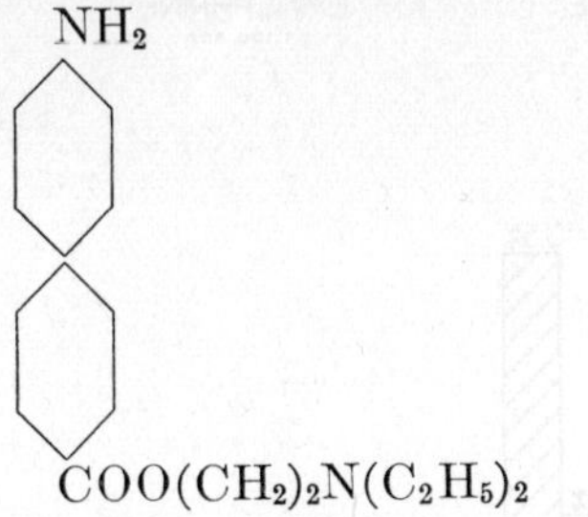

V
M.p., 78–79°C.

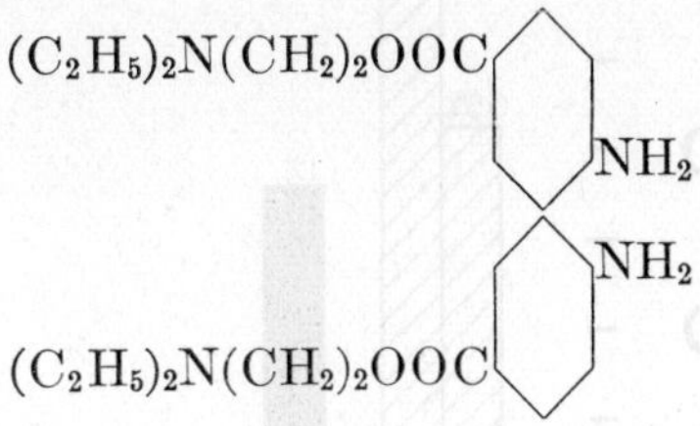

VI
M.p., 91–92°C.

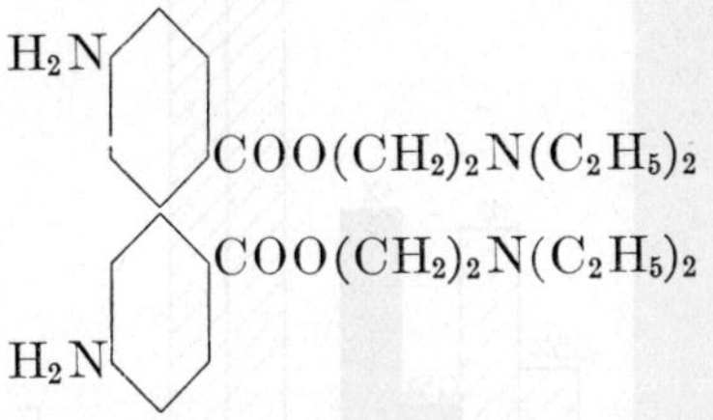

VII
M.p., 64–65°C.

The present experiments have been carried out primarily to determine if the three new biphenyl compounds (V, VI, VII) have local anesthetic properties and if so to ascertain if they possess any advantages over existing substances. The present studies also should yield information concerning the effect of position substitution on local anesthetic activity and toxicity. The criterion of their effectiveness was their ability to produce dermal anesthesia as studied by the technique described by Rose (5). Aqueous solutions of the compounds were injected in 0.1 cc. volumes intradermally in guinea-pigs shaved free of hair and the presence or absence of anesthesia tested by faradic stimulation of each area injected. Procaine served as the standard of comparison for duration of anesthesia.

In figure 1 it is shown that in the present experiments procaine in 0.1, 0.5 and 1.0 per cent concentrations produced anesthesia by intracutaneous injection in guinea-pigs for an average duration of 2, 19 and 31 minutes respectively. In spite of the low toxicity of procaine its use as an infiltration

[2] These compounds have been supplied by Dr. F. H. Case of the Department of Organic Chemistry, Temple University.

anesthetic would be limited except for Braun's (6) discovery that epinephrine intensifies and prolongs the action of certain anesthetics. In the present experiments 0.1, 0.5 and 1.0 per cent procaine in 1:100,000 epinephrine

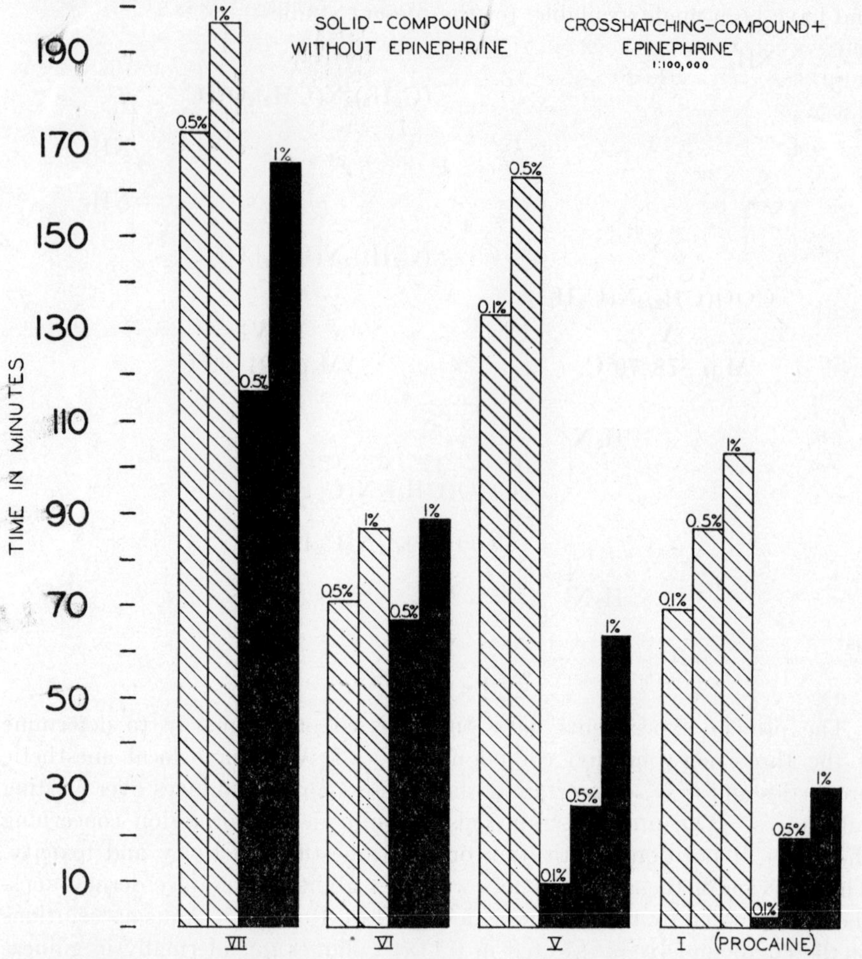

Fig. 1. Duration of Anesthesia after Intracutaneous Injection in Guinea-Pigs

The average figures for duration of anesthesia after procaine were obtained by 174 tests on 36 guinea-pigs; for compound V by 89 tests on 14 guinea-pigs; for compound VI by 137 tests on 30 guinea-pigs; for compound VII by 133 tests on 27 guinea-pigs.

produced an average period of anesthesia of 69, 87 and 103 minutes respectively.

β-diethylaminoethyl-4-amino-4′-biphenylcarboxylate hydrochloride (*compound V*). Compound V in 0.1, 0.5 and 1.0 per cent concentration produced anesthesia for an average duration of 10, 27 and 53 minutes as shown in figure 1.

In this figure it also is to be noted that 0.1 and 0.5 per cent concentrations of V in 1:100,000 epinephrine caused anesthesia for an average of 140 and 163 minutes respectively.

Di-(β-diethylaminoethyl) 2-2′-diamino-5-5′-biphenylcarboxylate hydrochloride (VI). In figure 1 it is shown that VI produced anesthesia of the skin in guinea-pigs in 0.5 and 1.0 per cent concentration for an average of 67 and 88 minutes. In 1:100,000 epinephrine these same concentrations of VI produced anesthesia for 71 and 84 minutes.

Di-(β-diethylaminoethyl)-5-5′-diaminodiphenate hydrochloride (compound VII). In figure 1 it is to be observed that VII in 0.5 and 1.0 per cent solutions produced an average duration of anesthesia in guinea-pigs of 117 and 168 minutes. A slight prolongation of anesthetic action of VII by epinephrine is shown by the fact that in 1:100,000 epinephrine, 0.5 per cent concentration of VII caused anesthesia for 172 minutes and in 1.0 per cent for 197 minutes.

TABLE 1

Subcutaneous toxicity in guinea-pigs

COMPOUND	DOSE	ANIMALS DIED/ANIMALS INJECTED
	mgm./kgm.	
V	200	5/9
	150	0/4
	100	0/6
VI	225	4/5
	200	6/6
	150	4/9
	100	0/3
	75	0/5
VII	100	10/10
	75	8/10
	50	1/9
Procaine	400	10/10
	375	8/10
	350	2/10

Corneal anesthesia. The presence or absence of corneal anesthesia was tested after aqueous solutions of the compounds had been instilled into the conjunctival sac of rabbits and allowed to remain in contact with the eye for exactly two minutes. Anesthesia was observed by touching the cornea with the rounded end of a fine glass rod. Absence of the winking reflex was taken as evidence of anesthesia.

It was found that the average duration of anesthesia after 1.0 per cent cocaine was 25 minutes and after 2.0 per cent, 37 minutes. The same concentrations of V produced 24 and 33 minute anesthesia. The average duration of anesthesia after 1.0 and 2.0 per cent VI was 45 and 54 minutes. In the case of 1.0 and 2.0 per cent VII, anesthesia was obtained for 63 and 71 minutes.

Toxicity. It was found that subcutaneously in guinea-pigs the M.L.D. of V was above 200 mgm. per kilogram of body weight and that of VI between 150 and 200 mgm. per kilogram of body weight (table 1). The M.L.D. of VII subcutaneously was 75 and that of procaine 375 mgm. per kilogram of body weight (table 1).

DISCUSSION

In consideration of possible advantages of the biphenyl compounds over local anesthetics in common use, certain facts are apparent. While the duration of anesthesia after intracutaneous injection of V in guinea-pigs is one and one-half times that observed after procaine the former is more toxic and causes tissue damage. Although the anesthetic potency of VI is greater than that of procaine it is also more than twice as toxic subcutaneously as the latter. The marked dermal anesthetic activity of VII is offset by the fact that it is 5 times more toxic than procaine.

While the duration of anesthesia of rabbit cornea produced by VI and VII was greater than that caused by cocaine, poor depth of anesthesia precludes their use as topical anesthetics. Despite its lower toxicity, V produces anesthesia of rabbit cornea which compares in depth and duration with that of cocaine but is inferior to the latter because it produces marked irritation in 2 to 3 per cent concentrations. It would appear, therefore, that the present biphenyl compounds are not superior either by injection or topical application to those agents in common use.

In a consideration of the effect of position substitution on anesthetic activity it should be recalled that in the present experiments V, which differs from III only in the position of the ester group, produces marked anesthesia, whereas Braker and Christiansen (3) state that III was relatively inactive. In the present studies it also was found that compound VII produced anesthesia in guinea-pigs of longer duration than VI and that the anesthesia of VII was slightly prolonged by epinephrine whereas that of VI was unaffected by the vasoconstrictor agent.

SUMMARY

1. The hydrochlorides of β-diethylaminoethyl-4-amino-4′-biphenyl carboxylate (compound V), di-(β-diethylaminoethyl)-2-2′-diamino-5-5′-biphenylcarboxylate (compound VI) and di-(β-diethylaminoethyl)-5-5′-diamino-diphenate (compound VII) were found to have marked local anesthetic properties.

2. The anesthetic activity of V after intradermal injection is slightly greater than that of the hydrochloride of p-amino-benzoyl-diethylamino ethanol

(procaine) but it is also more toxic subcutaneously and produces tissue damage. While the anesthetic potency of VI is somewhat greater it is also more than twice as toxic subcutaneously as procaine. The marked anesthetic activity of VII as compared with procaine is offset by a five fold increase in subcutaneous toxicity.

3. The irritant properties of V and the poor depth of anesthesia produced by VI and VII make the present biphenyl compounds inferior to cocaine as topical anesthetics.

4. Comparison of V with closely related substances discloses that position of the substituent groups on the biphenyl nucleus alters local anesthetic activity. This also was observed in the case of compounds VI and VII.

I wish to express my thanks to Dr. A. E. Livingston for the helpful suggestions and encouragement received.

REFERENCES

(1) Einhorn: Munch. Med. Wochnschr., **46**: 1218, 1899.
(2) Einhorn: Deutsch. Med. Wochnschr., **31**: 1668, 1905.
(3) Braker and Christiansen: J. Am. Phar. Assn., **24**: 358, 1935.
(4) Case and Koft: J. Am. Chem. Soc., **63**: 508, 1941.
(5) Rose: Journ. Lab. Clin. Med., **15**: 128, 1929.
(6) Braun: Arch. f. klin. Chir., **69**: 541, 1903.

THE EFFECT OF ATROPINE, PILOCARPINE, PROSTIGMINE, ESERINE, MECHOLYL AND EPHEDRINE ON THE TONUS AND CONTRACTION MECHANISMS OF THE URINARY BLADDER, WITH OBSERVATIONS ON THE CLINICAL APPLICATION OF THESE DRUGS

HARRY A. TEITELBAUM AND ORTHELLO R. LANGWORTHY

From the Sub-department of Neurology, the Johns Hopkins University, Baltimore, and the Neurological Service (Cornell Division) of Bellevue Hospital, New York

Received for publication February 25, 1941

Langley and Anderson (1) observed that atropine in very large doses (150 mgm. in the dog, 50 mgm. in the rabbit and cat) had some inhibitory effect on vesical contraction resulting from sacral nerve stimulation. Later Langley (2) confirmed the partial inhibitory effect of large doses of atropine, which also completely abolished the contractile effect of pilocarpine. Streuli (3) confirmed the inhibitory effect of atropine on the bladder contraction produced by pilocarpine. Henderson (4), contrary to Langley, could observe no inhibitory effect of large doses of atropine (100 mgm.) on bladder contraction induced by sacral nerve stimulation. Atropine did, however, lower both preexisting tone as well as tone due to pilocarpine. Henderson and Roepke (5, 6) suggested that the effects of pilocarpine and physostigmine were associated with the tonus mechanism, for they were abolished by atropine which had no effect on the contractile mechanism. While atropine could inhibit the peripheral tonic effect, it could not counteract the contractile effect referable to ganglionic stimulation. Henderson and Roepke (6) concluded that the tonus mechanism adjusts the intravesical pressure to inflow, and that the contractile mechanism is not weakened by a fall in tone. The poor inhibitory effect of atropine on the contractile action of the parasympathetic nerves and its good inhibitory effect on the action of parasympathomimetic drugs was subsequently confirmed in the intestine by Bayliss and Starling (7). Henderson (4), however, reported some weakening of the effect of vagus stimulation on the intestine by means of atropine. Le Heux (8) demonstrated that choline, which is liberated by the intestine, stimulates the latter organ. Atropine is able to inhibit choline action. However, if the choline is washed out, the antagonistic effect of atropine is absent. In the uterus, Cushny (9) observed that atropine abolished the response to pilocarpine and physostigmine, but the response due to nerve stimulation remained unaltered. Prostigmine, which has been employed to relieve post-operative urinary retention by Marden and Williamson (10), has been investigated by Myerson (11), and Greenberg, Loman and Myerson (12) in man. Myerson maintains that mecholyl and prostigmine have only a slight effect on the bladder when given separately, though a marked effect when given together. The slight effect of mecholyl is contrary to Levin's (13) observations in the cat, in which animal a very definite effect was produced. The findings to be described confirm Levin's report, and also contradict Myerson's conclusion that prostigmine has little effect on the bladder.

MATERIAL AND METHOD

Thirty-seven experiments were performed on eleven female cats under nembutal anesthesia. The apparatus used is similar to that described by Langworthy, Kolb and Lewis (14) but for the inclusion of the Marriotte mechanism. Instead of the repeated introduction of fixed increments (5 cc. for the cat, 50 cc. for man) of fluid until the bladder is filled, a constant flow of water into the bladder was adopted. The cystometer (fig. 1) is joined to a glass cannula (*5*) which is passed into the bladder through the urethral orifice. With the bladder empty, and the stopcock (*3*) adjusted to give the rate of flow desired, the other stopcock (*4*) is opened to allow a steady stream of water to pass from the reservoir (*2*) into the bladder. The pressure in the bladder can be read at all times on the manometer (*6*) which is joined to a recording tambour through the medium of rubber tubing (*7*). By means of a tube (*1*), the pressure of the receding column of water in the reservoir is kept constant in accordance with Marriotte's principle. The latter is discussed in greater detail by Teitelbaum and Harne (15). As soon as the water beings to leak around the catheter, the stopcock (*4*) is closed.

The apparatus described above permits the introduction of fluid into the bladder at a constant pressure. This is important because the tone of the vesical muscle varies with the pressure at which it is filled. When fluid is introduced rapidly under great pressure into the bladder, the resistance of the muscle is increased in response to stretch. With a constant pressure, the only variant present is the resistance to the introduction of fluid built up by the muscle tension during the process of filling.

For the purpose of stimulating the bladder subcutaneous injections of drugs were used as follows: pilocarpine hydrochloride, 1 to 2 mgm.; prostigmine methylsulphate, 0.5 to 1.5 mgm.; eserine sulphate, 5 to 7 mgm.; and mecholyl (Merck) (acetylbeta-methylcholine chloride), 2 to 5 mgm. Eserine sulphate in smaller doses of 1 to 3 mgm. was ineffective. In some cases combinations of prostigmine and mecholyl in small doses of 0.1 to 0.2 mgm. were used. All of these drugs showed definite stimulating effects on the bladder. In addition there were other responses such as salivation, lacrimation, nasal secretion, defecation and vomiting. Soon after the bladder responded to the particular stimulating drug being employed, atropine sulphate in doses varying from 0.1 to 1.0 mgm. was administered intramuscularly. In this manner some of the mechanisms brought into play by these mutually antagonistic forces could be studied. Since all of the stimulating drugs acted in a more or less similar manner, the data will be presented from the point of view of the different patterns of bladder behavior that could be discerned.

RESULTS

The normal bladder

The response of the cat's bladder to filling under constant pressure is not entirely uniform. There is considerable variation in different animals, and while individual animals generally repeat the patterns of their reaction, variations may be present here also.

Cats can be divided into two groups with regard to the contractile ability of their bladders as the result of filling. One group has poor or no contractile ability, as illus-

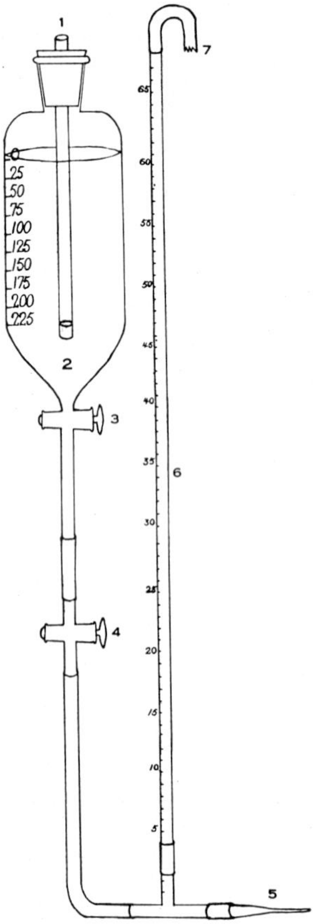

FIG. 1. DIAGRAMMATIC ILLUSTRATION OF CYSTOMETER

1, Glass tube. *2*, Reservoir. *3*, Stopcock for adjusting rate of flow. *4*, Stopcock for starting or stopping flow. *5*, Glass cannula used as catheter. *6*, Manometer. *7*, Connection to tambour. The arrangement of the glass tube, *1* to the reservoir, *2* is according to the Marriotte principle which maintains a constant head of pressure in a receding column of water.

trated in figure 2, *1*, while the other has good contractile ability as in figure 4, *1*. This agrees with the observations of Denny-Brown and Robertson (13) in man.

The problem of bladder tone is complex. Langworthy, Kolb and Lewis (14) refer to a number of "objective criteria by means of which it is possible to discuss tone in the urinary bladder. These are the capacity, the ability to accommodate to increased volumes, the resting pressure in the bladder empty and during filling, and the response of the muscle to sudden stretching." Because it was the most prominent criterion in the experiments to be described, the "resting pressure of the bladder" while empty or during filling will be adopted as descriptive of the tonus mechanism.

As with the contractile ability, there are two types of responses apropos of tone. In some animals the bladder can be filled to capacity and overflow occurs with very little rise in tone (fig. 2, *1*), while in others the tone increases considerably as the bladder fills. This confirms Henderson and Roepke's (6) conclusion that the tonus mechanism adjusts the intravesical pressure to inflow. That the contractile mechanism is not weakened by a fall in tone, as maintained by these authors, is also amply supported by the data to be presented.

While tone and contractile ability are dissociated from one another for purposes of discussion, it is generally conceded that the two phenomena as they occur in striated muscle, and probably also in smooth muscle, are manifestations of the same mechanism. Fulton (16) presents evidence "that the elements responsible for the maintenance of tension in a tonic muscle are those which contract when a motor nerve is stimulated." Tone, it is pointed out, is the asynchronous stimulation of individual muscle fibers. While various muscle fibers are affected alternately, a relatively uniform degree of tension can nevertheless be achieved. Movement, on the other hand, is the result of the synchronous contraction of large groups of muscle fibers. Denny-Brown and Robertson (17) interpret their results in the bladder in a manner that complies precisely with the principles set forth by Fulton (16). The tonic mechanism is of importance in the bladder because it can be regulated to permit the retention of various quantities of fluid at approximately the same pressure. Contractions as seen in the vesical muscle are of different types. Rhythmical waves are likely to appear during the process of filling. A well-sustained contraction may empty the bladder completely. It is actually not possible to separate the elements of vesical tension as recorded with the kymograph from one another and to refer to them as tone and contraction. However, in arranging the response of the bladder to drugs, this rather artificial distinction will be used for convenience.

The effect of drugs on bladders with low tone and poor normal contractile ability. In a bladder with low tone and poor contractile ability stimulating drugs can cause a decrease in capacity in association with only slight increases in tone and meager contraction of the bladder. Figure 2 presents such a case. The tone in the control record (*1*) averaged between 10 and 15 cm. of water, and leakage took place around the catheter at a pressure of 20 cm. after 75 cc. of water had been introduced into the bladder. There was no contraction at the time of leakage. After prostigmine and mecholyl (fig. 2, *2*) the tone varied between 15 and 20 cm. of water, which is only a slight rise, and the bladder capacity decreased to 45 cc. Leakage about the catheter occurred with only a minor contraction. Atropine was administered while record *2* was being taken, and twenty-three minutes later, record *3* was obtained. The tone was at about the original level, and there was less spontaneous activity than previously. The volume had increased to 115 cc. and leakage occurred without any sign of contraction following a gradual rise in tone to 22 cm. of water.

In the above experiment there is no striking correlation between tone (intravesical pressure) and the filling capacity. While the volume was decreased 40 per cent, there was only a slight and inconstant rise in tone. Atropine abolished the irregularities in the curve in figure 2, *1*, as well as the feeble contractions in figure 2, *2*. Atropine can, therefore, effectively oppose bladder contractility due to stimulating drugs. Other experiments have demonstrated this feature more strikingly than that illustrated in figure 2.

In another animal with low initial tone (fig. 3) the administration of pilocarpine reduced the volume from 75 to 18 cc., and at the same time elevated the tone and markedly accentuated the rhythmic fluctuations normally pres-

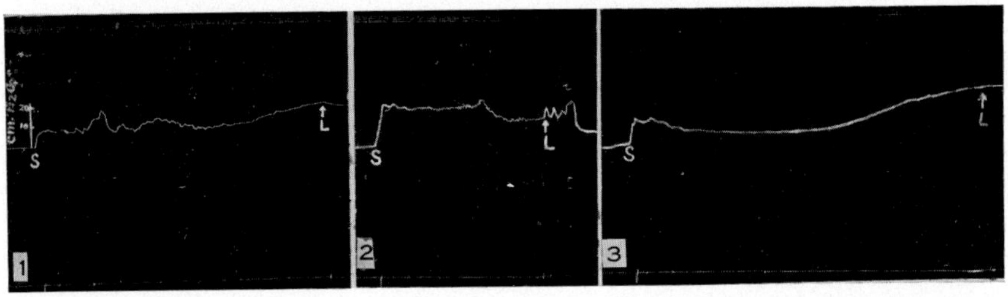

FIG. 2. Cat T 19. 7/22/40. Prostigmine and mecholyl decreased the volume and increased the tone, but only slightly increased the initially poor contractile power. Atropine decreased the tone, increased the volume, and abolished the poor contractile power. *S*, Start of inflow of fluid into bladder. *L*, Leak of fluid around catheter. Time, five seconds.

1, *S* at 1:05. *L* after introduction of 75 cc. Prostigmine 0.2 mgm. subcutaneously at 1:06. Mecholyl 0.2 mgm. subcutaneously at 1:07. *2*, *S* at 1:35. *L* after introduction of 45 cc. Atropine 1.0 mgm. intramuscularly at 1:37. *3*, *S* at 2:10. *L* after introduction of 115 cc.

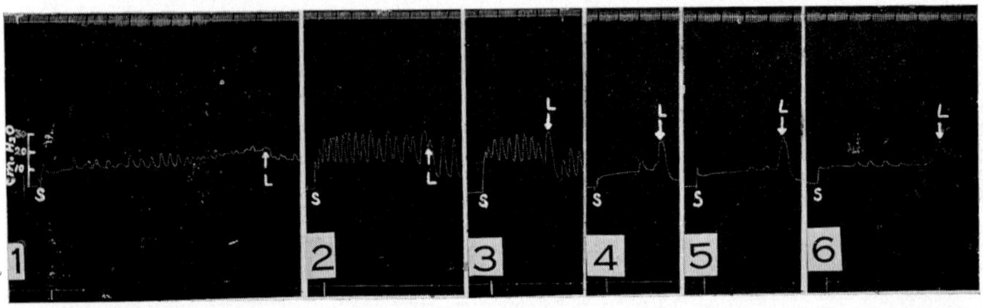

FIG. 3. Cat T 8. 4/9/40. Pilocarpine decreased the volume and increased the tone and rhythmic contractions. Atropine lowered the tone and increased the volume. The contractile ability, which was very poor initially, became good after the atropine, but was finally reduced. *S*, Start of flow of fluid into bladder. *L*, Leak of fluid around catheter. Time, five seconds.

1, *S* at 10:45. *L* after introduction of 75 cc. Pilocarpine 1.3 mgm. subcutaneously at 10:47. *2*, *S* at 11:00. *L* after introduction of 40 cc. *3*, *S* at 11:25. *L* after introduction of 18 cc. Atropine 0.2 mgm. intramuscularly at 11:30. *4*, *S* at 12:35. *L* after introduction of 25 cc. *5*, *S* at 12:45. *L* after introduction of 30 cc. *6*, *S* at 1:10. *L* after introduction of 40 cc.

ent. This experiment is particularly interesting because it can be seen in records *2* and *3* how leakage occurred along with one of these rhythmic fluctuations normally present. Following atropine the volume was gradually increased to 40 cc., the tone was lowered, and the rhythmic activity was almost completely abolished. However, leakage occurred in records *4* and *5* as the result of very definite contractions.

In the above experiment bladder contraction associated with leakage was induced by pilocarpine in a cat in which leakage occurred without contraction in the control. While this contractility was ultimately diminished by the atropine (fig. 3, *6*) it nevertheless persisted even after the increase in bladder tone had been reduced to normal.

The effect of drugs on bladders with low tone and good normal contractile ability. Just as the bladders of certain animals regularly show poor contractile ability, others present a constant picture of excellent contractile power. Some animals do, however, show variations in bladder contractility from time to time. In figure 4, *1*, the emptying contraction of the bladder had the pressure of 50 cm. of water though the initial tone was only 10 cm. Following small doses of mecholyl and prostigmine (fig. 4, *2*) the volume fell from 60 to 30 cc., and the tone rose to about 35 cm., while the contractility remained excellent.

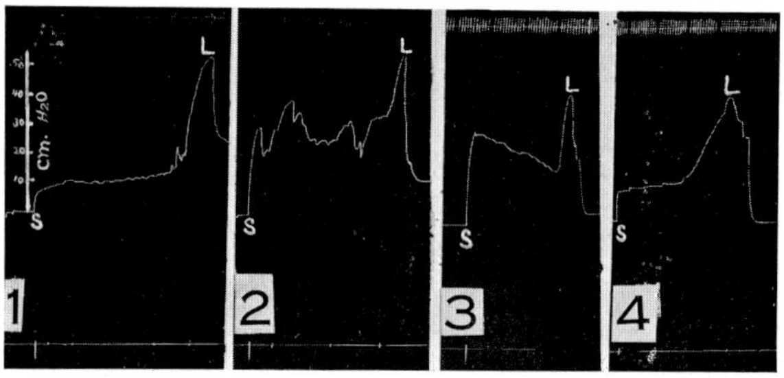

FIG. 4. Cat T 12. 7/8/40. Mecholyl and prostigmine caused an increase in tone and decrease in volume of the bladder. Atropine lowered the tone and increased the volume, but the contractile power remained good. *S*, Start of flow of fluid into bladder. *L*, Leak of fluid around catheter. Time, five seconds.

1, S at 11:45. *L* after introduction of 60 cc. Prostigmine 0.2 mgm. subcutaneously at 11:46. Mecholyl 0.2 mg. subcutaneously at 11:47. *2, S* at 11:50. *L* after introduction of 30 cc. Atropine 0.9 mgm. intramuscularly at 12:05. *3, S* at 12:18. *L* after introduction of 35 cc. *4, S* at 1:05. *L* after introduction of 55 cc.

After 0.9 mgm. of atropine the tone returned to its original pressure of 10 cm. of water and the volume increased to 55 cc. (fig. 4, *4*). The emptying contraction was reduced about 10 cm. of water. This reduction in normal contractile ability following atropine was seen on a number of occasions, though it is not constant by any means. This would indicate that atropine can partially oppose the normal contractile power of the bladder. In other experiments atropine in twice the dose used in the experiment illustrated in figure 4 was found to have no inhibitory effect on the normal contractile power (in the absence of stimulating drugs) of the bladder of the same cat. However, prostigmine, when administered after an adequate dose of atropine, was found to have no effect on the bladder.

The effect of drugs on bladders with normally high tone and good normal contractile ability. In the review of previously published work we pointed out that atropine is able to lower a high state of tone in the bladder, even when this is not due to drugs. This observation has been confirmed as is evident in figure 5. In the control record (fig. 5, *1*) the tone is of moderate height, and there is a good deal of spontaneous rhythmic activity. Following mecholyl (fig. 5, *2–3*) there was a reduction of the volume to 9 cc. from the original 25. The tone varied to some degree, as did the contractility (fig. 5, *1–3*). After the administration of atropine (fig. 5, *4–7*), the volume gradually rose to 23 cc. and the tone was lowered considerably with abolition of the rhythmic contractions. The contractile power remained good, however.

The action of ephedrine. Despite the clinical observation that this drug can produce urinary retention, doses varying from 30 to 350 mgm. had no inhibitory effect on either the tone or contractility of the bladder under the conditions of these experiments. Langworthy, Lewis, Dees and Hesser (18) were able to reduce the heightened tone of the bladder in Parkinsonian syn-

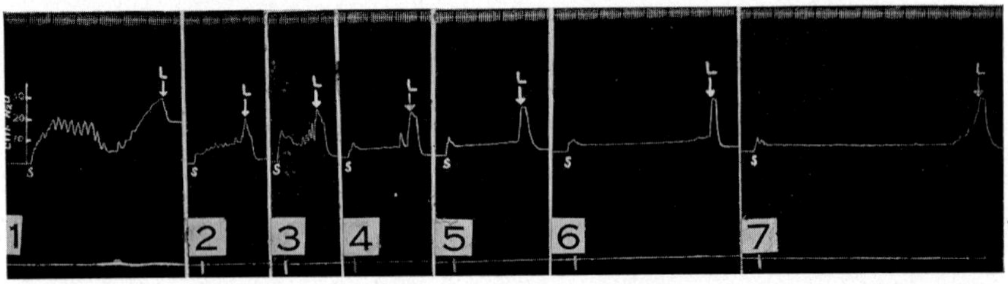

FIG. 5. Cat T 7. 4/23/40. Mecholyl caused a decrease in volume of the bladder. Atropine decreased the tone which was elevated in the control, and increased the volume, but the contractile power remained good. *S*, Start of flow of fluid into bladder. *L*, Leak of fluid around catheter. Time, five seconds.

1, *S* at 11:30. *L* after introduction of 25 cc. Mecholyl 2.5 mgm. subcutaneously at 11:56. *2*, *S* at 12:05. *L* after introduction of 15 cc. *3*, *S* at 12:25. *L* after introduction of 9 cc. Atropine 0.3 mgm. intramuscularly at 12:30. *4*, *S* at 12:55. *L* after introduction of 12 cc. *5*, *S* at 1:05. *L* after introduction of 17 cc. *6*, *S* at 1:15. *L* after introduction of 20 cc. *7*, *S* at 1:25. *L* after introduction of 23 cc.

drome by means of tincture of belladonna. Further reduction in tone was produced by the administration of ephedrine following the belladonna.

Clinical consideration. Langworthy, Lewis, Dees and Hesser (18) have described the state of the bladder in various clinical conditions of the nervous system such as tabes dorsalis, spina bifida, pyramidal tract damage, Parkinsonian syndrome and cerebellar abnormalities. Langworthy (19) has demonstrated the value of mecholyl in cases of tabes dorsalis in whom the bladder is overdistended and retention and overflow incontinence of urine are present. Dean (20) obtained satisfactory results with pilocarpine in cases of urinary retention due to injury of the nerve supply. The value of prostigmine in cases of post-operative urinary retention has been described by Marden and Williamson (10). Langworthy, Lewis, Dees and Hesser (18) demonstrated increased tone and small capacity of the bladder in cases of Parkinsonian syndrome. The contractility or emptying power of the bladder in such cases is apparently not impaired by drugs of the atropine series which relax the tone, for in some patients receiving hyoscine hydrobromide in doses as high as $\frac{1}{100}$ grain (0.0006 gram) twenty times a day, there have been no signs of urinary retention. This complies well with the selective activity of atropine de-

TABLE 1

The effect of pilocarpine on urinary retention in a case with a transverse spinal cord lesion of eighteen months duration

DATE	HOUR	DOSE OF PILOCARPINE	SPONTANEOUS	URINARY OUTPUT	CATHETERIZED RESIDUE
		mgm.		*cc.*	*cc.*
8/28/39	1:15 p.m.	10		30	300
	7:00 p.m.	10		180	30
8/29	11:30 a.m.	10		135	180
	6:30 p.m.	8		0	110
8/30	6:00 a.m.		x	90	
	9:20 a.m.		x	120	
	12:00 noon	8		180	45
	6:15 p.m.	8		90	30
	11:15 p.m.	8		0	150
8/31	11:30 a.m.	8		195	30
	6:15 p.m.	8		180	50
	11:10 p.m.	8		0	110
Injections continued irregularly through 9/8/39 with results similar to those recorded above					
9/9	1:00 a.m.		x	115	
	3:45 a.m.		x	120	
	5:30 a.m.		x	150	
	9:30 a.m.		x	150	
	1:55 p.m.		x	150	
	2:45 p.m.		x	150	
	8:50 p.m.		x	240	
9/10	6:45 a.m.		x	120	
	9:30 a.m.		x	180	
	?		x	120	
	2:30 p.m.		x	150	
	7:30 p.m.		x	120	
	9:30 p.m.		x	150	
9/11	6:55 a.m.		x	120	
	9:15 a.m.		x	150	
	5:00 p.m.		x	120	
	9:50 p.m.		x	150	

scribed above, in that it does not interfere with the normal contractile ability of the bladder while it does reduce the tone.

In order to demonstrate the value of the stimulating drugs of the bladder, the application of pilocarpine in several cases[1] of transverse cord lesion will be cited. Case 1 is of

[1] The cases reported are from the service of Dr. Foster Kennedy, Neurological Service, Bellevue Hospital, New York City.

TABLE 2

The effect of pilocarpine on urinary retention in a case with a transverse spinal cord lesion of two months duration

DATE	HOUR	DOSE OF PILOCARPINE	SPONTANEOUS	URINARY OUTPUT	CATHETERIZED RESIDUE
		mgm.		*cc.*	*cc.*
5/24	10:00 p.m.	10		230	250
5/25	4:00 a.m.	10		280	125
	11:30 a.m.	10		175	140
	6:00 p.m.	10		250	
	11:45 p.m.	10		220	
5/26	5:30 a.m.	10		300	
	11:35 a.m.	10		350	
	12:20 p.m.		X	50	300
	5:30 p.m.	10		500	
	11:30 p.m.	10		150	
5/27	5:30 a.m.	10		325	
	11:30 a.m.	10		30	550
	5:30 p.m.	10		180	
5/28	5:30 a.m.	10		?	
	11:30 a.m.	10		150	600
	5:30 p.m.	10		380	
	11:30 p.m.	10		150	
5/29	5:30 a.m.	10		220	
5/30	5:30 a.m.	10		350	
	11:30 a.m.		X	160	290
	5:30 p.m.	10		400	
	11:30 p.m.	10		400	
5/31	5:30 a.m.	10		520	
	12:00 noon	10		200	
	6:00 p.m.	10		400	
	12:30 a.m.	10		350	
6/1	? a.m.		X	?	
	12:00 noon		X	150	
	12:10 p.m.	10		225	25
	6:00 p.m.	10		200	
6/2	12:45 a.m.		X	425	
	7:15 a.m.		X	200	
	5:40 p.m.		X	100	200
6/3	? a.m.		X	55	
	? a.m.		X	225	
6/4	12:45 a.m.		X	450	
	8:30 a.m.		X	150	
	11:30 a.m.		X	425	
	4:30 p.m.		X	350	

particular interest because of the long duration of urinary retention without the spontaneous development of an automatic bladder, and because of the excellent response to pilocarpine.

Case 1. E. N., male adult with a history of a bullet wound suffered 9 months before admission on 1/25/39. The essential findings were complete anesthesia below T 4, spastic paraplegia with wasting of muscles in the legs, and other signs of bilateral pyramidal tract damage. There was urinary retention with overflow incontinence which required the use of a retention catheter. The retention catheter was withdrawn on 8/27/39, about 16 months after his injury, and subcutaneous pilocarpine injections were instituted, as indicated in table 1. A matter worthy of note was that after the development of spontaneous urination the patient was able to tell that he was going to urinate about 15 to 30 seconds before the flow started, for the latter would be preceded by a warm sensation passing up his spine. The improvement continued for the two months during which this case was followed.

Case 2. A. B., a 28 year old female, with a long history of pain in the lumbo-sacral region and legs, developed an almost complete paraplegia following an exploratory laminectomy on 4/18/39. On admission to Bellevue Hospital on 5/9/39, there was flaccid paralysis of the legs with only slight movement possible in the right thigh. Sensation was lost below L 2 on the right side and below T 12 on the left. All deep reflexes were absent in the legs, as were the plantar reflexes. Pathological reflexes could not be elicited. Urinary retention with overflow incontinence, and incontinence of stool were present.

As indicated in table 2, pilocarpine therapy for urinary retention was instituted on 5/24/39 and continued through 6/1/39 with some degree of regularity, four times daily in 10 mgm. doses by subcutaneous injection. The responses to the drug were excellent. On several occasions spontaneous automatic expulsion of variable quantities of urine occurred during the period of pilocarpine administration. However, on 6/2/39, spontaneous urination became much more effective, warranting the discontinuation of the pilocarpine. Fom that time on she was able to remain in a dry state without the use of either a retention catheter or pilocarpine. The automatic expulsion of urine was preceded by a normal sensation of bladder distension. She could not control the flow of urine once it had started. Also, she did not develop any awareness of the process of micturition, and she could not tell by means of pelvic or perineal sensation when it was completed.

DISCUSSION

The partial inhibition of bladder contraction due to sacral nerve stimulation, by atropine, as reported by Langley and Anderson (1) and Langley (2), was not confirmed by Henderson (4). The experimental data presented above do however support the observations of Langley and Anderson if the normal contractile ability in response to filling can be compared to the response of the bladder to nerve stimulation. Atropine was also found to counteract bladder contraction due to pilocarpine, prostigmine, eserine and mecholyl, thus confirming the observations of Langley (2) and Streuli (3) on pilocarpine.

Atropine, it has been shown, can lower a high state of tone in the bladder, as well as abolish rhythmic activity, either normal or drug induced. Henderson (4) contends that atropine does not inhibit bladder contractions due to nerve stimulation, but it does inhibit drug-induced contractions. Henderson and Roepke (5, 6) support this contention on the grounds that atropine is capable of counteracting the peripheral tonic effect but not the ganglionic contractile effect of acetylcholine. Whether this mechanism is similar to that brought into play by the drugs used in the experiments reported is difficult to state. It is more than likely that acetylcholine, which has a very distinct rôle as a humoral intermediary of nerve impulses in peripheral ganglia (Feldberg and Gaddum, 21), acts in an altogether different manner from the drugs studied above. There must be some reason why atropine can abolish contractions induced by pilocarpine, prostigmine, eserine, and mecholyl, and not those produced by acetylcholine. It is not at all unlikely that atropine, in its counteracting effect on the peripheral tonic mechanism, delays the response of the detrusor muscle to stretch and thus increases the capacity of the bladder. Its failure to oppose bladder contraction due to nerve stimulation is probably due to the fact that the stretch reflex is not involved in such contractions. The partial inhibitory effect of atropine on the normal contractile ability of the bladder in response to filling and its more marked inhibitory effect on contractions associated with filling following the administration of stimulating drugs, must be in some way related to the effect of atropine on the peripheral tonic mechanism.

The action of prostigmine, mecholyl, eserine and pilocarpine on the hypotonic bladder is of great value. While pilocarpine was used in the clinical cases reported, there is little doubt that any of the other stimulating drugs would be as effective. That these drugs can bring about the expulsion of urine from a hypotonic cord bladder is an interesting enough phenomenon in itself, but the ability of pilocarpine to produce an automatic bladder in a case that did not develop one spontaneously after a year and a half is indeed extraordinary. This observation indicates that pilocarpine is able to mobilize certain factors in the body which were not able to come into play by themselves.

The rôle of pilocarpine in facilitating the production of an automatic bladder is particularly significant in the light of recent observations made by Wolf (22). The latter author found that there was more rapid recovery from sciatic paralysis in cats given mecholyl, potassium chloride and prostigmine orally, than in cats not given these drugs. The experiments were repeated in rats with similar good results. These findings were applied clinically in cases of Bell's palsy, with prostigmine alone being given orally. The results were gratifying in some cases.

There can be little doubt that in the case of pilocarpine action on the bladder, the factor of nerve regeneration can be safely excluded. The bladder, as a result of the action of pilocarpine, was made reactive to the stretch reflex, to which it was insensitive prior to the use of this drug. That the pilocarpine was not the vital factor is evident from the fact that the automatic bladder persisted even after the pilocarpine was discontinued. Whether acetylcholine mobilization forms the basis of the mechanism brought into play is speculative, but this speculation is not only extremely interesting but also very suggestive of an inestimably valuable therapeutic procedure.

SUMMARY

1. Pilocarpine, prostigmine, eserine and mecholyl have a strong stimulating effect on both the tonus and contractility of the bladder.

2. Atropine has a selective inhibitory effect on the bladder. It can lower a high state of tone and abolish rhythmic activity, whether these states are present normally or are due to stimulating drug activity. Atropine can strongly inhibit bladder contractions due to drug action but only slightly inhibit bladder contractions that are normally present.

3. Ephedrine in large doses was not observed to have any effect on the bladder.

4. The value of atropine in relieving the symptoms of increased bladder tone without the danger of causing urinary retention is pointed out.

5. The stimulating parasympathomimetic drugs have a very beneficial effect on hypotonic bladders due to disease of the nervous system. Pilocarpine, it is shown, is able to stimulate the formation of an automatic bladder in cases with vesical distension and overflow incontinence due to transverse lesions of the spinal cord.

REFERENCES

(1) Langley and Anderson: J. Physiol., **19:** 71, 1895–96.
(2) Langley: J. Physiol., **43:** 125, 1911–12.
(3) Streuli, H.: Zeit. f. Biol., **66:** 167, 1916.
(4) Henderson: Arch. internat. de Pharm. et de Therap., **27:** 205, 1923.
(5) Henderson and Roepke: This Journal, **51:** 97, 1934.
(6) Henderson and Roepke: Ibid., **54:** 408, 1935.
(7) Bayliss and Starling: J. Physiol., **24:** 99, 1899.
(8) LeHeux: Pflüg. Arch. ges. f. Physiol., **179:** 177, 1920.
(9) Cushny: J. Physiol., **41:** 233, 1910–11.
(10) Marden and Williamson: Surg. Gyn. and Obst., **69:** 61, 1939.
(11) Myerson: Jour. Am. Med. Assoc., **110:** 101, 1938.
(12) Greenberg, Loman and Myerson: J. Urology, **40:** 280, 1938.
(13) Levin: This Journal, **62:** 449, 1938.
(14) Langworthy, Kolb and Lewis: Physiology of Micturition. The Williams & Wilkins Co., Baltimore, 1940.
(15) Teitelbaum and Harne: Jour. Lab. and Clin. Med. (in press).
(16) Fulton: Muscular Contraction and the Reflex Control of Movement. The Williams & Wilkins Co., Baltimore, 1926.
(17) Denny-Brown and Robertson: Brain, **56:** 149, 1933.
(18) Langworthy, Lewis, Dees and Hesser: Bull. Johns Hopkins Hosp., **58:** 89, 1936.
(19) Langworthy: Internat. Clin., **3:** 98, 1936.
(20) Dean: Bull. Neurol. Inst. of New York, **6:** 154, 1937.
(21) Feldberg and Gaddum: J. Physiol., **80:** 12p, 1934.
(22) Wolf: J. Nerv. and Ment. Dis., **92:** 614, 1940.

THE INFLUENCE OF GOLD SODIUM THIOMALATE (MYOCRYSIN) ON THE PREVENTION OF HEMOLYTIC STREPTOCOCCUS ARTHRITIS IN RATS[1]

SIDNEY ROTHBARD, D. MURRAY ANGEVINE AND RUSSELL L. CECIL

From the Department of Pathology, Cornell University Medical College, New York City

Received for publication February 27, 1941

Several investigators (1, 2, 3, 4, 5, 6) have shown the therapeutic value of gold preparations in experimental streptococcus infections. Heilman (7) demonstrated that gold sodium thiomalate protected mice against fatal doses of Streptobacillus monoliformis, and Findlay, Mackenzie, MacCallum and Klieneberger (8) reported that gold compounds prevented the development of polyarthritis in rats injected with pleuropneumonia-like organisms. Collier (3) has shown that gold prevents a polyarthritis in rats infected with an arthritis producing agent that he was unable to isolate but which Klieneberger (9) believes to be an organism of the pleuropneumonia-like group. Sabin and Warren (10) recently reported curative effects of inorganic and organic gold compounds on chronic arthritis of mice produced by pleuropneumonia-like organisms.

Because of the present interest in gold in the treatment of arthritis, it seemed desirable to study the effectiveness of gold sodium thiomalate (myocrysin) in the prevention and treatment of arthritis produced in the rat with a hemolytic streptococcus (11). Other investigations were carried out to compare the value of the gold compound with sulfanilamide and sulfathiazole in preventing arthritis. Since the toxic manifestations of gold are too often overlooked, studies were also performed to note what effect this gold salt might have on various organs.

METHODS

Male and female albino rats weighing from 90 to 110 grams were used.

A "matt" culture of a group A hemolytic streptococcus isolated from the blood stream of a patient with septicemia was employed for the production of arthritis. In most of the experiments, cultures were made from a strain that had been kept on artificial media

[1] Aided by a grant from the John and Mary R. Markle, and Ophthalmological Foundations.

for a period of 3 months. A more virulent form of this culture was obtained by injecting the streptococcus intravenously into rats and recovering the organism from the exudate of the joints. One passage only was necessary to increase the virulence of the organism.

The rats were injected into the tail vein with 0.5 cc. of an 18-hour blood broth culture and were examined daily for a period of about 10 to 12 days. Complete autopsies were performed on all the animals. In the experiments in which blood cultures were made, the animals were bled from the tail vein.

The organic gold compound used was an aqueous solution of gold sodium thiomalate (myocrysin) which contains 50 per cent metallic gold. Both the gold and the sulfonamide compounds used for treatment were injected by the subcutaneous route.

Single and multiple injections of gold in experimental arthritis

A group of 16 rats were injected intravenously with 0.5 cc. of streptococcus culture and 8 of them were treated at the time of infection with a subcutaneous injection of 2.5 mgm. of gold sodium thiomalate (table 1). This was repeated after 24 and 48 hours. All of the treated group that received 3 injections of the drug were protected while all the controls developed the disease. The treated animals did not appear ill at any time in the course of the experiment, whereas the controls, in addition to developing arthritis within 24 to 36 hours after infection, showed ruffled coats, were less active and lost weight.

TABLE 1

Arthritis in rats infected with 0.5 cc. of a hemolytic streptococcus culture and treated with 2.5 mgm. of myocrysin

	NUMBER OF RATS	NUMBER OF INJECTIONS	ARTHRITIS		AVERAGE NUMBER OF JOINTS PER RAT
			Number	Per cent	
Treated	8	3	0		0
Controls	8		8	100.0	3
Treated	39	2	13	33.3	1.7
Controls	28		26	92.9	3
Treated	8	1	5	62.5	3.6
Controls	8		7	87.5	4.9

A larger group of 67 animals were used in an experiment to determine whether two injections of gold would prevent the development of arthritis. Thirty-nine rats were treated with 2.5 mgm. of gold at the time of infection and again 24 hours later, while 28 animals were used as controls (table 1). In this experiment, 33.3 per cent of the group treated with 2 injections of myocrysin developed arthritis; only 66.7 per cent showed protection. The degree of protection was not so great as when 3 injections of gold were given but the average number of joints involved in the animals of the treated group was less than in the control group.

A third group of rats were infected in a similar manner and treated with one injection of 2.5 mgm. of myocrysin (table 1). Of the 8 treated animals, 5 or 62.5 per cent developed arthritis or only 37.5 per cent were protected. This experiment indicates that multiple injections of gold are more efficacious in preventing arthritis than single injections.

The effect of gold before infection with Streptococcus hemolyticus

Since the previous experiment showed that gold prevents arthritis when given after the inoculation of streptococcus, it appeared desirable to note the effect of gold when given prior to the infection. Three groups of 8 rats each were given a subcutaneous injection of 2.5 mgm. of gold on 2 successive days and then were infected with 0.5 cc. of hemolytic streptococcus culture at 6, 24 or 48 hours respectively following the last gold injection (table 2). When gold was injected 6 hours prior to infection, 3 of 8 animals did not develop arthritis. However, when it was given 24 or 48 hours before, no protection was demonstrable.

TABLE 2

Arthritis in rats infected with 0.5 cc. of a hemolytic streptococcus culture following 2 daily subcutaneous injections of 2.5 mgm. of myocrysin

NUMBER OF RATS	TIME INFECTED AFTER LAST GOLD INJECTION	ARTHRITIS		AVERAGE NUMBER OF JOINTS PER RAT
		Number	Per cent	
	hours			
8	6	5	62.5	1.4
8	24	8	100.0	3.2
8	48	8	100.0	3.3

The effect of gold on the hemolytic streptococcus made virulent by passage

During the course of these studies there was a slight diminution in the ability of this strain of streptococcus to produce arthritis. To increase the virulence of the organism, a rat was infected by intravenous injection and a hemolytic streptococcus was cultivated from the synovial membrane of an infected joint. This culture was used in the subsequent experiments. When it was injected, the arthritis appeared earlier and was more acute, but the number of involved joints in each animal was no greater than when a less virulent culture was used. To determine the influence of myocrysin on the more virulent or passage culture, 46 rats were infected intravenously with 0.5 cc. Twenty-five were treated at the time of infection and again at 24 hours with 2.5 mgm. of gold. Eighteen (72 per cent) of the 24 treated rats and 20 (95.5 per cent) of the untreated group developed arthritis (table 3). In other words, there was a protection of only 28 per cent in the treated animals whereas in an earlier group, similarly treated but infected with the less virulent culture, a 66.7 per cent protection was observed (table 1). This experiment demonstrated that when a more virulent culture is used, myocrysin is less effective in protecting the rat against the development of arthritis.

Because the amount of gold employed was not very effective against the virulent culture, the dosage of the drug was increased. Twenty-four rats were infected with the more virulent streptococcus, and half were treated immediately, at 24 and 48 hours with 10 mgm. of gold (table 3). Two of the treated group developed arthritis; there was a protection of 83.3 per cent.

TABLE 3

Arthritis in 3 groups of rats infected with 0.5 cc. of "virulent" hemolytic streptococcus culture and treated at various intervals after injection with different amounts of myocrysin

	NUMBER OF RATS	INJECTION OF GOLD		ARTHRITIS		AVERAGE NUMBER OF JOINTS PER RAT
		Amount	Time treated, hours	Number	Per cent	
		mgm.				
Treated	25	2.5(2x)	Immediately; 24	18	72.0	3
Controls	21			20	95.5	2.5
Treated	12*	10(3x)	Immediately; 24; 48	2	16.7	1.5
Controls	12			12	100.0	2.3
Treated	6	5(2x)	Immediately; 24	1	12.5	2
Controls	6			6	100.0	3

* 6 animals died 3 days after infection.

Although 6 of the 12 treated animals died 3 days after the injection of culture, sufficient time had elapsed for the development of arthritis, as it had appeared in all of the controls by this time. This amount of gold is usually well tolerated by a normal animal, but it will frequently kill an infected animal. A similar incidence of arthritis (12.5 per cent) was noted in a group of 6 rats which had received the same culture but were treated with two 5 mgm. doses of myocrysin immediately and 24 hours after the injection of bacteria. No deaths were noted among these animals.

Comparative value of gold and sulfonamide compounds

Sulfanilamide and sulfathiazole were selected for comparison with myocrysin in 2 experiments, in one of which the doses varied, while in the other they were the same. The animals were infected with 0.5 cc. of an 18-hour broth culture of hemolytic streptococci and treated at the time of infection and 24 hours later with subcutaneous injections of the drugs. Sulfanilamide and sulfathiazole afforded better protection than gold when adequate doses were given (table 4), but if equal amounts of the chemotherapeutic agents were used, gold appeared to be the most effective (table 5). However, the amount of the gold used in the second experiment was near the lethal dose while that of the other two drugs was far below this level. Therefore, one

TABLE 4

Arthritis in rats infected with 0.5 cc. of a hemolytic streptococcus culture and treated immediately and at 24 hours with various therapeutic agents

THERAPEUTIC AGENT	AMOUNT OF INJECTION	NUMBER OF RATS	ARTHRITIS	
			Number	Per cent
	mgm.			
Sulfanilamide	100	7	0	0
Sulfathiazole	35	9	0	0
Myocrysine	2.5	8	2	25
Controls		4	4	100

TABLE 5

Arthritis in rats infected with 0.5 cc. of a hemolytic streptococcus culture and treated immediately with various therapeutic agents

THERAPEUTIC AGENT	AMOUNT OF INJECTION	NUMBER OF RATS	ARTHRITIS	
			Number	Per cent
	mgm.			
Sulfanilamide	5	6	6	100.0
Sulfathiazole	5	6	6	100.0
Myocrysine	5	6	1	16.6
Controls		6	6	100.0

can safely give more sulfanilamide or sulfathiazole to obtain a favorable response, whereas it is not safe to increase the amount of gold beyond a certain level.

Since these three drugs were found to protect the rats from streptococcus arthritis, the question arose as to what effect they would have on the arthritis once it was present. Twelve of 18 rats that had developed arthritis were given daily subcutaneous injections of 2.5 mgm. of gold sodium thiomalate for a period of 7 days; the remaining 6 were not treated. Arthritis did not develop in any other joints of the treated animals nor was there any apparent alteration in the affected joints. The control rats, on the other hand, continued to develop arthritis in other joints. In another group of 13 rats with arthritis, 10 were treated subcutaneously with 0.1 gram of sulfanilamide in a 2.5 per cent solution for 4 days, and the findings were essentially the same as in the group injected with the gold salt. The same procedure was used for sulfathiazole, and similar results were obtained. These observations on a limited number of rats indicate that these compounds are not effective once the arthritis is established. However, further experiments of this nature are in progress.

The bactericidal effect of gold on the hemolytic streptococcus

Sealed glass tubes containing streptococci and gold, or streptococci alone, were placed in a mixing machine so that there was adequate contact of the gold with the streptococcus culture. Mixing machines of this nature have been used by the following investigators (12, 13, 14, 15). When the tubes were sealed, the contents were shown to be under anaerobic conditions (16) by the methylene blue method.

The tubes were fastened to a square box on the machine and rotated by a motor in an incubator at 37.5°C. at about 7 r.p.m. At 6-, 12-, 24- and 48-hour intervals, 0.1 cc. of the contents of the tubes were removed and mixed with agar and defibrinated horse blood. This mixture was poured into a Petri dish, and colony counts were made after 48 hours.

Myocrysin in a concentration of 1:2000 was found to have a bactericidal effect on hemolytic streptococci in a dilution of 10^{-6} and 10^{-7} (table 6). Dawson and Hobby (4) have recently described the bacteriostatic effects of this same gold compound on hemolytic streptococci, but the concentration of gold used was 1:10,000 which is considerably less than that used in these experiments.

Although this drug was bactericidal *in vitro*, experiments *in vivo* failed to yield as convincing results. A group of rats was infected with streptococci and half were treated with gold sodium thiomalate while the remainder were used as controls. All the animals were bled from the tail vein at varying intervals. Those which were treated with 2.5 mgm. of gold were killed at 24 hours after infection and those treated with 5 mgm. after 48 hours. The number of organisms found in the peripheral blood of the treated group was essentially the same as in that of the non-treated. Cultures of the bone marrow, spleen and liver made at autopsy also failed to show any marked differences (table 7).

The effect of gold on the peripheral blood and organs of rats

Four complete blood counts were made on each of 6 normal rats over a period of 10 days. The average red blood cell count was 6.6 million, the white blood cells 11,152 and the differential count: 27.8 per cent neutrophils, 0.39 per cent basophils, 0.61 per cent eosinophils, 59.8 per cent lymphocytes,

TABLE 6

Bactericidal action of myocrysin in a concentration of 1:2000 on the hemolytic streptococcus

DILUTION OF BACTERIA	COMPOUND USED	NUMBER OF ORGANISMS PER CC.				
		Original plate count	6 hours	12 hours	24 hours	48 hours
10^{-6}	Myocrysin	25	0	0	0	0
10^{-6}	Broth control	29	58	39,000	186,000	65,000
10^{-7}	Myocrysin	4	0	0	0	0
10^{-7}	Broth control	5	9	26,000	121,000	41,000

TABLE 7

Number of hemolytic streptococci recovered from the blood stream and organs of rats infected with 0.5 cc. of culture and treated immediately with myocrysin

	RAT NUMBER	AMOUNT OF MYOCRYSIN	COLONIES PER CC. OF BLOOD					TIME KILLED	BONE MARROW	SPLEEN	LIVER
			2 hours	4 hours	6 hours	24 hours	48 hours				
		mgm.						*hours*			
Treated	1	2.5	600	660	860	260		24	∞	4,230	6,640
	2	2.5	40	200	20	0		24	27	11,140	5,562
Controls	3		20	80	120	30		24	22	18,900	2,546
	4		120	540	800	2,700		24	37	7,575	9,981
Treated	5	5	100	20	40	980	0	48	0	520	0
	6	5	40	20	20	∞	20	48	0	200	520
	7	5	8,860	200	300	5,120	600	48	0	3,640	7,920
Controls	8		20	180	80	120	0	48	45	80	0
	9		1,000	10,220	140	10,060	220	48	0	1,440	1,012
	10		7,940	4,240	8,260	8,900	0	48	0	360	1,288

10.1 per cent monocytes, and 1.3 per cent unclassified forms. The rats were then injected subcutaneously with 2.5 mgm. of gold daily for 6 days, allowed to rest for 7 days and again treated for a 6-day period. An eosinophilia that ranged from 10 to 15 per cent developed in all the animals and was the only change observed in the peripheral blood picture. Eosinophilia increased shortly after the first injection of gold and returned to normal gradually when gold was stopped. Although platelets were not counted they did not appear to be diminished in the blood smears.

To determine the toxic effect of single doses of the gold compound, a group of 20 rats was injected subcutaneously with various doses of myocrysin. The animals injected with 50 to 100 mgm. died within 24 hours; those with 30 mgm. in 72 hours, and those with 20 mgm. in 96 to 120 hours. The animals that were injected with 15 and 10 mgm. lived for 7 days and then were sacrificed.

No abnormal changes were observed at necropsy in any of the organs with the exception of the kidneys and in these, severe lesions were noted in all animals that died within 120 hours. The kidneys were soft, large, and pale yellow-gray in color, and on hemisection the parenchyma bulged slightly. In the rats that received 20 mgm. of gold a narrow zone in the outer part of the medulla was conspicuous as a pale band (fig. 1, *B*, and fig. 2); with larger doses, the cortex had a gray-white pallor and was sharply demarcated from the medulla (fig. 1, *C*). Microscopic examination showed that with the 20 mgm. dose the greatest change was in the outermost zone of the medulla (fig. 2). This area corresponds to the part of the tubules designated by Cowdry (17) as the medullary segments of the proximal convoluted tubules in the mammalian kidney. Dible and Hay (18) have shown that fatty changes first appear in starved rabbits at the same site, but they describe this part of the tubule as the wide portion of the descending loop of Henle. It appears that both authors are referring to the same structure which is the distal part of the proximal convoluted tubule. It takes an approximately straight course through the outermost zone of the medulla and through the cortical rays (Cowdry (17)).

When the kidneys of rats that received 30 mgm. of gold were examined microscopically, both the medullary segments of the proximal convoluted and of the distal convoluted tubules, which occasionally extend to the capsule, were dilated and contained albuminous fluid, epithelial cellular debris and casts. The cells of these tubules were swollen, contained colloid droplets in many places and in part had undergone necrosis. The necrotic epithelium of some of the tubules took a deep blue stain with hematoxylin as the result of calcium deposits. The injured cells were still recognizable; in other places the lumen was indistinguishable. Coagulated albuminous material was present in subcapsular spaces of the glomeruli.

The extent of the renal damage was found to depend on the dosage of the drug. When 10 or 15 mgm. were injected, only the medullary segment of the proximal convoluted loops showed necrosis of the epithelial cells and the tubules contained albuminous material and casts. When 20 or 30 mgm. were used, many proximal, as well as distal convoluted tubules underwent necrosis and calcification. The loops of Henle contained albuminous material but the epithelial cells were apparently not involved. When 50 to 100 mgm. were injected, the necrosis was more extensive and included the loops of Henle as well as the proximal and distal parts of the convoluted tubules. The collecting tubules contained albuminous fluid and casts but the epithelium was not injured.

The selective action of a toxic agent for a specific part of the renal tubule is demonstrated in these experiments.

In order to note the effect of prolonged administration of gold, 14 rats were given repeated injections of 1.6 to 2.5 mgm. of gold over a period of 8 weeks, and the animals were killed after different intervals following the first injection. Those that lived longest had received 24 injections of gold. Practically all of the animals showed some nephrosis but it varied considerably in severity and in no instance caused the death of an animal. One rat that received 2 injections of gold developed severe icterus, but no changes were found in the liver.

DISCUSSION

Gold sodium thiomalate will prevent streptococcus arthritis in rats, but its ability to inhibit the disease varies with the amount of the drug and the number of injections that are given. If groups of rats are infected with bacteria after either 6, 24 or 48 hours following 2 daily subcutaneous injections of 2.5 mgm. of gold, only 37.5 per cent of the animals are protected in the first group, and none in the second and third groups. On the other hand, if the drug is given at the time of infection and again after 24 and 48 hours, all animals are protected. These observations indicate that the quantity of gold in the body must reach a certain level before the drug becomes effective against the bacteria. The effect of the gold is transient since it was found that in rats protected against streptococcus arthritis by gold treatments and re-infected with bacteria a second time the incidence of arthritis was as high as in the non-treated controls.

The effectiveness of gold was observed to vary with the virulence of the culture. When the more virulent "passage" strain was used, 3 doses of 10 mgm. each were necessary to protect 83.3 per cent of animals, whereas when the less virulent culture was injected, 3 doses of only 2.5 mgm. were adequate to inhibit the development of arthritis in all of the animals. Moreover, 50 per cent of the rats died after they had received 30 mgm. of gold, and the cause of death was found to be a severe renal lesion for which the gold was directly responsible. The larger doses did not protect animals against the virulent strain because they were lethal.

Although Smith (19) showed that it is not possible to block out completely the mononuclear phagocytes of the body, an attempt was made to determine if interference with these cells has any inhibitory influence on the protective action of gold injections in rats. The animals were injected intravenously with large doses of methylene blue or india ink. Twelve hours later cultures of streptococci were injected, and the animals were treated with gold. Myocrysin was found to be just as effective in preventing arthritis as in the experiments in which no dyes had been used.

CONCLUSIONS

1. Gold sodium thiomalate is an effective chemotherapeutic agent in the prevention of arthritis produced by a hemolytic streptococcus in rats. Its effectiveness is less against a more virulent strain of the same culture.
2. Sulfanilamide and sulfathiazole are more effective in the prevention of this disease than gold.
3. Neither gold nor the sulfonamide compounds cure arthritis once it is established.
4. *In vitro*, myocrysin is bactericidal under anaerobic conditions.
5. A severe renal injury resulting in death has been observed in rats weighing 100 grams after an injection of 20 mgm. or more of gold.
6. Myocrysin protects rats against hemolytic streptococcus arthritis but since the effective dose is so close to the lethal dose, great caution is necessary in its administration.

Acknowledgment is made to Merck and Company for supplying the Myocrysin.

REFERENCES

(1) Collier: Med. Klin., **29:** 1447, 1933.
(2) Collier and Verhoog: Ztschr. f. Immunitätsf., **90:** 174, 1937.
(3) Collier: Ztschr. f. Immunitätsf., **95:** 32, 1939.
(4) Dawson and Hobby: This Journal, **69:** 359, 1940.
(5) Feldt: Deutsch. med. Woch., **61:** 593, 1935.
(6) Schiemann and Feldt: Ztschr. f. Hyg., **106:** 83, 1926.
(7) Heilman: Science, **91:** 366, 1940.
(8) Findlay, Mackenzie, MacCallum and Klieneberger: Lancet, **2:** 7, 1939.
(9) Klieneberger: J. Hyg., **40:** 204, 1940.
(10) Sabin and Warren: J. Bact., **40:** 823, 1941.
(11) Rothbard: Proc. Soc. Exp. Biol. and Med., **44:** 379, 1940.
(12) Rosenow: J. Infect. Dis., **3:** 683, 1906.
(13) Fenn: J. Gen. Physiol., **3:** 439, 1920–21.
(14) Robertson and Sia: J. Exp. Med., **39:** 219, 1924.

(15) TODD: Brit. J. Exp. Path., **8:** 1, 1927.
(16) DEGARA: Personal communication, 1940.
(17) COWDRY: Special Cytology, Vol. II. Paul B. Hoeber, New York, 1932.
(18) DIBLE AND HAY: J. Path. and Bact., **51:** 1, 1940.
(19) SMITH: J. Exp. Med., **51:** 395, 1930.

PLATE 1

FIG. 1. *A*, kidney of a normal rat; *B*, showing moderate degeneration at the cortico-medullary junction of the kidney of a rat 96 hours after it had received 20 mgm. of gold; *C*, showing the grey white pallor of the cortex which is sharply demarcated from the medulla of the kidney of a rat 72 hours after it had received 30 mgm. of gold.

FIG. 2. Photomicrograph showing necrosis and calcification of the epithelium of the medullary segment of the proximal convoluted tubules at the cortico-medullary junction. × 15.

FIG. 3. Photomicrograph of kidney (fig. 1, *C*) showing edema, necrosis and calcification of the epithelium of proximal and distal convoluted tubules. The calcium is stained black in the photograph. The rat had received 30 mgm. of gold and died within 96 hours. × 80.

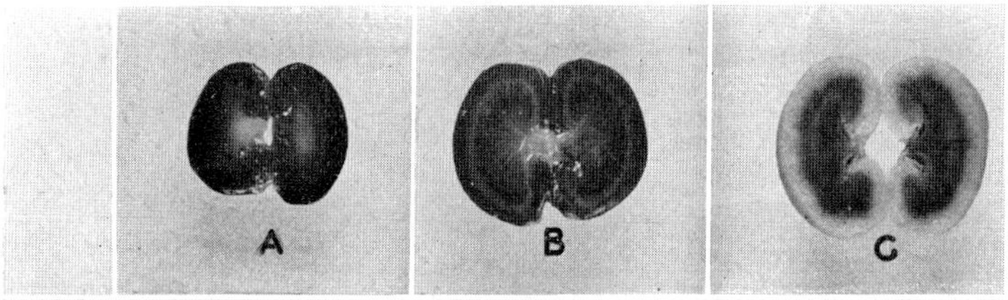

1

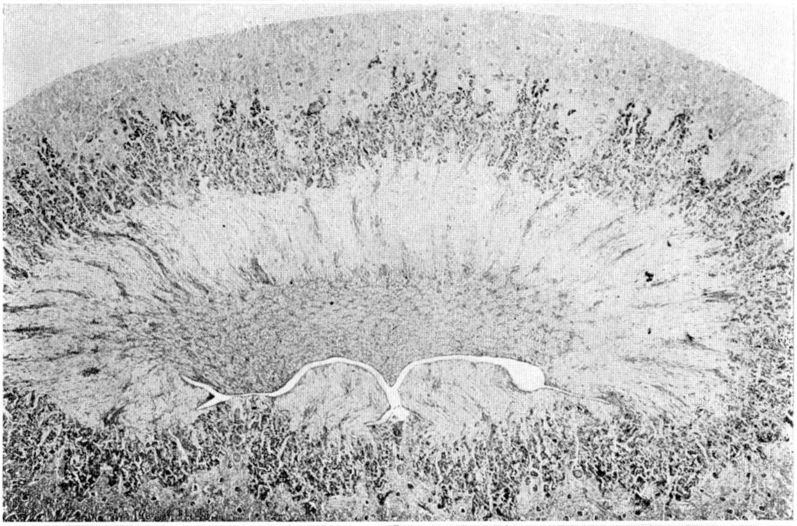

2

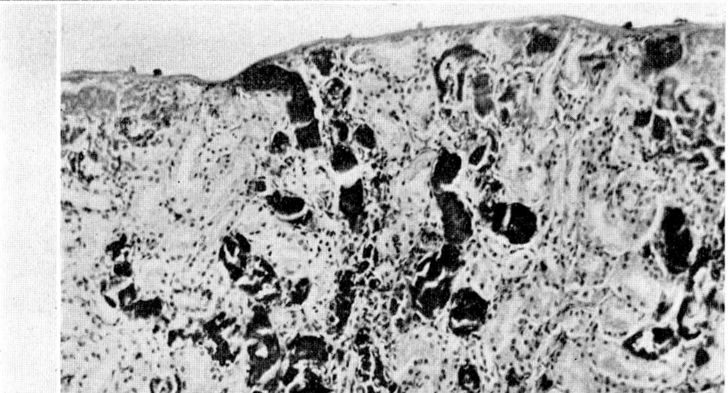

3

PLATE 1

THE EFFECT OF BARBITURIC AND THIOBARBITURIC ACID DERIVATIVES ON THE PYLORIC SPHINCTER AND STOMACH IN UNANESTHETIZED DOGS[1]

CHARLES M. GRUBER AND CHARLES M. GRUBER, JR.

From the Department of Pharmacology, Jefferson Medical College, Philadelphia, Pennsylvania

Received for publication March 1, 1941

The effects of barbituric and thiobarbituric acid derivatives on isolated segments of small intestine have been studied by numerous investigators (1), as have the actions of barbiturates on the intact stomach, small intestine and colon (2). Olmsted and Giragossintz (3) observed the effect of amytal anesthesia on glucose tolerance in dogs. They believed their "experiments show that under amytal the pyloric sphincter is maintained so tightly closed that sugar introduced into the stomach cannot pass into the duodenum." Although this work was reported in 1929, no one has attempted to determine whether or not the barbiturates have an action upon the pylorus which is opposite to their effect on the remainder of the gastro-intestinal system, nor have the thiobarbiturates been investigated as to their effect on the activity of the stomach.

METHODS

Six unanesthetized, trained dogs were used in this research. These animals, while under ether anesthesia, had been operated on to produce permanent gastric and duodenal fistulae according to the methods outlined by Thomas, Crider and Mogan (4). At the time of the experiments they had fully recovered from the operations. The changes in height of the contractions of the pyloric sphincter were recorded by means of a pressure tonometer (5) connected to a glass U-tube in which bromoform was used. The changes in general tonus and the force of the contractions of the stomach were recorded by means of a water manometer. Rubber balloons placed in the stomach and pylorus as described by Thomas, Crider and Mogan (6) were connected by means of rubber tubing to the respective manometers.

Sodium amytal, in 10 per cent solution, was injected slowly into the saphenous vein on 17 different occasions. The amount used in three of these was 15, in six 20, two each of 25 and 30, and in four 40 mgm. per kilogram. A 10 per cent solution of sodium pentobarbital was injected intravenously in doses of 20 mgm. per kilogram in three experiments and 30 mgm. per kilogram in eight. Sodium evipal was administered in doses of 30 mgm. per kilogram twice and 40 mgm. per kilogram six times. Sodium ortal was injected in doses of 20 mgm. per kilogram twice and 30 mgm. per kilogram six times.

[1] This research was made possible by a grant by Parke, Davis and Company for research in science.

Five per cent solutions of pentothal sodium (sodium thiopentobarbital) in 20 mgm. per kilogram doses and sodium thioethamyl in 40 mgm. per kilogram doses were injected 15 and 10 times each respectively. Each animal was used but once a week.

RESULTS

Barbiturates. The results of the 44 experiments performed on six trained dogs with the use of sodium amytal, sodium pentobarbital, sodium evipal, and sodium ortal are presented in table 1. Obviously all of the barbiturates had similar actions on the contractions of the pylorus and stomach. Sodium ortal appeared to be somewhat less depressant than the three other barbiturates tested. It will also be noted that sodium amytal caused the greatest excitation since 11 of the 17 experiments had to be discontinued before the

TABLE 1

	CONTRACTIONS INHIBITED			COMPLETE RECOVERY			EXPERIMENTS DISCONTINUED DUE TO EXCITATION	
	Number of experiments	Duration: Extremes	Duration: Average	Number of experiments	Time: Extremes	Time: Average	Number	Average time
		minutes	*minutes*		*minutes*	*minutes*		*minutes*
Pylorus:								
Amytal*	15	2-70	20	6	30-165	77	11	41
Pentobarbital	10	1-14	6	8	48-118	79	3	39
Evipal	8	9-78	24	4	70- 90	77	4	64
Ortal	8	1-15	7	6	40- 64	50	2	27
Stomach:								
Amytal	9	2-45	8	6	38-130	77	11	71
Pentobarbital	3	1-22	8	7	60-118	82	4	53
Evipal	5	5-12	9	5	37- 90	72	3	70
Ortal	4	2- 5	4	6	36- 64	47	2	27

* The sodium salts of the barbiturates were used.

organs returned to their normal state. All of the barbiturates tested caused a decrease in the tonus of the stomach. Usually the time of recovery in tonus paralleled the recovery of the contractions of the organ.

Our findings with the use of sodium amytal do not substantiate the direct observations on the pylorus made by Olmsted and Giragossintz (10). In the 17 experiments performed on our 6 dogs, except occasionally in one animal, sodium amytal in the doses used caused complete inhibition of the movements of the pylorus for a period varying from 3 to 63 (average 20) minutes. In 6 of the 17 experiments no visible activity of the stomach was observed for a period of 2 to 30 minutes following the injection. The height of the contractions and the general tonus of the stomach were decreased in every experiment. In only 6 experiments with the use of sodium amytal did we feel justified in continuing the observations until the functions of the organs returned to normal. In all of the other experiments of this series the animals as they recovered from the anesthetic action of the drug showed excitation and contracted their abdominal muscles so frequently and vigorously that the increased intra-abdominal pressure made it necessary to discontinue the experiments. It is evident that results obtained under such adverse experimental conditions must be inconclusive and worthless.

Figure 1 illustrates the characteristic responses of the pylorus and stomach to all of the barbiturates used. In this figure, at *1* between the arrows, 40

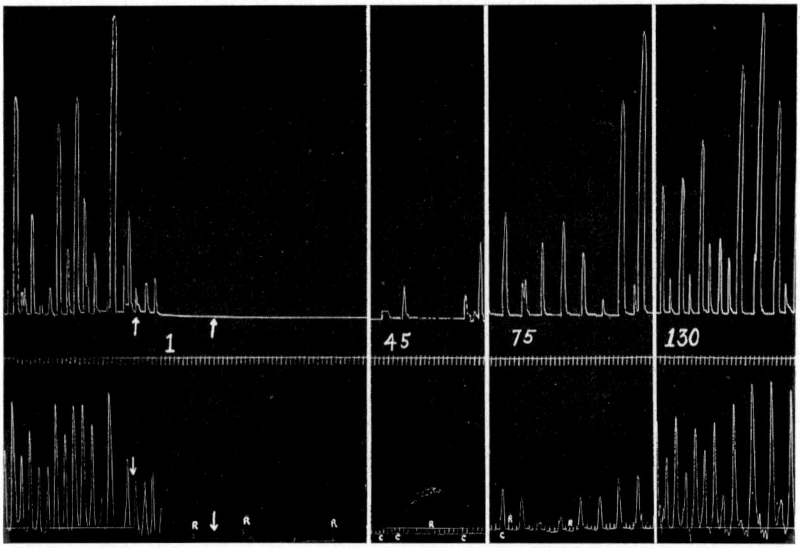

FIG. 1. Unless otherwise indicated in this and all following figures, the top curve records the action of the pylorus and the bottom one that of the stomach. Time in intervals of 6 seconds.

Nonanesthetized male dog weighing 24 kgm. with permanent fistulae of stomach and duodenum. Between the arrows at *1*, 40 mgm. per kilogram of a 10 per cent solution of sodium amytal were injected intravenously. The numerals 45, 75 and 130 indicate the number of minutes after the injection that the short sections shown were recorded. *R* indicates the influence of respiration on the record and *C* the contractions of the organ. Record reduced to one-fourth original size.

mgm. per kilogram of sodium amytal were injected intravenously in a 24 kgm. dog. Complete inhibition of movement of both the stomach and pyorus are seen. Forty-five minutes later, as seen in 45, insignificant contractions of the stomach occur, marked *C* in the record, and moderately strong contractions of the pylorus begin again. The pyloric contractions return to approximately their normal height 75 minutes after the injection at 75, and the contractions of the stomach became normal 130 minutes after the injection. Immediately after this record was taken the animal became excited and the experiment was discontinued.

A few curves like figure 2, which was the result of an injection of sodium evipal, were also obtained upon the injection of sodium amytal. In these cases the excitement occurred usually as the animal recovered from the anesthetic effect of the drug. In figure 2, 40 mgm. per kilogram of sodium evipal were injected intravenously at *1*. The letter *X* in the figure indicates changes in the record due to increased intra-abdominal pressure caused by deep

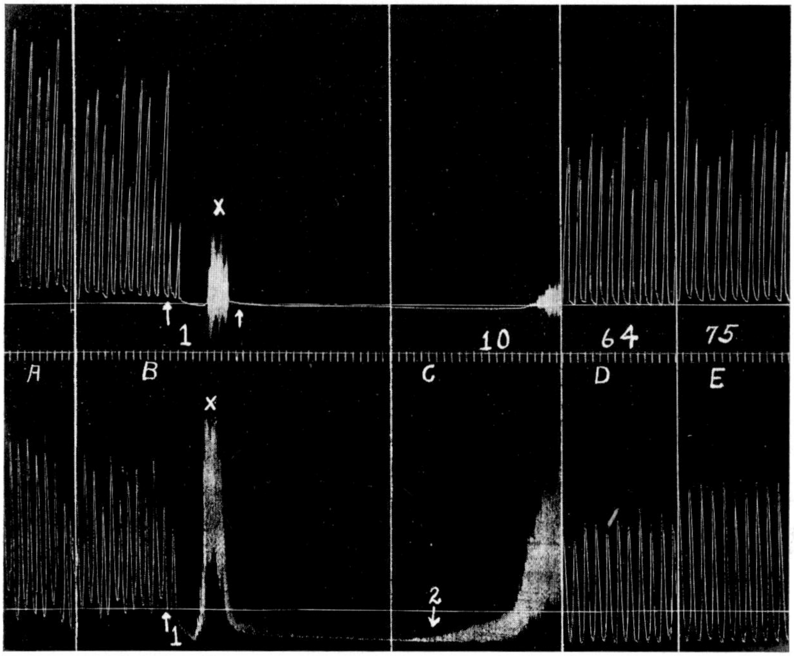

FIG. 2. Same dog as that used in figure 1. Time in intervals of 10 seconds. Section A of the control record was taken 5 minutes before section B. Between the arrows at *1*, 40 mgm. per kilogram of sodium evipal were injected intravenously. *X* records the movements of the writing points of the two levers due to excitation of the animal caused by the slow injection of the drug. The elevations of the writing points here are due to increased intra-abdominal pressure from the contractions of the thoracic and abdominal muscles. The small changes in the gastric record are due to superimposed respiratory contractions. Record C was taken 10 minutes after the injection. At *2*, the dog recovering from the anesthesia again showed excitation which lasted 50 minutes. Record D is a continuation of the experiment 64 minutes after the injection of the drug and E 11 minutes later. The general tonus of the stomach in E is still definitely below the level of the control. Following this, the experiment had to be discontinued. Record reduced one-half.

respirations and excitement. This is not always seen and is apparently dependent upon the rate of the injection of the drug, the dose administered, and the susceptibility of the animal. As the first excitation abated in this experiment, it is noted that the activity of both organs ceased and the general tonus of both is again below that of the control level and equal to that seen before the early excitement had set in. Eleven minutes after the injection at *2* in section C, the animal again became restless. Here, as in record B at *X*, the apparent elevation in the general tonus of the stomach is not due to an actual increase in the general tonus of the organ but due to increased intra-abdominal pressure, the result of the contractions of the abdominal muscles, thoracic muscles and the diaphragm. In this animal the second period of excitation lasted 50 minutes. Although the height of the muscular contractions of the organs had returned to approximately normal 75 minutes after the injection, nevertheless, 90 minutes later when the experiment had to be terminated the general tonus of the organs was still below that of the control level.

One dog was especially sensitive to all of the barbiturates. It required about two-thirds the usual dose to cause profound depression of the central nervous system. Moreover, the animal did not recover completely for hours

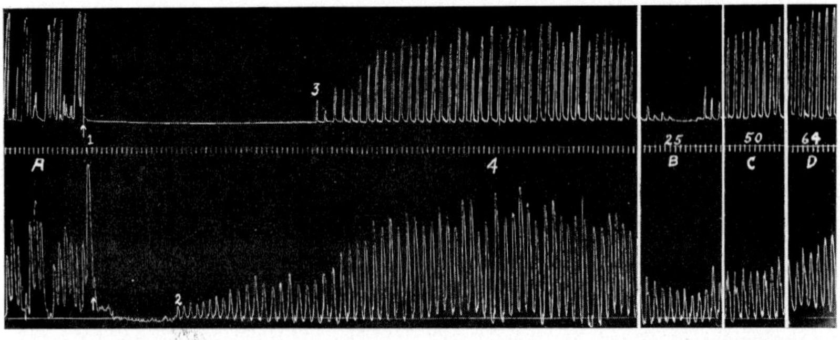

FIG. 3. Unanesthetized male dog weighing 14.5 kgm. A is the control record and B, C and D are sections taken 25, 50 and 64 minutes respectively after the injection of the drug. At *1*, 20 mgm. per kilogram of sodium ortal were injected intravenously. At *2*, the stomach began to contract with increasing force and at *3*, the pylorus began to contract similarly, both reaching their maximum heights at *4*, approximately 15 minutes after the injection of the drug. Following this the contractions decreased until they reached the height seen in section B. Record reduced to one-fourth original size.

after the injection of a small dose of sodium amytal. In some experiments on this dog an injection of any barbiturate produced in both organs, after a temporary inhibition, a temporary increase in activity like that seen in figure 3, here caused by an injection of sodium ortal. In this figure at *1*, 20 mgm. per kilogram of sodium ortal were injected intravenously. There resulted a temporary inhibition of all activity of the pylorus and decreased activity of the stomach. Two minutes after the injection of the drug, the stomach at *2*, and 6 minutes later the pylorus at *3*, began to contract with increasing force until a peak was reached at *4*, approximately 15 minutes after the injection of the drug. Subsequently a gradual reduction in the height of the contractions of the organs occurred, as seen in record B, 25 minutes after the injection. Complete recovery of the pylorus is seen in *D* 64 minutes after the dose was administered.

In some experiments with this animal complete inhibition of the pylorus occurred while the stomach, after a temporary inhibition, began to contract with increasing vigor, reaching a maximum 4 to 9 minutes after the injection and returning again to the depressed state equally as abruptly as it increased. The peak contractions were usually two-thirds as high as those of the control, although occasionally they were higher. In other experiments the stomach remained inactive and the pylorus showed this peculiar response to the drug.

Thiobarbiturates. The responses of the stomach and pylorus to intravenous injections of the thiobarbiturates were unpredictable. They varied not only from animal to animal but also in the same animal on different occasions and with varying dosages. Complete inhibition of the pylorus followed 7 of the 15 injections of pentothal sodium and all of the injections of sodium thioethamyl. In one animal one injection of 20 mgm. per kilogram of pentothal sodium caused complete inhibition of the pylorus lasting 237 minutes, whereas in the same animal on another occasion a similar injection only decreased the height of the contractions of the organ. In the former experiment the contractions became normal in 293 minutes and in the latter 96 minutes after the injection. In both instances the height of the contractions of the stomach was diminished. In the first experiment cited above the contractions became normal in 247 minutes, in the second experiment in 78 minutes. In the latter experiment the thiobarbiturate had no effect on the general tonus of the stomach but in the first it was still below that of the control level 5 hours after the injection.

In the remaining experiments with sodium thioethamyl and pentothal sodium, the height of the contractions of the pylorus, which was diminished by the thiobarbiturate, returned to normal in 12 to 82 (average 33) minutes. In the 18 experiments performed on these animals the contractions of the stomach were completely inhibited only three times. In all cases the height of the contractions of the stomach returned to normal 3 to 60 (average 28) minutes. In 19 of the 25 experiments the general tonus of the stomach was decreased, in the others it was either not affected or increased. The usual record was similar to that shown in figure 1.

In some of the experiments the injections of either pentothal sodium or sodium thioethamyl were followed by increased activity of both the pylorus and stomach, as seen in figure 4. This stimulation is usually followed by a depression lasting for several minutes. In this figure at *1*, 15 mgm. per kilogram of pentothal sodium were injected intravenously in a 13.9 kgm. dog. The general tonus and the height of the contractions of the stomach increased immediately after the injection of the drug, then diminished. The contractions of the pylorus increased in height and rate. Antiperistaltic contractions were noted at points *X* in the record, although the pylorus was again normal at the end of the record at *2*. The contractions of the stomach were still subnormal.

General tonus. There are reports in the literature showing an elevation in the general tonus and increased activity of the intestine and stomach following their relaxed state due to the action of barbituric acid derivatives (7). In our experiments on the pylorus and stomach there have been no such findings, instead the general tonus of the pylorus and stomach either returned to a normal level or remained subnormal one to 5 hours after the injection of the barbiturate. In no instance except in those experiments in which the animals showed excitement, thus causing increased intra-abdominal pressure, did we see an appreciable elevation in the writing points of the manometers. Moreover the mere fact that as the animal recovers from the anesthetic the abdominal muscles become taut would increase the intra-abdominal pressure and record an elevation in the writing lever. The elevation of the writing lever in these experiments we believe is a mechanical increase and is not due to

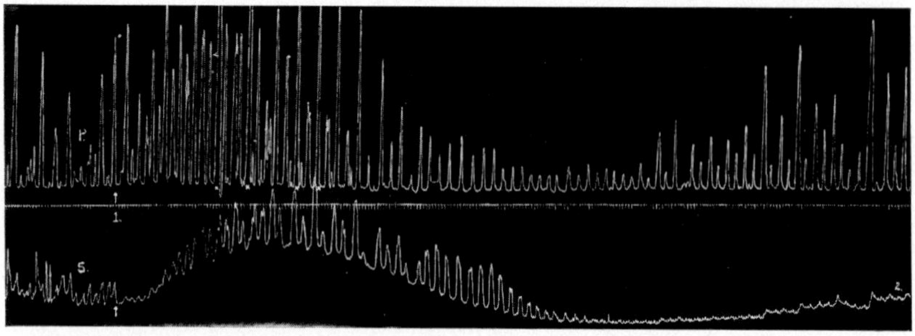

FIG. 4. Same dog as used in figure 3. At *1*, 15 mgm. per kilogram of pentothal sodium (sodium thiopentobarbital) in a 5 per cent solution were injected intravenously. Both the pylorus and stomach increase in general tonus and activity for a short time. Antiperistaltic contractions of the pylorus are observed at *X*. Following this temporarily increased activity, both organs show decreased activity. At *2* the height of the pyloric contractions is normal but the contractions of the stomach are still below normal. Shortly after *2* the experiment had to be ended. Record reduced to one-sixth original size.

increased general tonus of the organs. With the thiobarbiturates the results were inconsistent, some showing an increase in the general tonus as the animals recovered from deep anesthesia and others a decrease as the animals slept.

SUMMARY AND CONCLUSIONS

1. The increased emptying time of the stomach by amytal and other barbituric and thiobarbituric acid derivatives is not due to a contracted pyloric sphincter.

2. The sodium salts of amytal, ortal, pentobarbital, evipal, pentothal (thiopentobarbital), and thioethamyl when injected intravenously in anesthetic doses in unanesthetized dogs may cause complete cessation of action of the pylorus and stomach.

3. The height of the contractions of the pylorus and stomach muscles invariably decreases after the injection of the barbiturates but it may increase in some experiments with the thiobarbiturates.

4. The general tonus of the organs is always decreased with the barbiturates but it may in some animals be increased with the thiobarbiturates.

5. In those experiments in which the animal recovered from the anesthesia of the barbiturates without excitation and thus without producing increased intra-abdominal pressure, no increase in either the activity or the general tonus of the organs was noted.

We wish to thank Dr. J. Earl Thomas of the Department of Physiology for the use of two of the animals employed in this investigation. We also express our thanks to Abbott Laboratories for the pentothal, Eli Lilly and Company for the supply of sodium pentobarbital and sodium amytal, and Parke, Davis and Company for the remaining drugs used in this research.

REFERENCES

(1) Redonnet: Arch internat. de pharmacodyn. et de thérap., **30:** 322, 1925; Gruber: This Journal, **30:** 149, 1926; Arnell: Arch. internat. de pharmacodyn. et de thérap., **25:** 228, 1929; Reynolds: Proc. Soc. Exper. Biol. & Med., **28:** 656, 1931; Gruber, Scholten, De Note and Wilson: This Journal, **56:** 341, 1935; Gruber and Gruber: Arch. internat. de pharmacodyn. et de thérap., **63:** 243, 1939.

(2) Gruber, Crawford, Greene and Drayer: This Journal, **42:** 27, 1931; Quigley and Phelps: Ibid., **50:** 420, 1934; Quigley, Barlow and Himmelsbach: Ibid., **50:** 425, 1934; Gruber: Ibid, **56:** 432, 1936.

(3) Olmsted and Giragossintz: Proc. Soc. Exper. Biol. & Med., **27:** 103, 1929.

(4) Thomas, Crider and Mogan: Amer. J. Physiol., **108:** 683, 1934.

(5) Thomas: Amer. J. Physiol., **88:** 498, 1929.

(6) Thomas, Crider and Mogan: Ibid., p. 685.

(7) Quigley, Barlow and Himmelsbach: Loc. cit. p. 430; Burstein: Proc. Soc. Exper. Biol. & Med., **40:** 122, 1939.

THE TOXICITY OF OPTICALLY INACTIVE, *d*- AND *l*-SELENIUM-CYSTINE[1, 2]

A. L. MOXON, K. P. DU BOIS[3] AND R. L. POTTER[4]

South Dakota Agricultural Experiment Station, Brookings, South Dakota

Received for publication March 4, 1941

The toxicity of various organic selenium compounds is of interest because of the evidence indicating that the selenium in seleniferous plants occurs in organic compounds. As yet no organic selenium compounds isolated from plants have been definitely characterized but there have been indications and postulations that selenium-containing amino acids might exist in plants. In most of the work regarding toxicity of selenium, inorganic selenium compounds have been used. Franke and Moxon (1), Smith, Stohlman and Lillie (2), Jones (3), and others have worked on the toxicity of inorganic selenium when administered by intraperitoneal and intravenous injection. Franke (4), Franke and Potter (5), and Munsell, DeVaney and Kennedy (6), among others have described, in some detail, the effects of orally ingested seleniferous foodstuffs on experimental animals. In the above-mentioned work it was generally agreed that the symptoms were similar regardless of the form of selenium administered.

Painter and Franke (7) found that the selenium in cereals is in an organic form. Recently Painter *et al.* (8 and 9) have compared the chemical properties of selenium in seleniferous proteins and in a number of organic selenium compounds. Horn and Jones (10) have reported the isolation of a crystalline selenium containing compound from plant material. They have assigned the formula $C_7H_{14}N_2O_4Se$ based upon percentage composition and have suggested that the compound is a selenium ether of α-amino-butyric acid and α-amino-propionic acid.

[1] Approved for publication by the Director of the South Dakota Agricultural Experiment Station, as contribution No. 128 of the Journal Series.

[2] All three forms of selenium-cystine were synthesized by Dr. Arne Fredga, Upsala University, Upsala, Sweden. For information concerning preparation and properties of selenium-cystine see: Fredga, Svensk Kemisk Tidskrift, **48:** 160–165, 1936; **49:** 124–130, 1937 and **49:** 138–145, 1937.

[3] Present address, McArdle Memorial Institute for Cancer Research, University of Wisconsin, Madison, Wisconsin.

[4] Present address, Department of Biochemistry, University of Wisconsin, Madison, Wisconsin.

Moxon, Anderson and Painter (11) compared the toxicity of a number of organic selenium compounds representing three different types of organic selenium linkages and three different organic radicals linked to selenium. All of the compounds were much less toxic than sodium selenite. Moxon (12) investigated the toxicity of optically inactive selenium-cystine. When injected intraperitoneally into albino rats the toxicity of selenium-cystine was about equal to the toxicity of sodium selenite. It was much more toxic than any of the other organic selenium compounds that we have had an opportunity to study.

In this report the toxicity of selenium in optically inactive selenium-cystine was compared with selenium as it occurs in seleniferous wheat and as a common inorganic form of selenium, sodium selenite. All three of the rations contained the same concentrations of selenium. The toxicity of selenium in the optically active enantiomorphs, *d*- and *l*-selenium-cystine was also investigated.

THE TOXICITY OF OPTICALLY INACTIVE SELENIUM-CYSTINE

Two series of albino rats were used in the comparison of the toxicity of selenium-cystine, seleniferous wheat and sodium selenite. Toxicity measurements were based on food consumption, growth, pathological condition and selenium content of the various organs. The retention of the three forms of selenium was also compared by determining the amount of selenium excreted in the urine and in the feces in some metabolism studies.

The first series (series 145) consisted of 24 albino rats, which were divided into four groups of 6 rats each. The animals were twenty-eight days old when placed on experiment and the average weight of each group was within five grams of the average weight of the series.

The first group, the control group, received the following ration:

	per cent
Wheat	82
Casein	10
Lard	3
Dehydrated yeast	2
Cod liver oil	2
McCollum's salt mixture	1

The second group received the same ration except that seleniferous wheat was used in place of control wheat, and the resulting ration contained 18 p.p.m. of selenium. The third group received a ration containing optically inactive selenium-cystine added in such a quantity that the ration also contained 18 p.p.m. of selenium.

The animals remained on experiment for eighty days during which time 2 rats from each group (except the controls) died. The organs from these animals were examined and analyzed for selenium. Each liver showed necrosis, the degree of severity varying with the time of death. Hemochromatosis, atrophy, and necrosis of the liver, adhesions of the liver lobes and enlargement of the spleen were the most noticeable pathological conditions exhibited by these animals. No appreciable difference was noted in the

TABLE 1

Series 145

GROUP	SELENIUM USED	AVERAGE FOOD CONSUMPTION, GRAMS PER RAT PER DAY			
		40 days		80 days	
		Females	Males	Females	Males
1	None	8.4	12.50	12.0	14.5
2	18 p.p.m. selenium (wheat)	8.0	6.25	9.2	8.5
3	18 p.p.m. selenium (selenium-cystine)	7.8	6.5	8.4	8.25
4	18 p.p.m. selenium (Na_2SeO_3)	5.5	5.0	8.2	7.25

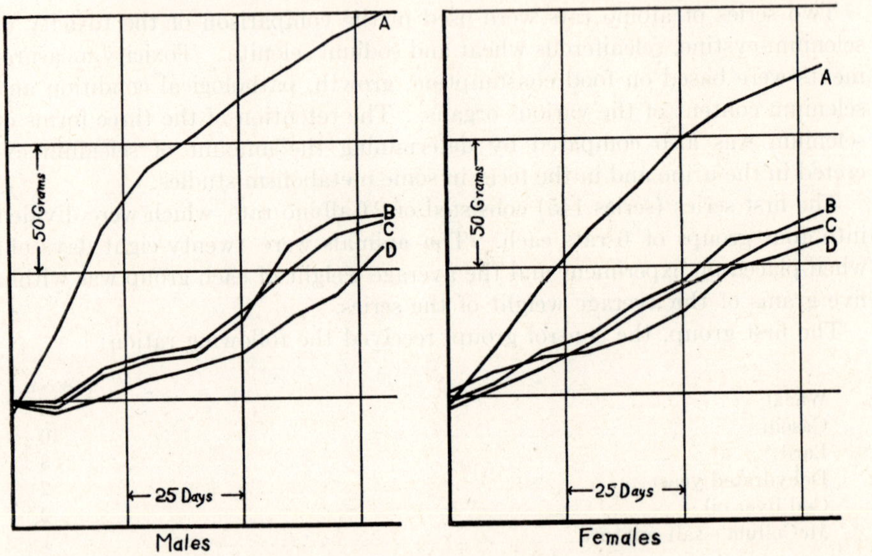

FIG. 1. GROWTH CURVES (SERIES 145)

A, control diet; *B*, seleniferous wheat diet (18 p.p.m. Se); *C*, selenium-cystine diet (18 p.p.m. Se); *D*, sodium selenite diet (18 p.p.m. Se).

degree of pathology which might be attributed to the different forms of selenium.

The daily food intake for the control males increased from 6 grams per rat, when the experiment started, to 14.5 grams at the time the animals were killed. The food intake of those rats receiving selenium-cystine, and those receiving seleniferous wheat was considerably lower than that for the controls, while the group which received sodium selenite had the lowest average food intake of the series.

The average weights for the males and females of each group was recorded at five-day intervals (fig. 1).

As will be noted (fig. 1) the control group showed a steady increase in body weight. The growth of all the other animals in the series was comparatively slow, since a diet containing 18 p.p.m. of selenium results in a severe inhibition of normal growth. It will also be noted that the average weight of the animals receiving selenium-cystine and seleniferous wheat paralleled each other quite closely from the beginning to the end of the experiment, showing a definite similarity in the toxicity of these two forms of selenium. The growth of the sodium selenite group was inhibited slightly more than the growth of the other two groups which received seleniferous diets.

At the end of eighty days the remaining animals were killed and autopsies were performed. Careful examination of the organs was made and the typical pathological conditions were noted in all rats receiving selenium. The livers were necrotic, atrophied and showed evidence of hemochromatosis. The spleens were enlarged in some of the animals.

TABLE 2

GROUP	SELENIUM USED
1	None
2	18 p.p.m. selenium (wheat)
3	18 p.p.m. selenium (selenium-cystine)
4	18 p.p.m. selenium (Na_2SeO_3)
5	18 p.p.m. selenium (selenium-cystine) + 10 p.p.m. As(Na_2HAsO_3) in drinking water

The organs of these groups of animals were analyzed for selenium as composite samples (table 3) by the digestion-distillation method (13).

For confirmation of these results a second series (series 146) of animals was employed to repeat the same study. This series consisted of 30 albino rats which were divided into five groups of 6 rats per group. These animals were selected for experimentation (as to age and weight) in exactly the same manner as the animals in series 145.

The first four groups received the same ration as the groups in the previous series (table 2). The fifth group received 18 p.p.m. of selenium-cystine but in addition it received 10 p.p.m. of arsenic as sodium arsenite in the drinking water. This level of arsenic had previously been found to give protection against 18 p.p.m. of selenium as seleniferous wheat (14), so this group was included to determine if arsenic would also give protection against selenium as selenium-cystine.

This series also remained on experiment for eighty days. Several animals in groups 2, 3 and 4 died during the experimental period. The pathological conditions observed by macroscopic examination of the organs resembled very closely the conditions observed in series 145, most noticeable were hemochromatosis of the liver, atrophy of the central liver lobes, necrosis of the liver, enlargement of the spleen and accumulation of ascitic fluid in the peritoneal cavity. Groups 2, 3 and 4 exhibited these conditions, while the animals in group 5, which received 10 p.p.m. of As in addition to 18 p.p.m. of selenium showed no degenerative effects from the selenium and their food intake and growth compared closely with the controls (group 1) indicating that arsenic gave good protection against the toxicity of selenium in this form.

TABLE 3

Selenium content of rats in series 145

GROUP	COMPOSITE SAMPLES OF HEART, LUNGS, SPLEEN, KIDNEYS	BRAIN	LIVER	CARCASS*
1. Control	0 p.p.m. Se	0 p.p.m. Se	0 p.p.m. Se	0 p.p.m. Se
2. Se-wheat	46.6	3.75	45.1	10.0
3. Se-cystine	40.0	3.33	37.5	10.0
4. Sodium selenite	40.0	3.00	37.2	11.0

* Entire carcass except the organs listed in tables and the contents of the G-I tract.

TABLE 4

Selenium content of rats in series 146

GROUP	COMPOSITE SAMPLES OF KIDNEYS, HEART, LUNGS, SPLEEN	BRAIN	LIVER	CARCASS*
1. Control	0 p.p.m. Se	0 p.p.m. Se	0 p.p.m. Se	0 p.p.m. Se
2. Se-wheat	50.0	2.15	51.0	8
3. Se-cystine	48.2	2.40	47.8	7
4. Sodium selenite	39.5	1.95	44.4	8
5. Se-cystine + As	16.6	2.25	19.6	4

* Entire carcass except organs listed in tables and contents of the G-I tract.

The daily food intake for the control group, and the group receiving selenium-cystine plus arsenic, increased steadily throughout the experimental period. The food intake for the selenium wheat group, and the selenium-cystine group was considerably lower while the sodium selenite group had the lowest food intake.

The animals receiving selenium-cystine plus arsenic grew normally as compared with the controls. The growth of the animals receiving selenium-cystine and those receiving seleniferous wheat was inhibited considerably (to about the same degree in each case). The growth of the sodium selenite group was inhibited slightly more than the growth of the selenium-cystine, and the seleniferous wheat groups.

At the end of eighty days the surviving rats were killed, the various organs from each animal were dried and their selenium content determined (table 4). The various results obtained from this series compared very closely with the results obtained in the previous series, which indicated that the toxicity of selenium is about the same in selenium-cystine and in seleniferous wheat.

SELENIUM CONTENT OF ORGANS AND TISSUES

The results of the analyses of the animals from the two series (145 and 146) are shown in tables 3 and 4.

The selenium content of various organs from the two series agrees very well. The organs from the rats receiving the seleniferous wheat diet (group 2 in each series) showed a slightly higher selenium content than those from the group which received sodium selenite. This is in agreement with the results of Smith, Westfall and Stohlman (15) although they did find a wider difference between the retention of organic and inorganic selenium in their experiments with cats. The selenium-cystine groups retained slightly less selenium than the seleniferous wheat groups but distinctly more than the inorganic selenium groups. The retention of selenium by the selenium-cystine group which received arsenic is considerably lower than the retention by the selenium-cystine group which did not receive arsenic. This is in agreement with our earlier observations on the influence of arsenic upon the metabolism of selenium. It could explain at least a part of the effect of arsenic in preventing selenium poisoning (14).

METABOLISM STUDIES

As a part of the biological comparison of the toxicity of the three sources of selenium, a group of metabolism trials were conducted. The amount of selenium ingested was calculated from the daily food intake, and the amount of selenium excreted was determined by selenium analysis of urine and feces after each seven day period, which was the time allotted for each trial.

Six rats, weighing approximately 110 grams each, were divided into three groups of two rats per group. The rats were five weeks old and had received a control (selenium-free) ration previous to the experiment. Two rats were given seleniferous wheat ration, two were fed selenium-cystine, and two were fed a sodium selenite ration. Each animal was kept in an individual metabolism cage, and removed into an individual feeding cage for two one-hour periods during the day.

At the end of each seven-day period selenium analyses were performed on the urine and feces samples, and subsequent calculation of the percentage excretion of selenium from the urine and feces was made.

TABLE 5

A comparison of excretion and retention of selenium administered as seleniferous wheat, selenium-cystine, and sodium selenite

Selenium content of diets = 18 p.p.m. in all cases

DIET	RAT NUMBER	TOTAL AMOUNT OF Se INGESTED	PER CENT OF INGESTED Se EXCRETED IN URINE	PER CENT OF INGESTED Se EXCRETED IN FECES	TOTAL PER CENT OF Se EXCRETED
First week					
		mgm.			
Se-wheat	6338	0.630	22.2	17.8	40.0
Se-wheat	6322	0.324	21.3	15.4	36.7
Se-cystine	6325	0.720	20.8	15.3	36.1
Se-cystine	6303	0.756	18.5	14.8	33.3
Sodium selenite	6315	0.594	16.9	17.4	34.3
Sodium selenite	6321	0.558	21.5	17.1	38.6
Second week					
Se-wheat	6338	0.702	25.6	16.9	42.5
Se-wheat	6322	0.540	29.6	18.4	48.0
Se-cystine	6325	0.684	32.1	14.6	46.7
Se-cystine	6303	0.792	25.2	16.1	41.3
Sodium selenite	6315	0.594	31.7	16.8	48.5
Sodium selenite	6321	0.612	29.3	14.7	44.0
Third week					
Se-wheat	6338	0.666	31.5	18.1	49.6
Se-wheat	6322	0.596	33.5	16.7	50.2
Se-cystine	6325	0.666	34.5	16.5	51.0
Se-cystine	6303	0.648	30.8	15.4	46.2
Sodium selenite	6315	0.450	37.7	15.5	53.2
Sodium selenite	6321	0.612	36.4	17.9	52.3
Fourth week					
Se-wheat	6338	0.396	36.5	20.2	56.7
Se-wheat	6322	0.342	34.6	23.2	57.8
Se-cystine	6325	0.594	30.4	19.6	50.0
Se-cystine	6303	0.630	35.3	18.9	54.2
Sodium selenite	6315	0.450	37.1	18.6	55.9
Sodium selenite	6321	0.396	38.2	20.5	58.7
Fifth week					
Se-wheat	6338	0.504	31.92	24.35	56.27
Se-wheat	6322	0.432	39.35	21.62	60.97
Se-cystine	6325	0.738	35.09	19.67	54.76
Se-cystine	6303	0.720	37.01	22.50	59.51
Sodium selenite	6315	0.576	34.72	24.81	59.53
Sodium selenite	6321	0.558	35.84	22.75	58.59
Sixth week					
Se-wheat	6338	(Died between fifth and sixth week)			
Se-wheat	6322	(Died between fifth and sixth week)			
Se-cystine	6325	0.594	35.8	20.5	56.3
Se-cystine	6303	0.612	38.2	21.6	59.8
Sodium selenite	6315	0.504	38.3	22.6	60.9
Sodium selenite	6321	0.468	39.7	23.7	63.4

As will be noted in tables 5 and 6 the total excretion for trial 1 was between 30 and 40 per cent of the selenium ingested. When the trials were completed the total selenium excretion ranged from 55 to 65 per cent of the amount ingested. There was only a small increase in selenium excreted in the feces. The percentage of selenium excreted in the feces was lower than that found by Gortner and Lewis (16) for the rats receiving sodium selenite. This can undoubtedly be explained by the higher selenium content of the diet which they used. The increase in total selenium excretion was, for the most part, due to an increase in selenium excreted in the urine. The percentage excretion of selenium in the urine was almost doubled in the last trial over the first trial. This decreased selenium retention may be due either to the increasing age of the rats, since old rats have been found more resistant to selenium poisoning, or it may be due to physiological factors which limit the amount of selenium retained on continued administration.

TABLE 6

Showing the total ingestion and excretion of selenium for six-week period

DIET	RAT NUMBER	TOTAL AMOUNT OF Se INGESTED	TOTAL AMOUNT OF Se EXCRETED	TOTAL AMOUNT OF Se RETAINED IN TISSUES	PER CENT OF TOTAL INGESTED Se RETAINED IN TISSUES
		mgm.	*mgm.*		
Se-wheat	6338	2.898	1.381	1.517	52.34
Se-wheat	6322	2.234	1.136	1.098	46.92
Se-cystine	6325	3.996	1.963	2.033	49.12
Se-cystine	6303	4.158	2.014	2.144	51.56
Sodium selenite	6315	3.168	1.632	1.536	48.48
Sodium selenite	6321	3.204	1.660	1.540	48.06

There was no significant difference in the amount of selenium excreted by the three different groups when expressed as per cent of the total selenium ingested during the duration of the trials.

THE TOXICITY OF OPTICALLY ACTIVE SELENIUM-CYSTINE

The toxicities of the two optically active forms of the selenium analogue of cystine have been compared. The results of two series of rats show that the *d*-form is only about one-third as toxic as the *l*-form. The comparative toxicities of selenium as *d*-selenium-cystine, *l*-selenium-cystine and sodium selenite is very well illustrated by the photographs in figures 2 and 3.

The livers in figure 3 are representative of the livers from the 16 rats on each diet. The *l*-selenium-cystine caused more severe atrophy of the central lobes than did the sodium selenite. Hypertrophy of the caudate and lateral lobes was also more prevalent in the livers from the *l*-selenium-cystine animals. As will be noted in animal C figure 2 the *l*-selenium-cystine caused considerable loss of hair from the flanks.

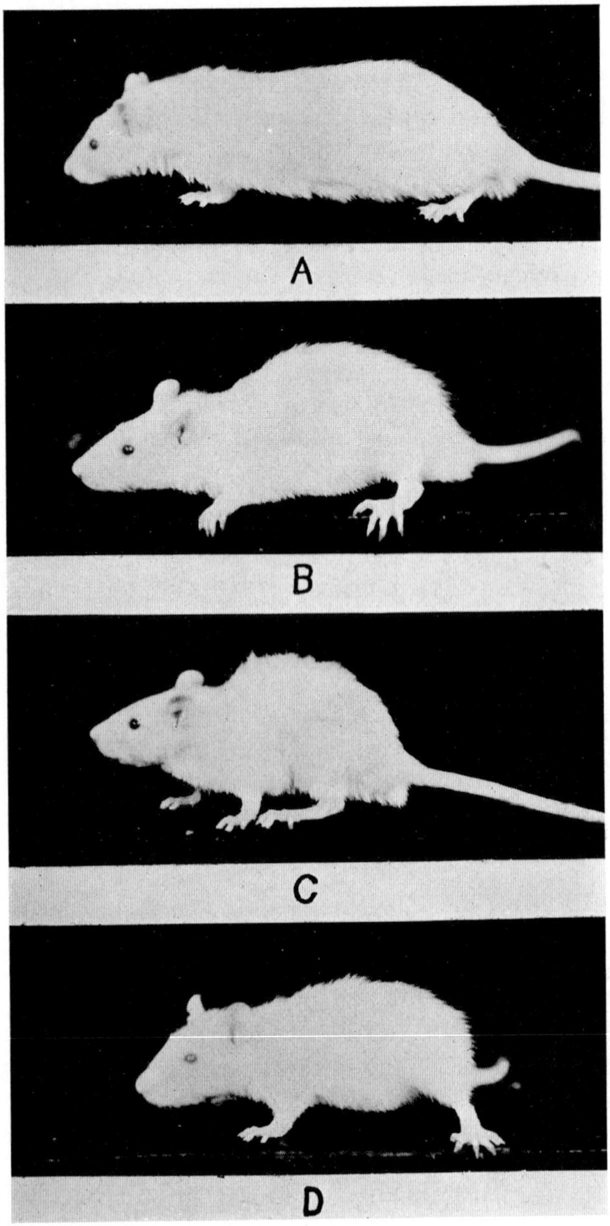

FIG. 2. *A*, control; *B*, 20 p.p.m. Se in diet (d-selenium-cystine); *C*, 20 p.p.m. Se in diet (l-selenium-cystine); *D*, 20 p.p.m. Se in diet (Na_2SeO_3).

Toxicities based on mortality rates, growth rates, pathological condition of organs and general symptoms show *l*-selenium-cystine to be considerably more toxic than *d*-selenium-cystine and even considerably more toxic than selenium as sodium selenite. *l*-Selenium-cystine is, in fact, the most toxic organic selenium compound that we have had occasion to work with while the toxicity of the *d*-selenium-cystine is about equal to that of such organic selenium compounds as β-selenodipropionic acid (11). It has been demonstrated that *d*-cystine cannot be utilized for growth by the rat in lieu of *l*-cystine (17). The difference in toxicity of the two optically active forms of selenium-cystine is probably related to the difference in the biological values of the corresponding enantiomorphs of cystine.

If the new selenium containing amino acid which Horn and Jones (10) have recently isolated from plant material is proven to have the structure

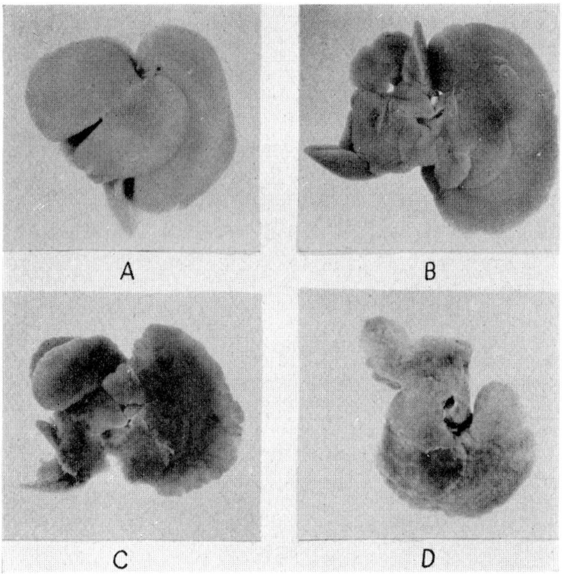

FIG. 3. LIVERS FROM RATS IN FIGURE 2

which they have suggested, it should be very toxic since it contains α amino groups and asymmetric carbon atoms. Moxon (12) has recently shown that the selenium in optically inactive selenium-cystine is six to seven times as toxic as selenium in the form of $\beta\beta'$ diselenodipropionic acid.

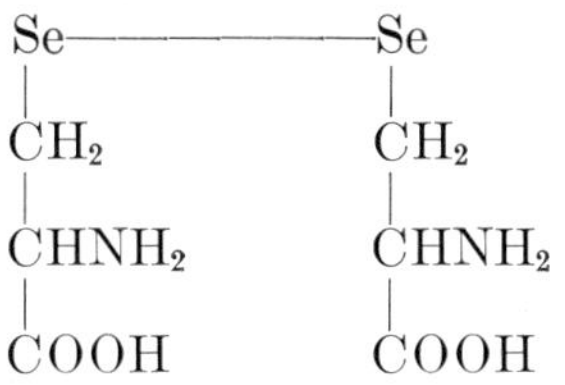

Selenium-cystine (optically inactive form)

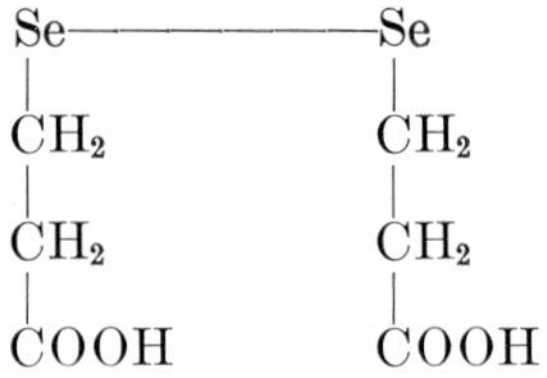

ββ′ diselnodipropionic acid

The minimum fatal doses of selenium-cystine when injected intraperitoneally into albino rats is 4.0 mgm. of selenium per kilogram of body weight while for ββ′ diselenodipropionic acid it is 25 to 30 mgm. of selenium per kilogram of body weight. This difference in toxicity is probably due to the asymmetric carbon atoms in the selenium-cystine since the *l*-form of selenium-cystine is so much more toxic than the *d*-form.

SUMMARY

In the first series (series 145) the toxicity of seleniferous wheat, selenium-cystine, and sodium selenite was compared by administering the different forms of selenium orally. Growth curves, daily food intake, macroscopic examination of the various organs, and selenium analysis all seemed to indiate that the toxicity of selenium-cystine was very similar to the toxicity of seleniferous wheat.

In the second series (series 146) the same compounds were compared and the same results obtained. However, this series contained an additional group which was fed a ration containing selenium-cystine and was given drinking water containing 10 p.p.m. of arsenic, in order to note whether arsenic would give protection against selenium-cystine toxicity as it had previously protected against the toxicity of selenium in seleniferous wheat. It was noted that arsenic gave full protection against the toxicity of selenium in selenium-cystine.

A third series of albino rats were used to compare the percentage excretion of selenium when the three seleniferous rations were administered. Both urine and feces selenium was determined and from the total amount of selenium ingested the percentage excretion was calculated. There was no significant difference in the amount of selenium excreted when the different rations were given.

d-Selenium-cystine was found to be moderately toxic while *l*-selenium-cystine appears to be the most toxic organic selenium compound that we have had occasion to feed to animals.

All results seemed to indicate that there could be a relationship between the compound which contains the selenium in cereal foods and selenium-cystine. Since it has been found that selenium in cereals is organic there may be a replacement of the sulfur by selenium in some sulfur containing compound or compounds which are present in the cereals.

REFERENCES

(1) Franke and Moxon: This Journal, **61**: 89, 1937.
(2) Smith, Stohlman and Lillie: Ibid., **60**: 449, 1937.
(3) Jones: Biochem. J., **4**: 405, 1909.
(4) Franke: J. Nutr., **8**: 597, 1934.
(5) Franke and Potter: J. Nutr., **10**: 213, 1935.
(6) Munsell, DeVaney and Kennedy: U. S. D. A. Tech. Bull., 534, 1936.
(7) Painter and Franke: J. Biol. Chem., **111**: 643, 1935.
(8) Painter and Franke: J. Biol. Chem., **134**: 557, 1940.
(9) Painter, Franke and Gortner: J. Organic Chem., **5**: 579, 1940.
(10) Horn and Jones: J. Am. Chem. Soc., **62**: 234, 1940.
(11) Moxon, Anderson and Painter: This Journal, **63**: 357, 1938.
(12) Moxon: J. Am. Pharm. Assoc., **29**: 249, 1940.
(13) Moxon: S. Dak. Ag. Expt. Sta. Bull., 311, 1937.
(14) DuBois, Moxon and Olson: J. Nutr., **19**: 477, 1940.
(15) Smith, Westfall and Stohlman: Public Health Reports, **53**: 1199, 1938.
(16) Gortner and Lewis: This Journal, **67**: 358, 1939.
(17) duVigneaud, Dorfmann and Loring: J. Biol. Chem., **98**: 577, 1932.

THE TOXICITY OF ORALLY-INGESTED TUNGSTEN COMPOUNDS IN THE RAT

F. W. KINARD AND JOHN VAN DE ERVE

From the Department of Physiology, Medical College of the State of South Carolina, Charleston, South Carolina

Received for publication March 7, 1941

The most extensive study of the toxicity of tungsten, the greater part of which is concerned with the subcutaneous injection of sodium tungstate, has been made by Bernstein-Kohan (1). In the one experiment devoted to the oral administration of sodium tungstate, 17 mgm. were given daily for 45 days to a 1400 gram rabbit with no effect except a constant diarrhea. From this it was concluded that sodium tungstate is slightly, if at all, absorbed from the gastro-intestinal tract. In a single experiment, Levin and Pouchet (2) observed no effect in a dog given 4 grams of ammonium tungstate. On the other hand, Karantassis (3, 4) produced death in 3 guinea pigs by the oral administration of sodium tungstate as follows:

575 grams body weight, dosage of 0.75 grams, death in 5 hours
632 grams body weight, dosage of 0.5 grams, death in 23 hours
640 grams body weight, dosage of 0.5 grams, death in 16 hours

Obviously these few experiments shed little light upon the toxicity of orally-ingested tungsten. Since rats are more readily available in our laboratory than are the other species mentioned, experiments were carried out in order to arrive at some approximation of the toxicity of several compounds of tungsten in the rat.

METHODS

Thirty-seven day old male and female rats from the College colony were caged separately in groups of 5 or 6. Ground Purina dog chow was fed to the control animals while the experimental animals were fed the control diet in which the powdered tungsten compound had been carefully mixed. Water and the diet were fed ad libitum.

The food was weighed every second day and the rats were weighed at intervals of 9 to 12 days. The food consumption values are not regarded as being exact for the rats on the experimental diets occasionally wasted the food despite the use of special food cups. All deaths were recorded and are designated upon the growth curves.

The groups were given the following diets:

Diet A. Purina dog chow.

Diet B. Purina dog chow + 0.1 per cent W as 0.1262 per cent tungstic oxide.

Diet C. Purina dog chow + 0.1 per cent W as 0.1795 per cent sodium tungstate.

Diet D. Purina dog chow + 0.5 per cent W as 0.8975 per cent sodium tungstate.

Diet E. Purina dog chow + 0.5 per cent W as 0.631 per cent tungstic oxide.

Diet F. Purina dog chow + 0.5 per cent W as 0.6912 per cent ammonium paratungstate.

Diet G. Purina dog chow + 2.0 per cent W as 2.756 per cent ammonium paratungstate.

Diet H. Purina dog chow + 2.0 per cent W as 3.59 per cent sodium tungstate.

Diet I. Purina dog chow + 3.96 per cent W as 4.99 per cent tungstic oxide.

Diet J. Purina dog chow + 5.0 per cent W as 6.912 per cent ammonium paratungstate.

All of the experiments were continued for 70 days unless they were terminated earlier by the death of the entire group.

The tungstic oxide, 99.84 per cent WO_3, was obtained from A. D. McKay Company; the sodium tungstate, 55.76 per cent W from Eimer and Amend; the ammonium paratungstate, 91.21 per cent WO_3, from the General Electric Company.

DISCUSSION OF RESULTS

Each of the compounds will be discussed separately.

Ammonium paratungstate. By reference to chart 1, it is evident that ammonium paratungstate, equivalent to 5.0 per cent W (diet J), is markedly toxic. One rat died on the sixth day after having ingested 1.50 grams of W, according to average figures of table 2. The remaining 4 rats died on the ninth and tenth days after having consumed 2.25 and 2.50 grams W respectively. The prompt loss of weight and the early death demonstrate conclusively that this concentration of W in the diet is highly toxic. No female rats were placed on this diet but it appears reasonable to assume that they would have reacted in a similar manner.

Charts 1 and 2 show that the 2.0 per cent W diet (diet G) produced an 80 per cent mortality after nineteen days. The first death among the males and females occurred at practically the same time, ten and nine days respectively, after the male had consumed, according to table 2, an average of 1.2 grams of W and the female an average of 0.32 gram of W. The last female death occurred on the eleventh day and the last male death on the nineteenth day. The surviving male and female, at the end of the 70-day experimental period, had consumed approximately 22.4 and 12.6 grams of W respectively. In view of the large quantity of wasted food, which could not be satisfactorily controlled, these figures of consumption are of doubtful value. The male, however, did begin to gain weight after about twenty days on the diet, and finally gained 100 grams more than the initial weight. Even though the actual quantity of W consumed cannot be ascertained with certainty, this rat must have consumed large quantities of the diet in order to attain the final weight. The female survivor never regained the initial weight.

The 0.5 per cent W diet (diet F) had only a slight effect upon growth as the males at the end of 70 days weighed 3.9 per cent less and the females 5.3 per cent less than the controls on diet A. The males had ingested a total of 5.25 grams W and the females a total of 3.15 grams W.

Tungstic oxide. On the 4.99 per cent tungstic oxide diet, equivalent to

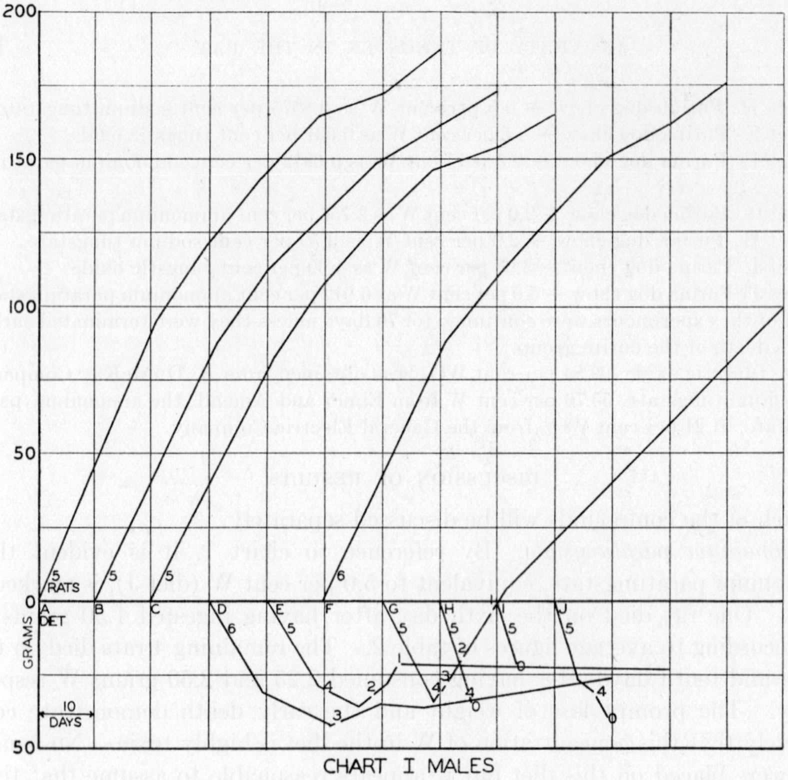

Chart 1. Gain in Weight and Deaths on Various Tungsten Diets

Diet A, control. Diet B, 0.1262 per cent tungstic oxide. Diet C, 0.1795 per cent sodium tungstate. Diet D, 0.8975 per cent sodium tungstate. Diet E, 0.631 per cent tungstic oxide. Diet F, 0.6912 per cent ammonium paratungstate. Diet G, 2.756 per cent ammonium paratungstate. Diet H, 3.59 per cent sodium tungstate. Diet I, 4.99 per cent tungstic oxide. Diet J, 6.912 per cent ammonium paratungstate.

Chart 2. Same as Chart 1

TABLE 1

Average weight and average food consumption on diets showing no mortality

DIET	SEX	AVERAGE WEIGHT 20TH DAY	AVERAGE DAILY CONSUMPTION		AVERAGE WEIGHT 50TH DAY	AVERAGE DAILY CONSUMPTION		AVERAGE WEIGHT 70TH DAY	AVERAGE DAILY CONSUMPTION	
			Food	W		Food	W		Food	W
		grams	*grams*	*grams*	*grams*	*grams*	*grams*	*grams*	*grams*	*grams*
Control	M	194	16.1	0.0	262	15.7	0.0	285	15.0	0.0
0.1262% tungstic oxide	M	180	13.6	0.014	243	14.5	0.014	267	13.7	0.014
0.1795% sodium tungstate	M	178	13.1	0.013	242	13.0	0.013	260	12.4	0.012
0.6912% ammonium paratungstate	M	186	17.0	0.085	249	16.0	0.08	274	15.3	0.076
Control	F	136	11.0	0.0	174	10.2	0.0	188	9.7	0.0
0.1262% tungstic oxide	F	127	10.0	0.01	150	10.0	0.01	174	9.7	0.009
0.1795% sodium tungstate	F	116	8.3	0.008	156	9.6	0.009	168	9.3	0.009
0.6912% ammonium paratungstate	F	136	12.0	0.06	163	10.0	0.05	178	9.3	0.046

TABLE 2

Average daily food consumption on diets showing mortality

DIET	SEX	UNTIL FIRST DEATH		UNTIL SECOND DEATH		UNTIL THIRD DEATH		UNTIL FOURTH DEATH		UNTIL FIFTH DEATH	
		Food	W	Food	W	Food	W	Food	W	Food	W
		grams	*grams*	*grams*	*grams*	*grams*	*grams*	*grams*	*grams*	*grams*	*grams*
6.912% ammonium paratungstate	M	5	0.25	7	0.35	7	0.35	7	0.35	7	0.35
4.99% tungstic oxide	M	3	0.119	3	0.119	3	0.119	3	0.119	3	0.119
	F	5	0.198	5	0.198	5	0.198	5	0.198	5	0.198
3.59% sodium tungstate	M	3	0.06	3	0.06	3	0.06	3	0.06	3	0.06
	F	4	0.08	3	0.06	3	0.06	3	0.06	3	0.06
2.756% ammonium paratungstate	M	6	0.12	6	0.12	4	0.08	4	0.08		
	F	2	0.04	2	0.04	8	0.16	8	0.16		
0.631% tungstic oxide	M	6	0.03	5	0.025	5	0.025	10	0.05		
	F	7	0.035	7	0.035	7	0.035	15	0.075	15	0.075
0.8975% sodium tungstate	M	7	0.035	7	0.035	7	0.035				
	F	7	0.035	7	0.035	7	0.035	7	0.035		

3.96 per cent W (diet I), all 5 of the males were found dead on the fourth day while 2 females were dead on the third day and the remaining 3 on the fourth day. In both cases much food was wasted so that the consumption values,

0.476 gram W for the males and 0.396–0.594 gram W for the females, are of doubtful value.

The 0.5 per cent W diet (diet E) produced the first death in the males on the tenth day, in 2 more on the eighteenth day, and in the fourth rat on the twenty-third day. The first death followed a total consumption of 0.3 gram W, the next 2 after a total consumption for each of 0.5 gram W, and the fourth death after the rat had consumed a total of 0.75 gram W. The sole survivor, during the entire 70 days of the experiment, consumed a total of 3.1 grams W and never regained its initial weight. In the females on this same diet, 1 died on the twelth day, 2 on the fourteenth, 1 on the seventeenth, and 1 on the eighteenth day. The consumption of W totaled 0.42 gram, 0.49 gram, 0.71 gram, and 0.79 gram respectively. The sole survivor, during the entire 70 days, consumed 2.61 grams W and never regained its initial weight.

The 0.1 per cent W (diet B) produced no deaths in 70 days. The males, at the end of this experimental period, weighed 6.3 per cent less than the controls, and had consumed a total of 0.98 gram W. The females weighed 7.4 per cent less than the controls and had consumed 0.68 gram W.

Sodium tungstate. 3.59 per cent sodium tungstate, equivalent to 2.0 per cent W (diet H), proved fatal to 1 male in five days (0.3 gram W total consumption), 3 more on the sixth day (0.36 gram W), and the last 1 on the seventh day (0.42 gram W). Of the females, the first died on the fourth day (0.32 gram W consumed) and the 4 remaining ones on the sixth day (0.44 gram W each).

On the diet of 0.5 per cent W (diet D), 3 males died on the twenty-second day after having consumed 0.77 gram W. The 3 survivors, at the end of 70 days had each consumed 2.45 grams of W. The first female died on the seventeenth day (0.595 gram W), 2 on the twenty-fourth (0.84 gram W), and 1 on the twenty-ninth day (1.01 grams W). At the end of the 70-day period, the 2 survivors had each consumed 2.45 grams of W. Both the males and females wasted an appreciable quantity of diet.

There were no deaths on the 0.1 per cent W diet (diet C). Each male, at the end of the experimental period, had consumed 0.65 gram W and weighed 8.8 per cent less than the control, while each female had consumed 0.61 gram W and weighed 10.6 per cent less than the control.

SUMMARY

In this type of feeding experiment, ammonium paratungstate is much less toxic in the rat than either tungstic oxide or sodium tungstate.

The diets of ammonium paratungstate, equivalent to 5.0 per cent W, the tungstic oxide, equivalent to 3.96 per cent W, and the sodium tungstate, equivalent to 2.0 per cent W, produced 100 per cent mortality in the rat while the ammonium paratungstate, equivalent to 2.0 per cent W, showed an 80 per cent mortality.

On the diets having a W equivalent of 0.5 per cent, the tungstic oxide produced death in 9 of 11 rats; sodium tungstate was fatal to 7 of 12 rats; while ammonium paratungstate produced no deaths. On the latter diet, at the end of 70 days, the males weighed 3.9 per cent less and the females 5.3 per cent less than the controls.

In the diets with a tungsten equivalent of 0.1 per cent, at the end of the 70-day experimental period on the tungstic oxide, the males weighed 6.3 per cent less and the females 7.4 per cent less than the controls. On the sodium tungstate diet, the males weighed 8.8 per cent less and the females 10.6 per cent less than the controls.

REFERENCES

(1) Bernstein-Kohan, J.: Arb. d. Pharmk. Inst. zu Dorpat, **5**: 42, 1890.
(2) Lewin and Pouchet: Traite de Toxicologie, Paris, 372, 1903.
(3) Karantassis, M. T.: Ann. de med., **5**: 44, 1925.
(4) Karantassis, M. T.: Bull. d. sc. pharmacol., **31**: 561, 1924.

STUDIES ON FAT METABOLISM AND SUSCEPTIBILITY TO CARBON TETRACHLORIDE

J. C. FORBES, B. E. LEACH AND E. L. OUTHOUSE

From the Department of Biochemistry, Medical College of Virginia, Richmond

Received for publication March 19, 1941

During the last few years a number of publications have appeared showing that xanthine and other relatively insoluble materials, when injected subcutaneously, render rats much more resistant to the poisonous action of carbon tetrachloride or chloroform. Since an understanding of the mechanism of protection might lead to developments of clinical significance in the prevention and treatment of certain liver conditions, we have conducted research on this problem for several years. Although the work so far has not led to a definite explanation of the protective mechanism, the results obtained are presented at the present time since they clearly eliminate certain possibilities as important factors in the process.

It was reported previously (1) that a decrease in the serum esterase (tributyrin hydrolyzing power) of normal rats went hand in hand with the increased resistance which results from the subcutaneous injection of xanthine and other protective substances. It was also shown (1, 2) that the state of increased susceptibility which follows the oral administration of fat was accompanied by an increase in the serum esterase concentration, while the administration of glucose, proteose-peptone and a balanced diet of Purina dog chow to similarly starved animals did not affect the esterase content. Furthermore, the administration of carbon tetrachloride was associated invariably with a rise in serum esterase rise, a definite increase being noted in as short a period of time as two hours after poisoning. Since these results suggested a definite correlation between the serum esterase concentration and the animal's resistance to carbon tetrachloride, it was decided to investigate the problem in greater detail. Two different approaches to the problem were made:

First, an attempt was made to lower the serum esterase concentration by the oral administration of suitable material and then to determine the animal's resistance to carbon tetrachloride; second, an attempt was made to raise the serum esterase concentration of rats in a protected state produced by xanthine administration and then to determine their susceptibility to carbon tetrachloride. The results, together with other data on the same general problem, are presented in this paper. The analytical procedures employed have been described previously (3).

EFFECT OF THE ORAL ADMINISTRATION OF VARIOUS SUBSTANCES ON SERUM ESTERASE

Although a variety of different substances such as quinine hydrochloride, malonic, tartaric, succinic and iodoacetic acids have been used, we have been unable to depress the serum esterase concentration through the oral administration of any of these compounds. Quinine hydrochloride is known to inhibit the tributyrinase activity of serum *in vitro*. Gajdos (4) reported that malonic, succinic and tartaric acids would do the same. Although able to confirm the *in vitro* inhibiting action of quinine, we have been unable to show any definite inhibiting effect of moderate concentrations of the above dicarboxylic acids, if the pH of the reacting medium is kept optimal for tributyrin hydrolysis by serum esterase. Laszt and Verzar (5) found that iodoacetic acid prevented the fatty infiltration of the liver which usually results from phosphorus poisoning; consequently we decided to test its effect on serum esterase activity. We found that its administration, in amounts comparable to those used by the above authors, had no demonstrable effect either on the serum esterase level or on the ability of the rat to respond to a feeding of fat by a marked increase in serum esterase.

EFFECT OF BUTTER FAT ON THE SERUM ESTERASE OF XANTHINE-PROTECTED RATS

Since the subcutaneous injection of xanthine reduces the serum esterase concentration and fat given orally increases it, we decided to determine whether the previous injection of xanthine would antagonize the effect of fat on the serum esterase. In these experiments rats were given an injection of xanthine in amount sufficient to reduce markedly the serum esterase concentration (75 mgm. per 100 grams of body weight). In about 2 days after the injection, when the serum esterase concentration should be at a minimum as determined by previous experiments, 2 cc. of butter fat were fed by stomach tube and the animals were sacrificed at various intervals thereafter. From the experimental data recorded in table 1, it will be seen that xanthine exerts no demonstrable antagonistic effect on the ability of fat to increase the serum esterase concentration.

In view of this lack of antagonism of xanthine to the serum esterase increase which follows fat administration, it was decided to determine whether xanthine injection would protect rats, which had been given fat, against carbon tetrachloride. The experimental results are presented in table 2. Clearly the protective action of xanthine was not inhibited by the prior administration of fat. Since the protective action is exerted in spite of a high initial serum esterase concentration, one must conclude that the protective mechanism must be associated with some phase of fat metabolism other than that particular phase responsible for the serum esterase increase which follows the feeding of fat or fatty acids. That some phase of fat metabolism is associated with susceptibility to carbon tetrachloride is evident from the well-known fact that the administration of fat to a normal animal definitely increases its susceptibility to carbon tetrachloride. This is also shown in the present experiments in which the unprotected animals receiving fat were definitely

TABLE 1

Effect of xanthine on the serum esterase response following fat administration

NUMBER OF RATS	AVERAGE WEIGHT	SERUM ESTERASE			REMARKS
		Minimum	Maximum	Average	
	grams				
4	197	12	18	13	75 mgm. xanthine per 100 mgm. of body weight, killed 44 hours after, no food for last 24 hours
5	177	18	33	24	Same as above but given 2 cc. of butter fat 2 hours, 30 minutes before sacrificing
2	204	31	36	34	Same as directly above but killed 3 hours after fat administration
6	180	23	46	34	Same as directly above but killed 3 hours, 30 minutes after fat administration
4	198	28	38	32	Same as directly above but killed 6 hours after fat administration

TABLE 2

Protective action of xanthine against liver damage from carbon tetrachloride administration to rats previously given butter fat

NUMBER OF RATS	NUMBER		REMARKS
	Lived	Died	
11	11*	0	75 mgm. xanthine subcutaneously 48 hours before CCl_4 administration
13	13*	0	Same as above but given 2 cc. of butter fat 3 hours before gassing
11	7†	4	Controls without xanthine
11	2†	9	Controls similar to above but given 2 cc. of butter fat 3 hours before gassing

* None of these rats looked ill at any time.

† Most of the rats which recovered looked extremely ill about 48 hours after poisoning.

more susceptible to the poisonous action of the carbon tetrachloride than were control animals starved for the same length of time but given no fat before gassing.

It has been suggested by various authors, and emphasized recently by

Ravdin, Goldschmidt and Vars (6), that the detrimental effect of fat administration in carbon tetrachloride or chloroform poisoning is due to the increased amount of liver fat which results therefrom. It was suggested that this increase in liver fat increases the absorption and retention of these fat-soluble poisonous substances by the liver cells and consequently causes greater cell destruction. In a previous publication (1) we presented data showing that the concentration of liver lipids was not changed when rats were protected against carbon tetrachloride by the subcutaneous injection

TABLE 3

Effect of fat content of the liver on susceptibility to carbon tetrachloride

EXPERIMENT NUMBER	HIGH FAT DIET				CONTROLS			2 CC. OF BUTTER FAT 3 HOURS BEFORE GASSING		
	Liver N.F. + chol.	Total number of rats	Number of rats lived	Number of rats died	Total number of rats	Number of rats lived	Number of rats died	Total number of rats	Number of rats lived	Number of rats died
	per cent									
1	22.8	3	3	0	2	1	1	2	0	2
2	23.2	17	4	13	15	3	12	15	0	15
3	17.2	5	2	3	5	2	3	5	3	2
4	31.0	5	2	3	4	1	3	5	0	5
5	19.5	5	4	1	5	4	1			
6	29.5	9	4	5	6	2	4			
7		4	2	2	4	4	0			
8		5	1	4	5	1	4			
9		5	3	2	5	4	1			
10		5	1	4	5	3	2			
								20 MGM. CHOLINE PER 10 GRAMS OF FOOD		
11	23.8	5	1	4	6	2	4	6	3	3
12	10.7	11	2	9	9	1	8	9	0	9
Total		79	29	50	71	28	43			

Note: The time on the high fat diet in the different experiments varied from 13 to 24 days. In experiment 12 fatty livers were produced by feeding a low choline-low fat-low protein diet.

of xanthine. Further evidence of the apparent unimportance of the actual lipid content of the liver is presented in table 3. In these experiments, unless otherwise specified, the animals were placed on a low choline diet of the following per cent composition: filtered butter fat 40, crude fibrin 10, salt mixture 4, sucrose 43, agar 2, cod liver oil 1, and thiamin chloride 0.2 mgm. After fatty livers were assured, as judged from previous experience with this diet, the animals were starved for approximately 24 hours together with a number of control animals on Purina dog chow.

In a few experiments, in order to determine whether the *degree* of active fat metabolism was important, normal animals were given 2 cc. of filtered butter fat, and after 3 hours they, along with the other animals, were anesthetized in the chamber described previously (7). The time of complete anesthesia was usually 65 minutes, the animals requiring about 20 minutes from the time they were placed in the box until they were anesthetized. Shortly

TABLE 4

Effect of a single feeding of fat on liver lipids

EXPERIMENT NUMBER	NUMBER OF RATS	AVERAGE RAT WEIGHT	LIVER T.P.L.	LIVER N.F. + Chol.	LIVER Chol.	REMARKS
		grams	*per cent*	*per cent*	*per cent*	
B-57	1	206	4.20	2.0	.28	1 cc. of butter fat. Killed 1 hour after
B-60	2	230	4.62	1.2	.26	1 cc. of butter fat. Killed 2 hours after
B-66	2	206	4.06	1.0	.29	1 cc. of butter fat. Killed 3 hours after
	3	200	4.39	0.9	.26	1 cc. of butter fat. Killed 4 hours after
	2	226	3.83	0.8	.25	1 cc. of butter fat. Killed 5 hours after
	2	190	4.47	2.4	.28	1 cc. of butter fat. Killed 6 hours after
	2	230	3.78	1.1	.28	1 cc. of butter fat. Killed 7 hours after
	1	238	4.91	1.4	.26	1 cc. of butter fat. Killed 8 hours after
	2	186	4.00	1.6	.25	1 cc. of butter fat. Killed 9 hours after
	1	220	4.45	1.2	.24	1 cc. of butter fat. Killed 10 hours after
	4	204	4.26	1.2	.25	Controls without fat
B-66a	1	200	4.62	1.6	.26	2 cc. of butter fat. Killed 1 hour after
	2	190	4.22	1.2	.26	2 cc. of butter fat. Killed 2 hours after
	1	183	4.06	0.7	.26	2 cc. of butter fat. Killed 4 hours after
	1	180	4.12	1.8	.26	2 cc. of butter fat. Killed 6 hours after
	1	170	4.09	1.8	.25	2 cc. of butter fat. Killed 9 hours after
	2	180	4.16	1.3	.26	Controls without fat
B-50	2	256	3.50	1.3	.37	5 grams of 40 per cent butter fat-Purina dog chow diet. Killed 3 hours after
	2	260	3.67	1.2	.34	Same amount of food. Killed 5 hours after
	2	256	3.55	1.1	.34	Same amount of food. Killed 7 hours after
	1	273	3.48	1.0	.31	Same amount of food. Killed 9 hours after
	2	243	3.74	1.1	.38	Control without food

T.P.L., total phospholipids; N.F. + chol., neutral fat plus cholesterol.

before the time of anesthesia one or two of the experimental animals on the high fat diet were killed, and the neutral fat plus cholesterol content of the livers was determined. The liver neutral fat plus cholesterol of the control animals on Purina dog chow was not determined, but our experience has been that in the rat this lipid fraction is not definitely increased by a 24 hour starvation period and remains approximately 1.0 to 2.0 per cent. Our experience has also been that the administration of 2 cc. of filtered butter fat leads to only an indefinite rise in liver lipids (cf. table 4). In experiments 11 and 12 sufficient choline was fed to some of the animals to prevent fatty livers. It will be seen that the rats so treated are apparently no more resistant to the poisonous action of carbon tetrachloride than the others.

In order to determine whether the concentration of serum lipids was of any significance in the protective mechanism, the serum lipids of rats in a resistant state following xanthine administration were determined and found not to differ from those of control animals. The experimental results are presented in table 5. In connection with these experiments, several others were carried out to determine whether xanthine affected the absorption of fat from the intestinal tract. In these experiments xanthine was injected, and after

TABLE 5

Effect of the subcutaneous injection of xanthine on serum lipids

WEIGHT OF RAT	SERUM T.P.L.	N.F. + CHOL.	REMARKS
	per cent	*per cent*	
207	.231	.195	Given 75 mgm. xanthine per 100 grams of body weight, killed 47 hours after. No food for last 24 hours
246	.231	.151	Same as above
216	.231	.184	Same as above
225	.227	.151	Same as above
225	.243	.162	Control starved same amount of time
204	.230	.151	Same as above
220	.223	.173	Same as above
217	.220	.141	Same as above

T.P.L., total phospholipids; N.F. + chol., neutral fat plus cholesterol.

44 hours 2 cc. of butter fat was given by stomach tube. No food was allowed 24 hours before the fat administration. The animals were killed at intervals up to six hours and their whole blood analyzed for neutral fat plus cholesterol, and phospholipids. No definite difference was found between the lipid content of the blood of these animals and that of similarly treated control animals without xanthine.

Since ketone body formation is increased in at least some of the conditions known to increase an animal's susceptibility to carbon tetrachloride and chloroform, such as starvation and fat administration, experiments were conducted to determine whether xanthine injections affected the concentration of ketone bodies in the blood. In some experiments normal animals were starved for a five day period and xanthine was injected 24 hours prior to starvation and every 48 hours thereafter. Blood from the tail vein was obtained at intervals and analyzed for total acetone bodies by Behre's method

(8) after preliminary distillation. Blood from an equal number of control animals, starved for the same period of time, was also analyzed. The increase in ketone bodies noted was very slight in each case and no difference between the control and xanthine-injected animals was evident. In other experiments, in order to obtain a more definite ketonemia, rats were given the high fat diet above described for 14 days before starving. Xanthine was injected as described previously, and blood ketone bodies were determined at intervals thereafter. Typical experimental results are shown in table 6. Although a certain degree of variation is noted between the different animals, it can be clearly seen that the xanthine injections exerted no apparent influence on

TABLE 6

Effect of xanthine injections on the ketonemia of fasting rats

SEX	XANTHINE INJECTED ANIMALS				CONTROL ANIMALS			
	Rat weight	Total acetone per 100 cc. after a fast of			Rat weight	Total acetone per 100 cc. after a fast of		
		24 hours	48 hours	72 hours		24 hours	48 hours	72 hours
	grams	*mgm.*	*mgm.*	*mgm.*	*grams*	*mgm.*	*mgm.*	*mgm.*
M	204	14.8	24.1	20.5	211	12.9	16.0	26.6
M	220	5.6	17.2	23.0	200	5.6	17.2	23.0
M	255	7.4	4.7		247	6.2	6.6	
M	212	13.5	12.0		218	12.0	12.0	
M	218	13.0	16.1		228	6.6	6.6	
M	230	10.3	8.5		180	13.7	18.5	
F	200	12.0	11.5		215	8.9	13.2	
F	203	5.2	11.6		213	11.8	19.2	
F	213	10.0	13.7		198	14.5	16.5	
F	190	30.3	35.1		205	16.5	24.0	
Average........		12.2	15.4			10.9	15.0	

Note: All animals were on a high fat-low choline diet for 2 weeks before starving.

the ketonemia of starving rats. Since a change in ketone body metabolism would probably be reflected by a change in the concentration of these substances in the blood stream, it seems apparent that the protective action of the subcutaneous injections of xanthine is not due to a change in ketone body metabolism.

DISCUSSION

The experimental results obtained in this investigation indicate quite conclusively that the concentration of neutral fat and cholesterol in the liver is not an important factor in the protective mechanism of the rat against carbon tetrachloride inhalation. On the other hand, a state of active fat metabolism, such as that resulting from the feeding of fat several hours prior to the time of poisoning, or through starvation, increases the animal's susceptibility. This detrimental effect of a high fat diet and of starvation has been recognized generally for some years. However, the most generally accepted explanation for the detrimental effect of fat seems to have been that its administration would lead to an increase in liver fat and in this way increase the animal's susceptibility. Since carbon tetrachloride is fat-soluble, it has been assumed that an increase in liver fat would increase the retention of carbon tetrachloride in the liver and consequently would result in a greater destruction of the liver cells. That such an explanation is untenable seems evident from the results which we have obtained. In a previous publication (1) it was shown that the concentration of liver lipids of animals in a protected state from xanthine administration did not differ from that of normal rats. In this paper data are presented showing that the administration of a single dose of butter fat, though it increases the animal's susceptibility, leads to only an indefinite rise in the concentration of liver fat. Furthermore, animals with very fatty livers, produced by low choline-high fat diets, starved for 24 hours, are apparently only very slightly, if any, more susceptible than normal animals starved for the same length of time.

In one of the experiments presented in table 3, the animals given fat several hours before the time of poisoning were not more susceptible than the control animals. However, in view of the results obtained in the other experiments and the experiences of others with a high fat diet, it seems safe to conclude that the lack of increased susceptibility in this case was due to the control animals being, as a whole, slightly more resistant than normal.

The apparent discrepancies between our results and those of Goldschmidt, Vars and Ravdin (6) with chloroform, are probably due to the fact that their animals were not starved prior to the time of anesthesia. Consequently their animals on a high fat diet not only had fatty livers but were probably in a state of active fat metabolism during the period of anesthesia, whereas their control animals on a normal diet were not. It is improbable that the results can be explained by a difference in the action of chloroform and carbon tetrachloride.

Since carbon tetrachloride is fat soluble, it might be supposed that increased susceptibility might be due to an increase in blood lipids, thus increasing its solubility in the blood and its transfer to the liver. That such is not the case is evident from the fact that rats in a protected state from xanthine administration do not differ in serum lipid content from normal rats. Also the serum lipids of protected animals following administration of butter fat by stomach tube show no apparent deviation from those of normal animals receiving the same amount of butter fat.

The question as to which phase of fat metabolism is involved remains to be answered. That it is not related to the phase responsible for the increase in serum esterase which follows the oral administration of fat is obvious from the fact that xanthine, though it does not prevent an increase of serum esterase following fat administration, nevertheless exerts its protective action in spite of fat administration. It also seems apparent that variations in ketone body metabolism play no significant part in the protective mechanism.

Any discussion as to the phase of metabolism involved, or any attempt to correlate theoretically the increased susceptibility following fat administration with the increased resistance of animals on high carbohydrate or protein diets or the administration of sulfur amino acids, expecially methionine, as recently reported by Miller, Ross and Whipple (9) seems superfluous until more is known about the processes involved. It is possible that the state of activity of the reticuloendothelial system, expecially of the Kupffer cells, is important in the protective mechanism. It is known that certain conditions which increase an animal's susceptibility, such as starvation and the feeding of fat, are also conditions in which fat tends to be deposited in the Kupffer cells. Experiments on the probable rôle played by these cells in the protective mechanism are now in progress. In unpublished experiments it have been shown that xanthine injection leads to marked liver stimulation as evidenced by an increased fibrinogen content of the blood.

SUMMARY

It has been shown that the protective action of xanthine against liver damage from carbon tetrachloride is not directly related to the decrease in serum esterase which follows its subcutaneous administration to normal rats.

Animals with fatty livers starved for twenty-four hours are very slightly, if at all, more susceptible to carbon tetrachloride than are normal rats starved for the same period of time. However, the oral administration of fat several hours before the time of poisoning increases markedly an animal's susceptibility irrespective of the concentration of liver fat.

Xanthine administration does not affect the concentration of serum lipids of fasting rats or the blood lipid concentration following the oral administration of butter fat.

Xanthine injections exert no demonstrable effect on the degree of ketonemia which results from starvation.

We gratefully acknowledge our indebtedness to the John and Mary R. Markle Foundation for a research grant in aid of this general research.

REFERENCES

(1) Forbes and Outhouse: This Journal, **68**: 185, 1940.
(2) Forbes, Outhouse and Leach: Proc. Soc. Exp. Biol. and Med., **43**: 523, 1940.
(3) Forbes and Outhouse: J. Lab. and Clin. Med., **25**: 1157, 1940.
(4) Gajdos: Compt. rend. Soc. Biol., **130**: 1566, 1939.
(5) Laszt and Verzar: Biochem. Z., **285**: 356, 1936.
(6) Goldschmidt, Vars and Ravdin: J. Clin. Inv., **18**: 277, 1939.
(7) Forbes and Neale and Scherer: This Journal, **58**: 402, 1936.
(8) Behre: J. Biol. Chem., **136**: 25, 1940.
(9) Miller, Ross and Whipple: Am. J. Med. Sci., **200**: 739, 1940.

THE QUANTITATIVE EFFECT OF FIFTEEN CHEMICALLY RELATED GLYCOSIDES AND GENINS ON THE EMBRYONIC CHICK HEART

ARTHUR C. DEGRAFF, GEORGE H. PAFF AND ROBERT A. LEHMAN

From the Department of Therapeutics, New York University College of Medicine; and the Department of Anatomy, Long Island College of Medicine

Received for publication March 24, 1941

The action of the digitalis glycosides on the embryonic chick heart has already been described (1, 2, 3, 4). The results indicate that this preparation may offer certain advantages for purposes of bioassay and for the study of the relationship between chemical structure and cardiac action. With this in view, the potency of the following pure crystalline glycosides and genins was studied and a procedure is proposed for their quantitative comparison: lanatosides A, B and C, K-strophanthoside, convallatoxin and all of the products of their hydrolysis, that is, digitoxin Merck, digitaline Nativelle, gitoxin, digoxin, K-strophanthin-β and cymarin, and the genins, digitoxigenin, gitoxigenin, digoxigenin and strophanthidin.

PROCEDURE

Embryonic chick hearts of 48 hours development (about 50 hours incubation) were dissected out and placed in drops of Tyrode solution containing the desired concentration of the drug to be studied. The Tyrode solution had the following percentage composition: NaCl 0.8, KCl 0.02, $CaCl_2$ 0.02, $MgCl_2 \cdot 6H_2O$ 0.01, NaH_2PO_4 0.005, and $NaHCO_3$ approximately 0.028 to give pH 7.4. The solution was placed in the well of a slide on the stage of a microscope which was mounted in a chamber maintained at 38 to 39°C. The well was covered during the experiment to prevent evaporation and the time from immersion of the heart in the solution until the first appearance of cardiac irregularities was measured with a stop watch. Atrio-ventricular block was, in the great majority of instances, the first event giving evidence of the action of the drug on the heart. Occasionally, however, dropped beats or diastolic arrest occurred first and in such cases these were taken as the end point. With continuous observation the end point is quite sharp; its reproducibility will be discussed below. A series of concentrations were chosen with which cardiac irregularities appeared on the average within the range of three to ten minutes. Usually about 20 hearts were used for each of four to six concentrations of the drug. Stock solutions of the glycosides[1] and genins were made up in 95 per cent alcohol. These concentrations were so chosen that never more than two per cent alcohol remained upon dilution with Tyrode solution. Control experiments

[1] Gitoxin was an exception and could only be brought into solution by warming 25 mgm. with 100 cc. of alcohol containing 30 per cent glycerol for 24 hours at 60°C. One to 100 was the least dilution of this stock solution used.

showed that Tyrode solution containing two per cent of alcohol (or glycerol) had no discernible effect on the hearts. Control experiments also showed (2) that many hearts could be poisoned by the same drop without diminution in the required time. A constant concentration gradient may therefore be assumed.

RESULTS AND DISCUSSION

General

Many of the variables inherent in either the frog or cat method of assay are eliminated by use of an isolated heart. Specifically the following sources of variation within an assay or between drugs are present in the method of Hatcher and Brody or its modifications: (*1*) the use of an arbitrary rate of infusion or of an arbitrary duration of life, (*2*) the use of an anesthetic and (*3*) the various possible causes of death, e.g., systolic arrest, ventricular fibrillation and so forth. For the methods using the intact frog we have, (*1*) the absorption of the drug from the lymph sac or muscle, (*2*) the use of an arbitrary environmental temperature and (*3*) the possible differences in response between the cold and warm blooded heart. The effect of the systemic circulation on the drug is, of course, operative in both the cat and the frog assay. This source of variation obtains also in man and it would therefore seem undesirable to eliminate it. Nevertheless it will be seen that this factor appears not to affect the significance of the results obtained with the chick heart. Naturally these arguments apply with equal force to any isolated heart but the embryonic chick heart seems to be the only preparation of this kind with sufficient economy of time and materials to make a statistically significant number of experiments feasible. It might be added that the mechanical and traumatic factors which are inherent in methods using older hearts are also avoided to a considerable extent. Furthermore the end point for the embryonic heart method is not the death of an animal, which, even under carefully controlled conditions, may be due to a summation of causes, but rather to the appearance of atrioventricular block. Since it has been shown (1), that no differentiated conducting tissue is present in a 48 hour heart, it may perhaps be assumed that the end point is the result of the direct cardiotonic action of the drug on the ventricle. Thus the end point depends upon that property of the digitaloids which is most important with respect to therapeutic use (5).

Calculations

The original data in terms of time and concentration are too voluminous to report in detail since about 1800 hearts were used in the investigation. Therefore the most logical procedure seemed to be to fit the results to an appropriate equation and express the action of each drug in terms of its parameters. It was found empirically that the time required for the appearance of irregularities of the heart was a linear function of the dilution, that is, the data approximately fit the equation

$$(t - t') = K(1/C) \qquad (1)$$

where t' is the intercept on the time axis and signifies the minimum time for an effect no matter how high the concentration, t is the elapsed time from immersion of the heart until the appearance of the end point, $1/C$ is the dilution of the drug in Tyrode solution and K is the slope and is a measure of the reciprocal of the potency. It might be pointed out here that for 10 of the 15 drugs studied, t' varied within the fairly narrow limits 1.2 to 1.6 minutes with extremes of 0.8 to 1.9 minutes. By analysis of the distribution of the individual time values within concentration groups it was found that the frequency curve is asymetric especially at high dilutions.

Trials with other functions showed that, with the exception of the highest concentrations, the data fit the expression

$$10^{a}C^{b} = 1/t \qquad (2)$$

equally well. In this case a is the intercept and b is the slope of the linear function

$$y = a + b \log C \qquad (3)$$

which is equivalent to equation (*2*). Here y equals log $1/t$. As would be expected, these curves flatten out sharply at high concentrations since a finite minimum time of about $1\frac{1}{2}$ minutes is required for an effect at any concentration. The concentration at which this flattening occurs thus is due to the same phenomenon which results in the time intercept, t', obtained by use of equation (*1*).

Equation (*3*) was adopted as a basis for the treatment of the time concentration data in this study. It has been recommended by Clark (6) and has a number of advantages. Most important is the fact that the values of y are more symetrically distributed about the mean than are the time values. Furthermore the data for the various drugs may now be expressed in the form of parallel lines and the log ratio of the potency of any two drugs will be given by their horizontal distance apart. An inherent property of this procedure is that the slopes of the lines are independent of the units in which time and concentration are expressed. Similar mathematical treatment has been worked out by Bliss and co-workers for a wide variety of bio-assays involving dosage-mortality and dosage response data (7, 8, 9). As noted above the concentrations were selected so that the end points appeared within 3 and 10 minutes. The lower time limit was adopted to avoid the flat portion of the curve. The upper limit is arbitrary and was chosen as the time beyond which the spread of the measured values becomes excessive.

In figures one to four are given the calculated regression lines for the drugs studied according to their chemically related groups. In table 1 the chemical relationships are reviewed and the values are given for log C (concentration in moles per liter $\times 10^9$), y (mean log $1000/t$ with time in minutes) and the number of experiments at each concentration. The statistics which seem

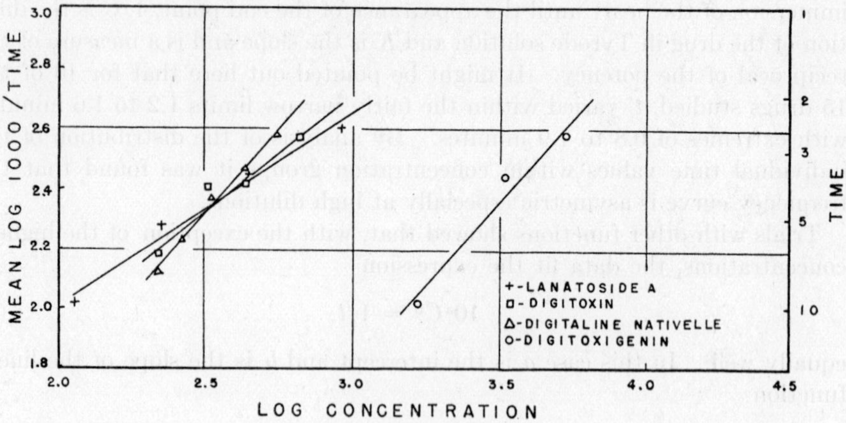

FIG. 1

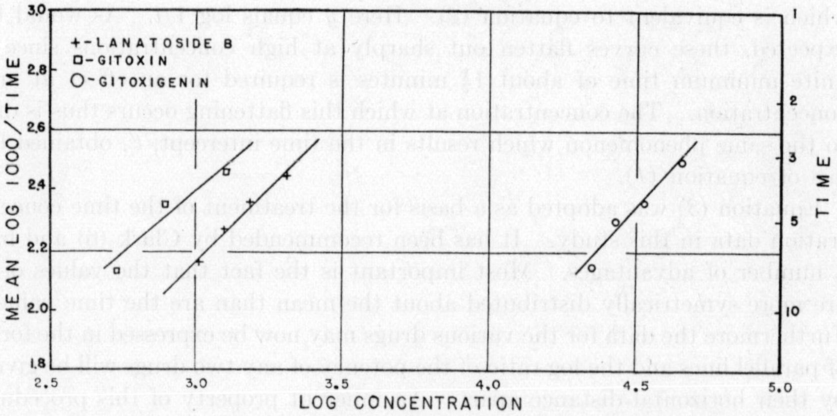

FIG. 2

useful are given in the table as follows: (σ) the standard deviations are listed for the distribution of the measured time values within concentration groups and are found to be somewhat greater at low than at high concentrations. In column (a) the y-intercepts for the regression lines are given in order to define the curves in figures one to four. In so far as the data are strictly defined by equation (*1*), the slopes or regression coefficients calculated on the basis of equation (*3*) will equal unity and equation (*2*) will then cease to be exponential in form. The values obtained for the slopes

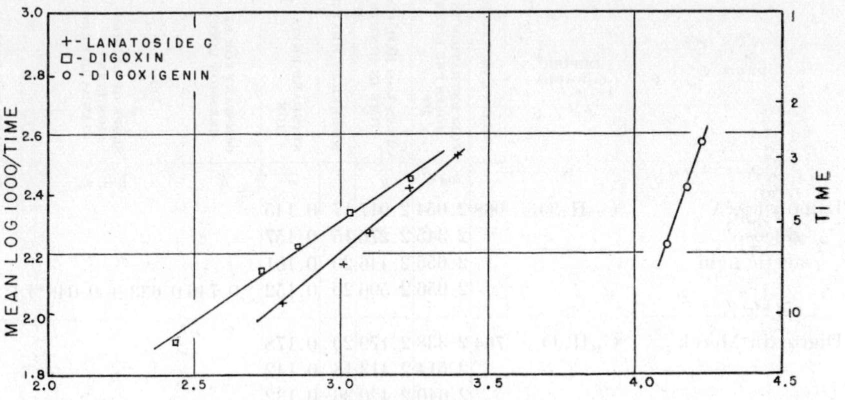

FIG. 3

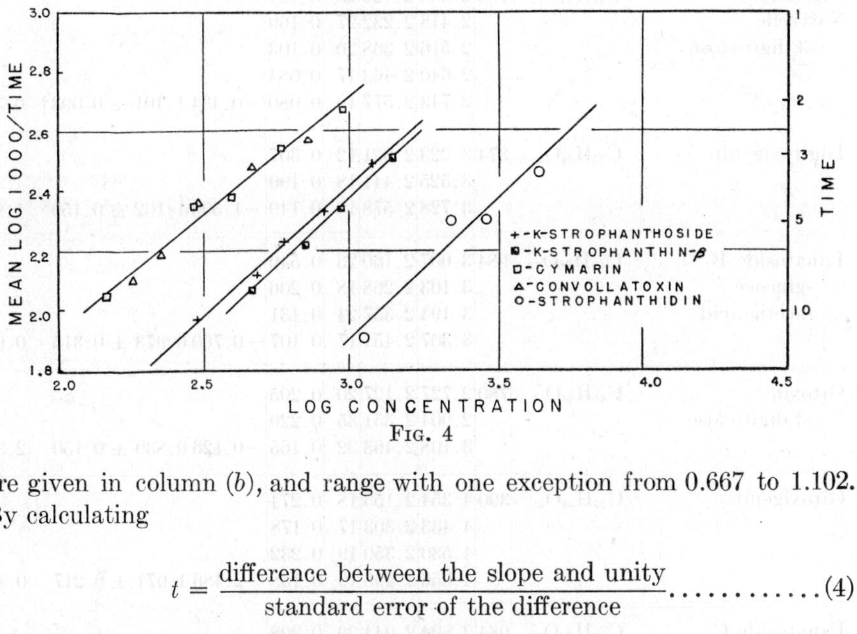

FIG. 4

are given in column (*b*), and range with one exception from 0.667 to 1.102. By calculating

$$t = \frac{\text{difference between the slope and unity}}{\text{standard error of the difference}} \qquad (4)$$

as described by Fisher (10), it was found that the slopes for only six[2] out of the 15 drugs differ significantly from unity. By a similar test it appeared that

[2] Indicated by a single asterisk in table 1.

TABLE 1

Chemical relationships of the glycosides and genins and summary of time-concentration data

DRUG	EMPIRIC FORMULA	MOLECULAR WEIGHT	CONCENTRATION IN MOLES PER LITER × 10⁹	MEAN LOG 1000/TIME (TIME IN MINUTES)	NUMBER OF HEARTS	STANDARD DEVIATION	CONSTANT FOR REGRESSION LINE	SLOPE OF REGRESSION LINE ± STANDARD ERROR	VARIANCE RATIO
			log C	*y*		σ	*a*	$b \pm s_b$	*F*
Lanatoside A	$C_{49}H_{76}O_{19}$	968	2.054	2.017	17	0.145			
-glucose			2.345	2.276	15	0.157			
-acetic acid			2.655	2.446	20	0.101			
↓			2.956	2.596	20	0.152	0.746	0.633 ± 0.049*†	1.45
Digitoxin Merck	$C_{41}H_{64}O_{13}$	764	2.338	2.179	20	0.178			
			2.514	2.413	18	0.142			
			2.640	2.420	36	0.132			
			2.816	2.571	20	0.089	0.411	0.768 ± 0.087*	3.28
Digitaline Nativelle	$C_{41}H_{64}O_{13}$	764	2.338	2.122	23	0.194			
			2.418	2.232	27	0.169			
-3 digitoxose			2.516	2.368	20	0.103			
			2.640	2.463	17	0.084			
↓			2.743	2.577	19	0.080	−0.434	1.101 ± 0.093†	0.56
Digitoxigenin	$C_{23}H_{34}O_4$	374	3.223	2.021	12	0.307			
			3.525	2.441	18	0.190			
			3.728	2.578	18	0.149	−1.500	1.102 ± 0.159	1.93
Lanatoside B	$C_{49}H_{76}O_{20}$	984	3.007	2.160	23	0.540			
-glucose			3.103	2.268	18	0.206			
-acetic acid			3.194	2.357	24	0.131			
↓			3.307	2.451	17	0.107	−0.760	0.973 ± 0.315	0.03
Gitoxin	$C_{41}H_{64}O_{14}$	780	2.727	2.127	20	0.205			
-3 digitoxose			2.904	2.351	35	0.229			
↓			3.108	2.463	32	0.165	−0.126	0.839 ± 0.150	2.30
Gitoxigenin	$C_{23}H_{34}O_5$	390	4.354	2.155	18	0.274			
			4.433	2.303	17	0.178			
			4.530	2.359	19	0.232			
			4.656	2.498	19	0.138	−2.486	1.071 ± 0.217	0.42
Lanatoside C	$C_{49}H_{76}O_{20}$	984	2.804	2.044	20	0.308			
-glucose			3.007	2.173	17	0.164			
-acetic acid			3.104	2.274	17	0.131			
			3.229	2.420	17	0.219			
↓			3.405	2.526	20	0.159	−0.304	0.834 ± 0.098	0.34

TABLE 1—*Concluded*

DRUG	EMPIRIC FORMULA	MOLECULAR WEIGHT	CONCENTRATION IN MOLES PER LITER $\times 10^9$	MEAN LOG 1000/TIME (TIME IN MINUTES)	NUMBER OF HEARTS	STANDARD DEVIATION	CONSTANT FOR REGRESSION LINE	SLOPE OF REGRESSION LINE ± STANDARD ERROR	VARIANCE RATIO
			$\log C$	y		σ	a	$b \pm s_b$	F
Digoxin	$C_{41}H_{64}O_{14}$	780	2.430	1.915	19	0.243			
-3 digitoxose ↓			2.730	2.155	17	0.233			
			2.857	2.230	20	0.133			
			3.032	2.345	20	0.136			
			3.236	2.450	17	0.134	0.312	0.667 ± 0.069*†	0.27
Digoxigenin	$C_{23}H_{34}O_5$	390	4.108	2.235	18	0.362			
			4.179	2.420	22	0.208			
			4.233	2.574	16	0.148	−8.75	2.67 ± 0.687*†	0.15
K-Strophanthoside	$C_{42}H_{64}O_{19}$	872	2.479	1.970	21	0.228			
-glucose ↓			2.688	2.122	13	0.214			
			2.780	2.227	20	0.097			
			2.906	2.331	16	0.201			
			3.081	2.494	23	0.121	−0.213	0.877 ± 0.083	0.10
K-Strophanthin-β	$C_{36}H_{54}O_{14}$	710	2.671	2.075	18	0.186			
-glucose ↓			2.848	2.222	17	0.112			
			2.975	2.339	17	0.195			
			3.149	2.516	17	0.119	−0.294	0.921 ± 0.107	0.09
Cymarin	$C_{30}H_{44}O_9$	548	2.171	2.054	20	0.242			
-cymarose ↓			2.472	2.352	20	0.154			
			2.597	2.379	15	0.140			
			2.772	2.539	15	0.117			
			2.979	2.667	7	0.083	0.407	0.768 ± 0.076*	0.73
Strophanthidin ↑	$C_{23}H_{32}O_6$	404	3.046	1.908	27	0.252			
			3.348	2.303	44	0.304			
-rhamnose			3.472	2.305	18	0.181			
			3.650	2.457	16	0.223	−0.878	0.930 ± 0.129	2.60
Convallatoxin	$C_{29}H_{42}O_{10}$	550	2.260	2.101	15	0.149			
			2.357	2.194	18	0.111			
			2.481	2.360	19	0.104			
			2.657	2.485	18	0.114			
			2.863	2.573	17	0.070	0.342	0.793 ± 0.059*	3.17

* Deviates significantly from unity.

† Deviates significantly from the weighted mean slope, 0.814.

the slopes of four[3] of the 15 drugs deviate significantly from the weighted mean slope of the series, 0.814, calculated according to Bliss (9). Qualitative identity in the mechanism of action of these latter four glycosides must naturally be regarded with some suspicion. There was, however, no apparent relationship between slope and potency or slope and chemical structure. In the last column (*F*) as a test of linearity the variance ratio was calculated as follows:

$$F = \frac{\text{variance due to lack of linearity}}{\text{variance within concentration groups}} \quad \text{(5)}$$

TABLE 2

Concentration ratios for the glycosides and genins

DRUG	RATIO OF CONCENTRATION OF DRUG TO THAT OF THE CORRESPONDING PROGENIN FOR END POINT AT CONSTANT TIME (RECIPROCAL OF POTENCY RATIO) ANTILOG OF M	LIMITS FOR ODDS OF 21 IN 22 ANTILOG OF M $\pm$ $2s_M$ EXPRESSED AS PERCENTAGE OF M
Lanatoside A	1.00	88–112
Digitoxin Merck	1	
Digitaline Nativelle	0.99	88–113
Digitoxigenin	8.91	88–116
Lanatoside B	1.77	82–123
Gitoxin	1	
Gitoxigenin	37.0	85–118
Lanatoside C	1.45	84–119
Digoxin	1	
Digoxigenin	11.7	78–129
K-Strophanthoside	2.50	86–116
K-Strophanthin-β	2.85	86–116
Cymarin	1	
Strophanthidin	9.03	82–122
Convallatoxin	1.00	88–113

The degrees of freedom used in entering Snedecor's table of "F" (11) will then be: n_1 equal to two less than the number of concentration groups, for the numerator of equation (*5*); n_2 equal to the number of time values minus the number of concentration groups, for the denominator. The variance ratios for digitoxin Merck and convallatoxin will be seen to lie between $P = 0.01$ and $P = 0.05$. In view of the good variance ratios ($P > 0.05$) obtained for the other 13 drugs, the justification for relating the variables linearly would seem to be ample.

In table 2 the most probable value is listed for the ratio of the concentra-

[3] Indicated by a dagger in table 1.

tions of each of the drugs to its progenin for the appearance of the end point at constant time (antilog of M). The weighted mean slope for the drugs in any group was used for the comparison within that group. The range, antilog of $M \pm 2s_M$, expressed as percentage of the concentration ratio is also given in the table. This represents the limits within which M will fall 21 times out of 22.

Significance of time

Any statement as to the meaning of the measured time values must necessarily be speculative. It seems likely that the initial lag before visible action begins regardless of concentration represents, among other factors, the time necessary for mechanical diffusion of the drug throughout the tissue. The consistent values obtained for this lag with all the drugs studied (t' = about $1\frac{1}{2}$ minutes) indicates that during this initial period the glycosides and genins are behaving nonspecifically. The latter portion of the measured time intervals probably depends upon a summation of effects. In view of recent work (13, 14, 15) which has emphasized the influence of the digitaloids on cell permeability to electrolytes, it is possible that a major part of this summation is the time required for the drug to produce a sufficient alteration in the electrolyte balance to give rise to the end point. The potency of the various glycosides might then stand in direct relation to their ability to cause the necessary membrane effect.

Significance of chemical structure

The general structure of the cardiac glycosides and genins used in this study is as follows (16):

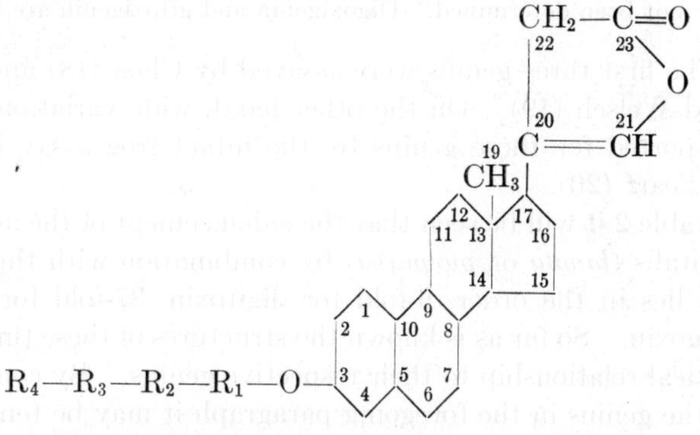

in which $R_1 \ldots R_4$ represent successive monosaccharide units of which R_1 at least, is always a desoxy sugar. The influence of chemical structure on cardiac action will be considered under three headings, (*1*) influence of the substituent groups on the steroid nucleus, (*2*) Influence of the desoxy sugars and (*3*) influence of glucose.

(*1*) The variations in the structures of the four genins are given in table 3. The evidence is consistent in showing that the unsaturated butyro-lactone ring on C-17 is essential for the characteristic action of the cardiac glycosides and the effect of various modifications of this ring has been determined by Chen and Elderfield (17). The importance of the sugars has also been emphasized, but the literature is not conclusive as to the influence of the substituents on the steroid nucleus. From table 3 it will be seen that the concentrations of the four genins causing an end point at constant time stand approximately in the order, 1 (digitoxigenin):1 (strophanthidin):4(digoxigenin):11 (gitoxigenin). A large enough series of the genins was not available to permit any conclusions as to the relative importance of the particular substituent groups. It is evident, however, that substitution on the nucleus is capable of producing profound changes in the potency of the genin for the embryonic heart. Such marked differences are not shown by the cat assay for which the ratios in terms of mols per kgm. for the four genins are 1:0.7:1:1.5 in the same order

TABLE 3

Variations in the structures of the genins (16) and comparison by the embryonic chick heart

GENIN	POSITIONS OF SUBSTITUENT GROUPS					CONCENTRATION RATIO	RANGE PER CENT
	C-3	C-5	C-10	C-14	C-16		
						M	$M \pm 2s_M$
Digitoxigenin	OH	H	CH_3	OH	H	1	
Gitoxigenin	OH	H	CH_3	OH	OH	10.6	83–120
Digoxigenin*	OH	?	CH_3	?	?	4.26	81–123
Strophanthidin	OH	OH	CHO	OH	H	0.93	81–124

* Digoxigenin bears three OH groups of which one is on C-3. The positions of the other two have not been determined. Digoxigenin and gitoxigenin are isomeric.

as above. The first three genins were assayed by Chen (18) and the last by Fromherz and Welsch (19). On the other hand, wide variations in potency have been reported for these genins by the intact frog assay (18) and the isolated frog heart (20).

(*2*) From table 2 it will be seen that the enhancement of the activity of the genins of digitalis (*lanata* or *purpurea*) by combination with three molecules of digitoxose lies in the order, 9-fold for digitoxin, 37-fold for gitoxin and 12-fold for digoxin. So far as is known the structures of these three progenins bear an identical relationship to their respective genins. By consideration of the data on the genins in the foregoing paragraph it may be tentatively concluded that the weaker the genin, the greater will be the enhancement of its activity on conjugation with desoxy sugar. This conclusion is further borne out by the strophanthus glycosides. Thus strophanthidin, which is equal in potency to digitoxigenin, is also enhanced 9-fold by conjugation with either cymarose or rhamnose to give cymarin or convallatoxin respectively. These latter observations lead to the conclusion that the nature of the desoxy sugar is of little or no importance in determining activity. This conclusion was predicted by Fieser and Jacobsen (21) who state, "... the early information indicated that the nature of the sugar residue is of relatively little importance in determining the potency of the glycosidic heart poisons in general. It is, therefore, surprising that convallatoxin possesses considerably greater physiological activity than cymarin, the cat and frog units being reported as 0.08 mgm. per kilogram and 0.00021 mgm. per gram for the rhamnoside and 0.13 mgm. per kilogram and 0.00060 mgm. per gram for the cymaroside. ..." It is evident that this difference in the potency of cymarin and convallatoxin, when determined in the cat or the frog, is due to the multiplicity of factors affecting these methods of assay. The chick heart procedure, which indicates that these two glycosides are of identical potency, would then seem to be fundamentally simpler, and therefore more useful than methods requiring intact animals, for the purpose of studying the effect of structural modifications on cardiac action. This of course implies that the results can be correlated with those obtained in man, a point which will be discussed below.

(*3*) Of the five glycosides containing glucose, lanatosides A, B and C, K-Strophanthin-β and K-Strophanthoside, all but one are weaker by 30 to 65 per cent than the corresponding progenins while lanatoside A is equal to its progenin.[4] The question arises as to whether this decrease in activity resulting from the introduction of glucose in position R_4 (in the case of digitoxin, gitoxin and digoxin) or R_2 (in the case of cymarin) is due to the inherent difference between glucose and the desoxy sugars or simply to the position which it takes up in the molecule. It seems probable that the former is the case, since (*a*) glucose added to one desoxy sugar unit as in K-Strophanthin-β produces roughly the same effect as when added to three digitoxose units as in lanatosides B and C, and since (*b*) there is no significant change in potency when an additional molecule of glucose is added to K-Strophanthin-β to give K-Strophanthoside. The answer to this question will depend upon the synthesis of glucosides of the various genins and the determination of their activity as compared with the rhamnosides, cymarosides and digitoxosides.

Application to bio-assay

It should be stated at once that it is not intended that the embryonic heart method should be used to establish a "chick unit" for digitalis assay. Whether or not it may be of service in comparing unknown with standard preparations may be judged from the considerations which follow:

While the use of a "relative" method, involving comparison with a widely accepted standard preparation, eliminates errors due to variations in pro-

[4] Quite the opposite is true for the cat assay results. Almost without exception the "genuine" glycosides are more potent in terms of moles per kgm. than their progenins (22).

cedure between laboratories and due to seasonal or other variations in experimental animals, it depends inherently on the qualitative identity of action of each of the drugs which enter into the comparison, whether galenical preparations or pure glycosides are to be compared with the same standard. The

TABLE 4

Comparison of the therapeutic dose of the individual glycosides with bio-assay data

GLYCOSIDE	TOTAL DOSE ORALLY FOR DIGITALIZATION	MAINTENANCE DOSE ORALLY	LETHAL DOSE FOR CAT, HATCHER AND BRODY METHOD	SYSTOLIC DOSE FOR FROG (U. S. P.)
	mgm.	*mgm.*	*mgm. per kgm.*	*mgm. per kgm.*
Digitaline nativelle	1.0–1.25	0.1–0.2 (Gold, 26)	0.42 (Gold, 26) 0.47 (Fromherz and Welsch, 20)	4.0 (Gold, 26)
Digoxin	3 –5	0.4 (Stroud, 27) 0.5 (Batterman, 28)	0.22 (Chen, 18) 0.33 (DeGraff, 23) 0.44 (White, 29)	2.5 (Chen, 18)
Lanatoside C	7.5–15. 6.25	1.5–2.5 (Gold, 30) 0.25 – 1.25 (Fahr, 31)	0.25 (Gold, 30) 0.28 (Rothlin, 32) 0.26 (DeGraff, 23)	1.6 (Gold, 30)

TABLE 5

Ratio of dosage (or concentration) of glycosides expressed in moles to digitaline nativelle by various methods of determination

DRUG	DIGITALIZING DOSE IN MAN—ORAL	MAINTENANCE DOSE IN MAN—ORAL	CAT INTRAVENOUS (AVERAGE)	FROG LYMPH SAC	EMBRYONIC CHICK HEART WITH RANGE IN PER CENT
Digitaline nativelle	1	1 (Gold)	1	1	1
Digoxin	3.5	2.6 (Stroud) 3.3 (Batterman)	0.73	0.61	3.07 (87–115)
Lanatoside C	7.8 4.3	10 (Gold) 3.9 (Fahr)	0.45	0.31	4.50 (87–115)

evidence is conclusive (19, 23, 24) that this requirement is not met in the case of the components of digitalis leaf or of the pure glycosides when administered by lymph sac or intramuscular injection in the frog or intravenous injection in the cat. The reason for this may be found largely in the great variation in the rate of dissipation of the lethal effect of the several glycosides (23, 24). It has been demonstrated (25), for instance, that a high rate of intravenous infusion in the cat will give rise to a smaller lethal dose for digitoxigenin and a greater lethal dose for digitoxin than is obtained with a slow rate. In other words, drugs which dissipate rapidly are favored by being introduced into the blood stream more rapidly than the organism can handle them. The frog methods are further complicated by variations in rate of absorption, but it seems likely that in both procedures the more rapidly dissipated drugs are given undue weight in the final result. Use of an isolated heart overcomes all variation due to this factor since no dissipation can occur except that brought about by the chemical processes in the heart itself. If the phenomenon of "cumulation" of the glycosides depends upon fixation by the heart, then it is not improbable that those drugs which are most rapidly dissipated in the intact animal will require the longest time (or conversely the highest concentration) to produce atrio-ventricular block in the isolated heart.

The validity of the above argument rests on the comparison of the results of the various methods of assay with the clinical dosages of the pure individual glycosides. Unfortunately the clinical data available at present are fragmentary. Nevertheless the order of magnitude of the therapeutic dose is known for a sufficient number of drugs to make certain preliminary conclusions possible. In table 4 are given data, taken from the literature, for the human and animal dosage of digitaline Nativelle, digoxin and lanatoside C. From this information the average ratio of dosages of the last two drugs to digitaline Nativelle have been calculated and appear in table 5. It should be noted that *mols* have been used in every case instead of *mgm.* This influences the absolute values somewhat but not the correlation between therapeutic and bio-assay dosage. It will be seen from table 5 that for these three drugs the order of magnitude of the clinical dosage ratios is the same as the concentration ratios for the embryonic chick heart. The ratios obtained by the cat and frog assay, on the other hand, do not even lie in the right direction. Thus lanatoside C and digoxin are both more potent than digitaline Nativelle for the cat and frog but much less potent when administered orally in man.

SUMMARY

1. A procedure has been described for the comparison of the digitaloids with respect to their ability to produce atrio-ventricular block in the embryonic chick heart. This preparation has been shown to offer a number of theoretical and practical advantages over those in general use. A method for expressing the results has been suggested.

2. Fifteen chemically related cardiac glycosides and genins have been studied by the chick heart procedure and the following tentative conclusions have been reached as to the influence of various structural configurations on cardiac action: (*a*) all other factors being constant, variation in the substitu-

ents on the steroid nucleus is capable of causing profound changes in activity; (*b*) the desoxy sugars give rise to marked enhancement in the activity of the genins, the weaker the genin the greater the enhancement, and this effect seems not to depend on the nature of the particular desoxy sugar; and (*c*) conjugation with glucose in addition to desoxy sugar never increases the potency of the glycoside and usually decreases it significantly.

3. The results obtained with the embryonic chick heart for digitaline Nativelle, digoxin and lanatoside C have been shown to correlate at least in order of magnitude, with the oral therapeutic dosage. On the other hand, the values for these three drugs by the cat and frog methods bear no apparent relationship to the clinical dose. The possible reasons for this have been discussed.

The authors wish to express their thanks to Dr. C. I. Bliss, Consulting Biometrician, and to Dr. E. J. DeBeer of Burroughs Wellcome and Company, Inc. for their helpful criticism of the manuscript, and to Dr. K. K. Chen of Eli Lilly and Company, Dr. Guy W. Clark of Lederle Laboratories, Inc., Professor Louis F. Fieser of Harvard University, Dr. Charles Henze of Sandoz Chemical Works, Inc., Dr. W. A. Jacobs of the Rockefeller Institute for Medical Research, Dr. Robert C. Page of Burroughs Wellcome and Company, Inc., Dr. E. M. Rothenberger of Sandoz Chemical Works, Inc., and Mr. Clyde G. Williams of the Laboratory Nativelle for their kind cooperation in supplying the glycosides and genins without which this study would have been impossible. The expenses of the investigation were defrayed, in part, by a grant from the John and Mary R. Markle Foundation.

REFERENCES

(1) Paff and Johnson: Am. J. Physiol., **122**, 753, 1938.
(2) Paff: This Journal, **69**, 311, 1940.
(3) Paff: Ibid., **70**, 235, 1940.
(4) Paff and Johnson: Proc. Soc. Exp. Biol. and Med., **44**, 155, 1940.
(5) Goodman and Gilman: The Pharmacological Basis of Therapeutics. Macmillan, N. Y., 1941, pp. 506–511.
(6) Clark: The Mode of Action of Drugs on Cells. Arnold, London, 1933, p. 78, 92.
(7) Bliss and Marks: Quart. J. Pharm. Pharmacol., **12**, 182, 1939.
(8) Miller, Bliss and Braun: J. Am. Pharm. Assoc., **28**, 644, 1939.
(9) Bliss: Ann. Entolmol. Soc. Am., **33**, 721, 1940.
(10) Fisher: Statistical Methods for Research Workers. Oliver and Boyd, London, 7th ed.; 1938, p. 140.
(11) Snedecor: Statistical Methods. Iowa State College Press, Ames, 2nd ed., 1940, p. 184.
(12) Irwin: J. Royal Statistical Soc., Suppl. 4, 1, 1937.
(13) Wedd: This Journal, **65**, 268, 1939.
(14) Boyer and Poindexter: Am. Heart J., **20**, 586, 1940.
(15) Cattell and Goodell: Science, **86**, 106, 1937.
(16) Elderfield: Chem. Reviews, **17**, 187, 1935.

(17) CHEN AND ELDERFIELD: THIS JOURNAL, **70,** 338, 1941.
(18) CHEN, ROBBINS AND WORTH: J. Am. Pharm. Assoc., **27,** 189, 1938.
(19) FROMHERZ AND WELSCH: Arch. f. exp. Path. Pharmakol., **161,** 266, 1931.
(20) CLOETTA: Arch. f. exp. Path. Pharmakol., **112,** 261, 1926.
(21) FIESER AND JACOBSEN: J. Am. Chem. Soc., **59,** 2335, 1937.
(22) STOLL: J. Am. Pharm. Assoc., **27,** 761, 1938.
(23) DEGRAFF AND LEHMAN: Proc. Soc. Exp. Biol. and Med., **45,** 323, 1940.
(24) GOLD: Arch. Int. Med., **32,** 779, 1923.
(25) ROTHLIN: Annale de l'Hosp. de la Santa Creu i Sant Pau, **9,** 586, 1935.
(26) GOLD, KWIT AND CATTELL: THIS JOURNAL, **69,** 177, 1940.
(27) STROUD AND VANDER VEER: J. A. M. A., **109,** 1808, 1937.
(28) BATTERMAN: Results to be published of a study on the Third (New York University) Division of Bellevue Hospital.
(29) WHITE: THIS JOURNAL, **52,** 1, 1934.
(30) KWIT, GOLD AND CATTELL: Ibid., **70,** 254, 1940.
(31) FAHR: Am. Heart J., **21,** 133, 1941.
(32) ROTHLIN: Schweiz. Med. Wochschr., **68,** 1336, 1938.

TOXICITY AND ACTIONS OF TRIMETHYLENE GLYCOL

W. VAN WINKLE, JR.

From the Department of Pharmacology, Stanford University School of Medicine, San Francisco

Received for publication February 20, 1941

Of the various glycols studied thus far, propylene glycol is the only one which is relatively non-toxic, and therefore useful as a solvent and vehicle for medicinal and food agents (1, 2, 3). The isomer of propylene glycol has not been previously investigated and nothing is known about its actions or possible toxicity. Since trimethylene glycol is isomeric with propylene glycol it was thought desirable to determine similarities in, or differences between, these two compounds. This report presents the results of such a study and shows that trimethylene glycol is entirely different pharmacologically from propylene glycol.

PROPERTIES OF TRIMETHYLENE GLYCOL

The chemical relationship between the propylene and trimethylene glycols is indicated by the following structural formulas:

Propylene Glycol   Trimethylene Glycol

Both compounds are closely related to naturally occurring body constituents such as glycerol, lactic acid and methyl glyoxal. Propylene glycol is converted to lactic acid and hence is burned or converted to glycogen (4). By analogy, it might be expected that trimethylene glycol would be converted physiologically to malonic acid. Since malonic acid forms an insoluble calcium salt, a somewhat higher toxicity might be expected from trimethylene glycol than from propylene glycol, and this was found to be the case.

Trimethylene glycol[1] is a viscous liquid which boils at 123 to 125°C. at 30 mm. pressure. When freshly distilled it is colorless, but it rapidly becomes

[1] The trimethylene glycol was obtained from the Eastman Kodak Company, Rochester, N. Y.

yellowish brown even when kept tightly stoppered in a dark bottle. The boiling point apparently does not change. It has a brackish, irritating taste, and the solvent and other properties common to glycols.

ACUTE TOXICITY

The criterion of acute toxicity was the rapidly fatal dose of trimethylene glycol according to different routes of administration in different species of animals.

Intravenous injection. A 50 per cent solution of trimethylene glycol in water was injected into the marginal ear veins of 19 rabbits, at least 3 rabbits being used for each dose tried. The surely fatal doses (which killed all of 6 rabbits injected) were 6 and 7 cc. per kilogram; 5 cc. per kilogram killed 60 per cent of 5; 4 cc. per kilogram killed 40 per cent of 5; and 3 cc. per kilogram was not fatal to 3. Accordingly, the 50 per cent fatal dose would be between 4 and 5 cc. per kilogram, which was the same for propylene glycol in the same species (1).

Intramuscular injection. Whole trimethylene glycol was injected into the gluteal musculature of 42 white rats, at least 4 animals being used for each dose tried. Surely fatal doses, which killed all of 9 rats injected, were 8 and 9 cc. per kilogram; 7.5 cc. per kilogram killed 75 per cent of 8 rats; 7 cc. per kilogram killed 80 per cent of 5; 6 cc. per kilogram killed 40 per cent of 5; and 3 and 5 cc. per kilogram were not fatal to any of 15. Thus the dose for 50 per cent mortality would be between 6 and 7 cc. per kilogram, which would indicate that trimethylene glycol is about twice as toxic as propylene glycol by the same route in the same species (1).

Gastric administration. Undiluted trimethylene glycol was administered gastrically with the aid of a suitable metal tube to 132 rats, in doses from 1 to 19 cc. per kilogram body weight. At least 5 rats were used for each dose. Surely fatal doses were 18 and 19 cc. per kilogram in 10 rats. Fifty per cent mortality in 6 rats was produced by 16 cc. per kilogram. However, 15 cc. per kilogram killed 64 per cent of 11 rats; 17 cc. per kilogram killed only 40 per cent of 5; 10 cc. per kilogram killed 47 per cent of 15; and doses of 11, 12, 13 and 14 cc. per kilogram killed only from 10 to 18 per cent of 6 to 11 rats in each group. No rats were killed with doses of from 1 to 9 cc. per kilogram among a total of 51 animals. The considerable variability in toxicity on oral administration might be expected because of the known variability in gastrointestinal absorption even under the most favorable conditions. Food had been withdrawn for 24 hours in all the rats used for gastric administrations. According to these results in rats, gastric toxicity of trimethylene glycol is about twice that of propylene glycol, in agreement with the results of intramuscular injection.

In cats, it was almost impossible to determine the fatal dose accurately. A single gastric administration of 3 cc. per kilogram to 3 cats produced no demonstrable effect within 48 hours. On the third day the animals refused to eat but craved water. Immediately after drinking water they vomited; they gradually lost weight and died within a week. Ten other cats were given trimethylene glycol in doses of from 1 to 48 cc. per kilogram as single or multiple doses. Doses of 1 cc. per kilogram were survived by 2 cats, but the remaining 8 cats died in from 1 to 16 days after receiving doses of 3, 5 and 15 cc. per kilogram. Multiple doses ranged from 2 to 16, but there was no relationship between multiplicity of dosage and survival time of animals, nor indeed between the total amount of the glycol given and survival time.

Cats are apparently rather sensitive to trimethylene glycol. Gastric doses of 3 cc. or more per kilogram were found to be fatal for all cats, but intravenous and intramuscular doses of 3 cc. per kilogram were not fatal to any. Whether death from gastric administration was due to the trimethylene glycol directly, or was the result of anorexia and starvation, was not determined. The lack of symptoms, and absence of pathological changes in the stomach, grossly and microscopically, suggest starvation, at least in the delayed deaths. The procedure of gastric administration could not have been responsible for any gastric intolerance or toxicity, since the same procedure gave high tolerances of propylene glycol. Owing to other unfavorable results it was not deemed worth while to continue further with this phase of the investigation.

The systemic symptoms from near-fatal doses of trimethylene glycol, and before death from fatal doses, were depression in all animals regardless of the method of administration, thus resembling propylene glycol in high doses.

CHRONIC TOXICITY

Seven groups of 5 rats each were maintained for 15 weeks on a stock diet[2] with additions as follows: Group 1, control diet alone; group 2, control diet containing 5 per cent trimethylene glycol; group 3, control diet containing 12 per cent trimethylene glycol; group 4, control diet plus 10 cc. water per kilogram, daily by stomach tube; group 5, control diet plus 10 cc. propylene glycol per kilogram, daily by stomach tube; group 6, control diet plus 5 cc. trimethylene glycol per kilogram, daily by stomach tube; and group 7, control diet plus 10 cc. trimethylene glycol per kilogram, daily by stomach tube. The food intake and body weight of all the animals were recorded weekly. The results are presented graphically in figure 1.

Of the 7 groups of rats, 3 groups showed definitely diminished growth rates,

[2] The constituents of this diet are as follows: corn meal 68 per cent, linseed oil cake 10 per cent, dried ground alfalfa 2 per cent, powdered casein 10 per cent, lard 5 per cent, cod liver oil 3 per cent, bone ash 1.5 per cent, and sodium chloride 0.5 per cent. The composition and caloric value were as follows: protein 18.6 per cent (19.4 calories), fat 11.8 per cent (26.9 calories), carbohydrate 51.5 per cent (53.7 calories), roughage 3.5 per cent, salts 3.9 per cent, and water 10.7 per cent.

3 grew normally, and 1 grew slightly less than normal. The 3 groups which grew at approximately normal rates were those on control diet and control diet plus water and control diet plus propylene glycol by stomach tube. The rats in these 3 groups consumed the same average amount (15 grams) of food daily. The 3 groups which showed diminished growth rates all received

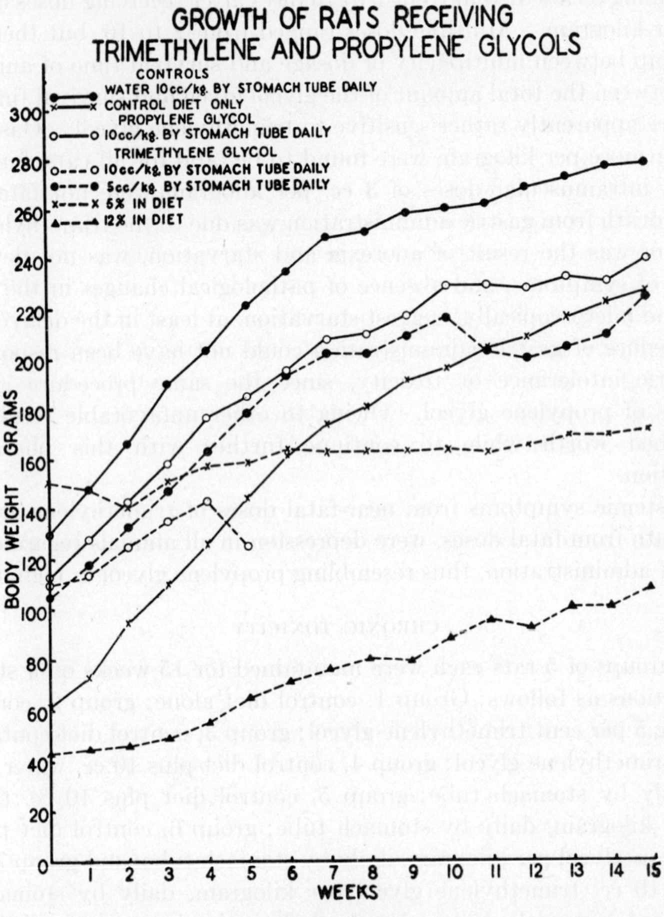

FIG. 1. GROWTH OF WHITE RATS ON CONTINUED ADMINISTRATION OF TRIMETHYLENE AND PROPYLENE GLYCOLS

trimethylene glycol, 2 groups receiving it in the diet and 1 receiving 5 cc. per kilogram by stomach tube daily. These 3 groups all showed a diminished food intake (10 to 11 grams daily) which probably accounted for the lessened growth rate. However, the trimethylene glycol exerted an additional toxic action, since all the rats receiving 10 cc. per kilogram by stomach tube died at the end of 5 weeks. The group which received 5 cc. trimethylene glycol per kilogram daily ate about as much food as the control unmedicated animals, but showed a lessened growth rate, particularly during the last 5 weeks. At this time, 2 of the rats lost weight rapidly and died. As compared with propylene glycol (2, 3), trimethylene glycol was about twice as toxic when given repeatedly to the same species and under the same conditions. This agreed well with the results on the comparative acute toxicity of these two compounds.

GLYCOGENIC ACTION

Forty rats of equal body weight were fasted for 48 hours and then given different doses of trimethylene glycol by stomach tube. After 3 hours the rats were killed by a rapid inhalation of chloroform and the liver glycogen was determined according to the method of Pflüger (5). Ten rats each received 3, 5, 10 and 15 cc. per kilogram body weight of trimethylene glycol, and the glycogen content of their liver was found to be 217, 237, 230 and 377 mgm. in 100 grams of liver, respectively. Ten other rats similarly treated received 10 cc. per kilogram of propylene glycol and the liver glycogen was 1202 mgm. in 100 grams of liver. Twenty additional rats received 10 cc. per kilogram of physiological saline solution, as controls, and the liver glycogen was 299 mgm. in 100 grams of liver. Clearly only the propylene glycol increased the liver glycogen, in confirmation of previous results (3, 4). Accordingly, trimethylene glycol has no demonstrable glycogenic action, an interesting difference from propylene glycol, which must be ascribed to the difference in chemical structure.

SUMMARY AND CONCLUSIONS

1. Trimethylene glycol, the chemical isomer of propylene glycol, was found to be about twice as toxic as propylene glycol according to acute fatal doses intramuscularly and gastrically in white rats. Intravenously in rabbits, the acute toxicity was about the same as that of propylene glycol.
2. Cats were found to be rather sensitive to trimethylene glycol gastrically, delayed death having occurred after single small doses of 3 cc. per kilogram of body weight which were well tolerated intravenously and intramuscularly in rats.
3. Trimethylene glycol exhibited a definite chronic toxicity, being about twice as toxic as propylene glycol in the same species and under the same conditions.
4. Trimethylene glycol showed no demonstrable glycogenic action in rats, a striking difference from propylene glycol.
5. Trimethylene glycol therefore has no usefulness as a vehicle or solvent in medicinal or food products and does not warrant further investigation. The higher acute and chronic toxicities, and absence of glycogenic action, indicate interesting fundamental differences between the trimethylene and

propylene glycols which are to be attributed to the difference in chemical structure of the 2 isomers, a difference which, in turn, determines the practical usefulness and comparative non-toxicity of propylene glycol.

REFERENCES

(1) SEIDENFELD: THIS JOURNAL, **44**: 109–121, 1932.
(2) HANZLIK, NEWMAN, VAN WINKLE, JR., LEHMAN AND KENNEDY: Ibid., **67**: 101–113, 1939.
(3) HANZLIK, LEHMAN, VAN WINKLE, JR. AND KENNEDY: Ibid., **67**: 114–126, 1939.
(4) NEWMAN, VAN WINKLE, JR., KENNEDY AND MORTON: Ibid., **68**: 194–200, 1940.
(5) PFLÜGER: Abderhalden's Handb. der biochem. Arbeitsmethod., **2**: 1070–1080, 1910.

ANESTHESIA

IV. THE ANESTHETIC ACTION OF CYCLOPROPYL ETHYL ETHER[1]

JOHN C. KRANTZ, JR., C. JELLEFF CARR, SYLVAN E. FORMAN, WILLIAM E. EVANS, JR., AND HENRY WOLLENWEBER

From the Department of Pharmacology, School of Medicine, University of Maryland, Baltimore

Received for publication March 29, 1941

In a previous communication (1) the authors reported their findings on the anesthetic properties of cyclopropyl methyl ether, designated as cyprome ether. Later its availability as a surgical anesthetic in man was demonstrated (2). In the chemical investigations which led to the synthesis of cyprome ether, its three homologs, namely, ethyl, propyl and butyl cyclopropyl ethers were prepared. The purpose of these studies is to investigate the pharmacology of the second member of this series of cyclopropyl aliphatic ethers, designated in this laboratory as "cypreth ether." Its relationship to ether and cyclopropane is apparent from the following formulas

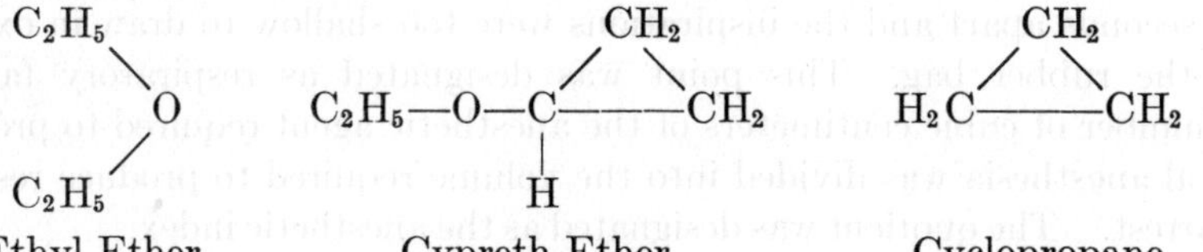

Ethyl Ether — Cypreth Ether — Cyclopropane

Cypreth ether is a volatile, colorless liquid, with a characteristic ethereal odor; it boils at 68°C. and has a specific gravity of 0.780 at 25°C.

Observation anesthesias (*monkey*). Five large Rhesus monkeys were each anesthetized twice with cypreth ether. The technic employed is described in detail in our previous communication (1). The induction period with cypreth ether was observed to be of short duration and frequently the monkeys passed into the plane of surgical anesthesia without appreciable struggle. During induction, salivation was not marked and the bronchial tree remained quite free from mucus throughout the anesthesia. Surgical anesthesia was uneventful. Breathing was often stertorous but deep and regular. Relaxation of the musculature of the abdomen and extremities was complete. Only

[1] The expense of this investigation was defrayed in part by a grant from the Ohio Chemical and Manufacturing Co. of Cleveland, Ohio. The authors are greatly indebted to Dr. Amos G. Horney of the technical staff of this company for making available comparatively large quantities of cypreth ether for us in the prosecution of these studies.

an occasional animal exhibited incoordinated muscular leg movements during anesthesia. Pain reflexes were abolished sufficiently for various surgical procedures such as abdominal and cervical incisions. Recovery from anesthesias of 15 to 20 minutes duration was as prompt as when ethyl ether was employed. There was some excitation during the recovery period, but less than with cyprome or ethyl ether. Incoordination of the extremities was observed for 10 to 15 minutes after recovery. During these 10 anesthesias the quantities of cypreth ether employed were approximately one-half those required for the same anesthetic plane with cyprome ether.

Anesthetic index (dog). The dogs used in these experiments were, as far as possible, of uniform weight. They were fed a standard laboratory ration during one week and fasted 12 hours before anesthesia. At least seven day intervals elapsed between anesthesias in the same animal. In a closed circuit the animal was permitted to breathe oxygen for 2 minutes. Two cubic centimeters of cypreth ether was then given, ejecting it from the needle of the syringe upon gauze contained in the mask. The mask was warmed to 37°C. to facilitate the volatilization of the agent. Thereafter 0.5 cc. was administered each minute until surgical anesthesia occurred. The point at which the corneal and the wink reflexes were abolished, concomitant with relaxation of the extremities and abdominal muscles, was considered as the the beginning of the plane of surgical anesthesia. The anesthetic was administered at the same rate until the respirations of the animal were from 6 to 10 seconds apart and the inspirations were too shallow to draw in oxygen from the rubber bag. This point was designated as respiratory failure. The number of cubic centimeters of the anesthetic agent required to produce surgical anesthesia was divided into the volume required to produce respiratory arrest. The quotient was designated as the anesthetic index.

In this series of 40 anesthesias with cypreth ether, only one animal succumbed; all others were revived by artificial respiration. For comparative purposes experiments were conducted with ethyl ether, cyprome ether, vinethene and chloroform on these same dogs. All technics were the same with the exception of warming the mask; this was not necessary with ethyl ether, cyprome ether or divinyl ether. With chloroform, the volumes were reduced one-half, owing to its greater density.

These data are shown in tables 1, 2, 3, 4 and 5.

The anesthetic index of cypreth ether is 2.0 times greater than the index of ethyl ether measured on these same dogs. The mean dose of cypreth ether required to produce respiratory arrest on a body weight basis is 1.2 times greater than that required of ethyl ether. Our value for the anesthetic index of ethyl ether of 2.07 is higher on this group of animals than was our previously determined value of 1.76. Likewise the value for cyprome ether is correspondingly higher. An examination of the data assembled indicates that within the error of this experiment the induction doses of cypreth ether

TABLE 1
Anesthetic index—cypreth ether

DOG NUMBER	SEX	WEIGHT	INDUCTION	RESPIRATORY FAILURE	ANESTHETIC INDEX
		kgm.	*cc./kgm.*	*cc./kgm.*	
1	M	10.8	0.42	1.54	3.70
2	M	7.8	0.45	1.79	4.00
3	M	6.6	0.45	1.82	4.00
4	M	6.1	0.41	1.47	3.60
5	F	7.0	0.43	1.43	3.33
6	F	9.3	0.54	1.72	3.20
6A	M	6.2	0.40	1.53	3.80
7	M	8.3	0.30	1.14	3.80
8	F	6.8	0.44	1.70	3.83
9	F	7.7	0.32	1.36	4.20
4	M	5.5	0.36	1.63	4.50
5	F	6.7	0.37	1.27	3.40
6	M	5.8	0.35	1.30	3.75
2	M	7.3	0.41	1.57	3.83
3	M	6.2	0.40	1.61	4.00
9	F	7.3	0.34	1.30	3.80
8	F	6.2	0.40	2.09	5.20
2	M	7.0	0.43	1.64	3.83
3	M	6.7	0.30	1.12	3.75
4	M	5.8	0.35	1.90	5.50
5	F	6.8	0.37	1.32	3.60
7	M	7.2	0.28	1.46	5.25
8	F	5.4	0.46	2.13	4.60
9	F	7.4	0.34	1.35	4.00
10	F	5.7	0.35	1.66	4.75
11	M	6.5	0.38	1.84	4.80
12	F	6.4	0.39	1.95	5.00
13	F	6.0	0.42	1.75	4.20
14	M	8.1	0.31	1.48	4.80
2	M	7.0	0.57	2.00	3.50
14	M	7.5	0.33	1.33	4.00
8	F	5.8	0.43	1.29	3.00
11	M	7.4	0.34	1.36	4.00
3	M	5.6	0.36	1.52	4.25
23	M	5.0	0.40	1.40	3.50
12	F	6.5	0.39	1.92	5.00
2	M	6.8	0.45	1.93	4.33
20	F	6.0	0.33	1.66	5.00
21	F	7.6	0.46	2.30	5.00
22	F	7.6	0.33	1.45	4.40
Mean			0.39	1.60	4.15
σ			0.07	0.27	0.61
C.V.			17.9	16.9	14.7

and divinyl ether are the same, and when correction is made for the specific gravity of chloroform, the potency of cypreth ether approaches that of

TABLE 2

Anesthetic index—ethyl ether

DOG NUMBER	SEX	WEIGHT	INDUCTION	RESPIRATORY FAILURE	ANESTHETIC INDEX
		kgm.	*cc./kgm.*	*cc./kgm.*	
1	F	11.6	0.99	2.24	2.26
2	M	8.3	1.38	1.80	1.30
3	M	7.3	0.69	1.50	2.20
4	M	5.8	1.12	2.50	2.22
5	F	6.8	1.10	2.06	1.86
9	F	7.7	1.04	1.76	1.69
6	M	5.7	1.40	2.36	1.69
7	M	7.0	0.78	2.28	2.91
8	F	5.5	0.91	2.09	2.30
3	M	6.5	0.62	1.77	2.87
2	M	7.0	1.07	1.85	1.73
5	F	7.1	1.20	2.10	1.75
9	F	6.3	0.55	1.59	2.87
2	M	6.8	1.25	2.21	1.76
8	F	5.5	1.00	2.09	2.09
12	F	6.5	1.08	2.15	2.00
14	M	7.7	0.78	1.43	1.83
11	M	5.4	1.11	2.31	2.08
15	M	6.1	1.15	2.46	2.14
17	M	7.5	0.93	1.66	1.78
Mean			1.00	2.00	2.07
σ			0.23	0.31	0.43
C.V.			23.0	15.5	20.8

TABLE 3

Anesthetic index—cyprome ether

DOG NUMBER	SEX	WEIGHT	INDUCTION	RESPIRATORY FAILURE	ANESTHETIC INDEX
		kgm.	*cc./kgm.*	*cc./kgm.*	
16	F	8.1	0.80	1.91	2.39
13	F	5.1	0.50	1.57	3.20
9	F	5.4	0.46	1.48	3.20
18	F	7.8	0.45	1.41	3.14
19	F	7.2	0.42	1.32	3.16
Mean			0.53	1.54	3.02

chloroform. The data on the relative margins of safety are self-explanatory and are diagramatically shown in the median values in chart 1.

Blood pressure studies (*dog*). The effect of cypreth ether on blood pressure

TABLE 4

Anesthetic index—divinyl oxide

DOG NUMBER	SEX	WEIGHT	INDUCTION	RESPIRATORY FAILURE	ANESTHETIC INDEX
		kgm.	*cc./kgm.*	*cc./kgm.*	
3	M	6.0	0.42	0.60	1.40
12	F	6.4	0.39	1.02	2.60
2	M	7.0	0.43	0.86	2.00
8	F	5.8	0.34	0.69	2.00
19	F	7.0	0.43	1.00	2.33
14	M	7.4	0.34	0.96	2.80
11	M	5.1	0.39	0.88	2.25
Mean..............................			0.39	0.86	2.00

TABLE 5

Anesthetic index—chloroform

DOG NUMBER	SEX	WEIGHT	INDUCTION	RESPIRATORY FAILURE	ANESTHETIC INDEX
		kgm.	*cc./kgm.*	*cc./kgm.*	
18	F	7.4	0.14	0.21	1.50
3	M	5.6	0.18	0.27	1.50
16	F	7.4	0.14	0.24	1.75
13	F	4.6	0.22	0.27	1.25
15	M	5.5	0.18	0.32	1.75
17	M	6.9	0.15	0.29	2.00
Mean..............................			0.17	0.27	1.62

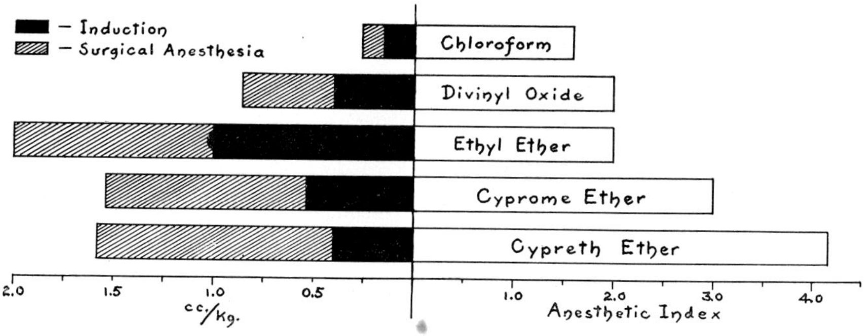

CHART 1. MEDIAN VALUES, ANESTHETIC INDEX

was determined by cannulating the femoral artery under procaine hydrochloride anesthesia and preparing the animal for a blood pressure tracing in the usual manner. The respiratory tracings were made by means of a chest tambour. After a normal tracing, cypreth ether was administered by the same technic employed to measure the anesthetic index. In six experiments the respiration ceased before cardiac arrest, and in one animal resuscitation was successful after 10 minutes of respiratory arrest. One animal was given the anesthetic and permitted to continue under surgical anesthesia for one hour. The amount of anesthetic agent was diminished so as not to induce respiratory failure. Portions of this typical tracing are shown in chart 2. The tracing in chart 2 shows a normal blood pressure and respiration during the hour period of surgical anesthesia.

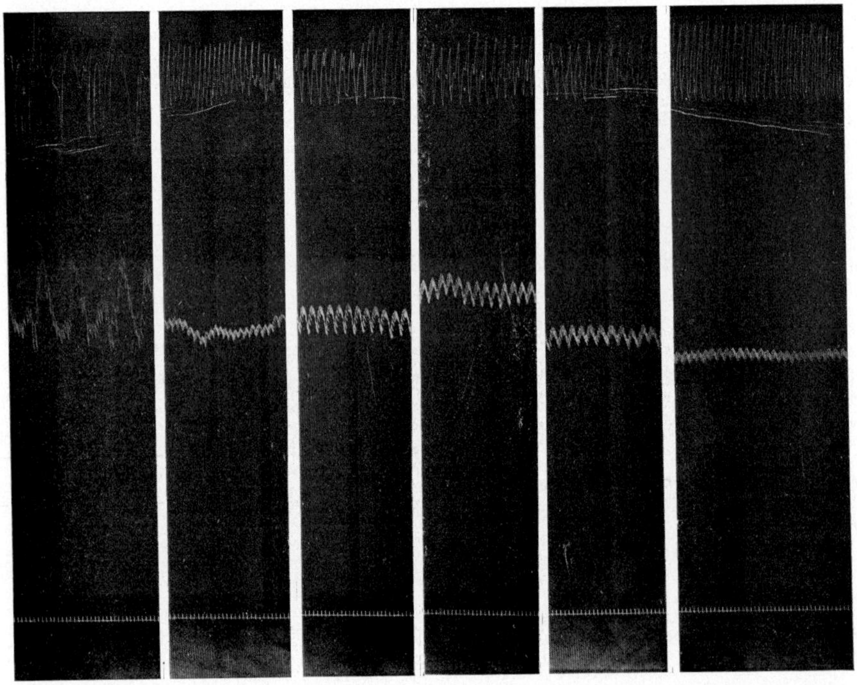

CHART 2. BLOOD PRESSURE OF THE DOG UNDER CYPRETH ETHER ANESTHESIA

The upper tracing is respiration. (*1*) is normal, (*2*) is the induction period, (*3*) light surgical anesthesia, (*4*) early surgical anesthesia (*5*) surgical anesthesia after ½ hour, (*6*) surgical anesthesia after 1 hour.

Electrocardiogram studies (*monkey*). Seven Rhesus monkeys were anesthetized with cypreth ether and maintained at the surgical level for 10 minutes. Just prior to anesthesia and during surgical anesthesia electrocardiograms were made. Five of these animals had been anesthetized repeatedly and in two, this anesthesia was the initial experiment.

Examination of the electrocardiographic records obtained in this series under normal conditions and under deep surgical anesthesia reveals no significant differences either in the form of the E.C.G. or in its regularity. In most cases there was a slight increase in rate during anesthesia although in two cases no change occurred. The average increase was about 10 per cent. The P-R interval held constant between 90 and 100 milliseconds, and the T wave was positive in all leads in all cases tested.

A typical E.C.G. Lead II record is shown in chart 3. Here the amplitude of the S wave increased slightly, the P-R interval remained constant at 0.094 seconds and the rate increased during anesthesia from 204 to 218 beats per minute. We are indebted to Dr. Robert H. Oster of the department of phys-

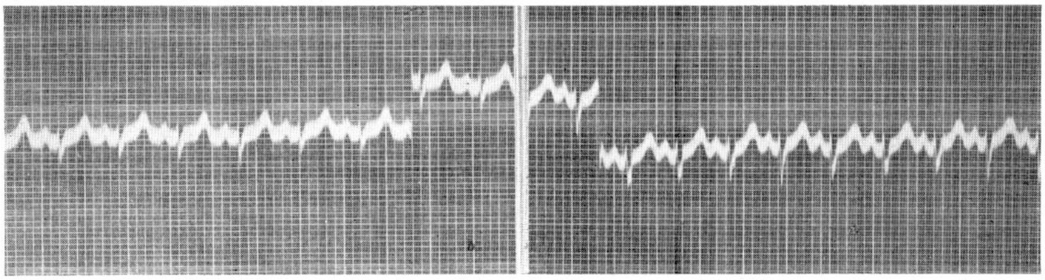

Normal Cypreth Ether Anesthesia

CHART 3. ELECTROCARDIOGRAMS, NORMAL AND UNDER CYPRETH ETHER ANESTHESIA

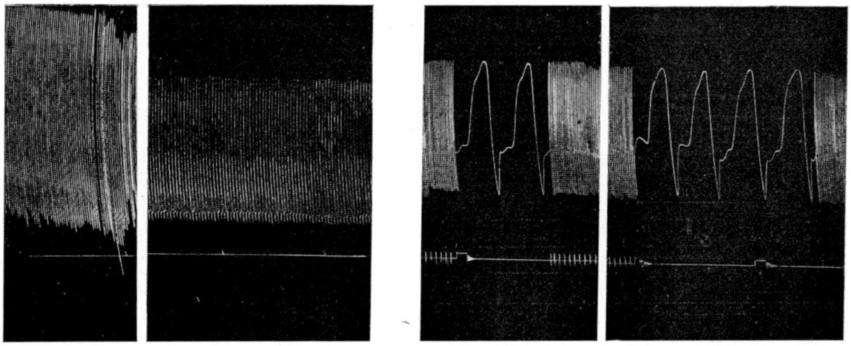

Normal After 1 hr.
Frog No. 8. Perfusion with 0.009M. Cypreth Ether.

Normal After 20 min.
Frog No. 12. Perfusion with 0.009 M. Cypreth Ether. Note lack of influence on auricular or ventricular beat.

CHART 4. EFFECT OF CYPRETH ETHER ON THE FROG'S HEART

iology for his assistance in conducting this study and for his advice in interpreting the findings.

Effect on the perfused heart (frog). Cypreth ether was dissolved in Howell-Ringer's solution and perfused through the frog's heart in situ. Several dilutions were employed to determine the threshold concentration required to cause demonstrable cardiac changes within a minute. In addition, the concentration of cypreth ether found in the dog's blood during surgical anesthesia, approximately 0.09 per cent or 0.009 molar, was perfused repeatedly for long periods of time. Typical tracings are shown in chart 4. The threshold concentration of cypreth ether required to produce cardiac effects in 15 animals was 0.035 molar. The tracings show that 0.009 molar cypreth ether did not significantly influence the rate or amplitude of the beat of the heart during one hour perfusion.

Liver function tests (monkey). Five Rhesus monkeys were subjected to the bromsulfonphthalein liver function test. The procedure for man was modified so that 1 cc. per kilogram of a 1 per cent solution of the dye was injected. After 15 minutes not more than 25 per cent of the injected dye remained in the blood of the unanesthetized healthy animals. The animals were anesthetized with cypreth ether and maintained at the level of surgical anesthesia for 10 minutes. This was repeated one week later and liver function tests performed the day following the second anesthesia and 4 days later. In no instance did the dye in the blood exceed 25 per cent of the total quantity injected.

TABLE 6

Effect of cypreth ether anesthesia on the blood chemistry of monkeys

MONKEY NUMBER	WEIGHT	BLOOD SUGAR			UREA NITROGEN			CARBON DIOXIDE COMBINING POWER OF PLASMA CC. PER CENT AT 0°C. AT 760 MM.		
		Normal	Anesthesia	24 hours later	Normal	Anesthesia	24 hours later	Normal	Anesthesia	24 hours later
	kgm.									
1	3.2	104	118	114	19.5	11.9	9.2	46.8	51.4	49.8
2	3.0	101	95	134	24.7	17.0	15.7	38.8	46.6	44.2
3	3.2	90	104	124	17.9	15.8	12.5	34.1	44.7	36.5
H	5.5	79	90	77	13.9	16.4	9.2	49.4	52.3	57.5
C	2.9	120	122	146	19.1	17.3	9.9	47.5	50.5	50.9

Blood chemistry studies (monkey). Rhesus monkeys were anesthetized to the surgical plane for 10 minutes with cypreth ether. Prior to anesthesia, during surgical anesthesia and 24 hours later blood samples were drawn for analysis. The data are shown in table 6.

Concentration required for anesthesia (mouse). The concentration of cypreth ether required to induce anesthesia was determined by typical partial pressure experiments previously described (1). The results are shown in table 7. With ethyl ether in our previous studies, 4 per cent partial pressure produced no anesthesias, and 5 per cent anesthetized 40 per cent of the animals.

Histological studies of important viscera (mouse, rat, dog and monkey). A group of 35 rats was used. Three control animals were killed by concussion. On consecutive days 3 animals were anesthetized with ethyl ether and cypreth ether respectively for a period of 10 minutes. Animals were sacrificed after 1, 2, 3 and 4 anesthesias for histological studies. Also 2 rats used in the delayed anesthetic death experiments were sacrificed after one week for histological study. No significant damage was present in the lungs, livers, kidneys and spleens in any of these animals.

Three of the mice used in the partial pressure experiments with cypreth ether were sacrificed and their livers, lungs and kidneys were examined histologically. The findings were negative.

Six dogs were anesthetized lightly with cyclopropane and liver biopsies performed. The anesthesia was changed to cypreth ether and maintained at the surgical level for one hour and a second biopsy performed. No pathological lesions were found that could be attributed to the effect of cypreth ether on the tissue. Rarefied hepatic cells seen often after cypreth ether anesthesia occurred in the animals normally and with an equal frequency. Frozen sections stained for fat by the Herxheimer method indicated that this rarefaction was due to a diminished amount of fat in the cytoplasm of the cells at the time of biopsy.

Five Rhesus monkeys, which over a period of 4 months had been anesthetized 10 times with cypreth ether for periods up to 30 minutes, were sacrificed

TABLE 7

Induction concentration in mice—cypreth ether

PARTIAL PRESSURE	CC. PER LITER	NUMBER OF MICE PER JAR	NUMBER OF MICE USED	ANESTHESIA	AVERAGE INDUCTION
per cent				*per cent*	*min.*
2	0.26	3	5	0	0.0
3	0.39	3	21	33	7.0
4	0.52	3	45	66	5.7
5	0.65	3	24	100	3.5

for histological studies at the termination of a 15 minute anesthesia. The lungs, kidneys and livers of 4 of the animals were normal. One monkey showed much rarefaction of the hepatic cells in the central area. Adrenals, cerebral cortex, sternal bone marrow and bladder of 2 of the monkeys were examined and found devoid of significant pathology.

Ten additional Rhesus monkeys were subjected to the foregoing biopsy procedure as performed on the dogs. The findings in this series coincide with those described with the dog anesthesias.

Clotting time and hemolysis (*monkey and dog*). The clotting time of blood was determined in 5 normal Rhesus monkeys by the capillary tube method. The average clotting time was approximately one minute. Within the error of the experiment this period was neither diminished nor increased under surgical anesthesia with cypreth ether.

Volumes of 20 cc. of cypreth ether in varying concentrations in normal salt solution were maintained at 25°C. To each of these was added 0.1 cc. of freshly drawn defibrinated dog's blood and the time required for hemolysis was observed. Two-tenths molar cypreth ether was the highest possible concentration. This concentration produced hemolysis within 15 minutes. One-tenth molar concentration did not produce hemolysis within an observation time of 5 hours. Nine-thousandths molar concentration cypreth ether, the mean level in the blood during anesthesia did not hemolyze red cells within an observation period of 2 days at 37°C.

Delayed anesthetic deaths (*rat*). Fifteen male adult rats were anesthetized with cypreth ether to the surgical plane and maintained in this condition for one-half hour. The same experiment was conducted with ethyl ether and effort was made to maintain the same depth of anesthesia. Fifteen unanesthetized rats taken from the same laboratory animal group served as controls. At the end of 3 weeks no animal in any group had died or appeared to be in an unhealthy condition.

Preanesthetic medication (*monkey*). With monkeys morphine-atropine medication influenced the anesthesia with cypreth ether in the same manner in which it affects the anesthesia of ethyl ether. In monkeys inducing cypreth ether anesthesia with nitrous oxide was uneventful. Preanesthetic medication with pentobarbital sodium was found to be entirely compatible with cypreth ether anesthesia. Twelve experiments were conducted.

Quantitative determination in blood (*dog*). The method used by Andrews et al. (3) for the determination of ethyl ether in the blood was employed with certain minor modifications. The method consists essentially of aspirating the cypreth ether from the blood by means of air into standard potassium dichromate solution in 7 molar sulfuric acid. The excess of oxidizing agent is determined iodimetrically. Recoveries from blood of known cypreth ether content were found to be complete. Fifteen determinations were made on dog's blood under surgical anesthesias of 10 minutes duration; the mean value in milligrams per cent was 76, high 92, low 55.

Excretion time (*monkey*). Four Rhesus monkeys were anesthetized with cypreth ether and maintained at the plane of surgical anesthesia for 15 minutes. At this period the blood and expired air were assayed for their cypreth ether content. The administration of the anesthetic was discontinued. At subsequent intervals during the excretion periods similar assays were made. The results are shown in table 8.

Physical Properties. Solubility in water: Ten cubic centimeters of cypreth ether was mechanically agitated with 100 cc. of water for 3 hours at 25°C. in a "Cassia Flask." The two liquids were allowed to separate for 12 hours and the volume of the supernatant cypreth ether measured. The solubility in these experiments was found to be 2.8 cc. in 100 cc. of water. The molar concentration of a saturated solution of cypreth ether in water is 0.25 at 25°C.

Oil/water coefficient: A 0.1 molar concentration of cypreth ether was prepared in corn oil (free fatty acids less than 0.03 per cent). Fifty cubic centimeters of this solution were agitated mechanically with an equal volume of water for 3 hours at 25°C. The immiscible liquids separated within 12 hours producing a clear aqueous layer. The cypreth ether was determined by the foregoing method in an aliquot portion of the aqueous solution. The molar concentration in water (9 experiments) at equilibrium was found to be 0.006. The oil/water coefficient of cypreth ether measured under these conditions is 15.7.

Inflammability range: Mixtures of cypreth ether vapor and air respectively were prepared at 25°C. and atmospheric pressure in an explosion pipette. The mixtures were exposed to the hot spark of an induction coil. Explosions occurred when the concentration of cypreth ether mixed with air was as low as 1.8 per cent. The minimal concentration for explosion with ethyl ether vapor under these conditions was found to be 2.5 per cent.

Vapor pressure: The vapor pressure of cypreth ether at 25°C. determined by means of a nitrometer, was found to be 147 mm., that of ethyl ether at the same temperature is 532 mm.

TABLE 8

Excretion of cypreth ether

NUMBER	BLOOD (MGM. PER CENT)					EXPIRED AIR (MGM. PER LITER)				
	End of anesthesia	½ hour	1 hour	2 hours	3 hours	End of anesthesia	½ hour	1 hour	2 hours	3 hours
1	23.0	2.5	2.0	0.0		0.32	0.21	0.03	0.00	
2	65.0	10.3	6.2	2.3	0.0	0.13	0.11	0.07	0.06	0.00
3	30.9	13.7	8.6	0.0		0.48	0.08	0.06	0.02	0.01
4	21.6	10.4	8.0	2.7	0.9	0.48	0.25	0.06	0.03	0.01

SUMMARY AND CONCLUSIONS

1. The union of the molecule of cyclopropane through an ether linkage with the alkyl radical, ethyl, results in the formation of a volatile liquid ("Cypreth Ether") exhibiting anesthetic properties in many species of animals.

2. Cypreth ether, which is a hybrid molecule between cyclopropane and diethyl ether, exhibits a potency which vies with chloroform and an anesthetic index double that of ether.

3. In the monkey, cypreth ether produces no functional liver damage as shown by the bromsulfonphthalein test. In these experiments in the mouse, rat, dog and monkey, anesthesias with cypreth ether produced no significant histopathological changes in important viscera.

4. The monkey's heart under cypreth ether anesthesia exhibited no arrhythmias. The frog's heart showed no effect when perfused with anesthetic concentrations of cypreth ether.

5. The explosive range of concentrations of cypreth ether and ethyl ether with air appears to be about the same. The oil/water coefficient of cypreth

ether is approximately 4 times greater than that of ethyl ether. The concentration in the respired air required to produce anesthesia is from one-third to one-half that required for ethyl ether. Anesthetic concentrations in the blood are about one-half those of ethyl ether.

6. Cypreth ether boils 33°C. higher than ethyl ether.

7. The blood pressure remains normal and the pulse good under deep surgical anesthesia in the dog.

8. We wish to emphasize that many studies reported in this communication are in their incipiency. More extensive investigations are in progress. The first approximation of the pharmacology of cypreth ether, in our opinion, warrants its careful and judicious trial in man by skilled anesthetists.

ADDENDUM

These experiments having been completed, we deemed that the properties of cypreth ether warranted its trial as an anesthetic agent in man. On January 29, 1941, at 3:30 p.m. cypreth ether was administered by the open drop method to one of us (J. C. K. Jr.). The induction period was one minute. Anesthesia was continued until 3:34 p.m. The induction was not unpleasant. Pain reflexes were abolished. The recovery was rapid and uneventful. Following this a similar trial anesthesia was conducted on (C. J. C.) with an analogous anesthetic syndrome.

REFERENCES

(1) Krantz, Carr, Forman and Evans: This Journal, **69**, 207, 1940.
(2) Black, Shannon and Krantz: Anesthesiology, **1**, 274, 1940.
(3) Andrews, Potter, Friedmann and Livingstone: J. Lab. Clin. Med., **25**, 966, 1940.

FURTHER STUDIES ON THE FATE OF SELENIUM IN THE ORGANISM

BENTON B. WESTFALL AND M. I. SMITH

From the National Institute of Health, Washington, D. C.

Received for publication April 1, 1941

The suggestion has frequently been made that the selenium in cereal grain grown on seleniferous soil and possibly that stored in animal tissues might be associated with and perhaps substituted for part of the organic sulfur. In keeping with this, Horn and Jones (1) have isolated from a plant source what appears to be the selenium analog as well as the sulfur containing amino-acid obtained by Küster and Irion (2) on hydrolysis of sheep wool after treatment with Na_2S. Painter and Franke (3) have presented evidence that a portion of the selenium of seleniferous protein and acid hydrolysates of such protein is with the lead sulfide following hydrolysis with alkaline plumbite. These findings make it appear that the excretion of ingested selenium might in part at least parallel that of the organic sulfur and factors influencing the metabolic mobilization of sulfur might also affect the mobilization of selenium from the tissues.

It was previously shown (4) that selenium fed in the form in which it occurs naturally in wheat or oats is stored in the body with the tissue proteins. Tryptic digestion of selenized livers liberated about 80 per cent of the contained selenium, apparently in organic combination but not associated with the small fraction of liberated cystine remaining undestroyed. Also data (5) have been presented indicating that urinary selenium from animals fed these grains or wheat protein behaves in such a manner as to make it appear that much of it is not inorganic in nature.

The present work includes an improved method for the fractionation of the urinary selenium, so as better to differentiate between the inorganic and organic forms, and data on the distribution of selenium in relation to the urinary sulfur. It also covers several measures used in an effort to influence the mobilization of selenium with particular attention to ridding the animal of that stored in the tissues. During the course of this work Moxon and associates (6) reported the favorable effect of administered brombenzene for this purpose and experiments are included bearing on this medication.

METHODS AND MATERIALS

Male rabbits, of mixed commercial stock, weighing about 2 kgm., fed wheat and cabbage, were used. The selenized animals had been kept for a minimum of 67 days with free access to seleniferous wheat containing 20 p.p.m. of selenium with cabbage as desired prior to the start of the experiment. Those animals used to furnish urine for the fractionation experiments and data of tables 1 and 2 had been maintained on the diet a minimum of 12 months. Under these conditions they ate about 500 grams cabbage and an average of from 15 to 35 grams of the wheat per day. Since the food intake in chronic selenosis is quite variable (7) it was not unusual for an animal to refuse the seleniferous wheat for one or more days at irregular intervals. Urines were collected in metabolism cages with thymol as preservative and residual bladder urine was drawn by catheter to terminate any period as desired.

Selenium estimations were made by the method previously employed (8), sulfur and sulfur partition by the usual gravimetric procedures (9).

The method used for examination of the protein-free filtrates from tryptic digests of liver tissue (4) was applied with some modification to the fractionation of the urinary selenium. Zinc hydroxide was used to clarify the urines after addition of a few drops of acetic acid, the excess zinc removed with sodium carbonate, and barium chloride with hydrochloric acid added to precipitate inorganic sulfate. For the remaining precipitations, barium was always in excess. The filtrate was adjusted to pH 7 and concentrated *in vacuo* at not over 50°C., to $\frac{1}{10}$ the original urine volume. It was then acidified with HCl to pH 2 and poured into ethyl alcohol sufficient to make 90 per cent by volume. The filtrate was adjusted to pH 7 and, after filtering off the small precipitate, the alcohol removed *in vacuo*. The concentrate was poured into 10 volumes of acetone, the filtrate from this forming fraction 7 of table 1. For each fractionation the 24-hour urine excreted by 8 selenized rabbits was used to give a volume of approximately 1 liter.

It was shown previously (5) that rabbits fed cabbage with oats containing 10 to 14 p.p.m. selenium eliminated approximately 50 per cent of the daily intake in the urine; those getting 20 p.p.m. with wheat excreted a somewhat greater portion, nearer 70 per cent.

The *p*-brom-phenyl-mercapturic acid was extracted from the urine by the method of McGuinn and Sherwin as used by Conway (10).

RESULTS

The distribution of selenium in the various crude fractions obtained as outlined is presented in table 1. Included with the results are experiments with sodium selenate, selenite, and diselenodiacetic acid added to normal rabbits' urine. It will be noted that the selenite is nearly completely removed by the zinc, whereas selenate is precipitated partly with the barium sulfate and partly in 90 per cent acid alcohol.[1] The urinary selenium of the experimental animals more nearly resembles diselenodiacetic acid than it does the others. Some 15 per cent of the urinary selenium is probably inorganic selenate, compared with a figure of 60 to 70 per cent for inorganic sulfate.[2]

[1] The best value from the literature for the aqueous solubility of $BaSeO_4$ is equivalent to 2300 micrograms selenium in 100 cc. at 25°C. (11). In urine it is somewhat greater, 2500 micrograms, due probably to the influence of the organic matter in producing a very fine colloid. There exist no data on its solubility in urine in the presence of excess $BaCl_2$, $BaSO_4$, HCl or 90 per cent ethyl alcohol.

[2] Sodium selenate given intravenously yielded results much like that added to normal urine. Eighty-five per cent of the selenium excreted in 24 hours was found in the $BaSO_4$, 90 per cent ethyl alcohol fractions. In this period 45 per cent of the injected dose was excreted, which is almost identical with that found by Aten and Hevesy for the isomor-

Sulfur distribution as between ethereal and neutral in the four fractions after inorganic sulfate was removed, indicated that both types were in each fraction. Hence selenium appears to be generally distributed, and not necessarily associated with any single portion of the sulfur. The completely arbitrary nature of the separation should, however, be borne in mind. It is possible to produce some differences in the amount of selenium in a given fraction by varying the extent to which concentration is carried.

A variety of procedures was employed in an attempt to alter the neutral or ethereal sulfur fraction of the urine with the hope that this might influence the urinary selenium output. Except as noted, 24-hour specimens of urine were analyzed for selenium and for the sulfur partition, and the findings compared with a similar period immediately before and one after the particular measure employed. Intravenous thiosulfate and oral brombenzene with cys-

TABLE 1

Fractionation of urinary selenium

FRACTION	PER CENT OF TOTAL SELENIUM									
	Chronic selenosis experiments							When added to normal urine as		
	1	3	4	6	7	8	Average	Na_2SeO_3	Na_2SeO_4	Diselenodiacetic acid
$Zn(OH)_2$	2	3	12	2	1	3	4	80	0	0
$ZnCO_3$	0	0	4	1	1	1	2	10	0	5
$BaSO_4$	4	2	2	2	2	1	2	1	50	0
90 per cent alcohol pH 2.0	20	20	4	4	2	9	10	1	57	0
90 per cent alcohol pH 7.0	6	15	14	14	5	20	12	1	1	70
Acetone precipitate	40	18	42	28	60	30	36	2	1	13
Acetone solution	28	35	18	42	24	44	32	2	1	10

tine increased the neutral sulfur. Intravenous calcium gluconate and oral menthol or brombenzene augmented the ethereal sulfur. None of these procedures, however, altered significantly the selenium output.

Moderate diuresis following water by mouth, or intense diuresis induced by 8 per cent sucrose in half Ringer's solution (13) failed to alter materially the selenium output. Normal saline or glucose infusion during a 5-hour period produced a moderate increase for the duration of the medication. For example, the selenium output during a 5-hour period of intravenous infusion of 10 cc. 10 per cent glucose per kilogram of body weight per hour with a

phous sodium sulfate (12). Intravenous selenite on the other hand gives about 15 per cent in the fractions where it appears when added *in vitro* and about 80 per cent with ethereal and neutral sulfur indicating a rapid working over of this compound. A small amount (about 5 per cent) appears where inorganic selenate would. About 30 per cent of the injected dose is excreted in the urine at the end of 24 hours.

fluid excretion of 7.3 cc. per kilogram per hour was increased from a normal of 3.5 to 5.5 micrograms per kilogram of body weight per hour. This last procedure also seemed to produce a slight increase in the neutral sulfur, but the nature and limited number of the experiments make this uncertain.

Since the greater part of the selenium eliminated from the body is excreted in the urine under the above condition of feeding, it is evident that the measures outlined must have had little influence on the selenium depots in the tissues. However, in view of the positive results reported by Moxon and coworkers (6), it was deemed necessary to do more work on the effect of brombenzene. Accordingly, an experiment was set up with six rabbits all on the seleniferous diet: three were given oral brombenzene, three served as controls. The experimental period covered nine days: first, three days' study of the

TABLE 2

The influence of brombenzene on the urinary excretion of selenium and its mobilization from the tissues of rabbits

Three animals in each group

PERIOD	AVERAGE DAILY OUTPUT OF URINARY SELENIUM	
	Controls	Treated
	micrograms	*micrograms*
1. Preliminary, November 4 to 7	217	160
2. Experimental, November 7 to 10; seleniferous wheat continued	230	200
3. Experimental, November 12 to 15; seleniferous wheat discontinued	198	160
Tissue selenium average micrograms, per cent		
1. Blood	200	183
2. Muscle	930	1010
3. Liver	867	1810

normal selenium output for all animals; then three days when one group was given brombenzene: finally, three days when the selenium wheat was replaced by normal wheat with brombenzene administration continued for the same three animals. This latter step was taken because there was considerable fluctuation in the individual intake of seleniferous grain which might obscure relationships. The animals were then bled under anesthesia and the blood, liver, and muscle analyzed for selenium. The data summarized in table 2 indicate no significant difference between the treated and untreated animals.

This essentially negative result prompted the extension of the experiment to cover a longer period with all the animals given the non-seleniferous diet. These were the animals noted as having been on the seleniferous diet for 67 days. As previously reported (5) when there are considerable stores of selenium in the body, discontinuance of ingestion is followed normally by a rapid fall in the amount excreted in the urine for about 18 days and then a very slowly diminishing excretion for months at a low level. Accordingly, these rabbits were followed for a minimum of 18 days. Three rabbits were continued as usual after transfer to the selenium-free diet and three were given brombenzene intragastrically daily.[3] In order to force the mobilization of cystine and, it was hoped, the associated selenium from the tissues, an additional six animals were fasted with free access to water, three serving as controls and three given brombenzene. Two animals died before the end of the experiment and are not included in this discussion. Charts 1 and 2 summarize the results including the selenium content of the blood, liver and

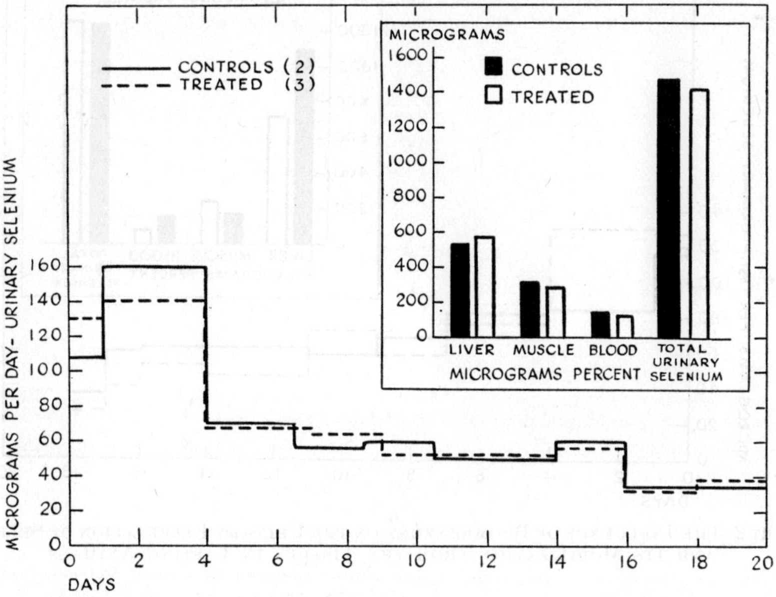

CHART 1. THE INFLUENCE OF BROMBENZENE ON THE URINARY ELIMINATION OF SELENIUM AND ITS MOBILIZATION FROM THE TISSUES IN RABBITS

muscle at the end of 18 and 20 days respectively for the fed and fasting groups.

Moxon and associates (6) suggested that the increased output of selenium following brombenzene administration in their experiments was due to the elimination of the tissue selenium in the mercapturic acid fraction, presumably as N-acetyl-Se-*p*-brom-phenyl cysteine. In the experiments reported here the crude *p*-brom-phenyl-mercapturic acid fraction isolated from rabbit urine

[3] Seventy-five to 110 mgm. brombenzene per kilogram of body weight per day in five per cent solution in 80 per cent alcohol. This is close to the maximum tolerated dose for these animals.

gave on analysis a maximum of no more than 10 per cent of the total urinary selenium. The yield of this product was low. Isolation of a relatively pure portion for identification by its melting point indicated only about 5 per cent conversion of the administered brombenzene to the sulfur derivative. Assuming that the selenium was conjugated in an analogous compound this would indicate that we might expect no more than a small portion of it to be so eliminated, if the two elements are metabolized in similar fashion.

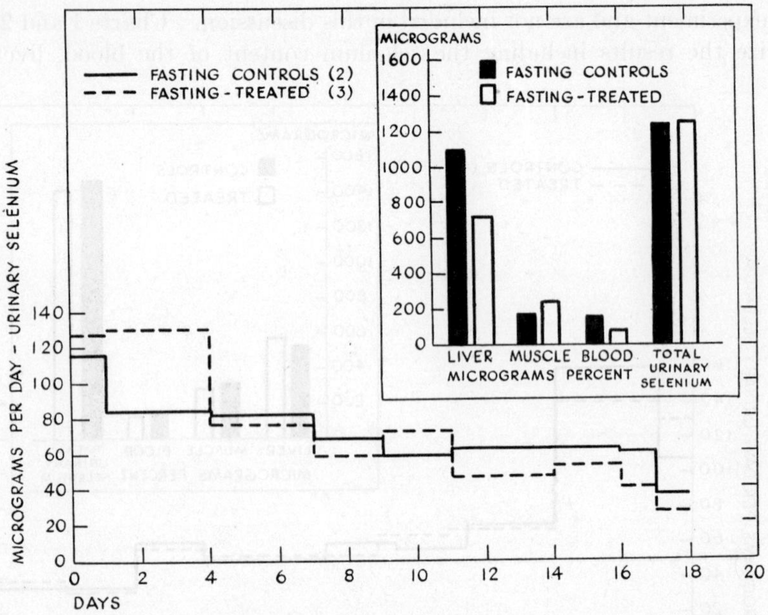

CHART 2. THE INFLUENCE OF BROMBENZENE ON THE URINARY ELIMINATION OF SELENIUM AND ITS MOBILIZATION FROM THE TISSUES IN FASTING ANIMALS

COMMENT

The results of the fractionation of the urinary selenium in chronic selenosis of rabbits indicate that most of it is associated with the neutral and ethereal sulfur and that mobilization from the tissues by administration of various agents including brombenzene is not markedly effective. The bromine compound has been used recently therapeutically in humans (14) but in view of the present work it would seem that so toxic an agent, if it is to be used at all, should be used with great reserve and caution, at least until there is a more substantial basis for the therapy.

SUMMARY

1. A method for the fractionation of urinary selenium which distinguishes sodium selenate and selenite from organic selenium has been presented.

2. Most of the urinary selenium excreted by rabbits fed on seleniferous wheat appears with the ethereal and neutral sulfur presumably as organic selenium, with only about 15 per cent as inorganic.

3. Various agents reputed to influence the sulfur partition of the urine produced no marked change in the urinary selenium output.

4. No significant increase in the output of urinary selenium or any decrease in the tissue selenium could be obtained by the oral administration of brombenzene.

5. No pronounced amounts of selenium could be found with *p*-brom-phenyl mercapturic acid isolated from the urine of brombenzene-treated selenized rabbits.

REFERENCES

(1) Horn and Jones: J. Am. Chem. Soc., **62:** 234, 1940.
(2) Küster and Irion: Hoppe-Seyler's Z. f. physiol. Chem., **184–185:** 225, 1939.
(3) Painter and Franke: J. Biol. Chem., **134:** 557, 1940.
(4) Westfall and Smith: Pub. Health Rep., **55:** 1575, 1940.
(5) Smith, Westfall and Stohlman: Pub. Health Rep., **53:** 1199, 1938.
(6) Moxon, Schaefer, Lardy, DuBois, and Olson: J. Biol. Chem., **132:** 785, 1940.
(7) Smith and Lillie: National Inst. Health Bull., **174:** 5, 1940.
(8) Westfall and Smith: National Inst. Health Bull., **174:** 45, 1940.
(9) Peters and Van Slyke: Quantitative Clinical Chemistry, II, 890, 1932.
(10) Conway: J. Biol. Chem., **121:** 27, 1937.
(11) Myer and Friedrich: Z. physik. Chem., **102:** 369, 1922.
(12) Aten and Hevesy: Nature, **142:** 952, 1938.
(13) Helmholz and Bollman: J. Lab. and Clin. Med., **25:** 1180, 1940.
(14) Lemley: J. Lancet, **60:** 528, 1940.

THE ABSORPTION AND ELIMINATION OF PHENOLPHTHALEIN IN NORMAL AND PATHOLOGIC STATES: WITH PARTICULAR REFERENCE TO LIVER AND KIDNEY DISEASES[1]

BERNARD FANTUS,* FREDERICK STEIGMANN AND J. M. DYNIEWICZ

From the Department of Pharmacology and Therapeutics and the Department of Internal Medicine, College of Medicine, University of Illinois, and the Department of Therapeutics and Internal Medicine, Cook County Hospital, Chicago, Ill.

Received for publication April 1, 1941

Textbooks of pharmacology and the older literature (1) state that very small amounts of phenolphthalein are excreted in the urine and that most of it appears in the stool. Fantus and Dyniewicz (2), who studied the elimination of phenolphthalein quite intensively, found that only a small proportion (1.4 to 19.7 per cent) was excreted in the urine in several days and after varying doses. (All discussions referred to are based on observations after the oral intake of powdered phenolphthalein.) In quantitative determinations of urinary phenolphthalein as part of the work on the validity of the Woldman test, (3) in which the patients studied received phenolphthalein in *alcoholic solution*, we were surprised to find large quantities of phenolphthalein in the urine (4). In some cases, (liver disease and sepsis) the amount of phenolphthalein in the urine was larger than that in the stool. By changing the mode of phenolphthalein administration we found it possible to make phenolphthalein elimination quite opposite to the statements in standard textbooks and in the literature. Not only are the quantitative results different from those previously reported, but the quantity of phenolphthalein excreted in the urine is not dependent solely upon the dose ingested. Other intrinsic factors are also involved. We found that certain diseases may modify the amount of phenolphthalein excreted in the urine, while others have no effect. Because of these observations, a study was planned to determine the circumstances that modify phenolphthalein excretion. Such a study with pure phenolphthalein is of importance, since it throws additional light upon the excretion of phenolphthalein compounds which are used in the diagnosis of diseases of the liver, (bromsulphalein and tetraiodophenolphthalein) and kidney (phenolsulphonphthalein).

Another reason for this study was the desire to comply with Rowland's request (5) to clarify and further to confirm certain observations as to the

[1] This work was assisted by a grant from Phenolphthalein Research, Inc.

* Deceased.

phenolphthalein absorption, conjugation and elimination, which were first observed during the preliminary work, in which phenolphthalein was given in an *alcoholic solution.* When phenolphthalein is given as a powder, it is dissolved by the intestinal juices before any is absorbed. The amount absorbed and later eliminated depends on how much phenolphthalein is dissolved. Since phenolphthalein is only slightly soluble, the amount dissolved and absorbed depends on the quantity of phenolphthalein ingested and on the amount of intestinal juice present. Not only does the amount of intestinal fluid influence the solubility of phenolphthalein, but also its composition, i.e., when bile is present the solubility is greater and *vice versa.* The administration of phenolphthalein *dissolved in alcohol* obviously does away with many of the factors that play a rôle in solubility and absorption when it is given as a powder.

Phenolphthalein absorbed from the gastrointestinal tract is normally excreted in the bile and urine, in which it can be determined quantitatively (2). The functional state of the liver and kidneys determines the relative amount excreted through each organ. In previous studies (6) we have shown that high concentrations of phenolphthalein in the bile are associated with low amounts in the urine and *vice versa,* hence the determination of the quantity in the urine alone may suffice for the evaluation of the functional status of either organ.

In the present work we used the reciprocal relationship between liver and kidney to estimate the functional activity or status of these organs. In addition, the clearance, (urine/plasma ratio) of phenolphthalein was also determined, and was compared with the endogenous creatinine clearance (7) to determine to what extent the two run parallel.

MATERIALS AND METHODS

Fasting individuals, both normal and diseased, (425 cases) were given, according to Woldman's (3) technic, 0.10 gram of white phenolphthalein, which had been dissolved in 10 cc. of high alcoholic elixir and diluted with water to 30 cc. just before administration. No food or fluids were allowed for two hours thereafter. The urine was collected for ten hours. Blood specimens were taken one and three hours after phenolphthalein ingestion. The free and conjugated (total) phenolphthalein in blood and urine was determined by a modification of the method of Fantus and Dyniewicz (2). The average of the two blood concentrates was taken.

Determination of phenolphthalein in urine. To five cc. of urine 15 cc. of 17 per cent hydrochloric acid were added and the mixture heated nearly to boiling for at least one hour. After cooling, the liberated phenolphthalein was extracted by shaking in a separatory funnel with 20 to 30 cc. portions of ether until the last washing gave no color with alkali. Interfering yellow coloring matter was removed from the ether extracts by adding just enough alkali solution to neutralize the acid; the colorless ether solution containing the phenolphthalein was then extracted with alkali solution until all pink color was removed. The phenolphthalein contained in the alkali solution was determined by finding the amount of phenolphthalein that had to be added to a volume of alkali solution equal to that used for extraction in order to make the colors equal; final reading was made with the aid of a colorimeter.

Determination of total phenolphthalein in bile was done by following the procedure outlined above, using five cc. of bile.

Determination of serum phenolphthalein. Five cc. of serum were first extracted with 25 cc. of ether, which was decanted and discarded if no free phenolphthalein was present in it. If phenolphthalein was present, it was extracted from the ether with five cc. of alkali solution.[2] Then ten cc. of concentrated HCl (sufficient to precipitate and dissolve the protein) was added to the serum and it was heated nearly to boiling on a hot plate for at least one hour. This procedure hydrolysed the conjugated phenolphthalein, and the freed phenolphthalein was then extracted and determined quantitatively as above. The accuracy of phenolphthalein determination depends on the successful ex-

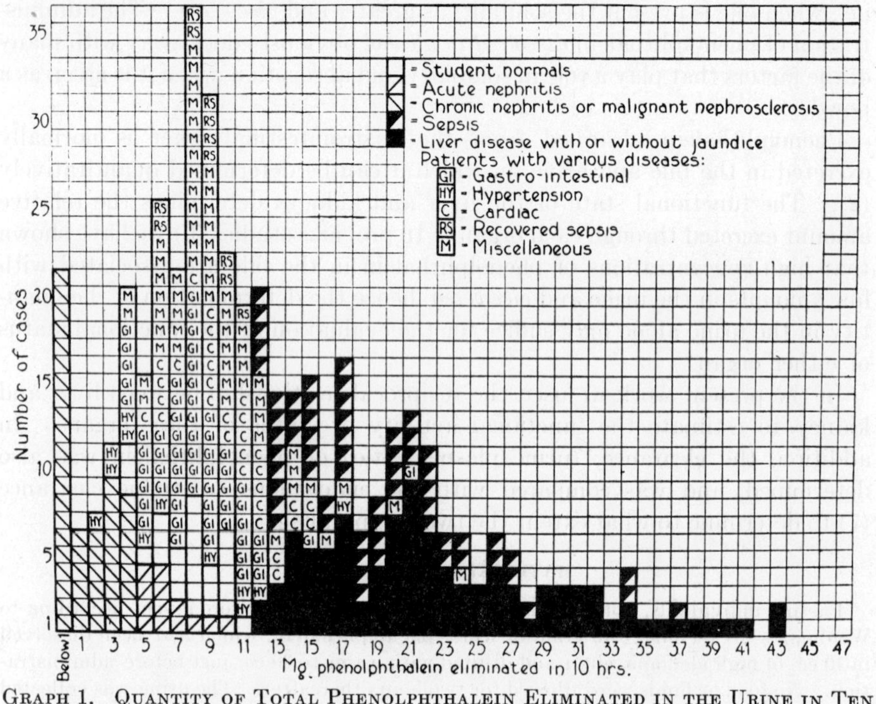

GRAPH 1. QUANTITY OF TOTAL PHENOLPHTHALEIN ELIMINATED IN THE URINE IN TEN HOURS IN NORMALS AND PATIENTS SUFFERING FROM VARIOUS AILMENTS

Summary of 425 case studies after 0.10 gram phenolphthalein in high alcoholic elixir

traction of interfering coloring matter. Since the amount of phenolphthalein (as conjugated), contained in serum is small, care had to be exercised when extracting the interfering yellow color to use just enough alkali, avoiding excess which would dissolve phenolphthalein.

RESULTS

1. *Normals*

Normal individuals, and patients without liver pathology and without sepsis, excrete more phenolphthalein in the bile than in the urine. In ten

[2] 4.0 gm. NaOH and 3.75 gm. ammonium sulfate per 1000 cc.

hours usually 5 to 10 mgm. were excreted in the urine (graphs 1 and 2). An elimination of over 12 mgm. or below 4 mgm. occurred only in cases with liver disease and sepsis or kidney disease respectively (table 1A, B, C, D). The average concentration of phenolphthalein in the serum, one and three hours after ingestion of phenolphthalein, varied from 0.18 to 0.23 mgm. per cent,

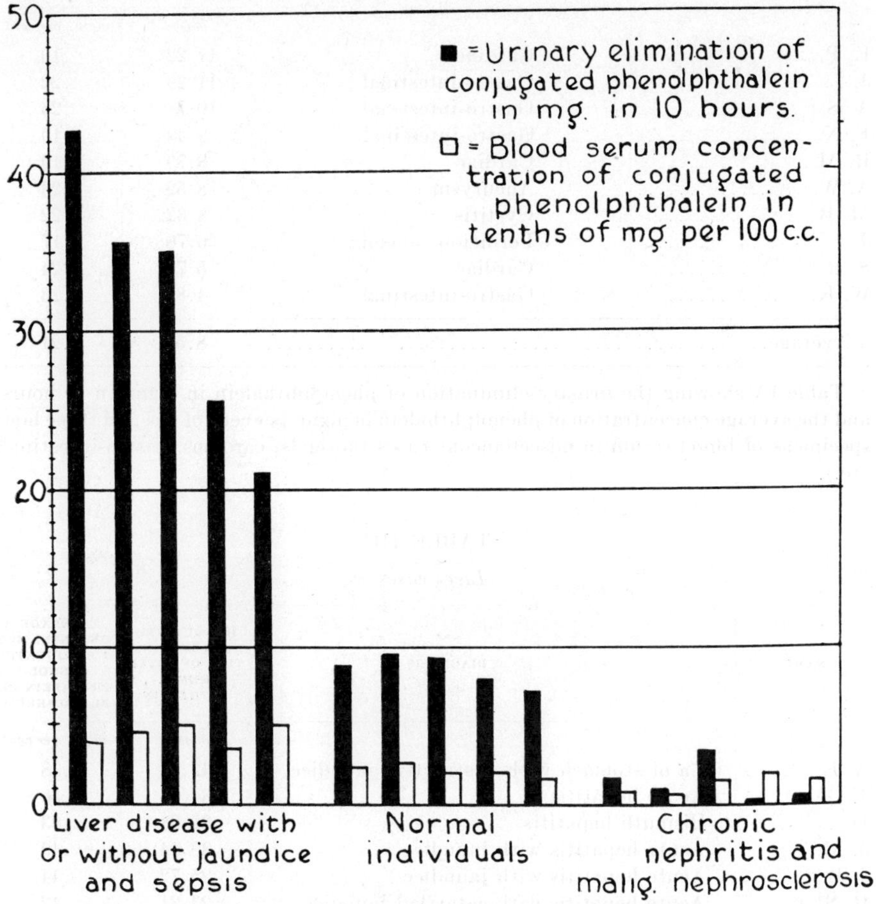

GRAPH 2. TYPICAL ELIMINATION OF PHENOLPHTHALEIN IN URINE AND CONCENTRATION IN BLOOD SERUM IN THE THREE DIFFERENT GROUPS

with an average normal of 0.2 mgm. per cent. Table 2 shows the number of cases studied in each group and their average phenolphthalein concentration.

2. Liver cases

In all cases of liver pathology, a marked increase (12 to 43 mgm.) in the urinary elimination of phenolphthalein was found (graphs 1 and 2). The

TABLE 1A

Miscellaneous

NAME	DIAGNOSIS	10-HOUR URINARY ELIMINATION OF TOTAL PHENOLPHTHALEIN	AVERAGE CONCENTRATION OF CONJUGATED PHENOLPHTHALEIN IN BLOOD SERUM
		mgm.	*mgm. per cent*
E. P.	Cardiac	11.22	.19
J. L.	Gastro-intestinal	11.29	.22
A. S.	Gastro-intestinal	10.78	.26
F. N.	Gastro-intestinal	9.49	.19
R. M.	Cardiac	8.79	.19
A. W.	Aneurysm	8.52	.23
M. B.	Cystitis	8.32	.22
J. F.	Pernicious anemia	6.76	.17
S. R.	Cardiac	5.75	.24
W. K.	Gastro-intestinal	4.82	.23
Average		8.57	.21

Table 1A showing the urinary elimination of phenolphthalein in mgm. in 10 hours, and the average concentration of phenolphthalein in mgm. per cent of one and three hour specimens of blood serum in miscellaneous cases (normals, cardiacs, gastro-intestinal, etc.).

TABLE 1B

Liver cases

NAME	DIAGNOSIS	10-HOUR URINARY ELIMINATION OF TOTAL PHENOLPHTHALEIN	AVERAGE CONCENTRATION OF CONJUGATED PHENOLPHTHALEIN IN BLOOD SERUM
		mgm.	*mgm. per cent*
A. E.	Ca of stomach with obstructive jaundice	42.68	.38
J. G.	Acute hepatitis	34.05	.56
D.	Bismuth hepatitis	32.38	.63
J. M.	Acute hepatitis with jaundice	30.04	.49
J. B.	Acute hepatitis with jaundice	25.72	.44
R. S.	Acute hepatitis with catarrhal jaundice	23.31	.42
G. W.	Cirrhosis	21.81	.54
J. A.	Cirrhosis	21.32	.43
E. S.	Obstructive jaundice due to cholelithiasis	19.95	.38
R. M.	Acute hepatitis with obstructive jaundice	14.35	.26
Average		26.56	.45

Table 1B showing the urinary elimination of phenolphthalein in mgm. in 10 hours, and the average concentration of phenolphthalein in mgm. per cent of one and three hour specimens of blood serum in liver cases.

TABLE 1C

Sepsis cases

NAME	DIAGNOSIS	10-HOUR URINARY ELIMINATION OF TOTAL PHENOLPHTHALEIN	AVERAGE CONCENTRATION OF CONJUGATED PHENOLPHTHALEIN IN BLOOD SERUM
		mgm.	*mgm. per cent*
G. T.	Tularemia	34.13	.40
C. L.	Infectious arthritis	26.96	.36
J. P.	Lung abscess	23.40	.28
C. K.	Blood dyscrasia + sepsis	21.62	.40
F. C.	Undulant fever	21.48	.32
S. H.	Dermat. exfoliativa	18.57	.41
S.	Subacute bacterial endocarditis	18.13	.29
D. D.	Malaria	16.93	.31
C. D.	Peritonitis	14.30	.31
F. B.	Pneumonia	12.74	.35
Average		20.83	.34

Table 1C showing the urinary elimination of phenolphthalein in mgm. in 10 hours, and the average concentration of phenolphthalein in mgm. per cent of one and three hour specimens of blood serum in sepsis cases.

TABLE 1D

Kidney cases

NAME	DIAGNOSIS	10-HOUR URINARY ELIMINATION OF TOTAL PHENOLPHTHALEIN	AVERAGE CONCENTRATION OF CONJUGATED PHENOLPHTHALEIN IN BLOOD SERUM
		mgm.	*mgm. per cent*
J. C.	Malignant nephrosclerosis	3.77	0.33
G. B.	Malignant nephrosclerosis	0.73	0.26
J. G.	Malignant nephrosclerosis	0.59	0.31
Average			0.30
L. P.	Chronic nephritis	4.56	0.06
R. S.	Chronic nephritis	2.69	0.06
J. K.	Chronic nephritis	1.88	0.07
N. Z.	Chronic nephritis	1.45	0.16
C. D.	Chronic nephritis	0.60	0.16
J. N.	Chronic nephritis	0.52	0.11
J. S.	Chronic nephritis	0	0.05
Average			0.09
Total average		1.68	

Table 1D showing the urinary elimination of phenolphthalein in mgm. in 10 hours, and the average concentration of phenolphthalein in mgm. per cent of one and three hour specimens of blood serum in kidney cases.

degree of this increase is related to the severity of the disease, and is usually parallel with the degree of jaundice. With improvement of the liver condition, the urinary elimination of phenolphthalein decreased (graph 3).

The increase in urinary phenolphthalein was associated with an increase in serum phenolphthalein (graph 4), though the increase of the serum concentration did not always coincide with the rise of the urinary level.

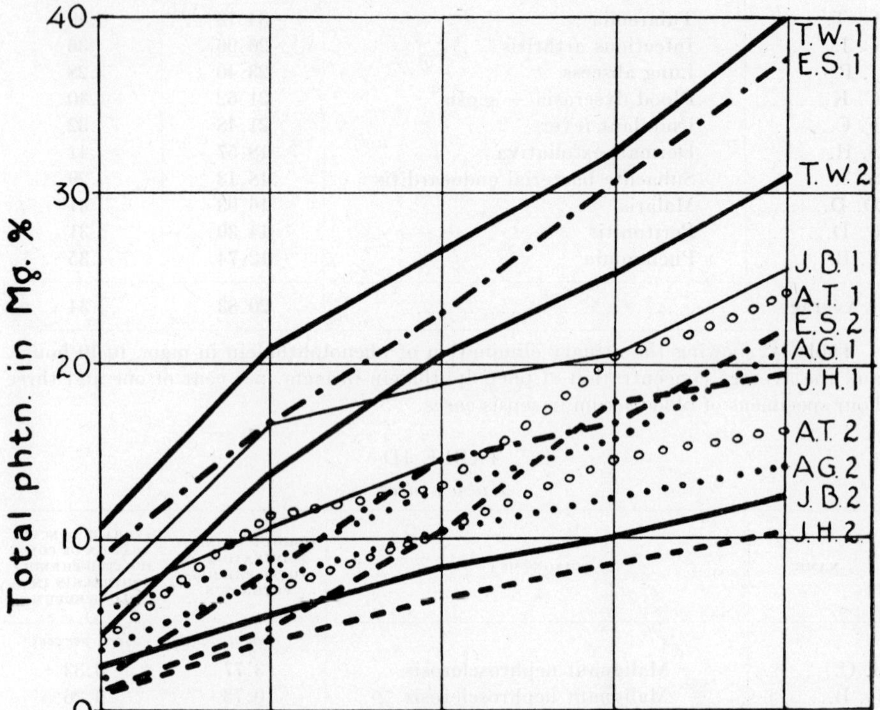

GRAPH 3. SHOWING URINARY ELIMINATION IN TEN HOURS AT HEIGHT OF JAUNDICE (1) AND DURING RECOVERY STAGE (2)

The previous study of excretion of phenolphthalein in urine and bile after oral administration in patients with gall bladder or common duct fistula was augmented by studies of cases with duodenal drainage following the intake of *alcoholic solution* of phenolphthalein. The previously reported results after oral phenolphthalein administration were more marked in these latter studies in which low quantities of phenolphthalein in the bile were associated with high phenolphthalein in the urine (graph 5), and *vice versa* (graph 6). If no phenolphthalein was present in the bile, the urinary phenolphthalein was usually above 25 mgm. in ten hours (graph 7). In subsiding jaundice

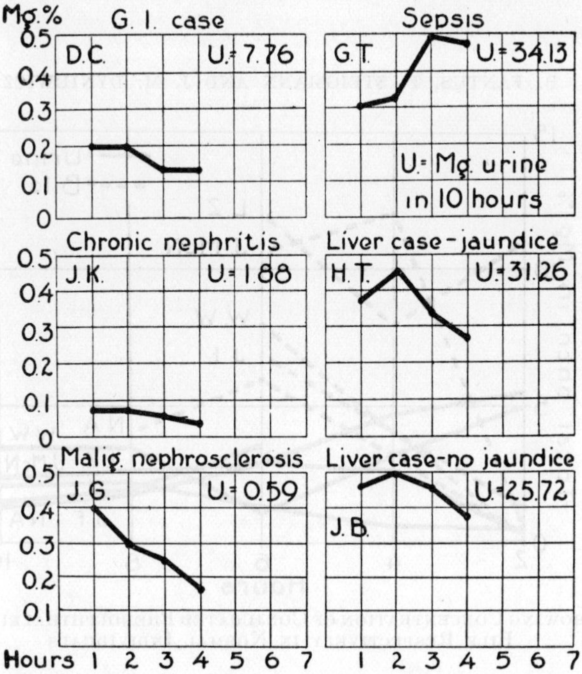

GRAPH 4. CONCENTRATION OF CONJUGATED PHENOLPHTHALEIN IN BLOOD SERUM IN TENTHS OF MILLIGRAMS AT HOURLY INTERVALS AFTER 0.100 GRAM PHENOLPHTHALEIN IN ALCOHOLIC ELIXIR

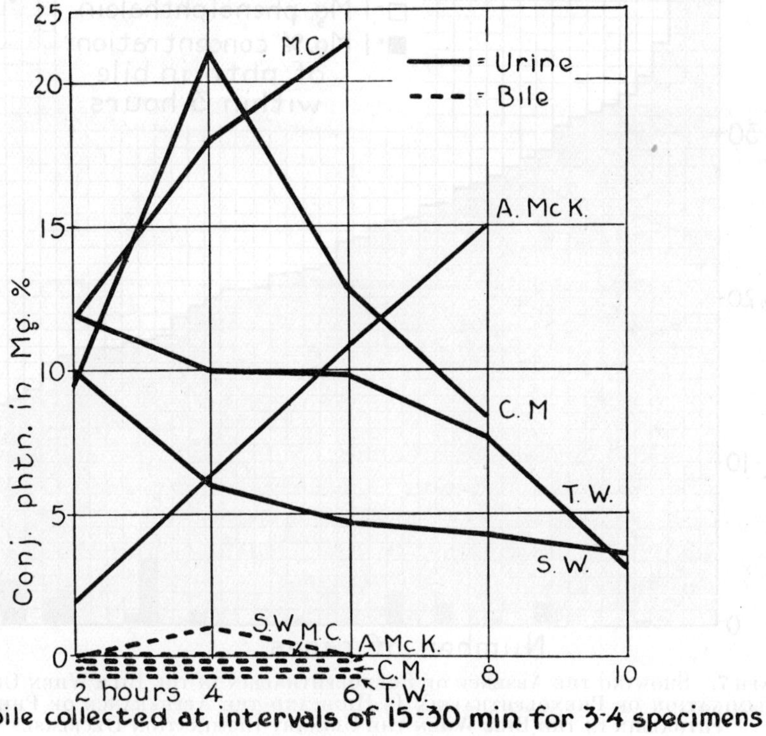

GRAPH 5. SHOWING CONCENTRATION OF CONJUGATED PHENOLPHTHALEIN IN URINE AND BILE RESPECTIVELY IN JAUNDICE CASES

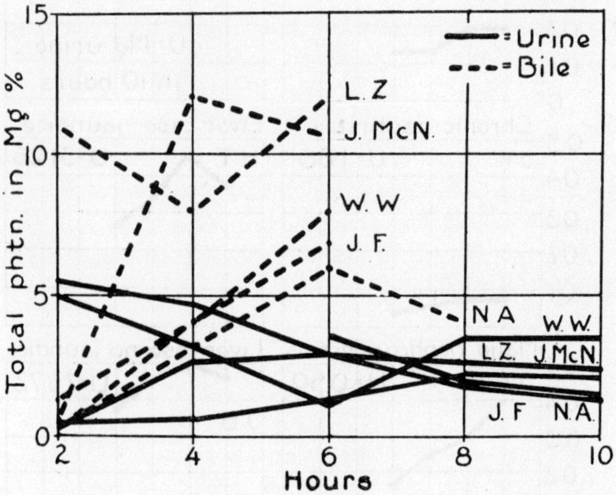

GRAPH 6. SHOWING CONCENTRATION OF CONJUGATED PHENOLPHTHALEIN IN URINE AND BILE RESPECTIVELY IN NORMAL INDIVIDUALS

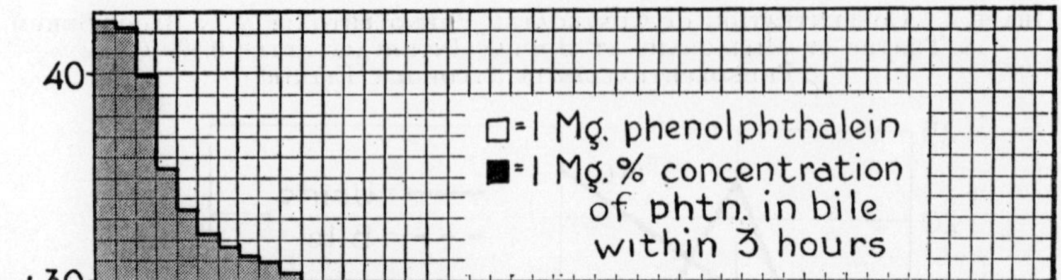

GRAPH 7. SHOWING THE ABSENCE OF PHENOLPHTHALEIN IN THE BILE WHEN URINARY ELIMINATION OF PHENOLPHTHALEIN IS HIGH AND THE APPEARANCE OF PHENOLPHTHALEIN IN THE BILE WHEN THE URINARY ELIMINATION DECREASES

when phenolphthalein was found in bile, the urinary phenolphthalein excretion was around 10 mgm. in ten hours.

3. Sepsis cases

In various septic conditions (pneumonia, abscess, etc.), the urinary phenolphthalein elimination curves are similar to those of the jaundice patients (above 12 mgm.). The phenolphthalein concentration in the blood of these cases was similar to the blood phenolphthalein concentration found in jaundice patients (table 1C).

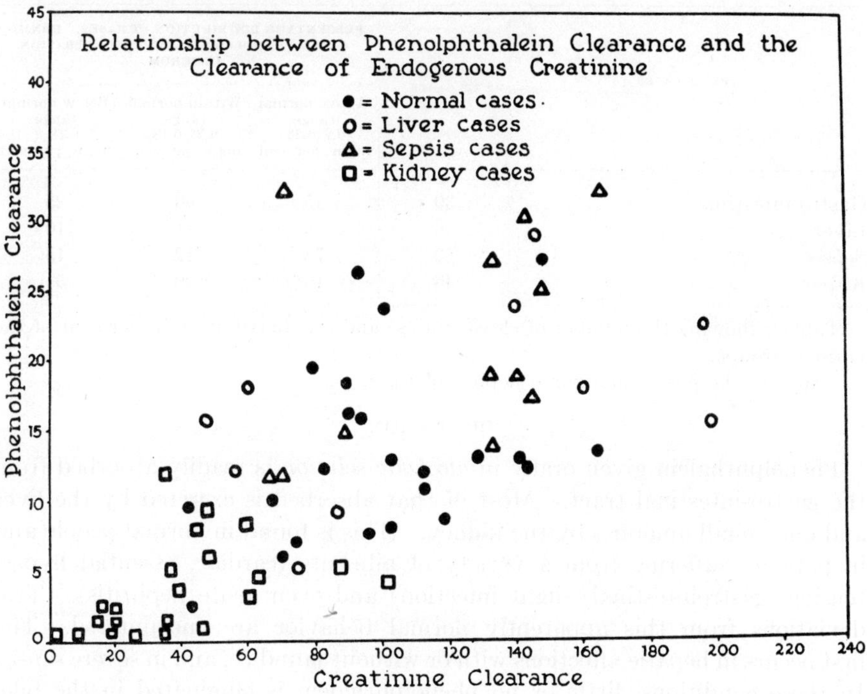

GRAPH 8

4. Kidney cases

All cases of chronic nephritis or malignant nephrosclerosis eliminated less than 5 mgm. of phenolphthalein in the urine within the ten hour test period. Most cases excreted only about 1 to 2 mgm. of phenolphthalein. In acute nephritis (without nitrogen retention), the phenolphthalein excretion was within normal limits.

The concentration of phenolphthalein in the blood of patients with chronic nephritis was less than the average normal, although here too, the decrease in the amount did not coincide with the drop of the phenolphthalein elimination in the urine. In cases of malignant nephrosclerosis, the concentration of blood phenolphthalein was higher than normal, in some instances being equal to that found in cases with liver pathology or sepsis.

Clearance. The phenolphthalein clearance was studied during the period in which phenolphthalein was demonstrable in the blood. The phenolphthalein clearance was much lower than the creatinine clearance. In cases in which the creatinine clearance was reduced, e.g., kidney pathology, the phenolphthalein clearance dropped proportionately (graph 8).

TABLE 2

TYPE OF CASES	NUMBER OF CASES	PERCENTAGE DISTRIBUTION OF CASES. CONJUGATED PHENOLPHTHALEIN CONCENTRATION IN SERUM		
		Above normal range 0.7–0.24 mgm. per cent	Within normal range 0.23–0.18 mgm. per cent	Below normal range 0.18–0 mgm. per cent
Gastro-intestinal	30	15	60	25
Liver	46	79	11	10
Sepsis	52	73	12	15
Kidney	48	19*	30	51

Table 2 showing the number of cases studied and the distribution in per cent of the various groups.

* Most of these were malignant nephrosclerosis.

DISCUSSION

Phenolphthalein given orally in *alcoholic solution* is readily absorbed from the gastro-intestinal tract. Most of that absorbed is excreted by the liver and only small amounts by the kidney. This is found in normal people and in patients suffering from a variety of ailments (cardiac, essential hypertension, gastrointestinal, slight infections and even acute nephritis). Two deviations from this apparently normal behavior are encountered. The first occurs in hepatic affections with or without jaundice, and in severe sepsis. In these conditions, little or no phenolphthalein is eliminated in the bile, hence the concentration of phenolphthalein in the blood is markedly increased and consequently more phenolphthalein appears in the urine. Because of the impaired elimination of phenolphthalein through the bile no absorbed phenolphthalein finds its way back into the intestinal tract, so that in these cases little phenolphthalein is found in the stool. Thus in some cases of jaundice or sepsis the amount of phenolphthalein excreted in the urine was much greater than that found in the stool, (e.g., 2.7 mgm. in stool and 59.2 mgm. in urine; 21.1 mgm. in stool and 45.9 mgm. in urine).

The other deviation consists in a reduction of the urinary excretion; this is found in chronic nephritis or malignant nephrosclerosis. In these cases, more phenolphthalein is found in the stool than in the urine.

In cases with the first type of deviation (hepatic pathology with or without jaundice), the reduced excretion through the bile is due either to dysfunction of the hepatic epithelial cells, the Kupffer's cells (reticulo-endothelial system), or both. The impaired excretion, however, was found not only in hepatitis with or without jaundice, but also in jaundice without hepatitis (obstructive jaundice).

In the cases of obstructive jaundice without hepatitis, tests for liver function (galactose tolerance, hippuric acid excretion) and the blood chemistry (cholesterol–cholesterol-ester ratio, phosphatase, and albumin-globulin ratio) did not reveal impaired hepatic function. Hence the status of the liver parenchyma is not the only factor responsible for the reduction of phenolphthalein in bile. The assumption may be made that the accumulation of bile pigments in the Kupffer's cells may in itself be responsible for the lack of phenolphthalein excretion in the bile (*yellow block*).

A similar condition is found both in the Graham-Cole test (in which tetraiodophenolphthalein is used to produce a roentgenologically demonstrable gall bladder shadow) and in the bromsulphalein test. In most instances of jaundice, there is no visualization of the gall bladder, even when the gall bladder is normal. Similarly, there is a marked retention of bromsulphalein in jaundice, with or without hepatitis. The phenolphthalein excretion indicates solely the status of the liver excretory function for dyes and does not necessarily indicate the condition of the hepatic parenchyma.

If increased phenolphthalein excretion through the urine (concomitant with reduced excretion through the bile) is found in sepsis disturbances in the hepatic excretory function can be assumed analogously (*white block*). The exact site of the block—liver parenchyma or Kupffer's cells—is not definitely established. The presence of this block in sepsis may be in favor of the latter site. We may assume that in jaundice the Kupffer's cells are blocked by bile pigments and in sepsis by the particular infectious "agents." Both may impair the passage of phenolphthalein.

The reduced urinary excretion in kidney disease is apparently due to two causes. One is the excretory inefficiency of the kidney parenchyma. The phenolphthalein in the blood is not normally excreted. The reduction of the phenolphthalein clearance parallel with that of the creatinine clearance indicates this etiologic factor. In accordance with the behavior of other substances (8), the phenolphthalein resorption is probably not increased, but possibly even decreased; a disturbance of phenolphthalein filtration through the glomeruli may, therefore, be assumed. Decreased urinary excretion should lead to retention and increase of the phenolphthalein level in the blood. This was not found to be the case; in fact, the blood level was even lower than in normal persons. This phenomenon points to a second factor responsible for the reduced urinary excretion, namely a decreased offering of phenolphthalein for excretion. This condition was only found in chronic nephritis and not in malignant nephrosclerosis. A possible explanation for it is a reduced phenolphthalein absorption from the gastrointestinal tract.

SUMMARY AND CONCLUSIONS

1. Phenolphthalein given in *alcoholic solution*, in contrast to that given in powder form, is readily absorbed from the gastrointestinal tract. The absorbed phenolphthalein is excreted chiefly through bile and partly through urine.

2. In liver damage with or without jaundice, in jaundice without liver damage and in severe sepsis, the biliary excretion is impaired; the urine excretion and the blood level of phenolphthalein are consequently much increased. The impaired biliary excretion in all these cases is probably due to a block of the excretory function of the Kupffer's cells.

3. In chronic nephritis, the urinary excretion is decreased, but the blood level is normal, or lower than normal.

4. In malignant nephrosclerosis, the urinary excretion is decreased, but the blood level is normal, or higher than normal.

5. Comparison of the phenolphthalein clearance with the endogenous creatinine clearance indicates that the reduction in phenolphthalein excretion is partly due to filtration damage. The low blood level in chronic nephritis may be due to impaired intestinal absorption.

6. The determination of the blood and urinary phenolphthalein gives evidence of the excretory function of liver and kidney respectively.

REFERENCES

(1a) SOLLMANN, T.: A Manual of Pharmacology. Philadelphia and London, W. B. Saunders Company, 221, 1936.

(1b) CUSHNY, A. R., EDMUNDS, C. W., AND GUNN, J. A.: Pharmacology and Therapeutics. 12th Edition. Lea and Febiger, 270, Philadelphia, 1940.

(1c) VON VAMOSSY, Z.: Therapie Der Gegenwart, Munchen. Med. Wchnschr., May, 1902.

(1d) FLEIG, U. C.: Arch. Internat. de Pharmacodynam., **18**: 327, 1908.

(2) FANTUS, B., AND DYNIEWICZ, J. M.: J. A. M. A., **110**: 796, 1938.

(3) WOLDMAN, E. E.: Am. J. Digest. Dis., **5**: 221, 1938.

(4) STEIGMANN, F., AND DYNIEWICZ, J. M.: Am. J. Digest. Dis., **6**: 120, 1939.

(5) ROWLAND, V. C.: Editorial. Am. J. Digest Dis., **6**: 396, 1939.

(6) STEIGMANN, F., BARNARD, R. D., AND DYNIEWICZ, J. M.: Am. J. Med. Sci., **196**: 673, 1938.

(7) POPPER, H., AND MANDEL, E.: Ergeb. d. inn. Med. u. Kinderheilk., **53**: 685, 1937.

(8) ARKIN, A., AND POPPER, H.: Arch. Int. Med., **65**: 627, 1940.

COMPARATIVE PHYSIOLOGICAL ACTIONS OF PHENYL-, THIENYL- AND FURYLISOPROPYLAMINES

GORDON A. ALLES AND GEORGE A. FEIGEN

From the Pharmacological Laboratory, University of California Medical School, San Francisco, and the William G. Kerckhoff Laboratories of the Biological Sciences, California Institute of Technology, Pasadena

Received for publication April 2, 1941

Corresponding derivatives of benzene, thiophene and furan differ notably in their chemical composition and structure, but since the time of Victor Meyer (6) the close similarity of the chemical and physical properties of benzene and thiophene derivatives has been recognized. The similarities between thiophene and furan compounds were early recognized, and thiophene was designated as thiofuran in some of its literature. The aromatic properties of furan have been emphasized by Gilman and coworkers (4), and Pauling (7) has recently presented pertinent resonance data and structural interpretations for thiophene and furan that are in keeping with the known physical and chemical similarities of these compounds with benzene.

Closely related to some of the work here reported are the observations of Tainter (10) that *β-2*-thienylethylamine (referred to as thiophenylethylamine) has about the same order of pressor activity in cats as does *β*-phenylethylamine, and that pretreatment with cocaine diminished the pressor activity of both compounds. Burn also studied the pressor effects of *β-2*-thienylethylamine synthesized by Barger and Easson (2), and reported that its effects were qualitatively and quantitatively indistinguishable from those of *β*-phenylethylamine. Observations of the effects of *β-2*-thienylethylamine (referred to as thiophenethylamine) and *β*-phenylethylamine in producing increased motor activity in rats have recently been reported by Schulte, Reif, Bacher, Laurence and Tainter (9). Thienyl aminoethyl ketones were found to have some local anesthetic activity by Sinha in working with the compounds of Levvy and Nisbet (1938).

Furylmethylamine and *β*-furylethylamine were prepared by Windaus and Dalmer (1920) and Impens found them to cause a transient fall in blood pressure when injected into cats, without notable effect on pulse rate or respiration. On isolated guinea-pig uterus, these compounds caused a marked increase in tone. These same compounds were studied by Fujii (3) who reported furylmethylamine to be depressor in cats, but pressor in rabbits; and *β*-furylethylamine to cause an initial fall, then a rise, then a prolonged fall of blood pressure in rabbits. Both compounds acted to contract a considerable number of isolated smooth muscle preparations from various species of animals, and this action was considered to be upon the parasympathetic endings in small doses, and upon the muscle itself with large doses. Judging from the effects of approximately lethal doses in mice, Fujii concluded that furylmethylamine acts principally upon the central nervous system as a depressant, while β-furylethylamine acts as a stimulant. Kanao (1927) synthesized a large number of furylalkanolamines, but they were investigated only with respect to their mydriatic action, which was found to be inversely proportional to the number of carbon atoms in the side chain. Levvy and Nisbet (1939) found that several of a series of furyl aminoethyl ketones had some local anesthetic action on the rabbit's cornea, but all proved to be highly irritant.

The present studies were carried out to determine the similarities and differences in certain physiological actions of identical aminoalkyl derivatives of benzene, thiophene and furan. These isopropylamines have both peripheral and central actions and certain of these actions that may be measured with some quantitative precision were studied.

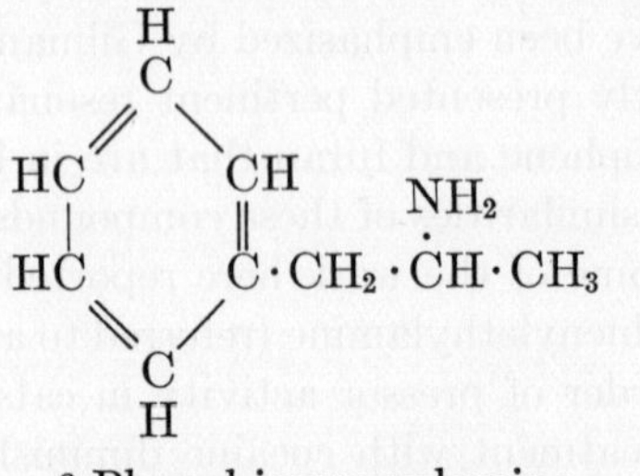

β-Phenyl isopropylamine

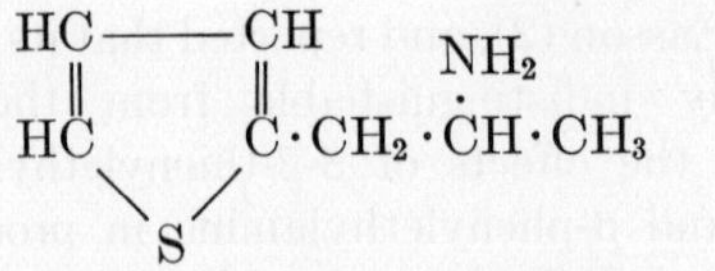

β-(2-Thienyl) isopropylamine

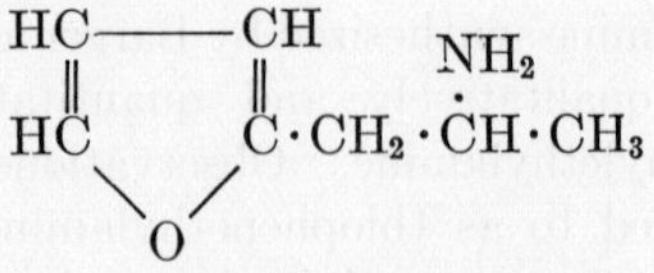

β-(2-Furyl) isopropylamine

EXPERIMENTAL STUDIES IN ANIMALS

Phenethylamine and phenisopropylamine (β-phenylisopropylamine) were used in the form of their sulfates, and one or both were used as primary comparison standards when such was needed and possible of use.

The β-2-thienylisopropylamine, in the form of its sulfate, was prepared from the corresponding ketone by Dr. Glenn E. Ullyot, and the SO_4 content analyzed 25.26 and 25.14 per cent, the calculated value being 25.25 per cent. The sulfate of β-2-furylisopropylamine was obtained from the amine product of the reduction of the corresponding furylnitropropylene by Dr. George H.

Connitt, and the SO_4 content analyzed 27.48 and 27.16 per cent, the calculated value being 27.57 per cent.

Pressor effects in dogs

Dogs under anesthesia with ether or sodium pentobarbital were used, and phenethylamine was used as the primary comparison standard, though responses to epinephrine were also usually studied in the same animals. The threshold dose for any considerable pressor activity of the thienyl- and furyl-isopropylamines is the same as for phenethylamine or phenisopropylamine (about 5×10^{-7} to 10^{-6} mol./kgm. intravenously) and in freshly prepared animals the intensity of the pressor response to 10^{-6} mol./kgm. is comparable to that of about 10^{-8} mol./kgm. of epinephrine. The duration of pressor effect of the thienyl- and furyl-isopropylamines is comparable to that of phenisopropylamine, and is very much more prolonged than that following injection of phenethylamine. Like phenisopropylamine, the thienyl- and furyl-isopropylamines exhibit marked tachyphylactic effect in serial injections, and fairly precise comparisons of the relative pressor activities of all of these compounds require the use of phenethylamine, or similar substance, as a standard.

As found in earlier work by Alles (1), the intensity of pressor effect of phenisopropylamine is quite comparable to that of phenethylamine, and within the limits of the observational technic, the same is true for thienylisopropylamine. The effect of furylisopropylamine, however, is definitely less, the best comparisons indicating this compound to be but about one-third as active as phenethylamine. In some preparations an initial depressor effect of short duration precedes the long-lasting pressor effect of furylisopropylamine, particularly with doses above 10^{-6} mol./kgm., and atropine in a dose of 10^{-6} mol./kgm. appears to diminish this initial depressor effect. Vagal slowing of the heart at times of maximal pressor response did not appear to be different with the three isopropylamines or phenethylamine. It was not determined whether such vagal effects were due to blood pressure reflexes or due to direct medullary stimulation of the vagus by the compounds.

Effects on isolated rabbit intestine

Ileum strips suspended in a medium of 0.9 per cent NaCl, 0.042 per cent KCl, 0.018 per cent $CaCl_2$, 0.015 per cent $NaHCO_3$ and 0.10 per cent glucose, at 37°C., were used for study, and effective bath concentrations for particular responses were determined. The effects of phenisopropylamine and of thienylisopropylamine were nearly the same, both being "di-phasic" in that minimally active doses (5×10^{-4} or 10^{-3} molal) showed increases in tonus with some decrease in amplitude, while higher doses (2 to 8×10^{-3} molal) showed a progressive decrease in tone and abolition of amplitude. Furylisopropylamine differed from the other two compounds in that over the same dosage range (5×10^{-4} to 10^{-2} molal) there was dominantly an increase in tonus, and while inhibition of amplitude was notable with doses of around 10^{-3} molal, about five to ten times this dose was necessary to abolish ampli-

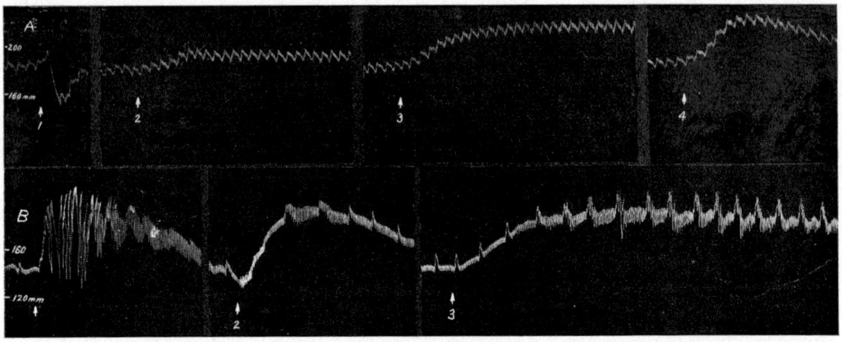

FIG. 1. DOGS, Na-PENTOBARBITAL. CAROTID ARTERIAL PRESSURE

A. 16 kgm. *1*, 10^{-9} mol./kgm. epinephrine. *2*, 10^{-6} mol./kgm. B-furylisopropylamine. *3*, 10^{-6} mol./kgm. B-thienylisopropylamine. *4*, 10^{-6} mol./kgm. phenethylamine.

B. 9 kgm. *1*, 10^{-8} mol./kgm. epinephrine. *2*, 10^{-6} mol./kgm. phenethylamine. *3*, 3×10^{-6} mol./kgm. B-furylisopropylamine.

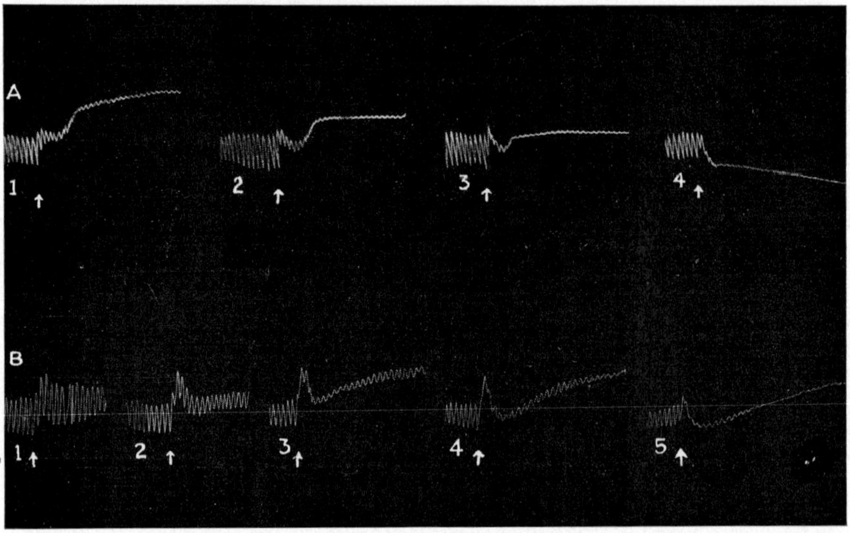

FIG. 2. ISOLATED RABBIT ILEUM

A. Thienylisopropylamine in the following concentrations: *1*, 10^{-3} molal.

B. Furylisopropylamine in the following concentrations: *1*, 5×10^{-4} molal; *2*, 10^{-3} molal; *3*, 2×10^{-3} molal; *4*, 5×10^{-3} molal; *5*, 10^{-2} molal.

tude. On colon strips the effect of all the compounds studied was more dominantly to increase tone than with ileum strips, as has been noted by Alles (1b) for the optically isomeric phenisopropylamines.

The increased tonus effect of the phenyl-, thienyl- and furylisopropylamines on isolated ileum or colon strips was found to be antagonized by atropine in approximately equal molal concentration. Concentrations of 2 to 5 $\times 10^{-4}$ molal atropine usually caused some decrease in the tonus responses to 10^{-3} molal of these isopropylamines, but 10^{-3} molal atropine was usually required to effectively abolish the tonus responses. In several experiments it appeared that furylisopropylamine was somewhat more readily antagonized by atropine than were the phenyl- and thienyl-isopropylamines, but the differences were not great (about two-fold).

The effects of epinephrine and acetylcholine on isolated intestinal strips may be diminished or abolished by suitable mol ratio concentrations of phenisopropylamine (see 1b), and with the thienyl- and furyl-isopropylamines this is also true. The antagonism of the relaxing effect of 10^{-6} molal epinephrine by 1 to 2 $\times 10^{-3}$ molal thienyl-isopropylamine is comparable to the effect of phenisopropylamine in the same concentrations, but furylisopropylamine is less effective, and even 5 $\times 10^{-3}$ molal may not abolish the relaxant responses to 10^{-6} molal epinephrine. Antagonism of the stimulant effect of 10^{-6} molal acetylcholine is marked, though not complete, by 1 to 2 $\times 10^{-3}$ molal of phenyl-, thienyl- or furyl-isopropylamine, and there does not appear to be any difference among these compounds in their antagonism to acetylcholine. However, the considerable stimulant effect of furylisopropylamine itself, in all concentrations used, does diminish the conclusiveness of interpretation of its antagonism to acetylcholine.

Motor effects and lethal toxicity in mice

Three groups of 10 mice each were injected intraperitoneally with phenyl-, thienyl- or furyl-isopropylamine in a dose of 10^{-4} mol./kgm. (about 20 mgm./kgm. of sulfates), and placed in adjacent cages. Phenisopropylamine and thienylisopropylamine caused very similar stimulant effects, but the group injected with phenisopropylamine was active for about 4 hours, as compared with 2 hours with the thienyl compound. Furylisopropylamine showed practically no motor stimulant effect, and caused no deaths, while two out of ten died with both phenisopropylamine and thienylisopropylamine with this dose.

Similar observations with a dose of 2 $\times 10^{-4}$ mol./kgm. of the three compounds showed furylisopropylamine to exert a stimulant action for only 15 to 30 minutes. Phenisopropylamine and thienylisopropylamine caused much longer-lasting stimulant effects which were very similar, and some of the animals injected with phenisopropylamine were active after 5 hours, whereas none with thienylisopropylamine was active after 3½ hours. There was one death with phenisopropylamine, but none with furyl- or thienyl-isopropylamine.

Observations made after a dose of 4 $\times 10^{-4}$ mol./kgm. showed very similar stimulant effects from all three compounds. However, most of the effect from the furyl compound had worn off in 2 hours, but with phenisopropylamine six of the group of ten were still active after 5 hours, while none with thienylisopropylamine was active after 5 hours. There were no deaths with furylisopropylamine, while four out of ten died with both phenisopropylamine and thienylisopropylamine.

To determine an approximate LD_{50}, the thienyl and furyl compounds were also administered in larger doses. With thienylisopropylamine, four out of ten died from 6×10^{-4} mol./kgm., and eight out of ten died from 8×10^{-4} mol./kgm., the LD_{50} thus being about 6×10^{-4} mol./kgm., or 114 mgm./gm. of sulfate. Furylisopropylamine was appreciably less toxic, and its LD_{50} was found to be about 20×10^{-4} mol./kgm., or 348 mgm./kgm. of sulfate. Respiratory arrest was the primary cause of death from the furylisopropylamine, as the heart continued to beat for some time after respiration had ceased. Marked intestinal peristalsis was often a noteworthy finding at prompt autopsy, but no macroscopic histologic changes were noted in the organs. With the thienylisopropylamine, autopsy occasionally showed the lungs to be hemorrhagic, and there was often a finding of considerable gas in the stomach, both findings being common with acute lethal doses of phenisopropylamine.

Although phenyl-, thienyl- and furyl-isopropylamine at the dosage level of 4×10^{-4} mol./kgm. all showed very similar stimulant effects, there was a striking difference between the three at the level of 10^{-4} mol./kgm., with the furyl compound being definitely less active than the other two. The relationship of these doses to the LD_{50} for the same compounds should, however, be considered, for while 4×10^{-4} mol./kgm. of phenisopropylamine or thienylisopropylamine is approximately the LD_{50} for these two compounds, this dose represents but about one-fifth the LD_{50} for furylisopropylamine, at which dose the surviving animals were active for 2 to 2.5 hours.

EXPERIMENTAL STUDIES IN MAN

The comparative valuation of the central nervous system effects of compounds in man may well be expected to be quite different than in animals having lesser degrees of integration of the central nervous system. Compounds that exhibit a considerable degree of action upon the cerebral cortex might be expected to act more evidently in man, in whom cortical control exerts a greater dominance, than in the usual laboratory animals. The more complete cooperation of the experimental subject in remaining in a steady state may also be expected to contribute to the precision of such studies.

Observations on circulatory effect and subjective impressions of central effect were carried out with two normally healthy persons who lay supine during the period of observation of blood pressure and pulse rate. The compounds were administered completely dissolved in water, about two hours

TABLE 1

Activity after Oral Administration in Man

COMPOUND	DOSE	INITIAL B.P./PULSE	MAXIMUM B.P./PULSE	B.P. RETURN TO NORMAL	C.N.S. EFFECT
G. A.					
	mgm.			*hours*	
Phenylisopropylamine sulfate	10	114–64/74	130–84/64 (120 min.)	4	Stimulation
	20	114–68/72	136–84/64 (120 min.)	4	Stimulation, sleeplessness
	50	118–72/68	170–94/52 (100 min.)	>8	Stimulation, sleeplessness
Thienylisopropylamine sulfate	10	114–64/68	122–78/62 (120 min.)	3	No stimulation, no sleeplessness
	20	116–68/74	120–70/74 (40 min.)	3	No stimulation, no sleeplessness
Furylisopropylamine sulfate	20	120–70/68	126–78/72 (50 min.)	3	No effect
	50	122–68/70	114–74/68 (60 min.)	2	No effect
G. F.					
Phenylisopropylamine sulfate	10	126–82/72	134–86/70 (30 min.)	1	No marked stimulation
	20	124–74/76	128–82/88 (80 min.)	2	Some stimulation
	40	128–72/70	146–90/74 (160 min.)	>5	Stimulation, then depression during maximum B.P. effects
Thienylisopropylamine sulfate	10	116–94/70	120–92/70 (40 min.)	1	No stimulation
			108–90/90 (160 min.)	>3	
	20	120–86/70	116–76/72 (180 min.)	>3	No stimulation
	50	124–90/74	142–100/78 (100 min.)	4	No stimulation
Furylisopropylamine sulfate	20	124–90/66	114–78/66 (30 min.)	1	Temporary stimulation during maximum rise of B.P. (ca. 1 hr.)
			130–98/76 (100 min.)	2.5	
	50	122–88/70	110–76/80 (140 min.)	>3	No stimulation

after a light morning meal, and lunch was postponed until the end of the observations. Both persons have had considerable experience with administration of phenisopropylamine in various dosages, and their subjective impressions were comparative to this compound. Alertness, talkativeness, feelings of awareness, and anti-sleep effects were considered as the indices of the central stimulant effects.

The data in table 1 indicate the thienyl- and furyl-isopropylamines to be much less active as pressor agents than is phenisopropylamine Indeed, in the case of G. F., there was a doubtfully significant lowering of blood pressure during the periods following administration of the furyl- or thienyl- com-

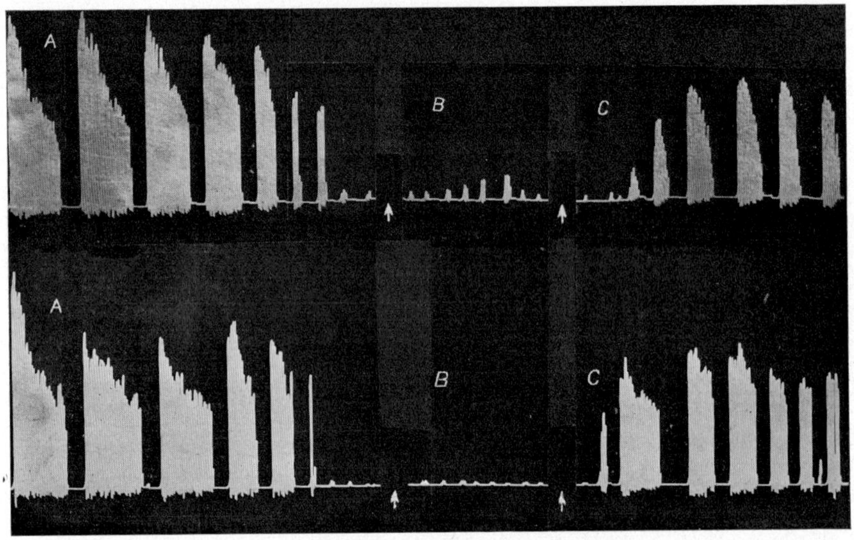

FIG. 3. ERGOGRAPH FATIGUE RECORDS. REPEATED AT 15 MINUTE INTERVALS AND CONTINUED FOR SIX HOUR PERIOD. MIDDLE FINGER OF LEFT HAND

Upper tracing: *A*, initial 2 hour control period. *B*, 2 hour period following 20 mgm. thienylisopropylamine sulfate. *C*, subsequent 2 hour period following 10 mgm. phenisopropylamine sulfate.

Lower tracing: *A*, initial 2 hour control period. *B*, 2 hour period following 50 mgm. furylisopropylamine sulfate. *C*, subsequent 2 hour period following 10 mgm. phenisopropylamine sulfate.

pounds. There were no notable central nervous system stimulant effects in G. A. following the thienyl or furyl compounds. In G. F., whose circulatory stability is not great, a slight effect from 20 mgm. of the furyl compound did appear to result in the trial reported, though no effect was apparent following 50 mgm. of the same compound, or after 20 mgm. when sitting up during the observational period. It is clear from these observations that neither thienyl- nor furyl-isopropylamine are at all closely comparable to phenisopropylamine in their circulatory or central effects in man.

To confirm subjective observations as to the relative lack of central nervous system effect of the thienyl- and furyl-isopropylamines, observations were made with regard to the effect of these substances and of phenisopropylamine upon patellar reflex (knee-jerk) activity, and also upon voluntary muscular fatigue of the middle finger of the hand, as measured upon an ergograph. The studies of Reid (8) on the mechanism of voluntary muscle fatigue appear to establish the cause of such fatigue to be a depression of central nervous system mechanisms. For the present studies, records of knee-jerk activity and rate of voluntary fatigue of the middle finger of the hand were made at fifteen-minute intervals for a two-hour initial control period, then for two hours following the compound to be tested, and then for two hours following the administration of phenisopropylamine sulfate in an amount which had previously been established as an effective dosage of this compound.

Knee-jerk activity records on both experimental persons showed no changes following the administration of as much as 20 mgm. of thienylisopropylamine sulfate, or of as much as 50 mgm. of furylisopropylamine sulfate. In contrast to this, an increase in knee-jerk activity was commonly observed following 20 mgm. phenisopropylamine sulfate.

As shown in figure 3 for G. A., no definite effects of 20 mgm. thienylisopropylamine sulfate or of 50 mgm. furylisopropylamine sulfate upon ergographic work production were observed, though a following administration of but 10 mgm. of phenisopropylamine sulfate caused a marked increase in ergographic work output after about 30 minutes, and the effect lasted more than 2 hours. Similar observations were made with G. F., and there can be no doubt that the thienyl- and furyl-isopropylamines are relatively ineffective central nervous system stimulants with respect to voluntary muscle fatigue phenomena.

DISCUSSION

If we use pressor activity following intravenous injection in anesthetized dogs as the criterion for relative physiological activity, phenisopropylamine and thienylisopropylamine are very comparable, or possibly identical, as was stated for the relationship between phenethylamine and thienylethylamine by Gunn. Furylisopropylamine, however, is less active as a pressor agent than the other two isopropylamines, and its initial depressor effect that can be diminished by atropine suggests that it also has a parasympathetic type of activity, and this type of activity is very notable when the compound is studied with respect to its actions upon isolated intestine.

Upon isolated rabbit ileum and colon, all three isopropylamines in proper concentrations cause contraction effects which may be considered to be a parasympathetic stimulant type of activity, particularly because the response may be abolished by pretreatment with a proper mol ratio of atropine. This type of activity is most notable with furylisopropylamine, and this compound differs quite considerably from thienyl- or phenyl-isopropylamines in respect to its action upon isolated intestine. As with phenisopropylamine or its optical isomers (1b), the mechanism of action of furylisopropylamine is not clear because it also exhibits antagonism to the relaxant effects of epinephrine or the stimulant effects of acetylcholine in about the same dosage range in which it appears to exert a direct parasympathetic stimulant effect.

The most noteworthy aspect of the physiological activities of phenisopropylamine is its notable stimulation of functional parts of the central nervous system in man with doses that exert a relatively slight action upon the circulation or upon the intestinal musculature. Several attempts have been made to establish experimental technics with laboratory animals that would be analogous to effects in man and serve to value quantitatively such activities of phenisopropylamine and related compounds. A most extensive study of this kind is that of Schulte, Reif, Bacher, Lawrence and Tainter (9) who mechanically recorded the motor activity of rats following subcutaneous injection of some seventy-five compounds. Among these compounds, phenethylamine and thienylethylamine (thiophenethylamine) were reported upon, and from the data it would appear that although thienyl in any dosage did not cause as much motor effect as did phenethylamine, the threshold dose of the thienyl compound was only one-eighth that of the phenyl compound. A greater and longer-lasting effect was obtained with thienylethylamine with but one-quarter the optimum dose of phenethylamine, and in terms of a calculated therapeutic margin (fatal dose/threshold dose), thienylethylamine was found to be about sixteen times as effective as a central stimulant agent.

Our own observations with small animals were carried out in a manner similar to that used by Gunn and Gurd (5), using mice and making simultaneous visual observations of the motor activity effects of the control and studied compounds. Satisfactory precision of observation is obtained under such conditions, but no great difference was observed between the intensity of the effects of the phenyl- and thienyl-isopropylamines, although the duration of action of the thienyl compound was definitely less prolonged. Also, contrary to the relationship reported by Schulte et al., the calculation of therapeutic margins for the phenyl- and thienyl-isopropylamines would show them to be nearly the same.

In any case, since the central stimulant effects in mice or rats can only be noted with dosages that closely approach the lethal range, such animal experiments can only doubtfully be translated to indicate probable central effects in man, and the direct experiments in man are of special interest. In these direct experiments, it became apparent that there are very considerable differences in the central nervous system effects of phenyl-, thienyl- and furyl-isopropylamines. It may be that a further increase in the amounts administered of the thienyl- and furyl-isopropylamines would establish some detectable central stimulant or depressant effects of these compounds, but the observations were sufficiently extended to conclude with certainty that these compounds are considerably less active agents than phenisopropylamine on the central nervous system of man when using the reported methods of observation.

SUMMARY

1. In dogs under ether or pentobarbital anesthesia, phenyl- and thienyl-isopropylamines injected intravenously induce pressor effects very closely similar as to intensity and duration. About three times as much furyl-isopropylamine is required to produce an equally intense pressor response, and a preceding depressor effect, which can be antagonized by a proper mol ratio of atropine, may occur.

2. On isolated rabbit intestinal strips, these three isopropylamines in minimally active concentrations induce an increase in tone that may be prevented by pretreatment with equal molal concentrations of atropine. With greater concentrations, all three compounds act to decrease tone, but the range of dosage in which furyl-isopropylamine acts only to increase tone is much greater than for phenyl- or thienyl-isopropylamine.

3. Phenyl- and thienyl-isopropylamines injected intraperitoneally into mice in nearly lethal dosages are more active motor stimulants than furyl-isopropylamine, and the thienyl compound has a shorter duration of action than phenisopropylamine.

4. Thienylisopropylamine injected intraperitoneally into mice is slightly less toxic than the phenyl compound, and furylisopropylamine is but about one-fourth as toxic as the other two compounds.

5. Orally administered to man, phenisopropylamine is very considerably more active as a circulatory stimulant and as a central nervous system stimulant, though these two activities appear unrelated.

The authors wish to express here their indebtedness and thanks to Drs. Glenn E. Ullyott and George H. Connitt, of the Smith, Kline & French Laboratories, Philadelphia, for samples of the furyl- and thienyl-isopropylamines, and to Mildred A. Shull, Pasadena, for much help with the experimental studies here presented.

REFERENCES

(1) Alles: (a) This Journal, **47:** 339, 1933. (b) Univ. Calif. Publ. Pharmacol., **1:** 101, 1939.
(2) Barger and Easson: Jour. Chem. Soc., p. 2100, 1938.
(3) Fujii: Folia pharmacol. japon., **2:** 1; in Jap. Jour. Med. Sci., **2:** 4, 1926. Folia pharmacol. japon., **2:** 29; in Jap. Jour. Med. Sci., **2:** 5, 1926.
(4) Gilman and Wright: Chem. Rev., **11:** 323, 1932.
(5) Gunn and Gurd: Jour. Physiol., **97:** 453, 1940.
(6) Meyer: Die Thiophene Gruppe (Viewig und Sohn, Braunschweig) p. 276, 1888.
(7) Pauling: The Nature of the Chemical Bond (Cornell Univ. Press, Ithaca) pp. 130, 208–9, 1939.
(8) Reid: Jour. Exper. Physiol., **19:** 17, 1928.
(9) Schulte, Reif, Bacher, Lawrence and Tainter: This Journal, **71:** 62, 1941.
(10) Tainter: Quart. Jour. Pharm. Pharmacol., **3:** 584, 1930.

A METHOD FOR THE DETERMINATION OF *5,5* DIPHENYLHYDANTOIN IN BIOLOGICAL MATERIAL[1]

F. L. KOZELKA AND C. H. HINE

From the Department of Pharmacology and Toxicology, University of Wisconsin, Madison

Received for publication April 11, 1941

While *5,5* diphenylhydantoin is extensively employed for the treatment of epilepsy, the only information available on its distribution in the tissues and rate of disappearance from the body is the preliminary report from this laboratory (1). In order to study this problem, a method for the quantitative determination of this drug was developed. In a preceding report (2), a brief description of the method was presented. The technic is based upon the early observations of Harries and Weiss (3) and Biltz and Behrens (4) who reported that the chlorine derivative of the hydantoin nucleus can be prepared by treatment with sodium hypochlorite. They also demonstrated that the chlorine could be removed and the original compound recovered with relative ease by boiling the derivative in alcohol or treatment with potassium iodide in the presence of sodium bicarbonate. Preliminary work on the isolation and purification of the drug and its dichloro derivative by sublimation indicated that this technic would not be satisfactory for quantitative purposes. However, for qualitative purposes, most of the drug can be isolated by sublimation and identified by melting point and mixed melting point determinations. For quantitative determinations, the technic described below was developed.

CHEMICAL REACTIONS

The chemical reactions involved in the determinations are:

(*1*) $$2Cl_2 + 2H_2O \rightarrow 2HOCl + 2HCl$$

(*2*)

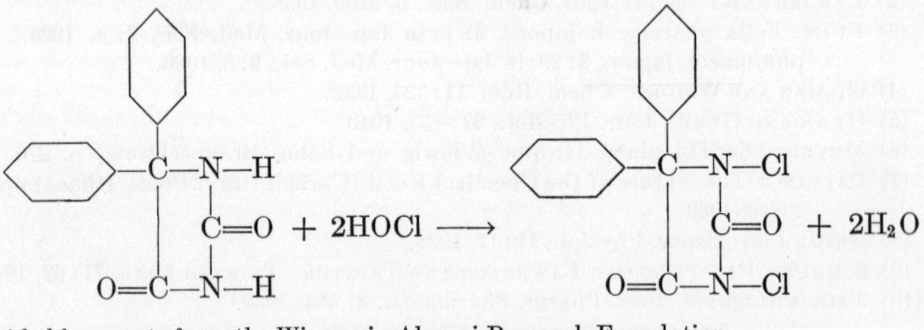

[1] Aided by grants from the Wisconsin Alumni Research Foundation.

(3)

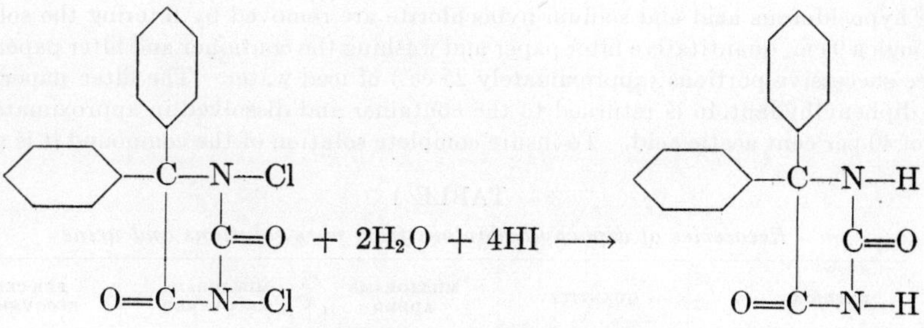

$$+ 2HCl + 2H_2O + 2I_2$$

(4) $$4Na_2S_2O_3 + 2I_2 \rightarrow 4NaI + 2Na_2S_4O_6$$

The reaction equilibrium in equation (2) is toward the right but when hydriodic acid is present (potassium iodide dissolved in acetic acid) to take up the chlorine, the reaction is reversed in the following manner:

$$-\underset{|}{N}-Cl + H_2O \longrightarrow -\underset{|}{N}-H + HOCl$$

and $$HOCl + 2HI \longrightarrow HCl + H_2O + I_2$$

It follows that:

$$\frac{\text{Mol. wt. of diphenylhydantoin}}{\text{Wt. of diphenylhydantoin}} = \frac{4 \text{ Mol. wt. of } Na_2S_2O_3}{\text{Wt. of } Na_2S_2O_3 \text{ per cc.}}$$

From the above equations it will be noted that one cubic centimeter of a .01 N solution of sodium thiosulfate is equivalent to .6377 milligram of diphenylhydantoin.

PROCEDURE

Urine specimens are acidified and the diphenylhydantoin extracted directly with ether in a continuous extractor without previous treatment with a precipitating agent. Tissue specimens are macerated and digested in 40 per cent acetic acid for 24 hours. After the precipitation of the proteins with sodium tungstate, the material is filtered through a Büchner funnel using ordinary filter paper. The residue is again digested in 40 per cent acetic acid for 24 hours and filtered. This process is repeated a third time to remove the last trace of the drug. It is usually necessary to add a small amount of sodium tungstate before the second and third filtrations. The combined filtrates are treated with concentrated sodium hydroxide until they are but slightly acid to litmus and then are extracted with ether in a continuous extractor. The crude extract is evaporated to dryness on a water bath and transferred by washing with a minimum amount of chloroform to a 200-cc. centrifuge cup or a large test tube. Chloroform is preferred to ether for this transfer, because of the low solubility of water in this solvent, and consequently a minimum amount of salts are transferred with the diphenylhydantoin. The chloroform is then completely evaporated and the diphenylhydantoin is dissolved in a minimum amount (approximately 5 cc.) of dilute sodium hydroxide solution. Chlorine gas is passed slowly through the solution for approximately one-half hour to insure complete chlorination. The excess chlorine is removed by directing a jet of air over the surface of the solution.

The hypochlorous acid and sodium hypochlorite are removed by filtering the solution through a 9 cm. quantitative filter paper and washing the container and filter paper with three successive portions (approximately 25 cc.) of iced water. The filter paper with the diphenylhydantoin is returned to the container and dissolved in approximately 50 cc. of 40 per cent acetic acid. To insure complete solution of the compound it is advisable to stopper the container and shake it vigorously until the filter paper is completely broken up into a fine pulp. The material adhering to the stopper and the sides of the container is washed down with water. Forty per cent acetic acid was found to be the optimum concentration which would insure the complete solution of the compound and not liberate iodine from potassium iodide. Approximately 0.3 gram of potassium

TABLE 1

Recoveries of diphenylhydantoin from pure solutions and urine

MATERIAL	QUANTITY	MILLIGRAMS ADDED	MILLIGRAMS RECOVERED	PER CENT RECOVERED
	cc.			
Water	500	20.0	20.0	100.0
Water	500	25.0	24.2	96.8
Water	500	50.0	48.6	96.4
Water	1000	6.8	6.4	94.5
Water	1000	36.4	36.6	100.4
Urine	1000	20.0	20.2	100.9
Urine	1000	10.0	10.1	101.0
Urine	1000	15.0	14.5	96.7
Urine	1000	20.0	18.9	94.5
Urine	1000	30.0	28.6	95.3
Urine	1000	15.0	14.6	97.3

TABLE 2

Recoveries of diphenylhydantoin from tissues

MATERIAL	QUANTITY	MILLIGRAMS ADDED	MILLIGRAMS RECOVERED	PER CENT RECOVERED
	grams			
Blood	20	5	4.3	86.0
Blood	20	10	8.6	86.0
Blood	20	1	1.05	105.0
Blood	20	5	4.34	86.8
Blood	20	4	4.12	103.0
Blood	20	5	4.78	95.6
Blood	20	3	3.01	100.3
Blood	20	4	3.72	93.0
Blood	20	5	5.24	104.8
Blood	120	10	10.2	102.0
Muscle	300	25	23.0	92.0
Liver	100	10	11.5	115.0
Liver	107	15	15.0	100.0
Brain	16	5	5.0	100.0
Kidney	41	5	4.7	94.0

iodide (free from iodates) is added and the liberated iodine is titrated with 0.01 N sodium thiosulfate. One cubic centimeter of the sodium thiosulfate is equivalent to 0.6377 mgm. of diphenylhydantoin.

Diphenylhydantoin and the dichloro derivative are very soluble in ether, chloroform and acetic acid and relatively insoluble in water. One milligram of the dichloro derivative is soluble in 100 cc. of water at 25°C. Its low solubility in water permits the removal of the excess chlorine and hypochlorous acid by washing with water without a significant loss. It also permits the separation of the diphenylhydantoin from certain other interfering compounds, such as uric acid, theobromine, theophylline, and the common barbiturates. The chlorine derivatives of these latter compounds are quite soluble in water and remain in solution during the chlorination process. Twenty milligrams of uric acid, theobromine or theophylline gave negative results, while quantities of luminal or barbital up to ten milligrams added to the specimens did not increase the readings. Larger amounts of the barbiturates will produce high results, but not in proportion to the amount of barbiturate present. Blank determinations on ether extracts of one liter of normal urine vary between zero and one milligram of diphenylhydantoin. Similar determinations on two hundred grams of normal tissue gave negative results.

RESULTS

The technic was tested by recovering known quantities of diphenylhydantoin from pure solutions, urine, and tissues. The recoveries from pure solutions and urine are given in table 1. Table 2 gives the recoveries from blood and other tissues to indicate the adequacy of the method for clinical and experimental purposes. While the percentage error is relatively large in some cases when dealing with less than 10 mgm., the absolute error is within ±1 (one) mgm. and should meet the requirements for clinical use.

CONCLUSIONS

1. A method for the determination of *5,5* diphenylhydantoin is described. Recoveries of ±one milligram are obtainable, which should meet the requirements for clinical and experimental studies.

2. The technic is specific for the drug under conditions in which it will usually be employed.

3. If circumstances require that the compound be identified specifically, the diphenylhydantoin or its dichloro derivative can be purified by sublimation.

REFERENCES

(1) Kozelka and Hine: This Journal (Proc.), **69**: 292, 1940.
(2) Hine and Kozelka: This Journal (Proc.), **69**: 290, 1940.
(3) Harries and Weiss: Justus Liebig's Annalen der Chemie, **327**: 355, 1903.
(4) Biltz and Behrens: Ber. d. deut. Chem. Gesellschaft, **43**: 1984, 1910.

DISTRIBUTION AND RATE OF METABOLISM OF 5,5 DIPHENYLHYDANTOIN[1]

C. H. HINE AND F. L. KOZELKA

From the Department of Pharmacology and Toxicology, University of Wisconsin, Madison

Received for publication April 11, 1941

No analytical data are available on the rate of detoxification of 5,5 diphenylhydantoin or on its distribution in the tissues except that contained in the preliminary report from this laboratory (1). Data on laboratory animals pertinent to the question of whether or not a predilection of any tissue for the drug exists and whether or not there is a tendency of the drug to accumulate in the body after repeated doses should be of value in connection with the occasional development of manifestations of toxicity noted in its clinical use. To investigate this problem, the method of analysis described by Kozelka and Hine (2) was employed.

PROCEDURE

To insure a quantitative administration of the drug, a purified acid form (M.P. 296°C.) was employed and the solution checked titrimetrically with the technic previously described. This solution contained 10 mgm. of the drug per cc. and had a pH of approximately 10.5. Dosages of 50 mgm. per kilogram of body weight were administered intravenously. Two groups of six rabbits each were sacrificed at one-half, four, eight and twelve hours, respectively, after the injection. The tissues from each group were pooled and duplicate determinations were made on each tissue except the brain. Only one determination was made on the pooled brain tissue from each group because of the limited amount of material available. It has been our experience that when freshly removed tissues containing diphenylhydantoin were permitted to remain at room temperature for several hours, some of the drug disappears. It was necessary, therefore, that the tissues be treated with 40 per cent acetic acid immediately after removal from the body to prevent this postmortem destruction.

In order to determine whether or not the drug accumulates in the body after repeated doses, five groups of eight rabbits each were used. Each animal in the first group (controls) received 300 mgm. of diphenylhydantoin orally and was sacrificed twenty-four hours after the administration. Each animal in groups 2, 3, 4 and 5 received orally 300 mgm. of the drug daily for seven days. Groups 2 and 3 were sacrificed twenty-four hours after and groups 4 and 5 forty-eight hours after the last administration. The tissues from each group were pooled and duplicate analyses made on each tissue except the brain.

RESULTS

The concentration of the drug in the tissues at the various time intervals is shown graphically in figure 1. Each point on the graph represents an aver-

[1] Aided by grants from the Wisconsin Alumni Research Foundation.

age of four determinations on two groups of animals. Excellent checks were obtained on the duplicate determinations. The maximal variation was 0.5 mgm. per cent on the larger quantities (10 mgm. or more of diphenylhydantoin) and 0.1 to 0.3 mgm. per cent when smaller quantities were involved.

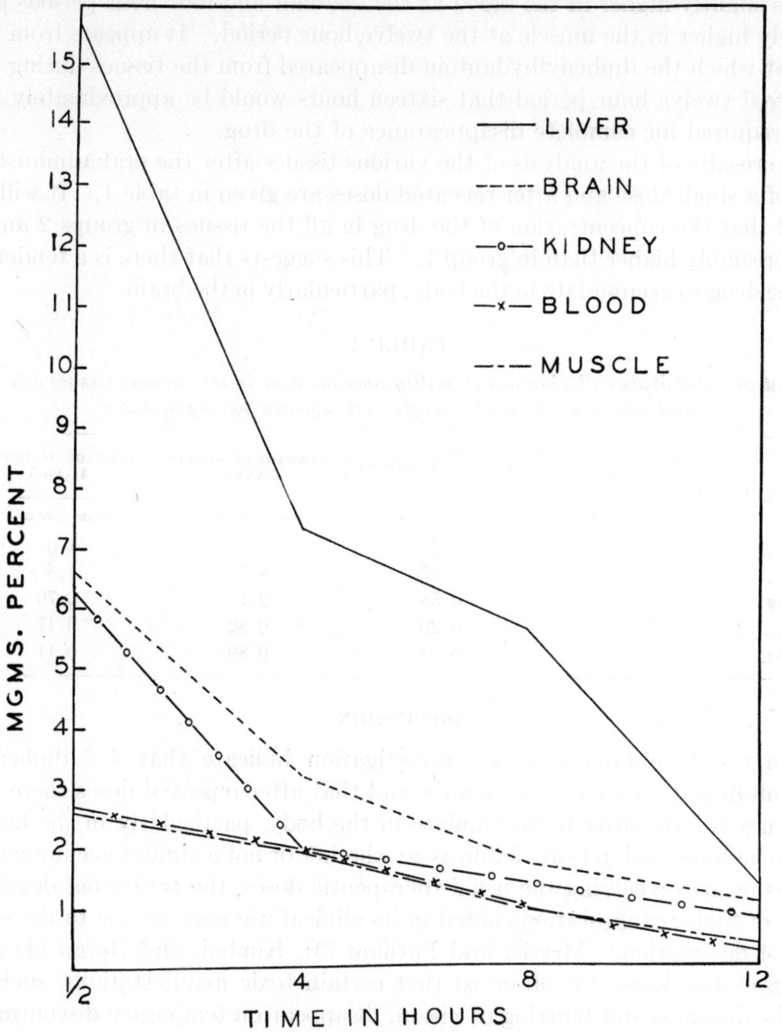

FIG. 1. CONCENTRATION OF DIPHENYLHYDANTOIN IN THE TISSUES AT THE VARIOUS TIME INTERVALS AFTER THE INTRAVENOUS ADMINISTRATION OF 50 MGM. PER KILOGRAM

It will be noted that at the one-half and four hour intervals after the injection, the relative concentrations decrease in the various tissues in the order listed, viz., liver, brain, kidney, blood and muscle.

The concentration of the drug in the liver was considerably higher than in the other tissues during the first ten hour period; in the brain and kidney it decreased rapidly from the early peak during the first four hour period but continued to remain slightly higher than in the blood and muscle. The concentration of the drug found in blood and muscle was approximately the same; it was slightly higher in the blood at the one-half and four hour periods and slightly higher in the muscle at the twelve hour period. It appears from the rate at which the diphenylhydantoin disappeared from the tissues during the observed twelve hour period that sixteen hours would be approximately the time required for complete disappearance of the drug.

The results of the analysis of the various tissues after the oral administration of a single dose and after repeated doses are given in table 1. It will be noted that the concentration of the drug in all the tissues in groups 2 and 3 is appreciably higher than in group 1. This suggests that there is a tendency for the drug to accumulate in the body, particularly in the brain.

TABLE 1

Concentration of diphenylhydantoin in milligrams per cent in the various tissues after the oral administration of a single and repeated 300 mgm. doses

	AVERAGE OF GROUP I	AVERAGE OF GROUPS 2 AND 3	AVERAGE OF GROUPS 4 AND 5
	mgm. per cent	*mgm. per cent*	*mgm. per cent*
Liver	1.23	4.2	1.6
Brain	1.27	8.7	1.8
Kidney	0.58	2.1	0.79
Blood	0.20	0.82	0.17
Muscle	0.24	0.89	0.11

DISCUSSION

The results obtained in this investigation indicate that *5,5* diphenylhydantoin is destroyed rather slowly and that after repeated doses there is a tendency for the drug to accumulate in the body, particularly in the brain. While no information is available as to whether or not a similar accumulation occurs in man receiving the usual therapeutic doses, the occasional development of toxic manifestations noted in its clinical use may be due to the slow rate of destruction. Merritt and Putnam (3), Kimball and Horan (4) and Hodgson and Reese (5) observed that certain toxic manifestations, such as ataxia, dizziness and blurring of vision, disappear on temporary discontinuation of the drug. Merritt and Putnam report that 0.6 gram is the maximal quantity which can be detoxified in a twenty-four hour period since this amount is tolerated by only a small percentage of the patients when given daily. These observations indicate that the drug is eliminated rather slowly in man and that it may accumulate in the body if a certain dose is exceeded. That the accumulation of the drug may be exceedingly slow is indicated by the fact that some of the toxic manifestations occur only after several months of therapy.

SUMMARY

Data on the relative distribution of diphenylhydantoin in rabbit tissue and the rate of its disappearance from the body are presented. The relative concentrations in the various tissues decrease in the order listed, viz., liver, brain, kidney, blood and muscle. Approximately sixteen hours are required for the drug to disappear from the body when administered intravenously in a dose of 50 mgm. per kilogram of body weight. After the repeated oral administration of relatively large daily doses, there is evidence that the drug accumulates in the tissues, particularly in the brain.

REFERENCES

(1) Kozelka and Hine: This Journal (Proc.), **69:** 292, 1940.
(2) Kozelka and Hine: This Journal (in press).
(3) Merritt and Putnam: Arch. Neurol. & Psychiat., **42:** 1053, 1939.
(4) Kimball and Horan: Annals Int. Med., **13:** 787, 1939.
(5) Hodgson and Reese: Wis. Med. J., **38:** 968, 1939.

DISTRIBUTION, EXCRETION, AND RATE AND SITE OF DETOXIFICATION OF METRAZOL[1]

H. J. TATUM AND F. L. KOZELKA

From the Department of Pharmacology and Toxicology of the University of Wisconsin, Madison

Received for publication April 11, 1941

Metrazol is being used rather extensively in clinical medicine both as an analeptic and as a convulsant drug for the treatment of schizophrenia. For this reason, it seemed pertinent to study the distribution of this drug in the body and to obtain some information concerning the factors influencing its detoxification and elimination. In order to make such a study, it was essential to have available a satisfactory method for the quantitative determination of metrazol in biological material.

Leppert (1) reported a method utilizing the precipitation of metrazol with mercuric chloride; however, we found that this mercuric chloride-metrazol complex is not sufficiently insoluble to permit satisfactory quantification from biological material when small quantities are involved. Esser and Kühn (2) extracted metrazol with alcohol from tissues acidified with sulfuric acid. The metrazol was then purified by reextractions with chloroform from aqueous solutions of the drug. Since alcohol is a rather general organic solvent this method lacks the specificity required for such a study. Zwikker (3) observed that metrazol combines with cuprous chloride to form a relatively insoluble compound and used this reaction as a basis for the determination of the drug. According to Hinsberg (4), this method is not applicable to organic extracts since pure precipitates cannot be obtained. This author found that precipitation of metrazol with phosphotungstic acid effected a complete precipitation of the drug and was quite satisfactory for quantification when employed on pure solutions of the drug but was unsuitable when applied to extracts of biological material. Stewart (5) modified the Zwikker method, using cupric chloride in place of cuprous chloride which formed characteristic crystals with metrazol. He applied this method only to qualitative determinations.

In a search for an adequate method, it was found that with a few modifications the method for the determination of barbiturates reported by Kozelka,

[1] Aided by grants from the Wisconsin Alumni Research Foundation. Preliminary reports before the American Pharmacological Society at Toronto (1939) and New Orleans (1940).

Nelson and Tatum (6) could also be used for the determination of metrazol. The tissues are digested in 20 per cent acetic acid and the proteins precipitated with sodium tungstate. The metrazol[2] is extracted from the neutralized tissue filtrate by continuous extraction with ether and purified by micro-distillation under reduced pressure in the sublimation apparatus. The small amounts of lipoidal material present are removed by dissolving the metrazol in 5 to 10 cc. of distilled water and filtering this solution through a wet filter paper. The water is then evaporated and the pure metrazol weighed. Melting points of the recovered products corresponded with the accepted value for metrazol. When the quantities found were too small to be accurately

TABLE 1

Recoveries of metrazol from 200 gram rats after the intraperitoneal injection of varying quantities of the drug and from tissues to which known quantities have been added

RATS	AMOUNT INJECTED	PER CENT RECOVERED
	mgm.	
1	100	95.8
2	50	96.4
3	10	89.0
4	50	99.0
5	50	90.6
6	50	92.0
7	46	93.7
8	46	95.8
9	70	97.0
10	93	94.1

TISSUE	WEIGHT OF TISSUE	AMOUNT ADDED	PER CENT RECOVERED
	grams	*mgm.*	
Blood	200	35	94.3
Muscle	200	50	96.0
Muscle	200	75	96.6
Liver	180	100	93.7

determined gravimetrically, the mouse bio-assay method was employed. The results which were obtained with this method are indicated on the graphs. It was found that one milligram is the minimal convulsant dose when injected intraperitoneally into a 20-gram mouse. Recoveries ranging from 89 to 99 per cent were obtained by the gravimetric technic when rats were injected intraperitoneally with varying amounts of the drug and sacrificed within five minutes after the injection. Recoveries were also made from tissues to which different quantities of metrazol were added. The recoveries from rats and from the tissues are summarized in table 1.

[2] The metrazol used in these studies was generously donated by The Bilhuber-Knoll Corporation.

DISTRIBUTION AND RATE OF DETOXIFICATION

In order to determine the distribution and rate of detoxification of metrazol, the drug content of pooled specimens of blood, liver, muscle and brain from rabbits in groups of five was estimated at hourly intervals ranging from 15 minutes to 4 hours and 15 minutes after the injection of the drug. The metrazol was given intravenously in doses of 50 mgm. per kilogram. Two groups of animals were employed at each time interval and duplicate determinations were made on the blood, liver and muscle in each group. The results of these analyses are shown in figure 1. From these data it is apparent that metrazol is uniformly distributed in the tissues analyzed and that none

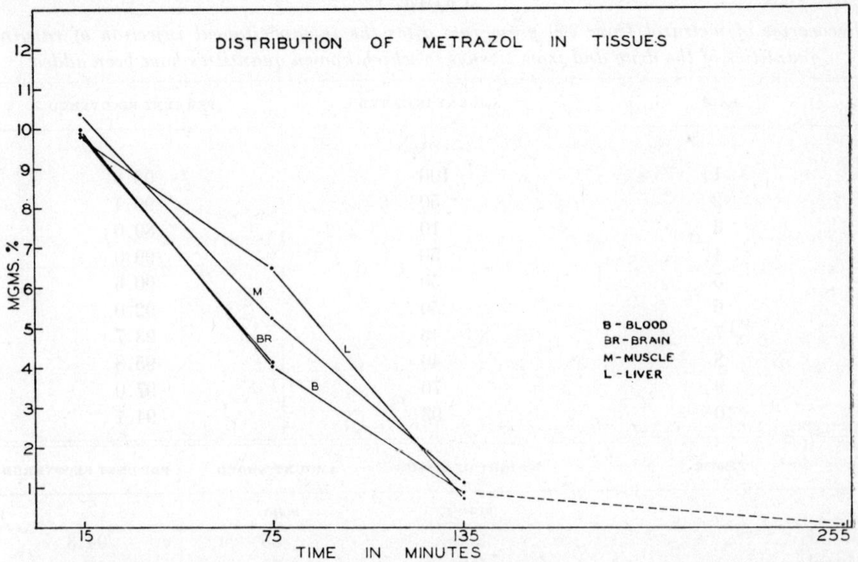

FIG. 1. CONCENTRATION OF METRAZOL IN THE TISSUES AT THE 135 AND 255 MINUTE PERIODS WAS DETERMINED BY THE MOUSE BIO-ASSAY METHOD

of them shows any particular affinity for the drug. This uniform distribution was found to be maintained as long as metrazol could be detected in the tissues.

RATE OF DETOXIFICATION

Hildebrandt and Mügge (7) determined the rate of detoxification of metrazol in the rabbit by means of continuous intravenous injection. They obtained a rate of 0.85 mgm. per kilogram per minute, whereas Werner and Tatum (8), in a similar type of experiment, reported a rate of 0.21 mgm. per kilogram per minute. The latter investigators employed a longer period of injection than did Hildebrandt and Mügge and consequently a lower average concentration of the drug was maintained in the animals during the period of observation.

By means of the concentration of metrazol found in the tissues at hourly intervals, we were able to calculate the rate of detoxification during these intervals. For the first period (between 15 minutes and 1 hour and 15 minutes after the drug had been given), the rate was found to be 0.86 mgm. per kilogram per minute. During the second hour the rate dropped to 0.65 mgm. per kilogram per minute, and during the third and fourth hours it averaged 0.08 mgm. per kilogram per minute. Thus, it can be seen that the rate decreased as the concentration of the drug in the tissues decreased and that the rates reported by Hildebrandt *et al.* and Werner *et al.* are within this range.

EXCRETION OF METRAZOL

Leppert (1), Granér and Santesson (9), and Schulte (10) concluded that in the dog and man little, if any, metrazol is excreted unchanged by the kidney. Hinsberg (4) reported that the drug was probably excreted by way of the gastrointestinal tract, possibly in combination with colloidal material. This conclusion is not supported by experimental data.

In order to reinvestigate this question, urine and feces from both dogs and man were examined for the presence of metrazol. One dog received 3.1 grams of the drug in the course of 72 hours by repeated subcutaneous injections. The urine was collected throughout the 72-hour period and for 24 hours after the last injection of the drug had been given. No metrazol could be detected in the urine. The second dog received a total of 9.5 grams of the drug within a period of 15 hours. This animal was protected against convulsions by barbital. Both the urine and the fecal material were collected for a period of 36 hours after the last metrazol had been injected. The urine contained only traces of the drug. Since it has been suggested that metrazol might be excreted in a conjugated form, this urine was hydrolyzed by boiling for two hours with 10 per cent HCl after the first ether extraction and was then reextracted. This second extract contained no metrazol. The fecal material was dried prior to its extraction with ether and with absolute alcohol. No metrazol could be detected in this material.

The urine of six patients receiving from 400 to 1800 mgm. of the drug within a 10-hour period was collected for 48 hours and examined for metrazol. Only traces could be detected. Metrazol added to normal urine was recovered quantitatively. The 48-hour fecal specimens from two of the patients receiving 1200 and 1800 mgm., respectively, were examined and no trace of metrazol could be detected.

SITE OF DETOXIFICATION

The site of detoxification of metrazol has been the subject of considerable controversy. This question is of clinical importance since preëxisting pathology of the organ or systems responsible for the detoxification might contraindicate the use of this drug. Voss (11) reported that the kidney was the principal site of detoxification. This conclusion was based on the fact that when 50 per cent of the convulsant dose was administered twice at intervals of three hours to bilaterally nephrectomized rats, convulsions were observed in all of the animals. He concluded further that the kidney was not the only site of detoxification because when the interval between the injections was increased to six hours, only 50 per cent of the rats developed convulsions. Ridder (12) was unable to show any detoxification of metrazol by perfusing a solution of this drug through livers of either warm- or cold-blooded animals and concluded that the liver was not the site of detoxification. These results are indecisive because controls were not made with substances known to be destroyed by the liver.

To study this problem, four series of six rabbits each were used. All the animals received 200 mgm. of paraldehyde per kilogram intravenously followed by 125 mgm. of metrazol per kilogram by the same route. The paraldehyde was used for the purpose of raising the tolerated dose of metrazol in order that more of the material might be available for the analyses. To determine the rate of detoxification under these conditions, the rabbits in the first series were sacrificed 10 minutes after the administration of the drug, and those of the second series 3 hours after the injection of the metrazol. The metrazol content of the blood, liver and muscle was determined at these two time intervals. These values were considered as the controls for this particular study. To study the rôle played by the kidney, the rabbits in the third series were bilaterally nephrectomized during ether anesthesia. After the animals had completely recovered from the effects of the ether, they received the same dose of paraldehyde and metrazol as the control series, and the metrazol content of the tissues was determined 3 hours after the drug was injected. In the fourth series, the animals received orally 0.5 cc. per kilogram carbon tetrachloride for three consecutive days. In previous work (13) it was found that this procedure produced a 50 per cent decrease in the functioning capacity of the liver as measured by the bromsulphalein test. On the fourth day these animals received the paraldehyde and metrazol and the concentration of the metrazol was determined 3 hours later. Results of these experiments are shown in figure 2. It will be noted in the control group that there is a marked drop in the concentration of the drug during the three hour interval after the injection, indicating a rather rapid detoxification of the drug during this period. Similarly, the concentration of metrazol found in the tissues of the nephrectomized animals at the end of three hours is practically the same as that found in the control group at the same time interval, indicating that the detoxification mechanism had been uninfluenced by the removal of the kidneys. On the other hand, the concentration in the tissues from the rabbits which had been treated with carbon tetrachloride was only slightly lower at the end of the three hour period than that found in the controls ten minutes after the injection. This would indicate that the detoxification mechanism had been drastically interfered with and that very little metrazol had disappeared from the tissues during the three hour period. This evidence indicates conclusively that the kidneys have little or no effect on the detoxification of metrazol, while parenchymatous injury, such as produced by carbon tetrachloride, which is known seriously to affect the liver, practically abolishes the process of detoxification. These data, previously reported by us in 1939 and 1940, were later confirmed by Dille and

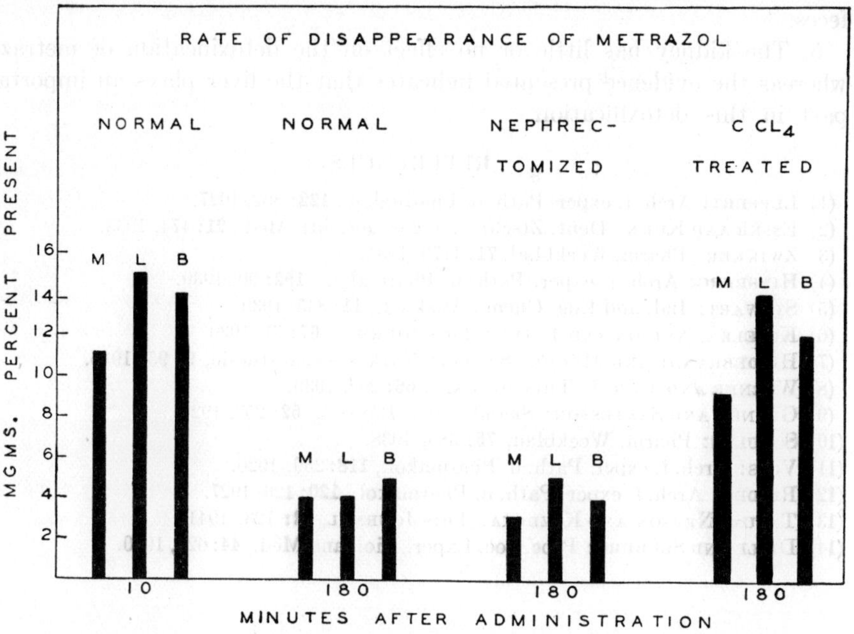

FIG. 2. CONCENTRATION OF METRAZOL IN THE TISSUES OF NORMAL AND NEPHRECTOMIZED RABBITS AT THE 180 MINUTE PERIOD WAS DETERMINED BY THE MOUSE BIO-ASSAY METHOD

Seeburg (14) who employed biological rather than chemical methods of analysis.

SUMMARY

1. A method for the quantitative determination of metrazol in biological material is described. Recoveries of 89 per cent or better were obtained from rats given varying amounts of the drug. The duplicate analyses of the different tissues analyzed were within 2 mgm. per cent of the mean, the majority of the determinations being within 1 mgm. per cent of the mean. The recovered metrazol was checked by melting point and mixed melting point determinations and found to agree with the accepted value for this drug.

2. The distribution of metrazol in the blood, liver, muscle and brain was determined at hourly intervals and found to be equally distributed in these tissues. No tissues analyzed appeared to have any particular affinity for the drug.

3. The rate of detoxification of metrazol was directly proportional to the concentration of the drug in the tissues.

4. Only traces (less than 3 mgm. per 24-hour specimen) of metrazol were excreted unchanged in the urine of dogs or man following relatively large doses of the drug. No evidence was found which would indicate that metrazol was excreted in a conjugated or easily hydrolyzable form in the urine or feces.

5. The kidney has little or no effect on the detoxification of metrazol, whereas the evidence presented indicates that the liver plays an important part in this detoxification.

REFERENCES

(1) Leppert: Arch. f. exper. Path. u. Pharmakol., **122**: 362, 1927.
(2) Esser and Kühn: Deut. Ztschr. f. d. ges. gerichtl. Med., **21**: 474, 1933.
(3) Zwikker: Pharm. Weekblad, **71**: 1170, 1934.
(4) Hinsberg: Arch. f. exper. Path. u. Pharmakol., **192**: 90, 1939.
(5) Stewart: Ind. and Eng. Chem., Anal. ed., **11**: 345, 1939.
(6) Kozelka, Nelson and Tatum: This Journal, **67**: 71, 1939.
(7) Hildebrandt and Mügge: Schmerz Narkose-Anaesthesie, **9**: 95, 1936.
(8) Werner and Tatum: This Journal, **66**: 260, 1939.
(9) Granér and Santesson: Skand. Arch. Physiol., **52**: 253, 1927.
(10) Schulte: Pharm. Weekblad, **75**: 386, 1938.
(11) Voss: Arch. f. exper. Path. u. Pharmakol., **118**: 259, 1926.
(12) Ridder: Arch. f. exper. Path. u. Pharmakol., **120**: 126, 1927.
(13) Tatum, Nelson and Kozelka: This Journal, **72**: 123, 1941.
(14) Dille and Seeburg: Proc. Soc. Exper. Biol. and Med., **44**: 624, 1940.

THE MODE OF ACTION OF NEOPRONTOSIL IN STREPTOCOCCUS INFECTIONS IN MICE[1]

J. T. LITCHFIELD, JR., H. J. WHITE AND E. K. MARSHALL, JR.

From the Department of Pharmacology and Experimental Therapeutics, The Johns Hopkins University, Baltimore

Received for publication April 16, 1941

The hypothesis that prontosil and neoprontosil had no action as such but acted only after reduction in the body to sulfanilamide was advanced by the Tréfouels, Nitti and Bovet (1). Fuller (2) showed conclusively (by isolation from urine) that a considerable amount of sulfanilamide is formed when the "prontosils" are administered, but did not feel that sufficient data were available to prove that their activity was due entirely to the sulfanilamide formed. Gley and Girard (3) found that molecular equivalents of prontosil and sulfanilamide were equally effective on a streptococcus infection in mice, but that a carboxy derivative of prontosil was more active. They used this as an argument against the theory that prontosil acts entirely through sulfanilamide. Others (4, 5, 6) have found the "prontosils" as active as sulfanilamide, weight for weight. Feinstone, Bliss, Ott and Long (7, 8) showed that molecule for molecule neoprontosil and sulfanilamide were equal in therapeutic efficiency in a mouse streptococcus infection. They also found that four hours after a single dose of molecular equivalents of the two drugs the blood concentrations of sulfanilamide were the same although the blood concentration from sulfanilamide was much higher than that from neoprontosil before the fourth hour. They concluded that in the mouse the action of neoprontosil is due to its breakdown to sulfanilamide.

The difficulty in interpreting all of the above observations is due to the fact that the drugs were given in a single daily dose. Under these conditions the blood concentration-time curves of sulfanilamide, obtained when the "prontosils" or sulfanilamide are given, are markedly different. Since we do not know the relative effectiveness of these two types of blood concentration-time curves, the mode of action of the "prontosils" cannot be determined from such data. To prove that the "prontosils" act solely through the sulfanilamide formed from them in the body, it is necessary to compare the therapeutic response of the "prontosils" with that of sulfanilamide when the drugs are administered in such a manner as to give identical blood concentration-

[1] This investigation has been aided by a grant from The John and Mary R. Markle Foundation.

time curves of sulfanilamide. By the use of the drug-diet method to maintain a more or less constant blood concentration of sulfanilamide throughout the period of treatment of a streptococcus infection in mice, we have compared the activity of neoprontosil (sodium *4*-sulfonamido-phenyl-*2*-azo-*7*-acetyl-amino-*1*-hydroxynaphthalene *3*, *6*-disulfonate) and sulfanilamide.[2] In addition, we have established the fact that in mice essentially the same blood concentration-time curve of sulfanilamide may be obtained when either sulfanilamide or neoprontosil is fed in the diet.

METHODS

In order to obtain data relating the blood concentration-time curves of sulfanilamide resulting from neoprontosil and sulfanilamide diets two groups of 30 mice each were used. One group received 0.1 per cent of sulfanilamide, the other 0.4 per cent of neoprontosil-diet. Each group was subdivided into 3 lots of 10 mice each. Each mouse was kept in a separate cage in order to measure drug-diet intake per mouse. After 48 hours of feeding with the drug-diets, a tail blood sample for estimation of blood concentration of sulfanilamide was taken from each of the 10 mice in the first lot in each group. Four hours later samples were taken from the 10 mice in the second lot in each group; eight hours later the third lot in each group was used, and 12 hours later a second set of samples was obtained from the mice in the first lot in each group. This procedure was continued for 24 hours so that two blood samples (12 hours apart) were obtained from each mouse. Thus, 120 blood samples for the determination of sulfanilamide were obtained in 12 lots of 10 samples each, six lots from each drug. The drug-diet intake was measured for each mouse for each 4 hour period.

The procedure for the collection and treatment of chemotherapeutic data was similar to that previously described (9, 10). Three comparisons of the activity of the two drugs were made. In the first comparison, 60 mice (CF1 strain) were used for each drug; in the second and third comparison, 50 and 80 mice (CFCW) respectively were used for each drug. Equal numbers of males and females were used on each drug in each experiment. The mice ranged from 14 to 22 grams in weight but in any one comparison variation in weight was ± 2 grams. Our former method of treating chemotherapeutic data was modified in the present study as follows. The drug intakes from any one diet were averaged and this mean value was plotted logarithmically against the probit value of the percentage survival of mice on the same diet. This simple procedure eliminated the laborious arrangement of individual drug intakes from high to low and their correlation with survival or death of the corresponding mice. However, if there is wide variation of drug intakes within diet groups, this procedure may be somewhat less accurate. The Median Survival Dose (SD_{50}) was obtained by calculation of the regression of probit percentage survival on the logarithm of the dose according to the method of Bliss (11).

The C 203 strain of β-hemolytic streptococcus was used to produce the experimental infection. After three days of preliminary feeding with the drug-diet, infection was obtained by intraperitoneal injection of 0.5 cc. of suitably diluted culture. Drug-diet therapy was carried out for three days following infection and surviving mice were kept under observation for an additional 27 days. The infections in experiments 1, 2 and 3 consisted of 200, 3,000 and 7,000 lethal doses, respectively. The average time of death

---

[2] We wish to thank the Winthrop Chemical Company for the neoprontosil and the Eli Lilly and Company for the sulfanilamide used in this study.

of control mice was 18 hours, ranging from 15 to 31 hours. Mice whose heart culture at the time of death was negative for β-hemolytic streptococcus have been excluded from the present data. Mice whose intake of the drug-diet after infection was less than 0.3 gram have also been excluded. The survival time of these latter mice was the same as that of the untreated control mice (15 to 31 hours).

Blood concentrations of sulfanilamide were determined as previously described (10). Since filtrates obtained from the blood of mice receiving neoprontosil by mouth did not contain this drug, sulfanilamide could be accurately determined.[3] In the first therapeutic experiment the factors used to convert Median Survival Doses ($S.D._{50}$'s) to Median Survival Blood Concentrations ($S.B.C._{50}$'s) were determined by the previously described procedure (10). In the other two experiments the factors were determined during the 24 hour period immediately preceding infection, and on the same mice used in the therapeutic experiment. Factors were determined in the second experiment only on the mice receiving the drug-diet expected to produce 50 per cent survival, but in the last experiment factors were determined on all four diets of each drug.

RESULTS

In figure 1 are shown the completely different blood concentration-time curves of sulfanilamide obtained when single doses of equimolecular amounts of sulfanilamide and neoprontosil are given per os to mice.

In figure 2 are shown the results of the experiment designed to compare the blood concentration-time curve of sulfanilamide from a sulfanilamide-diet with that of sulfanilamide from a neoprontosil-diet. Simple harmonic curves were fitted by the method of least squares to the data obtained in this experiment.[4] It is evident that with properly chosen drug-diets of sulfanilamide and neoprontosil, essentially identical blood concentration time curves of sulfanilamide are obtained.

The essential data of the therapeutic experiments are given in tables 1 and 2. From these data are derived the values given in table 3. The $S.D._{50}$'s of sulfanilamide and neoprontosil are expressed as milligrams per mouse per day[5] but the $S.B.C._{50}$'s are expressed as milligrams per cent of *sulfanilamide*

[3] The method for the estimation of sulfanilamide is not specific; it determines any arylamine. All of the evidence available indicates that the free arylamine present in blood after giving neoprontosil is mainly, if not entirely, sulfanilamide.

[4] It was found that when the logarithm of the drug intake per four hour period in this experiment was plotted against time of day a series of points on a sine curve was obtained. This sine curve with a 24 hour cycle had a maximum value at 12:20 a.m. and a minimum value at 12:20 p.m. The blood concentrations in this experiment followed the same type of curve within experimental error.

[5] When the Median Survival Doses of sulfanilamide and neoprontosil are calculated on a molar instead of a weight basis, the values obtained for neoprontosil for the three experiments are: 92, 97, and 90 per cent of the corresponding values for sulfanilamide (weighted mean 93 ± 14). Thus in the mouse the conversion of neoprontosil to sulfanilamide is complete or nearly so when the drug is fed in the diet.

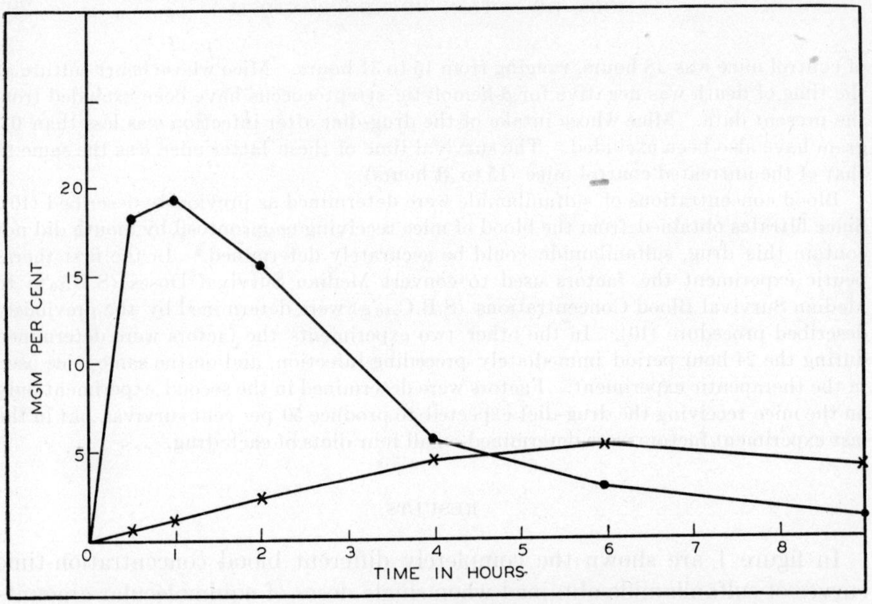

Fig. 1. Blood Concentration-Time Curves of Sulfanilamide Obtained by per Oral Administration at Zero Hours to Mice of Equimolecular Doses of Sulfanilamide (6 mgm.) and Neoprontosil (20.5 mgm.)

Each curve represents the average of 8 individual curves, each determined on a single mouse. Curve with dots (●—●) sulfanilamide from administration of sulfanilamide; curve with crosses (×—×) sulfanilamide from the administration of neoprontosil.

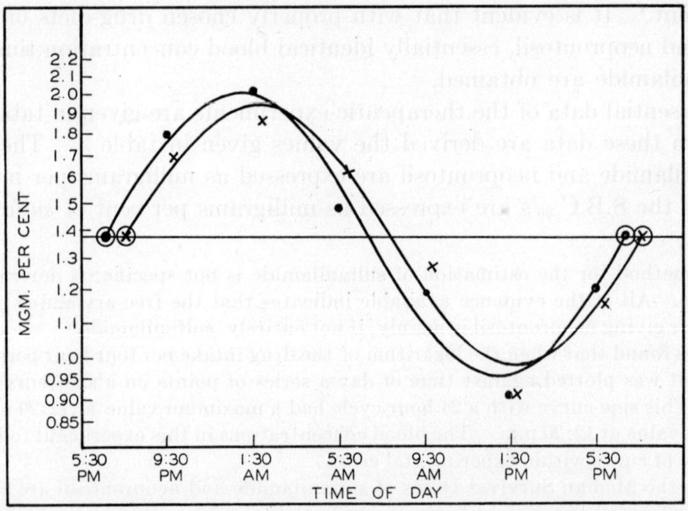

Fig. 2. Blood Concentration-Time Curves of Sulfanilamide Obtained from Mice Receiving 0.1 per cent Sulfanilamide-Diet and 0.4 per cent Neoprontosil-Diet

The blood concentration is plotted logarithmically against time of day. The curve running between encircled dots (⊙) is sulfanilamide from administration of sulfanilamide-diet; curve running between encircled crosses (⊗) sulfanilamide from administration of neoprontosil-diet. The six points on each blood concentration-time curve were obtained by averaging the determinations from 10 mice at that time of day.

TABLE 1

Summary of therapeutic data

DATE	SULFANILAMIDE				NEOPRONTOSIL			
	Number of mice	Drug in diet	Drug intake per mouse per day	Per cent survival	Number of mice	Drug in diet	Drug intake per mouse per day	Per cent survival
		per cent	*mgm.*			*per cent*	*mgm.*	
6/ 4/40	19	0.25	7.71	63	20	1.00	28.3	75
	19	0.12	3.60	37	19	0.50	14.2	10
	14	0.06	1.79	14	17	0.25	7.5	35
10/ 8/40	10	0.25	10.53	80	10	1.00	42.2	100
	20	0.12	4.93	65	18	0.50	21.0	78
	19	0.06	2.61	32	18	0.25	10.7	33
11/12/40	20	0.14	6.39	70	20	0.54	23.1	65
	20	0.10	4.28	55	19	0.38	16.6	53
	20	0.07	2.46	10	20	0.27	10.5	30
	19	0.05	1.73	21	20	0.19	6.8	15

TABLE 2

*Relation of blood concentration to drug intake**

DATE	NUMBER OF MICE EACH DRUG	DRUG INTAKE		BLOOD CONCENTRATION		FACTOR: BLOOD CONC. / DRUG INTAKE	
		Sulfanilamide	Neoprontosil	Sulfanilamide	Neoprontosil	Sulfanilamide	Neoprontosil
6/ 4/40	10	8.52 ± 1.78	15.9 ± 4.6	3.44 ± 1.44	1.68 ± 0.68	0.404 ± 0.064	0.106 ± 0.018
10/ 8/40	20	4.94 ± 0.64	21.6 ± 2.5	2.53 ± 0.72	2.60 ± 0.87	0.512 ± 0.039	0.120 ± 0.009
11/12/40	10	6.75 ± 1.16	23.0 ± 3.6	1.54 ± 0.24	1.98 ± 0.55	0.228 ± 0.017	0.086 ± 0.009
	10	4.52 ± 0.53	17.8 ± 2.1	1.29 ± 0.24	1.28 ± 0.35	0.285 ± 0.020	0.072 ± 0.007
	10	3.15 ± 0.51	11.9 ± 1.5	0.96 ± 0.49	0.84 ± 0.09	0.305 ± 0.052	0.071 ± 0.004
	10	2.55 ± 0.30	8.4 ± 1.4	0.77 ± 0.17	0.58 ± 0.15	0.302 ± 0.024	0.069 ± 0.007

* Figures for drug intake and blood concentration represent milligrams per mouse per day and milligrams per cent respectively. The standard deviation is given after each figure. Figures for factors are given with their standard errors.

TABLE 3

Activity ratios

DATE	DRUG	$\beta \pm$ S.E.*	S.D.$_{50}$†	S.B.C.$_{50}$‡	ACTIVITY RATIO	STANDARD ERROR OF LOGARITHMS OF:		
						S.D.$_{50}$	S.B.C.$_{50}$	Activity ratio
6/ 4/40	Sulfanilamide	2.18 ±0.77	5.32	2.15	**1.00**	0.092	0.115	
	Neoprontosil	1.66 ±3.09	19.82	2.10	**1.02**	0.307	0.317	0.337
10/ 8/40	Sulfanilamide	2.32 ±0.89	3.87	1.98	**1.00**	0.083	0.089	
	Neoprontosil	4.41 ±1.20	13.58	1.64	**1.21**	0.052	0.061	0.108
11/12/40	Sulfanilamide	2.84 ±0.78	4.30	1.23	**1.00**	0.060	0.062	
	Neoprontosil	2.70 ±0.78	16.26	1.23	**1.00**	0.061	0.062	0.088

* Slope constant ± standard error.

† Median survival dose.

‡ Median survival blood concentration.

in all cases. The activity ratios are calculated from the S.B.C.$_{50}$'s. The slope constants (β's) of the sulfanilamide experiments do not differ significantly in any case from those of the neoprontosil experiments. Furthermore, the slope constant of the combined sulfanilamide data does not differ significantly from that of the neoprontosil data. Comparison of the dosage response curves of the two drugs is therefore justified. *In no case did the activity of neoprontosil on the basis of the blood concentration of sulfanilamide obtained from it differ significantly from that of sulfanilamide.*

DISCUSSION

The curves given in figure 1 clearly show that the blood concentration-time curves of sulfanilamide obtained from single doses of the two drugs are unrelated. Therefore, data based on single dose therapy provide no basis for determining whether or not sulfanilamide is entirely responsible for the therapeutic effect of neoprontosil. However, when the activities of the two drugs are compared under conditions where one obtains essentially the same blood concentration-time curve of sulfanilamide from either drug, it is possible to determine whether or not the activity of neoprontosil is due entirely to the sulfanilamide formed from it.

Figure 2 shows that essentially the same blood concentration-time curve of sulfanilamide may be obtained from either of the two drugs by use of the drug-diet method. Under these established conditions of identical blood concentration-time curves of sulfanilamide, the activity of neoprontosil is the same as that of sulfanilamide. Therefore one can only conclude that the therapeutic activity of neoprontosil in a streptococcus infection in the mouse is entirely due to the sulfanilamide formed from it.

SUMMARY

The therapeutic activity of neoprontosil has been compared to that of sulfanilamide in a streptococcus infection in mice. Essentially the same blood concentration-time curve of sulfanilamide was obtained from both drugs by use of the drug-diet method of therapy. The results show that the entire therapeutic activity of neoprontosil depends on the sulfanilamide formed from it.

REFERENCES

(1) Tréfouel, Tréfouel, Nitti and Bovet: Presse med., **45**²: 839, 1937.
(2) Fuller: Lancet, **1**: 194, 1937.
(3) Gley and Girard: Presse med., **44**²: 1775, 1936.
(4) Buttle, Gray and Stephenson: Lancet, **1**: 1286, 1936.
(5) Mayer: Biol. Med. 27 (supplement): **45**: 1937.

(6) RAIZISS, SEVERAC, MOETSCH AND CLEMENCE: J. Chemotherapy, **14:** 91, 1938.
(7) FEINSTONE, BLISS, OTT AND LONG: Bull. Johns Hopkins Hospital, **62:** 565, 1938.
(8) LONG: "Chemistry and Medicine" (Papers presented at the 50th Anniversary of the Founding of the Medical School of the University of Minnesota) p. 185. University of Minnesota Press, Minneapolis.
(9) LITCHFIELD, WHITE AND MARSHALL: THIS JOURNAL, **67:** 437, 1939.
(10) MARSHALL, LITCHFIELD AND WHITE: Ibid., **69:** 89, 1940.
(11) BLISS: Quart. J. Pharmacy and Pharmacology, **11:** 192, 1938.

THE EFFECT OF SULFANILAMIDE AND SOME OF ITS DERIVATIVES ON THE REACTION OF MICE TO ANESTHETICS[1]

THOMAS C. BUTLER, H. L. DICKISON, WM. M. GOVIER, C. M. GREER AND PAUL D. LAMSON

From the Department of Pharmacology, Vanderbilt University School of Medicine, Nashville, Tennessee

Received for publication April 14, 1941

Adriani (1) has reported that the daily injection of sulfanilamide in rats for three days renders them more easily anesthetized and killed by various derivatives of barbituric acid. He failed to find any difference between the sulfanilamide and control rats when they were anesthetized with tribromethanol, nitrous oxide, ether, cyclopropane, or chloroform. From his experiments, Adriani draws the conclusion that "the combination of sulfanilamide and barbiturates may be unwise in human therapy," the thiobarbituric acids being the "worst offenders."

A statistical examination of Adriani's published data indicates that sulfanilamide exerted a significant effect on the number of rats anesthetized by each of the barbituric acids studied, but the effects on the mortality[2] can be considered significant only for thioethamyl and pentothal. This fact, however, does not support the conclusion that these two drugs are the "worst offenders." Failure to show a significant difference is in no way an indication that there is no difference. This same reasoning is applicable to Adriani's experiments with the gases and tribromethanol. The experiments with the gases, particularly, were performed in such a way that it would scarcely be expected that a difference could be detected unless it were very great.

Since the amount by which the anesthetic and lethal doses were reduced was not determined, the conclusion that "the combination of sulfanilamide and barbiturates may be unwise in human therapy" is unjustified. A further objection to the drawing of any clinical conclusions from this study is that the levels of sulfanilamide that prevailed in the blood of the rats shortly after the injections, although not determined, must have been far higher than any

[1] This work was supported by grants from the Mallinckrodt Chemical Works and the National Research Council. The sulfadiazine was supplied through the kindness of Lederle Laboratories, Inc.

[2] The mortalities tabulated for nembutal and amytal in the control groups seem remarkable in comparison with other published data on the lethal doses of these drugs for rats (e.g. (2)).

employed in human therapy. Adriani failed to find any effect with daily injections of less than .25 mgm. per gram.

In a similar study, Glaubach (3, 4) reported that sulfapyridine intensifies the effects of codeine, morphine, and papaverine in animals. The doses of sulfapyridine given were high (4 and 5 grams per kilogram). The blood levels in the rats and mice were not reported, but those reported for the rabbits were considerably above the therapeutic range.

Because of the frequent desirability of treating surgical patients with sulfanilamide, it seemed that more evidence was needed to justify a warning against the dangers of combining anesthetics with sulfanilamide. At the request of the National Research Council we have undertaken a reinvestigation of the problem.

METHODS

Animals

Male white mice were used in all of the experiments.

Feeding of the sulfonamides

Purina "Layena" was ground and sifted to produce a fine powder. The various sulfonamides were thoroughly mixed with this basic feed in the concentrations shown in table 1. Mice were given these mixtures and no other food from the afternoon of one day until the morning of the third day following, when the anesthetic was given (about 65 hours). They were allowed free access to the feeding mixture and to water until they were given the anesthetic. The anesthetic experiments were usually performed between 9 a.m. and 11 a.m. The blood analyses shown in table 1 were made at this time of day.

The animals designated "controls" were fed the powdered "Layena" without any drug. Otherwise they were treated as nearly as possible like those receiving the drugs.

Blood analyses

The concentrations of the sulfonamides in blood were determined by Hoffman's (5) modification of the method of Bratton and Marshall.

Randomization of mice

In each experiment, mice were assigned strictly at random to the different treatments that were to be compared. The randomization was accomplished by means of shuffled cards. For example, in table 2, a group of 12 mice was divided at random into 2 groups of 6. One group was fed sulfanilamide. The other group served as controls. On the day of injection, the 6 sulfanilamide mice were assigned at random to the 6 doses of pentobarbital shown in table 2. Likewise, the 6 control mice were assigned to their 6 doses. Twenty such groups of 12 were used. In the first experiments before the range of dosage was located, other doses than those shown in the table were included and correspondingly larger groups of mice were used.

In the same manner, for table 3, a group of 15 mice was divided at random into 5 groups of 3, the 5 groups being assigned at random to the control feed, sulfapyridine, sulfathiazole, sulfadiazine, and acetylsulfanilamide. On the day of injection the 3 mice in each group were assigned at random to their 3 doses. Twenty such groups of 15 were used.

Likewise, mice in groups of 4 were assigned at random to the 4 treatments of table 4, and in groups of 6 to the 6 treatments of table 5.

Administration of anesthetics

Pentobarbital was given intraperitoneally as a freshly prepared solution of the sodium salt. The solution used for the doses in the anesthetic range contained 2 mgm. per cubic centimeter; that for the doses in the lethal range, 5 mgm. per cubic centimeter. All doses of pentobarbital shown in the tables are expressed in terms of the acid form.

The volatile anesthetics were introduced in liquid form into a bottle of capacity 2.7 liters. After the liquid had evaporated, a mouse was introduced into the bottle in such a way as to cause the least possible loss of vapor. The tabulated concentrations of ether are those present before the mouse was put in the bottle. No effort was made to find how much ether was removed from the air by the mouse during the course of an experiment.

Criteria of anesthesia

Pentobarbital. A mouse was considered anesthetized if it could not gain and maintain the standing posture after stimulation by repeated pinching of the tail.

Volatile anesthetics. The glass bottle, the inside diameter of which was 12 cm., was rotated mechanically at a speed of 14 revolutions per minute from the time the mouse was put in until anesthesia had come about. The mouse was considered anesthetized when it lost the ability to maintain the standing posture and rolled over continuously for 15 seconds.

Estimation of median doses

The median anesthetic and lethal doses were estimated by interpolation on the assumption that the curve relating log dose and proportion anesthetized is the integrated normal frequency curve. The standard errors of the medians were calculated by the equations given by Bliss (6).

RESULTS

Effect of the feeding of sulfonamides on the reaction of mice to pentobarbital

The sulfonamides were fed for two and one-half days prior to the injection of the pentobarbital. The composition of the feeding mixtures and the final blood levels are indicated in table 1.

Both the anesthetic and lethal doses of pentobarbital were determined after the feeding of sulfanilamide. The results are shown in table 2. Comparison of the estimated median doses shows that for the sulfanilamide group both the anesthetic dose and lethal dose are significantly lower than for the control group.[3] Within the limits of error of the measurements, the median

[3] The same conclusion may be reached by direct comparison of the effects produced by a single dose in the two groups without reference to the interpolated median values. Thus if the two groups of mice be assumed to be equally sensitive to pentobarbital, the probability of a difference as great as that shown for dose 40 mgm. per kilogram arising as a fluctuation of simple sampling is 10^{-7}. From the same premises, the probability of a difference as great as that found for dose 105 mgm. per kilogram is .118; for dose 116 mgm. per kilogram, .056. The probability of both of the latter events occurring is $.118 \times .056 = .007$.

Such a direct comparison has the logical advantage of involving none of the queslethal dose is reduced by the same absolute amount as is the median anesthetic dose. Despite the rather large standard errors of the median lethal doses, it is clear that the lethal dose is not reduced by nearly the same proportion as is the anesthetic dose. Thus the ratio of lethal dose to anesthetic dose is higher for the sulfanilamide mice than for the control mice. This is

TABLE 1

DRUG	CONCENTRATION OF DRUG IN FEED	NUMBER OF MICE ANALYZED	MEAN BLOOD CONCENTRATION WITH STANDARD ERROR OF MEAN	
			Free	Conjugated
	per cent		*mgm. per cent*	*mgm. per cent*
Sulfanilamide	1.0	20	5.1 ±0.5	1.0 ±0.1*
Sulfapyridine	0.8	20	7.7 ±0.9	0
Sulfathiazole	1.5	23	5.0 ±0.3	0
Sulfadiazine	0.4	26	15.2 ±0.6	0
N^4-Acetylsulfanilamide	2.0	19	0.8 ±0.1	6.4 ±0.7*

* Expressed in terms of sulfanilamide.

TABLE 2

Anesthetic and lethal effects of pentobarbital after the feeding of sulfanilamide

DOSE OF PENTOBARBITAL	NUMBER OF MICE ANESTHETIZED/TOTAL		DOSE OF PENTOBARBITAL	NUMBER OF MICE KILLED/TOTAL	
	Sulfanilamide	Control		Sulfanilamide	Control
mgm. per kgm.			*mgm. per kgm.*		
30	9/20		96	5/20	
35	18/20		105	6/20	2/20
40	20/20	4/20	116	13/20	7/20
46		18/20	127		14/20
			140		18/20

Estimated median doses with their standard errors

	SULFANILAMIDE	CONTROL	DIFFERENCE
AD 50	30.4 ±0.8	42.3 ±0.7	11.9 ±1.1
LD 50	110.5 ±3.5	120.5 ±2.2	10.0 ±4.1

the same effect that would have been produced if a preliminary dose of pentobarbital itself had been given instead of sulfanilamide.

The effects of four derivatives of sulfanilamide on the anesthetic dose of pentobarbital were investigated. The results are shown in table 3. It is obvious that all of the drugs had a significant effect in lowering the anesthetic

tionable assumptions used in estimating median doses. Moreover, it may furnish a more sensitive test of difference than does the comparison of median doses (e.g., see table 4).

dose of pentobarbital. Although these experiments were not done at the same time as those on sulfanilamide, it may be legitimate to infer that the derivatives have less effect than sulfanilamide itself. In comparing the effects of sulfadiazine with those of the other drugs, it must be kept in mind that the blood level of this drug was higher than those of the other drugs.

Effect of intravenously injected sulfanilamide on the reaction of mice to pentobarbital

A dose of 100 mgm. per kilogram of sulfanilamide was injected intravenously in the half of the animals assigned to this treatment. Pentobarbital

TABLE 3

Anesthetic effects of pentobarbital after the feeding of sulfanilamide derivatives

DOSE OF PENTOBARBITAL	NUMBER OF MICE ANESTHETIZED/TOTAL				
	Control	Sulfapyridine	Sulfathiazole	Sulfadiazine	N^4-Acetyl-sulfanilamide
mgm. per kgm.					
30		1/20	2/20	1/20	7/20
35	4/20	12/20	15/20	16/20	15/20
40	11/20	18/20	16/20	20/20	20/20
46	19/20				

Estimated median doses with their standard errors

DRUG	AD 50	DIFFERENCE FROM CONTROL
	mgm. per kgm.	*mgm. per kgm.*
Control	38.8 ±0.8	
Sulfapyridine	34.7 ±0.7	4.1 ±1.1
Sulfathiazole	34.1 ±0.9	4.7 ±1.2
Sulfadiazine	33.3 ±0.5	5.5 ±0.9
Acetylsulfanilamide	31.8 ±1.0	7.0 ±1.3

was given intraperitoneally between 20 and 35 minutes later (mean interval 28 minutes). Table 4 shows the numbers anesthetized. Although the effects produced by dose 46 mgm. per kilogram in the two groups do differ significantly (probability of chance occurrence = .022), the estimated median doses do not differ significantly. Some effect has made itself evident in half an hour, but comparison with the feeding experiments indicates that it has not reached its full intensity in this time.

Effect of the feeding of sulfanilamide on the reaction of mice to diethyl ether and chloroform

Sulfanilamide was fed in the same manner as for the pentobarbital experiments.

Ether. Since the animal's tissues do not become equilibrated with ether for a long time, the concentration of ether in the air necessary to anesthetize will be dependent on the time the animal is exposed to the vapor. In these experiments, the mice were observed for only 20 minutes. Table 5 shows the

TABLE 4

Anesthetic effects of pentobarbital after the intravenous injection of sulfanilamide

DOSE OF PENTOBARBITAL	NUMBER OF MICE ANESTHETIZED/TOTAL	
	Sulfanilamide	Control
mgm. per kgm.		
40	3/20	4/20
46	19/20	13/20

Estimated median anesthetic doses with their standard errors

Sulfanilamide	42.2 ±0.6
Control	44.0 ±1.1
Difference	1.8 ±1.3

TABLE 5

Anesthetic effects of diethyl ether after the feeding of sulfanilamide

CONCENTRATION OF ETHER	NUMBER OF MICE ANESTHETIZED/TOTAL					
	In 10 min.		In 15 min.		In 20 min.	
	Control	Sulfanilamide	Control	Sulfanilamide	Control	Sulfanilamide
millimoles per liter						
0.95		4/20		7/20		11/20
1.09	0/20	7/20	2/20	15/20	4/20	20/20
1.25	4/20	12/20	10/20	18/20	16/20	20/20
1.44	16/20		20/20		20/20	

Estimated median concentrations of ether necessary to anesthetize (mM./l.)

	CONTROL	SULFANILAMIDE	DIFFERENCE
In 10 min.	1.34 ±.03	1.19 ±.06	.15 ±.07
In 15 min.	1.25 ±.04	0.99 ±.04	.26 ±.06
In 20 min.	1.17 ±.02	<0.95	>.22

number anesthetized at three different times. At each time there was a significantly greater number anesthetized in the group that had received sulfanilamide. At 15 minutes there is a 21 per cent reduction of the median anesthetic concentration, as compared with the 28 per cent reduction of the median anesthetic dose of pentobarbital (table 2).

Eleven sulfanilamide mice and eleven of the corresponding controls that were used in these experiments were reserved and both groups given untreated food for 24 hours. At the end of this time they were again given ether. Six of the original control group and six of the original sulfanilamide group were exposed to a concentration of 1.09 millimoles per liter. None of either group were anesthetized in 15 minutes. Five of the original control group and five of the original sulfanilamide group were exposed to a concentration of 1.25 millimoles per liter. In 15 minutes, one of the sulfanilamide group and three of the control group were anesthetized.

With neither concentration of ether is there any significant difference between the two groups, nor between these small groups and the corresponding control groups of table 5. Yet there is a significant difference between the proportions anesthetized in these groups and in the sulfanilamide groups of table 5.

These experiments furnish no evidence that any of the effect of sulfanilamide remains after 24 hours. They do indicate that at least a part of the effect has disappeared in this time. When the second experiment with ether was performed, the mice that had originally had sulfanilamide were still noticeably cyanotic.

Chloroform. No effort was made to determine the median anesthetic concentration. Enough mice were used to establish that those fed sulfanilamide were anesthetized in a significantly shorter time than the controls. With the concentration of .25 millimoles per liter, the times of onset of anesthesia for five sulfanilamide mice were: 16, 12, 11, 10, 9 minutes; for five control mice: 105, 75, 60, 60, 45 minutes.

DISCUSSION

Sulfanilamide renders mice more easily anesthetized by pentobarbital, ether, and chloroform. Since the effect is found with each of these three narcotics, which are widely different chemically and pharmacologically, we think that it might be expected with any type of anesthetic. It is evidently not limited to the barbituric acids as was claimed by Adriani.

The mechanism by which this action of sulfanilamide is brought about is still obscure. Although sulfanilamide alone in high levels will cause definite signs of depression, it is not clear that this is the same phenomenon that we are encountering here with low levels. Sulfanilamide at a blood level of 6 mgm. per cent can replace 28 per cent of the anesthetic dose of pentobarbital, but a level four times as high does not produce anesthesia alone. The fact that the effect does not develop immediately after intravenous injection might suggest that some slowly progressive chemical change is produced in the cells secondary to some such reaction as the inhibition of an enzyme system. However, the recently reported inhibition of carbonic anhydrase (7, 8) probably is not involved, since substitition on the amide nitrogen does not abolish the effect.

So far as the practical implications of this work are concerned, we do not think that there is any reason to believe that anesthesia as generally carried out should be either more or less dangerous in the presence of sulfanilamide. Whether the anesthetic is given intravenously or by inhalation, surgical anesthesia is produced by the gradual addition of the agent until the patient reaches the desired level. If the anesthetic dose and the lethal dose of the anesthetic are lowered equally by sulfanilamide as was found for pentobarbital in these experiments, the danger of such a procedure should not be increased by sulfanilamide. If a predetermined amount of narcotic is to be given in one dose, the situation is of course different.

SUMMARY

Feeding of sulfanilamide, sulfapyridine, sulfathiazole, sulfadiazine, or N^4-acetylsulfanilamide to mice for two and one-half days causes them to be anesthetized by smaller amounts of pentobarbital than are normal mice. The final mean blood levels of the five sulfonamides were respectively, 6, 8, 5, 15, and 7 mgm. per cent (total).

Sulfanilamide reduces the median lethal dose of pentobarbital by about the same absolute amount as the median anesthetic dose.

Sulfanilamide also reduces the concentration of ether and chloroform necessary to anesthetize mice.

Twenty-four hours after the withdrawal of sulfanilamide, the effect on the reaction to ether has at least in part disappeared.

One-half hour after the intravenous injection of sulfanilamide, there is much less effect on the anesthetic dose of pentobarbital than after two and one-half days of feeding of sulfanilamide.

REFERENCES

(1) Adriani: J. Lab. & Clin. Med., **24,** 1066, 1939.
(2) Swanson and Fry: J. Am. Pharm. A., **29,** 509, 1940.
(3) Glaubach: Proc. Soc. Exper. Biol. & Med., **42,** 325, 1939.
(4) Glaubach: Proc. Soc. Exper. Biol. & Med., **46,** 53, 1941.
(5) Hoffman: Photelometric Clinical Chemistry (Wm. Morrow & Co., New York, 1941).
(6) Bliss: Quart. J. Pharm. & Pharmacol., **11,** 192, 1938.
(7) Mann and Keilin: Nature, **146,** 164, 1940.
(8) Locke, Main and Mellon: Science, **93,** 66, 1941.

FURTHER OBSERVATIONS ON THE ACTION OF DRUGS ON THE CALIBER OF CORONARY VESSELS[1]

PAPAVERINE HYDROCHLORIDE, DIGITALIS DERIVATIVES, AMINOPHYLLIN, CAFFEIN, GLUCOSE, CALCIUM GLUCONATE AND METRAZOL

E. LINDNER AND L. N. KATZ

From the Cardiovascular Dept., Michael Reese Hospital, Chicago, Ill.

Received for publication April 25, 1941

In a previous communication (1) we described a method in which the direct action of drugs on the caliber of the coronary vessels could be determined. In principle, this consisted of an isolated fibrillating heart in which the coronary vessels were perfused under constant pressure with defibrinated-heparinized dogs' blood of constant temperature (37°C.). It is a modified Langendorff preparation. In all preparations, 3 cc. of 10 per cent calcium gluconate and 1 gram of dextrose were added to each liter of the perfusate. Changes in caliber of the coronary vessels were indicated by changes in the coronary outflow from the pulmonary artery. Drainage of the left heart by means of a cannula passed through the ventricular wall, along with the drainage of the right heart, prevents the extravascular effects which arise from changes in the tension in the walls of the heart when these chambers are permitted to become distended. We have already shown that in this preparation changes in the character of the fibrillation are without effect on the coronary flow (2), and that the drainage from the left ventricle is always less than 10 per cent, usually less than 5 per cent of that *via* the pulmonary artery (3). In all instances the drug to be tested was injected into the coronary inflow tube.

PAPAVERINE HYDROCHLORIDE

Nine injections in six preparations were made of 0.5 to 1 cc. of a 1:30 dilution of papaverine hydrochloride (Lilly). In 7 instances there was an increase in coronary flow of more than 100 per cent and this lasted on the average 21 minutes (range 7 to 60 minutes). The concentration of the drug reaching the heart varied from 1:120 to 1:1190. There was no correlation between the concentration of the drug and the duration of the dilatation; however, the briefest effects were obtained when the initial flows were the

[1] Aided by the A. D. Nast Fund for Cardiac Research and a grant from the Committee on Scientific Research of the American Medical Association.

smallest. In one experiment the second injection gave a large and long-lasting increase in coronary flow; the third injection, however, caused a marked constriction; apparently the concentration of papaverine in this instance had become so great as to reverse the effect. In another experiment the second injection gave only a slight increase in flow lasting seven minutes, indicating again that larger doses of the drug above a certain level are less effective and may even be constricting.

Macht (4) was the first to report an increase in coronary flow with papaverine. This has been confirmed in the trained unanesthetized dog by Essex *et al.* (5). Our results show that this is due, probably in large part, to a direct dilator action on the coronary vessels.

This, together with its antifibrillatory action which we recently noted (6), explains the usefulness of this drug in pulmonary embolism and coronary flow insufficiency.

DIGITALIS DERIVATIVES

Three injections of *K*-strophanthin (Abbott), six of digifoline (Ciba), and 10 of ouabain (Lilly) were made. Twenty-five milligrams of *K*-strophanthin were injected in each case, $\frac{1}{4}$ cat unit of digifoline, and from 0.04 to 0.1 mgm. of ouabain. *K*-strophanthin gave a definite constriction twice, and a fleeting dilatation once. Digifoline caused constriction 3 times, no effect twice and dilatation once. Ouabain gave a constriction 4 times, no effect 5 times, and a varying response, dilatation-constriction-dilatation, once. The dilatation occurred with the first 2 drugs when the concentration of the drug reaching the heart was minimal; this correlation could not be made with ouabain, the lowest concentrations causing constriction at times, where on other occasions greater concentrations were without effect. In no instance with these digitalis derivatives was the response marked.

Our experience suggests that the response to digitalis derivatives is a variable and unpredictable one in moderate doses. In view of the numerous derivatives used in the past and the differences in preparations and methods of measuring coronary flow, controversy as to the effect would be expected, but our results show that even with the same type of preparation and the same derivative the results are variable. Other investigators, too, have reported variable results with a single preparation and with a single digitalis derivative. Thus Sakai and Saneyoshi (7) in the cat, Gilbert and Fenn (8) in the isolated beating perfused dog heart, Rühl and Wiehler (9) on the dog heart-lung preparation, Essex, Herrick and Visscher (10) on the trained unanesthetized dog, and Ginsberg and Stoland (11) on the dog, all obtained variable responses. Our results show that this variability is due, in part at least, to a variable direct action on the coronary vessels. Kountz and Smith (12) have suggested that the variability may be due to the degree of anoxia present in the heart. The occasional coronary constrictor action of these digitalis preparations suggests that, on occasion, therapeutic doses in man may have this effect. In coronary disease this possibility of such action occurring takes on considerable importance.

AMINOPHYLLIN AND CAFFEIN SODIUM BENZOATE

Aminophyllin (Dubin) was injected 12 times into 8 preparations and caffein sodium benzoate (Endo) 5 times, once in each of 5 preparations. The dose of aminophyllin was 24 to 48 mgm., that of the caffein sodium benzoate was 125 to 500 mgm. In every instance a lasting noticeable dilatation was noted, that of aminophyllin being by far the more marked. Aminophyllin increased the flow 75 per cent for 10.6 minutes on the average; the corresponding figures for caffein were 35 per cent and 6.3 minutes.

Our results are thus in accord with the consistent reports in the literature that the xanthine derivatives are coronary dilators (cf. Fowler, Hurevitz and Smith (13) for review). Our results, however, indicate that the action is directly on the coronary vessel calibre.

DEXTROSE

The sugar was injected seven times in seven preparations; 4 times as 3 to 5 cc. of a 5 per cent solution, once as 7 cc. of a 2 per cent solution, once as 55 cc. of a 27 per cent solution and once as 250 cc. of a 50 per cent solution. Twice the 5 per cent solution was without effect. The injection of the large amount of 50 per cent solution caused an immediate marked diminution which in six minutes led to complete stoppage of flow. The other three injections of 2 and 5 per cent glucose caused a noticeable increase in coronary flow, on the average amounting to 40 per cent and lasting 5.5 minutes. The 27 per cent glucose caused a more marked increase in flow amounting to 200 per cent and lasted $3\frac{1}{2}$ minutes. Thus except for the extreme amount and concentration used (250 cc. of a 50 per cent solution) glucose has a definite tendency to dilate the coronary vessels by a direct action. It is thus possible that among the clinical benefits derived from intravenous glucose is this potential coronary dilating action. Furthermore, these findings give support to the impression we have obtained over years of experience with this preparation, that glucose added to the perfusing blood results in better flow and a longer lasting experiment.

CALCIUM GLUCONATE

From 1 to 3 cc. of a 10 per cent solution of calcium gluconate (Hoffman-LaRoche) were injected 5 times in five preparations. No definite effect was observed; this is entirely unlike the marked dilator effect we previously noted with calcium chloride (2). Apparently the gluconate prevents the full action of calcium exhibited when it is given as the chloride salt. Whether this would also be true if calcium gluconate had not already been added (3 cc. of

10 per cent solution per liter of blood) we have not determined. The effect of the addition of this initial larger quantity of calcium gluconate was determined twice; both times, it caused a slight dilatation. Our results indicate clearly that it is the chloride salt of calcium which should be employed when a coronary dilator effect is desired. The benefit derived from calcium gluconate in this preparation must be due to an action other than coronary dilatation.

METRAZOL

This commonly employed drug was tested five times in our preparation; each time 100 mgm. of the drug (Bilhuber-Knoll) was used. In all five cases a temporary increase in coronary flow was obtained, on the average amounting to 26 per cent and lasting only 2 minutes. Our results are in accord with those of Stoland and Ginsberg (14) on the dog heart-lung, but not with their results in the entire dog. However, their results were based on coronary sinus outflow measurements, which we have shown are subject to serious errors (3, 15).

Our results show that metrazol has a mild temporary direct coronary dilator action. Whether or not the other actions of the drug on the animal tend to neutralize this effect remains to be demonstrated.

SUMMARY

1. The digitalis derivatives, *K*-strophanthin, ouabain and digifoline at times have a direct coronary constrictor action even in therapeutic doses.

2. Metrazol and glucose are mild direct coronary dilators.

3. Calcium gluconate, in contrast with the chloride salt which is a powerful dilator of the coronary vessels, does not cause any constant or striking change in coronary caliber except that a mild dilatation occurs with large doses.

4. Aminophyllin and caffein sodium benzoate are consistently direct coronary dilators, the aminophyllin being the more powerful.

5. Papaverine hydrochloride is a powerful long-lasting direct coronary dilating agent. This and its tendency to prevent ventricular fibrillation probably explain its clinical benefits.

We are indebted to Dr. S. R. Elek and Mr. R. Asher for assistance in these experiments.

REFERENCES

(1) Katz, Lindner, Weinstein, Abramson and Jochim: Arch. Int. d. Pharm. et Thèrap., **59:** 399, 1938.
(2) Katz and Lindner: Am. J. Physiol., **124:** 155, 1938.
(3) Katz, Jochim and Weinstein: Am. J. Physiol., **122:** 252, 1938.
(4) Macht: J. A. M. A., **44:** 1489, 1915.
(5) Essex, Wégria, Herrick and Mann: Am. Heart J., **19:** 554, 1940.

(6) LINDNER AND KATZ: Am. J. Physiol. (in press).
(7) SAKAI AND SANEYOSHI: Arch. exp. Path. u Pharmak., **78**: 331, 1915.
(8) GILBERT AND FENN: Arch. Int. Med., **50**: 668, 1932.
(9) RÜHL AND WIEHLER: Arch. f. exp. Path. u Pharmak., **175**: 665, 1934.
(10) ESSEX, HERRICK AND VISSCHER: Am. Heart J., **16**: 143, 1938.
(11) GINSBERG, STOLAND AND SILER: Am. Heart J., **16**: 663, 1938.
(12) KOUNTZ AND SMITH: J. Clin. Invest., **17**: 147, 1938.
(13) FOWLER, HUREVITZ AND SMITH: Arch. Int. Med., **56**: 1242, 1935.
(14) STOLAND AND GINSBERG: THIS JOURNAL, **60**: 396, 1937.
(15) KATZ, JOCHIM AND BOHNING: Am. J. Physiol., **122**: 236, 1938.

Reprinted from The Journal of Pharmacology and Experimental Therapeutics
Vol. 72, No. 4, August, 1941

THE RESPONSE OF SULFAPYRIDINE-RESISTANT PNEUMOCOCCI TO HYDROXYETHYLAPOCUPREINE

L. H. SCHMIDT and CLARA L. SESLER

From the Institute for Medical Research, Christ Hospital, and the Department of Biological Chemistry, College of Medicine, University of Cincinnati, Cincinnati, Ohio

Received for publication June 23, 1941

Experiments performed both *in vivo* and *in vitro* have shown that pneumococci become resistant ("fast") to sulfapyridine when exposed for a considerable time to concentrations of that drug which do not inhibit growth completely (1–8). According to the observations of several investigators (7–9), these "fast" pneumococci are resistant not only to sulfapyridine but also to other sulfonamides. In view of this finding, it seemed of interest to determine whether chemotherapeutic substances of different chemical structure are effective against sulfonamide-resistant pneumococci. Such a study was carried out with hydroxyethylapocupreine, which has a structure entirely different from that of the sulfonamides and, according to Maclachlan and coworkers (10, 11), is effective against both experimental and clinical pneumococcal infections.

METHODS

A comparative study was made of the effectiveness of sulfapyridine and hydroxyethylapocupreine against infections with parent and sulfapyridine-fast strains of types I, II, and III pneumococci. The parent strains were stock organisms that had been passed daily through mice until maximum virulence and invasiveness had been obtained. The sulfapyridine-fast strains were prepared from the parent organisms by methods described heretofore (3–5).

Similar experiments were performed with each of the parent and fast organisms. Groups of 40 mice were infected intraperitoneally with 10^{-6} cc. of a 12- to 14-hour blood broth culture of the desired organism. Ten mice were kept as untreated controls. The remaining 30 were treated with either sulfapyridine or hydroxyethylapocupreine base.[1] These drugs, suspended in 10 per cent acacia, were administered by stomach tube 2, 8, 14, and 22 hours after infection and at eight-hour intervals thereafter for five additional days. Sulfapyridine was given in doses of 20 mgm. on the basis of earlier work (12) which showed this to be the most effective amount. Hydroxyethylapocupreine was administered in 10 mgm. quantities, since experiments indicated this to be the most effective dose that could be tolerated at the above intervals. Even this dosage of hydroxyethylapocupreine produced some toxic symptoms, as Greey had observed previously (13). It was not lethal, however, and, as table 1 shows, 10 mgm. doses were much more effective against infections with parent strains of pneumococci than were the smaller doses of 5 and 2.5 mgm.

[1] We are indebted to Dr. Alice G. Renfrew and the Mellon Institute for the hydroxyethylapocupreine used in this study.

Male white mice, all of the same stock, weighing 18 to 22 grams, were used throughout this study. In the comparison experiments described below, animals were kept under observation for thirty days after infection. A prolonged observation period is necessary in determining the curative action of hydroxyethylapocupreine, since mice receiving this drug may be essentially normal for ten to fourteen days after infection and die subsequently with an overwhelming pneumococcal infection, as shown by cultures of heart blood.

TABLE 1

Response of parent strains of pneumococcus to varying amounts of hydroxyethylapocupreine

ORGANISM	NUMBER OF ORGANISMS IN INFECTING DOSE	NUMBER OF MICE INFECTED	TREATMENT	NUMBER OF DEATHS DAYS AFTER INFECTION							HOURS SURVIVAL OF MICE THAT DIED	10-DAY SURVIVORS	
				1	2	3	4	5	6	7–10		Number	Per cent
			mgm. HEC.										
I, McGovern, parent	830	20	2.5*	0	17	3	0	0	0	0	41	0	0
	830	20	5*	0	0	4	3	6	4	2	101	1	5
	830	20	10*	0	0	0	0	0	3	2	157	15	75
	830	10	None	1	8	1	0	0	0	0	32	0	0
II, CH, parent	450	20	2.5	0	19	1	0	0	0	0	37	0	0
	450	20	5	0	6	2	2	9	0	0	82	1	5
	450	20	10	0	0	0	0	3	2	0	117	15	75
	450	10	None	0	10	0	0	0	0	0	30	0	0
III, CHA, parent	360	20	2.5	1	19	0	0	0	0	0	31	0	0
	360	20	5	1	16	3	0	0	0	0	40	0	0
	360	20	10	0	1	7	7	3	1	0	83	1	5
	360	10	None	2	8	0	0	0	0	0	30	0	0

* These doses of hydroxyethylapocupreine were administered at 2, 8, 14, and 22 hours after infection and at 8-hour intervals thereafter for five additional days.

RESULTS

The response to sulfapyridine of infections with parent and fast organisms is shown in table 2. It is apparent from these data that the same treatment which had a marked curative or life-prolonging action against infections with parent organisms had little effect on infections with sulfapyridine-fast organisms. For example, in the experiment with type I McGovern, 26 of 30 mice recovered from infections with the parent strain, whereas the animals infected with the "fast" organisms lived, on the average, 38 hours—only nine hours longer than the untreated controls. Similar differences were observed in the responses of the parent and fast strains of types II CH and III CHA.

The effects of hydroxyethylapocupreine on infections with the above organisms are shown in table 3. These data show that *this drug was almost equally effective against infections with the parent and sulfapyridine-fast strains.* Thus in the experiment with type I McGovern, 6 of 30 mice recovered from infections with the parent organism, and 6 of 29 recovered from infections with the sulfapyridine-fast organism. The average survival times of the mice that did not recover were 230 and 221 hours for the respective groups. The parent and "fast" strains of type III CHA responded similarly. In the

TABLE 2

Response of parent and sulfapyridine-fast strains of pneumococcus to sulfapyridine

STRAIN	NUMBER OF ORGANISMS IN INFECTING DOSE	NUMBER OF MICE INFECTED	TREATMENT	NUMBER OF DEATHS DAYS AFTER INFECTION								AVERAGE HOURS SURVIVAL OF MICE THAT DIED	30-DAY SURVIVORS	
				1	2	3	4	5	6	7–10	11–30		Number	Per cent
Type I, McGovern														
Parent	280	30	S.P.*	0	0	1	1	1	0	1	0	113	26	87
		10	None	2	8	0	0	0	0	0	0	35	0	0
Fast	290	30	S.P.	0	26	4	0	0	0	0	0	38	0	0
		10	None	0	10	0	0	0	0	0	0	29	0	0
Type II, CH														
Parent	260	29	S.P.	0	0	0	0	1	0	12	0	173	16	55
		10	None	0	10	0	0	0	0	0	0	32	0	0
Fast	280	30	S.P.	0	30	0	0	0	0	0	0	38	0	0
		10	None	1	9	0	0	0	0	0	0	31	0	0
Type III, CHA														
Parent	690	29	S.P.	0	0	0	0	0	0	29	0	171	0	0
		10	None	0	10	0	0	0	0	0	0	28	0	0
Fast	760	29	S.P.	3	25	1	0	0	0	0	0	36	0	0
		10	None	4	6	0	0	0	0	0	0	25	0	0

* 20 mgm. doses of sulfapyridine were administered at 2, 8, 14, and 22 hours after infection and at eight-hour intervals thereafter for five additional days.

experiment with type II CH, the curative action of hydroxyethylapocupreine was the same against parent and "fast" organisms; however, of the mice that did not recover, those infected with the parent organism lived somewhat longer than those infected with the "fast" strain.

Although hydroxyethylapocupreine was equally effective against infections with parent and sulfapyridine-fast pneumococci, it should be noted that in only one case was it as effective as sulfapyridine against infections with the parent strains. This point will be discussed later.

DISCUSSION

As pointed out previously, it is now well established that under suitable experimental conditions pneumococci can become highly resistant to sulfapyridine. Evidence is accumulating that this may occur also during the use of sulfapyridine and other sulfonamides in treating clinical pneumococcal infections (7, 14). Up to the present time, however, the development of sulfonamide-resistant pneumococci has not seriously limited the clinical effectiveness of these drugs.[2] The importance of this problem may increase in the future since these resistant organisms are carried in the respiratory tracts of apparently healthy individuals, just as are other pneumococci (14). Infections caused by such organisms would not respond to treatment with other sulfonamides since pneumococci resistant to one sulfonamide are

TABLE 3

Response of parent and sulfapyridine-fast strains of pneumococcus to hydroxyethylapocupreine

STRAIN	NUMBER OF ORGANISMS IN INFECTING DOSE	NUMBER OF MICE INFECTED	TREATMENT	NUMBER OF DEATHS DAYS AFTER INFECTION								AVERAGE HOURS SURVIVAL OF MICE THAT DIED	30-DAY SURVIVORS	
				1	2	3	4	5	6	7–10	11–30		Number	Per cent
Type I, McGovern														
Parent	520	30	HEC*	0	0	1	0	3	1	1	18	230	6	20
		10	None	1	9	0	0	0	0	0	0	35	0	0
Fast	540	29	HEC	0	1	3	1	0	0	5	13	221	6	21
		10	None	0	10	0	0	0	0	0	0	35	0	0
Type II, CH														
Parent	160	30	HEC	0	1	2	0	0	1	1	10	225	15	50
		10	None	0	10	0	0	0	0	0	0	29	0	0
Fast	290	30	HEC	0	0	1	5	5	0	0	3	135	16	53
		10	None	0	10	0	0	0	0	0	0	28	0	0
Type III, CHA														
Parent	330	30	HEC	2	3	12	4	9	0	0	0	72	0	0
		10	None	3	7	0	0	0	0	0	0	27	0	0
Fast	340	30	HEC	0	2	9	8	8	1	1	0	86	1	3
		10	None	2	8	0	0	0	0	0	0	27	0	0

* 10 mgm. doses of hydroxyethylapocupreine were administered at 2, 8, 14, and 22 hours after infection and at eight-hour intervals thereafter for five additional days.

[2] The development of sulfonamide-resistant gonococci occurs frequently during treatment of gonococcal infections with sulfanilamide and its derivatives. According to the work of Schmith and Reymann (15) this may be one of the hazards of such therapy.

resistant to the others as well (7–9); moreover, serotherapy would be relatively ineffective if delayed until indications of sulfonamide resistance were obtained. For that reason, it is of practical interest to know that sulfonamide-resistant organisms respond to hydroxyethylapocupreine.

Although hydroxyethylapocupreine may be useful in treating infections with sulfonamide-resistant pneumococci, our observations indicate that it would not be as satisfactory as sulfapyridine or sulfathiazole for routine treatment of pneumococcal infections. In the first place, therapeutically effective doses of hydroxyethylapocupreine are more toxic than similarly effective amounts of sulfapyridine or sulfathiazole. Secondly, the latter drugs seem to have a higher therapeutic activity—or at best hydroxyethylapocupreine is no more effective than sulfapyridine.

There is little experimental data available on the relative activities of hydroxyethylapocupreine and sulfapyridine. According to our data (tables 2 and 3), sulfapyridine was distinctly more effective than hydroxyethylapocupreine against infections with types I and III pneumococci; this agrees with the results of Greey, MacLaren and Lucas (13) in type I infections. On the other hand, the two drugs were about equally effective against type II infections—an observation similar to that of Bracken *et al.* (11). Thus there is a possibility that some strains (or types) of pneumococcus may respond equally well to either drug, but indications are that sulfapyridine is generally more effective than hydroxyethylapocupreine.

In conclusion, it should be pointed out that the finding that sulfonamide-resistant pneumococci respond to hydroxyethylapocupreine indicates that different mechanisms are involved in the action of these drugs.

SUMMARY

A comparison was made of the activity of hydroxyethylapocupreine and sulfapyridine against infections in mice with parent and sulfapyridine-fast pneumococci. Infections with the parent organisms were susceptible to treatment with sulfapyridine, whereas infections with the "fast" organisms were not. On the other hand, hydroxyethylapocupreine was equally effective against infections with parent and sulfapyridine-resistant strains. However, hydroxyethylapocupreine was less effective than sulfapyridine against infections with most of the parent organisms.

REFERENCES

(1) MacLean, Rogers and Fleming: Lancet, **1,** 562, 1939.
(2) MacLeod and Daddi: Proc. Soc. Exper. Biol. & Med., **41,** 69, 1939.
(3) Schmidt and Dettwiler: J. Biol. Chem., **133,** lxxxv, 1940.
(4) Dettwiler and Schmidt: J. Bact., **40,** 160, 1940.
(5) Schmidt, Sesler and Dettwiler: To be published.
(6) Mulder, Van Den Berg and Eimer: Nederl. tijdschr. v. geneesk, **84,** 923, 1940.
(7) Lowell, Strauss and Finland: Ann. Int. Med., **14,** 1001, 1940.

(8) SCHMITH: Nord. Med., **8**, 2211, 1940.
(9) SCHMIDT, CLAUGUS AND STARKS: Proc. Soc. Exper. Biol. & Med., **45**, 256, 1940.
(10) MACLACHLAN, JOHNSTON, BRACKEN AND PIERCE: Am. J. Med. Sc., **201**, 367, 1941.
(11) BRACKEN, JOHNSTON, CRUM, PATRICK, PERMAR AND MACLACHLAN: THIS JOURNAL, **68**, 259, 1940.
(12) SCHMIDT AND HILLES: Proc. Soc. Exper. Biol. & Med., **40**, 611, 1939.
(13) GREEY, MACLAREN AND LUCAS: Canad. M. A. J., **40**, 319, 1939.
(14) HAMBURGER, SESLER, SCHMIDT AND RUEGSEGGER: To be published.
(15) SCHMITH AND REYMANN: Nord. Med., **8**, 2493, 1940.

STUDIES ON SHOCK INDUCED BY HEMORRHAGE[1]

I. EFFECT OF THIAMIN ON SURVIVAL TIME

WM. M. GOVIER AND C. M. GREER

From the Department of Pharmacology, Vanderbilt University School of Medicine, Nashville, Tennessee

Received for publication June 27, 1941

In beginning our studies on shock induced by hemorrhage, we were impressed by the magnitude of the changes observed in the blood potassium level by Scudder (1) and co-workers. Inasmuch as hyperglycemia with depletion of hepatic glycogen following certain types of shock, including shock due to hemorrhage, has been observed by many investigators, among them Wertheimer *et al.* (2), Aub and Wu (3), Aggazzotti (4), Lundberg (5), Scarpello (6), Robertson (7), and others, it seemed reasonable to us that at least part of the increase in blood potassium could be due to the liberation of potassium ions along with phosphate ions and hexose during hepatic glycogenolysis. A series of experiments was undertaken on dogs under ether anesthesia in which shock was induced by hemorrhage according to the technique described below, in an effort to confirm the results of the above-mentioned investigators and to attempt to replace the hepatic glycogen which had been depleted and, at the same time, to bind potassium ions. In these experiments we noted the hyperpotassemia described by Scudder (1), and the hyperglycemia and hepatic glycogenolysis shown by the other workers mentioned above. However, the results of attempts to produce glycogenesis and lowering of blood potassium were inconclusive. The work of Tonutti and Wallraff (8), showing that the B_1-avitaminotic mouse liver is unable to store glycogen, suggested to us that thiamin might be a necessary factor in glycogenesis in shock. In addition, Blotevogel and Tonutti (9) have reported beneficial results from the administration of thiamin to cases of severe burns. Preliminary experiments in which thiamin was given to dogs in shock indicated that survival time may thus be significantly prolonged and impelled us to investigate the question more thoroughly by comparing the survival time of a series of control dogs in shock with that of a series of thiamin-treated animals. The results of these experiments are reported below.

[1] This work was supported by grants from the Mallinckrodt Chemical Company and the National Research Council.

METHODS

After considerable experimentation the following uniform procedure was adopted for the induction of shock. Fractional bleedings at thirty-minute intervals were carried out until the dog's blood pressure remained within the arbitrarily selected range

TABLE 1

Thiamin-treated dogs

DOG	WEIGHT	DATE	TOTAL BLEEDING (PER CENT BODY WEIGHT)	BLOOD PRESSURE AT ONSET OF SHOCK	MAXIMUM RISE IN BLOOD PRESSURE OVER SHOCK LEVEL	SURVIVAL TIME
	kgm.			*mm.* Hg	*mm.* Hg	*hours*
1	7.6	3/19	2.0	55	20	14.66
2	7.95	3/19	3.0	55	0	3.00
3	7.2	3/24	2.0	55	10	7.66
4	5.9	3/24	2.25	60	0	12.33
5	12.2	3/25	3.5	60	5	6.00
6	9.7	3/25	3.0	60	25	7.25
7	7.6	3/26	3.0	60	50	6.25
8	8.7	3/26	3.5	60	10	8.0
9	13.5	3/28	4.0	60	0	4.75
10	16.0	3/28	2.75	50	15	18.00
Average			2.8			8.79

TABLE 2

Controls

DOG	WEIGHT	DATE	TOTAL BLEEDING (PER CENT BODY WEIGHT)	BLOOD PRESSURE AT ONSET OF SHOCK	MAXIMUM RISE IN BLOOD PRESSURE OVER SHOCK LEVEL	SURVIVAL TIME
	kgm.			*mm.* Hg	*mm.* Hg	*hours*
1	11.6	3/18	3.75	50	Fall	4.33
2	7.2	3/19	5.00	50	Fall	1.00
3	9.1	3/24	2.50	50	Fall	1.50
4	5.6	3/24	2.50	55	10	8.80
5	6.1	3/25	3.25	55	10	4.16
6	5.7	3/26	3.25	55	10	4.16
7	20.0	3/26	2.625	55	Fall	3.66
8	20.4	3/27	3.50	60	Fall	4.83
9	15.2	3/27	4.75	60	Fall	1.83
10	25.4	3/28	1.0	50	Fall	2.00
Average			3.2			3.63

of 45 to 60 mm. Hg for one-half hour. The first two bleedings usually consisted of 1.0 per cent of the dog's body weight, the next two of 0.5 per cent of body weight, and subsequent bleedings of 0.25 per cent of body weight. The magnitude of successive bleedings after the first was determined by the blood pressure level produced by the previous hemorrhage. Bleedings were stopped when the blood pressure remained at the above-mentioned level for thirty minutes. In the 40 to 50 dogs in which shock has been induced by this method, no spontaneous recoveries have occurred.

Twenty healthy dogs, selected at random, were placed under continuous ether anesthesia by means of tracheal cannula and ether bottle. Cannulae were tied in the left carotid artery for recording blood pressure, in the left femoral artery for bleeding. The right femoral vein was exposed for intravenous injections. Shock was then induced in all of these animals by the method described above. Ten of these dogs were regarded as controls and nothing further was done to them. The remaining ten dogs, after having been left at the above-mentioned blood pressure level for thirty minutes, were given 1.0 mgm./kgm. thiamin chloride intravenously and 2.0 mgm./kgm. thiamin chloride intramuscularly. Thereafter at two-hour intervals they were given 0.5 mgm./kgm. thiamin chloride intramuscularly. The thiamin was administered as a 1.0% solution in distilled water. All of the animals were allowed to succumb and the time of death was noted.

The results of this study are summarized in tables 1 and 2.

DISCUSSION

The average survival time of the thiamin-treated animals was found to be 2.4 times that of the controls. The probability of chance occurrence of this increase in survival time is calculated to be less than 0.01.

A rise in blood pressure, ranging from 5 to 50 mm. Hg, was seen in 70 per cent of the treated animals. This increase began about thirty minutes after thiamin administration and lasted at least one hour, after which time the blood pressure gradually fell until the death of the animal. In the remaining 30 per cent of the treated animals the blood pressure did not rise but was sustained for a considerable time at the original shock level before declining as the animal died. In 30 per cent of the controls a rise in blood pressure was seen, but this was transient and only 10 mm. Hg in each case. The blood pressure of the remaining controls decreased steadily until the animal died. No attempt was made to administer fluids or to restore blood volume in any of these animals.

It should be noted that the dogs were anesthetized with ether. In view of the improvement brought about in alcoholic patients by administration of vitamin B_1, there is a possibility that part of the beneficial effects seen in this series of animals may have been due to counteraction of some of the effects of the anesthetic. This point has been investigated and the result of this study, as well as data on the effect of thiamin administration on carbohydrate metabolism in shock, are found in the paper which follows.

SUMMARY

1. The survival time of dogs, anesthetized with ether, in which shock has been induced by hemorrhage, is significantly greater in those animals treated with thiamin than in untreated animals.

2. This increase in survival time is in most cases accompanied by a significant sustained rise in blood pressure.

REFERENCES

(1) Scudder, John: Shock, Lippincott, Philadelphia, 1940.
(2) Wertheimer, Fabre, and Clogne: Soc. de Chir. de Paris, 1919, p. 8.
(3) Aub and Wu: Am. J. Physiol., **54**: 416, 1920-21.
(4) Aggazzotti: Boll. d. Soc. ital. di Biol. Sper., **2**: 870-883, 1927.
(5) Lundberg: C. R. Soc. de biol., **101**: 931, 1929.
(6) Scarpello: Rif. med., **46**: 1198, 1930.
(7) Robertson: J. Physiol., **84**: 393, 1935.
(8) Tonutti and Wallraff: Zeitschr. f. Mikro-Anat. Forsch., **44**: 532, 1938.
(9) Blotevogel and Tonutti: Klin. Wchnschr., **18**: 471, 1939.

STUDIES ON SHOCK INDUCED BY HEMORRHAGE[1]
II. EFFECT OF THIAMIN ON DISTURBANCES OF CARBOHYDRATE METABOLISM

WM. M. GOVIER AND C. M. GREER

From the Department of Pharmacology, Vanderbilt University School of Medicine, Nashville, Tennessee

Received for publication June 27, 1941

In the preceding paper (1) we have presented evidence which indicates that administration of thiamin to etherized dogs in which shock was induced by repeated hemorrhages results in a marked prolongation of survival time. Lohmann and Schuster (2) have shown thiamin, as a coenzyme, to be essential in the metabolism of pyruvic acid. Platt and Lu (3) have shown that the increase of blood pyruvate values may be correlated with the degree of vitamin B_1 deficiency in cases of beri-beri, and that the blood pyruvate determination may be used as a diagnostic test in this disease. Evidence that diphosphothiamin may catalyze the decarboxylation of other keto acids than pyruvic, such as α ketobutyric and α ketovaleric, has been obtained by Long and Peters (4) in their work on pyruvate oxidation in brain tissue.

On the basis of the above work, it was decided to determine blood keto acids, blood sugars, and blood lactic acids in animals in a state of shock due to hemorrhage, before and after treatment with thiamin, in order to determine whether or not any correlation might be found between blood levels of these substances and the improvement noted in thiamin-treated animals or the failure of improvement noted in the controls. Since it was suspected that ether as an anesthetic might have been responsible for some of the disturbances seen in the animals reported in our previous paper, and that thiamin might be simply remedying toxic effects of ether, the present experiments were carried out on dogs anesthetized locally with procaine, as well as on animals anesthetized with ether. The above determinations were also carried out on etherized animals which were not bled or otherwise traumatized, and on dogs the femoral arteries of which were cannulated under procaine anesthesia, but which were not otherwise traumatized or bled.

The results of these several sets of experiments are presented below.

Group I. Six dogs were selected at random and divided into two groups of three each. Shock was produced in all of these animals by fractional

[1] This work was supported by grants from the Mallinckrodt Chemical Company and the National Research Council.

bleedings (1) at 30 minute intervals after cannulation of both femoral arteries under infiltration anesthesia by procaine. One group of three animals was allowed to expire without treatment; the other three were given thiamin. The thiamin was administered as a 1.0 per cent solution in distilled water and was given in the following amounts: 1.0 mgm./kgm. intravenously and 2.0 mgm./kgm. intramuscularly after the blood pressure had remained between 45 and 60 mm. Hg for 30 minutes, followed by 0.5 mgm./kgm. intramuscularly every hour thereafter.

Blood samples were drawn from the right femoral artery, the left femoral artery being cannulated for blood pressure recording. The samples were used for keto acid, blood sugar, and lactic acid determinations. Keto acids were determined by the method of Lu (5) with the modification of Bueding and Wortis (6), (using 3.0 N NaOH), blood sugars by the Hoffman (7) modification of the Folin-Wu technique, and blood lactic acids by the method of Dische and Laszlo (8).

Several check analyses for keto acids with a single blood sample indicated that the method, as used by us, yielded values accurate to within about 5 per cent.

The results of these determinations are summarized in tables 1 and 2.

It may be seen from tables 1 and 2 that the values for blood keto acids rise progressively as the animal sinks into shock and, in the case of the controls, remain high until the death of the animal. The same rise occurs in the thiamin-treated animals, followed by a slow decline in keto acid values during the first few hours after thiamin administration. Twenty-four hours later the keto acids are seen to have returned almost to the normal level. It is interesting that all three of the thiamin-treated animals recovered, whereas the maximum survival time of the untreated animals was 5.5 hours. Hyperglycemia was seen in four of these dogs. All of the control animals died with a hypoglycemia. Blood lactic acid values increased markedly as these animals went into shock, as has been reported by other investigators (9). In the case of the thiamin-treated animals these values decline as the animals recover.

Group II. The six dogs of this group were treated as were the dogs of Group I, with the exception that they were placed under ether anesthesia by means of tracheal cannula and ether bottle. The animals were kept in full surgical anesthesia as judged by abolition of reflexes and muscular relaxation, but no attempt was made to estimate the blood ether concentration or to relate it to the blood keto acid level. Three animals were regarded as controls and the remainder were treated with thiamin, as were those of Group I. Results obtained from this series of animals are shown in tables 3 and 4.

A rise in blood keto acids, hyperglycemia, and high blood lactic acid values were seen in these animals, as in those of Group I. The blood keto acid values appeared to be somewhat lowered after thiamin administration coincident with the blood pressure rise attendant on the improvement of these dogs. When the keto acid levels after 30 minutes of shock are compared with those at death, the average rise of the control animals is 0.7 mgm./100 cc., whereas the average fall seen in the treated dogs is 0.4 mgm./100 cc.

TABLE 1

Procaine—hemorrhage—thiamin

TIME	KETO ACIDS	BLOOD SUGAR	LACTIC ACID	
	mgm./100 cc.	*mgm./100 cc.*	*mgm./100 cc.*	
Before experiment	1.4	140.0	62.0	19.2 kgm., ♂, 4/28. Procaine anesthesia. Total bleeding 3.0 per cent of body weight. Survival time—recovered. *Thiamin, 1.0 mgm./kgm. IV and 2.0 mgm./kgm. IM; 0.5 mgm./kgm. IM every hour thereafter. Total = 5.5 mgm./kgm.
After 30 minutes shock	3.3	210.0	139.0	
*Thiamin:				
1 hour	4.1	186.0	182.0	
2 hours	4.1	122.0	158.0	
3 hours	3.5	113.0	158.0	
4 hours	3.1	110.0	212.0	
5 hours	Dog's wounds sutured			
24 hours	2.2	90.0	38.0	
Before experiment	1.9	110.0	74.0	11.8 kgm., ♂, 5/19. Procaine anesthesia. Total bleeding 1.25 per cent of body weight. Survival time—recovered. *Thiamin, 1.0 mgm./kgm. IV and 2.0 mgm./kgm. IM; 0.5 mgm./kgm. IM every hour thereafter. Total = 5.5 mgm./kgm.
After 30 minutes shock	4.5	104.0	134.0	
*Thiamin:				
1 hour	4.9	86.0	139.0	
2 hours	4.9	94.0	145.0	
3 hours	4.7	80.0	139.0	
4 hours	4.6	94.0	139.0	
5 hours	Dog's wounds sutured			
6 hours	4.3	90.0	133.0	
24 hours	2.3	112.5	104.0	
Before experiment	1.6	125.0	84.0	12.9 kgm., ♂, 5/13. Procaine anesthesia. Total bleeding 2.0 per cent of body weight. Survival time—recovered. *Thiamin, 1.0 mgm./kgm. IV and 2.0 mgm./kgm. IM; 0.5 mgm./kgm. IM every hour thereafter. Total = 6.0 mgm./kgm.
After 30 minutes shock	4.3	158.0	122.0	
*Thiamin:				
1 hour	5.2	138.0	126.0	
2 hours	5.3	112.0	95.0	
3 hours	4.7	120.0	126.0	
4 hours	5.2	100.0	126.0	
5 hours	4.3	106.0	126.0	
6 hours	Dog's wounds sutured			
24 hours	2.4	62.0	94.0	

The probability of chance occurrence of these values is less than 0.05. Survival times of the thiamin-treated dogs averaged slightly greater than those of the controls but this was not significant in view of the small number of animals.

Group III. Eight dogs were used in this group. They were placed on

TABLE 2

Procaine—hemorrhage

TIME	KETO ACIDS	BLOOD SUGAR	LACTIC ACID	
	mgm./ 100 cc.	*mgm./ 100 cc.*	*mgm./ 100 cc.*	
Before experiment	1.1	100.0		22.7 kgm., ♂, 4/25. Procaine anesthesia. Total bleeding 3.5 per cent of body weight. Survival time from onset of shock—3.5 hours
After 30 minutes shock	3.6	225.0		
1 hour	4.5	126.0		
2 hours	4.3	111.0		
3 hours	4.2	80.0		
At death	4.9	55.0		
Before experiment	1.7	135.0	79.0	8.95 kgm., ♀, 5/20. Procaine anesthesia. Total bleeding 3.0 per cent of body weight. Survival time from onset of shock—5.5 hours
After 30 minutes shock	4.1	210.0	148.0	
1 hour	4.0	130.0	135.0	
2 hours	4.1	133.0	124.0	
3 hours	4.8	126.0	130.0	
4 hours	5.1	95.0	158.0	
5 hours	5.1	81.0		
At death	5.3	62.0	280.0	
Before experiment	2.1	115.0	64.0	7.65 kgm., ♀, 5/14. Procaine anesthesia. Total bleeding 1.03 per cent of body weight. Survival time from onset of shock—1.66 hours
After 30 minutes shock	2.9	118.0	122.0	
1 hour	4.6	110.0	126.0	
At death	4.5	86.0	158.0	

TABLE 3

Ether—hemorrhage

TIME	KETO ACIDS	BLOOD SUGAR	LACTIC ACID	
	mgm./ 100 cc.	*mgm./ 100 cc.*	*mgm./ 100 cc.*	
Before experiment	2.3	83.0	102.0	7.3 kgm., ♂, 5/22. Ether anesthesia. Total bleeding 2.5 per cent of body weight. Survival time—5.5 hours
After 30 minutes shock	4.8	150.0	280.0	
1 hour	3.9	64.0	280.0	
2 hours	3.7	70.0	216.0	
3 hours	3.8	50.0	234.0	
4 hours	3.8	43.0	216.0	
5 hours (at death)	5.3	38.0	256.0	
Before experiment	1.9	67.0	76.0	9.9 kgm., ♂, 5/23. Ether anesthesia. Total bleeding 3.0 per cent of body weight. Survival time—3.5 hours
After 30 minutes shock	3.9	164.0	216.0	
1 hour	5.2	154.0	234.0	
2 hours	5.1	90.0	170.0	
3 hours	5.7	86.0	234.0	
3½ hours (at death)	5.1	103.0	280.0	
Before experiment	2.1	120.0	79.0	12.0 kgm., ♀, 4/30. Ether anesthesia. Total bleeding 3.0 per cent of body weight. Survival time—4.5 hours
After 30 minutes shock	2.7	285.0	200.0	
1 hour	2.4	253.0	230.0	
2 hours	2.5	240.0	178.0	
3 hours	3.0	180.0	250.0	
4 hours (at death)	3.2	146.0	290.0	

the dog-boards and kept under continuous ether anesthesia by tracheal cannula and ether bottle. The left femoral artery was cannulated for the withdrawal of blood samples and the right femoral vein was exposed by a small incision. These dogs were not bled or traumatized in any other way than that necessary for cannulation of the above-mentioned structures. Three animals were regarded as controls and nothing further was done to them

TABLE 4

Ether—hemorrhage—thiamin

TIME	KETO ACIDS	BLOOD SUGAR	LACTIC ACID	
	mgm. /100 cc.	*mgm. /100 cc.*	*mgm. /100 cc.*	
Before experiment	1.8	86.0	60.0	7.1 kgm., ♀, 5/6. Ether anesthesia. Total bleeding, 3.25 per cent of body weight. Survival time—4 hours. *Thiamin, 1.0 mgm./kgm. IV and 2.0 mgm./kgm. IM; 0.5 mgm./kgm. IM every hour thereafter. Total = 4.5 mgm./kgm.
After 30 minutes shock	3.9	170.0	140.0	
*Thiamin:				
1 hour	4.2	153.0	142.0	
2 hours	3.8	137.0	136.0	
3 hours	4.0	115.0	158.0	
At death	4.1	93.0	230.0	
Before experiment	2.3	95.0	118.0	6.55 kgm., ♂, 5/7. Ether anesthesia. Total bleeding, 3.0 per cent of body weight. Survival time—5 hours. *Thiamin, 1.0 mgm./kgm. IV and 2.0 mgm./kgm. IM; 0.5 mgm./kgm. IM every hour thereafter. Total = 5.0 mgm./kgm.
After 30 minutes shock	3.9	156.0	96.0	
*Thiamin:				
1 hour	3.7	107.0	138.0	
2 hours	3.1	100.0	135.0	
3 hours	3.0	105.0	146.0	
4 hours	3.1	97.0	139.0	
At death	3.1	90.0	139.0	
Before experiment	2.8			6.2 kgm., ♀, 5/12. Ether anesthesia. Total bleeding 2.0 per cent of body weight. Survival time—7.0 hours. *Thiamin, 1.0 mgm./kgm. IV and 2.0 mgm./kgm. IM; 0.5 mgm./kgm. IM every hour thereafter. Total = 6.0 mgm./kgm.
After 30 minutes shock	4.4	300.0	232.0	
*Thiamin:				
1 hour	3.9	300.0	230.0	
2 hours	4.2	300.0	300.0	
3 hours	4.3	290.0	284.0	
4 hours	4.1	280.0	288.0	
5 hours	4.2	168.0	284.0	
6 hours	3.9	138.0	284.0	
At death	3.8	107.0	185.0	

save for the withdrawal of 8.0 cc. of blood for analysis every hour for 6 hours in two animals, for 3 hours in the remaining one. The other five dogs were treated as were the controls with the exception that thiamin was given after three hours had elapsed.

The results obtained in this group are summarized in tables 5 and 6.

It will be seen from these tables that moderate rises in blood keto acids occurred in six of the eight dogs under anesthesia. A hyperglycemia of variable magnitude and a hyperlactacidemia occurred in all of the animals in which these substances were determined. Blood keto acids of the controls remained somewhat elevated until the animals were killed at the end of the experiment. In the dogs whose keto acid values rose under ether, thiamin administration was followed by a slow decline in these values.

It is noteworthy that the rise in blood keto acids in these animals did not

TABLE 5

Ether

	KETO ACIDS	BLOOD SUGAR	LACTIC ACID	
	mgm./ 100 cc.	*mgm./ 100 cc.*	*mgm./ 100 cc.*	
→Ether begun				5.5 kgm., ♀, 5/27. Ether anesthesia. No hemorrhage. No thiamin
Five minutes after ether	2.4	135.0	108.0	
1 hour	2.3	137.0	126.0	
2 hours	2.6	150.0	111.0	
3 hours	2.0	170.0	117.0	
4 hours	2.1	280.0	158.0	
5 hours	2.4	260.0	178.0	
6 hours	2.6	220.0	135.0	
→Ether begun				7.0 kgm., ♂, 5/27. Ether anesthesia. No hemorrhage. No thiamin
Five minutes after ether	2.3	124.0	126.0	
1 hour	2.5	156.0	158.0	
2 hours	3.3	177.0	255.0	
3 hours	3.0	223.0	280.0	
4 hours	3.3	240.0	234.0	
5 hours	3.2	225.0	216.0	
6 hours	3.4	172.0	158.0	
Before experiment	2.6			10.2 kgm., ♂, 6/20. Ether anesthesia. No hemorrhage. No thiamin
15 minutes later	2.3			
→Ether begun:				
1 hour	2.8			
2 hours	3.9			
3 hours	4.1			

approach the magnitude seen in those in shock. It seems reasonable to suppose that an animal which has not suffered depletion of circulating blood volume or tissue anoxia would be better able to cope with an increased blood keto acid content than would one which has suffered the results of hemorrhage shock. However, it is evident that thiamin may be of value in reducing blood keto acid increments in uncomplicated ether anesthesia.

Group IV. Two dogs were allowed to remain tied down for three hours

TABLE 6

Ether—thiamin

	KETO ACIDS	BLOOD SUGAR	LACTIC ACID	
	mgm./100 cc.	*mgm./100 cc.*	*mgm./100 cc.*	
→Ether begun				6.3 kgm., ♂, 5/26. Ether anesthesia. No hemorrhage. *Thiamin, 1.0 mgm./kgm. IV and 2.0 mgm./kgm. IM; 0.5 mgm./kgm. IM every hour thereafter. Total = 4.0 mgm./kgm.
Five minutes after ether	2.3	70.0	80.0	
1 hour	3.0	162.0	126.0	
2 hours	3.6	188.0	126.0	
3 hours	3.5	205.0	150.0	
*Thiamin:				
4 hours	2.3	208.0	133.0	
5 hours	2.3	247.0	144.0	
6 hours	2.1	215.0	126.0	
→Ether begun				11.3 kgm., ♂, 5/26. Ether anesthesia. No hemorrhage. *Thiamin, 1.0 mgm./kgm. IV and 2.0 mgm./kgm. IM; 0.5 mgm./kgm. IM every hour thereafter. Total = 4.5 mgm./kgm.
Five minutes after ether	1.9	80.0	73.0	
1 hour	2.6	118.0	139.0	
2 hours	3.6	108.0	200.0	
3 hours	3.6	104.0	200.0	
*Thiamin:				
4 hours	3.1	117.0	200.0	
5 hours	2.7	133.0	171.0	
6 hours	2.4	126.0	148.0	
Before experiment	1.8			8.4 kgm., ♀, 6/18. Ether anesthesia. No hemorrhage. *Thiamin, 1.0 mgm./kgm. IV and 2.0 mgm./kgm. IM; 0.5 mgm./kgm. IM every hour thereafter. Total = 5.0 mgm./kgm.
15 minutes later	1.9			
→Ether begun:				
1 hour	2.0			
2 hours	1.7			
3 hours	1.7			
*Thiamin:				
4 hours	1.9			
5 hours	1.7			
6 hours	2.1			
7 hours	2.0			
8 hours	1.7			
Before experiment	2.0			7.1 kgm., ♂, 6/19. Ether anesthesia. No hemorrhage. *Thiamin, 1.0 mgm./kgm. IV and 2.0 mgm./kgm. IM; 0.5 mgm./kgm. IM every hour thereafter. Total = 5.0 mgm./kgm.
15 minutes later	2.2			
→Ether begun:				
1 hour	2.9			
2 hours	2.9			
3 hours	3.5			
*Thiamin:				
4 hours	3.4			
5 hours	3.1			
6 hours	2.7			
7 hours	2.2			
8 hours	2.3			

TABLE 6—*Concluded*

	KETO ACIDS	BLOOD SUGAR	LACTIC ACID	
	mgm./ 100 cc.	*mgm./ 100 cc.*	*mgm./ 100 cc.*	
Before experiment	2.1			8.7 kgm., ♂, 6/20. Ether anesthesia. No hemorrhage. *Thiamin, 1.0 mgm./kgm. IV and 2.0 mgm./kgm. IM; 0.5 mgm./kgm. IM every hour thereafter. Total = 5.0 mgm./kgm.
15 minutes later	2.0			
→Ether begun:				
1 hour	2.2			
2 hours	3.5			
3 hours	3.4			
*Thiamin:				
4 hours	3.1			
5 hours	3.1			
6 hours	2.8			
7 hours	2.7			
8 hours	2.8			

TABLE 7

Procaine

	KETO ACIDS	BLOOD SUGAR	LACTIC ACID	
	mgm./ 100 cc.	*mgm./ 100 cc.*	*mgm./ 100 cc.*	
→Procaine←				6.7 kgm., ♂. Procaine anesthesia. No hemorrhage
Sample I	1.5	80.0	72.0	
1 hour	0.9	73.0	71.0	
2 hours	0.9	72.0	72.0	
3 hours	1.0	66.0	72.0	
→Procaine←				6.0 kgm., ♂. Procaine anesthesia. No hemorrhage
Sample I	1.3	73.0	58.0	
1 hour	0.7	72.0	108.0	
2 hours	1.3	73.0	83.0	
3 hours	1.0	75.0	81.0	

after cannulation of the right femoral artery under procaine anesthesia for removal of blood samples. These samples were withdrawn at hourly intervals. At the end of the three hours the dogs' wounds were repaired and the animals were returned to their cages. They were not subjected to hemorrhage.

The results of analyses of blood samples from this group are summarized in table 7.

It will be seen from this table that no increase in blood keto acids or blood sugar occurred in this group. Moderate increases in blood lactic acid values may be attributed to the dogs' struggling.

DISCUSSION

The chain of events following hemorrhage, namely: Tissue anoxia → Epinephrine secretion → Hepatic glycogenolysis → Hyperglycemia, is well known in these animals, as is the hyperlactacidemia occurring after hemorrhage. The data also indicate (*1*) that blood keto acids (which may include pyruvic, acetoacetic, α ketoglutaric, and oxaloacetic) are increased in hemorrhage shock, (*2*) that there is a fall in these elevated values after thiamin administration, (*3*) that along with this fall a rise of blood pressure and an increase of survival time occur, and (*4*) that similar but much less marked changes in blood keto acid values usually occur in etherized animals in which shock has not been produced.

It is recognized that the need for thiamin is increased when increasing quantities of carbohydrate are metabolized. Thus, our animals, in view of their increased blood sugar levels, may be assumed to have an increased thiamin requirement. In those dogs subjected to hemorrhage, bleeding itself may have reduced the available tissue thiamin content significantly.

Lu (10) believes that, although the increase of pyruvic acid in circulating blood provides a measurable index of avitaminosis B_1, this increase is detrimental only in so far as due to "secondary changes caused by the efforts of the organism to remove such an unexpected load of pyruvate." These secondary changes, according to her, are the conversion of pyruvic acid into other bisulphite-binding compounds which may be toxic.

In considering the increase in blood keto acids occurring in shock due to hemorrhage and the fall of keto acid levels with increased longevity after thiamin treatment, one must take account of several factors: First, it must be emphasized that we are probably dealing with an increase in several keto acids (other than pyruvic) which may be of varying toxicity. Another possibility is that, as Lu (10) suggests, pyruvic acid may be converted into other bisulphite-binding substances which are toxic. A third possibility is that the increase of keto-acids in shock and the decrease following thiamin administration are entirely unrelated to the symptomatology and pathology of the shock syndrome. It is important to note that our animals were subjected to generalized tissue anoxia by hemorrhage and subsequent shock, and that the possibility exists that these keto acids or substances formed from them may be much more toxic to the cardiovascular and nervous system in these animals than in the non-shocked normal and B_1-avitaminotic animals of Platt and Lu. Further studies on this point are planned.

In view of the fact of anaerobic muscle glycogen ↔ lactic acid conversion in skeletal muscle, the accumulation of large amounts of lactic acid in the blood of the tissue-anoxic animal in shock is not surprising. We do not believe this accumulation to be as significant in producing toxic effects as the keto acid increase, since large amounts of lactic acid may accumulate temporarily in the blood without detrimental effects after violent exercise.

Hepatic glycogenolysis and hyperglycemia under ether anesthesia are well recognized. It is significant that blood keto acids may also increase and that thiamin administration results in reduction of these values. A mechanism probably operates here which is similar to that discussed above for hemorrhage shock. It has been noted above that, although a keto acid increase usually occurred in these dogs, the values did not often become as high as those in the animals which were bled. However, since the rise in keto acids may occur under ether and does not occur under local anesthesia, this would emphasize the fact that the anesthetic for shocked patients should be carefully chosen. Work in progress at the present time suggests that anesthetics vary greatly in their properties of producing a keto-acidosis.

The studies reported here also suggest that if glucose be given to shocked patients, it should be accompanied by thiamin.

SUMMARY

1. A marked increase in blood keto acids occurs in dogs in which shock has been induced by hemorrhage. This increase is accompanied by hyperglycemia and hyperlactacidemia.

2. Administration of thiamin to these animals is followed by a delayed fall in the elevated blood keto acid values.

3. The increase in survival time and elevation of blood pressure following thiamin administration is much more marked in the locally anesthetized animal than in the animal anesthetized with ether.

4. Ether anesthesia alone may produce a moderate increase in blood keto acids, a hyperglycemia and increased blood lactic acid values. In these dogs also, elevated keto acid values usually fall after thiamin administration.

5. Animals locally anesthetized with procaine solution and not subjected to shock show no rise in keto acids, blood sugar or blood lactic acid.

REFERENCES

(1) Govier and Greer: This Journal, **72**: 317, 1941.
(2) Lohmann and Schuster: Biochem. Ztschr., **294**: 188, 1937.
(3) Platt and Lu: Quart. J. Med., **5**: 355, 1936.
(4) Long and Peters: Biochem. Jour., **33**: 759, 1939.
(5) Lu: Biochem. Jour. **33** (1): 249, 1939.
(6) Bueding and Wortis: J. Biol. Chem., **133**: 585, 1940.
(7) Hoffman: Photelometric Clinical Chemistry, New York, 1941.
(8) Dische and Laszlo: Biochem. Z., **187**: 344, 1927.
(9) Gutmann, Olson, et al: Am. J. Physiol. **133**: P308, 1941.
(10) Lu: Biochem. Jour., **33**(1): 774, 1939.

Reprinted from THE JOURNAL OF PHARMACOLOGY AND EXPERIMENTAL THERAPEUTICS
Vol. 72, No. 4, August, 1941

HISTONE ZINC INSULIN—ITS PHARMACOLOGIC CHARACTERISTICS AND ITS APPLICATION IN THE TREATMENT OF DIABETES MELLITUS

CHARLES A. BARNES, TRACY D. CUTTLE, AND GARFIELD G. DUNCAN

From the Medical Service, Pennsylvania Hospital, Philadelphia

Received for publication January 14, 1941

The use of protamine zinc insulin has simplified the treatment of diabetes mellitus, but three limitations impair its usefulness. First, the slow rate at which the drug is absorbed delays the onset of a pronounced fall in blood sugar until six to eight hours after the injection; many diabetic patients may therefore require an additional injection of a more quickly acting insulin preparation. Second, the apparent maximum blood sugar lowering effect of protamine zinc insulin is reached during the second twelve hours after injection, a period which usually corresponds with the night hours of fasting; hypoglycemic reactions are therefore most likely to occur between midnight and breakfast. Third, the insulin action may persist for more than twenty-four hours, which causes the effect of one day's dose to be carried over into the second day and opens the way for cumulative effects.

Hagedorn (1), in his search for an insoluble protein to combine with insulin, tried histone, which is prepared from thymic tissue, but he was unable to produce a stable compound. Biasotti, Deulefeu, and Mendive (2) in 1927 reported that their preparation, in which crystalline insulin was combined with histone at a pH of 7–7.2 had a more prolonged action than crystalline insulin. Later the same year, Gray, Bischoff, and Sansum (3) reported the use of a histone insulin which had an action similar to protamine zinc insulin. Their product was a suspension, but the crystals had a marked tendency to clump.

The histone zinc insulin used in this study was prepared by the Eli Lilly Company. Insulin, histone, and zinc are mixed in a suitably buffered solution. When brought into a uniform suspension, each cubic centimeter contains 40 units of insulin, approximately 1.3 mgm. of histone, and approximately 0.08 mgm. of zinc. The pH of the solution is about 7.0. Phenol 0.25 per cent is added as a preservative and glycerine 1.6 per cent as an agent for achieving isotonicity.

The essential difference in the composition of the original histone insulin and the present histone zinc insulin lies in the addition of zinc, which has the same sort of stabilizing effect on this precipitate as it has on that of protamine insulin. The effect of zinc in further prolonging the action of the product turns out to be about what would be expected in view of the experience with the original protamine insulin. Data on the effect of histone zinc insulin in animals have been collected and will be reported in a separate publication. The results are similar to those obtained in man.

METHODS

Twelve patients suffering from diabetes mellitus and one normal subject were studied at the Pennsylvania Hospital during the course of this investigation. The aim was to contrast the time of onset, the duration, and the degree of the hypoglycemic effects produced by single doses of each of four types of insulin—protamine zinc insulin, zinc insulin crystals in solution,[1] unmodified insulin, and histone zinc insulin.

At intervals of not less than one week, the patients received equal quantities of protamine zinc insulin, and either unmodified insulin or crystalline insulin. (It has been shown by Marble and Vartiainen (4a), Ricketts and Wilder (4b), and Duncan, Cuttle, and Jewesbury (4c) that there is no appreciable difference in the action of unmodified insulin and crystalline insulin as now commercially available in the United States.) After a suitable control period, during which the patient received a weighed diet and insulin, the insulin was discontinued for a length of time considered sufficient for its action to have become exhausted. After a fasting period of twelve hours venous blood was obtained for determinations of the sugar level,[2] and a dose of insulin was given. The amount of insulin prescribed for each patient was based upon the severity of his diabetes, with due consideration for age, general body stature, and the amount of insulin which experience had shown to be necessary to maintain the level of the blood sugar within normal limits. In order to maintain a constant intake of carbohydrate throughout the period of observation each patient was given fruit juice containing 20 gm. of carbohydrate concurrently with the insulin and at two-hour intervals thereafter until the effect of the insulin was exhausted. Determinations of the blood sugar level were made every two hours, coinciding with the time of the administration of the carbohydrate.

CASE REPORTS

Case 1. D. C., a white male, aged 55 years, height 162 cm. (64 inches), weight 61.2 kgm. (135 pounds), was admitted on August 28, 1939, with a history of diabetes of two years' duration. His diet contained protein 90 grams, fat 116 grams, and carbohydrate 200 grams (2200 calories). He was given 80 units of protamine zinc insulin a day. After a period of six weeks, during which other investigations were pursued, and after a control period of five days, the insulin was withheld for forty-eight hours. He was then given 78 units of unmodified insulin. A prompt decrease in the blood sugar from a fasting level of 180 to 41 mgm. per cent was observed (see fig. 1) during the first four hours, but thereafter the level rose until after twelve hours it was 216 mgm. Four weeks later insulin was again withheld and observations were made after the administration of 78 units of protamine zinc insulin. The sugar concentration in the blood rose from a fasting level of 183 to 209 mgm. per cent during the first four hours, but fell, particularly between the sixth and tenth hours, so that levels below 100 mgm. per cent were main-

---

[1] Zinc insulin crystals in solution is designated crystalline insulin for the sake of brevity.

[2] Determinations of the blood sugar level were made using Benedict's (5) modification of the macromethod of Folin and Wu.

tained from the twelfth to the twenty-sixth hour. After an interval of six weeks, he once more received no insulin for forty-eight hours and was given 78 units of histone zinc insulin. The fasting level of 202 mgm. fell to 146 mgm. per cent in two hours. It remained within the normal range for eighteen hours, rising to 182 mgm. at the twenty-second hour.

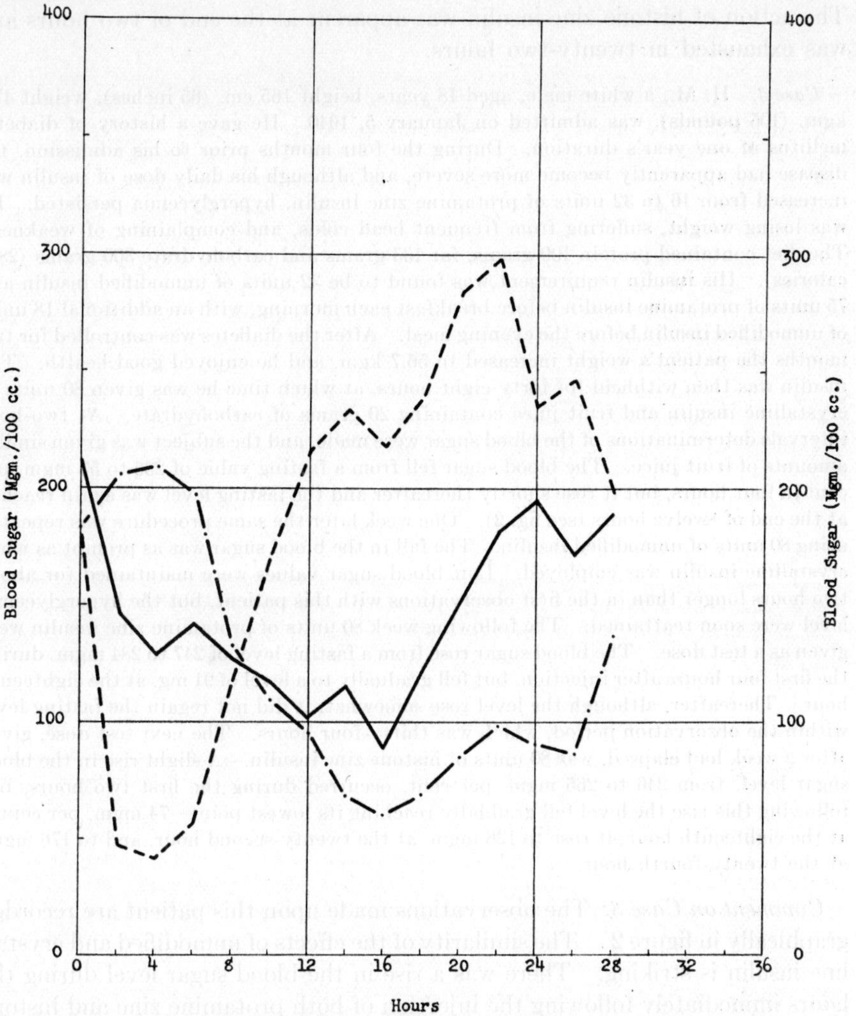

FIG. 1. CASE 1. DEPICTS THE RELATIVE EFFECTS OF 78 UNITS OF EACH, UNMODIFIED, PROTAMINE ZINC, AND HISTONE ZINC INSULIN, ON THE BLOOD SUGAR CONCENTRATION UNDER CONTROLLED CONDITIONS

Histone Zinc Insulin, ——; Protamine Zinc Insulin, .—.; Unmodified Insulin — — —

Comment on Case 1: The effect of unmodified insulin persisted for about eight hours (see fig. 1). The protamine zinc insulin apparently became effective only after four hours but its effect was continued for twenty-eight hours. The preliminary rise, while not great, nevertheless is of clinical significance in the routine treatment of diabetes, since one must give a quickly acting insulin (crystalline insulin or unmodified insulin) in addition to protamine zinc insulin to maintain a normal blood sugar level during this period. The action of histone zinc insulin was apparent at the end of two hours and was exhausted in twenty-two hours.

Case 3. H. M., a white male, aged 18 years, height 165 cm. (65 inches), weight 47.6 kgm. (105 pounds), was admitted on January 5, 1940. He gave a history of diabetes mellitus of one year's duration. During the four months prior to his admission, the disease had apparently become more severe, and although his daily dose of insulin was increased from 16 to 32 units of protamine zinc insulin, hyperglycemia persisted. He was losing weight, suffering from frequent head colds, and complaining of weakness. The diet contained protein 100 grams, fat 133 grams and carbohydrate 300 grams (2800 calories). His insulin requirement was found to be 32 units of unmodified insulin and 75 units of protamine insulin before breakfast each morning, with an additional 18 units of unmodified insulin before the evening meal. After the diabetes was controlled for two months the patient's weight increased to 56.7 kgm. and he enjoyed good health. The insulin was then withheld for forty-eight hours, at which time he was given 80 units of crystalline insulin and fruit juice containing 20 grams of carbohydrate. At two-hour intervals determinations of the blood sugar were made, and the subject was given similar amounts of fruit juice. The blood sugar fell from a fasting value of 236 to 53 mgm. per cent in four hours, but it rose shortly thereafter and the fasting level was again reached at the end of twelve hours (see fig. 2). One week later the same procedure was repeated using 80 units of unmodified insulin. The fall in the blood sugar was as prompt as when crystalline insulin was employed. Low blood sugar values were maintained for about two hours longer than in the first observations with this patient, but the hyperglycemic level were soon reattained. The following week 80 units of protamine zinc insulin were given as a test dosc. The blood sugar rose from a fasting level of 247 to 284 mgm. during the first four hours after injection, but fell gradually to a level of 91 mg. at the eighteenth hour. Thereafter, although the level rose somewhat, it did not regain the fasting level within the observation period, which was thirty-four hours. The next test dose, given after a week had elapsed, was 80 units of histone zinc insulin. A slight rise in the blood sugar level, from 246 to 265 mgm. per cent, occurred during the first two hours, but following this rise the level fell gradually reaching its lowest point—74 mgm. per cent—at the eighteenth hour; it rose to 126 mgm. at the twenty-second hour, and to 176 mgm. at the twenty-fourth hour.

Comment on Case 3: The observations made upon this patient are recorded graphically in figure 2. The similarity of the effects of unmodified and crystalline insulin is striking. There was a rise in the blood sugar level during the hours immediately following the injection of both protamine zinc and histone zinc insulin but this was less pronounced and briefer with the histone zinc preparation. Clinically, this rise can be prevented by giving the histone zinc insulin at a slightly longer interval before breakfast than is customary and by dividing the diet as follows: one fifth for breakfast, two fifths for lunch and two fifths for supper. It has not been necessary, in our experience, to give an additional dose of unmodified or crystalline insulin to prevent this brief rise except in rare instances.

Case 8. G. G., a white female, aged 60 years, height 162 cm. (64 inches), weight 54 kgm. (119 pounds), was admitted to the hospital suffering from arteriosclerotic heart disease and diabetes mellitus. The diabetes was of ten years' duration and was well

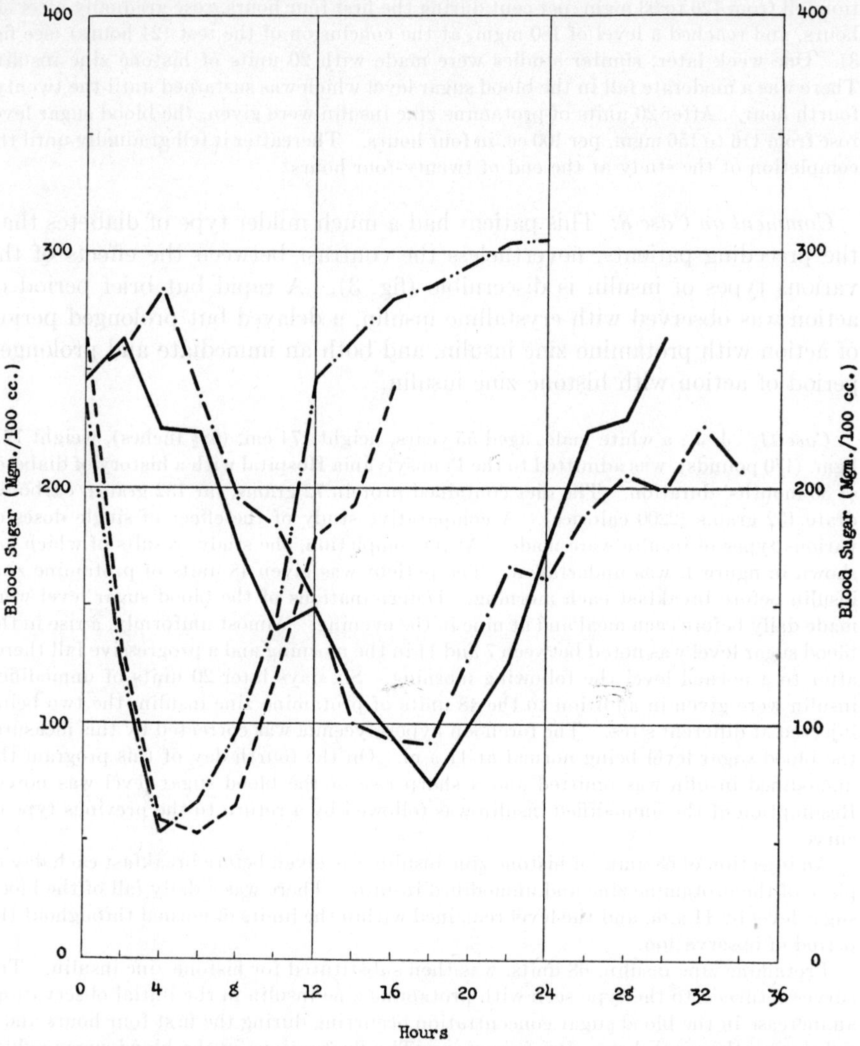

FIG. 2. CASE 3. THE CONTRAST OF THE EFFECTS OF 80 UNITS EACH OF FOUR DIFFERENT INSULINS REVEALS: (*1*) A REMARKABLE SIMILARITY IN THAT OF THE UNMODIFIED AND CRYSTALLINE INSULIN, (*2*) THE DELAYED AND PROLONGED ACTION OF PROTAMINE ZINC INSULIN, (*3*) THE PROMPTNESS AND LONG DURATION OF THE EFFECT OF HISTONE ZINC INSULIN

Histone Zinc Insulin, ——; Protamine Zinc Insulin, .—.; Unmodified Insulin, — — —; Crystalline Insulin, —..—

controlled at the time of admission. The diet contained protein 70 grams, fat 58 grams, and carbohydrate 150 grams (1400 calories). She received 20 units of crystalline insulin before each meal. At the time of admission she was suffering from cardiac decompensation, but with rest and the administration of digitalis the extreme dyspnea, edema, and hydrothorax subsided. A period of freedom from signs or symptoms of cardiac decompensation having elapsed, the initial test dose to 20 units of crystalline insulin was administered after the fasting blood sugar level was obtained. The blood sugar concentration fell from 126 to 93 mgm. per cent during the first four hours, rose gradually after six hours, and reached a level of 180 mgm. at the conclusion of the test (24 hours) (see fig. 3). One week later, similar studies were made with 20 units of histone zinc insulin. There was a moderate fall in the blood sugar level which was sustained until the twenty-fourth hour. After 20 units of protamine zinc insulin were given, the blood sugar level rose from 116 to 156 mgm. per 100 cc. in four hours. Thereafter it fell gradually until the completion of the study at the end of twenty-four hours.

Comment on Case 8: This patient had a much milder type of diabetes than the preceding patients, nevertheless the contrast between the effects of the various types of insulin is discernible (fig. 3). A rapid but brief period of action was observed with crystalline insulin, a delayed but prolonged period of action with protamine zinc insulin, and both an immediate and prolonged period of action with histone zinc insulin.

Case 11. J. J., a white male, aged 55 years, height 174 cm. (68½ inches), weight 77.1 kgm. (170 pounds), was admitted to the Pennsylvania Hospital with a history of diabetes of 30 months' duration. The diet contained protein 72 grams, fat 132 grams, carbohydrate 132 grams (2200 calories). A comparative study of the effect of single doses of various types of insulin were made. At its completion, the study, results of which are shown in figure 4, was undertaken. The patient was given 48 units of protamine zinc insulin before breakfast each morning. Determinations of the blood sugar level were made daily before each meal and at nine in the evening. Almost uniformly, a rise in the blood sugar level was noted between 7 and 11 in the morning and a progressive fall thereafter to a normal level the following morning. Six days later 20 units of unmodified insulin were given in addition to the 48 units of protamine zinc insulin, the two being injected at different sites. The forenoon hyperglycemia was corrected by this measure, the blood sugar level being normal at 11 a.m. On the fourth day of this program the unmodified insulin was omitted and a sharp rise of the blood sugar level was noted. Resumption of the unmodified insulin was followed by a return to the previous type of curve.

An injection of 68 units of histone zinc insulin was given before breakfast each day in place of the protamine zinc and unmodified insulin. There was a daily fall of the blood sugar level by 11 a.m. and the level remained within the limits of normal throughout the period of observation.

Protamine zinc insulin, 68 units, was then substituted for histone zinc insulin. The curves returned to the type seen with protamine zinc insulin in the initial observation, an increase in the blood sugar concentration occurring during the first four hours and a fall during the ninth hour after injection. The fluctuations in the blood sugar values were less marked than were observed when smaller doses of protamine zinc insulin were employed.

Comment on Case 11: A single injection of histone zinc insulin was sufficient to replace the combined effect of a dose of protamine zinc insulin and a dose of unmodified insulin in this patient. Most patients with diabetes mellitus, when given a single injection of histone zinc insulin each morning one hour before breakfast, will have a normal blood sugar concentration and no glycosuria throughout the day. Some patients with severe diabetes will require a second injection before the evening meal in order to bridge the period

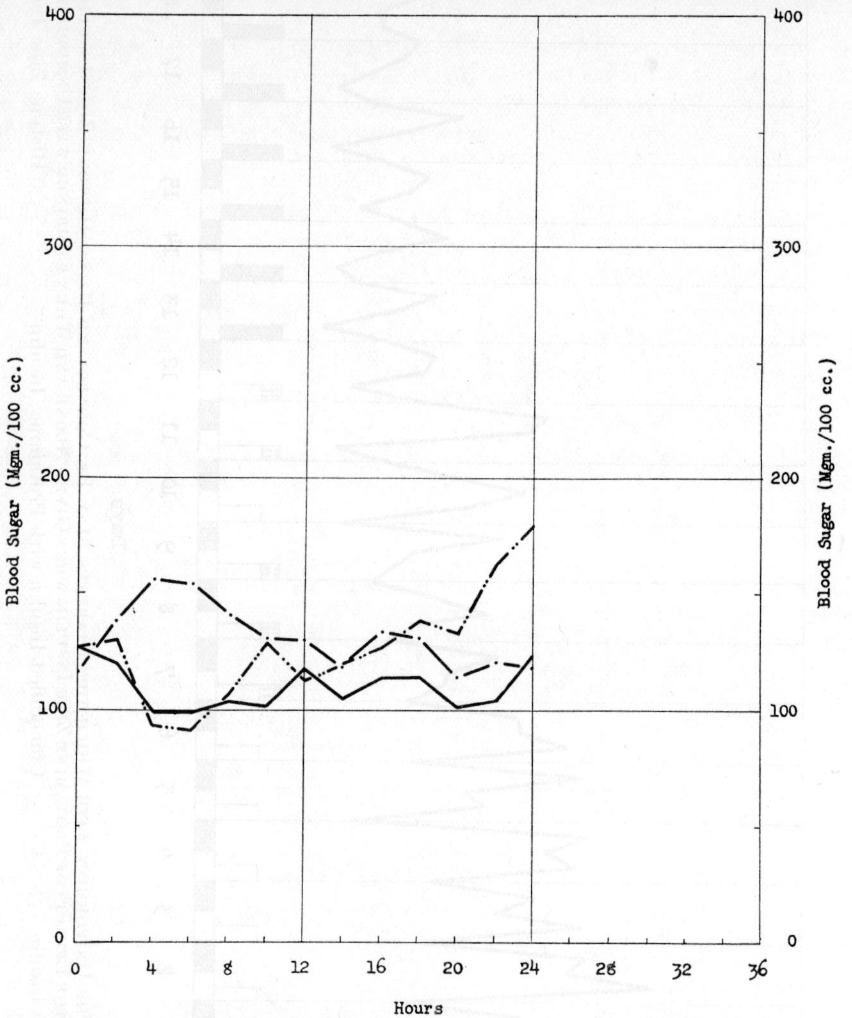

FIG. 3. CASE 8. ILLUSTRATES THE PROMPT EFFECTS OF SMALL DOSES (20 UNITS EACH) OF CRYSTALLINE AND HISTONE ZINC INSULIN AND THE DELAYED EFFECT OF THE SAME AMOUNT OF PROTAMINE ZINC INSULIN UPON THE BLOOD SUGAR LEVEL AS THEY OCCUR IN A PATIENT WITH MILD DIABETES

Note the apparent prolonged effect of the histone zinc insulin in this type of patient Histone Zinc Insulin, ——; Protamine Zinc Insulin, .—.; Crystalline Insulin, — . . —

of from four to six hours between the time when one day's dose is exhausted and the next day's dose is given. In most adult patients, however, this is unnecessary, as this period coincides with the early morning fasting hours.

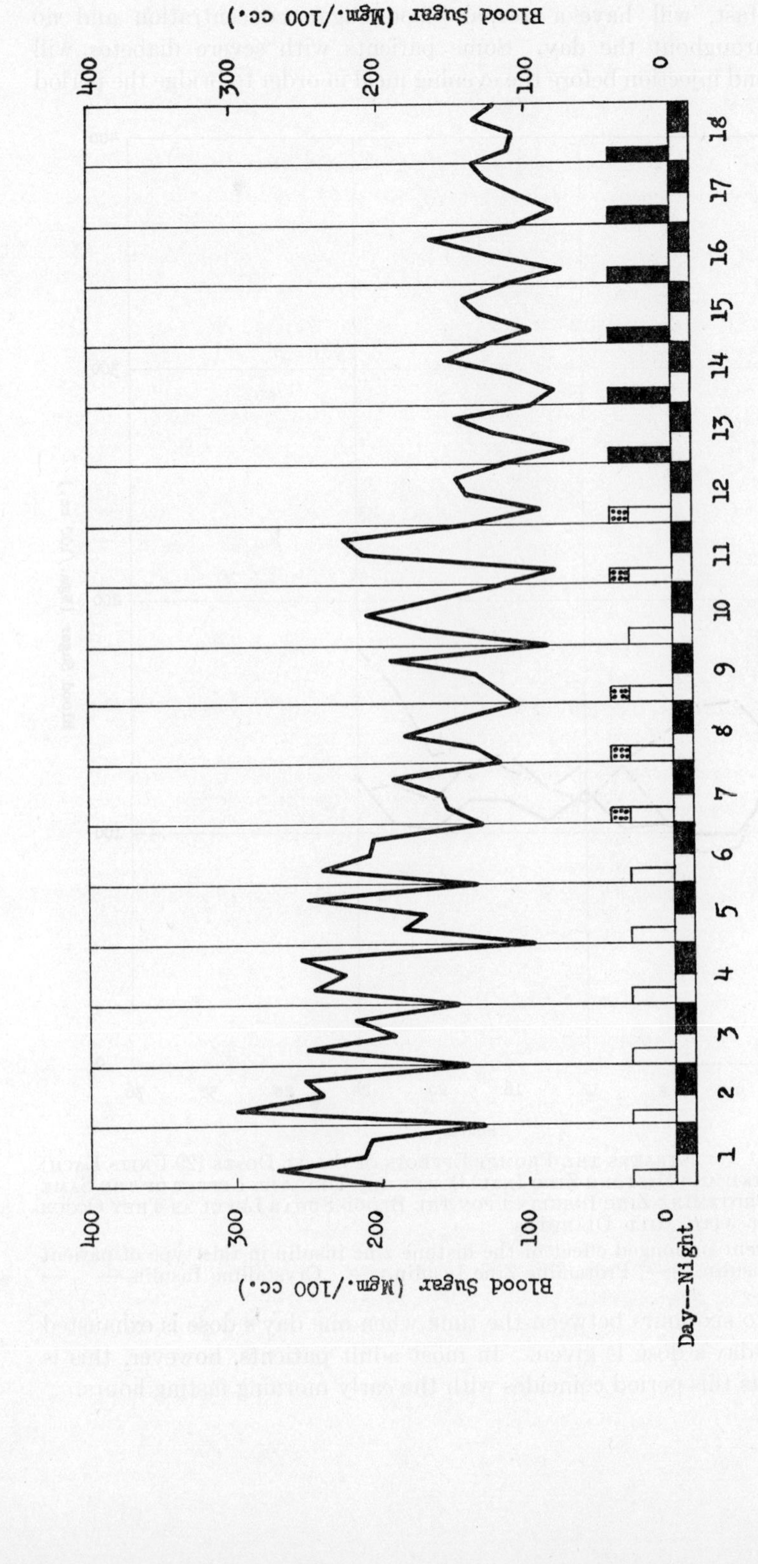

FIG. 4. CASE 11. THE UNIFORMITY WITH WHICH THE DIABETES MAY BE CONTROLLED USING HISTONE ZINC INSULIN ALONE IS CONTRASTED WITH THE EFFECTS OF PROTAMINE ZINC INSULIN WHEN GIVEN ALONE AND WHEN COMBINED WITH UNMODIFIED INSULIN

Protamine Zinc Insulin □ Unmodified Insulin with Protamine Insulin ⊞ Histone Zinc Insulin ■

DISCUSSION

From the data obtained in observations made on twelve diabetic patients and one nondiabetic patient, it was found that they fell into two groups (see table 1). Six of the patients (2, 6, 8, 9, 10, 13) may be classified as having mild diabetes. As a group they were older and more obese than the individuals with severe diabetes. Clinically they required no insulin or only small doses, providing they were maintained on diets suitably restricted in total caloric content. These patients without exception had normal fasting blood sugar levels. The point of maximum hypoglycemic effect following the injection of each of the various types of insulin was readily observed. It was much more difficult, however, to determine the point at which the action of insulin was exhausted, as these patients do not tend to have a rapid elevation of the blood sugar level as soon as the insulin is no longer effective. Patient 12 is a nondiabetic subject but shows essentially the same type of blood sugar curves as observed in patients with mild diabetes.

Patients 1, 3, 4, 5, 7, and 11 fall into another group. The fasting blood sugar level in every instance was markedly elevated, the average for the six patients being 226 mgm. per cent. Blood sugar rapidly returned to hyperglycemic levels after the action of the insulin was exhausted. The resulting curves obtained by averaging the blood sugar values of these six patients when given crystalline or unmodified insulin, protamine zinc insulin, and histone zinc insulin are presented in figure 5. Each curve has been corrected so that the fasting blood sugar level in each is 226 mgm. per cent. The rapid but evanescent action of crystalline and unmodified insulin is clearly shown, as is the failure of protamine zinc insulin to prevent a morning rise in the blood sugar level following breakfast. The curve secured with histone zinc insulin is slightly delayed but falls more quickly than does that with protamine zinc insulin. The action of histone zinc insulin is most apparent between the second and twentieth hours after injection.

SUMMARY

The comparative effects of identical doses of histone zinc, unmodified, crystalline, and protamine zinc insulin were observed under strictly controlled conditions in twelve diabetic patients and in one nondiabetic subject. The hypoglycemic effects of unmodified and crystalline insulin disappeared between six and eight hours after administration, whereas those of histone zinc insulin subsided in eighteen to twenty-two hours, and those of protamine zinc insulin between twenty-four and thirty-six hours.

The blood sugar lowering effect of histone zinc insulin is less abrupt and more prolonged than that of unmodified and crystalline insulin but more prompt than that of protamine zinc insulin. These qualities make it possible

TABLE 1

A presentation of the comparative effects which four different kinds of insulin exerted on the blood sugar levels in twelve diabetic patients and one non-diabetic subject, under carefully controlled conditions

CASE NUMBER	INITIALS	SEX	AGE	HEIGHT	WEIGHT	TYPE OF INSULIN	DOSAGE	BLOOD SUGAR (MGM./100 CC.) Fasting	2	4	6	8	10	12	14	16	18	20	22	24	26	28	30	32	34
									Hours																
				cm.	*mgm.*		*units*																		
1	D. C.	M	53	162	61.2	Unmodified	78	180	47	41	56	117	172	216	233	217	239	283	298	235	246	198			
						Protamine zinc	78	183	205	209	197	132	109	95	68	60	68	85	98	90	86	137			
						Histone zinc	78	212	146	128	142	127	117	102	115	89	122		182	195	171	189			
2	M. V.	F	64	157.5	70.3	Unmodified	60	96	81	61	69	82	89	98	113	123	100	148	180	173					
						Crystalline	60	85	80	55	46	68	75	103	134	144	187	171		231					
						Protamine zinc	60	85	96	109	134	118	127	146	135		131	145	151	159					
						Histone zinc	60	126	88	80	103	94	103	95	97	117	103	103	122	134					
3	H. M.	M	18	165	56.7	Unmodified	80	264	130	58	53	65	118	178	193	243									
						Crystalline	80	236	125	53	67	97	145	246		280	286		303	305					
						Protamine zinc	80	247	258	284	238	195	183	152	100	93	91		167	161	189	205	199	226	207
						Histone zinc	80	246	263	225	224	173	139	148	114	94	74		126	176	224	229	263		
4	L. W.	F	43	165.1	74.8	Unmodified	50	179	42	53	62	58	46	63	82	109		139	144	207	249	229			
						Protamine zinc	50	251	280	300	264	203	245	253	234	198	200		186	178	217	200			
						Histone zinc	50	208	229	190	143	147	144	193	193	207	203	209	233	260	243	243			
5	F. S.	F	46	152.4	59.0	Unmodified	50	259	141	88	92	108	90	138	152	182	197	210	223	235	243	233			
						Protamine zinc	50	254	294	288	254	256	246	262	254	254	245	245	266	278	295	256			
						Histone zinc	50	239	262	207	153	150	125	131	132	130	114	146	154	173	200	187			
6	L. O.	F	58	162.5	68.9	Unmodified	40	83	62	51	63	62	72	92	113	96	115	92	95	129					
						Protamine zinc	40	97	88	96	89	88	83	83	87	103	98	96	100	111	113	106			
						Histone zinc	40	78	88	77	66	62	85	56	51	104	110	107	98	91					

7	J. V.	F	50	157.5	54.4	Unmodified	80	217	117	52	61	64	105	139	146	152	144	171	178	200	210	214		
						Protamine zinc	80	302	316	320	293	234	244	234	205	209	195	237	197	212	209	221		
						Histone zinc	80	225	283	214	210	142	150	142	145	138	182	212	239	234	224	187		
8	G. G.	F	60	162.5	54.9	Crystalline	20	126	130	93	92	107	129	112	119	127	138	133	163	180				
						Protamine zinc	20	116	138	156	154	141	131	130	118	133	131	114	121	118				
						Histone zinc	20	127	120	99	99	103	102	118	105	114	114	101	104	123				
9	S. S.	M	58	165.1	70.3	Unmodified	55	124	86	48	62	82	105	113	130	187	146	152	113	125	135	145		
						Protamine zinc	55	114	173	144	150	152	118		123	81	77	109	99	92	99	148		
						Histone zinc	55	91	139	140	90	78	77	86	101	82	77	81	84	96	118	141		
10	J. B.	M	65	157.5	63.5	Unmodified	22	91	106	131	90	76	69	85	82	102	78	102	98	97	129	157		
						Protamine zinc	22	95	133	148	163	138	140	102	135	106	105	143	122	124	144	169		
						Histone zinc	22	86	102	123	111	106	129	121	157	136	122		100	102		128		
11	J. J.	M	56	174	77.1	Unmodified	48	189	91	72	76	87	109	120	142	159	163	207	209	219	224	203		
						Protamine zinc	48	209	224	203	134	117	89	103	149	181	197	200	203	216	229	225		
						Histone zinc	48	189	193	150	138	111	93	84	118	104	111	136	146	169	166	171		
12*	T. B.	M	47	172.7	70.8	Unmodified	15	92	60	76	80	89	92	101	92	105								
						Crystalline	15	84	51	49	65	77	90	96	101	89								
						Protamine zinc	15	97	89	89	88		77	81	78	74	76		76	87	114			
						Histone zinc	15	101	85	71	80	71	75	91	91	98	89		117	99	101	111		
13	A. Z.	M	62	165.7	61.2	Unmodified	30	90	84	51	52	81			93									
						Crystalline	30	113	47	56	56	88	90	118	118	107								
						Protamine zinc	30	90	81	102	77	73	77		63	59	53		67		80	85		
						Histone zinc	30	94	98	76	66	71	77	73	71	72	71		82	90	78	96	82	84

* Non-diabetic subject.

to secure a continuously normal blood sugar level and a freedom from glycosuria in a larger number of patients after a single morning injection of histone zinc insulin than is possible when other preparations are employed.

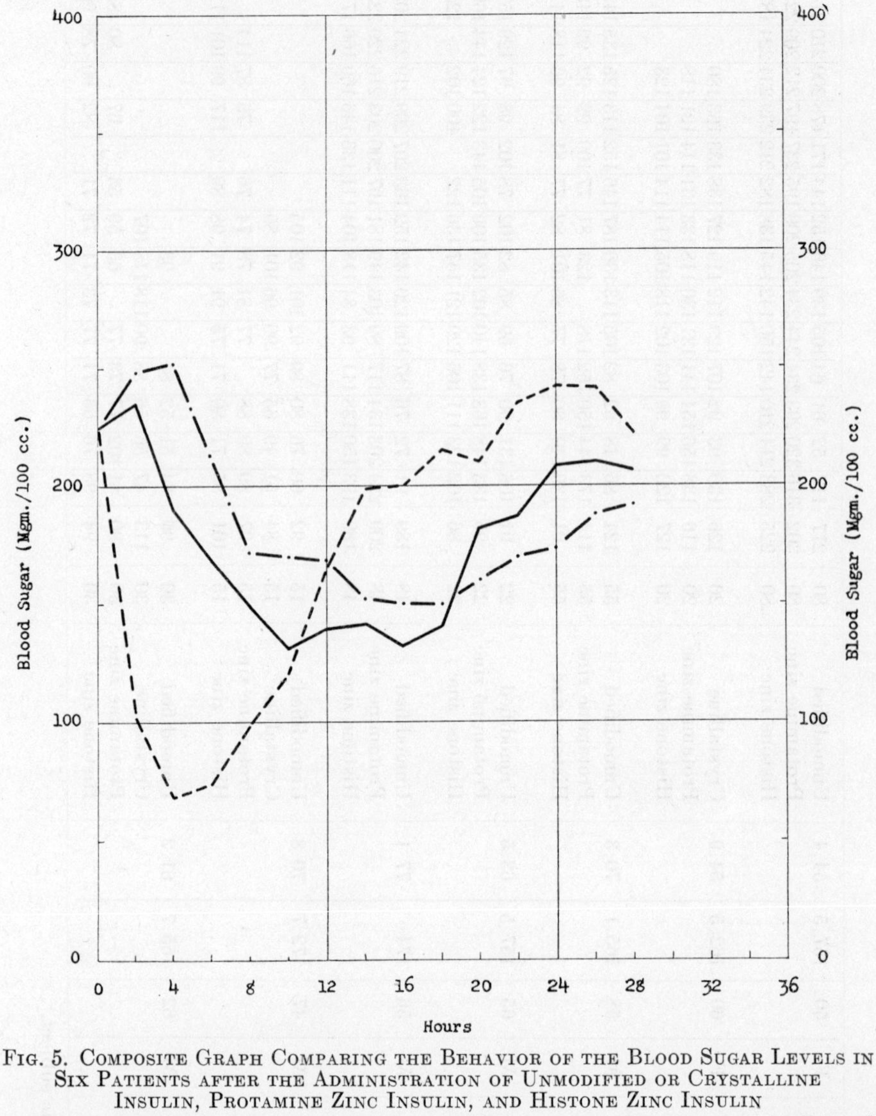

FIG. 5. COMPOSITE GRAPH COMPARING THE BEHAVIOR OF THE BLOOD SUGAR LEVELS IN SIX PATIENTS AFTER THE ADMINISTRATION OF UNMODIFIED OR CRYSTALLINE INSULIN, PROTAMINE ZINC INSULIN, AND HISTONE ZINC INSULIN

The rapid and short lived effect of the unmodified or crystalline insulin, the delayed but prolonged action of the protamine zinc insulin, and the effect of histone zinc insulin, which falls between these two, are apparent.

Histone Zinc Insulin, ——; Protamine Zinc Insulin, .—.; Unmodified or Crystalline Insulin, — — —

We are indebted to the Eli Lilly Company for their generous supply of histone zinc insulin used in this investigation and to Harry P. Trueman, Harry F. Dickenson and Allan Mitchell for their technical assistance.

BIBLIOGRAPHY

(1) Hagedorn, Jensen, Krarup and Wodstrup: J. A. M. A., **106**: 177, 1936.
(2) Biasotti, Deulefeu and Mendive: Prensa. med. argent., **24**: 1122, 1937.
(3) Gray, Bischoff and Sansum: Ann. Int. Med., **11**: 274, 1937.
(4a) Marble and Vartiainen: J. A. M. A., **113**: 1303, 1939.
(4b) Ricketts and Wilder: Ibid., **113**: 1310, 1939.
(4c) Duncan, Cuttle and Jewesbury: Bull. Ayer Clin. Lab., Pennsylvania Hospital, **3**: 293, 1939.
(5) Benedict: J. Biol. Chem., **76**: 457, 1938.

QUANTITATIVE GASTROINTESTINAL ABSORPTION AND RENAL EXCRETION OF PROPYLENE GLYCOL

W. VAN WINKLE, JR.

From the Department of Pharmacology, Stanford University School of Medicine, San Francisco, California

Received for publication April 14, 1941

Propylene glycol is practically a non-toxic solvent or vehicle and preservative for medicinal and food products, and possesses a definite glycogenic action. These collective properties are not shared by other glycols thus far investigated, or by ethyl alcohol (1, 2, 3). These desirable properties have resulted in an extensive and increasing utility in the pharmaceutical and food industries and in medicine for drugs, chemicals, vitamins, and hormones for internal use, and recently it has been proposed as an antiseptic aerosol (9). Oral administration of propylene glycol has frequently resulted in such rapid, spectacular absorption that it was thought desirable to obtain more data according to more direct criteria of quantitative absorption and excretion than the indirect criteria used heretofore. It appeared especially desirable to determine how the absorption from the alimentary canal compared with that of ethyl alcohol, which obeys fairly definite laws. This was deemed essential for a further and more complete understanding of this glycol before its general use in pharmaceutical products and foods is officially approved. This report presents the results of extensive studies of the quantitative aspects of gastrointestinal absorption and of renal excretion of this glycol.

Most of the data on absorption were obtained on cats, comparisons with rats and rabbits being made where indicated. Differences between species will be pointed out where such differences occurred. In general, ligated intestinal loops were employed for the determination of absorption, variable amounts and concentrations of propylene glycol being injected directly into the loop.

ABSORPTION

Absorption according to anatomical site of the gastrointestinal tract

A total of 48 cats, 72 rats and 16 rabbits was used for this purpose. In some experiments loops of intestine 15 cm. long were ligated, in others the entire stomach or colon was ligated and the absorption from these regions determined. Ten cc. of 10 per cent propylene glycol per kilo of body weight were injected into the loops. At the end of the absorption period each loop was removed and washed with 150 cc. of distilled water. The volume of washings was made up to 200 cc. and the propylene glycol determined in an aliquot portion according to the method of Lehman and Newman (4). The results on cats are shown in figure 1 as curves of average absorption from different anatomical regions of the alimentary canal. The results on rabbits and rats were tabulated, but the tabulations are omitted to save space. For one thing, the absorption in rabbits and cats was the same, and therefore, figure 1 suffices to illustrate the actual, quantitative results in both species.

Rats showed a somewhat more rapid absorption of the glycol than cats and rabbits, but the quantitative relations were similar. For instance, absorption from the jejunum was complete within 20 to 30 minutes in rats, but was only 91 per cent in cats and rabbits at the end of 1 hour. All animals showed

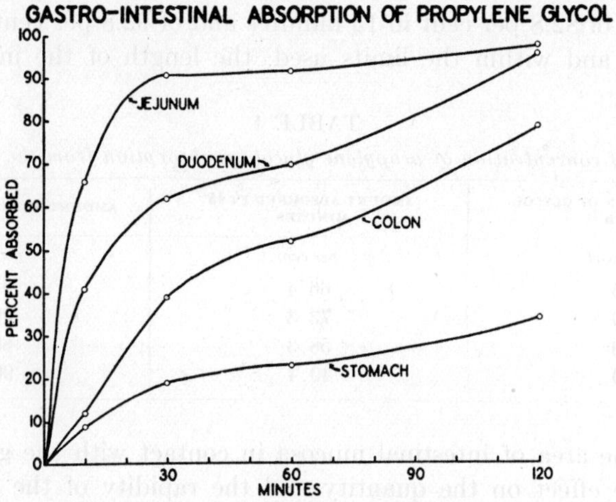

FIG. 1. GASTROINTESTINAL ABSORPTION OF PROPYLENE GLYCOL ACCORDING TO ANATOMICAL SITE

absorption of this glycol from both the stomach and colon, in agreement with the absorption of ethyl alcohol reported by Hanzlik and Collins (5). No difference between the absorption of propylene glycol from the jejunum and ileum could be detected and the results were lumped together.

Effect of concentration on absorption

Ten cats were used. Four equal loops of jejunum were tied off and the glycol introduced in concentrations of 5, 10, 50 and 100 per cent. Care was taken to keep the absolute quantity of the glycol the same in each loop. In half the cats the absorption period was 15 minutes, in the others one hour. The results obtained are shown in table 1.

It is seen that the lower concentrations of propylene glycol were more rapidly absorbed than the higher, the difference between the per cent absorbed from a 10 per cent concentration and a 100 per cent concentration being more than twice the variation between the absorption of the same concentration in different animals. This is different from phenol and alcohol where concentration made no difference in absorption. At the end of one hour all concentrations were about equally absorbed.

Effect of area of absorbing surface on intestinal absorption

Ten cats were used. Two loops of jejunum, one 15 cm. and one 75 cm. long, were tied off. Equal quantities of 10 per cent propylene glycol were injected into each loop. In half the cats the absorption period was 15 minutes, in the others one hour. The average per cent absorption from the shorter loops (smaller area) was 83.7 per cent in 15 minutes and 91 per cent in one hour. The results were almost the same for the intestinal loops 5 times longer, i.e., averages of 82.8 per cent in 15 minutes and of 92.8 per cent in one hour. Accordingly, and within the limits used, the length of the intestinal loop,

TABLE 1

Effect of concentration of propylene glycol on absorption from the jejunum

CONCENTRATION OF GLYCOL USED	AMOUNT ABSORBED IN 15 MINUTES	AMOUNT ABSORBED IN 1 HOUR
per cent	*per cent*	*per cent*
5	66.4	91.5
10	73.3	95.2
50	58.3	88.2
100	49.4	90.7

and hence the area of intestinal mucosa in contact with the glycol, had no demonstrable effect on the quantity and the rapidity of the absorption of glycol. This was also true for alcohol (5).

Inhibition of absorption

The results on the effects of concentration of propylene glycol on absorption suggested that the higher concentrations might cause an inhibition of absorption. Inhibition of absorption has been shown for alcohol, phenol and iodide (5, 6, 7). Experiments similar to those used for alcohol were made with propylene glycol. In each of 5 cats, 4 equal loops of jejunum were tied off. Five cc. of 10 per cent propylene glycol per kilogram body weight were injected into the first loop. After 15 minutes a blood sample was taken from the mesenteric vein of this loop and the loop excised. The second loop was then injected with the same quantity of propylene glycol, and immediately 2.5 cc. of 50 per cent propylene glycol per kilogram were injected rapidly into the saphenous vein. At the end of another 15 minutes, a blood sample was taken, as before, and the loop excised. The third loop was injected next with propylene glycol, as before, and a slow intravenous infusion of 50 per cent propylene glycol begun. After 15 minutes, a blood sample was taken from a mesenteric vein and the infusion stopped. Both the third and fourth loops were excised, the latter loop being a control on possible re-excretion of propylene glycol into the intestine. The results are shown in table 2.

It is seen that, with a rising concentration of propylene glycol in the intestinal venous blood, there was a decrease in rate of absorption of the glycol from the lumen of the same intestine. The saturation of the blood might be responsible for the inhibition of absorption. However, the effect might be due to a decreased blood flow through the intestine resulting either from a local damaging effect produced by the handling of the loops, to the operation involved in removing portions of the gastrointestinal tract, or to the intravenous injection of a presumably hypertonic solution resulting in a fall of blood pressure, splanchnic pooling, and decreased blood flow through the intestine.

To test this, a second series of loops was used exactly similar to those

TABLE 2

*Increasing mesenteric blood concentration of propylene glycol on absorption of the glycol from loops of small intestine**

	LOOP 1	LOOP 2	LOOP 3	LOOP 4
Glycol absorbed (per cent)	85.4	78.5	70.4	0
Mesenteric blood concentration of glycol (mgm. per cent)	345	869	1321	

* The loops were injected with glycol and removed in the order numbered in the table, Loop 1 being first, and Loop 4, last.

described above but substituting another substance for the intravenous injection. It was thought desirable to use some naturally occuring body constituent in an equivalent osmotic concentration for this injection. In order to choose such a substance, it was first necessary to determine how propylene glycol behaved osmotically. This was tested simply by determining the concentration necessary to produce hemolysis in cat's blood. To a series of tubes containing 5 cc. quantities of various concentrations of propylene glycol in distilled water, or in 0.9 per cent sodium chloride, 0.02 cc. of cat's blood was added. The mixture was shaken, allowed to stand for 40 minutes, centrifuged, and the hemoglobin estimated in the supernatant liquid with a photoelectric colorimeter.

Propylene glycol was found to hemolyze blood in all concentrations in distilled water. However, in 0.9 per cent saline solution, hemolysis did not commence until the concentration of propylene glycol reached 38 per cent, and was complete at 45 per cent. Hence propylene glycol acted much like urea in its osmotic behavior. For this reason a 40 per cent solution of urea was used as the control injection fluid. A 40 per cent aqueous urea solution is the moledular equivalent of a 50 per cent aqueous propylene glycol solution. The results with the urea solution used intravenously, instead of the propylene glycol solution, are presented in table 3.

It is seen that the mesenteric blood glycol concentrations did not rise above those found without the injection of urea (table 2). Whereas the blood concentration of propylene glycol was increased four-fold and the rate of absorption from the intestine decreased 15 per cent, without the use of urea (table 2), the blood concentration of propylene glycol remained low and the absorption rate was decreased only 3 per cent, when urea was used (table 3). Therefore these results suggested an inhibition of absorption. This inhibition was most probably related to a high blood concentration of propylene glycol rather than to the effects of operative procedure, intravenous injection, or change of blood flow resulting from these procedures. This is true because the two sets of experiments were identical as to operative and injection

TABLE 3

*Effect of intravenous injection of 40 per cent urea solution on absorption of 50 per cent propylene glycol from loops of small intestine**

	LOOP 1	LOOP 2	LOOP 3	LOOP 4
Glycol absorbed (per cent)	72.3	67.4	69.5	0
Mesenteric blood concentration of glycol (mgm. per cent)	231	314	342	

* The loops were used in the same way as in Table 2.

procedures, the only difference being in the solution used for injection. These results do not rule out the possibility that the inhibition of absorption might have resulted from a slowing of the circulation caused by the presence of a high blood concentration of propylene glycol. The blood pressure was not recorded, but judging from the results of previous experiments (4) we believe that it was probably lowered somewhat.

A further test of this explanation of the inhibition of absorption was made on 10 cats in which the operative procedure was less extensive. Following a rapid intravenous injection of 2.5 cc. of 50 per cent propylene glycol per kilogram, a loop of jejunum of 15 cm. length was ligated and 5 cc. of 10 per cent propylene glycol per kilogram placed into the loop. After 15 minutes, a sample of blood was removed from a mesenteric vein and the loop excised. The average blood concentration of glycol was 1032 mgm. per cent, the average absorption of glycol 56 per cent. This was the smallest absorption ever demonstrated for a 15-minute absorption period, which supports the explanation that an inhibition of absorption resulted from a high concentration of propylene glycol in the blood stream. The physical factor in the absorption was important in that an evenness of the glycol concentration on the opposite sides of the absorbing surface tended to limit or arrest the absorption.

Effect of variations in absolute amount of glycol in intestine on absorption

In order to determine whether the absolute quantity of propylene glycol in a loop of intestine altered the rate of absorption, the following experiment was performed: In each of 5 cats, 3 loops of jejunum 15 cm. in length were ligated. Into the first loop 0.5 cc. of 50 per cent propylene glycol per kilogram was introduced, into the second loop 1.0 cc. per kilogram, and into the third loop 2.0 cc. per kilogram. After 15 minutes the loops were excised and the residual propylene glycol determined. The results are presented in table 4.

It is seen that, although the actual quantity of absolute propylene glycol absorbed increased as the amount of glycol in the intestine increased, i.e., 0.4 cc., 0.69 cc. and 1.14 cc., the percentage absorbed decreased. This was consistent with an inhibition of absorption described in the previous section.

TABLE 4

Effect of different quantities of 50 per cent propylene glycol on absorption from intestine

	LOOP 1	LOOP 2	LOOP 3
Quantity of glycol introduced (cc. per kgm.)	0.5	1.0	2.0
Average absolute amount of glycol absorbed (cc.)	0.4	0.69	1.14
Average per cent absorbed	79.5	68.8	57.0

Effect of iodoacetic acid and chloral on the intestinal absorption

It is claimed by Verzár and co-workers (8) that iodoacetic acid specifically inhibits the absorption of dextrose, galactose, glycerol, fats, lipoids, and certain other substances, reducing their rate of absorption as compared with pentose sugars and other substances which are absorbed by "non-specific" mechanisms. Since propylene glycol is absorbed with great rapidity, like dextrose and glycerol, it was of interest to determine whether iodoacetic acid decreased the absorption rate of this polyalcohol. Since iodoacetic acid must be given in very large doses for any inhibitory effects, the inhibition might be due to a general non-specific depression. Therefore the tests with this acid were controlled with large doses of chloral, a well known general and protoplasmic depressant. The dose of iodoacetic acid used was 100 mgm. per kilogram, that of chloral 300 mgm. per kilogram, both being injected subcutaneously. In all, 8 cats were used. The results were negative throughout, no difference in absorption being demonstrable between the poisoned animals (both iodoacetic and chloral) and the unpoisoned controls. We conclude that the absorption of propylene glycol was not mediated through some specific mechanism which might be inhibited by iodoacetic acid.

DISTRIBUTION OF PROPYLENE GLYCOL IN THE CIRCULATION DURING ABSORPTION FROM THE GASTROINTESTINAL TRACT

The concentration of propylene glycol in the portal and venous bloods (right heart) was determined in 48 cats during absorption of propylene glycol from different regions of the gastrointestinal tract. The doses and method of administration of the glycol used have been described in the first section of this report. The average results are presented in figure 2.

It is seen that there were considerable variations in the blood concentration of the glycol during absorption from the stomach and colon. This was not

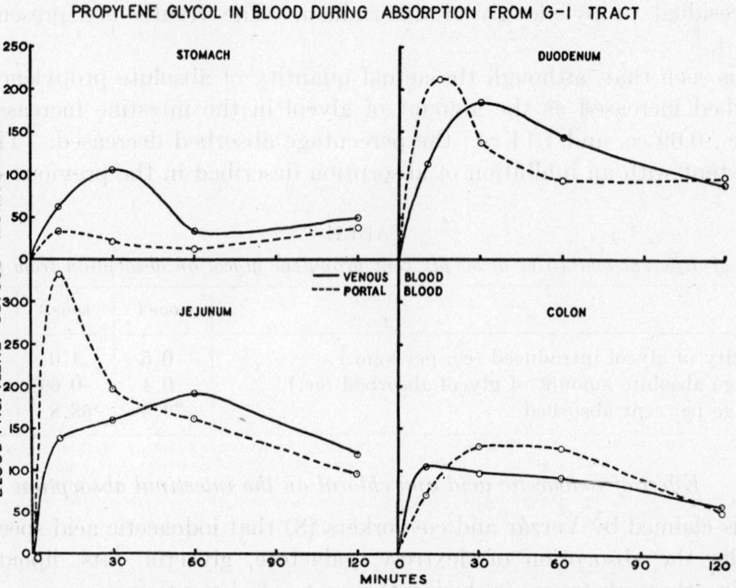

FIG. 2. BLOOD CONTENT OF GLYCOL DURING ABSORPTION OF PROPYLENE GLYCOL FROM DIFFERENT REGIONS OF THE GASTROINTESTINAL TRACT

surprising, since there are two possible venous paths from these organs, one to the general venous system directly, another to the portal system. In general the results indicated a higher concentration in the caval system than in the portal, this difference becoming less as absorption was completed. The reverse was true for the jejunum and duodenum, the portal concentration being initially much higher than the caval, and later the caval being slightly higher than the portal. In general the distribution of propylene glycol in the blood stream was found to be about as might be expected anatomically and physiologically.

RENAL EXCRETION OF PROPYLENE GLYCOL

Five rats were placed in individual cages suspended above funnels in such a way that the urine could be collected quantitatively, free from feces. Food and water were allowed freely. After a control period of 8 or 9 days, during which fluid intake and fluid output were recorded daily, the drinking water was changed to a solution of propylene glycol, the concentrations used being 5, 10, 15 and 20 per cent. Daily records were made of fluid intake and output,

TABLE 5

Fluid balance in rats drinking different concentrations of propylene glycol

RAT	CHANGE IN* MEAN FLUID INTAKE	CHANGE IN* MEAN FLUID OUTPUT	BODY WEIGHT CHANGE DURING GLYCOL PERIOD	BODY WEIGHT CHANGE IN THE FIRST 24 HOURS ON WATER†
	5 per cent propylene glycol			
	cc. per diem	*cc. per diem*	*grams*	*grams*
1	−7 ±2.01	−2.7 ±0.37	−4	0
2	−3 ±1.10	−1.3 ±0.69	+7	+1
3	−1 ±1.61	−0.2 ±0.18	+5	+2
4	0	+0.1 ±0.50	+2	+1
5	−2 ±4.76	+0.2 ±0.25	+1	−1
	10 per cent propylene glycol			
1	0	+1.2 ±0.92	+3	+1
2	+9 ±1.45	+6.7 ±1.49	−5	+3
3	−1 ±2.08	+0.7 ±0.56	+2	+0
4	+6 ±2.11	+6.1 ±2.09	−3	+2
5	0	+2.9 ±0.79	−5	+4
	15 per cent propylene glycol			
1	−3 ±1.83	+4.4 ±1.46	−28	+20
2	+4 ±2.55	+10.7 ±3.40	−39	+23
3	+3 ±1.50	+4.8 ±0.66	−17	+15
4	−1 ±2.56	+3.1 ±1.27	−29	+5
5	+3 ±1.14	+6.0 ±1.94	−41	+23
	20 per cent propylene glycol			
1	−6 ±1.46	+2.7 ±0.79	−65	+36
2	−9 ±1.58	+2.6 ±1.68	−64	+35
3	−6 ±1.76	+3.4 ±0.87	−59	+35
4	−16 ±2.76	0	−97	+44

* Mean change ± standard error of mean.

† Change in body weight during first 24 hours after glycol period was terminated; − = decrease, + = increase.

and daily analyses of urine for glycol content. After one week on the glycol the solution was replaced by water and the observations continued. When this second control on fluid balance was obtained the rats were given another concentration of propylene glycol and the observations repeated. The results obtained are presented in table 5.

It is seen that when the rats drank a concentration of 5 per cent propylene glycol they showed little, if any, change in fluid balance. On 10 or 15 per cent propylene glycol the fluid intake was only slightly increased. However, the fluid output was uniformly increased in all these rats and the net result was a dehydrating action, especially with 15 per cent propylene glycol. On the 20 per cent concentration the disagreeable taste of the mixture reduced the fluid intake markedly, but at the same time the fluid output was increased. As a result the animals lost nearly one-third their body weight in 1 week. That this was largely due to loss of water was shown by the fact that one-half this weight loss was regained within 24 hours when water was substituted for the glycol solution, and 90 per cent was regained within 48 hours. The relationship between fluid intake and output is indicated by the summary in table 6, which also shows the urinary excretion of propylene glycol.

TABLE 6

Renal excretion of propylene glycol in rats

CONCENTRATION OF GLYCOL IN DRINKING WATER	RATIO: INTAKE TO OUTPUT		CONCENTRATION OF GLYCOL IN URINE
	Fluid	Glycol	
per cent			*per cent*
0	4.1	—	—
5	3.6	4.5	3.6
10	2.7	3.1	8.4
15	2.2	3.1	10.6
20	1.9	3.5	10.0

This summary shows that, as the concentration of propylene glycol in the drinking water increased, the ratio between the fluid intake and output decreased. However, the ratio between glycol intake and output remained quite constant, indicating that, regardless of the concentration of glycol drunk, the kidneys excreted approximately one-third the amount ingested. The remaining two-thirds of the glycol must have been metabolized by the body. Apparently the rats, under the conditions used, were unable to concentrate the glycol beyond 10 per cent in the urine. No hematuria occurred.

SUMMARY AND CONCLUSIONS

1. Propylene glycol was found to be readily absorbed from all anatomical regions of the gastrointestinal tract of rabbits, rats, and cats, i.e., from the stomach, duodenum, jejunum and colon, the absorption being particularly rapid from the jejunum.

2. The following quantitative characteristics of the intestinal absorption of this glycol were demonstrated: absorption was more rapid with low concentrations than high; rate of absorption was not affected by variations in

the area of the intestinal surface; inhibition of absorption occurred during high blood concentrations of the glycol; rate of absorption decreased as the absolute amount of glycol in a given region increased; iodoacetic acid and chloral had no demonstrable effects on the absorption, thus differing from dextrose, glycerol, fats and lipoids; during absorption, large differences in concentration of the glycol occurred in different parts of the venous circulation of the gastrointestinal tract.

3. Propylene glycol in distilled water hemolyzed blood in all concentrations, but, in 0.9 per cent sodium chloride, hemolysis did not occur until the concentration reached 38 per cent, and was complete at 45 per cent.

4. A marked dehydrating action occurred in rats drinking concentrations above 5 per cent of this glycol, the ratio of intake to output remaining constant in rats drinking freely various concentrations.

5. Approximately one-third the administered propylene glycol was excreted by the kidneys, the remaining two-thirds being metabolized in the body.

6. The concentration of propylene glycol in the urine did not exceed 10 per cent, after the drinking of highest tolerated doses by rats.

7. In general, the quantitative gastrointestinal absorption of propylene glycol agreed in several respects with that demonstrated by others previously for alcohol, phenol and iodide, except that absorption of propylene glycol was more rapid and complete.

REFERENCES

(1) Hanzlik, Newman, Lehman, Van Winkle and Kennedy: This Journal, **67**: **101**, 1939.
(2) Hanzlik, Lehman, Van Winkle and Kennedy: Ibid., **67**: 114, 1940.
(3) Newman, Van Winkle, Kennedy and Morton: Ibid., **68**: 194, 1940.
(4) Lehman and Newman: Ibid., **60**: 312, 1937.
(5) Hanzlik and Collins: Ibid., **5**: 185, 1913.
(6) Sollman, Hanzlik and Pilcher: Ibid., **1**: 409, 1910.
(7) Hanzlik: Ibid., **3**: 387, 1912.
(8) Verzar and MacDougall: Absorption from the Intestine. Longmans Green and Co., London, 1936.
(9) Robertson, Bigg, Miller and Baker: Science, **93**: 214, 1941.

THE PRODUCTION IN CULTURES CONTAINING SODIUM PARANITROBENZOATE OF A SUBSTANCE THAT AFFECTS THE ACTION OF SULFATHIAZOLE

JOHN K. MILLER

From the Division of Laboratories and Research, New York State Department of Health, Albany

Received for publication April 17, 1941

In a previous investigation (1), a temporary growth-retarding action of sodium paranitrobenzoate on a strain of *Streptococcus viridans* (no. 40108) was observed. This bacteriostatic effect could be inhibited by the addition of 0.05 mgm. per cent of sodium para-aminobenzoate to the medium. The growth of a second strain (no. 4022) was affected little, if at all, by sodium paranitrobenzoate. When growth of these strains did occur in the presence of the paranitrobenzoate, it was accompanied by the appearance in the medium of a substance, presumably a primary aromatic amine, that was detectable by diazotization and coupling with dimethyl-alpha-naphthylamine, following the method of Marshall (2, 3). Also, it was noted that plain broth cultures of these strains contained a substance similarly detectable but occurring in lesser concentrations and after longer incubation.

Since one aromatic amine derivative, para-aminobenzoic acid, has been found to inhibit the bacteriostatic action of sulfanilamide (4), these observations raised the question whether the amine produced in cultures of streptococcus grown in broth alone or in broth containing sodium paranitrobenzoate can likewise affect the bacteriostatic effect of sulfanilamide or any of its derivatives on *Streptococcus viridans*. Preparatory to the experiments directed toward answering this question, it was necessary to determine the susceptibility of the two strains to the sulfanilamide compounds, and to ascertain whether para-aminobenzoic acid or similar compounds affected the growth-retarding action of the drugs on our strains.

MATERIALS AND METHODS

Two strains of streptococcus isolated from the blood of two cases with a clinical diagnosis of subacute bacterial endocarditis were used; both are insoluble in bile and produce a greenish discoloration of blood agar. Strain no. 40108 is a Gram-positive coccus that grows in chains and forms small, gray, glistening colonies on blood agar. Strain no. 4022, a Gram-positive oval coccus, has a more mucoid growth and ferments lactose, mannite, and salicin, whereas strain no. 40108 ferments lactose but not mannite or salicin.

Culture medium. Beef-infusion broth containing 2-per-cent peptone and 0.02-per-cent dextrose.

Cultures. Serial dilutions in broth were made of a 15-hour infusion-broth culture of the test strain. Duplicate blood-agar poured plates containing 10^{-6} and 10^{-8} cc. of the culture were incubated for 48 hours and the colonies counted. Each colony was considered to represent one microorganism.

(*a*) To determine the susceptibility of the streptococci to sulfanilamide derivatives and the effect of sodium para-aminobenzoate on any growth-retarding action, 9.5 cc. of broth or broth containing 5, 25, or 100 mgm. per cent of the compound to be tested were inoculated with 0.5 cc. of a 1 to 5000 or 1 to 500,000 dilution of a 15-hour broth culture of each strain. To a second similar series of cultures, 0.05 or 0.005 mgm. per cent of sodium para-aminobenzoate was added. After 20, 26, and 48 hours' incubation at approximately 37°C., 0.5 cc. of each culture, appropriately diluted in broth, was plated in blood agar (15–16 cc.) and incubated for 144 hours; in addition, 0.005 mgm. (approximately 0.03 mgm. per cent) of sodium para-aminobenzoate was added to duplicate plates of all cultures containing a sulfanilamide compound alone. In such plates inoculated with 0.1 cc. or more of culture, distinct colonies appeared after 24 hours' incubation, as will be demonstrated later, whereas in the absence of the para-aminobenzoate, colonies were detectable, if at all, only after 72 hours' incubation. Colonies were counted every 24 hours. In this manner the action of sulfanilamide, sulfapyridine, sulfadiazine, sulfathiazole, and sulfamethylthiazole was tested.

By similar methods, the effect of 0.2-mgm.-per-cent concentrations of para-aminophenol, para-aminoacetophenone, para-aminophenylacetic acid, meta-aminobenzoic acid, and glycine on the bacteriostatic action of sulfanilamide was studied.

(*b*) To demonstrate the production of the aromatic amine substance in cultures of each strain of streptococcus grown in plain broth as compared with broth containing 10 or 400 mgm. per cent of sodium paranitrobenzoate, the same procedure was followed. After 6, 12, and 24 hours' incubation, blood agar poured plates were made, and samples of each culture were taken for determination by Marshall's method of the presence of the aromatic amine substance. Broth solutions of sodium para-aminobenzoate were used as standards. Recovery of from 90 to 95 per cent or more of the added drug was obtained in control determinations of these standards.

(*c*) To investigate the effect of the aromatic amine substances produced in these cultures on the action of a sulfanilamide derivative, 48-hour cultures of each strain grown in broth alone and in broth containing 25 mgm. per cent of sodium paranitrobenzoate were passed through a Mandler filter, and the amount of aromatic amine substance in each filtrate determined. Amounts of each filtrate sufficient to give at least 0.05 mgm. per cent of each amine compound, computed as sodium para-aminobenzoate, were added to cultures of strain no. 40108 in broth alone, and in broth containing 25 mgm. per cent of sulfathiazole; control cultures included broth cultures with and without sulfathiazole and broth cultures containing sulfathiazole in combination with 0.05 mgm. per cent of sodium para-aminobenzoate. After 20 and 26 hours' incubation at approximately 37°C., 0.5-cc. amounts of each culture, appropriately diluted, were plated in blood agar. Plates were incubated for 144 hours and counted every 24 hours.

(*d*) To observe the effect on the growth-retarding action of sulfathiazole of different concentrations of sodium paranitrobenzoate (a possible precursor of the aromatic amine substance found in cultures growing in its presence), cultures of strain no. 40108 in plain broth, in broth with 25 mgm. per cent of sulfathiazole, and in broth with 25 mgm. per cent of sulfathiazole plus 10 or 400 mgm. per cent of sodium paranitrobenzoate were incubated and the amount of growth at 12, 20, 26, and 48 hours determined by the usual methods.

RESULTS

Growth-retarding action of sulfanilamide derivatives on Streptococcus viridans and the effect of various compounds on this action. Sulfanilamide, sulfapyridine, sulfadiazine, sulfathiazole, and sulfamethylthiazole, even in 100-mgm.-per-cent concentrations, had no demonstrable effect on the growth of strain no. 4022. On the other hand, 25- and 100-mgm.-per-cent concentrations of sulfathiazole, sulfamethylthiazole, sulfapyridine, and, to a lesser extent, sulfanilamide and sulfadiazine had a growth-retarding action on strain no. 40108.

TABLE 1

The effect of sodium para-aminobenzoate on the growth-retarding action of sulfanilamide compounds on Streptococcus viridans, strain no. 40108

COMPOUND: 25 MGM. PER CENT	SODIUM PARA-AMINO-BENZOATE	COLONIES PER CC. OF CULTURE		
		Before incubation	Incubated at ±37°C. for	
			20 hours	48 hours
	mgm. per cent			
Control		2050	125,000,000	100,000,000
Sulfanilamide		2050	124,000	850,000
"	0.05	2050	155,000,000	130,000,000
Control		1900	365,000,000	
Sulfapyridine		1900	190,000	2,000
"	0.05	1900	180,000,000	
Control		1900	365,000,000	
Sulfamethylthiazole		1900	175,000	400
"	0.05	1900	42,000,000	70,000,000
Control		1100	255,000,000	
Sulfathiazole		1100	65,000	10
"	0.05	1100	13,500,000	35,000,000
Control		1750	150,000,000	
Sulfadiazine		1750	365,000	
"	0.05	1750	170,000,000	

Five-milligram-per-cent concentrations of these compounds were less effective.

This bacteriostatic action of these sulfanilamide compounds was inhibited by 0.05 mgm. per cent of sodium para-aminobenzoate. The results with 25 mgm. per cent of the sulfanilamides are shown in table 1. However, 0.005-mgm.-per-cent concentrations of sodium para-aminobenzoate did not affect materially the growth-retarding action of 25 mgm. per cent of sulfathiazole during 48 hours' incubation.

During the studies it was observed that, in blood-agar poured plates inoculated with 0.1 cc. or more of cultures containing 25 mgm. per cent or more of growth-inhibiting sulfanilamide compounds, colonies began to appear, if at all, only after 72 hours' incubation. If approximately 0.03 mgm. per cent of sodium para-aminobenzoate was added to the blood agar at the time such cultures were plated, distinct colonies appeared after 24 hours' incubation. Table 2 illustrates this effect in cultures containing 25 mgm. per cent of sulfathiazole. Hence, in all studies in which cultures containing a sulfanilamide derivative were plated in amounts of 0.1 cc. or more, duplicate plates containing sodium para-aminobenzoate were also made.

TABLE 2

The effect of sodium para-aminobenzoate on the appearance of colonies of strain no. 40108 in blood agar containing sulfathiazole

AMOUNT OF CULTURE PLATED*	SODIUM PARA-AMINOBENZOATE ADDED TO BLOOD AGAR	COLONIES IN BLOOD AGAR POURED PLATES INCUBATED AT ±37°C. FOR				
		24 hours	48 hours	72 hours	96 hours	144 hours
	mgm.					
Control no. 1 No sulfathiazole 10^{-7} cc.		11, 19	11, 19	11, 19	11, 19	11, 19
Culture no. 1 Sulfathiazole 0.5 cc.	 0.005	0, 0 small colonies	0, 0 776, 728	0, 0 776, 728	0, 0 776, 728	0, 0 776, 728
Culture no. 1 Sulfathiazole 10^{-1} cc.	 0.005	0, 0 small colonies	0, 0 190, 170	0, 0 190, 170	42, 54 190, 170	99, 89 190, 170
Culture no. 1 Sulfathiazole 10^{-2} cc.	 0.005	16, 16 15, 17	16, 16 15, 17	16, 16 15, 17	16, 16 15, 17	16, 16 15, 17

* Culture after 20 hours' incubation at ±37°C. in infusion broth containing 25 mgm. per cent of sulfathiazole; 0.5 cc. of undiluted or diluted culture plated in approximately 15 cc. of melted agar to which 0.5 cc. of normal defibrinated blood had been added. Control cultures contained no sulfathiazole.

The antisulfanilamide effect of para-aminobenzoic acid was not duplicated by certain other amine compounds. In concentrations of 0.2 mgm. per cent para-aminophenol, para-aminoacetophenone, para-aminophenylacetic acid, meta-aminobenzoic acid, and glycine did not interfere with the growth-retarding action of 25 mgm. per cent of sulfathiazole in strain no. 40108.

As a result of these observations, it was evident that the bacteriostatic effect of a 25-mgm.-per-cent concentration of sulfathiazole on broth cultures of strain no. 40108 provided a favorable system for the study of possible antisulfathiazole action of the amine compounds produced by both strains of streptococcus growing in plain broth and in broth containing paranitrobenzoate.

The rate of production of aromatic amine substance by each strain of Streptococcus viridans in plain broth and in broth containing sodium paranitrobenzoate is shown in table 3. In plain broth cultures no amine compound detectable by Marshall's method was produced by either strain after 24 hours' incubation; but in other experiments after 48 hours, filtrates of cultures of strain

TABLE 3

The production of amine compound in cultures of Streptococcus viridans with and without sodium paranitrobenzoate

INOCULUM, NUMBER OF STREPTOCOCCI	SODIUM PARA-NITRO-BENZO-ATE	PERIODS OF INCUBATION AT ±37°C.					
		6 hour		12 hour		24 hours	
		Colonies per cc.	Amine compound	Colonies per cc.	Amine compound	Colonies per cc.	Amine compound
	mgm. per cent		*mgm. per cent*		*mgm. per cent*		*mgm. per cent*
Strain no. 40108							
115		19,000	0.00	105,600,000	0.00	260,000,000	0.00
11500		2,200,000	0.00	230,000,000	0.00	340,000,000	0.00
115	10	150	0.00	350	0.00	550,000	0.01
11500	10	35,000	0.00	50,000	tr	230,000,000	0.08
115	400	450	tr	10,700	0.01	115,000,000	0.25
11500	400	50,000	tr	1,835,000	0.01	140,000,000	0.50
Strain no. 4022							
500		2,660,000	0.00	300,000,000	0.00	460,000,000	0.00
50000		279,000,000	0.00	400,000,000	0.00	440,000,000	0.00
500	10	2,055,000	tr	185,000,000	0.04	360,000,000	0.05
50000	10	135,000,000	tr	340,000,000	0.08	400,000,000	0.10
500	400	535,000	tr	160,000,000	0.25	390,000,000	0.40
50000	400	60,000,000	0.05	250,000,000	0.28	420,000,000	0.45

tr = trace.

no. 40108 contained 0.21 mgm. per cent and those of strain no. 4022, 0.27 mgm. per cent. In broth cultures containing sodium paranitrobenzoate, on increase in bacterial multiplication, the aromatic amine substance was detectable before 24 hours and occurred in greater concentrations as growth continued. It was formed in larger amounts in the presence of higher concentrations of sodium paranitrobenzoate and the larger inocula of streptococci. In cultures of strain no. 4022, the growth of which was not inhibited by paranitrobenzoate, the aromatic amine compound appeared earlier and in larger amounts than in cultures of strain no. 40108 on which sodium paranitrobenzoate had a growth-retarding action. This may be the result of earlier and more rapid growth of no. 4022. The final concentration of aromatic amine compound was not greater in the cultures of the resistant strain than in those of the susceptible strain.

Effect of filtrates of streptococcus cultures grown in broth alone or in broth containing sodium paranitrobenzoate on the action of sulfathiazole. The addition of filtrates of the plain broth cultures of each strain to cultures of strain no. 40108 containing 25 mgm. per cent of sulfathiazole did not affect the growth-retarding action of sulfathiazole. In fact, in control cultures containing filtrate alone, there was some retardation of growth. The results are shown in table 4.

TABLE 4

The effect of filtrates of cultures of Streptococcus viridans grown in broth alone on the action of sulfathiazole on strain no. 40108

SULFATHIAZOLE	FILTRATES OF STRAIN NUMBER: 40108	FILTRATES OF STRAIN NUMBER: 4022	COLONIES PER CC. OF CULTURE: Before incubation	Incubated at ±37°C. for 20 hours	Incubated at ±37°C. for 48 hours
	Mgm. per cent of amine compound*				
mgm. per cent					
			12	270,000,000	
25			12	2,550	7,750
	0.0945		12	115,000	12,800,000
25	0.0945		12	800	750
		0.113	12	375,000	23,000,000
25		0.113	12	1,150	900

* Computed as sodium para-aminobenzoate.

On the other hand, as may be noted in table 5, filtrates of cultures of either strain grown in broth containing 25 mgm. per cent of sodium paranitrobenzoate, diluted to give a final concentration of 0.05 mgm. per cent of the aromatic amine substance, interfered with the growth-retarding action of sulfathiazole. This inhibitory effect was similar to that produced by 0.05 mgm. per cent of sodium para-aminobenzoate.

The results summarized in table 6 indicate that the growth-retarding action of sulfathiazole was affected only in cultures containing 400 mgm. per cent of sodium paranitrobenzoate inoculated with the larger number (2000 per cc.) of streptococci of strain no. 40108. A comparison of tables 3 and 6 shows that the action of sulfathiazole was demonstrably affected at a time when the aromatic amine substance might be expected to appear in cultures containing paranitrobenzoate, as noted in table 3. This substance appeared first in those cultures containing the greater concentration of sodium paranitrobenzoate and the larger inoculum of streptococci, and it was in similar

TABLE 5

The effect of filtrates of cultures of Streptococcus viridans containing 25 mgm. per cent of sodium paranitrobenzoate on the bacteriostatic action of sulfathiazole

INOCULUM, NUMBER OF STREPTOCOCCI, STRAIN NUMBER 40108	SULFATHIAZOLE	SODIUM PARA-AMINOBENZOATE	CULTURE FILTRATES OF STRAINS NUMBER 40108	CULTURE FILTRATES OF STRAINS NUMBER 4022	PERIODS OF INCUBATION AT ± 37°C. 20 hours	PERIODS OF INCUBATION AT ± 37°C. 26 hours
			Mgm. per cent amine compound*		Colonies per cc.	Colonies per cc.
	mgm. per cent	*mgm. per cent*				
80					170,000,000	150,000,000
80	25				1,600	3,700
80	25	0.05			13,000,000	40,000,000
80			0.05		140,000,000	130,000,000
80	25		0.05		26,500,000	60,000,000
80				0.05	130,000,000	200,000,000
80	25			0.05	16,900,000	55,000,000

* Computed as sodium para-aminobenzoate.

TABLE 6

The effect of sodium paranitrobenzoate on the growth-retarding action of sulfathiazole on strain no. 40108

SULFATHIAZOLE	SODIUM PARANITROBENZOATE	COLONIES PER CC. OF CULTURE: Before incubation	Incubated at ±37°C. for 12 hours	20 hours	48 hours
mgm. per cent	*mgm. per cent*				
		20	11,000,000	280,000,000	
		2000	125,100,000	210,000,000	
25		20	1,300	1,550	2,690
		2000	190,000	255,000	323,500
25	10	20	2,100	2,500	4,760
		2000	125,000	200,000	423,000
25	400	20	1,900	3,350	30,760
		2000	125,000	480,000	4,948,000

cultures that interference with the action of sulfathiazole was demonstrated first, as noted in table 6.

DISCUSSION

Swain (5) has reported that two strains of *Streptococcus viridans*, isolated from cases of subacute bacterial endocarditis that had been favorably influenced but not cured by chemotherapy, were susceptible to sulfapyridine *in vitro*, but that two other strains from cases unaffected by chemotherapy were sulfapyridine-resistant *in vitro*. This variation in susceptibility of strains of *Streptococcus viridans* to sulfanilamide compounds *in vitro* was observed in our studies. One strain was resistant to all five sulfanilamide compounds tested; with the other strain, sulfapyridine, sulfathiazole and its methyl derivative were about equally effective in retarding growth, while sulfanilamide and sulfadiazine retarded growth but to a lesser degree.

As Woods (4), Landy and Wyeno (6), and Strauss, Lowell, and Finland (7) have shown, para-aminobenzoic acid inhibits the bacteriostatic action of sulfanilamide. We have found that the sodium salt of para-aminobenzoic acid interferes with the action of all five sulfanilamide compounds tested. The earlier appearance of colonies in blood-agar poured plates inoculated with cultures of *Streptococcus viridans* containing sulfathiazole when sodium para-aminobenzoate was added to the plates is similar to the results obtained by the addition of para-aminobenzoate to cultures containing paranitrobenzoate (1).[1] Landy and Wyeno found that with decreasing amounts of para-aminobenzoic acid there was a decrease in the amount of growth in the presence of sulfanilamide compounds. This is in accord with our findings that 0.05 mgm. per cent was effective but that 0.005 mgm. per cent of sodium para-aminobenzoate was much less effective in inhibiting the action of 25 mgm. per cent of sulfathiazole.

Woods, and Landy and Wyeno, also observed that, of the various aromatic amine compounds tested, only para-aminobenzoic acid inhibited sulfanilamide to any degree. Our studies confirm this observation and suggest, as did the work of Woods, that both the amine and the carboxylic groups in the para position in the benzene ring appear to be necessary for interference with the bacteriostatic action of sulfanilamide by this type of inhibitor.

Concerning the nature of the substance in filtrates of streptococcus cultures grown in broth alone, little can be concluded. The production of a color by diazotization and coupling with a compound such as dimethyl-alpha-naphthylamine strongly suggests that it may be a primary aromatic amine.

On the other hand, filtrates of streptococcus cultures containing sodium paranitrobenzoate not only produced a color on diazotization and coupling with dimethyl-alpha-naphthylamine after from 6 to 12 hours' incubation, but also inhibited the growth-retarding action of sulfathiazole. The inhibiting effects were produced only by filtrates of cultures containing sodium paranitrobenzoate, and the diazo color reaction produced in cultures was more

[1] Since the completion of this work, Janeway (8) has reported similar observations.

marked with increased concentrations of the paranitrobenzoate. Since reduction of the nitro group in the paranitrobenzoate would yield para-aminobenzoate, the presence of which imparts to the cultures both the diazo color reaction and the capacity to inhibit sulfathiazole, these results suggest that para-aminobenzoate is formed by reduction of the sodium paranitrobenzoate in the cultures of *Streptococcus viridans.*

SUMMARY

Sulfapyridine, sulfathiazole, sulfamethylthiazole, and to a lesser degree, sulfanilamide, sulfadiazine, and sodium paranitrobenzoate had a growth-retarding action on one strain of *Streptococcus viridans;* a second strain was resistant to all these compounds. Sodium para-aminobenzoate interfered with their growth-retarding action.

Filtrates of cultures of both strains of streptococcus grown in broth alone and in broth to which sodium paranitrobenzoate had been added contained a substance, presumably a primary aromatic amine, that gave a color on diazotization and coupling with dimethyl-alpha-naphthylamine. The filtrates of plain broth cultures did not affect the growth-retarding action of sulfathiazole on the susceptible strain, but filtrates of either strain grown in broth containing sodium paranitrobenzoate interfered with the bacteriostatic action of sulfathiazole.

REFERENCES

(1) Miller: This Journal, **71**: 14, 1941.
(2) Marshall: J. Biol. Chem., **122**: 263, 1937.
(3) Marshall and Litchfield: Science, **88**: 85, 1938.
(4) Woods: Brit. J. Exper. Path., **21**: 74, 1940.
(5) Swain: Brit. M. J., **1**: 722, 1940.
(6) Landy and Wyeno: Proc. Soc. Exper. Biol. & Med., **46**: 59, 1941.
(7) Strauss, Lowell and Finland: J. Clin. Investigation, **20**: 189, 1941.
(8) Janeway: J. A. M. A., **116**: 941, 1941.

THE EFFECT OF POSTERIOR PITUITARY PREPARATIONS ON THE LARGE INTESTINE OF THE UNANESTHETIZED DOG[1]

EDWARD LARSON

From the Department of Pharmacology, Temple University School of Medicine, Philadelphia

Received for publication February 19, 1941

The experiments reported in this paper were undertaken in the hope of explaining some of the discrepancies in the literature on this subject. With reviews by Steggerda *et al.* (1) and by Wolff (2) available, it is necessary to mention only a few of the reports most directly concerned. Elmer *et al.* (3) reported that vasopressin stimulates the intestine more than pituitary extract and that the effects of vasopressin were antagonized by oxytocin. L. M. Larson and Bargen (4) found that solution of pituitary increased activity in the middle portion but had little or no effect on distal portions of a Thiry-Vella fistula of the large intestine. From Roentgen ray studies on unanesthetized dogs, Melville and Stehle (5) concluded that intravenous injection of their postlobin-V (pressor) extract produced shortening of the large bowel whereas the postlobin-O (oxytocic) extract had no definite effects. Melville (6) observed defecation following intravenous injections of pitressin or pitocin in the unanesthetized dog but concluded that the oxytocic hormone may inhibit the typical effects of the pressor constituent. Reagan and Puestow (7) reported that pitressin intramuscularly in dogs did not stimulate contractions but did increase slightly the tonus of exteriorized segments of the colon. Wolff (2) injected pituitrin, pitocin or pitressin subcutaneously or intravenously into dogs with either Thiry or Vella fistulas of the colon and observed inhibition in most instances.

METHODS

Ten normal dogs and seven dogs each having an appendicostomy were used in the present experiments. After a dog had been trained to lie quietly, a condom-balloon 10 cm. long on a catheter was inserted into the large intestine. In normal dogs the balloon was inserted through the anus about 7 or 8 inches (lower portion). In dogs having an appendicostomy the balloon was inserted 7 or 8 inches through the fistula (upper portion) or through the anus as in the normal dogs; in some instances both approaches were used simultaneously. The balloon contained water at 15 cm. pressure and was connected to a bellows for a graphic record. After a control period of about

[1] A part of these results were presented before the American Society for Pharmacology and Experimental Therapeutics in March, 1940. THIS JOURNAL, **69**, 293, 1940.

one-half hour, injections were made and the record was continued for an hour and a half. In some of the 39 control experiments contractions were recorded for periods of about two

TABLE 1

*Effects of posterior pituitary preparations on the large intestine and heart rate of dogs**

PREPARATION AND DOSE PER KGM.	METHOD OF INJECTION	POSITION OF BALLOON	MOVEMENTS			TONE			HEART RATE	
			No effect	Decrease	Increase	No effect	Decrease	Increase	No effect	Decrease
Sol. post. pit. 2.5 or 5 M.U.	I.V.	Upper	14	5	0	9	10	0	2	32
		Lower	14	20	0	7	27	0		
Sol. post. pit. 10 M.U.	I.V.	Upper	1	18	1	0	20	0	0	25
		Lower	1	24	0	1	24	0		
Sol. post. pit. 100, 250 or 500 M.U.	I.V.	Upper	0	19	1	0	19	1	0	17
		Lower	0	17	1	0	18	0		
Sol. post. pit. 100 M.U.	S.C. or I.M.	Upper	3	1	10	11	1	2	18	5
		Lower	10	8	7	18	7	0		
Sol. post. pit. 250 M.U.	S.C. or I.M.	Upper	6	5	15	10	11	5	18	14
		Lower	15	13	8	18	16	2		
Sol. post. pit. 500 M.U.	S.C. or I.M.	Upper	4	1	17	2	9	11	11	22
		Lower	6	12	8	12	13	1		
Pitocin 10 M.U.	I.V.	Upper	0	7	0	0	7	0	14	0
		Lower	0	14	0	0	14	0		
Pitocin 250 or 500 M.U.	S.C.	Upper	14	6	1	7	13	1	38	1
		Lower	18	21	0	22	17	0		
Pitressin 10 M.U.	I.V.	Upper	7	0	1	6	1	1	0	13
		Lower	12	1	0	9	4	0		
Pitressin 250 or 500 M.U.	S.C. or I.M.	Upper	3	2	17	9	6	7	14	28
		Lower	27	1	15	34	4	5		
Pitressin 10 M.U. plus Pitocin 10 M.U.	I.V.	Upper	0	5	0	0	5	0	0	12
		Lower	0	12	0	0	12	0		

* From the results observed on the lower portion of the large intestine of ten normal dogs and seven dogs each having an appendicostomy, no distinction could be made on either the basis of sex or operative procedure. All dogs were used several times at various intervals for a period of about eighteen months. Usually more results were obtained from the intestine than from the heart because sometimes more than one portion of the intestine was used.

hours without any injections; in others injections of 0.9 per cent sodium chloride were made. If external evidence of oestrus was present the dog was not used at that time either for control or drug injection. Several days were allowed between experiments to assure recovery. The dogs were not fed for 12 hours before experiments and were allowed to defecate before being brought into the laboratory.

Solution of posterior pituitary was prepared according to the U.S.P. XI. The pitocin and pitressin were N.N.R. preparations. *All doses mentioned are per kilogram of body weight.* When the milliunit dose was 10 or less, the preparations were diluted with 0.9 per cent sodium chloride solution to facilitate measurement. The injections

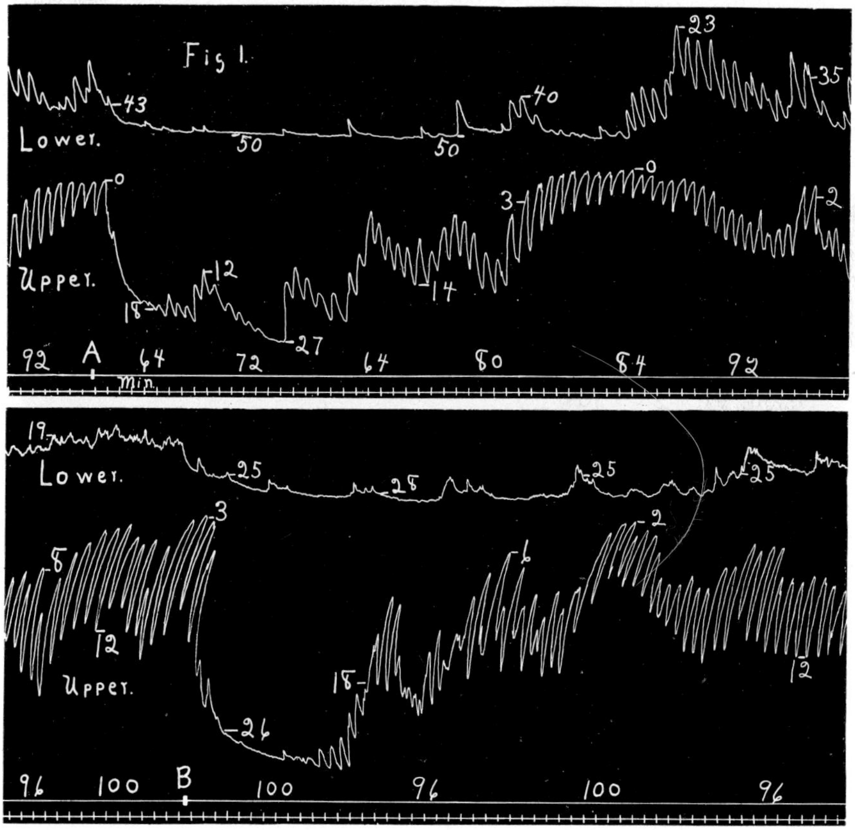

FIG. 1. *A*, intravenous injection of 10 M.U. of solution of posterior pituitary per kilogram in an 18.2 kgm. dog having an appendicostomy. The figures on the tracings indicate the number of cubic centimeters in the balloons at 15 cm. water pressure. The figures above the signal lines are heart rates per minute. *B*, intravenous injection 10 M.U. pitocin per kilogram in the same dog.

were made intravenously into one of the leg veins, subcutaneously into the back near the shoulders, or intramuscularly into the thigh as indicated. The results are summarized in table 1.

RESULTS

Control records showed no significant changes in motility and only occasional diminution of tone. Intravenous injections (I.V.) of solution of posterior pituitary (sol. post. pit.) in a very small dose, such as 2.5 or 5 milliunits (1 M.U. means $\frac{1}{1000}$ of a unit, U.S.P. XI, 2nd Supp., p. 138) might or might not cause decrease in tone and motility of the large intestine but a slightly larger dose (10 M.U.) usually depressed both tone and motility for about 20 minutes (fig. 1, *A*). Large intravenous doses such as 100, 250 or 500 M.U. depressed the tone and motility for 45 minutes or more. The heart rate was reduced by these injections in nearly all cases. Subcutaneous (S. C.) or intramuscular (I.M.) injections of 100, 250 or 500 M.U. tend to stimulate the motility of the upper portion of the large intestine by causing either an in-

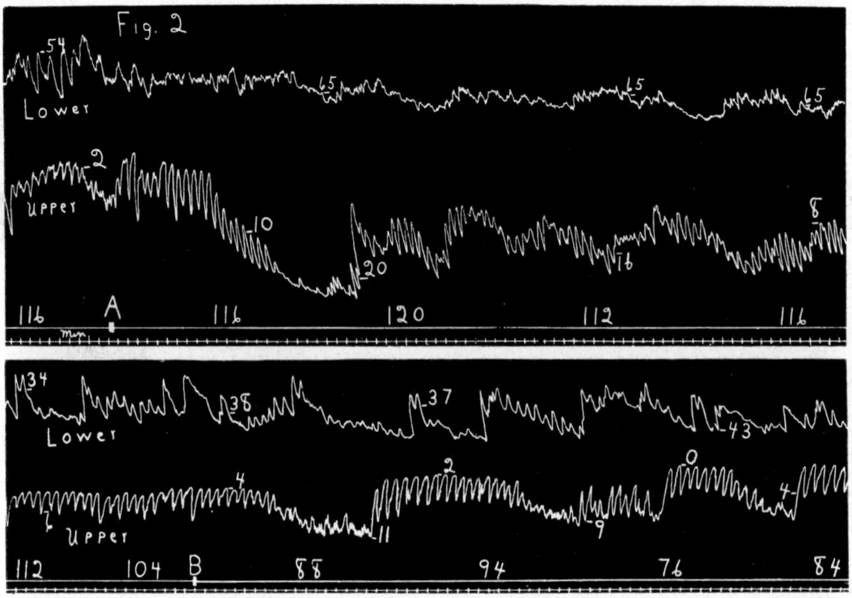

FIG. 2. *A*, subcutaneous injection 250 M.U. pitocin per kilogram into a 20.8 kgm. dog having an appendicostomy. *B*, subcutaneous injection 250 M.U. pitressin per kilogram into a 17.6 kgm. dog having an appendicostomy.

crease in the rhythmic movements or waves of contraction with no definite effect on the motility or tone of the lower portion. In most cases the tone of the upper portion was not affected by the 100 M.U. dose but 500 M.U. tended to cause an increase in tone. Doses smaller than 100 M.U. subcutaneously or intramuscularly did not give any definite results.

Pitocin injected intravenously in a 10 M.U. dose (N.N.R. 1940, p. 385) depressed the tone and motility of the large intestine with no effect on heart rate (table 1, fig. 1, *B*). Pitocin injected subcutaneously in either a 250 or 500 M.U. dose sometimes had no effect and sometimes decreased the motility and tone (table 1, fig. 2, *A*).

Pitressin intravenously in a small dose (10 M.U., N.N.R. 1940, p. 386) had no definite effect on the motility or tone of the upper large intestine (table 1) but occasionally depressed the tone of the lower portion. The heart rate was reduced by pitressin when this dose was given intravenously. Subcutaneous injections of pitressin usually stimulated the motility of the upper portion of the large intestine (table 1, fig. 2, *B*) with no definite trend on the motility of the lower portion or tone of either. Combination of pitressin and pitocin, in the same concentration as in solution of the posterior pituitary, produced similar results to those of the posterior pituitary (table 1).

DISCUSSION

Depression of motility and tone of the large intestine by a small but effective intravenous dose (10 M.U.) of solution of posterior pituitary is due to the pitocin present since equivalent amounts of pitocin have similar and perhaps identical effects whereas equivalent amounts of pitressin do little or nothing. Evidently the vascular constriction induced in the large intestine, or any other circulatory effects produced by these small doses of pitressin, are not sufficient to affect the motility; the tone however, which is influenced more easily, was depressed in a few cases. Larger intravenous doses of pitressin were not injected because the amount of oxytocic principle present as a contaminant (8) might be sufficient to produce definite effects. Both Elmer *et al.* (3) and Melville (6), using other procedures, have found that pitocin depresses the large intestine though Melville and Stehle (5) reported that their oxytocic preparation (postlobin-O) had no definite effect.

The marked depression of tone and rhythmic movements produced by the larger intravenous doses (100, 250 or 500 M.U.) of solution of posterior pituitary are very similar to those observed by Wolff (2) in loops of the colon. In addition to the depressant action of the pitocin fraction, vascular constriction by the pitressin fraction, which blanches the exteriorized portions of the fistula with an attendant anoxia and carbon dioxide accumulation, probably contributes to the depression. In 2 of these 38 results there were increased movements and in several there was vomiting or retching which might be regarded as evidence of temporary stimulation of the gastro-intestinal tract. This occasional temporary stimulation may be secondary to the effects on the circulatory and respiratory systems as suggested by Steggerda *et al.* (1).

The effects of the subcutaneous or intramuscular injections of the solution of posterior pituitary (100, 250 or 500 M.U.) or pitressin (250 or 500 M.U.) usually is an increased motility of the upper portion of the large intestine (fig. 2, *B*) with less or no definite effect on the lower portion, which is in accordance with results of L. M. Larson and Bargen (4) with Thiry-Vella fistulae of the colon. Deviations from these usual results may be due to the counteracting effects of the following factors: vascular constriction of the intestinal vessels by pitressin, depressant action of the pitocin fraction, inactivation (9) and adsorption (10) of the injected preparation by the various tissues of the body. The increased activity on the upper with less or no effect on the lower portion of the large intestine (effects characteristic of defecation (11)) might explain the defecation (6) and passage of flatus (12) induced by pitressin.

Pitocin, injected subcutaneously or intramuscularly, either had no effect or depressed the large intestine; this confirms the results reported by Elmer *et al.* (3). The failure of pitocin to cause depression in all cases may at least be partially explained by inactivation (9) and adsorption (10) of the injected pitocin by the various tissues of the body and by the presence of small amounts of pitressin (8).

Tone and motility of the large intestine were depressed less easily in the upper than in the lower portion and if depressed, the upper portion recovered more rapidly (fig. 1, *A* and *B*). Also the tone of the upper portion, as indicated by content of the balloon, was greater than that of the lower (fig. 1, *A* and *B*; 2, *A* and *B*). Like Templeton and Lawson (13) and L. M. Larson and Bargen (4), the author has observed greater motility in the upper than in the lower portion. Motility was depressed less easily than tone.

CONCLUSIONS

1. Intravenous injection of solution of posterior pituitary U.S.P. or pitocin in a dose of 10 M.U. (Milliunits) per kilogram usually produced a decrease in tone and motility of the upper and lower portions of the large intestine in the unanesthetized dog. Larger doses, 100 to 500 M.U. of solution of posterior pituitary, produced the same effect except that the duration was greater and in a few cases a short initial period of increased movements was sometimes seen. Tone was depressed more easily than movements.

2. Pitressin, 10 M.U. per kilogram intravenously usually had no effect on either the movements or tone of the large intestine in these unanesthetized dogs.

3. Subcutaneous or intramuscular injections of 100, 250 or 500 M.U. of solution of posterior pituitary or 250 or 500 M.U. of pitressin per kilogram usually caused an increase of movements in the upper portion of the large intestine with no significant effect on tone. On the lower portion in about half of the cases, no effect was produced on either tone or movement by these injections.

4. Subcutaneous injections of 250 or 500 M.U. pitocin per kilogram usually had either no effect or decreased the tone and motility of the large intestine.

The author wishes to extend his thanks to Dr. A. E. Livingston for many helpful suggestions.

REFERENCES

(1) Steggerda, Gianturco and Essex: Am. J. Physiol., **123,** 400, 1938.
(2) Wolff: Am. J. Dig. Dis., **6,** 243, 1939.
(3) Elmer and Ptaszek: Comp. rend. Soc. de biol., **104,** 540, 1930.
Elmer, Ptaszek and Scheps: Klin. Wchnschr., **9,** 1765, 1930.
(4) Larson and Bargen: Arch. Surg., **27,** 1130, 1933.
(5) Melville and Stehle: This Journal, **50,** 165, 1934.
(6) Melville: J. A. M. A., **106,** 102, 1936.
(7) Reagan and Puestow: *Surg.*, **6,** 663, 1939.
(8) New and Nonofficial Remedies, Am. Med. Assoc., 385, 1940.
(9) Larson: This Journal, **62,** 346, 1938; **67,** 175, 1939.
(10) Geiling and Oldham: J. A. M. A., **116,** 302, 1941.
(11) Templeton and Borkin: Am. J. Dig. Dis., **5,** 809, 1939.
(12) Kenning and Lofstrom: Am. J. Roentgenol., **37,** 28, 1937.
(13) Templeton and Lawson: Am. J. Physiol., **96,** 667, 1931.

INFLUENCE OF COCAINE ON THE UTERINE REACTIONS INDUCED BY ADRENALIN AND HYPOGASTRIC NERVE STIMULATION[1]

JOHN S. LABATE

From the Departments of Anatomy and of Obstetrics and Gynecology, New York University

Received for publication February 24, 1941

The origin, course and distribution of the sympathetic and sacral nerves were studied in detail for the first time in the cat and rabbit by Langley and Anderson (9, 10). They demonstrated that stimulation of the hypogastric nerves caused inhibition of uterine activity in the non-pregnant cat and excitation of the uterus in the non-pregnant rabbit. Later Cushny (2) Dale (3) and Kehrer (7) independently observed the phenomenon of "pregnancy reversal" in the cat. Adrenalin and hypogastric nerve stimulation provoked inhibition of the uterus in the non-pregnant cat but during pregnancy an excitatory effect was observed. In the rabbit these stimuli induced uterine excitation in both the pregnant and non-pregnant animal. It became obvious at this time that the type of hypogastric innervation to the uterus differed in the cat and rabbit. A third variation in the hypogastric innervation was observed later for the uterus of the rat and guinea pig. In these animals adrenalin and nerve stimulation produced an inhibitory effect on the uterus in the pregnant as well as in the non-pregnant state (5, 13). The monkey (3) was found to resemble the rabbit in that adrenalin provoked an excitatory effect on the non-pregnant uterus.

The present study was undertaken to determine, by a pharmacological approach, the reason for the species differences observed in the uterine reactions of hypogastric nerve stimulation and adrenalin. Since the information concerning the uterine effects of nerve stimulation and adrenalin has been gathered by various investigators under different experimental conditions, it was necessary to obtain corroborative evidence of the uterine effects of these stimuli in each of the animal species. The species differences observed in the uterine reactions of nerve stimulation and adrenalin may be due to the fact that whereas adrenergic effects prevail in one species, cholinergic effects may predominate in another. This possibility has been studied by observing the influence of cocaine on the uterine response of hypogastric nerve stimulation and of adrenalin. Cocaine is a sympathomimetic drug which is able

[1] Supported by a Fellowship granted by the Commonwealth Fund.

to potentiate the peripheral excitability of adrenergic nerves. If in the course of this study augmentation of the uterine effects of nerve stimulation and adrenalin results after cocaine it should afford evidence that the sympathetic uterine innervation to the particular animal is predominantly adrenergic.

METHODS

Female cats, rabbits, rats and monkeys were used in these experiments. In all of the animals except the monkeys, observations were made during the pregnant and non-pregnant state. Some of the non-pregnant animals were ovariectomized 7 days to 3 months previously under nembutal anaesthesia in order to eliminate any ovarian hormonal influence on uterine activity.

The animal was placed upon a heated operating table and laparotomy was performed through a midline suprapubic incision. The intestines were walled off into the upper abdomen with gauze, allowing complete freedom for the uterine horns. The hypogastric nerves were dissected free and cut between two ligatures. A shielded electrode was then attached to the peripheral segment of each severed nerve and connected to a Harvard inductorium. In a few of the earlier experiments the electrode was placed on the intact hypogastric nerves. Movements of the uterus were recorded mechanically by a fine silk thread stitched through the outer layer of the muscularis of the right uterine horn (cat, rabbit, rat) approximately one third the distance from the tubal extremity; in the monkey the thread was inserted in the middle of the superior surface of the *fundus uteri*. The thread was attached to a light lever which recorded every contraction of the uterus on a revolving kymograph. The abdomen was closed incompletely with interrupted sutures allowing a small opening to remain, through which could be observed the loop of the uterus with its attached recording thread.

In a number of experiments visual observations of uterine activity were made simultaneously with the mechanical recording. In these instances the closure of the abdomen was less complete. During later experiments the animal was kept in a cabinet the internal temperature of which could be kept within the range of 37 to 40°C. by means of electric light bulbs, and steam was allowed to circulate intermittently through its interior in order to maintain a high degree of moisture.

The reactivity of the uterus to adrenalin was tested by an initial dose of 0.00005 mgm. of adrenalin injected into the right femoral or right jugular vein. The amount of adrenalin was successively increased to 0.0005, 0.005 and 0.05 mgm., each dose being given after complete recovery from the effect of the previous administration. In animals with unresponsive uteri larger quantities of the drug, up to 0.9 mgm., were used.

The reactivity of the uterus to hypogastric stimulation was next determined, using threshold and slightly greater intensities. Each stimulus was applied for a period of 2 minutes and was not repeated until complete recovery of the uterus occurred.

Following this cocaine hydrochloride (8 to 10 mgm. per kilogram of body weight of a freshly prepared solution) was injected intravenously and five to ten minutes later the response of the uterus to adrenalin and to threshold and slightly greater intensities of nerve stimulation again was determined. Thus it was possible to compare the uterine effects of nerve stimulation and adrenalin before and after the administration of cocaine hydrochloride.

RESULTS

The uterine effects of hypogastric nerve stimulation vary in different animal species. These effects also vary with the depth of anaesthesia and with the frequency and strength of current used for stimulation and statements made here necessarily apply to one particular type of stimulation.

Cats

A. Non-pregnant. There were nine animals in this group, three of which had been ovariectomized 6 weeks previously. Stimulation of the hypogastric nerves in this group of cats provoked relaxation of the uterus and inhibition of uterine contractions (fig. 1, Table 1). The inhibitory effect was associated with definite vasomotor constriction as shown by intense pallor of the uterine horns.

The response of the uterus to adrenalin closely paralleled that produced by stimulation of the hypogastric nerves (table 1). There occurred relaxation of the uterus and inhibition of uterine activity (fig. 1), and vascular constriction became strikingly visible to the naked eye. It was observed that the uterus which reacted poorly to stimulation of the hypogastric nerves was also resistant to adrenalin. Ovariectomy did not appear to effect the response of the uterus to adrenalin and nerve stimulation (table 1).

Cocaine hydrochloride produced a variable response on the non-pregnant uterus of the cat (table 1). The drug failed to cause any alteration in uterine activity in four of the animals. An inhibitory and vasomotor effect occurred in four cats although this was less pronounced than the inhibition and vasoconstriction induced by adrenalin or hypogastric nerve stimulation. In several of these animals the inhibitory effect was preceded by a transient increase in the amplitude of uterine contractions. In one animal a short period of uterine excitation followed the administration of cocaine (fig. 1).

Augmentation of the uterine effects of adrenalin and nerve stimulation was observed after cocaine in six of the cats (table 1, fig. 1). In one cat (*#21*) accentuation of the effect of nerve stimulation was induced by cocaine without any alteration in its reactivity to adrenalin. In the other two animals, one of which was a castrate, a decrease in these uterine effects followed the injection of cocaine. The augmenting influence of cocaine was demonstrated further by combining small amounts of the drug with either adrenalin or hypogastric nerve stimulation. The inhibitory effect of adrenalin and nerve stimulation on the uterus of one animal persisted two to three times as long when 0.3 mgm. of cocaine was given at the onset of nerve stimulation and immediately after the adrenalin. Similar combinations failed to show accentuation of the effect of nerve stimulation on the uterus of two castrate cats although in one animal a prolongation of the adrenalin effect was observed.

B. Pregnant. There were eight animals in this group. Complete reversal from inhibition to excitation occurred in the uterine effects of hypogastric nerve stimulation in five of the pregnant animals (table 1). In these cats stimulation of the nerves caused an elevation in tonus, vasoconstriction and an increase in the amplitude and frequency of contractions of the uterus. The duration of the pregnancy had no apparent influence on the appearance

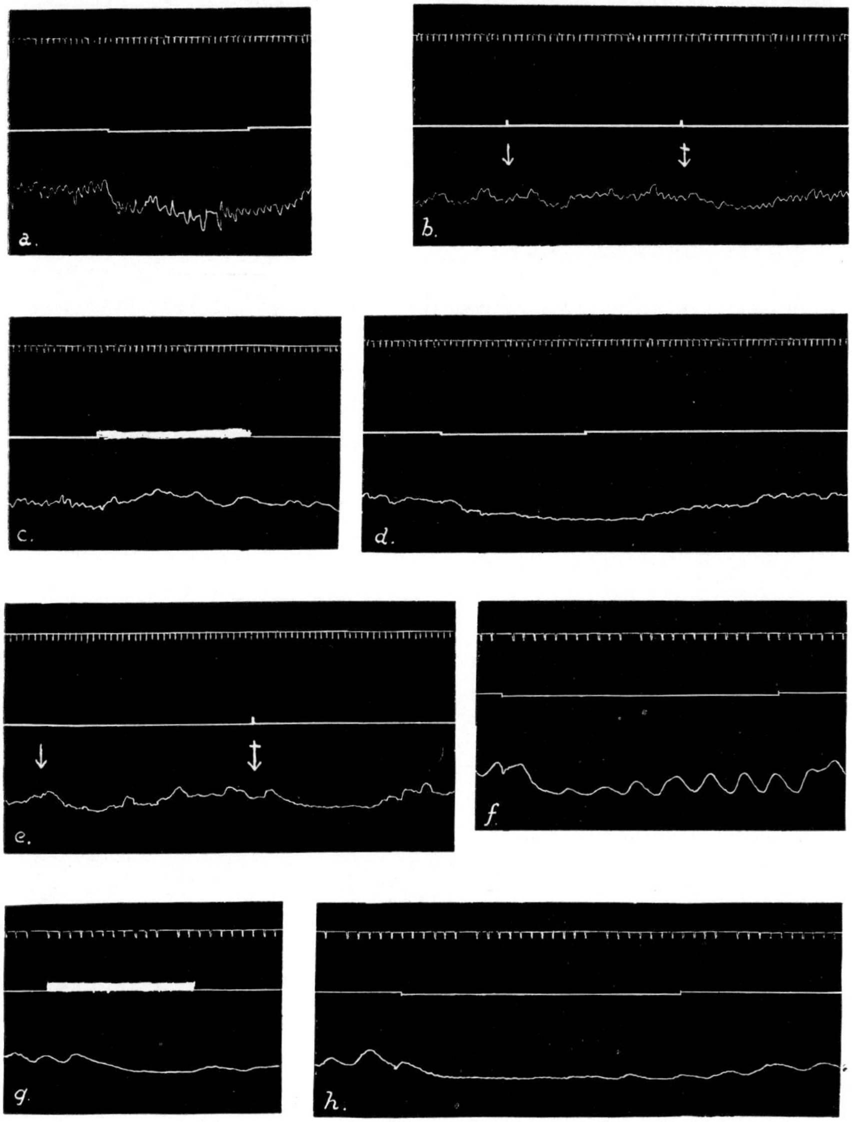

FIG. 1. Virgin cat #14. Effect on uterine activity from nerve stimulation (sec. coil 12 cm.) *a*, before cocaine (12.5 mgm.) injection; *d*, after cocaine injection. Note the accentuation of the inhibitory effect.

Effect on uterine activity from adrenalin (0.0005 mgm. ↓), (0.005 mgm. ‡) *b*, before cocaine. *e*, after cocaine injection. Note the accentuation of inhibitory effect.

Virgin cat #21. Effect on uterine activity from nerve stimulation (sec coil 6 cm.). *f*, before cocaine (7.68 mgm.); *h*, after cocaine. Note augmentation of inhibitory effect.

Effect on uterus of cocaine. *C*, excitatory in cat #14; *g*, inhibitory in cat #21.

of the phenomenon of pregnancy reversal since this was observed during the early as well as the late period of pregnancy. In two other pregnant animals, near term, stimulation of the hypogastric nerves failed to influence uterine activity. In one, however, adrenalin produced an excitatory effect. A slight inhibitory response of the uterus was observed with stimulation of the hypogastric nerves at high intensities in one cat. This animal was believed to have a pregnancy of less than two weeks duration.

TABLE 1

Cats

NUMBER	BEFORE COCAINE		AFTER COCAINE		
	Nerve stimulation	Adrenalin	Nerve stimulation	Adrenalin	Accentuation
			Non-pregnant—normal		
12	– –	– –	– –	– –	Yes
16	– –	– –	0	0	No (prolonged experiment)
17	– –	– –	– –	– –	Yes
20	– –	– –	– –	– –	Yes
21	– –	– –	– –	– –	Yes (no for adrenalin)
22	– –	– –	– –	– –	Yes
			Castrate		
2	– –	– –	0	– –	Decreased
4	– –	– –	– –	– –	Yes
5	– –	– –	– –	– –	Yes
			Pregnant		
10	–	–	–	0	No
25	++	++	++	++	Yes
30	++	++	++	++	Yes
34	++	++	++	++	Yes (no for adrenalin)
35	++	++	++	++	Yes (no for adrenalin)
37	++	++	++	++	Yes
40	0	0	0	0	No
45	0	++	0	Not tested	No

Explanation of symbols for all tables: +, excitatory; –, inhibitory; 0, no reaction.

Adrenalin produced vasoconstriction and excitation of the uterus in six pregnant cats (table 1). The uterus of one animal failed to show any change in its activity following the administration of adrenalin. In one cat, a slight inhibitory effect was observed with large amounts (0.01 mgm.) of the drug. This was the same animal in which stimulation of the hypogastric nerves provoked slight inhibition of uterine activity.

Cocaine hydrochloride caused an elevation in uterine tonus and an increase in amplitude and frequency of contractions in four pregnant animals. In three others no alteration in uterine activity could be detected following the administration of the drug. In only one cat did cocaine induce inhibition of the uterus. This was the same animal in which pregnancy reversal of the uterine effects of adrenalin and nerve stimulation failed to occur. Cocaine appeared to be strongly sympathomimetic, reproducing the pregnancy reversal effects of adrenalin and nerve stimulation.

The uterine effects of nerve stimulation were accentuated by the administration of cocaine in five pregnant cats. In three of these augmentation of

TABLE 2

Rabbits

NUMBER	BEFORE COCAINE		AFTER COCAINE		
	Nerve stimulation	Adrenalin	Nerve stimulation	Adrenlin	Accentuation
Non-pregnant—Normal					
10	0	+	0*	Not tested	No
11	++	++	++	0	Decrease
12	++	++	++	++	No
13	+	+	0	Not tested	No
14	++	++	++	++	Yes
16	+	+	0*	0	Decrease
17	++	++	++	++	Yes
Castrate					
2	0	0	0	Not tested	No
3	++	++	+	++	No
5	++	++	0	++	No
6	++	++	++	++	Decrease
Pregnant					
22	0*	0*	0*	0*	No
15	++	0	0	0	No
20	0	*	0	0	No
21	++	++	+	++	No
18	++	++	+	++	Decrease
18	0	0	0	0	No

* Occasional +.

the uterine effects of adrenalin also occurred. The remaining three pregnant animals failed to develop any sensitization to either adrenalin or stimulation of the hypogastric nerves.

Rabbits

A. Non-pregnant. Of the eleven animals comprising this group, four had been overiectomized 76 to 88 days previous to the day of the experiment. Both adrenalin and stimulation of the hypogastric nerves in the rabbit caused excitation and vasoconstriction of the uterus (table 2). Nerve stimulation induced excitatory uterine effects in nine of these animals; it was ineffective in two rabbits, one of which had been castrated. Adrenalin produced a similar excitatory uterine effect in ten of these rabbits; one of the ovariectomized animals failed to show any uterine response. The period of excitation frequently was followed by inhibition of uterine activity. Thus while the prevailing action was excitatory, the inhibition of spontaneous activity which often followed excitation suggests the possibility that the hypogastric nerves in the rabbit contain both excitatory and inhibitory fibers. The spontaneous activity of the uterus and its reactivity to adrenalin and nerve stimulation were markedly reduced in the castrate rabbits. This may be due largely to atrophy of uterine muscle and connective tissue following the removal of the ovaries.

Cocaine hydrochloride caused excitation of uterine activity in four of these animals. No effect on the uterus was observed from its administration in seven rabbits, three of which were castrates. Augmentation of the uterine effects of nerve stimulation and adrenalin after cocaine occurred in only two normal rabbits.

B. Pregnant. There were six animals in this group, of which three were 7 to 10 days pregnant and the rest 19 to 25 days pregnant. The reactivity of the pregnant rabbit's uterus following hypogastric nerve stimulation and adrenalin varied in different animals. Stimulation of the hypogastric nerves in three pregnant rabbits resulted in excitation of the uterus characterized by an increase in the tone and in the amplitude of contractions. A fourth animal showed an occasional excitatory effect on the uterus only after stimulation of the hypogastric nerves with strong current. The uteri of the two remaining rabbits, 19 and 20 days pregnant, were unresponsive to electrical stimulation of the hypogastric nerves. After the tenth day of pregnancy the rabbit's uterus appears to become increasingly resistant to nerve stimulation.

Adrenalin caused an excitatory uterine effect in two animals, 7 and 25 days pregnant, and an occasional excitatory effect on two others, 10 and 19 days pregnant. The remaining two rabbits failed to show any uterine effects from the drug. There was no apparent relationship between the period of gestation and the reactivity of the rabbit's uterus to this drug (table 2).

Cocaine hydrochloride induced an excitatory response on the pregnant uterus of three rabbits. The remaining three animals showed no uterine effects from the drug. Cocaine failed to cause any accentuation of the uterine effects of nerve stimulation and adrenalin in all of the six pregnant rabbits. Its injection, however, was followed by a decrease in the reactivity of the uterus to these stimuli in three animals (table 2).

Rats

A. Non-pregnant. There were six animals in this group, three of which had been ovariectomized for some time preceding the day of the experiment.

The response of the uterus to nerve stimulation and adrenalin in the normal non-pregnant rat is similar to the effect observed in the non-pregnant cat. Both stimulation of the hypogastric nerves and adrenalin provoked inhibition and relaxation of the uterus. Cocaine, however, caused an inhibitory effect in only one of these animals, whereas no alteration in uterine activity was observed in the other two. Augmentation of the uterine effects of nerve stimulation and adrenalin followed the administration of cocaine in all three of the normal rats (table 3).

TABLE 3

Rats

NUMBER	BEFORE COCAINE		AFTER COCAINE		
	Nerve stimulation	Adrenalin	Nerve stimulation	Adrenalin	Accentuation
			Non-pregnant—Normal		
15	— —	— —	— —	— —	Yes
19	0 or —	—	—	— —	Yes
20	—	—	— —	Not tested	Yes
			Castrate		
2	0	0	0	0	No
3	0	0	0	0	No
106	0	0	— —	— —	Yes
			Pregnant		
101	++	++	0	0	Decreased
104	0 or —	— —	++	0 or +	Yes
105	++*	—	†	— —	Yes
108	0 or —	— —	0	— —	No
111	—	—	— —	— —	No

* Followed by inhibition.

† After second dose of cocaine, +.

The spontaneous activity as well as the reactivity of the uterus of the rat was found to be greatly diminished after castration. Neither adrenalin, nerve stimulation nor cocaine produced any effect on the uterus of two animals whose ovaries had been removed 116 and 117 days previously. These rats did not develop any augmentation of the uterine effects of nerve stimulation or adrenalin after cocaine (table 3). One rat, which had been castrated 7 days previously, failed to show any uterine response to nerve stimulation and adrenalin before the injection of cocaine. Ten milligrams per kilogram of this latter drug, however, produced a slight excitatory effect on the uterus, and following its administration nerve stimulation, with the secondary coil of the inductorium at a 6 cm. distance, and 0.00005 mgm. of adrenalin provoked uterine inhibition and relaxation (table 3). This affords an excellent example of the accentuating effect of cocaine on the uterine responses resulting from stimulation of the hypogastric nerves and from adrenalin.

B. Pregnant. These experiments were performed on five pregnant animals which had been allowed to mate 10 to 14 days before. The reaction of the pregnant uterus to stimulation of the hypogastric nerves was characterized by either inhibition or excitation. Inhibition of the contractions and relaxation of the uterus was observed in three animals, although in two of these the uterus was more resistant to nerve stimulation since only an occasional

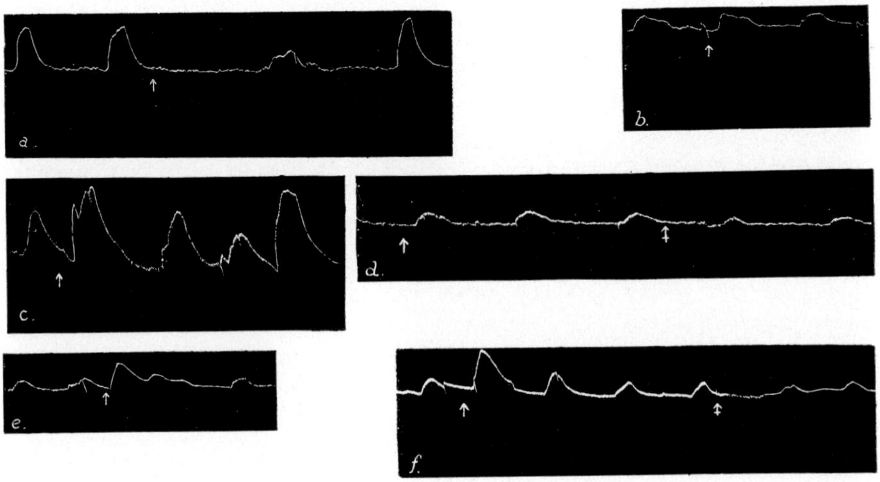

FIG. 2. Pregnant rat #104. Effect on uterine activity from nerve stimulation (sec. coil 12 cm.); *b*, before cocaine no effect; *e*, after cocaine excitatory effect.

Effect on uterine activity from adrenalin; *a*, 0.0001 mgm. ↑ before cocaine—note inhibition; *d*, 0.0001 mgm. ↑ and 0.0005 mgm. ↨ after cocaine—note decrease in inhibitory effect.

f, Excitatory effect of nerve stimulation ↑ and slightly inhibitory effect of adrenalin 0.005 mgm. ↨ after cocaine. Note that adrenalin effect has been reduced but not reversed. *c*, Excitatory effect of cocaine (2 mgm.).

inhibitory effect could be induced. The uterus of another pregnant rat responded to nerve stimulation by an initial excitatory phase which was followed occasionally by inhibition. In the fifth pregnant animal a definite and predominant excitatory uterine effect followed electrical stimulation of the hypogastric nerves (table 3).

The effect of adrenalin on uterine activity was more constant in this group of rats. Inhibition and relaxation followed the administration of adrenalin in four of these animals. In only one, the rat whose uterus showed an excitatory response to nerve stimulation, was excitation provoked by the adrenalin. From these observations, although inconstant, it appears that reversal of uterine effects may develop during pregnancy, since one of our animals showed an initial excitatory uterine effect from nerve stimulation alone.

Definite excitation of uterine motility followed the injection of cocaine in three of these animals. Two, however, showed no uterine reaction to the drug (table 3). In this group of pregnant rats accentuation of the uterine effects of nerve stimulation and adrenalin after cocaine was characterized by the occurrence of pregnancy reversal in rats #104 and #105. It appears that cocaine may have sensitized in some way, the excitatory fibers contained in the hypogastric nerves of these animals. Whereas before cocaine inhibition of uterine motility resulted from nerve stimulation and adrenalin, after the administration of 10 mgm. of cocaine per kilogram of body weight these same stimuli provoked an excitatory response (table 3, fig. 2).

Monkeys

Non-pregnant. Observations of the uterine effects of adrenalin, hypogastric nerve stimulation and cocaine were made on three virgin female monkeys. Stimulation of the hypogastric nerves and adrenalin caused excitation of uterine motility which was characterized by a gradual increase in tonus and by vasomotor constriction. During this period of increased tone frequent small uterine contractions were observed. Not infrequently the period of excitation was followed by a period of diminished uterine activity. The spontaneous activity of the tubes was also increased by stimulation of the hypogastric nerves.

Cocaine produced an excitatory effect on the uterus of all three monkeys. Excitation was represented by an increase in the rate of uterine contractions. None of the monkeys showed any accentuation of the uterine effects of nerve stimulation and adrenalin following cocaine.

DISCUSSION

Stimulation of the hypogastric nerves and adrenalin provoked an excitatory effect on the uterus of the non-pregnant and pregnant rabbit and of the virgin monkey. The reaction of the uterus in the cat to nerve stimulation and adrenalin varies, depending on whether the animal is pregnant or not (table 4). These stimuli produce inhibition of uterine motility in the non-pregnant state, whereas excitation occurs during pregnancy (3, 2, 7, 16). The reason for such pregnancy reversal phenomenon has been ascribed to the influence of the corpus luteum hormone (6, 8).

Gunn and Gunn (5) first observed that adrenalin provoked relaxation of the uterus of the rat in the pregnant or non-pregnant state. Similar observations were obtained with the guinea pig. Later Fleming (4) noted relaxation of the non-pregnant uterus of these animals after the administration of adrenalin. In this series of experiments nerve stimulation and adrenalin induced inhibitory uterine effects in the non-pregnant rat. But during pregnancy, the uterus, although more refractory to nerve stimulation, responded by either inhibition or excitation (table 4). Adrenalin too, was found to provoke an occasional excitatory uterine response in the pregnant rat. An occasional excitatory effect from adrenalin also has been observed on the pregnant uterus of the guinea pig (7, 13, 17).

The occurrence of the phenomenon of pregnancy reversal is not limited to the cat alone, since in the rat a similar reversal in the uterine effects of nerve stimulation and occasionally adrenalin has been observed during pregnancy. Although pregnancy reversal occurs more constantly in the cat than in the rat one can see points of similarity between the uterine reactions of both animals following nerve stimulation and adrenalin.

The reactions of the uterus observed in these four animal species are of two main types. The first type of uterine response is characterized by the reversal of inhibition during the non-pregnant state to excitation during pregnancy. This occurred in the cat and occasionally in the rat (table 4).

TABLE 4

Summary of effect of nerve stimulation and adrenalin on uterine activity and the influence of cocaine on this activity

	NON-PREGNANT			PREGNANT		
	Nerve stimulation	Adrenalin	Accentuation following cocaine	Nerve stimulation	Adrenalin	Accentuation following cocaine
Cats	−	−	Yes (77.7%)	+ (occasional − or 0)	+ (occasional − or 0)	Yes (62.5%)
Rats	−	−	Yes (100%)	− (occasionally +)	− (occasionally +)	Yes (40%)
Rabbits	+	+	No (81.8%)	+ (occasionally 0)	+ (occasionally 0)	No (100%)
Monkeys	+	+	No (100%)	?	?	?

−, inhibition, +, excitation.

The second type of uterine reaction was observed in the rabbit and is characterized by excitation of the uterus, pregnant or non-pregnant, on stimulation of the hypogastric nerves or on administration of adrenalin. The reactions of the uterus in the monkey probably are of this same type although we have no information concerning the uterine effects of nerve stimulation and adrenalin during pregnancy (table 4).

A similar subdivision into two main groups can be made depending on whether cocaine does or does not augment the uterine effects of nerve stimulation and of adrenalin. It has been demonstrated that cocaine causes augmentation of the uterine effects of adrenalin and nerve stimulation in the cat and rat and no augmentation in the rabbit and monkey (table 4).

Rosenblueth (15) also observed augmentation of the adrenalin effect on the uterus *in situ* of the non-pregnant cat. Burn and Tainter (1) and MacGregor (12) investigated the behavior of excised uterine strips of the virgin cat and found that the inhibition caused by adrenalin was reduced or abolished by cocaine. Lindblom (11) and Thienes and Hackett (18) reported sensitization of the adrenalin effect after cocaine on excised strips of uterus from the virgin rabbit. The contradictory results observed by *in vitro* experiments are probably due to the differences in the experimental conditions and in the dosage of the drugs used. Excised tissues deteriorate rapidly and experiments of this type are likely to show wide variations in reactivity.

It is generally conceded that cocaine potentiates the peripheral activity of adrenergic nerve fibers. The hypogastric nerve presumably contains both cholinergic and adrenergic nerve fibers. Both Dale (3) and Cushny (2) assumed the existence of a mixture of motor and inhibitory elements in the hypogastric nerves, one or the other becoming functionally active according to whether the cat is pregnant or not. The results of the present series of experiments show that cocaine has accentuated the uterine effects of hypogastric nerve stimulation in both the cat and in the rat. On this basis it appears possible that the hypogastric nerves in these animals may contain a predominantly higher percentage of adrenergic fibers.

The rabbit and monkey, however, failed to show any potentiation of the effects of nerve stimulation after cocaine. This is the result to be expected if the hypogastric nerves of these animals consist predominantly of cholinergic elements. Recently Reynolds and Foster (14) found that estrogen has a cholinergic action on the uterus of the castrate rabbit whereas this substance is devoid of cholinergic action on the uterus of the castrate cat and rat. This would tend to support the present findings which indicate that two types of sympathetic innervation to the uterus may exist, depending upon the animal species.

SUMMARY

1. Experiments were performed on cats, rats, rabbits and monkeys to show the effect of adrenalin and nerve stimulation on the non-pregnant and pregnant uterus. Cocaine was then administered and the influence of this drug on the uterine reactions induced by the adrenalin and nerve stimulation was determined.

2. Stimulation of the hypogastric nerves and adrenalin both resulted in inhibition of uterine activity in the non-pregnant cat and rat. During pregnancy reversal of this effect to one of excitation developed. This pregnancy reversal was more constant in the cat than in the rat.

3. Stimulation of the hypogastric nerves and adrenalin both caused excitation of the pregnant and non-pregnant uterus of the rabbit and of the non-pregnant uterus of the monkey.

4. Accentuation of the effect of nerve stimulation and adrenalin was observed after cocaine on the uterus of the cat and rat. No augmentation of such uterine effects followed the administration of cocaine in the rabbit and monkey.

5. From the results of cocaine accentuation it is suggested that the fibers contained in the hypogastric nerves of the cat and rat are predominantly adrenergic, whereas in the rabbit and monkey the hypogastric nerves contain a relatively higher percentage of cholinergic elements.

LITERATURE

(1) BURN AND TAINTER: J. Physiol., **71**: 169, 1931.
(2) CUSHNY: J. Physiol., **35**: 1, 1906–07.
(3) DALE: J. Physiol., **34**: 163, 1906.
(4) FLEMING: Trans. Roy. Soc. Edin., 1927, 55, p. 11; no. 22, p. 507.
(5) GUNN AND GUNN: THIS JOURNAL, **5**: 527, 1914.
(6) GUSTAVSON AND VAN DYKE: Ibid., **41**: 139, 1931.
(7) KEHRER: Arch. f. Gynäk., **81**: 160, 1907.
(8) KENNARD: Am. J. Physiol., **118**: 190, 1937.
(9) LANGLEY AND ANDERSON: J. Physiol., **19**: 122, 1895–6.
(10) LANGLEY AND ANDERSON: J. Physiol., **20**: 372, 1896.
(11) LINDBLOM: Compt. Rend. Soc. Biol., **95**: 1070, 1926.
(12) MACGREGOR: THIS JOURNAL, **66**: 394, 1939.
(13) QUAGLIARIELLO: Arch. de ostet. e. ginec., 5, series 2: 377, 1916.
(14) REYNOLDS AND FOSTER: Am. J. Physiol., **131**: 200, 1940.
(15) ROSENBLUETH: Ibid., **98**: 186, 1931.
(16) ROSS: Ibid., **119**: 527, 1937.
(17) SUGIMOTO: Arch f. exper. Path. u. Pharmakol., **74**: 27, 1914.
(18) THIENES AND HACKETT: Proc. Soc. Exp. Biol., **25**: 793, 1928.

THE EFFECTS OF SODIUM DIPHENYL HYDANTOINATE (DILANTIN) ON THE BLOOD ASCORBIC ACID LEVEL IN GUINEA PIGS[1]

MILES E. DRAKE, CHARLES M. GRUBER, VICTOR G. HAURY AND E. ROSS HART

From the Department of Pharmacology, Jefferson Medical College, Philadelphia, Pennsylvania

Received for publication March 8, 1941

The recent investigations of Merritt and Foster (1) indicated that dilantin sodium had little or no effect upon the plasma ascorbic acid level in humans, but Kimball (2) believes that the gingival hyperplasia in his dilantin-treated patients was due to a deficiency in ascorbic acid. Gruhzit (3), working with animals, found that the administration of dilantin sodium had no effect on the absorption or utilization of this vitamin. In the albino rat Drake, Gruber and Haury (4) found that dilantin produced a sharp rise in the urinary excretion of Vitamin C and an abrupt decrease in the ascorbic acid content of the brain, adrenal glands, blood, liver and striated muscle. These conflicting reports have led us to make additional studies on the blood ascorbic acid level in guinea pigs which, as far as is known, cannot synthesize their own Vitamin C and can, therefore, be rendered quickly vitamin deficient.

METHODS

Thirty-six young, female guinea pigs weighing between 150 and 250 grams were used in this work. Throughout the experiments the animals were on a diet of Purina Rabbit Chow (5) and were given subcutaneously 5 mgms. of ascorbic acid daily. On the 14th and 21st days of this diet the ascorbic acid level was determined for each animal and then was used as the control level. Twenty-seven of these animals were then given orally each day, except Sunday, a capsule containing 13 mgms. dilantin per kilogram (which is equivalent to the human dose). The remaining 9 animals were kept as controls. Following this blood was taken once a week from each animal by cardiac puncture and the ascorbic acid level determined. After 3 weeks of dilantin administration, the drug was discontinued and the blood examinations were made each week as before.

The blood was prepared for titration by adding 1 cc. of freshly drawn blood to 3 cc. of a mixture containing 6.7 per cent metaphosphoric acid and 13.3 per cent trichloracetic acid. This mixture was centrifuged and 1 cc. of the clear supernatant fluid titrated with 2-6 dichlorophenolindophenol which was accurately standardized each time before using.

[1] This research was made possible by a grant from Parke, Davis and Company.

RESULTS

In figure 1 is presented the average weekly ascorbic acid levels of both the treated and the control animals. In this figure it is seen at once that the administration of 13 mgm. of dilantin per kilogram daily to guinea pigs produced a rapid and progressive decrease in the blood ascorbic acid level. The control animals, however, maintained their blood ascorbic acid level throughout the course of the experiment. It will also be noted that within three weeks after the discontinuation of dilantin the ascorbic acid levels of the treated animals returned to their original values. These observations support our previous findings that oral administration of dilantin decreases the blood ascorbic acid level in rats (4).

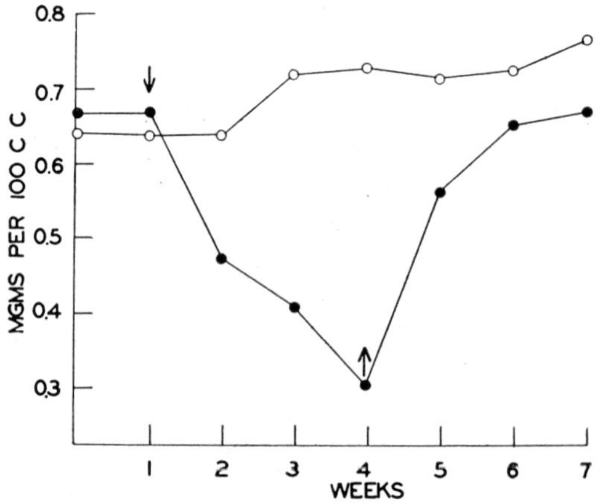

FIG. 1. A graph showing the average weekly blood ascorbic acid level in 27 dilantin-treated and 9 control guinea pigs on a Vitamin C free diet supplemented by a daily subcutaneous injection of 5 mgm. of ascorbic acid. The curve with the open circles pertains to the control animals that with the dots to the dilantin-treated animals. The ordinate shows the blood ascorbic acid in mgm. per 100 cc., and the abscissa is time in weeks. The symbol ↓ indicates the beginning of the daily oral administration of 13 mgm. dilantin per kilogram to 27 animals. At the second arrow (↑) the dilantin was discontinued.

From our experiments it will be noted that 5 mgm. of ascorbic acid given daily to normal animals, on a diet of Purina Rabbit Chow (5), free of Vitamin C, are adequate to maintain the blood ascorbic acid levels in otherwise normal animals over a period of at least 9 weeks. However, animals kept on this same routine are unable to maintain their blood Vitamin C levels while receiving dilantin. It will also be noted that after the withdrawal of the dilantin the daily dose of 5 mgm. of ascorbic acid is sufficient to restore the blood ascorbic acid level to its original value within 3 weeks.

CONCLUSIONS

1. Dilantin sodium given orally in daily doses of 13 mgm. per kilogram (equivalent to human dose) to guinea pigs on a Vitamin C free diet, supple-

mented with 5 mgm. ascorbic acid daily, produces a rapid and progressive fall in the blood ascorbic acid level.

2. The blood ascorbic acid level in the animals which had received dilantin returned to normal within 3 weeks after withdrawal of the drug.

REFERENCES

(1) Merritt and Foster: Am. J. Med. Sc., **200:** 541, 1940.
(2) Kimball: J. Am. Med. Assn., **112:** 1244, 1939.
(3) Gruhzit: Arch. Path., **28:** 761, 1939.
(4) Drake, Gruber and Haury: In press.
(5) Ecker and Pillemer: Proc. Soc. Exp. Biol. and Med., **44:** 262, 1940.

ANTAGONISTIC EFFECT OF ASPHYXIA TO CURARE PARALYSIS OF THE VAGUS NERVE

HANS MAUTNER AND ALDO LUISADA

From the Department of Pharmacology of the Middlesex University Medical School, Waltham, Mass.

Received for publication March 17, 1941

The induction of asphyxia restores excitability to the vagus nerve paralysed by curare. The purpose of this paper is to report the results of experiments designed to investigate this phenomenon.

MATERIAL AND METHODS

The experiments were performed on dogs (8 to 15 kg.) anesthetized by morphine sulfate (10 mgm. per kg. subcutaneously) followed 30 minutes later by urethane given by stomach tube (1 gm. per kg.). In a few instances cats or rabbits were used. In all experiments tracheotomy was performed and a T-cannula introduced before the various blood vessels were prepared. This allowed the immediate starting of artificial respiration. In most experiments the right vagus nerve was then isolated and severed. The left vagus nerve was treated similarly, but the peripheral end was bound on two curved electrodes. The exposed nerves were covered with gauze soaked in Ringer's solution. The stimulation of the nerve was accomplished by means of a Harvard inductorium and a dry cell of 1.5 volts. The secondary was usually placed at number 6 of the scale.

Three different samples of curare were tried, all supplied by Merck and Co. The solutions were prepared in the following way: to 50 mgm. of curare 10 cc. of distilled water were added; then the ampule was sealed and shaken for two hours, heated to 100°C. for one hour and allowed to settle overnight at room temperature. The next day the solution was filtered, 1 cc. of the filtrate containing approximately (according to a statement of Merck and Co.) 3 mgm. of dissolved curare. The initial dose of curare solution was 0.05 to 0.1 cc. per kg. The same dose was again injected, if required, up to a total of 1 to 2 cc. per kg.

The action of curare was compared with that of Erythroidine (tetrahydroerythroidine hydrobromide) (1) supplied by Merck and Co. A 5 per cent solution was used.

An increase of CO_2 in the blood of curarized animals was obtained by interrupting the artificial respiration. In animals with normal breathing it was obtained: (*1*) by rebreathing from an extensible rubber balloon filled with air applied to the tracheal cannula; (*2*) by closing the trachea with a clamp.

All the drugs used in these experiments, potassium chloride, physostigmine salicylate, atropine sulfate, nicotine sulphate, acetylcholine chloride, and acetyl-beta-methylcholine, were given intravenously, almost always in the right jugular vein. The blood pressure was measured in the right carotid artery. Lead 2, using needle electrodes, of the electrocardiogram was recorded in some experiments.

RESULTS

1. Effect of vagal stimulation before and after curare administration. It is well known that electrical excitation, either of the peripheral cut end or of the intact vagus nerve, is quickly followed by bradycardia and by a fall in blood pressure. The bradycardia is often preceded by complete asystole, apparently due to sino-auricular block. The drop in blood pressure is sudden and dramatic. The electrocardiogram may show the following changes: sino-auricular block, sinus bradycardia or auriculo-ventricular block; there are usually also a decrease in the height of, or an inversion of, the T-wave and a depression of the S-T segment.

The injection of curare produces in the dog a more or less lasting drop in blood pressure. In cats, however, the effect is less uniform and in some experiments hypertension is noted. The electrocardiogram shows no changes after the administration of curare.

The injection of a small dose (0.05 to 0.1 cc. per kg.) of curare solution does not always alter the excitability of the vagus nerve. However, when the dose of curare is large enough to impair the diaphragm, stimulation of the peripheral cut end of the vagus nerve is followed by a drop in blood pressure which is smaller and may even be reduced to less than one-half that occurring in the non-curarized dog. When the injected dose is increased from 0.3 to 0.5 cc. per kg. of the curare solution the diaphragm becomes paralyzed and following vagal stimulation the drop in blood pressure is reduced to approximately one-third of that occurring in a non-curarized dog. Upon increasing the dose to 1 to 2 cc. per kg. of the curare solution a stage is reached in which no changes in the blood pressure occur upon stimulating the vagus nerve (figs. 1, 2, and 5). That the paralysis of the vagus nerve is not related to the low level of blood pressure induced by curare can be demonstrated by the fact that injection of epinephrine increases the blood pressure in a curarized animal but does not influence the induced vagal paralysis. In cats often no blood pressure drop precedes the paralysis of the vagus caused by curare.

Analysis of the electrocardiogram shows that when the dose of curare is insufficient to cause paralysis of the diaphragm, the usual changes noted after vagal stimulation in a non-curarized animal still occur, but to a lesser degree. In fully curarized animals, stimulation of the vagus nerve no longer produces electrocardiographic changes.

Erythroidine, on the contrary, showed a much weaker action on the vagus. A dose sufficient to paralyze the diaphragm (1.5 mgm./kg.) is without effect on the vagus nerve. A dose three times as large is able to change the function of the vagus nerve, but complete paralysis is obtained only by injection of 10 mgm. per kg. or more (fig. 6).

Acetylcholine and acetyl-beta-methylcholine cause bradycardia, often heart block, and hypotension when injected into normal dogs. After curarization

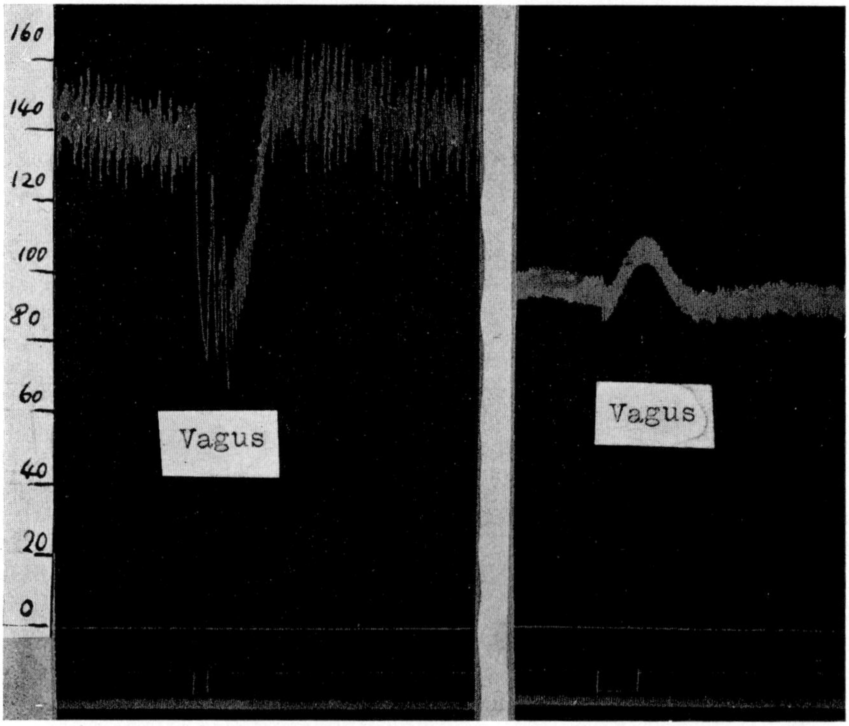

FIG. 1. DOG, 8 KG. INTACT VAGI

a, blood pressure drop by stimulation of the left vagus; *b*, blood pressure rise by same stimulation after 2.5 cc. of curare solution.

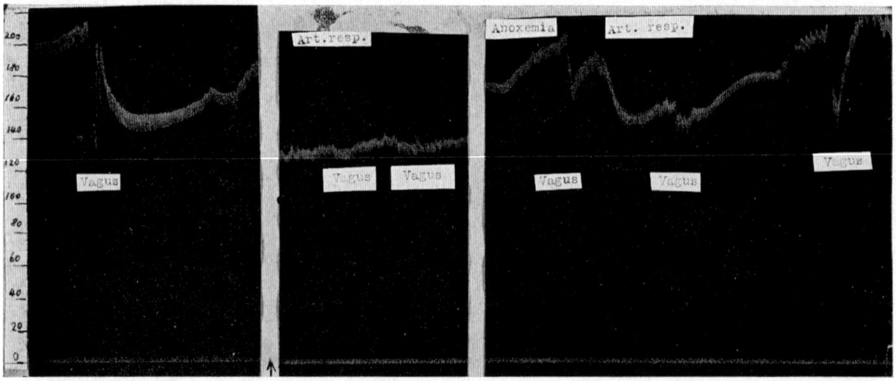

FIG. 2. DOG, 4.3 KG. CUT VAGI. STIMULATION OF THE PERIPHERAL END OF LEFT VAGUS

a, blood pressure drop before curare; *b*, no change in blood pressure after 3 cc. of curare solution; *c*, the excitability of the vagus is increased by anoxemia, then depressed by artificial respiration, then increased again by anoxemia (not marked).

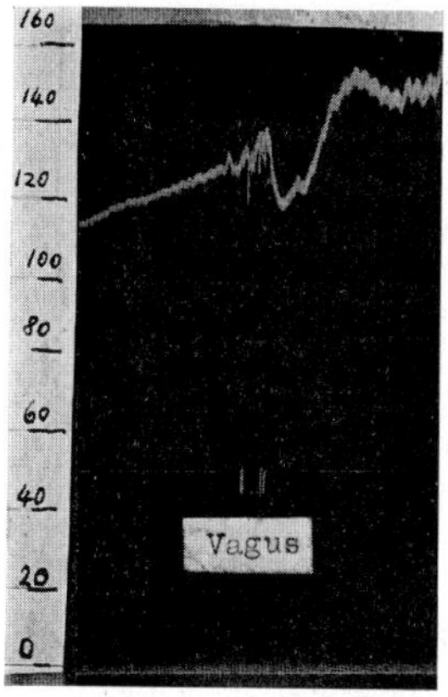

a

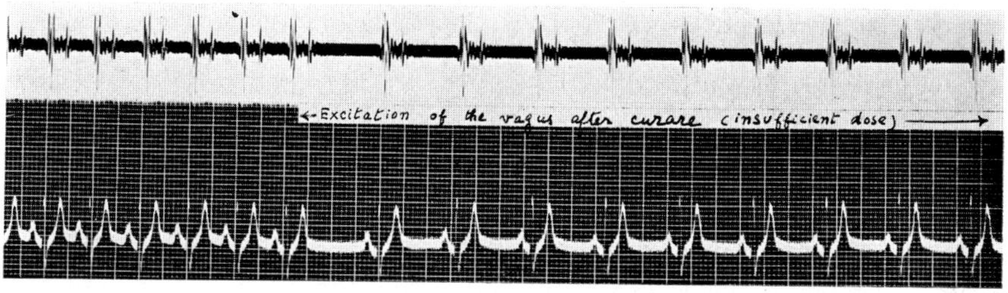

b

FIG. 3. DOG, 16 KG. CUT VAGI. STIMULATION OF THE PERIPHERAL END OF LEFT VAGUS AFTER 10 CC. OF CURARE SOLUTION

a, effect on blood pressure; *b*, effect on heart sounds and electrocardiogram.

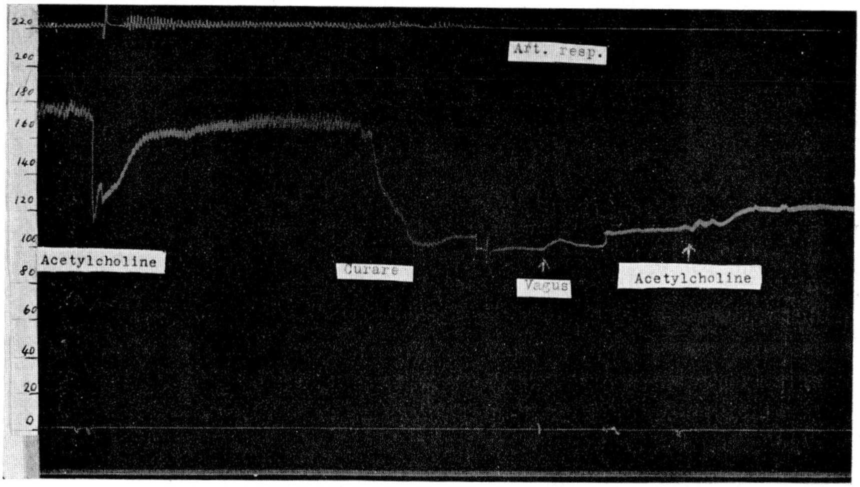

FIG. 4. DOG, 7.3 KG. INTACT VAGI. RESPIRATORY CURVE AND BLOOD PRESSURE CURVE

Action of acetylcholine (0.05 mg.) before and after curare solution (10 cc.). After curare as well vagus stimulation as acetylcholine cause a slight rise of blood pressure.

small doses of acetylcholine chloride (0.05 mgm. per kg.) and of acetyl-beta-methylcholine, (0.25 mgm. per kg.) become ineffective (fig. 4). Much larger doses still lower the blood pressure, but the intensity of the action is markedly decreased, so that only one-half or one-third of the original drop in pressure is obtained.

2. Effect of asphyxia, potassium, and physostigmine on the vagal paralysis caused by curare, erythroidine, nicotine, or atropine. That the paralysis of the vagus nerve caused by curare can be abolished is demonstrated by the following experiments. If, in a curarized animal, artificial respiration is stopped, the blood pressure rises. If now the peripheral cut end of the vagus nerve is

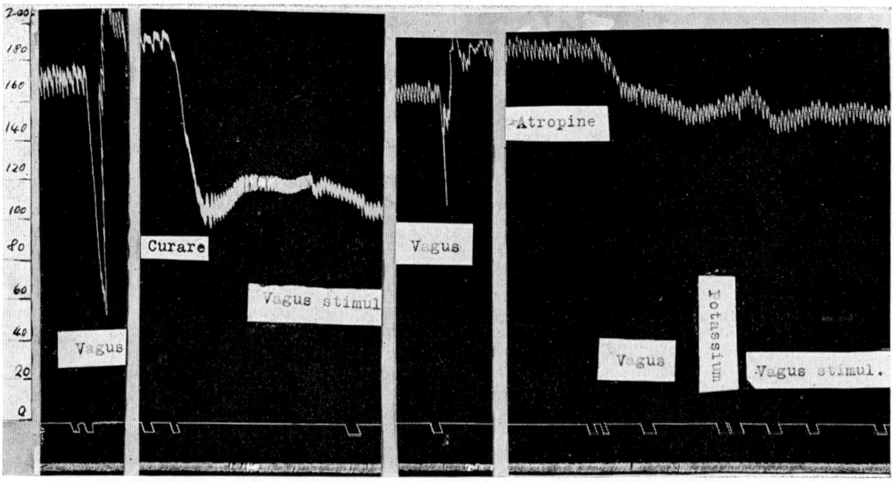

FIG. 5. DOG, 5.3 KG. CUT VAGI. STIMULATION OF PERIPHERAL END OF LEFT VAGUS

a, blood pressure drop before curare; *b*, curare solution (2 cc.) causes hypotension; after the injection vagus stimulation has no effect; *c*, after potassium chloride (3 cc. 1 per cent solution) the vagus nerve is excitable again; *d*, atropine sulphate (0.3 mg.) is injected causing paralysis of the vagus; reinjection of potassium chloride in the same dose does not affect the paralysis.

stimulated, excitability can be demonstrated, though to a lesser degree, than before curare administration (fig. 2). This newly awakened excitability lasts for some minutes, even though artificial respiration is restored. Asphyxia will likewise renew the excitability of a vagus nerve paralyzed by erythroidine.

To demonstrate that this is a specific effect for curare and erythroidine, in an atropinized animal, on the other hand, anoxemia produces no change in the peripheral paralysis of the vagus nerve. Furthermore, if a curarized animal (vagal excitability present after anoxemia) is atropinized, the vagus nerve can no longer be rendered excitable by asphyxia. In nicotinized animals we were also able to show that the induced paralysis of the vagus nerve is not affected by asphyxia.

In a curarized animal the intravenous injection of 20 to 50 mgm. per kg. of potassium chloride in 1 per cent solution partly re-establishes the excitability of the paralyzed vagus nerve (fig. 5). The maximal effect is obtained 1 to 2

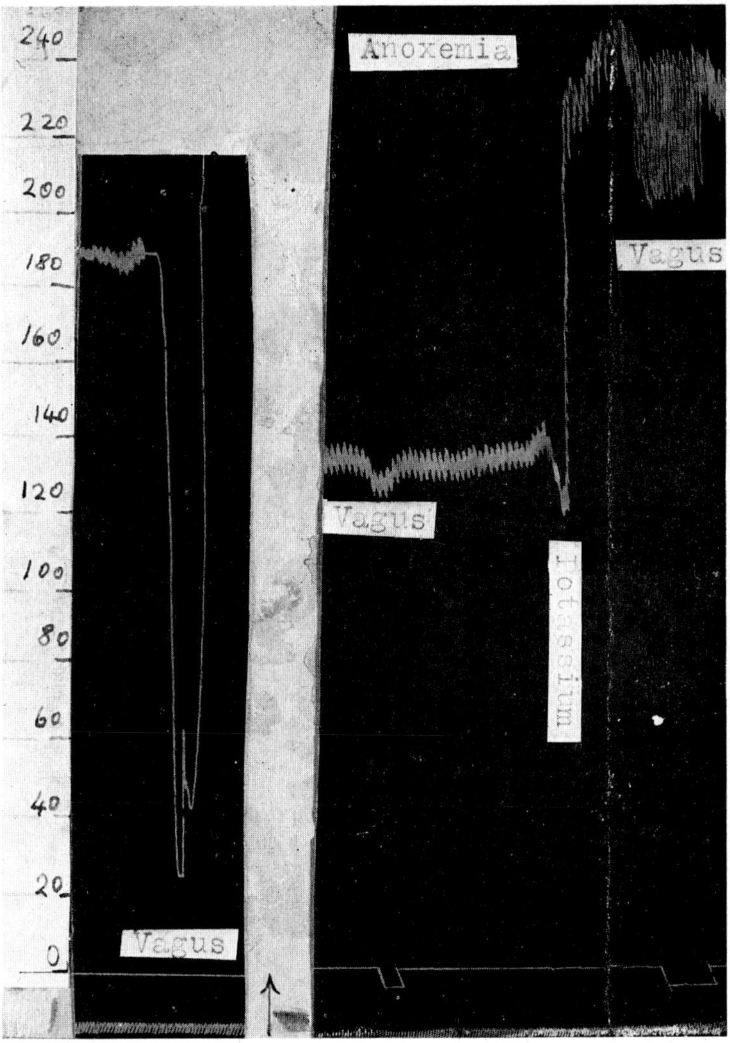

FIG. 6. DOG, 18 KG. CUT VAGI. STIMULATION OF PERIPHERAL END OF LEFT VAGUS
a, blood pressure drop before erythroidine; *b*, very slight reaction after 225 mg. of erythroidine (25 mg. were sufficient for paralyzing the diaphragm). Injection of 25 cc. of potassium chloride 1 per cent restores partly the excitability of the vagus, so that bradycardia follows excitation of the nerve.

minutes after the intravenous injection of the drug and then it gradually subsides. Paralysis of the vagus nerve due to erythroidine is also overcome by potassium chloride (fig. 6).

Physostigmine salicylate (1 mgm. per kg.) is likewise able to overcome completely the paralysis of the vagus nerve due to curare (fig. 7). Its action seems to be even more effective than that of potassium.

Acetylcholine chloride (0.05 mgm. per kg.) has no effect in a curarized dog. If, however, potassium chloride is injected into this animal, the previously ineffective dose of acetylcholine will now lower the blood pressure and cause bradycardia.

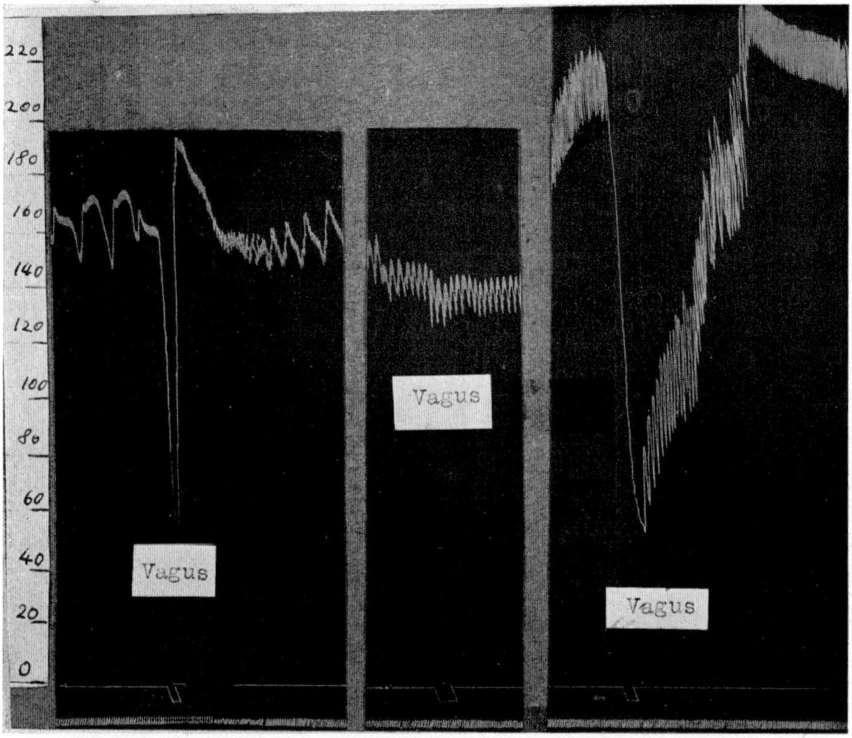

FIG. 7. DOG, 9 KG. CUT VAGI. STIMULATION OF PERIPHERAL END OF LEFT VAGUS
a, before curare; *b*, after repeated injections of curare solution up to a total of 5 cc. (paralysis of the vagus nerve); *c*, after a single injection of physostigmine salicylate (9 mg.) the vagus excitability is restored.

The paralysis of the vagus nerve induced by atropine sulfate (fig. 5) or nicotine sulfate is unaffected either by potassium chloride or by physostigmine salicylate injection.

COMMENT

It is evident that curare paralysis of the vagus nerve can be overcome by asphyxia. This is specific for curare paralysis since asphyxia has no influence upon atropine or nicotine paralysis of the vagus nerve. Since we have demonstrated that the injection of potassium chloride has the same effect as asphyxia, although not so marked, it is theoretically possible that asphyxia, in some unknown way, causes the liberation of potassium. This was actually described by previous workers (2, 3, 4, 5, 6).

Physostigmine is able to restore completely the excitability of the vagus nerve (7, 8) and its action is even more intense than that of asphyxia or potassium. In curarized animals spontaneous respiration is observed after physostigmine administration. It is known that both substances, acetylcholine and potassium, work in the same direction on the vagus nerve and on voluntary muscle tissue (9). Normally acetylcholine liberates potassium (10, 11) and is quickly destroyed by choline esterase. One of the possibilities is that curare prevents the liberation of potassium (12). This does not explain, however, why spontaneous respiration is only seen after the injection of physostigmine, but never after the induction of asphyxia or the injection of potassium.

SUMMARY AND CONCLUSIONS

1. Curare causes a peripheral paralysis of the vagus nerve. The effect on the vagus nerve becomes noticeable with a dose which is not sufficient to cause paralysis of the diaphragm, but is complete only when doses sufficient to produce diaphragmatic paralysis are used. Stimulation of the peripheral cut end of the vagus nerve is without effect after curarization.

2. Erythroidine has an effect on the vagus nerve similar to that of curare, but this effect is obtained only by very large doses, which are much greater than those necessary to paralyze the diaphragm.

3. The paralysis of the vagus nerve induced by curare is partly relieved by asphyxia; this is not due to the resulting hypotension, since hypertension induced by epinephrine in the curarized animals does not re-excite the vagus nerve.

4. The injection of potassium or physostigmine has the same effect as asphyxia upon curare paralysis of the vagus nerve.

5. Curare paralysis of the vagus nerve differs from atropine or nicotine paralysis in that the latter are unaffected by asphyxia and potassium or physostigmine.

REFERENCES

(1) UNNA: Am. J. Phys., **126:** 644, 1939.
(2) HOUSSAY, MARENZI AND GERSCHMAN: Compt. rend. Soc. Biol. **124:** 382, 1937.
(3) ZWEMER AND PIKE: Ann. N. Y. Acad. Sc., **37:** 257, 1938.
(4) DENNIS AND MOORE: Am. J. Physiol., **123:** 443, 1938.
(5) MULLIN, DENNIS AND CALVIN Am. J. Physiol., **124:** 192, 1938.
(6) CATTELL AND CIVIN: J. Biol. Chem., **126:** 633, 1938.
(7) PAL: Zbl. f. Physiol., **14:** 255, 1900.
(8) ROTHBERGER: Pflügers Arch. ges. Physiol., **87:** 117, 1901.
(9) HOWELL: Am. J. Physiol., **15:** 280, 1906.
(10) BROWN AND FELDBERG: J. Physiol., **86:** 290, 1936.
(11) CAMP AND HIGGINS: THIS JOURNAL, **57:** 376, 1936.
(12) WOOD, COLLINS AND MOE: Am. J. Physiol. **128:** 635, 1940.

THE EFFECT OF DIGOXIN ON THE COLD BLOODED HEART AND ITS BEARING ON THE MECHANISM OF DIGITALIS ACTION

A. M. WEDD, H. A. BLAIR AND G. K. DWYER

From the Department of Physiology, School of Medicine and Dentistry, University of Rochester

Received for publication April 4, 1941

The exact manner in which digitalis exerts its beneficial effect on the failing heart is still a moot question, and extreme divergence of opinion exists even among present day investigators. Gold and Cattell (1) maintain that by direct action on muscle the drug enables the heart to develop greater tension during systolic contraction without primary change in the diastolic length of the muscle. Katz, Rodbard, Friend and Rottersman (2), on the other hand, concluded from experiments on dogs that the chief site of action of therapeutic doses of digitalis is not the heart but peripheral vessels, particularly those of the liver. To avoid certain difficulties of interpretation of observations made on the intact animal or the isolated whole heart we have investigated the action of digitalis on small strips cut from the cold blooded heart. Interest has been centered for the most part on the alteration in time relations brought about the drug. These include changes in the conduction rate, the rate of spontaneous beating and the Q-T interval of the electrocardiogram. Since the Q-T interval was shown previously (3) to be equal to the refractory period this latter quantity also has been measured indirectly. Mechanical records were taken simultaneously with electrical in certain cases to see whether the linear relation between the duration of the beat and the Q-T interval previously established in normal heart strips (3) held also when Q-T was shortened by the drug. The threshold strengths of electrical stimuli were studied with a view to the possibility of relating them to changes in the spontaneous rhythm.

The method and the theoretical basis for the interpretation of the electrograms obtained have been described in detail elsewhere by Blair, Wedd and Young (3), (or see Craib (4), Wilson, Macleod and Barker (5) or Ashman, Wilde and Drawe (6)). Strips of muscle were placed on filter paper or a paraffin block and bathed with phosphate-buffered Ringer's solution. The tissues were rhythmically stimulated by condenser discharges; the stimulating electrodes were placed transversely at one end and two recording electrodes lay along the muscle; the latter were paired with indifferent electrodes placed about two inches from the muscle. Potential differences were amplified and recorded by a piezoelectric crystal ink writer. With this type of recording a diphasic wave is obtained when the tissue depolarizes and also when it repolarizes at the region under a contiguous electrode (fig. 1). The muscle strip represented twice at the top of this figure is stimulated through two electrodes at A. The passage of the wave of excitation is evidenced by progressive depolarization which is equivalent in its external electrical effects to the passage along the strip of the polarized cap shown underneath. If electrode P' is distant, the potential changes recorded between P and P' will be due essentially to changes at the region P alone. The polarized cap as it approaches and recedes from P will make it positive and negative respectively giving a diphasic record

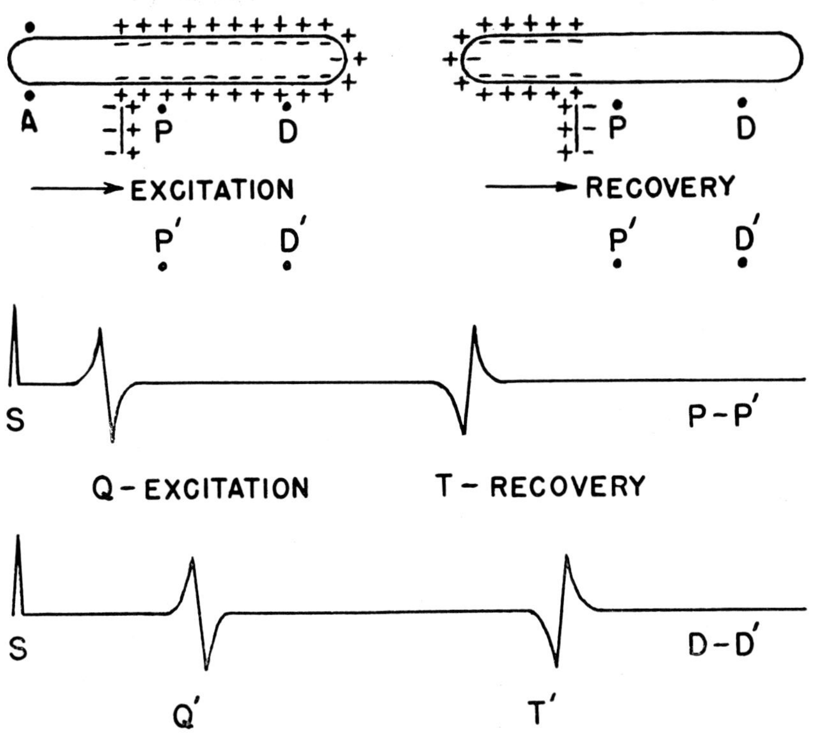

FIG. 1. A SCHEMATIC REPRESENTATION OF THE METHOD AND RECORDS

At the top is represented a heart strip during excitation and recovery. The dots A represent the stimulating electrodes. P and P' represent one pair of recording electrodes, and D and D' represent another pair. Each pair gives a record of the type represented below in which S is due to the stimulus, Q to depolarization of the strip and T to repolarization. The tissue is refractory at a given region while it is depolarized there, that is from the middle of Q to the middle of T in the record.

like Q in the diagram marked P-P'. The repolarization or recovery of the strip will be equivalent electrically to the passage of a similar but oppositely directed polarized cap as shown in the top right. This will make the electrode P first negative and then positive as represented by the diphasic wave T in the middle diagram. The changes at electrode D will be the same as at P but later in occurrence as shown by the lowest diagram. The velocity of the excitation wave may be measured by dividing the distance AP by the time SQ, S being the record of the stimulus; or by dividing the distance PD by the time QQ'. The interval between depolarization and repolarization at a given electrode is called *Q-T* in conformity with customary electrocardiographic nomenclature. To determine the refractory period the muscle was driven rhythmically, and test shocks five times the threshold strength were placed successively closer to the repolarization wave until an extra response failed to occur. To record mechanical systole the muscle was placed in a small well in a paraffin block and was attached at one end to a fine glass rod which served as an isometric lever whose movements were photographed. The stimulating shock was recorded on both camera and ink writer to permit accurate timing. The drug used in all experiments was digoxin, a pure glucoside obtained from Digitalis lanata. Observations were made with varying concentrations. In general, the concentration 2×10^{-6} proved most useful by producing definite effects promptly without appearing to be unduly toxic.

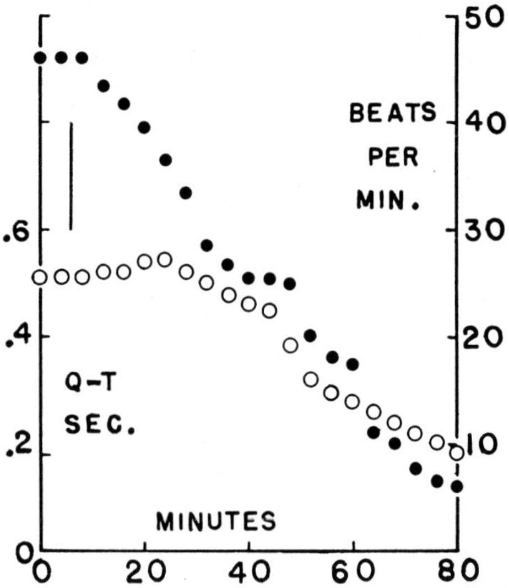

FIG. 2. FROM A SPONTANEOUSLY BEATING STRIP OF TURTLE AURICLE

Digoxin 1×10^{-6} was added at the time indicated by the vertical bar. Slowing of rate began almost immediately. At first *Q-T* tended to lengthen in accord with rate slowing but this was soon overcome by the characteristic action of the drug to shorten this interval.

DRUG EFFECTS

Rate of beating

Spontaneously beating strips of frog and of turtle auricle were used to determine the effect of the drug on the rate. In these the rate was measured from electrical records taken at intervals of a few minutes. The strips were bathed with Ringer's solution until the rate was found to be stable, and then the drug was added. Fall in rate usually occurred promptly with concentrations of 1×10^{-6} or greater. In figure 2 is a typical example of a turtle auricular strip in which the rate fell nearly linearly for 80 minutes after which time the beating ceased. Exceptions to this were observed, however, in two cases of freshly excised strips of turtle auricle. In these the rate of beating increased to about twice its initial value during the first hour after the drug, 2×10^{-6} in one case and 1×10^{-6} in the other. This result may have been due to injury as it was never observed in strips which had been dissected some hours before using and kept cold—the procedure commonly followed. On the other hand this rise in rate may be due to the same factors which sometimes give rise to spontaneous tachycardia in rhythmically driven turtle ventricular strips.

Threshold

The threshold strengths of electrical stimuli applied at regular rates were measured to see if their variations could be related to the change in spontaneous rhythm produced by the drug. The reason for doing this is as follows: The natural rhythm can be regarded as due to the spontaneous development of an excitatory state in the pacemaker region. When it reaches a given threshold value the tissue responds locally and conduction to other regions ensues. Following the refractory period this process is repeated. The rate will decrease if the excitatory state develops more slowly, if the refractory period lengthens, or if the threshold becomes higher. It will be shown later that the drug always shortens the refractory period. Consequently the rate would be expected to increase if the other factors remained constant. Since it actually decreases a rise in threshold was looked for as a possible cause. A rise in this threshold of the spontaneously developed excitatory state is measurable in terms of the threshold for externally applied stimuli according to generally accepted views.

To study threshold changes the heart strip was suspended in Ringer's solution in a U-tube and driven at a constant rate. Non-polarizable electrodes of the Zn-Zn SO_4 type were used. The drug was introduced by changing the solution without disturbing the muscle, or by continuous irrigation with Ringer's solution to which digoxin had been added. The threshold was determined by reducing the strength of the stimulus until the response just failed to appear. The results of these experiments are shown in table 1. Here the percentage change in threshold found at various times in hours following the addition of the drug is given for a number of different drug concentrations. In approximately one-half the experiments the change was less than 10 per cent. Two additional experiments with a concentration of 4×10^{-6} caused a fourfold rise in one hour; the effects of this high concentration are therefore more consistent. In a few cases the lowering of a threshold may be sufficient to account for a considerable increase in rate and therefore for the occasional tachycardias induced by the drug which were mentioned above. Because the threshold changes are usually relatively small at the time the rate has changed considerably it is concluded from these results that the usual marked slowing of rate cannot be due principally to threshold changes but rather to a slowing of the rate of development of excitation at the pacemaker.

Effect on the refractory period and the Q-T interval

We have shown already (3) that in this type of experiment practically identical values are obtained for the Q-T interval and the absolute refractory period when both are measured at the same region, that is, at a region such as that adjacent to electrode *P* or to electrode *D* of figure 1. The importance of this restriction is due to the fact that the refractory period is intrinsically a local property while the Q-T interval or electrical systole may be measured either locally by the method of figure 1 or for the whole strip or organ as is

TABLE 1

The columns give the changes in threshold strengths of electrical stimuli in per cent of the normal as measured at one-half hour intervals following administration of digoxin of the concentrations in parts per million given by the top row

TISSUE	TIME	DIGOXIN CONCENTRATION													
		.15	.25	.3				1			2				4
	hours														
Turtle ventricle	0.5	0		+60	0	0	0	−10	+50		−25	−55	−5		+100
	1.0	+150		+70	0	+10	−10	−5	+300		+80	−55	0		+300
	1.5					+15	−15	0	+800				0		+1300
	2.0					+20	−15	+10							
Turtle auricle	0.5			0	+75		−20	0	+5	+150	0	+20	0	−30	
	1.0				+75		−5	0	+20	+300		+30	−5	−5	
	1.5								+10			+20	0		
	2.0								+5						
Frog ventricle	0.5		+10	−5	0						−15				
	1.0		+10	−5							−15				
	1.5			0											

done in clinical electrocardiography. Obviously the latter method measures electrical systole from its beginning in the region first excited to its ending in the region last to recover. Equality of refractory period and Q-T was obtained after digoxin as well as with normal strips (3). Digoxin invariably shortens the Q-T interval and the refractory period if the rate is kept constant and it usually does so even when the rate is slowed considerably. In figure 2 it will be seen, for example, that only a very transient increase of Q-T occurred with slowing of the rate of the spontaneously beating strip. Figure 3 shows how Q-T becomes shorter when the rate is kept constant. In *A* a weak concentration produced a slow shortening. In *B* a strong concentration acted much more rapidly. In either case the ultimate shortening was more than 50 per cent. Results of this kind were invariably obtained with both auricular and ventricular strips. These observations on the relation of Q-T to refractory period, and its shortening by digitalis confirm those of Macleod for the whole frog heart (7).

Earlier observations which reported lengthening of refractory period by digitalis failed to take sufficiently into account its depressant action on conduction. When the point of electrical recording is some distance from the stimulating electrode, or more especially when mechanical recording alone is used, slowing of conduction will account for the delay in response to the test shock after the drug. The controversial aspects of this question have been discussed by Lewis and Drury (8) and by Macleod (7).

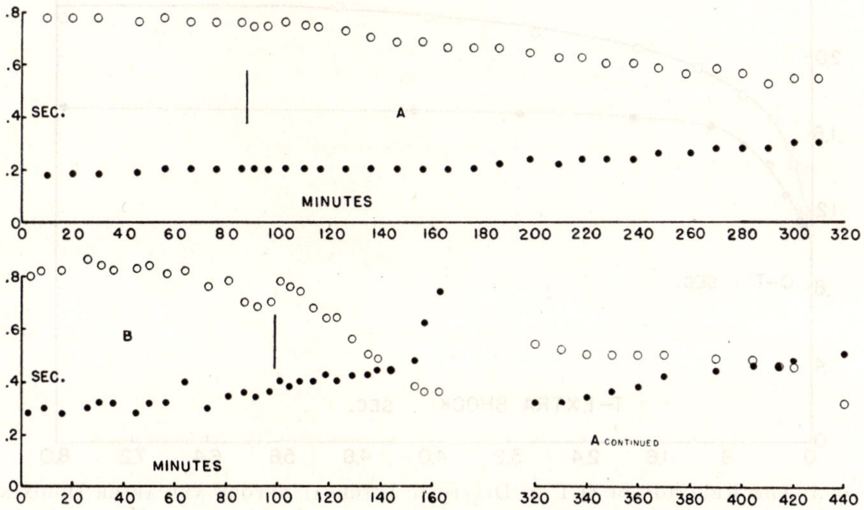

FIG. 3. THE EFFECT OF DIGOXIN ON RHYTHMICALLY DRIVEN STRIPS OF TURTLE VENTRICLE

Open circles represent *Q-T* intervals; solid dots, conduction time (shock to *Q*). Stimulation rate 17 per minute. Ringer solution containing digoxin was begun at the vertical bars. In *A* the digoxin concentration was 0.5×10^{-6}; in *B*, 4×10^{-6}. The abscissae are times measured from the beginning of the experiment.

It was shown previously (3) that Q-T of the beat following a single shortened diastolic interval, introduced during steady driving, was shorter the shorter the diastolic interval until a limit was reached with zero diastolic interval. The upper curve of figure 4 represents an experiment of this kind on a normal turtle ventricular strip. The records in figure 6A represent the data for a single point of this curve. Digoxin was then added while driving at the steady rate of 7.5 per minute and the experiment was repeated after substantial shortening of Q-T had occurred. The resulting data are plotted in the lower curve of figure 4. It will be seen that Q-T shortened as before with decrease of diastolic interval to the same limiting value. Thus although a long Q-T at the slow steady rate is markedly shortened by the drug its further shortening by an extra very early beat cannot be carried beyond the normal minimal value which appears to be fixed and independent of the drug action. The analogous effect determined by increasing the rate of beating will be discussed now.

Many observations were made on the response of the muscle to various rates of beating before and after digoxin. In general, the Q-T interval varied with the rate of beating, and usually the longer the initial Q-T the greater was the shortening produced by the drug. However, exceptions were noted. In

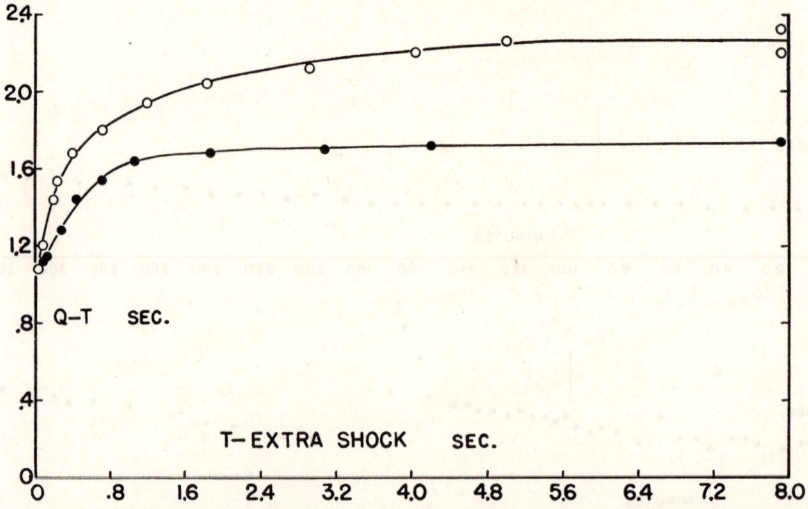

FIG. 4. THE RELATION OF Q-T TO DIASTOLIC INTERVAL BEFORE AND AFTER DIGOXIN

While stimulating a strip of turtle ventricle at intervals of 8 secs. single extra shocks were introduced to determine the relation of the *Q-T* interval of the extra beat to the preceding diastolic interval. The upper curve is the control. The lower was obtained one hour after digoxin 2×10^{-6} had been added. It will be seen that the *Q-T* interval for the regular driving was considerably shortened by the drug but the maximal *Q-T* shortening for the shortest possible diastolic interval was the same as that recorded before the drug. One of the actual records of this experiment is given in figure 6A.

one experiment in which two strips from the same heart were studied on the same day, for the one driven at a rate of 21 per minute the Q-T interval shortened 45 per cent; its mate driven at a rate of 9 shortened but 23 per cent; all conditions for both were the same as far as could be determined. One of a group of experiments in which the tissue was driven at increasing rates, holding it for a short time at each rate to allow Q-T to stabilize, is illustrated in figure 5. Comparison of the response before and after digoxin shows that before the drug the maximal shortening of Q-T was reached at a rate of 54 per minute and it then became unstable and alternating. After the drug, the same minimal Q-T was reached at a lower rate of beating, 37 per minute, followed by similar instability. Thus it is found that by driving at increasing rates as well as following single early beats the Q-T interval of a given tissue

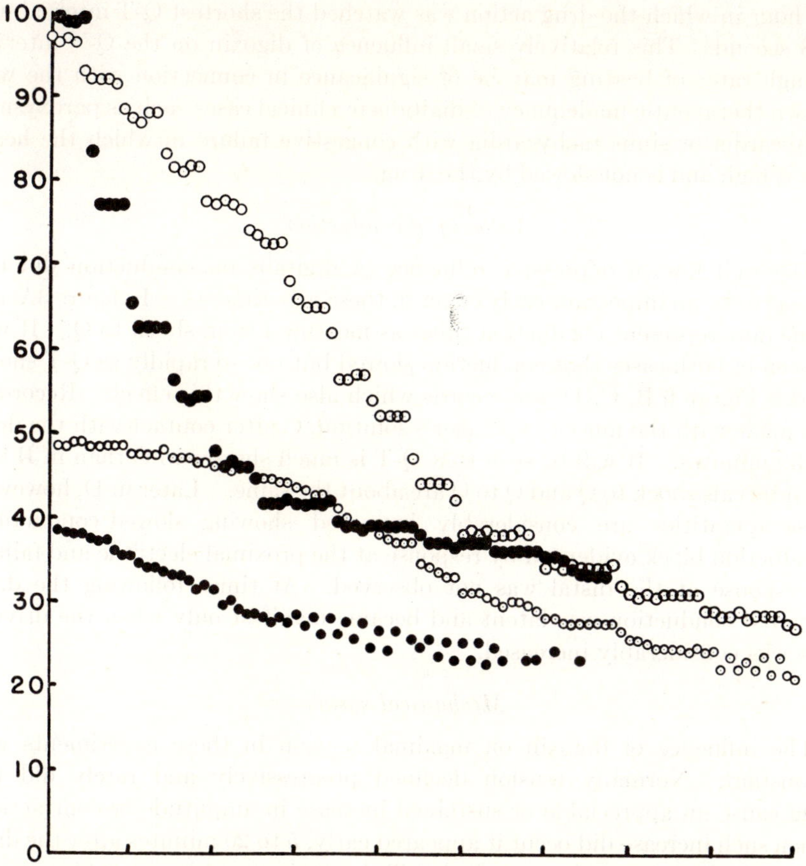

FIG. 5. RESPONSE OF THE Q-T INTERVAL IN A STRIP OF TURTLE VENTRICLE TO INCREASING RATES OF BEATING, BEFORE AND AFTER DIGOXIN

The uppermost circles represent the shock to shock intervals before digoxin, and the corresponding *Q-T* intervals are given by the smaller open circles below. The abscissae are successive beats. At the extreme right, alternation of *Q-T* is seen; just after this point block occurred. The procedure was repeated 45 minutes after digoxin 2×10^{-6}. These beat and *Q-T* intervals are represented by the larger and smaller dots, respectively. *Q-T* has been considerably shortened by the drug, even for the low rate. On increasing the rate *Q-T* began to alternate when it had attained the same degree of shortening as before the drug, and likewise block occurred with the same *Q-T* value, but both of these appeared earlier and the strip could not be driven as fast after digoxin as before it. Both sets of intervals are plotted in millimeters and 25 mm. equal 1 second.

cannot be shortened beyond a minimal value which is the same with or without the drug. Therefore the drug cannot shorten significantly Q-T which already has been greatly shortened by high rate. This is demonstrated in a single experiment in which the muscle was driven at a rate of 31 per minute for one hour and in which the Q-T interval alternated between 1.22 and 1.26 second; digoxin, 2×10^{-6} was then added; alternation continued, and during the hour in which the drug action was watched the shortest Q-T interval was 1.18 second. This relatively small influence of digoxin on the Q-T interval at high rates of beating may be of significance in connection with the well known therapeutic inadequacy of digitalis in clinical cases such as paroxysmal tachycardia or sinus tachycardia with congestive failure in which the heart rate is high and is not slowed by the drug.

Velocity of conduction

The well known depressive influence of digitalis on conduction did not appear to be an important early effect in these experiments. In figure 3A and B the dots represent conduction times as measured from shock to Q. It will be seen in both cases that conduction slowed but not so rapidly as Q-T shortened. Figure 6 B, C, D, are records which also show this effect. Record B was made with the muscle in Ringer's solution, C after contact with the drug for 30 minutes. It will be seen that Q-T is much shorter in C than in B but the intervals shock to Q and Q to Q are about the same. Later in D, however, these quantities are considerably increased showing slowed conduction. Conduction block evidenced by response at the proximal electrode and failure of response at the distal was not observed. At times following the drug impaired conduction was latent and became manifest only when the driving rate was considerably increased.

Mechanical systole

The influence of digoxin on maximal tension in these experiments was inconstant. Normally tension declined progressively and rarely did the drug cause an appreciable or sustained increase in amplitude of contraction. When such increase did occur it appeared early, 5 to 20 minutes after the drug was applied, always before marked Q-T shortening, and it was seldom maintained more than one-half hour. Failure to obtain the tension increase usually expected from digitalis action may be due in part to the slow rate of beating and the relatively long diastole of the tissue studied. Since repolarization appears to terminate contraction (3), marked shortening of Q-T may limit tension development unless there is some other direct action which tends to increase it. That tension is not necessarily related to rate of beating or to the Q-T interval was seen in numerous experiments, with or without digoxin, in which, following a period of rapid stimulation and then a pause, there appeared an unusually large beat with a short Q-T interval. An illustration of this interesting phenomenon is seen in figure 7, and further details of this experiment are given in table 2. This effect has been observed in single fibers of skeletal muscle by Ramsey and Street (11).

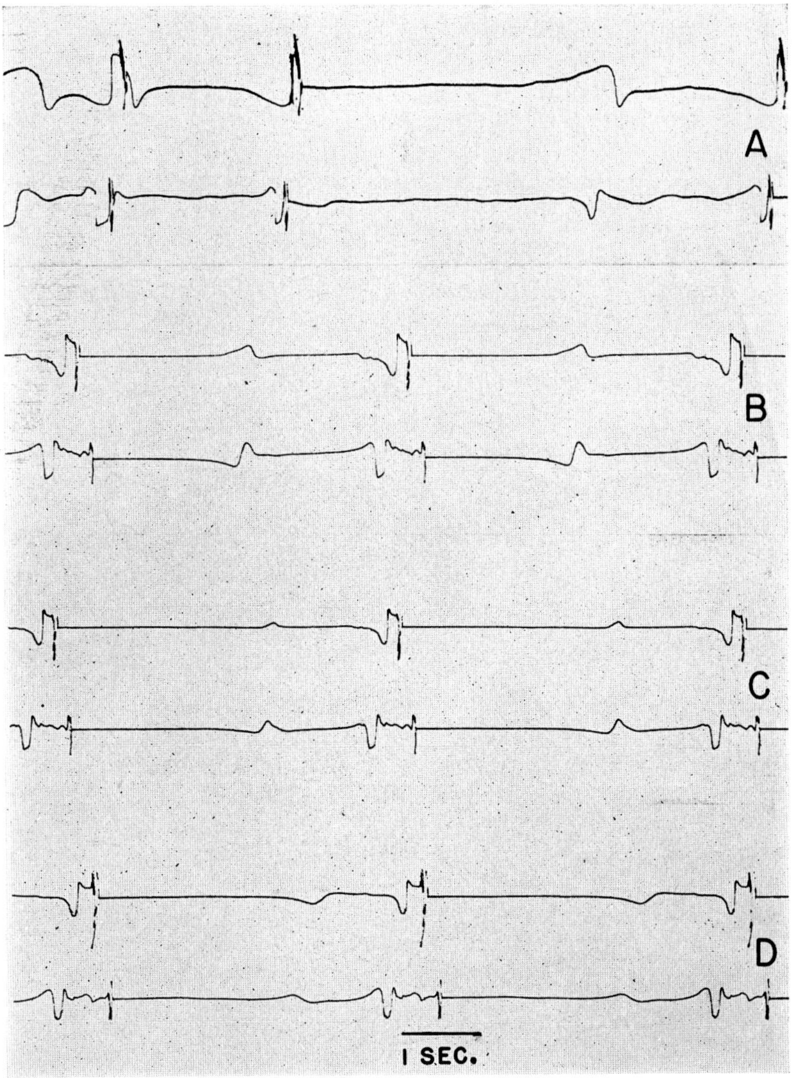

FIG. 6. A. To illustrate the relation between Q-T and diastolic interval and the method of relating the refractory period to Q-T. Read from right to left. Upper line complexes recorded near stimulating electrodes; lower line, distal complexes. The first stroke is due to the shock. This is followed by a diphasic Q, which is better separated from the shock in the distal record. The T wave is similar in form but opposite in phase. At the left an extra shock placed just after the middle of T gives rise to a beat with a very short Q-T interval. A complete experiment of this type is shown in figure 4.

B, *C*, *D* is a series obtained just before, and 30 and 50 minutes, respectively, after digoxin; drug concentration 2×10^{-6}. Upper line complexes were recorded 11 mm. and lower line 28 mm. from the stimulating electrodes; length of muscle strip, 40 mm. The difference between the lower and the upper shock to Q intervals gives Q-Q, the conduction time over the 17 mm. between the two recording electrodes. In *C*, marked shortening of Q-T has occurred without much change in Q-Q. In *D*, conduction is noticeably slower. The wave forms in these records are somewhat different from the expected types, more closely realized in *A*, because of muscle movements which occur in the long strip.

The duration of mechanical systole was regularly shortened by the drug. As already mentioned, since repolarization appears to be the factor which terminates contraction, and since Q-T is regularly shortened by the drug, this shortening of mechanical systole is to be expected. The relation between Q-T and the width of the mechanogram measured at about half relaxation was found to be a linear one in normal tissue (3). In figure 8 this relation is plotted for a strip in which Q-T was first shortened by driving at increasing rates. The rate was then slowed to its original value and the drug administered. During the following 30 min. Q-T was shortened by the drug alone. Then it was shortened further by fast driving. All the points except the first three after the drug fall closely on the same line. From this it is concluded that the duration of mechanical systole varies as the duration of electrical

TABLE 2

Data for beats shown in figure 7. The second to last beat is enhanced greatly in height by the preceding high rate and the lengthened diastolic pause

SHOCK TO SHOCK INTERVAL	Q-T INTERVAL	BEAT DURATION	BEAT HEIGHT
sec.	*sec.*	*sec.*	*mm.*
6.32	1.28		
6.32	1.28		
6.32	1.28	1.20	36
6.32	1.28	1.20	36
18.9	1.28	1.24	33.5
2.8	1.26	1.24	38
2.8	1.26	1.24	40.5
2.8	1.20	1.22	41.5
2.8	1.20	1.22	41.5
16 beats at increasing rates omitted			
1.2	.66	.76	24
1.2	.66	.76	24
4.7	.90	1.04	48
4.4	.96	.94	35

systole and that it does so in the same way after the drug as before. The first three points taken at 5 min. intervals after drug administration show a decrease in duration of mechanical systole before Q-T is shortened. We have no explanation for this minor exception to the rule but it may be associated with the progressive weakening of contraction usually observed following the drug. If so, fast driving tends to relieve this depression. Enhanced beats, such as that in figure 7 are sometimes off the line also in either direction depending on the pause preceding them.

COMMENT

The failure in these experiments to observe a significant and sustained increase in the height of mechanical contraction cannot be considered to have any bearing on the experiments of Gold and Cattell (1) or their interpretation of the mechanism of digitalis action. We, too, have observed that action, and have also shown that mechanical effects may be independent of electrical. It is possible that under certain conditions digitalis does have a direct stimu-

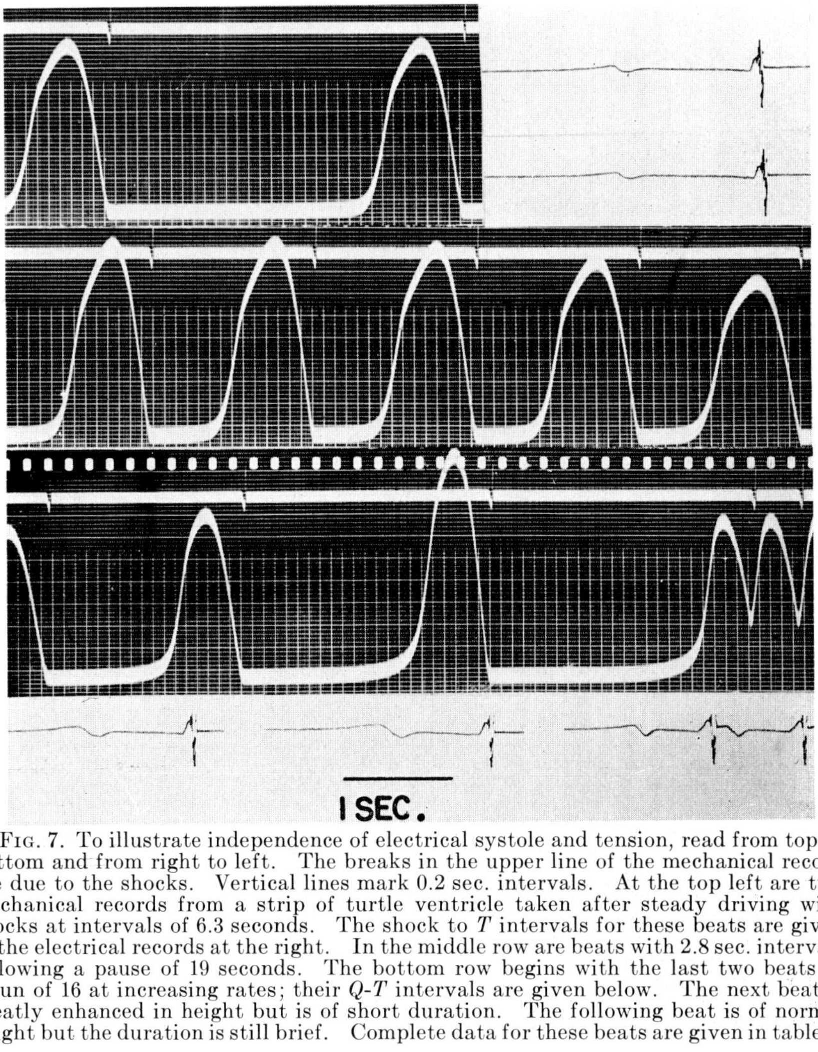

FIG. 7. To illustrate independence of electrical systole and tension, read from top to bottom and from right to left. The breaks in the upper line of the mechanical record are due to the shocks. Vertical lines mark 0.2 sec. intervals. At the top left are two mechanical records from a strip of turtle ventricle taken after steady driving with shocks at intervals of 6.3 seconds. The shock to *T* intervals for these beats are given in the electrical records at the right. In the middle row are beats with 2.8 sec. intervals following a pause of 19 seconds. The bottom row begins with the last two beats of a run of 16 at increasing rates; their *Q-T* intervals are given below. The next beat is greatly enhanced in height but is of short duration. The following beat is of normal height but the duration is still brief. Complete data for these beats are given in table 2.

lating action on contraction. In our experiments the invariable action of the drug was to shorten systole, both electrical and mechanical. This same effect has also been observed in man. Cheer and Dieuaide (9) found a consistent decrease in the length of the Q-T in relation to the R-R interval and Berliner

(10) in a small series of patients with normal rhythm, found Q-T shortening in every instance, while change in the form of T and slowing of rate occurred less frequently. It would seem logical to seek, at least in part, the explana-

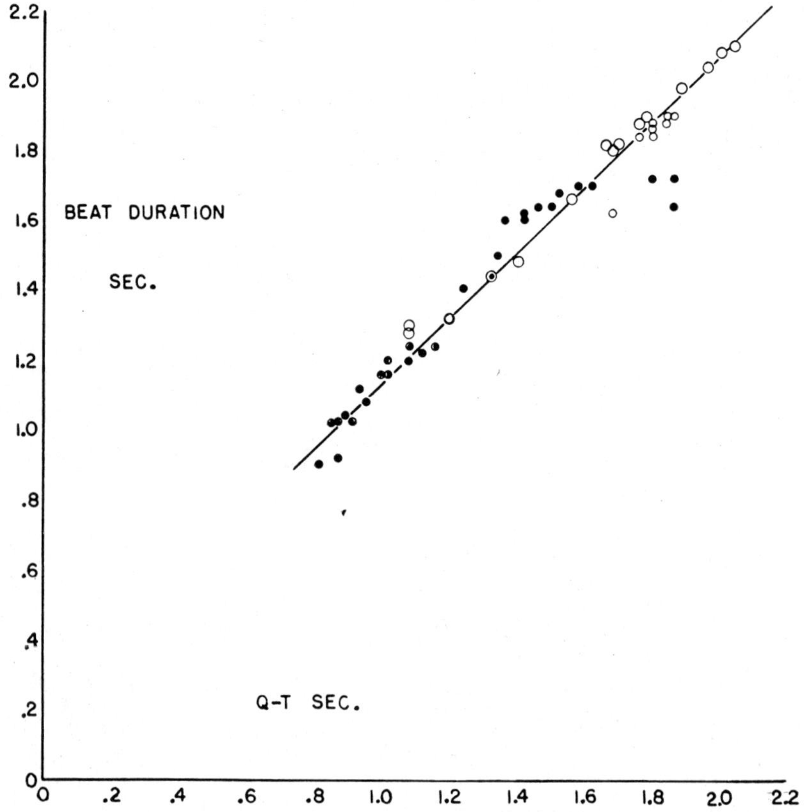

FIG. 8. TO ILLUSTRATE THE RELATION BETWEEN Q-T AND THE DURATION OF MECHANICAL SYSTOLE IN A STRIP OF TURTLE VENTRICLE AT DIFFERENT RATES OF BEATING BEFORE AND AFTER DIGOXIN

The large circles represent consecutive *Q-T* intervals at increasing rates, and the small circles at decreasing rates before drug action. Black dots are for similar *Q-T* intervals after digoxin except that the seven dots to the right just above the 1.6 position were obtained at 5 min. intervals during the initial 30 minute period of regular driving. The remainder are the data for successive beats while driving at increasing rates. These latter points fall around the same line as that determined for the norm al tissue. During the initial period the beat duration often shortens somewhat before *Q-T* has begun to shorten; this is shown by the three dots farthest to the right.

tion of the desired drug effect in this constant action. If there were greater agreement with the view of Cheer and Dieuaide that prolongation of Q-T is an accompaniment of congestive heart failure the importance of Q-T shortening by digitalis would be obvious.

Shortening of the Q-T interval, the refractory period and mechanical systole may indicate that recovery is more rapid, or, on the other hand, the shortening of systole may contribute to recovery by permitting longer diastole. If so, the powerful contraction of a well recovered muscle, though brief, is probably more effective than the longer, weaker contraction of a partially recovered muscle. Whether the ultimate action of digitalis consists in increasing oxygen consumption, or favoring the building up of a greater creatine reserve, or influencing some other metabolic activity, it would seem highly probable that such action would be furthered by the increasing of diastole, which is accomplished by shortening of systole, and at times also by desirable slowing of rate of beating. Certainly the maintenance energy requirement is reduced by such changes.

Cheer and Dieuaide have pointed out that excessive shortening of Q-T is followed by toxic symptoms, but it should be emphasized that Q-T shortening itself is not a toxic manifestation and it appears well before therapeutic dosage has been administered to patients.

A brief description of the principal action of digitalis is that its effect on systole is similar to that of increase in heart rate. This is true in regard to the increase in muscle tension and to the shortening of Q-T, the refractory period and the duration of the beat. It is not true in regard to conduction which is usually slowed rather than improved by the drug.

SUMMARY

The effect of digoxin has been studied on spontaneously beating strips of auricle from the frog, Rana pipiens, and the turtle, Pseudomys elegans, and rhythmically driven strips of ventricle from the turtle. The spontaneous rhythm was usually slowed markedly by the drug. Measurements were made on the driven strips of the Q-T interval, the conduction time, the maximal tension, the duration of systole, the effect of a single short diastole on the ensuing Q-T, the effect of different rates on Q-T, the relation of Q-T to the duration of systole and variations of the threshold to electric stimuli. Mechanical systole is proportional to electrical systole and both are invariably shortened by the drug. The shortening is less at higher rates of beating because the Q-T of a given tissue cannot be shortened beyond a certain limit, either by single early beats or rapid driving and this limit is the same with or without the drug. Since the refractory period which is equal to Q-T is shortened by the drug and the threshold does not regularly change markedly, the slowing action of the drug is ascribed to the slowing of the development of excitation at the pacemaker region. Slowing of conduction usually occurred but later than Q-T changes. Tension increases were irregular and when seen occurred early. The amplitude of contraction may be independent of the duration of systole and the diastolic interval. The possible significance of the shortening of systole for the therapeutic action of digitalis was discussed briefly. It seems reasonable to suppose that the final action of digitalis is related to the lengthened diastole which it produces. There is reduction in the maintenance energy requirement, and longer time for recovery from contraction is given.

REFERENCES

(1) Gold and Cattell: Arch. Int. Med., **65**: 263, 1940.
(2) Katz, Rodbard, Friend and Rottersman: This Journal, **62**: 1, 1938.
(3) Blair, Wedd and Young: Am. J. Physiol., **132**: 157, 1941.
(4) Craib: Heart, **14**: 71, 1927.
(5) Wilson, MacLeod and Barker: The Distribution of the Currents of Action and of Injury Displayed by Heart Muscle and other Excitable Tissues. Ann Arbor, Univ. of Mich. Press, 1933.
(6) Ashman, Wilde and Drawe: Am. J. Physiol., **128**: 547, 1939.
(7) Macleod: Am. Heart J., **17**; 294, 1939.
(8) Lewis and Drury: Heart, **13**: 95, 1926.
(9) Cheer and Dieuaide: J. Clin. Investigation, **11**: 1241, 1932.
(10) Berliner: Am. Heart J., **7**: 189, 1931.
(11) Ramsey and Street: Biological Symposia, **3**: (in press) 1941.

THE EFFECTS OF SEDATIVE DRUGS ON THE PIAL VESSELS*

THEODORE P. SOHLER, GLADYS N. LOTHROP AND JOAN WILKINSON

From the Departments of Neuropathology and Neurology, Harvard Medical School, Boston

Received for publication April 12, 1941

The present paper deals with the effect of dial,[1] avertin fluid,[2] avertin crystals,[3] amylene hydrate, acetanilide and sodium bromide on the cerebral vessels of anesthetized cats. The method of observation, briefly, was as follows: A cranial window was inserted over the parietal cortex, and the diameters of pial vessels were observed and measured by microscope. Recordings of blood pressure from the femoral artery and of cerebrospinal fluid pressure from the cisterna magna were obtained by photokymograph (1). Various drugs: dial, avertin (with or without amylene hydrate), nembutal or ether were used for surgical anesthesia. When the animal was ready for observation, successive doses of the drug to be tested were injected intravenously. Sometimes the same drug as that used for the initial anesthesia was studied, sometimes a different drug. Forty-two cats were studied.

1. DIAL

The results compiled from individual records are shown in figure 1. Dial itself was used as the initial anesthetic eight times and ether once. Subsequent intravenous injections of dial, in doses ranging from 0.036 to 0.32 cc. per kilogram, caused a variable response (fig. 1). In two animals a dilator effect was clear. In four others the situation was complicated by periods of apnea or of low blood pressure, and either of these conditions alone would have been sufficient cause for the dilation (1). With the three remaining animals there was no constancy in the vascular response. The first injection of dial often was followed by apnea. In the uncomplicated experiments the degree of dilation was never large; it began about twenty-five seconds after the injection and lasted only a minute or so. The four constrictions shown

* This study was aided by a grant from the Institute for the Study of Analgesic and Sedative Drugs.

[1] Dial—each cc. contains diallylmalonylurea, 0.1 gram.; urethane, 0.4 gram and monethylurea in distilled water. The dial was contributed for experimental purposes by the Ciba Co., Lafayette Park, Summit, N. J.

[2] Avertin fluid—tribromethanol (sat. sol.) in amylene hydrate diluted with water to make a 2.5 per cent solution of the "original fluid." (Winthrop Chem. Co.)

[3] Avertin crystals—a 2.5 per cent solution in distilled water.

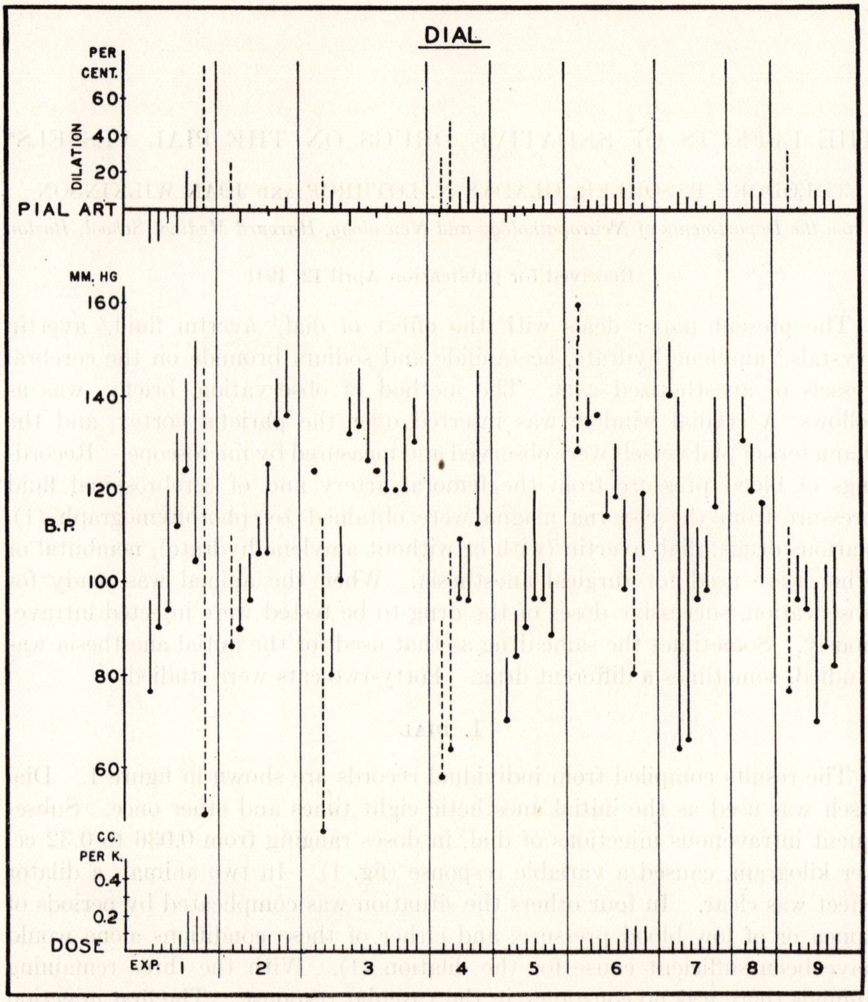

In figures 1–6 the arrangement and symbols are the same. At the top, labelled "Pial Art," each line charted represents the percentage change in diameter of a pial artery following a single intravenous injection of the drug. Below, labelled "B.P.", each line charted represents the total amount of rise or fall of pressure in the femoral artery; the terminal point reached is signified by the black dot at the end of the line. In a few instances both a rise and a fall in blood pressure occurred. This is shown by a crook in the line and a dot at either end, designating the extent of rise or fall. At the bottom, labelled "Dose", each line represents the amount of drug given at each injection. The injections are arranged in chronological order. Experiments on thirty-three cats are shown in these charts. The thin vertical lines separate the results pertaining to one cat (experiment 1) from those of the next (experiment 2). The dotted lines indicate that the changes recorded were complicated by a long period of asphyxia following that particular injection.

in experiment 1 (fig. 1) occurred in a cat anesthetized with ether. After the ether was omitted the pial artery under observation became slowly narrower during the next few hours. It was in this period that the test injections of dial were given. The results therefore may have been affected by the previous etherization. Three intracarotid injections of dial caused prompt dilation. On the whole dial seemed to act as a dilator but this action was neither powerful nor consistent.

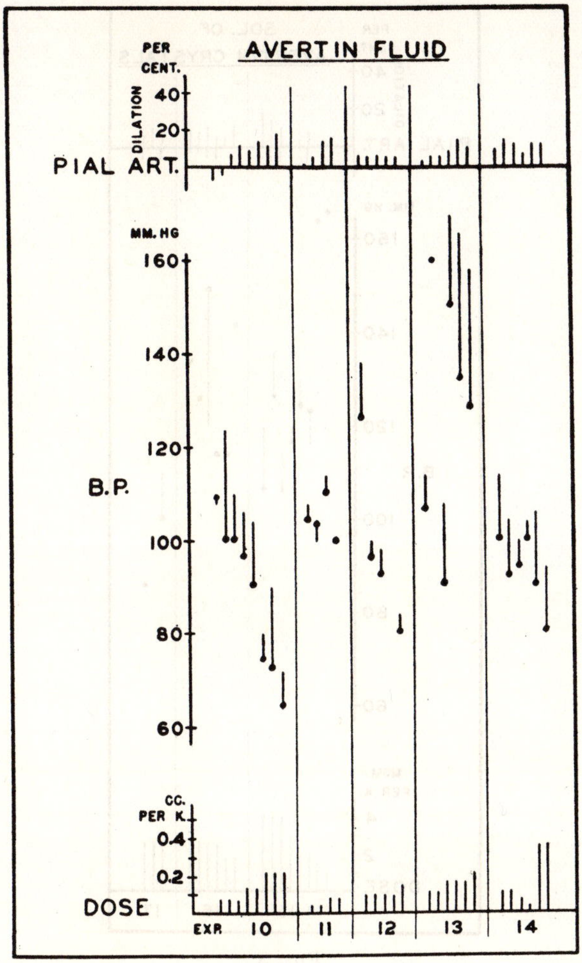

FIG. 2

2. AVERTIN FLUID

Avertin fluid was used as the initial anesthetic. Subsequent intravenous doses ranged from 0.038 to 0.358 cc. per kilogram. The pial arteries dilated in all experiments. The latent period, between the end of the injection and the onset of the dilation, varied from ten to twenty seconds and the duration of the dilation averaged forty seconds. The blood pressure often fell a few millimeters, but not enough to affect the pial artery. No important fluctuation in cerebrospinal fluid pressure or in respiration occurred. Sometimes the respiration became a little slower but artificial respiration was employed during most of the experiments. See figure 2.

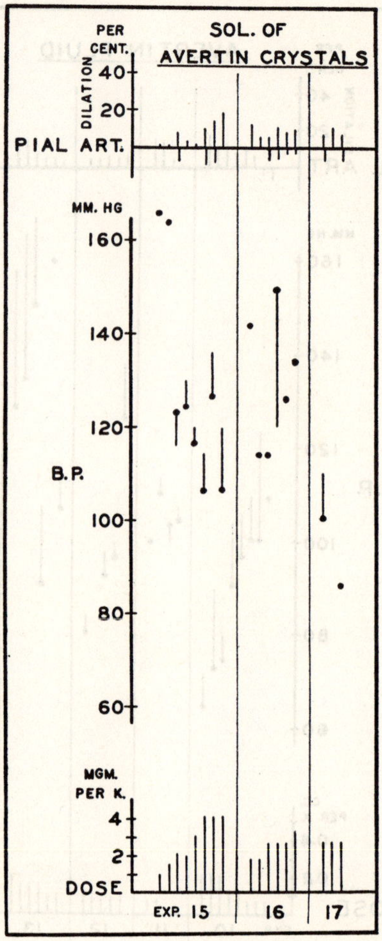

Fig. 3

3. avertin crystals

Twice the initial anesthetic was avertin, once ether. Intravenous injections of the drug, in doses ranging from 1.05 to 4.2 mgm. per kilogram, caused a dilation lasting about forty seconds, and this in turn was often followed by a constriction. Sometimes the constriction did not start until several minutes after the injection, and the artery then remained constricted for six or eight minutes. No complicating fluctuations of blood pressure or of respiration were encountered. Changes in cerebrospinal fluid pressure were negligible. See figure 3.

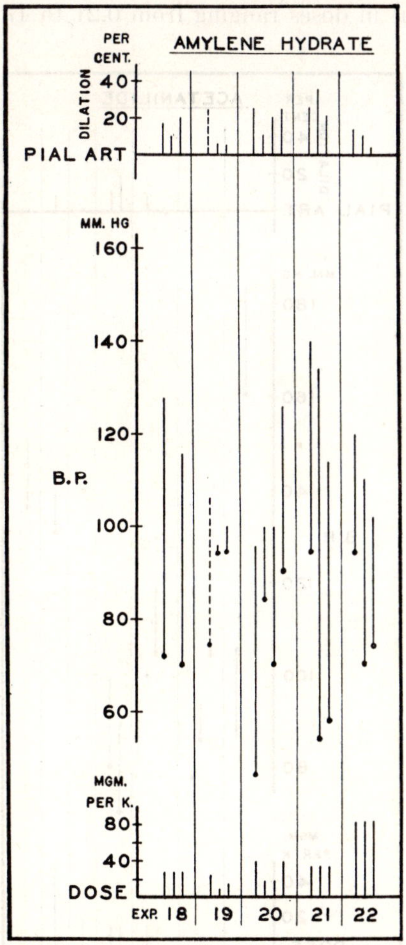

FIG. 4

4. AMYLENE HYDRATE

Nembutal, dial or amylene hydrate were given as initial anesthetics. Intravenous injections of amylene hydrate in doses ranging from 10.2 to 81.4 mgm. per kilogram were given. Following most of the injections the pial arteries dilated. However, in many of the trials a large dilation was preceded or accompanied by a large fall in blood pressure. The cerebrospinal fluid pressure showed a slight tendency to rise. See figure 4.

5. ACETANILIDE

The initial anesthetic was dial except in one animal when ether was given. There were no conspicuous changes in diameter of the pial arteries or in blood pressure following these injections. A 0.5 per cent solution was given (by intravenous injection) in doses ranging from 0.21 to 47 mgm. per kilogram.

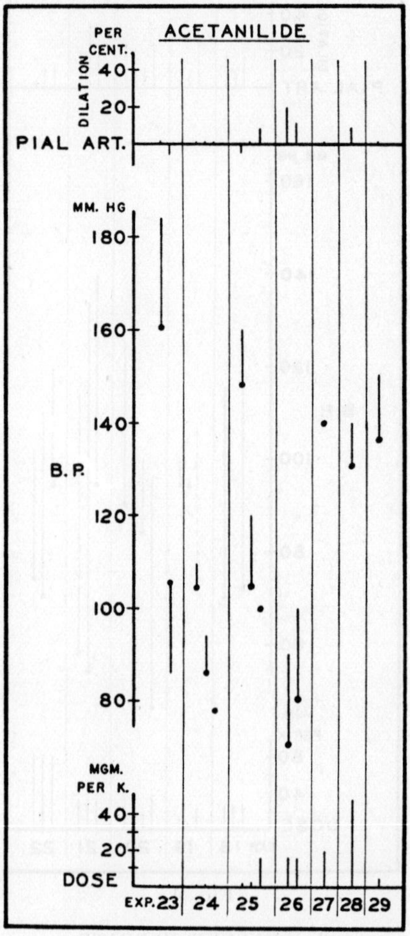

FIG. 5

The most striking observation was the appearance of a purplish brown color in the pial circulation. This color change increased with successive doses and affected arterioles and venules alike. It was noticed about eighty minutes after a small intravenous dose of acetanilide (as small as 10 mgm. per kilogram). See figure 5.

6. SODIUM BROMIDE

Dial was used as the initial anesthetic. There was no change in diameter of the pial arteries after these injections except for an occasional dilation following a rapid injection or a very large dose of the solution. The doses given ranged from 5 to 1000 mgm. per kilogram. The blood pressure and

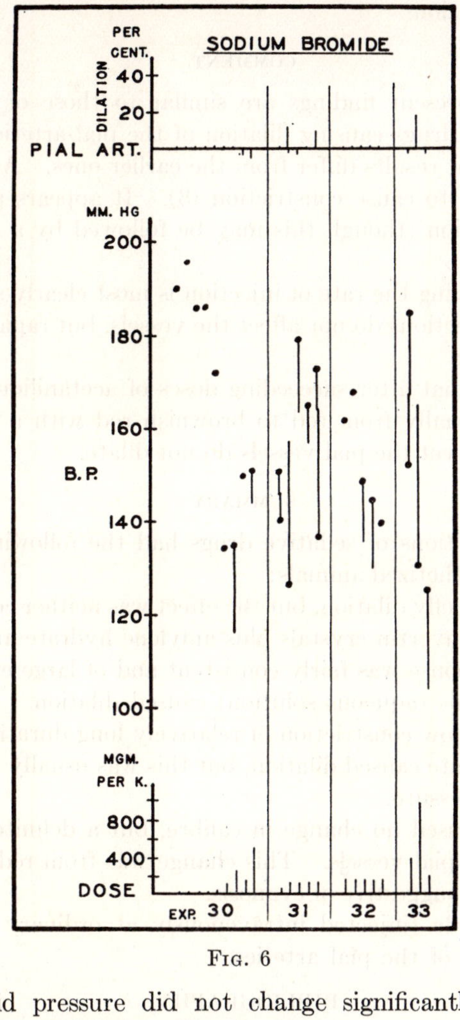

FIG. 6

cerebrospinal fluid pressure did not change significantly, the respiration occasionally increased slightly. See figure 6.

7. OTHER EXPERIMENTS

For purposes of comparison nine additional experiments were carried out with drugs which had already been studied by this method: intravenous alcohol (2 experiments), intravenous or inhaled ether (3 experiments), inhaled CO (2 experiments), inhaled CO_2 (1 experiment) and intravenous salt solution (0.9 per cent NaCl + HCl) of pH 5 (one experiment).[4] Alcohol was followed by dilation of the pial arteries (preceded sometimes by a small constriction); ether, CO and CO_2 were all followed by dilation. These results are in agreement with the results of earlier experiments (2, 3, 4). There was no change after the NaCl solution.

COMMENT

In general the present findings are similar to those of previous experiments, most of the drugs causing dilation of the pial arteries. In regard to one drug the present results differ from the earlier ones. Avertin crystals in 1935 were reported to cause constriction (3). It appears now that avertin causes mainly dilation (though this may be followed by a slow constriction of moderate degree).

The effect of varying the rate of injection is most clearly seen with sodium bromide. Slow injections do not affect the vessels, but rapid injections occasionally dilate them.

It is interesting that after succeeding doses of acetanilide the color of the blood changes gradually from red to brownish red with a purple tint, suggestive of cyanosis, yet the pial vessels do not dilate.

SUMMARY

Intravenous injections of sedative drugs had the following effects on the pial arteries of anesthetized animals:

1. Dial caused chiefly dilation, but the effect was neither constant nor large.
2. Avertin fluid (avertin crystals plus amylene hydrate and water) caused dilation. This response was fairly consistent and of large extent.
3. Avertin crystals (aqueous solution) caused dilation. Occasionally this was followed by a slow constriction of relatively long duration.
4. Amylene hydrate caused dilation, but this was usually complicated by a change in blood pressure.
5. Acetanilide caused no change in calibre, but a definite change in color of the blood in the pial vessels. This change was from red to brownish red with a purple tint—suggestive of cyanosis.
6. Sodium bromide (injected intravenously at ordinary rate) caused no change in diameter of the pial arteries.

BIBLIOGRAPHY

(1) Forbes, Nason and Wortman: Arch. Neurol. & Psychiat., **37:** 334 (Feb.) 1937.
(2) Thomas: Ibid., **38:** 321 (Aug.) 1937.
(3) Finesinger and Cobb: This Journal, **53:** 1 (Jan.) 1935.
(4) Wolff and Lennox: Arch. Neurol & Psychiat., **23:** 1097 (June) 1930.

[4] This was the approximate pH of the solutions of dial, of avertin and of amylene hydrate.

INDEX

Adrenalin; Action of, and potential changes in cat uterus, 63
and pitocin, Action of, on different segments of rabbit uterus, 90
Alles, Gordon A., and Feigen, George A. Comparative physiological actions of phenyl-, thienyl- and furylisopropylamines, 265
Aminophyllin, Action of, on caliter of coronary vessels, 306
Anemia and cyanosis, Comparative effects of sulfonamide compounds as to, 99
Angerine, D. Murray, Cecil, Russell L., and Rothbard, Sidney. Influence of myocrysin on prevention of hemolytic streptococcus arthritis in rats, 164
Anesthesia. IV. Anesthetic action of cyclopropyl ethyl ether, 233
Anesthetic, local, activity and toxicity of three new biphenyl derivatives, 146
Anesthetics, reaction of mice to, Effect of sulfanilamide and some of its derivatives on, 298
Atrhritis, hemolytic streptococcus, in rats, Influence of myocrysin on prevention of, 164
Asphyxia, Antagonistic effect of, to curare paralysis of vagus nerve, 386
Atropine, pilocarpine, prostigmine, eserine, mecholyl and ephedrine, Effect of, on tonus and contraction mechanisms of urinary bladder, with observations on clinical applications of these drugs, 152

Balassa, G., and Gurd, M. R. Action of adrenaline and potential changes in cat uterus, 63
Barbituric and thiobarbituric acid derivatives, effect of, on pyloric sphincter and stomach in unanesthetized dogs, 176
Barnes, Charles A., Cuttle, Tracy D., and Duncan, Garfield G. Histone zinc insulin, pharmacologic characteristics and application in treatment of diabetes mellitus, 331
Biphenyl derivatives, three new, Toxicity and local anesthetic activity of, 146
Blair, H. A., Dwyer, G. K., and Wedd, A. M. Effect of digoxin on cold blooded heart and its bearing on mechanism of digitalis action, 394
Bonnycastle, D. D., and Ferguson, J. K. W. Action of pitocin and adrenalin on different segments of rabbit uterus, 90
Bratton, A. Calvin, Litchfield, J. T., Jr., Marshall, E. K., Jr., and White, H. J. Relationship between *in vitro* and *in vivo* activity of sulfonamide compounds, 112
Butler, Thomas C., Dickison, H. L., Govier, W. M., Greer, C. M., and Lamson, Paul D. Effect of sulfanilamide and some of its derivatives on reaction of mice to anesthetics, 298

Caffein, Action of, on caliber of coronary vessels, 306
Calcium gluconate, Action of, on caliber of coronary vessels, 306
Carbon tetrachloride and morphine, Effects of, on rate of disappearance of ethyl isoamyl barbiturate acid, 123
susceptibility to, and Fat metabolism, 202
Carr, C. Jelleff, Forman, Sylvan E., Evans, William E., Jr., Wollenweber, Henry, and Krantz, John C., Jr. Anesthesia. IV. Anesthetic action of cyclopropyl ethyl ether, 233
Chick heart, embryonic, quantitative effect on, of fifteen chemically related glycosides and genins, 211
Circulatory system, Action of prostigmine, 80
Cocaine, Influence of, on uterine reactions induced by adrenalin and hypogastric nerve stimulation, 370
Cold, Effects of certain drugs on temperature regulation, and changes in their toxicity, in rats exposed to, 130

Cornoary vessels, Action of drugs or Caliber of, 306
Curare paralysis of vagus nerve, Antagonistic effect of asphyxia to, 386
Cuttle, Tracy D., Duncan, Garfield G., and Barnes, Charles A. Histone zinc insulin, pharmacologic characteristics and application in treatment of diabetes mellitus, 331
Cyanosis and anemia, Comparative effects of sulfonamide compounds as to, 99
Cyclopropyl ethyl ether, Anesthetic action of, 233

D'Amour, Fred E., and Smith, Donn L. Method for determining loss of pain sensation, 74
deGraff, Arthur C., Paff, George H., and Lehman, Robert A. Quantitative effect of fifteen chemically related glycosides and genins on embryonic chick heart, 211
Diabetes mellitus, Application of histone zinc insulin in treatment of, 331
Dickison, H. L., Govier, W. M., Greer, C. M., Lamson, Paul D., and Butler, Thomas C. Effect of sulfanilamide and some of its derivatives on reaction of mice to anesthetics, 298
Digitalis action, mechanism of, bearing on, of Effect of digoxin on cold blooded heart, 394
derivatives, Action of, on caliber of coronary vessels, 306
Digoxin, Effect of, on cold blooded heart, and its bearing on mechanism of digitalis action, 394
Dilantin, Effects of, on blood ascorbic acid level in guinea pigs, 383
5,5 diphenylhydantoin, Distribution and rate of metabolism of, 280
Method for determination of, in biological material, 276
Drake, Miles E., Gruber, Charles M., Haury, Victor G., and Hart, E. Ross. Effects of dilantin on blood ascorbic acid level in guinea pigs, 383
duBois, K. P., Potter, R. L., and Moxon, A. L. Toxicity of optically inactive *d*- and *l*-selenium cystine, 184
Duncan, Garfield G., Barnes, Charles A., and Cuttle, Tracy D. Histone zinc insulin, pharmacologic characteristics and application in treatment of diabetes mellitus, 331
Dwyer, G. K., Wedd, A. M., and Blair, H. A. Effect of digoxin on cold blooded heart and its bearing on mechanism of digitalis action, 394
Dyniewicz, J. M., Fantus, Bernard, and Steigmann, Frederick. Absorption and elimination of phenolphthalein in normal and pathologic states: with particular reference to liver and kidney diseases, 252

Ephedrine and eserine, Comparison of, 48
atropine, pilocarpine, prostigmine, eserine and mecholyl, Effect of, on tonus and contraction mechanisms of urinary bladder, with observations on clinical application of these drugs, 152
Esserine and ephedrine, Comparison of, 48
mecholyl, ephedrine, atropine, pilocarpine and prostigmine, Effect of, on tonus and contraction mechanisms of urinary bladder, with observations on clinical application of these drugs, 152
Ethyl isoamyl barbituric acid, rate of disappearance of, effects of morphine and carbon tetrachloride on, 123
Evans, William E., Jr., Wollenweber, Henry, Krantz, John C., Jr., Carr, C. Jelleff, and Forman, Sylvan E. Anesthesia. IV. Anesthetic action of cyclopropyl ethyl ether, 233

Fantus, Bernard, Steigmann, Frederick, and Dyniewicz, J. M. Absorption and elimination of phenolphthalein in normal and pathologic states: with particular reference to liver and kidney diseases, 252
Fat metabolism and susceptibility to carbon tetrachloride, 202
Feigen, George A., and Alles, Gordon A. Comparative physiological actions of phenyl-, thienyl- and furylisopropylamines, 265
Fellows, Edwin J. Toxicity and local anesthetic activity of three new biphenyl derivatives, 146
Ferguson, J. K. W., and Bonnycastle, D. D.

Action of pitocin and adrenalin on different segments of rabbit uterus, 90
Forbes, J. C., Leach, B. E., and Outhouse, E. L. Studies on fat metabolism and susceptibility to carbon tetrachloride, 202
Forman, Sylvan E., Evans, William E., Jr., Wollenweber, Henry, Krantz, John C., Jr., and Carr, C. Jelleff. Anesthesia. IV. Anesthetic action of cyclopropyl ethyl ether, 233
Furyl-, phenyl- and thienylisopropylamines, Comparative physiological actions of, 265

Glycosides and genins, Quantitative effect of fifteen chemically related, on embryonic chick heart, 211
Glucose, Action of, on caliber of coronary vessels, 306
Govier, W. M., and Greer, C. M. Studies on shock induced by hemorrhage. I. Effect of thiamin on survival time, 317
II. Effect of thiamin on disturbances of carbohydrate metabolism, 321
Govier, W. M., Greer, C. M., Lamson, Paul D., Butler, Thomas C., and Dickison, H. L. Effect of sulfanilamide and some of its derivatives on reaction of mice to anesthetics, 298
Graham, J. D. P., and Gurd, M. R. Comparison of ephedrine and eserine, 48
Greer, C. M., and Govier, W. M. Studies on shock induced by hemorrhage. I. Effect of thiamin on survival time, 317
II. Effect of thiamin on disturbances of carbohydrate metabolism, 321
Greer, C. M., Lamson, Paul D., Butler Thomas C., Dickison, H. L., and Govier, W. M. Effect of sulfanilamide and some of its derivatives on reaction of mice to anesthetics, 298
Gross, E. G., and Thompson, Vincent. Excretion of combined morphine in tolerant and non-tolerant dog, 138
Gruber, Charles M., and Gruber, Charles M., Jr. Effect of barbituric and thiobarbituric acid derivatives on pyloric sphincter and stomach in unanesthetized dogs, 176
Haury, Victor G., Hart, E. Ross, and Drake, Miles E. Effects of dilantin on blood ascorbic acid level in guinea pigs, 383
Gurd, M. R., and Balassa, G. Action of adrenaline and potential changes in cat uterus, 63
and Graham, J. D. P. Comparison of ephedrine and eserine, 48

Hart, E. Ross, Drake, Miles E., Gruber, Charles M., and Haury, Victor G. Effects of dilantin on blood ascorbic acid level in guinea pigs, 383
Haury, Victor G., Hart, E. Ross, Drake, Miles E., and Gruber, Charles M. Effects of dilantin on blood ascorbic acid level in guinea pigs, 383
Hemorrhage, shock induced by; Effect of thiamin on disturbances of carbohydrate metabolism, 321
Shock induced by; effect of thiamin on survival time, 317
Herrmann, Julian B. Effects of certain drugs on temperature regulation, and changes in their toxicity in rats exposed to cold, 130
Hine, C. H., and Kozelka, F. L. Distribution and rate of metabolism of *5,5* diphenylhydantoin, 280
and Kozelka, F. L. Method for determination of *5,5* diphenylhydantoin in biological material, 276
Histone zinc insulin, pharmacologic characteristics and application in treatment of diabetes mellitus, 331
Hydroxyethylapocupreine, Response to, of sulfapyridine-resistant pneumococci, 311

Katz, L. N., and Lindner, E. Action of drugs on caliber of coronary vessels, 306
Kinard, F. W., and van de Erve, John. Toxicity of orally ingested tungsten compounds in rat, 196
Kozelka, F. L., and Hine, C. H. Distribution and rate of metabolism of *5,5* diphenylhydantoin, 280
and Hine, C. H. Method for determination of *5,5* diphenylhydantoin in biological material, 276
and Tatum, H. J. Distribution, excre-

tion, and rate and site of detoxification of metrazol, 284
Tatum, H. J., and Nelson, D. E. Effects of morphine and of carbon tetrachloride on rate of disappearance of Ethyl isoamyl barbituric acid, 123
Krantz, John C., Jr., Carr, C. Jelleff, Forman, Sylvan E., Evans, William E., Jr., and Wollenweber, Henry. Anesthesia. IV. Anesthetic action of cyclopropyl ethyl ether, 233

Labate, John S. Influence of cocaine on uterine reactions induced by adrenalin and hypogastric nerve stimulation, 370
Lamson, Paul D., Butler, Thomas C., Dickison, H. L., Govier, W. M., and Greer, C. M. Effect of sulfanilamide and some of its derivatives on reaction of mice to anesthetics, 298
Langworthy, Orthello R., and Teitelbaum, Harry A. Effect of atropine, pilocarpine, prostigmine, eserine, mecholyl and ephedrine on tonus and contraction mechanisms of urinary bladder, with observations on clinical applications of these drugs, 152
Larson, Edward. Effect of posterior pituitary preparations on large intestine of unanesthetized dog, 363
Leach, B. E., Outhouse, E. L., and Forbes, J. C. Studies on fat metabolism and susceptibility to carbon tetrachloride, 202
Lehman, Robert A., deGraff, Arthur C., and Paff, George H. Quantitative effect of fifteen chemically related glycosides and genins on embryonic chick heart, 211
Lindner, E., and Katz, L. N. Action of drugs on caliber of coronary vessels, 306
Litchfield, J. T., Jr., Marshall, E. K., Jr., White, H. J., and Bratton, A. Calvin. Relationship between *in vitro* and *in vivo* activity of sulfonamide compounds, 112
White, H. J., and Marshall, E. K., Jr. Mode of action of neoprontosil in streptococcus infections in mice, 291
Lothrop, Gladys N., Wilkinson, Joan, and Sohler, Theodore P. Effects of sedative drugs on pial vessels, 409
Luisada, Aldo, and Mautner, Hans. Antagonistic effect of asphyxia to curare paralysis of vagus nerve, 386

Marshall, E. K., Jr., Litchfield, J. T., Jr., and White, H. J. Mode of action of neoprontosil in streptococcus infections in mice, 291
White, H. J., Bratton, A. Calvin, and Litchfield, J. T., Jr. Relationship between *in vitro* and *in vivo* activity of sulfonamide compounds, 112
Mautner, Hans and Luisada, Aldo. Antagonistic effect of asphyxia to curare paralysis of vagus nerve, 386
Mecholyl, ephedrine, atropine, pilocarpine, prostigmine and eserine, Effect of, on tonus and contraction mechanisms of urinary bladder, with observations on clinical application of these drugs, 152
Mendez, Rafael, and Ravin, Abe. Action of prostigmine on circulatory system, 80
Metabolism, carbohydrate, disturbances of, Effect of thiamin on, in shock induced by hemorrhage, 321
Metrazol, Action of, on caliber of coronary vessels, 306
Distribution, excretion, and rate and site of detoxification of, 284
Miller, John K. Production in cultures containing sodium paranitrobenzoate of a substance that affects action of sulfathiazole, 354
Morphine and carbon tetrachloride, effects of, on rate of disappearance of ethyl isoamyl barbituric acid, 123
combined, Excretion of, in tolerant and non-tolerant dog, 138
Moxon, A. L., duBois, K. P., and Potter, R. L. Toxicity of optically inactive *d*- and *l*-selenium cystine, 184
Myocrysin, Influence of, on prevention of hemolytic streptococcus arthritis in rats, 164

Nelson, D. E., Kozelka, F. L., and Tatum, H. J. Effects of morphine and of carbon tetrachloride of rate of disappear-

ance of ethyl isoamyl barbituric acid, 123
Neoprontosil, Mode of action of, in streptococcus infections in mice, 291

Outhouse, E. L., Forbes, J. C., and Leach, B. E. Studies on fat metabolism and susceptibility to carbon tetrachloride, 202

Paff, George H., Lehman, Robert A., and deGraff, Arthur C. Quantitative effect of fifteen chemically related glycosides and genins on embryonic chick heart, 211
Pain sensation, Method for determining loss of, 74
Papaverine hydrochloride, Action of, on caliber of coronary vessels, 306
Phenolphthalein, Absorption and Elimination of, in normal and pathologic states: with particular reference to liver and kidney diseases, 252
Phenyl-, thienyl- and furylisopropylamines, Comparative physiological actions of, 265
Pial vessels, Effects on, of sedative drugs, 409
Pilocarpine, prostigmine, eserine, mecholyl, ephedrine and atropine, Effect of, on tonus and contraction mechanisms of urinary bladder, with observations on clinical applications of these drugs, 152
Pitocin and adrenalin, Action of, on different segments of rabbit uterus, 90
Pneumococci, sulfapyridine-resistant, Response of, to hydroxyethylapocupreine, 311
Posterior pituitary preparations, Effect of, on large intestine of unanesthetized dog, 363
Potter, R. L., Moxon, A. L., and duBois, K. P. Toxicity of optically inactive *d*- and *l*-selenium cystine, 184
Proceedings of the American Society for Pharmacology and Experimental Therapeutics, Incorporated, 1
Proceedings of the American Society for Pharmacology and Experimental Therapeutics, Incorporated, 1
Anesthetic potency and biochemical effects of 1 and 2 chlor-propene-1 and 1 and 2 brom-propene-1. B. E. Abreu, S. A. Peoples, C. A. Handley and D. F. Marsh, 1
The determination of chloral hydrate in blood and the absorption curve of chloral hydrate. W. Lloyd Adams, 1
Effects of chlorination of alkyl cresols on their local and systemic activity. Hamilton H. Anderson and M. H. Hu, 2
Side chain oxidations and their possible pharmacological significance. Georg Barkan, 2
Pharmacological studies on levo-n-ethylephedrine hydrochloride (nethamine hydrochloride). I. Toxicity and effect on the respiratory and circulatory systems. T. J. Becker, M. R. Warren, D. G. Marsh, and R. S. Shelton, 3
Attempted immunization of canaries against plasmodium cathemerium by injection with filtered whole mosquito substance. Harry Beckman, 3
Nitrophenol as an antiseptic. R. Beutner, A. Cohen, and K. R. Beutner, 4
The effect of narcotics on diuresis. R. C. de Bodo and H. I. Bloch, 4
Metabolic fate of evipal. Milton T. Bush and Thomas C. Butler, 5
The action of ergot alkaloids on the virgin rat uterus. R. A. Bussabarger, L. D. Seager and O. S. Gibbs, 5
The delay in onset of action of intravenously injected anesthetics. Thomas C. Butler, 6
The effect of ethyl yohimbine in experimental hypertension. H. F. Chase, F. F. Yonkman and A. J. Lehman, 6
The effect of posterior pituitary extract on the water uptake in frogs after complete or partial hypophysectomy, infundibular lesions and thyroidectomy. Graham Chen, 7
The LD_{50}s of neoarsphenamine and thiobismol for mice and Chinese hamsters. Y. P. Chen and H. Y. Soong, 7
The comparative narcotic potency of 1-diethylacetyl-5,5-cyclopentamethylene biuret, paraldehyde and sodium barbital. Charles H. Cheng, Hamilton H. Anderson and S. Y. P'an, 7
The effect of hydro-alcoholic solutions of

pyrethrum on drosophila flies. Yin-ch'ang Chin, 8
The acute effects of aniline on circulation and blood of dogs. Byron B. Clark, E. J. Van Loon and R. W. Morrissey, 9
The similarity in basic functions of various bismuth compounds used in the therapy of syphilis. N. M. Clausen, B. J. Longley and A. L. Tatum, 9
Sweat responses to drugs with a nicotine-like action. Julius M. Coon and Stephen Rothman, 9
A comparison of blood pressure effects and toxicity of ephedrine and racephedrine. Elizabeth M. Cranston, 10
The pharmacology of certain derivatives of phenyl triazole carboxylic acid. Raymond W. Cunningham, Edwin J. Fellows and A. E. Livingston, 10
Vioform-N.N.R. and "diodoquin": animal toxicity and iodine absorption in man. Norman A. David, Nilkanth Phatak and F. B. Zener, 11
Correlation of the structure of the cardiac glycosides with their action on the embryo chick heart. Arthur C. DeGraff, George H. Paff and Robert A. Lehman, 11
Sodium citrate as a protective agent against injury by a heavy metal. G. L. Donnelly and R. L. Holman, 12
Effects of irritation of the upper airway on spleen volume. M. S. Dooley, 12
The determination of the pH of the skin of man and common laboratory animal. John H. Draize, 12
A pharmacologic and toxicologic study of mannitol and sorbitol. Fred W. Ellis and C. Jelleff Carr, 13
The anesthetic action of methyl allyl ether and n-propyl ethyl ether. William E. Evans, Jr., 13
A roentgenkymographic study of the effect of intravenous lanatoside C upon the diastolic volume and stroke output on the failing heart. George Fahr and John S. La Due, 14
The local anesthetic activity of three new biphenyl derivatives. Edwin J. Fellows, 14
The pharmacology of piperidine and morpholine derivatives of α and β-naphthol. Edwin J. Fellows, Raymond W. Cunningham and A. E. Livingston, 14
The chronic toxicity of cadmium. O. Garth Fitzhugh and Fred H. Meiller, 15
The elimination of prostigmine. Dale G. Friend and Otto Krayer, 15
Yohimbine and the estrous cycle in rats. N. W. Fugo and E. G. Gross, 16
Toxicological studies on ammoniated mercury. O. S. Gibbs, H. Pond and G. A. Hansmann, 16
Are the results of the U.S.P. frog method for the assay of Digitalis applicable to man? Harry Gold, McKeen Cattell, Nathaniel T. Kwit and Milton Kramer, 17
Effect of dilantin on metrazol convulsions. Louis Goodman and Björn Lih, 18
Further studies on the mechanism of the vasomotor reversal. Melvin W. Green, 18
The effect of barbituric and thiobarbituric acid derivatives on the pyloric sphincter and stomach in unanesthetized dogs. Charles M. Gruber and Charles M. Gruber, Jr., 18
N-allyl-norcodeine and N-allyl-normorphine, two antagonists to morphine. E. Ross Hart, 19
The influence of aloe and podophyllum on the flow of bile. Lloyd W. Hazleton, 20
The atropine-like action of pilocarpine. Robert P. Herwick and Theodore Koppanyi, 20
Studies on the metabolism of diphenylhydantoin. C. H. Hine and F. L. Kozelka, 20
Anthelmintic properties of alkyl cresols and their chlorinated derivatives. M. H. Hu, Peter P. T. Sah and Hamilton H. Anderson, 21
Acute fatal insulin poisoning. Eugene L. Jackson, 21
The rôle of blood cells in the anaphylactic histamine release. Gerhard Katz, 22
Some effects of potassium salts in man. N. M. Keith, A. E. Osterberg and H. B. Burchell, 22

Effect of drugs on blood lipids. F. E. Kelsey, 23
The effect of sparteine on the autonomic nervous system. Theodore Koppanyi and Charles R. Linegar, 23
Anesthetic action of cyclopropyl aliphatic ethers. John C. Krantz, Jr., and Sylvan E. Forman, 24
Interrelations of pharmacodynamic properties of morphine and its derivatives. Hugo Krueger, 24
Effect of sulfanilamide and some of its derivatives on the sensitivity of mice to anesthetics. Paul D. Lamson, Thomas C. Butler, H. L. Dickison, Wm. M. Govier and C. M. Greer, 25
The effect on the blood picture of the 11 day embryo of liver extract injected into the pregnant rat. Jules H. Last and Edwin E. Hays, 25
The influence of autonomic drugs and of nerve stimulation on the spasm of the cardiac sphincter following bilateral vagotomy. G. Lehmann, 25
The effect of "vitamin P" on the circulatory system. A. J. Leser, C. F. Lombard, C. H. Thienes, Cecil Wawra and J. L. Webb, 26
Intravenous toxicity of the acetins in dogs and rabbits. R. C. Li and Hamilton H. Anderson, 26
The mode of action of neoprontosil in streptococcus infections in mice. J. T. Litchfield, Jr., H. J. White and E. K. Marshall, Jr., 26
Cathartic effectiveness of parenterally administered phthalein laxatives in the monkey. S. Loewe, 27
The action of chemical components of cannabis extracts. S. Loewe and W. Modell, 27
Damage to the optic tract produced in monkeys by tryparsamide. B. J. Longley, N. M. Clausen, F. A. Davis, M. E. Nesbit and A. L. Tatum, 27
Correlation between structure and the ratio of inhibitory to pressor activity of sympathomimetic amines. Amedeo S. Marrazzi, 28
Effect of quinine on urinary metabolites of fasting dogs. A. T. Milhorat and W. E. Bartels, 28
Effect of quinine on metabolism in patients with muscular wasting and creatinuria. A. T. Milhorat and V. Toscani, 29
The use of digitalis to prevent the exaggerated acceleration of the heart during physical exercise in patients with auricular fibrillation. Walter Modell and Harry Gold, 29
Organotropy of tribromoethanol, tribromoacetaldehyde and tribromoacetic acid. James L. Morrison and G. A. Emerson, 30
A simple and rapid qualitative test for barbiturates. Hurley L. Motley, 30
The liver histamine in canine anaphylaxis. Gaylord Ojers, Carl A. Holmes and Carl A. Dragstedt, 30
Distribution of sulfapyridine and its sodium salt in ocular fluids and tissues after local application. S. Y. P'an, 31
A method for determining the solubility of gases and vapors in liquids by means of the Van Slyke-Neill apparatus. S. Anderson Peoples, 3
The effect of varying the intake of dietary salts on the formation of galactose cataracts. Carl Pfeiffer, Howard G. Glass and Robert H. Dreisbach, 31
Addiction potentialities of "seconal" and sodium amytal in rats. Nilkanth M. Phatak, John R. Hill and Norman A. David, 32
The effect of high fat-low protein diets on the nitrogen and fat metabolism of hypophysectomized and normal rats. Roger M. Reinecke, Leo T. Samuels and Howard A. Ball, 32
Toxicity of theophylline-ephedrine-barbiturate mixtures. R. K. Richards, 33
Comparative effects of sulfonamide compounds in producing cyanosis and anemia. Arthur P. Richardson, 33
The influence of metrazol on the "neurotic pattern" in rats. Jacob Sacks, Norman R. F. Maier and Nathan M. Glaser, 33
Balance studies in hypophysectomized rats fed high carbohydrate and high fat diet. Leo T. Samuels, Roger M. Reinecke and Howard A. Ball, 34
The action of various agents on the gall

bladder of the frog. Lloyd D. Seager, 35
On the oxidative metabolism of skeletal muscle from chronically morphinized rats. M. H. Seevers and F. E. Shideman, 35
Morphine on the "in vitro" respiration of certain tissues of the rat, rabbit and cat. F. E. Shideman and M. H. Seevers, 36
Some "in vitro" effects of morphine on the respiratory metabolism of skeletal muscle. F. E. Shideman and M. H. Seevers, 36
Further observations on the pharmacological effects of trypsin. M. Rocha e Silva and Carl A. Dragstedt, 36
Effect of pentothal-sodium on urine output under various experimental conditions. Herbert Silvette, 37
Some new aspects of morphine action: influence on excretion and blood level by prostigmin. Donald Slaughter, C. R. Treadwell and J. W. Gales, 37
The oxytocic assay of posterior pituitary fractions. Blackwell Smith, Jr., 38
The ratio of bromide to chloride in body fluids. Paul K. Smith, Alexander W. Winkler and Anna J. Eisenman, 38
The effect of morphine and certain new derivatives upon the fetus. Franklin F. Snyder and Kha Ti Lim, 39
The toxicity of bismuth salts by intravenous injection. Torald Sollman and Joseph Seifter, 39
Effect of convulsants at low body temperatures. R. T. Stormont and W. E. Hook, 40
Further studies on substituted oxazolediones. Roger W. Stoughton and J. H. Baxter, Jr., 40
Effects of chronic nicotine poisoning of rats on viability of the young and on the adrenal gland. C. H. Thienes, C. F. Lombard and A. J. Leser, 40
The transfer of bismuth into the fetal circulation after the maternal administration of sobisminol. H. E. Thompson, Jr., Ph.D., L. T. Steadman, Ph.D. and W. T. Pommerenke, M.D., 41
Studies on the absorption of some digitalis preparations from the gastro-intestinal tract in the cat and man. Janet Travell and Harry Gold, 41
Solubility experiments with posterior lobe pituitary powder in 0.25 per cent acetic acid. John A. Vaichulis, 41
Effects of anterior pituitary like substance on carbohydrate metabolism. Ben Vidgoff and Rosa Kubin, 42
On the mechanism of carbon monoxide poisoning. W. F. von Oettingen, D. D. Donahue and P. J. Valaer, 42
Effect of acetylcholine, derivatives, and certain other drugs upon artificially induced auricular fibrillation in the intact dog. Edward W. Wallace, 43
Observations on kation shifts following magnesium and calcium injections. George B. Wallace and Bernard B. Brodie, 44
Pharmacological studies on levo-N-ethyl ephedrine hydrochloride (nethamine hydrochloride). II. Effect on bronchioles, uterus, small intestine, stomach, and pupil. M. R. Warren, T. J. Becker, D. G. Marsh and R. S. Shelton, 44
Oxygen therapy in the relief of fatigue in relation to flying. R. A. Waud and Ward Smith, 45
The effects of benzedrine, coramine, metrazol and picrotoxin on body temperature and gaseous metabolism in rabbits depressed by alcohol. H. W. Werner, 45
The inactivation of choline esterase by morphine and derivatives. Charles I. Wright, 45
A study of the possible toxic effects of prolonged formaldehyde ingestion. F. F. Yonkman, A. J. Lehman, C. C. Pfeiffer and H. F. Chase, 46
Effect of lipoiodine-N.N.R. therapy on maternal and fetal blood iodine. F. B. Zener, Nilkanth Phatak and Norman A. David, 47
Propylene glycol, Quantitative gastrointestinal absorption and renal excretion of, 344
Prostigmine, Action of, on circulatory system, 80
eserine, mecholyl, ephedrine, atropine and pilocarpine, Effect of, on tonus and

contraction mechanisms of urinary bladder, with observations on clinical application of these drugs, 152
Pyloric sphincter and stomach, Effect of barbituric and thiobarbituric acid derivatives, in unanesthetized dogs, 176

Ravin, Abe, and Mendez, Rafael. Action of prostigmine on circulatory system, 80
Richardson, Arthur P. Comparative effects of sulfonamide compounds as to anemia and cyanosis, 99
Rothbard, Sidney, Angevine, D. Murray, and Cecil, Russell L. Influence of myocrysin on prevention of hemolytic streptococcus arthritis in rats, 164

Schmidt, L. H., and Sesler, Clara L. Response of sulfapyridine-resistant pneumococci to hydroxyethylapocupreine, 311
Sedative drugs, Effects of, on pial vessels, 409
d- and *l*-selenium cystine, Toxicity of optically inactive, 184
Selenium, Fate of, in the organism, 245
Sesler, Clara L., and Schmidt, L. H. Response of sulfapyridine-resistant pneumococci to hydroxyethlyapocupreine, 311
Shock induced by hemorrhage; Effect of thiamin on disturbances of carbohydrate metabolism, 321
  induced by hemorrhage; Effect of thiamin on survival time, 317
Smith, Donn L., and D'Amour, Fred E. Method for determining loss of pain sensation, 74
Smith, M. I., and Westfall, Benton B. Fate of selenium in the organism, 245
Sodium paranitrobenzoate, Production in cultures containing, of a substance that affects action of sulfathiazole, 354
Sohler, Theodore P., Lothrop, Gladys N., and Wilkinson, Joan. Effects of sedative drugs on pial vessels, 409
Steigmann, Frederick, Dyniewicz, J. M., and Fantus, Bernard. Absorption and elimination of phenolphthalein in normal and pathologic states: with particular reference to liver and kidney diseases, 252
Streptococcus infections in mice, Mode of action of neoprontosil in, 291
Sulfanilamide and some of its derivatives, Effect of, on reaction of mice to anesthetics, 298
Sulfapyridine-resistant pneumococci, Response of, to hydroxyethylapocupreine, 311
Sulfathiazole, Production in cultures containing sodium paranitrobenzoate of a substance that affects action of, 354
Sulfonamide compounds, Comparative effects of, as to anemia and cyanosis, 99
  Relationship between *in vitro* and *in vivo* activity of, 112

Tatum, H. J., and Kozelka, F. L. Distribution, excretion, and rate and site of detoxification of metrazol, 284
  Nelson, D. E., and Kozelka, F. L. Effects of morphine and of carbon tetrachloride on rate of disappearance of ethyl isoamylbarbituric acid, 123
Teitelbaum, Harry A., and Langworthy, Orthello R. Effect of atropine, pilocarpine, prostigmine, eserine, mecholyl and ephedrine on tonus and contraction mechanisms of urinary bladder, with observations on clinical applications of these drugs, 152
Temperature regulation, Effects of certain drugs on, and changes in their toxicity, in rats exposed to cold, 130
Thiamin, Effect of, on disturbances of carbohydrate metabolism, in shock induced by hemorrhage, 321
  Effect of, on survival time, in shock induced by hemorrhage, 317
Thienyl-, phenyl- and furylisopropylamines, Comparative physiological actions of, 265
Thiobarbituric and barbituric acid derivatives, Effect of, on pyloric sphincter and stomach in unanesthetized dogs, 176
Thompson, Vincent, and Gross, E. G. Excretion of combined morphine in tolerant and non-tolerant dog, 138
Toxicity and local anesthetic activity of three new biphenyl derivatives, 146
  changes in, in certain drugs affecting temperature regulation, in rats exposed to cold, 130

of optically inactive *d*- and *l*-selenium cystine, 184
of orally ingested tungsten compounds in rat, 196
Trimethylene glycol, Toxicity and actions of, 227
Tungsten compounds, orally ingested, in rat, Toxicity of, 196

Urinary bladder, tonus and contraction mechanisms of, Effect on, of atropine, pilocarpine, prostigmine, eserine, mecholyl and ephedrine, 152
Uterine reactions induced by adrenalin and hypogastric nerve stimulation, Influence of cocaine on, 370
Uterus of cat, potential changes in, and Action of adrenaline, 63
rabbit, Action of pitocin and adrenalin on different segments of, 90

van de Erve, John, and Kinard, F. W. Toxicity of orally ingested tungsten compounds in rat, 196
Van Winkle, W., Jr. Quantitative gastrointestinal absorption and renal excretion of propylene glycol, 344

Toxicity and actions of trimethylene glycol, 227

Wedd, A. M., Blair, H. A., and Dwyer, G. K. Effect of digoxin on cold blooded heart and its bearing on mechanism of digitalis action, 394
Westfall, Benton B., and Smith, M. I. Fate of selenium in the organism, 245
White, H. J., Bratton, A. Calvin, Litchfield, J. T., Jr., and Marshall, E. K., Jr. Relationship between *in vitro* and *in vivo* activity of sulfonamide compounds, 112
Marshall, E. K., Jr., and Litchfield, J. T., Jr. Mode of action of neoprontosil in streptococcus infections in mice, 291
Wilkinson, Joan, Sohler, Theodore P., and Lothrop, Gladys N. Effects of sedative drugs on pial vessels, 409
Wollenweber, Henry, Krantz, John C., Jr., Carr, C. Jelleff, Forman, Sylvan E., and Evans, William E., Jr. Anesthesia. IV. Anesthetic action of cyclopropyl ethyl ether, 233